Stella
20 Clarendon Road.
Dover .

PRACTICAL COOKERY

Victor Ceserani
MBE, CPA, MBA, FHCIMA
Formerly Head of
The School of Hotelkeeping and Catering,
Ealing College of Higher Education
(now Thames Valley University)

Ronald Kinton
BEd (Hons), FHCIMA
Formerly of
Garnett College, College of Education for Teachers
in Further and Higher Education
(now University of Greenwich)

David Foskett
BEd (Hons), FHCIMA
Programmes Manager
Thames Valley University

Eighth Edition

Hodder & Stoughton

A MEMBER OF THE HODDER HEADLINE GROUP

British Library Cataloguing in Publication Data

Ceserani, Victor
    Practical Cookery. – 8Rev.ed
    I. Title   II. Kinton, Ronald
    III. Foskett, David
    641.5

    ISBN 0 340 62068 4

First published 1962
Second edition 1967
Third edition 1972
Fourth edition 1974
Fifth edition 1981
Sixth edition 1987
Seventh edition 1990
Eighth edition 1995

Impression number   10   9   8   7   6   5   4   3
Year   1999   1998   1997

Typeset by Wearset, Boldon, Tyne and Wear.
Printed in Great Britain for Hodder & Stoughton Educational,
a division of Hodder Headline Plc, 338 Euston Road,
London NW1 3BH by Butler & Tanner Ltd, Frome.

CONTENTS

Introduction to the eighth edition   v

Acknowledgements   vi

Metric conversion tables and oven temperature chart   vii

1   The working environment   1
     Maintain a safe and secure working environment   2
     Maintain a professional and hygienic appearance   16
     Maintain effective working relationships   17
     Contribute to the development of self and others   23
     Selection, use and care of knives and small equipment   26
     Cleaning of cutting equipment   34
     Maintain clean food production areas, equipment and utensils; food hygiene   37

2   Nutrition and healthy eating   57

3   Methods of cookery   73
     Boiling   77
     Poaching   80
     Stewing   81
     Braising   83
     Steaming   86
     Baking   89
     Roasting   91
     Pot roasting   94
     Grilling   96
     Shallow frying   99
     Deep frying   102
     Paper bag cooking   106
     Microwave cooking   106

4   Stocks, soups and sauces   109

5   Hors-d'oeuvre, salads, cooked/cured/prepared foods   153

6   Eggs   197

7	Pasta and rice	213
8	Fish and shellfish	240
9	Meat and poultry	286
	Lamb	296
	Beef	324
	Veal	355
	Pork	374
	Bacon	384
	Poultry	389
	Game	397
10	Ethnic dishes	420
	Caribbean	425
	Chinese	426
	Greek	433
	Indian and Pakistan	440
	Indonesian	456
	Japanese	459
	Mexican	466
	Middle Eastern and Israeli	469
	Israeli kosher	474
	Spanish	480
	Thai	482
	USA	484
11	Vegetarian dishes	489
12	Vegetables and pulses	516
13	Potatoes	561
14	Pastry	581
	Desserts	586
	Dough products	638
	Pastry dishes	650
	Cakes and biscuits	693
15	Snacks, light meals, savouries and convenience foods	721
	Glossary of culinary terms	743
	Index	750

INTRODUCTION TO THE
EIGHTH EDITION

The purpose of this book is to provide a sound foundation of professional cookery knowledge for students taking City and Guilds and BTEC courses, Advanced and Intermediate GNVQ Food Preparation and Cooking courses and the examinations of the HCIMA. In addition, it identifies the underpinning knowledge and skills required by those wishing to be assessed at NVQ/SVQ Levels 1, 2 and 3. We also think that the book will assist students of catering other than those taking these courses and examinations.

We consider that the following points are important:

- to develop a professional attitude and appearance, acquire professional skills and behave in a professional manner;
- to develop knowledge and understanding of the commodities available: how to select for quality, cost and availability and to compare fresh, part-prepared, commercial and convenience products;
- to understand the methods of cookery and in which circumstances they are used for specific foods; with this knowledge to be able to produce a variety of dishes suitable for the various types of establishments;
- to understand recipe balance and be able to follow recipes to produce dishes of the required quality, colour, consistency, seasoning, flavour, temperature and presentation;
- once confidence and competence to produce satisfactory dishes from set recipes has been achieved, to learn to adjust recipes when required to meet specific situations; to learn how variations to set recipes can be produced and develop recipes by using original ideas;
- to understand the principles of healthy catering, to be aware of basic nutrition and the requirements of vegetarians and vegans;
- to understand fully the essential necessity for healthy, hygienic and safe procedures at all times in the preparation, storage, cooking and serving of food.

NVQ/SVQ Workbook Level 2 – Food Preparation and Cooking is available to accompany this book, for those readers who wish to check their own knowledge by means of self assessment.

Questions and Answers for Practical Cookery 8th edition is also available, for those wishing to test their knowledge more widely across the contents of the book.

Readers wishing to take the additional qualifications: Handle and store food; Cook chill foods; Cook freeze foods, will find the necessary information in *The Theory of Catering*, eighth edition.

ACKNOWLEDGEMENTS

The authors wish to acknowledge and thank the following:

- The publishers for enabling this book to be illustrated
- Jane Cliff BSc (Nutrition), and Jenny Poulter, BSc, PhD, for their section on nutrition/healthy eating in Chapter 2 and for the nutritional data supplied alongside many of the recipes; and Margaret Brookes, Senior Lecturer, Thames Valley University, for her valuable contribution
- Wendy Doyle, Research Nutritionist for her help with the nutritional analysis
- Colleagues and students of the TVU, including Maddalena Bonino, and to the Potato Marketing Board for recipe 23, page 572.

The authors and publishers would like to thank the following:

- The photographer Ian O'Leary and his assistant Tim Ridley for their helpful advice and co-operation
- David Foskett for use of kitchens and staff help at Thames Valley University
- Glynn Johnson, Cert Ed, and Frank McDowell, Cert Ed, FHCIMA, for the interest, helpful suggestion and care taken in the preparation and presentation of the food required for the photographs
- The Milk Marketing Board for generously sponsoring the work of Jane Cliff, Jenny Poulter and Wendy Doyle
- *For Copyright material*: Winch and Associates *pages* 1, 73; Chubb Fire Ltd, 1.1, 1.2; Ted Poole, The College, Swindon, fig. 1.2; The Department of Health, pl. 1.4; Comark Ltd, pl. 1.5; Rentokil Ltd, fig. 1.13; The British Heart Foundation, pl. 2.1; The Health Education Authority, pl. 2.2; The Flour Advisory Bureau and The Dunn Nutrition unit, pl. 2.3; IDS Foods Ltd, pl. 7.1; Anthony Blake Photo Library, pl. 7.4, 10.5, 10.6, 12.6, *page 57*; Robert Harding Photo Library, pl. 10.1, 10.7, 10.8; Marshall Cavendish Photo Library, 10.2–4, 12.1, 15.1, *page 420*.

— *Metric equivalents* —

	APPROXIMATE EQUIVALENT	EXACT EQUIVALENT
$\frac{1}{4}$ oz	5 g	7.0 g
$\frac{1}{2}$ oz	10 g	14.1 g
1 oz	25 g	28.3 g
2 oz	50 g	56.6 g
3 oz	75 g	84.9 g
4 oz	100 g	113.2 g
5 oz	125 g	141.5 g
6 oz	150 g	169.8 g
7 oz	175 g	198.1 g
8 oz	200 g	227.0 g
9 oz	225 g	255.3 g
10 oz	250 g	283.0 g
11 oz	275 g	311.3 g
12 oz	300 g	340.0 g
13 oz	325 g	368.3 g
14 oz	350 g	396.6 g
15 oz	375 g	424.0 g
16 oz	400 g	454.0 g
2 lb	1 kg	908.0 g
$\frac{1}{4}$ pt	125 ml	142 ml
$\frac{1}{2}$ pt	250 ml ($\frac{1}{4}$ litre)	284 ml
$\frac{3}{4}$ pt	375 ml	426 ml
1 pt	500 ml ($\frac{1}{2}$ litre)	568 ml
$1\frac{1}{2}$ pt	750 ml ($\frac{3}{4}$ litre)	852 ml
2 pt (1 qt)	1000 ml (1 litre)	1.13 litre
2 qt	2000 ml (2 litre)	2.26 litre
1 gal	$4\frac{1}{2}$ litre	4.54 litre

APPROXIMATE EQUIVALENTS

$\frac{1}{2}$ cm = $\frac{1}{4}$ in   10 cm = 4 in

1 cm = $\frac{1}{2}$ in   12 cm = 5 in

2 cm = 1 in   15 cm = 6 in

4 cm = $1\frac{1}{2}$ in   16 cm = $6\frac{1}{2}$ in

5 cm = 2 in   18 cm = 7 in

6 cm = $2\frac{1}{2}$ in   30 cm = 12 in

8 cm = 3 in   45 cm = 18 in

— *Oven temperature chart* —

	°C	GAS REGULO	°F
slow (cool)	110	$\frac{1}{4}$	225
	130	$\frac{1}{2}$	250
	140	1	275
	150	2	300
	160	3	325
moderate	180	4	350
	190	5	375
	200	6	400
hot	220	7	425
	230	8	450
very hot	250	9	500

THE WORKING ENVIRONMENT

Maintain a safe and secure working environment

1   Carry out procedures in the event of fire.
2   Maintain a safe environment for customers, staff and visitors.
3   Maintain a secure environment.

CARRY OUT PROCEDURES IN THE EVENT OF FIRE

The reader should be able to:

- explain when to raise the alarm;
- explain how to use the fire fighting equipment;
- demonstrate knowledge in the understanding of all safety and emergency signs and ensure notices are adhered to;
- demonstrate the correct evacuation procedures and ensure that these are followed in a calm and orderly manner;
- be able to reach the nominated assembly point.

Fire precautions

Fires in hotel and catering establishments are fairly common and all too often can result in injury to the employee, colleagues or customers. All employees must be aware of any specific procedures laid down for the establishment and be ready to comply with them at all times. A roll call should always be taken to ensure that everyone is safely out of the building.

Three components are necessary for a fire to start:

- fuel – something to burn
- air – oxygen to sustain combustion
- heat – gas, electricity, etc.

To extinguish a fire the three principal methods are:

- starving – removing the fuel
- smothering – removing the air
- cooling – removing the heat.

Procedure in the event of a fire

- The fire brigade must be called immediately a fire is discovered.
- Do not panic.
- Warn other people in the vicinity and sound the fire alarm.
- Do not jeopardise your own safety or that of others.
- Follow the fire instructions of the establishment.
- If the fire is small, use appropriate fire extinguisher.
- Close doors and windows, turn off gas, electricity and fans.
- Do not wait for the fire to get out of control before calling the fire brigade.

It is important that in all catering establishments, passageways are kept clear and that doors open outwards. Fire escape doors and windows should be clearly marked and fire fighting equipment must be readily available and in working order. Periodic fire drills should occur and be taken seriously since lives may be endangered if a fire should start. Fire alarm bells must be tested at least four times a year and staff should be instructed in the use of fire-fighting equipment. All extinguishers should be refilled immediately after use.

All *fire extinguishers* should be manufactured in accordance with British Standard specifications; they should be coloured, with a code to indicate the type and with operating instructions on them.

Red – water
Blue – dry powder
Cream – foam
Green – halon (vapourising liquid)
Black – carbon dioxide

Fire blankets must also conform to British Standards specifications.

Fire hoses are used for similar fires to those classified under water fire extinguishers. You should be familiar with the instructions displayed by the fire hose before using it.

Water sprinkler system consists of an array of sprinkler heads at ceiling level connected to a mains water supply. In the event of a fire, the nearest sprinkler head above the fire operates when the temperature at ceiling level reaches a preset level (e.g. 68°C). Additional heads operate later if necessary to control the fire.

Plate 1.1: Fire blanket

Plate 1.2: Types of fire extinguishers

CARRY OUT PROCEDURES ON DISCOVERY OF A SUSPICIOUS ITEM OR PACKAGE

The reader should:

- know that suspicious items and packages are left untouched;
- understand that suspicious items and packages are reported in accordance with laid-down procedures;
- demonstrate the correct safety and security procedures and that these are followed in a calm and orderly manner.

In all areas of every type of catering establishment vigilance is necessary at all times regarding suspicious items. It is wiser to be safe than sorry, so that any item which is left unattended in public areas should not be ignored. Any item which may be in full view, hidden or partially hidden in a strange or unusual place should be treated with suspicion. The item or items may contain a bomb or an incendiary device and be concealed in a package, bag, box, holdall, briefcase, etc. Anything which is out of the ordinary must not be ignored. Particular attention should be paid to exits, yards, corridors, stores, changing rooms, staircases, toilets, etc., which may be unattended for some of the time.

It is also necessary to be alert to persons frequenting the establishment or part of the premises who have no business to be there. If you are suspicious, make sure you can give an accurate description to your employer.

The procedure in the event of finding a suspicious item, even though it proves not to be harmless is as follows:

- do not panic;
- calmly warn others in the vicinity;
- do not touch the item or allow others to do so;
- immediately inform your employers;
- move to a safe place.

It is the employer's responsibility to ensure that employees are aware of the procedures to be taken at that establishment and for the employee to fully understand them.

CARRY OUT PROCEDURES IN THE EVENT OF AN ACCIDENT

The reader should:

- know the laid down procedures for contacting emergency services and identify persons responsible for first aid;
- demonstrate knowledge of appropriate action to be taken to ensure safety of injured and non-injured persons with laid down procedures;
- know how to comfort and reassure injured persons;
- demonstrate how accidents are recorded or documented in accordance with laid down procedures.

In the event of an accident the person responsible for First Aid must be called immediately. If it is a serious accident then an ambulance must be obtained by phoning 999 and asking for the ambulance service. Meanwhile comfort the injured person or persons and reassure them by explaining that help is on the way and assist in making them as comfortable as possible, according to the nature of the injury. Never give the injured person any alcoholic liquid, e.g. brandy. Should the accident involve or appear to involve broken bones on no account move the injured person until the injury has been secured and immobilised. If a person has fallen or had an accident whereby they are on the ground, do not attempt to lift them up until it is certain no further damage will occur. In due course the details of the accident must be documented.

It is better to prevent accidents than have to deal with them. Ensure that any specific procedures relevant to the establishment are complied with.

Should it be necessary to obtain the services of an ambulance:

- dial 999, state you require an ambulance;
- state exact location of the incident;
- give both address and telephone number of location;
- describe the accident; if a heart attack is suspected, say so immediately;
- indicate age of casualty or casualties.

Accidents

It is essential that people working in the kitchen are capable of using the tools and equipment in a manner which will neither harm themselves nor those with whom they work. Moreover, they should be aware of the causes of accidents and be able to deal with any that occur.

Accidents may be caused in various ways:

- excessive haste
- distraction
- failure to apply safety rules.

It should be remembered that most accidents could be prevented.

- Excessive haste – the golden rule of the kitchen is *never run*. This may be difficult to observe during a very busy service but excessive haste causes people to take chances which inevitably lead to mishaps.
- Distraction – accidents may be caused by not concentrating on the job in hand, through lack of interest, personal worry or distraction by someone else. The mind must always be kept on the work so as to reduce the number of accidents.

Reporting accidents

Any accident occurring on the premises where the employee works must be reported to the employer and a record of the accident must be entered in the Accident Book.

Full name of injured person:			
Occupation:		Supervisor:	
Time of accident:	Date of accident:	Time of report:	Date of report:
Nature of injury or condition:			
Details of hospitalisation:			
Extent of injury (after medical attention):			
Place of accident or dangerous occurrence:			
Injured person's evidence of what happened (include equipment/items/or other persons): *Use separate sheets if necessary*			
Witness evidence (1):		Witness evidence (2):	
Supervisor's recommendations:			
Date:	Supervisor's signature: *This form must be sent to the company health and safety officer*		

Fig 1.1: Sample in-house record of accidents and dangerous occurrences

Any accident causing death or major injury to an employee or member of the public must be reported by the employer to the Environmental Health Department. Accidents involving dangerous equipment must also be reported even if no one is injured.

First aid

As the term implies this is the immediate treatment on the spot to a person who has been injured or is ill. Since 1982 it has been a legal requirement that adequate first-aid equipment, facilities and personnel to give first aid are provided at work. If the injury is serious, the injured person should be treated by a doctor or nurse as soon as possible.

First aid equipment

A first aid box, as a minimum, should contain:

- a card giving general first-aid guidance
- 20 individually wrapped, sterile, adhesive, waterproof dressings of various sizes
- $4 \times 25\,g$ (1 oz) cotton wool packs
- 1 dozen safety pins
- 2 triangular bandages
- 2 sterile eye pads, with attachment
- 4 medium-sized sterile unmedicated dressings
- 2 large sterile unmedicated dressings
- 2 extra large sterile unmedicated dressings
- tweezers
- scissors
- a report book to record all injuries.

First-aid boxes must be easily identifiable and accessible in the work area. They should be in the charge of a responsible person, checked regularly and refilled when necessary.

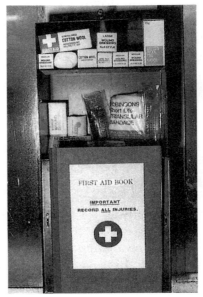

Fig 1.2: First aid kit and book

Shock

The signs of shock are faintness, sickness, clammy skin and a pale face. Shock should be treated by keeping the person comfortable, lying down and warm. Cover the person with a blanket or clothing, but do not apply hot water bottles.

Fainting

Fainting may occur after a long period of standing in a hot, badly ventilated kitchen. The signs of an impending faint are whiteness, giddiness and sweating. A faint should be treated by raising the legs slightly above the level of the head and, when the person recovers consciousness, putting the person in the fresh air for a while and making sure that the person has not incurred any injury in fainting.

Cuts

All cuts should be covered immediately with a blue coloured waterproof dressing, after the skin round the cut has been washed. When there is considerable bleeding it should be stopped as soon as possible. Bleeding may be controlled by direct pressure, by bandaging firmly on the cut. It may be possible to stop bleeding from a cut artery by pressing the artery with the thumb against the underlying bone; such pressure may be applied while a dressing or bandage is being prepared for application but not for more than 15 minutes.

Nose bleeds

Sit the person down with the head forward, and loosen clothing round the neck and chest. Ask them to breathe through the mouth and to pinch the soft part of the nose. After 10 minutes release the pressure. Warn the person not to blow the nose for several hours. If the bleeding has not stopped continue for a further 10 minutes. If the bleeding has not stopped then, or recurs in 30 minutes, obtain medical assistance.

Fractures

A person suffering from broken bones should not be moved until the injured part has been secured so that it is immobile. Medical assistance should be obtained.

Burns and scalds

Place the injured part gently under slowly running water or immerse in cool water, keeping it there for at least 10 minutes, or until the pain ceases. If serious, the burn or scald should then be covered with a clean cloth or dressing (preferably sterile) and the person sent immediately to hospital.

Do *not* use adhesive dressing, apply lotions or ointments or break blisters.

Electric shock

Switch off the current. If this is not possible, free the person by using a dry insulating material such as cloth, wood or rubber, taking care not to use bare hands otherwise the electric shock may be transmitted. If breathing has stopped, give artificial respiration and send for the doctor. Treat any burns as above.

Gassing

Do not let the gassed person walk, but carry them into the fresh air. If breathing has stopped, apply artificial respiration and send for a doctor.

Artificial respiration

There are several methods of artificial respiration. The most effective is mouth-to-mouth (mouth-to-nose) resuscitation and this method can be used by almost all age groups and in almost all countries.

It is stressed that all students should preferably complete a first-aid course run by the St John Ambulance, St Andrew's Ambulance Association or British Red Cross Society. Further information can be obtained from St John Ambulance Association, 1 Grosvenor Crescent, London SW1X 7EF.

MAINTAIN A SAFE ENVIRONMENT FOR CUSTOMERS, STAFF AND VISITORS

The reader should:

- know which hazards and potential hazards are to be identified;
- appreciate that preventative action is taken immediately where appropriate, in accordance with laid down procedures;
- appreciate hazards and report potential hazards to the appropriate person;
- recognise that all safety and emergency signs and notices are adhered to.

Prevention is better than cure. It is essential that everyone entering, staying in, working in or leaving an establishment can be certain they will not be exposed to (unnecessary) risks, accidents, dangers or rashness. Hazards and potential hazards should be identified and eliminated, thus preventing the occurrence of accidents.

Legislation

Every year in the UK a thousand people are killed at work, a million people suffer injuries and 23 million working days are lost annually because of industrial injury and disease. As catering is one of the largest employers of labour the catering industry is substantially affected by accidents at work.

In 1974 the *Health and Safety at Work Act* was passed with two main aims:

- to extend the coverage and protection of the law to all employers and employees;
- to increase awareness of safety amongst those at work, both employers and employees.

The law imposes a general duty on an employer 'to ensure so far as is reasonably practicable, the health, safety and welfare at work of all his employees'. The law also imposes a duty on every employee while at work to:

- take reasonable care for the health and safety of himself or herself and of other persons who may be affected by his or her acts or omissions at work;
- co-operate with his or her employer so far as is necessary to meet or comply with any requirement concerning health and safety;
- not interfere with, or misuse, anything provided in the interest of health, safety or welfare.

It can be clearly seen that both health and safety at work is everybody's responsibility. Furthermore the Act protects the members of the public who may be affected by the activities of those at work.

Penalties are provided by the Act which include improvement notices, prohibition notices and criminal prosecution. The Health and Safety Executive has been set up to enforce the law and the Health and Safety Commission will issue codes of conduct and act as advisers.

Responsibilities of the employer
The employer's responsibilities are to:

- provide and maintain premises and equipment that are safe and without risk to health;
- provide supervision, information and training;
- issue a written statement of 'safety policy' to employees to include:
  a general policy with respect to health and safety at work of employees;
  b the organisation, to ensure the policy is carried out;
  c how the policy will be made effective;
- consult with the employees' safety representative and to establish a Safety Committee.

Responsibilities of the employee
Employees, for their part, should:

- take reasonable care to avoid injury to themselves or to others by their work activities;
- co-operate with their employer and others so as to comply with the law;
- refrain from misusing or interfering with anything provided for health and safety.

Enforcement of the Act

Health and safety inspectors and local authority inspectors (Environmental Health Officers) have the authority to enforce the requirements of the Act. They are empowered to:

- issue a *prohibition notice* which immediately prevents further business until remedial action has been taken;
- issue an *improvement notice* whereby action must be taken within a stated time, to an employee, employer or supplier;
- *prosecute* any person breaking the Act. This can be instead of or in addition to serving a notice and may lead to a substantial fine or prison;
- seize, render harmless or destroy anything that the inspector considers to be the cause of imminent danger.

Preventive action

Anywhere that could be hazardous should be clearly indicated with appropriate signs and/or notices giving warning and, where suitable, the procedure to follow. It is everyone's responsibility to be on the look-out for hazards or potential hazards and report them to the appropriate person. Ensure that any specific procedures which may apply within the establishment are complied with. It is essential that all safety and emergency signs are followed. Notices and signs must never be tampered with.

Examples of notices which must be complied with are those sited by electrical machines with moving parts. Signs showing exit routes in the event of fire and notices that lifts must not be used if there is a fire must be clearly visible and situated in appropriate places. Exits must at all times be clear of obstruction with an illuminated exit sign over the door.

Safety

Identifying hazards, assessing risks and taking action to remove hazards is the concern of every employer and employee. Serious accidents must be reported. Most accidents in the catering industry are caused by:

- slips, trips and falls
- incorrect lifting
- burns, scalds and cuts.

It is desirable to develop a sense of awareness of potential hazards, in order to prevent accidents. Examples of hazards include:

- power plug 'on' when cleaning electrical equipment
- trailing electrical flexes
- faulty sockets (electrical)
- overloaded plugs (electrical)
- failure to replace lighting, bulbs or tubes
- not using correct steps to replace bulbs
- having wet hands when handling equipment and plugs
- gas pilot not alight
- main gas not igniting.

Precautions to obviate accidents or hazards include the following advice.

- Floors must be in good repair and free from obstacles.
- Spillages must be cleaned up at once.
- Warning notices of slippery floors need to be well displayed.
- Guards on machinery should be in place.
- Extra care is needed when guards are off during cleaning.
- Only one person at a time should operate machine.
- Never put hand or arm into bowl of electric mixer or cutter until stopped.
- Only dry untorn gloves or cloths should be used to handle hot pans, etc.
- Pan-handles should not protrude over the stove.
- Lift heavy items correctly to prevent back injury.
- Use a trolley to move heavy items.
- Finger guards and safety aprons may assist in preventing accidents.
- Never place knives in sinks.
- Use knives correctly so as to prevent accidents; if you have to carry knives, carry with points down; always lay down knives flat, not with blade pointing up.
- Signs must indicate potentially hazardous machinery and chemicals.
- Protective clothing should be worn, sleeves down, apron on.
- Protective footwear should be in good state of repair.

The Health and Safety at Work Act requires employers to have a procedure for reporting potential hazards; serious accidents must be reported to the HASAWA inspectors based usually at the Environmental Health Office.

MAINTAIN A SECURE ENVIRONMENT FOR CUSTOMERS, STAFF AND VISITORS

The reader should know:

- that establishment property is secured in accordance with laid down procedures;
- how customer, staff and storage areas are secured against unauthorised access;
- that keys are secured form unauthorised access at all times;
- that missing establishment staff or customers' property is reported to the appropriate person;
- that suspicious individuals are politely challenged or reported in accordance with laid down procedures;
- that lost property is dealt with in accordance with laid down procedures.

It is in the interests of everyone employed on the premises or using them that they should be safe and secure and feel safe and secure. Security applies to both the person and to their property and possessions. Risks to security can be caused by criminals such as thieves, muggers, rapists and terrorists and also by disturbed and possibly violent people. Therefore all areas and property should be secured from unauthorised access at all times so as to comply with the law and to prevent crime on the premises. It is the management's responsibility to install the procedures necessary and for employees to use the security system correctly.

Staff areas and facilities

Work areas that have lockable cupboards and drawers should be kept locked and the keys kept in a safe place. Personal items should be kept in a locker and the key kept on the person; however, money and items such as watches, rings, etc. are best kept on the person. Items of real or considerable value should not be brought into the workplace. Lockers can be broken into by a determined thief.

Storage areas

The food, drink and equipment stored in hotel and catering establishments are tempting to both the sneak thief and the practised criminal. Therefore all items must be kept under control by a secure system with a strict control procedure. This control would apply to all items in the dry stores, refrigerator and freezers since the more effective the control is, then the less temptation there is, and pilfering and stealing is reduced. Particular attention should be paid to expensive foods and to those most easily taken away on the person. Alcoholic drink is an item which is particularly tempting to those who may have a drink problem; strict control of stock is essential to reduce stealing.

Public areas

Places used by the public such as reception areas, lounges, restaurants, bars, toilets, etc. are where people may leave bags, brief cases or handbags on a seat or on the floor whereby an alert thief could steal them. Secure storage areas for luggage and safe deposit facilities should be available for valuables.

In all establishments providing accommodation, the keys and lock should be secure and the system of collecting and handing in of keys when entering or leaving the establishment is controlled and secure. If a key is lost then for security the lock must be changed. At all times keys should not be left in odd places such as in drawers but in a secure key cupboard. Keys should only be issued to authorised people, for example the person or persons who have booked accommodation in an hotel, the storekeeper, barman, or whoever is responsible for the contents and issuing of goods.

A sound effective security system is dependent on the responsible attitude and practice of the staff which in turn benefits everyone using the establishment.

Lost and missing property

Most establishments will have a procedure for dealing with such items. Details will be needed of:

- what is lost;
- when it was discovered that it was missing;
- where it was missing from;
- what action is taken to find the items should be known. When valuable or large quantities of items are missing then the police should be informed. Items which are found should be handed in to the management.

Other points to note

- Where cash is handled, for example in a canteen or store's restaurant, then extra vigilance is required, for example when the till is open, and when the takings are transported to the office after the service time. Cash should be kept in a secure place away from the public.
- Security procedures should be kept confidential and followed.
- If the security staff's role is to check on the possessions of employees leaving the premises in case of theft, then co-operation is expected.

- In the interests of security, do not ignore a person who may have mislaid the way, ask if they need help. If a stranger is being sought on the premises, and you are suspicious, do not endanger yourself immediately but report the incident to your supervisor.

Maintain a professional and hygienic appearance

1   Understand that clean, smart and appropriate clothing, footwear and head gear are worn in accordance with laid down procedures.
2   Identify that personal cleanliness and hygiene is maintained in accordance with laid down procedures.
3   Understand that hair, moustaches and beards are neat and tidy.
4   Know that jewellery, perfume and cosmetics are worn in accordance with laid down procedures.
5   Understand how cuts, grazes and wounds are treated in accordance with laid down procedures.
6   Know that illness and infections are reported in accordance with laid down procedures.

APPEARANCE

A *professional appearance* is one that conveys to other people the fact that the employee has pride in the job, pride in how they look and that their attitude to learning indicates interest, willingness and keenness as well as that they care. A *hygienic appearance* is indicated by high standards of personal cleanliness and is shown by cleanliness of hair, hands, face, clothing and shoes.

It is most important not only in the self-interest of the individual, but also to other food handlers and consumers, and in the interest of the reputation of the establishment, that professional and hygienic standards are practised. It is also a legal requirement that all involved in the preparation and cooking of food comply with the Food Hygiene Regulations.

PERSONAL HYGIENE

Good personal hygiene is essential to help prevent food-borne disease. Therefore the following points must be put into practice.

- Shower or bath daily.
- Wear clean uniform.

- Do not work if suffering from a communicable disease.
- Handle food as little as possible.
- Wash hands before and during work and after using the toilet.
- Keep hair clean and do not touch with hands.
- Keep fingernails clean and short.
- Do not touch nose and mouth with hands.
- Do not cough or sneeze over food; use a tissue.
- Do not wear rings, jewellery or watches.
- Do not smoke or allow smoking in food areas.
- Taste foods with a clean teaspoon.
- Do not sit on work surfaces.

Other points to note

- *Footwear* should be clean, safe, kept in good repair and be able to give protection should anything spill onto the feet.
- Suitable *head gear* should be worn at all times when food is handled.
- Hair, moustaches and beards should be neat, tidy and clean. An unshaven appearance indicates lack of care.
- Cuts, grazes, burns, etc. must be covered with a blue waterproof dressing, coloured so that, should it come off, it can be easily retrieved.
- Know whom you should inform if you are ill and liable to pass on infection.
- Persons suffering from vomiting, diarrhoea, sore throat or a head cold must not handle food.
- As soon as a person becomes aware that they are suffering from, or is a carrier of, typhoid, paratyphoid fever, salmonella or staphylococcal infection, the person responsible for the premises must be informed. This person must then inform the Medical Health Officer.

Maintain effective working relationships

1 Deal with members of staff in a polite and helpful manner at all times.
2 Deal with requests from other members of staff promptly and accurately, taking into account current work priorities.
3 Communicate essential information required by the organisation accurately to the appropriate personnel.
4 Reach agreement with colleagues regarding the division of work and work responsibilities.

5   Deal with any differences of opinion with other members of staff in a manner that maintains good will and respect and avoids offence and conflict.

6   Inform the immediate line manager in an appropriate level of detail about activities, progress and results.

7   See that difficulties affecting one's own ability to meet allocated responsibilities are promptly brought to the attention of immediate line manager.

8   Seek information and advice on matters within allocated area of responsibility from immediate line manager where necessary.

9   Treat line managers' comments constructively.

10   Check one's own understanding of points made by line managers actively and confirm.

WORKING WITH OTHERS

Working in the hotel and catering industry means that you will be working closely with other people; you are required to work with people not only in your own department but with people from other areas of the company or organisation.

Colleagues should aim to support each other. If someone is under pressure then you should try to lend a hand. This help, if freely and cheerfully given, will no doubt be reciprocated at a later date. Because of your actions, the customer may receive a better service or product.

Each member of staff is dependent on others successfully completing his or her job. Equipment will be used by a number of different people and it is important that each person keeps it in the appropriate condition for the next user. People who do their job badly make extra work for others.

WORKING WITH THE SUPERVISOR AND MANAGER, THE SECTIONAL CHEF AND HEAD CHEF

Your immediate boss whether it is the sectional chef, sous chef or head chef will need to know that they can rely on you. Part of their job is to delegate the work to others under their control: that could be you! You must be able to follow their instructions as well as to complete the tasks that they set. You must be able to accept constructive criticism from them. You should learn to recognise that positive criticism is valuable to improve working standards and customer care; it should not be taken personally.

BE POSITIVE

Being positive is really an attitude of mind. Positive thinkers make a habit of looking on the bright side, no matter how difficult the situation. It is a quite deliberate conscious process.

BE ASSERTIVE

Even for a positive thinker, it is often quite difficult to deal with people who are rude, short, get angry, interrupt you, blame you or keep you waiting. Faced with this problem some people give way submissively, others act aggressively.

The assertive person will openly and directly express their point of view and should also understand the other person's point of view.

COMMUNICATING WITH FELLOW WORKERS, SUPERVISORS AND MANAGERS

Some people find communicating with others easy, others find it more difficult. Communication involves the following:

- *Speaking* Verbal communication using the voice. You may have to give instructions or messages to other members of staff.
- *Listening* Aural communication using the ears. You will have to listen to instruction, take orders, attend briefings, meetings, etc.
- *Body language* Visual communication using the eyes.

Talking

Speech has certain characteristics which affect the message that is being spoken. 'Have a good day' can seem insincere or even sarcastic depending on how it is said, it should be communicated in a friendly positive way.

Volume
Loud speech often sounds bossy, while quiet speech can be interpreted as being 'soft'.

Pitch
An unnatural pitch usually sounds false so it is best for people with particularly high or deep voices not to try and disguise them. Some people's voices get higher in pitch if they become agitated or overexcited; this can turn into an irritating whine.

Tone

Warm tones if overdone can sound as if you are grovelling, while cool tones are very unwelcoming. A natural friendly tone will often yield results. It is not only *what* is said but *how* it is said.

Pace

Fast speech is not easy to follow but very slow speech is unwelcome – it has the effect of making the speaker sound stupid or can give the listener the impression that the speaker thinks that they are slow and not particularly bright. It is therefore important to communicate in a polite effective tone of speech which makes you both feel comfortable.

Listening

It is not only important for supervisors to be able to give orders but they must also be able to listen. People want to be listened to, they feel valued and at ease if someone is willing to listen to their views. You as a listener will also benefit, it will help you form better relationships with your fellow workers and supervisors.

Listening is a skill which has to be learnt. It involves the following:

- Maintain eye contact giving full attention and respect to the speaker. Do not let your mind wander or let it become distracted.
- Interest must be shown in full in what the speaker is saying. Interpretation or attempts to upstage the speaker should be avoided.
- Note the important information, points, criticisms, ignore all irrelevant detail.
- Act on what has been said, on the instruction and criticisms given. If necessary notes may be taken; you may also have to communicate to other staff in order for action to be taken.

Body language

Body language is an important vehicle of communication. Three quarters of all communications take place without words through body language. As a chef or manager if you become aware of it and identify the way you and others use it, it will give you more of an idea of what others' needs are, including customers'. You will have more control over your own behaviour and it will assist you in understanding your work colleagues.

You understand body language by watching others and then trying to relate this to yourself.

Facial expression

When people say to you 'you look tired', 'you look frightened', they are reading your body language. Your face is a powerful communicator: you may look happy, sad, joyful. It is telling others about your attitudes and feelings. People will receive messages during the conversation from your face and eyes, so there is no point in welcoming a new member of staff saying 'pleased to welcome you, looking forward to working with you', with dull eyes, corners of your mouth turned down, anger in your face because you fear he/she may threaten your position.

Remember 'friendship begins with a smile'.

Gestures

Gestures are also important. People use their hands in different ways to emphasise what they are saying. Some people use their hands more than others. Often gestures are used by some people in place of words. For example pointing as a means of communicating directions. It is unwise and rude to use gestures without words.

Gaze

Look at people when you are communicating, it will help you read the expression on the other person's face and will assist them in getting the message across.

Space

It is advisable not to stand too close to the person you are talking to; you will soon realise that the person is too close because they will begin to back off and look uncomfortable.

Obstacles are often used by people to display attitudes and feelings. Such obstacles could be the office desk to separate you and the person that you are speaking to. Some people use this to demonstrate their authority. Where possible this should be avoided as it can make junior members of staff uneasy and this will not promote good communication and understanding.

It is important to understand body language because it helps:

- to identify the leader in a group;
- to notice when someone is unsure of what to do and where to go;
- to notice when someone is tired, frustrated, impatient or angry;
- to identify a suspicious character;
- to know when to make a suggestion;
- to know when to give an order, command or direction.

If working in a food service situation, it helps:

- to know when to present the menu and to whom;

- to know when to present the bill to the customer;
- to identify the host;
- to know when to serve the next course or to clear the table;
- to notice when a customer is unhappy or not pleased but is reluctant to complain.

Remember body language is not a list of hard and fast rules; it varies according to situations, to customs and to the culture. Body language does vary amongst individual groups and races, sex, age and individual personality.

Chefs and managers use body language to instruct, give direction and to train people within their department. The trainee or student will in turn often match this body language to create a good atmosphere and to demonstrate understanding.

Examples of information used in Food Production that has to be communicated to others in order to achieve an effective working relationship.

- Number of meals needed to be prepared, special orders, parties, functions, etc.
- Problems associated with equipment, staffing, food orders.
- Details relating to health and safety, in particular food safety.
- Details of future planning, bookings, holiday dates.

People working in teams can achieve far more than individuals. Winners will often be working for the team whose function is critical to the success of the operation. Teamwork is essential in a busy kitchen to achieve the goals. Teamwork can be identified as the following:

- Everyone working to the same objective.
- Everyone pulling their weight.
- Each member of the team ready to support one another.
- Every member of the team accepts the others.
- Going to do something that an individual has overlooked and finding it has already been done.
- Getting help when it is needed.
- Everyone getting 'stuck in' to retrieve a disaster.
- Everyone pitching in without complaint when there is a crisis.
- Enjoying each other's successes, commiserating with others' setbacks.
- Sharing success and failure.
- Having people, who understand, to talk to.
- Enjoying working with the team.
- All dancing to the same tune.

Contribute to the development of self and others

1   Welcome new staff to the work area and familiarise them with relevant facilities.
2   Explain basic work routines and local procedures accurately and in sufficient detail to enable understanding.
3   Encourage new staff to ask relevant questions and seek clarification of areas of which they are unsure.
4   Advise and assist new staff constructively in the initial performance of allocated work activities.
5   Respond to requests for support willingly and courteously.
6   Justify the extent and nature of support in terms of the requirements of the work activities and the individual.
7   Review the individual's own performance and competence level against identified requirements.
8   Make constructive contributions to discussions concerning issues relating to work.
9   Identify current competence and potential areas for development in conjunction with the supervisor.
10 Make sure the objectives set are achievable, realistic and challenging.
11 Review progress and performance in achieving set objectives regularly with the line manager.
12 Use feedback from the supervisor to enhance future development.

FAMILIARISE NEW STAFF WITH THE WORKPLACE

Any new member of staff must be given a good induction programme and should immediately begin to feel part of the team and organisation. An induction programme should include a briefing on the organisation or company with discussion on:

- organisation chart
- conditions of employment
- benefits
- customers
- fire procedures and evacuation
    fire exits
    access and egress procedures
    first aid procedures.

With an introduction to all members of staff, the induction may also require the person to undertake the food hygiene and health and safety course. When the new member of staff enters the kitchen they should be introduced to the menu and daily requirements. Instruction will need to be given on:

- what has to be done;
- how it has to be done;
- when it had to be done;
- where it has to be done.

The individual will need to familiarise him/herself with the work area and the kitchen flow for each preparation and service area, how the raw material enters the kitchen and how it is processed. The methods of communication need to be explained: these may feature on staff notice boards or company bulletin, but how the orders are communicated to the kitchen staff is important.

SUPPORT OTHERS IN THE PERFORMANCE OF THEIR WORK

We have already discussed how important teamwork is (page 22) to achieve the organisational goals. In developing the team we have also said how important it is to support one another.

Support can be given to others by:

- knowing the skills that are required in the team and assisting others to achieve these skills;
- generating enthusiasm and commitments by believing in yourself and others;
- establishing standards and working to them;
- building good relationships and developing a positive polite manner; accepting different points of view and listening carefully;
- developing a common working language that can be easily understood.

Our personal relationships at work depend heavily in the quality of our communications:

- Know the amount and the limitations of the support you can give.
- Assess your performance against the other members of the team.

Examples of these relationships include:

- Have you been pulling your weight in the team?
- Have you given assistance and support when it has been required?
- Has the day shift left sufficient mise en place for the evening shift?

- Is the team working as a team? Are some individuals deliberately disrupting the team in order to seek attention or recognition?
- Give careful consideration to proposals different from your own.
- Review your progress over time and assess your own further training needs with your supervisors.

DEVELOPING SELF WITHIN THE JOB ROLE

Self knowledge is invaluable to any one seriously intent on choosing the right career path. A good chef needs a range of skills and knowledge which comes with experience. You will need to practise your food preparation skills, seek advice, use others' strengths and work hard. Self assessment is always a good starting point.

To know how you function in the workplace, what you are best at and what you are worst at, is all part of knowing yourself.

To an employer first impressions are important. It will begin to form their attitude towards you and towards your place of work. Personal hygiene is of paramount importance when working in food preparation (see pages 16–17). What you look like can say a great deal about you and your attitude to:

- your work
- your place of work
- your colleagues
- yourself.

The way you stand, the way you sit will also have an effect on the first impression. You should aim at being:

- tidy
- smart
- friendly
- helpful.

A tidy posture is controlled, an untidy posture is fidgety and often fussy. A smart posture is upright, the opposite is a shuffle. A friendly posture is welcoming, an unfriendly posture is where you are not facing the customer. A helpful posture is an attentive one, an unhappy posture is being in a world of your own.

KNOWING YOURSELF

This is important if you are to develop within your role. It enables you to arm yourself with the equipment to make correct choices concerning your role, your job and your life.

Question yourself about your needs, your personality, your strengths and weaknesses and your values.

Be aware that your body, your thoughts, your attitudes may be changing. It is important to keep up-to-date with yourself. Be prepared to change, concentrate on your strengths; winning is about putting your strengths to the forefront, without ignoring your weaknesses.

Constructive feedback on your performance from your colleagues and supervisor is important, if acted upon positively. This feedback can assist you in your personal development. From this you may be able to set yourself tasks and objectives that will eventually help you with your self development.

Remember:

- Believe in yourself.
- List your strengths and weaknesses.
- Listen to feedback.
- Set yourself objectives.
- Practise your skills.
- Concentrate on your personal hygiene and appearance.
- Avoid personal bad habits.
- Create good impressions.
- Be polite and friendly.
- Be assertive.
- Become a team player.
- Be determined to reach your career goal.

Selection, use and care of knives and small equipment

1   Keep knives clean to satisfy food hygiene regulations.
2   Keep knives sharp to satisfy health and safety regulations.
3   Clean and sharpen knives in accordance with laid down procedures.
4   Handle and store knives in accordance with laid down procedures.
5   Take appropriate action to deal with unexpected situations within an individual's responsibility.
6   Explain that all work is carried out in an organised and efficient manner taking account of priorities and laid down procedures.

Knives must be handled with respect, used correctly and taken care of so that a professional performance can be achieved. Blunt knives are likely to be the cause of accidents since more pressure has to be applied than if a sharp knife is used. Sharp knives enable the work to be completed more quickly with less expenditure of energy and with better finish, thus giving greater job satisfaction.

SAFETY RULES

Always observe the rules of safety for the benefit of yourself and others.

- If carried, the knife point must be held downwards.
- Knives on the table must be placed flat so that the blade is not exposed upwards.
- Do not allow knives to project over the edge of the table.
- When using knives keep your mind and eye on the job in hand.
- Use the correct knife for the correct purpose.
- Always keep knives sharp.
- After use, always wipe the knife with the blade away from the hand.
- Keep the handle of the knife clean when in use.
- Never leave knives lying in the sink.
- Never misuse knives; a good knife is a good friend but it can be a dangerous weapon.
- After use, knives should be carefully washed in warm water with detergent, thoroughly rinsed and dried, and safely put away.

To assist in preventing cross-contamination, colour coding of knife handles can be used, eg:

- *Brown* for cooked meat.
- *Blue* for raw fish.
- *Red* for raw meat.
- *Yellow* for cooked fish.
- *Green* for vegetables.

The establishment's procedures must be checked and followed.

SELECTING THE RIGHT KNIFE FOR THE CORRECT PURPOSE

Specific tools have been designed for certain functions to be performed in the kitchen so that work can be done successfully.

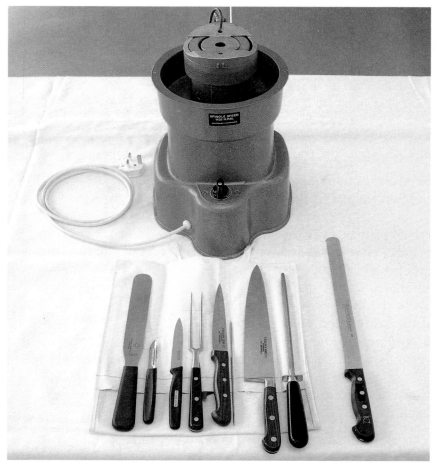

Plate 1.3: Knives and small equipment

A basic set of tools could comprise the following:

1   vegetable peeler – peeling vegetables and fruit;
2   vegetable knife 10 cm (4 inch) blade – general use, vegetables and fruit;
3   filleting knife 15 cm (6 inch) blade – filleting fish (flexible);
4   medium large knife 25 cm (10 inch) blade – shredding, slicing, chopping;
5   carving knife – in addition when and if needed for carving;
6   boning knife – in addition when and if needed for butchery;
7   palette knife – spreading, turning items over and lifting;
8   trussing needle – trussing poultry and game;
9   fork – lifting and holding joints of meat;
10   steel – sharpening knives.

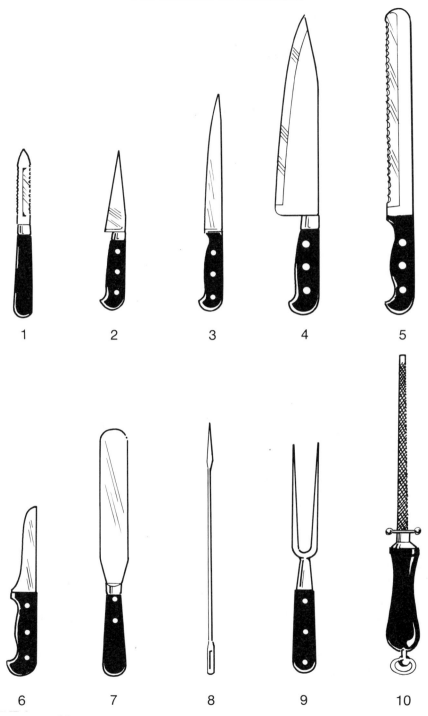

Fig 1.3: A basic set of knives

Even with the correct tool there are occasions when extra care needs to be taken.

- There will be less control with the use of a knife to cut side-ways than to cut downwards, e.g. cross-cuts when chopping onion or slicing long sandwich loaves lengthwise.
- When shredding or chopping keep the finger tips and nails clear of the blade since they are not visible all the time. When chopping, keep the fingers of the hand, which is not holding the handle, on top of the blade.
- Never bone out or fillet frozen meat or fish in the frozen state; however, when thawed the centre may still be very cold and cause the fingertips to numb. Cuts are then more likely to occur.
- When using a large knife use the thumb and first finger on the sides of the blade near the handle so as to control the sideways as well as the downward movement of the knife.
- When using a trussing needle take extra care when drawing the needle and string upwards towards the face.
- When scoring pork rind take care lest the surface being scored offers varying degrees of resistance, causing the knife to go out of control.

SHARPENING

Two tools are available for sharpening knives: a steel, which should be well grooved, and a carborundum stone, which should not be too coarse as a saw edge may result. Periodically knives will require to be ground which is usually done by a knife grinder.

When using a stone *always* draw the blade of the knife away from the hand holding the stone because few stones are provided with a guard. When using a steel, for preference use one with a guard. Should you however have a steel with no guard *always* draw the knife being sharpened away from you. When using a stone or a steel, angle the blade of the knife to 45° and sharpen alternate sides of the knife using considerable pressure and drawing almost the whole length of the blade edge along the stone or steel. Having used the stone always follow up by using the steel and then wipe the knife on a cloth before use. The reason for drawing the knife across at an angle is to produce an edge to the blade, and to obtain a sharp edge it is necessary to apply both sides of the blade to the steel or stone. As the stone produces a rough edge it is necessary to follow with a steel to provide a smooth sharp edge. The knife must be wiped after use of the stone since small particles of the stone will adhere to the blade.

The steel may be used in three ways. Whichever way is chosen, take care to sharpen the knife safely.

1   Holding the steel in one hand and the knife in the other (right-handed people will hold the knife in the right hand), draw the blade down the steel at an angle of 45° some six or seven times on each side of the steel (thus both sides of the blade), exerting pressure. Before doing so, *check* that the steel has a guard.

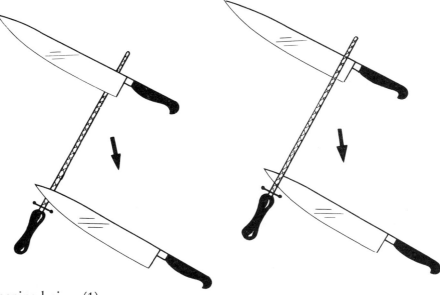

Fig 1.4: Sharpening knives (1)

2   Holding the steel and knife as (1), draw the knife away from you towards the end of the steel at an angle of 45° some six or seven times on each side of the steel (thus both sides of the blade), exerting pressure.

Fig 1.5: Sharpening knives (2)

3 Placing the pointed end of the steel on the wooden block or heavy board, draw the knife downwards towards the block at an angle of 45° exerting pressure and making certain the steel does not slip. As with the two previous methods, both sides of the blade are drawn down the steel some six or seven times for each side.

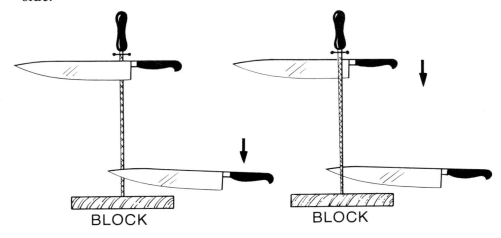

Fig 1.6: Sharpening knives (3)

To test for sharpness, slice the skin of a tomato as a good indicator. To retain sharpness always use a wooden surface or suitable cutting surface of a cutting board. Never cut on stainless steel. Clean knives during and after use and particularly after using on acid items such as lemon. Stains on the blade can be cleaned with a fine cleaning powder or abrasive pad.

Stainless steel knives for professional cooks are available which may need less sharpening as they retain their sharpness and of course do not stain.

A good craftsman or craftswoman never blames their tools, since they always take care of them.

SMALL EQUIPMENT

In addition to the range of chef's knives, there are a number of other small implements in general use. It is important always to buy good quality equipment and to wash and dry it thoroughly after each use. Some examples include:

Cook's forks

These are obtainable in several shapes and sizes and are used:

- for holding hot and cold meats in place whilst carving; it is sensible practice to use a fork with a guard for this purpose in case the knife should slip;
- for turning large pieces of meat or poultry being roasted or braised; do not pierce the meat if possible otherwise the meat juices will seep out, resulting in loss of flavour and moisture.

Cook's tongs

These are used:

- for turning small pieces of food during cooking;
- in place of hands or forks when removing foods for dressing-up ready for service; tongs are more efficient than forks for handling small items of food and, in addition, there is no risk of piercing the foods.

Vegetable peelers

These are obtainable in several patterns, for example:

- fixed blade, English type;
- fixed blade, French type – this usually removes a thinner skin from the vegetable or fruit;
- swivel blade – this takes a little practice to use effectively but, once mastered, it can be used very swiftly and economically;
- combined peeler and apple corer.

Vegetable groovers

These are usually obtainable in two types and are used for grooving and decorating lemons, oranges, limes and carrots:

- top cutter
- side cutter.

Vegetable cutters

These are scoop-shaped implements obtainable usually in five shapes:

- pea-shaped round (referred to as a Solferino cutter);
- small ball-shaped round (referred to as a Parisienne cutter);
- slightly larger ball-shaped round (referred to as a Noisette cutter);
- plain oval shape (referred to as an Olivette cutter);
- fluted oval shape.

The last four are generally used for cutting potatoes, hence Parisienne, Noisette and Olivette potatoes.

Trussing and larding needles

These are obtainable in several sizes suitable for large and small joints of meat or different sizes of poultry or game (e.g. 20 kg (40 lb) turkey; 500 g (1 lb) grouse).

Kitchen scissors and secateurs

Scissors are chiefly used for trimming fish and secateurs for jointing game and poultry.

Pastry cutting wheels

These are obtainable with plain or fluted edges and are used for cutting ravioli, canneloni and other pastry shapes.

Citrus fruit zesters

These are obtainable in several types and used for removing the zest-filled top layer of citrus skin in ribbons ranging in width from fine filaments to thicker sized twists.

Cleaning of cutting equipment

1 Demonstrate that equipment is correctly turned off and dismantled before and during cleaning.
2 Plan work and allocate time appropriately to meet daily schedules.
3 Clean equipment in accordance with laid down procedures.
4 Use correct cleaning equipment and materials and store after use.
5 Make sure that cleaned equipment is dry and ready for use to satisfy health, safety and hygiene regulations.

GENERAL

When cleaning machines used for cutting, both manual and electrically driven, great care must be taken to prevent accidents. Persons under 18 years of age must not use or clean any mechanical machine and this is a legal requirement. A notice must be displayed by each machine stating instructions for use and safety precautions.

- Equipment must be correctly turned off before dismantling for cleaning.
- Cleaning should occur at a time convenient to working schedules.
- If guards have to be removed to facilitate cleaning, extra care must be taken so as to avoid accidents.
- Cleaning procedures must be followed where specified.
- Correct cleaning materials and equipment should be used.
- Having cleaned, washed and dried the equipment, re-assemble correctly and check that it is ready for use.
- Any attachments should be cleaned, dried and stored correctly.
- The area around machines should be left clean and dry.

Cutting blades are sharp and can easily cause serious cuts; however, machines must be thoroughly cleaned otherwise food particles left in machines will contaminate other foods when the machine is next used.

Power driven machines include mixing machines, mincers, choppers, slicers. The cleaning procedure is as follows:

- Switch off the machine and remove the plug.
- Remove particles of food with a cloth, palette knife, needle or brush as appropriate.
- Thoroughly clean with hand-hot detergent water all removable and fixed parts, paying particular attention to threads and plates with holes on mincers.
- Rinse thoroughly.
- Dry and re-assemble.
- While cleaning see that exposed blades are not left uncovered or unguarded.
- Guards must be replaced when cleaning is completed.
- Any specific makers' instructions should be observed.
- Test that the machine is properly assembled by plugging in and switching on.

Mandolin

This piece of equipment must be used with care since the very sharp cutting blade can cause a nasty accident. When using the mandolin for slicing vegetables or potatoes such as game chips or wafers, it is essential to be extra careful when the items being sliced have nearly all been sliced. Constantly make certain that no part of the hand, thumb or fingers come into contact with the blade. Do not exert too much pressure and use water on the article being sliced to enable it to move smoothly. Take particular care when cleaning the mandolin and, as a precaution, close the blade so that the cutting edge is not exposed.

Graters

Graters should be used with care particularly when the item being grated becomes small and the fingers are close to the grater. It is important to clean graters thoroughly since food particles could become lodged in the holes. This is best done by holding under a water tap with pressure and using a brush to clean thoroughly.

MECHANICAL EQUIPMENT

Listed under the Prescribed Dangerous Machines Order 1964 are:

Power-driven

- Worm-type mincing machines.
- Rotary knife bowl-type chopping machines.
- Dough mixers.
- Food mixing machines when used with attachments for mincing, slicing, chipping or other cutting operations or for making breadcrumbs.
- Pie and tart machines.
- Vegetable slicing machines.

Power-driven or manual

- Circular knife slicing machines for cutting bacon and other foods.
- Potato chipping machines.

The document giving manufacturers instructions must be available and a record of maintenance should be sited near the machine.

SAFETY PRECAUTIONS

Machines should not be overloaded since this will affect the effectiveness of the machine and may cause it to breakdown. Signs of overloading will be an abnormal sound and slowing down. Should this occur switch off immediately and reduce the load.

When liquidising hot foods, allow to cool and make certain the cover or lid is firmly in place before switching on. When using food slicers ensure that:

- no bone is included in the food to be sliced;
- guards are in place;
- only one person operates the machine;

- only persons instructed in the use of the machine are allowed to use it;
- handles are free of grease.

Maintain clean food production areas, equipment and utensils; food hygiene

1   Plan all work and allocate time appropriately to meet daily schedules.
2   Maintain all food surfaces in a clean and tidy manner to satisfy health, safety and food hygiene legislation.
3   Dispose all rubbish and waste food correctly and make sure that containers are clean and ready for use.
4   Take appropriate action to deal with unexpected situations using an individual's responsibility.
5   Demonstrate that all work is carried out in an organised and efficient manner.
6   Maintain, clean and reassemble all equipment and utensils in accordance with health, safety and food hygiene regulations.
7   Store equipment and utensils properly after use.

Hygiene is the science and practice of maintaining health and preventing disease and is one of the most important subjects for anyone working in the hotel and catering industry. It should be studied, understood and practised in every working day. Personal hygiene is as important as food hygiene. This is covered on pages 16–17.

In every catering establishment providing food it is essential that:

- persons employed are hygienic in themselves and work hygienically;
- ingredients to be used arrive, are stored and prepared in a hygienic manner;
- premises, equipment and utensils are kept clean and maintained hygienically.

Therefore kitchen, personal and food hygiene are interrelated factors in a clean and safe environment for food production. It is essential that a plentiful supply of hot water is always available and cleaning equipment, brushes, cloths, etc., as well as suitable detergent and bactericide are provided. Unsuitable and inadequate provisions of suitable cleaning equipment and materials would be contrary to legal health and safety requirements and would jeopardise the health of customers and staff. Should premises not come up to legal requirements of the Health and Safety at Work Act, the Environmental Health Officer can enforce a closure order.

CLEAN FOOD PRODUCTION AREAS

Hygiene in the kitchen is of paramount importance. Initially the premises should be constructed in a manner that eases maintenance and cleaning. It is essential that the areas where food is prepared and cooked are well lit and ventilated, that the layout of equipment enables floors and walls and also ceilings to be cleaned easily. A maintenance and cleaning rota should be produced so that systematic cleaning is ensured.

Sinks, handbasins, drains, gullies, traps and overflows must at all times be kept clean; failure to do so could lead to blockages and flooding and to the multiplication of harmful bacteria. Gullies and overflows can also be passageways for vermin. Any evidence of vermin such as droppings or run marks should be reported immediately to a supervisor.

Work surfaces should be thoroughly cleaned and as far as practicable, kept clean during use; the maxim 'clean as you go' is particularly apt. A sterilising solution according to manufacturer's instructions should be used to clean the work surfaces in order to prevent the growth or spread of germs.

Shelves, cupboards and drawers should be kept clean, particularly cupboards and drawers, since out of sight corners can be breeding grounds for insects and pests. Cupboards and drawers used for keeping clean materials and equipment need particular attention since they may be overlooked, whereas drawers containing tools are used frequently. Harmful cleaning materials, such as bleach, should be stored clearly marked, away from other items.

Knives should be kept in a clean drawer with blades all facing the same way. 'A place for everything and everything in its place' should enable tidy, clean storage areas to assist those at work in being methodical and not wasting time.

Food waste and refuse disposal areas should always be kept clean and tidy. Frequent clearing away of rubbish is essential so as to prevent smells and infestation by flies. The production area should not have an accumulation of food waste since smells may attract pests. Disposable containers are best used as they are easily handled. Plastic sacks are not porous and do not readily break. Bins and lids should be kept clean and the lid should always be used so that the bin contents are covered. Rubbish and waste food bins should be scrubbed and scoured clean inside and out. Wastemasters, where installed, should be used only for soft kitchen waste which will be disposed of in the machine. Bones, tins and any other firm rubbish should not be disposed of in this manner.

The area around food waste and rubbish containers must be kept clean at all times. Commonsense should be used. If, for example, bins have not been emptied, employees should inform their employer of such a situation.

Good ventilation will provide fresh air, remove smells and hot air, thus making a more hygienic and congenial atmosphere in which to work.

Signs should be sited in areas cordoned off in the event of the floor being flooded; in any case a warning sign should indicate that a floor is wet. Any spillage should be cleared up as quickly as possible.

All cleaning should be done efficiently in an organised way so as not to interrupt the smooth working of a kitchen. Correct cleaning and handling of waste helps prevent:

- accidents
- contamination
- fire hazard
- pest infestation
- unpleasant odours
- pollution of the environment.

It also complies with the law.

Cleaning of surfaces

- *Metal*: wash with hot detergent water; rinse with hot water containing a sterilising agent; alternatively use a chemical which acts as both detergent and steriliser in hot water.
- *Tiles*: thoroughly wash with hot water containing detergent and dry.
- *Paint*: wash with hot detergent and dry with a cloth.
- *Glass*: wash well using a leather or clean cloth; a window-cleaning agent may be used in accordance with manufacturers instructions; polish with a clean cloth.
- *Vinyl or linoleum*: clean well with a machine or by hand using hot detergent water and dry off; when wet put up warning notices.
- *Laminate*: use hot water containing combined detergent and sterilising agent then dry with clean cloth.

Anti-bacterial cleansers which do not require rinsing are available in spray containers for cleaning surfaces.

CLEANING FOOD PRODUCTION EQUIPMENT

Food production equipment which may be operated by gas or electricity must be used with care, properly cleaned and maintained in efficient working order. This assists in the smooth running of the kitchen, helps prevent accidents and enables the premises to have a good standard of hygiene. If equipment does not work effectively then planning schedules cannot be met. An organised kitchen needs skilled, efficient staff but also sufficient clean and well maintained equipment such as ovens, ranges, fryers, grills and hot plates.

After each use, large equipment items such as ranges, salamanders, hot plates, etc. should be cleaned. This should be done without disturbing the smooth working of the kitchen and carried out at convenient times. Gas or electricity supply must be turned off before equipment is dismantled and cleaned and turned on only when the equipment has been re-assembled. Turn the equipment on then to test that the supply is working correctly. This will prevent accidents and complies with the law.

The procedure for cleaning large equipment is as follows:

- Turn off the fuel supply.
- Wash with hot water containing detergent; do not use more water than necessary.
- Soak any foods adhering to the equipment then gently scrape off without scratching the surfaces.
- Rinse, using sufficient water.
- Dry the equipment.
- Re-assemble any parts that had been removed.
- Test that equipment is functioning.

Other points to note include:

- Use cleaning equipment and materials according to the establishment's procedures and manufacturer's instruction.
- Store cleaning equipment and materials in the appropriate place.
- Do not damage surfaces to be cleaned by scratching with wire wool or bleaching pads.
- In the event of equipment not working satisfactorily, do not ignore it; report the fault. Should you inadvertently damage any part or parts, inform your supervisor or tutor.

Ovens, hobs, ranges

For *electrical* equipment, turn off the electricity supply. Remove the plug. Do not use more water than necessary to clean the surfaces. Use a hot detergent water and dry when clean. Do not scratch surfaces. Replace plug and check that supply is available.

For *gas* equipment, turn off taps that supply fuel to the appliance. Clean thoroughly with hot detergent water. Remove those parts of hobs which can be cleaned separately. Clean these and the hob tops; replace and check that they fit correctly. Check that pilot lights are functioning; test by turning on gas taps only if pilot is alight. If pilot light is off, inform your supervisor at once.

Grills, salamanders, griddles

Check that fuel supply is off. Thoroughly clean grill bars (in a suitable sink if convenient) by scrubbing or scraping the bars clean. Ensure that the tray or area beneath the bars is clean. Re-assemble correctly and check fuel supply.

With salamanders, ensure that the top is clean. Take care not to clean salamanders when hot.

Griddles should be cleaned very carefully; scrape gently with a plastic scraper, clean with a cloth very thoroughly and oil lightly.

Fryers

Ensure that the fuel supply is off. When cool, drain off the oil and *close* the tap. Clean interior by removing any small particles in the base of the fryer and wipe clean. Hot detergent water may be needed to clean the exterior. Finally rinse and dry. Ensure that the drain tap is closed and add clean oil.

Bains-marie

After use, remove all containers and drain off the water; clean thoroughly with hot water containing detergent; rinse and dry. *Close* the drain tap. Refill with clean water or leave empty ready for use.

Hotplates

Check that the hot plate has cooled down before cleaning. Remove any food and wipe top shelves and base with hot water with detergent; rinse and dry. Ensure that door runners are clean.

CLEANING FOOD PRODUCTION UTENSILS

All small equipment used in the kitchen must be clean and maintained in a hygienic manner so that it can be used effectively. It must be stored so that it is readily available, and also stay clean when not in use. Cleaning methods should not damage items, e.g. do not bang sieves or conical strainers to clear the holes. Items which are damaged and may cause accidents, e.g. a broken mandolin, should not be used but reported to your supervisor or tutor; likewise a broken sieve, which cannot be properly cleaned.

Items which require particular attention when being cleaned include sieves, conical strainers and colanders because food particles are difficult to dislodge. Therefore, they should be cleaned immediately after use.

Pots and pans

Remove any food particles; if any food sticks to the pan, soak to soften in cold water. Clean in very hot washing-up water containing detergent, rinse, dry and store so that the pans remain clean.

Bowls, dishes, moulds

Remove any food and wash thoroughly in hot water containing detergent; rinse, dry and store in a clean place.

Whisks

The whole item including the handle should be thoroughly cleaned in hot water containing detergent. Particular attention should be paid to where the wires meet at the base.

Sieves, strainers, colanders

Wash immediately after use. Use the full power of water from the tap to wash through the mesh. Move up and down in the sink of hot water so that the water goes through the mesh. The bristles of a stiff brush may be used to dislodge obstinate food particles. Wash thoroughly, rinse and dry.

Graters

Food particles are likely to lodge in graters. Wash under the running tap and use a stiff brush to clean. Wash well, rinse and dry.

Peelers, zesters, corers

After use wash thoroughly, rinse and dry. A brillo pad can be used to clean peelers.

Tin openers

Extra care is needed to clean the cutting edge of tin openers as food or metal particles can get caught between the blade and the part of the opener by the blade. Wash well, rinse and dry.

Stainless steel items

Wash with hot water containing detergent, rinse with hot water containing a sterilising agent. Do not use abrasive or wire wool or material which could scratch the surface.

Teflon items

Care should be taken when cleaning teflon-coated items. Avoid abrasives which scratch and remove teflon, causing the containers to lose their non-stick quality.

Wooden items

Scrub with a bristle brush and hot water containing detergent; rinse and dry thoroughly. If items are left wet, cracks can appear in the surface.

Plastic items

Wash in reasonably hot water containing detergent and rinse.

Porcelain and earthenware

Soak if necessary; remove all food particles with a brush. Avoid extreme heat and do not clean with an abrasive. Wash in hot water and rinse in very hot water.

FOOD HYGIENE

Unless preserved, foods deteriorate; to keep them in an edible condition it is necessary to know what causes food spoilage. In the air, there are certain micro-organisms called moulds, yeasts and bacteria which cause food to decompose, putrefy and go sour; the food then discolours, smells unpleasant and/or becomes sticky or slimy.

Moulds

These are simple plants which appear like whiskers on foods, particularly sweet foods, meat and cheese. To grow they require warmth, moisture, air, darkness and a medium; they are killed by heat and sunlight. Moulds can grow where there is too little moisture for yeasts and bacteria to grow. Correct storage in a cold dry store prevents moulds from forming.

Yeasts

These are single-cell plants or organisms, larger than bacteria, that grow on foods

DEPARTMENT OF HEALTH

ASSURED SAFE CATERING · CRITICAL CONTROL POINTS

Step	Hazard		Action
1 **Purchase**	High-risk* (ready-to-eat) foods contaminated with food-poisoning bacteria or toxins (Poisons produced by bacteria).		Buy from reputable supplier only. Specify maximum temperature at delivery.
2 **Receipt of food**	High-risk* (ready-to-eat) foods contaminated with food-poisoning bacteria or toxins.		Check it looks, smells and feels right. Check the temperature is right.
3 **Storage**	Growth of food poisoning bacteria, toxins on high-risk* (ready-to-eat) foods. Further contamination.		High-risk* foods stored at safe temperatures. Store them wrapped. Label high-risk foods with the correct 'sell by' date. Rotate stock and use by recommended date.
4 **Preparation**	Contamination of High-risk* (ready-to-eat) foods. Growth of food-poisoning bacteria.		Wash your hands before handling food. Limit any exposure to room temperatures during preparation. Prepare with clean equipment, and use this for high-risk* (ready-to-eat) food only. Separate cooked foods from raw foods.
5 **Cooking**	Survival of food-poisoning bacteria.		Cook rolled joints, chicken, and re-formed meats eg. burgers, so that the thickest part reaches at least 75°C. Sear the outside of other, solid meat cuts (eg. joints of beef, steaks) before cooking.
6 **Cooling**	Growth of any surviving spores or food poisoning bacteria. Production of poisons by bacteria. Contamination with food-poisoning bacteria.		Cool foods as quickly as possible. Don't leave out at room temperatures to cool, unless the cooling period is short, eg place any stews or rice, etc, in shallow trays and cool to chill temperatures quickly.
7 **Hot-holding**	Growth of food-poisoning bacteria. Production of poisons by bacteria.		Keep food hot, above 63°C.
8 **Reheating**	Survival of food-poisoning bacteria.		Reheat to above 75°C.
9 **Chilled storage**	Growth of food-poisoning bacteria.		Keep temperature at right level. Label high-risk ready-to-eat foods with correct date code.
10 **Serving**	Growth of disease-causing bacteria. Production of poisons by bacteria. Contamination.		COLD SERVICE FOODS - serve high-risk foods as soon as possible after removing from refrigerated storage to avoid them getting warm. HOT FOODS - serve high-risk foods quickly to avoid them cooling down.

A. *High-risk foods are those which may easily support the growth of food poisoning organisms and won't be cooked any further before you serve them, for example; cooked fish, meat patés, cooked egg dishes, pre-prepared dairy products that may only be re-heated.
B. Some food-poisoning bacteria can form spores which may survive cooking.

If cooling is delayed or takes a long time, these spores may grow or produce toxins (poisons). After cooking, food should be cooled quickly to prevent or reduce this. The list above is not exhaustive but shows some of the hazards likely to be present in any operation. In your catering operation you may be able to identify other hazards not listed above. If you do so make sure you control these as well.

Plate 1.4: Control of hygiene in food preparation (courtesy of Department of Health)

containing moisture and sugar. Foods containing a small percentage of sugar and a large percentage of liquid such as fruit juices and syrups are liable to ferment because of yeasts. Yeasts increase food spoilage, therefore food stuffs should be refrigerated. The ability of yeast to feed on sugar and produce alcohol is the basis of the beer and wine-making industry. Yeasts are destroyed by heat.

Bacteria

Bacteria (or germs), which cause disease, are one-celled plants that can grow and spread. There are two kinds of bacteria which concern the caterer:

- helpful bacteria which assist in the manufacture of items such as cheese and yoghurt;
- harmful bacteria which caterers, cooks and other food handlers must be aware of, understand, and most importantly develop positive procedures and attitudes in their place of work to counteract the risks.

Transference of bacteria

Bacteria cannot move on their own. They must be carried by any of the following:

- hands
- cuts, sores and burns
- coughs and sneezes
- other foods
- unclean equipment, utensils and work surfaces
- air
- water
- insects or birds
- vermin
- poor waste disposal.

Cross-contamination means that unaffected food becomes contaminated by transference of bacteria from another item or medium.

Types of bacteria

Salmonella is food poisoning caused by the actual bacteria. The source is bacteria present in the intestines of animals and human beings. Foods affected include poultry, meat, eggs, raw foods and shellfish from contaminated waters. Prevention should include:

- good standards of personal hygiene;
- elimination of insects and rodents;

25 hospital kitchens ban fresh eggs

FRESH eggs have been banned from the kitchen of 25 hospitals in one area because of fears that they may be a source of salmonella infection.

The health authority is switching its weekly order for 7,200 eggs to liquefied, pasteurised eggs after an outbreak of 78 cases of food poisoning.

The Government warned people last week against eating raw or undercooked eggs and researchers have since found that even cooked eggs may be a source of infection by a strain of bacteria called salmonella enteritidis.

A spokesman for the health authority said 'Until we get much clearer guidelines we are not going to take chances with the sick and the elderly.'

Farming practices had changed in recent years, he said, "and this bacterium is now a lot stronger that it was and is finding itself in a lot more places than before".

A spokesman for the Ministry of Agriculture said the risks from eggs were very small and described the area's action as "rather alarmist".

A Health Department spokesman said that caterers were advised to use pasteurised liquid egg.

The advice is reinforced by a study by Public Health Laboratory doctors of four cases of Salmonella enteritidis poisoning.

The foods blamed for the outbreaks included home-made ice cream containing raw egg, scrambled eggs, egg sandwiches and Scotch egg.

Writing in the *Lancet*, the doctors say all eggs should be regarded as possibly infected.

Fig 1.7: Newspaper report on *Salmonella* and egg

- washing hands and equipment and surfaces after handling raw poultry;
- use of shellfish from reputable sources;
- not allowing carriers of the disease to handle food.

Staphylococcus aureus causes food poisoning due to poisons produced in the food. The source includes human hands and other parts of the skin; sores, spots, etc.; nose and throat. Foods affected include those which are handled a lot and brawn, pressed beef, pies, custards, etc. Prevention includes good hygiene habits: ensure that cuts are covered and handle food as little as possible. Pay particular attention to washing the hands after using the toilet.

Clostridium perfringens lives in the intestines of humans and animals, and in the soil. Foods affected include raw meats and poultry. Bacteria are liable to survive light cooking; therefore, foods need to be cooked thoroughly.

Growth of bacteria

Bacteria multiply by splitting in half and under favourable conditions for growth can double in numbers every 20 minutes so that, in about six hours, 1 000 000 could be produced from one bacterium! Favourable conditions for growth are warmth, moisture, time and a suitable food on which to multiply. Food contaminated by bacteria is the most common cause of food poisoning (see page 53).

Most foods are easily contaminated. Those most likely to cause food poisoning and needing extra care are:

- stock, sauces, gravies, soups;
- meat and meat products (sausages, pies, cold meats);
- milk and milk products;
- eggs and egg products;
- all foods which are handled;
- all foods which are reheated.

Temperature conditions

- Bacteria grow between 7°C (45°F) and 63°C (145°F).
- Food poisoning bacteria multiply rapidly at body temperature.
- A badly ventilated kitchen is ideal for bacterial growth.
- Luke warm water is also ideal for bacterial growth.
- Hot water must be used for washing up.
- Foods should be kept in a refrigerator or larder.
- Extra care should be taken in warm weather.
- Foods for reheating must be reheated thoroughly.

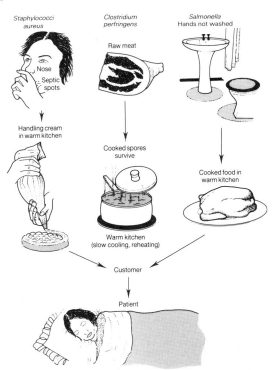

Fig 1.8: How food poisoning may be caused

Plate 1.5: Using a hand-held digital thermometer (courtesy of Comark Ltd)

Whilst boiling kills most bacteria, it is important that a sufficient length of time is allowed at a high temperature to be sure of safe food. For further information on temperature aspects of food handling, see pages 51–53 and chapter 3.

Moisture conditions
Bacteria require moisture as they cannot multiply on dry food. Ideal foods for their growth are jelly with meats, custards, cream and sauces.

Time conditions
Small numbers of bacteria may have little effect but because they multiply rapidly under ideal conditions, in a short time sufficient numbers can be produced to cause food poisoning.

Foods should therefore be in a warm kitchen for as short a time as is practical. There is a time lag whilst bacteria are adjusting to the conditions before they multiply; during this time foods are relatively safe and can be worked on in the warm kitchen.

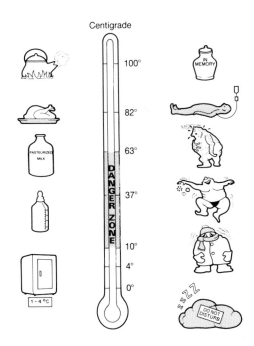

Fig 1.9: Germometer

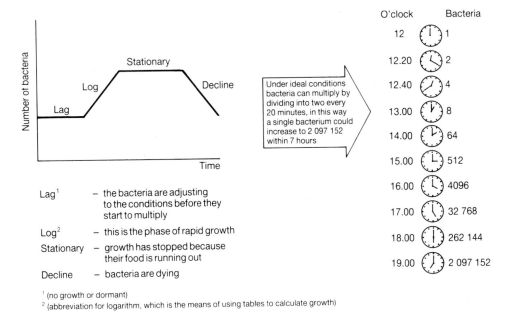

Lag[1] — the bacteria are adjusting to the conditions before they start to multiply

Log[2] — this is the phase of rapid growth

Stationary — growth has stopped because their food is running out

Decline — bacteria are dying

[1] (no growth or dormant)
[2] (abbreviation for logarithm, which is the means of using tables to calculate growth)

Fig 1.10: Germs multiplying over time

Control of bacteria

There are three methods of controlling bacteria.

- To prevent bacteria from spreading, do not allow food to come into contact with anything that may contain disease-producing bacteria. Protect food from bacteria in the air by keeping foods covered as much as possible. To prevent cross-contamination, use separate boards and knives for cooked and uncooked foods. Use different coloured boards for particular foods, e.g. red for meat, blue for fish and yellow for poultry. Store cooked and uncooked foods separately. Wash hands frequently, especially between handling raw and cooked foods.

- To prevent the growth of bacteria, do not keep foods in the danger zone between 8° and 63°C (48–141°F) for longer than absolutely necessary.

- To kill bacteria, subject bacteria to a temperature of 77°C (170°F) for 30 seconds or a higher temperature for less time. (Certain bacteria develop into spores and can withstand higher temperatures for longer periods of time.) Certain chemicals also kill bacteria and can be used for cleaning equipment and utensils.

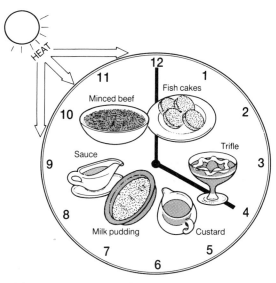

Fig 1.11: Germs multiplying in moist foods in warm temperature over time

Other points to be observed:

- ensure that food is obtained from reliable sources;
- handle foods as little as possible; when practicable use tongs, palette knives, plastic gloves, etc.;
- ensure utensils and work surfaces are spotlessly clean;
- pay particular attention when handling raw poultry meat and fish;
- wash raw fruits and vegetables;
- clean methodically and as frequently as necessary;
- thoroughly reheat made-up dishes.

Food Hygiene (Amendments) Regulations 1990/1991

These amendments specify the temperature controls for certain foods. They also apply to foods in transit and catering operations using mobile facilities. The main points are

- Certain foods should be kept at 8°C (46°F) or under.
- Certain foods should be kept at 5°C (41°F) or under.
- All hot food must be kept above 63°C (145°F).
- Although chilling extends shelf life of foods, high standards of hygiene and control of storage life is essential.
- Storage temperature of below 5°C (41°F) for all perishables should be achieved as quickly as possible.
- The regulations relate to the temperature of the food not to the air temperature of the chiller units or hot cupboards.
- To comply with the regulations regular and frequent checks must be made to monitor temperatures.

Practical implications

- On receipt of deliveries, cool the goods to the proper temperature as soon as possible.
- To account for defrost cycle or breakdown of refrigeration, an allowance of 2°C (35°F) is permitted.
- A maximum time of 2 hours for cold food preparation in the kitchen is tolerated provided there is no more than two degrees rise above the 5°C (41°F) or 8°C (46°F) specified temperature.
- Food intended to be served hot at 63°C (145°F) or above can be held at a temperature below this but for no more than 2 hours.
- Exception is made for foods served warm, e.g. hollandaise sauce. They may be kept for no more than 2 hours; any remaining must be discarded.
- Foods intended to be served cold at 5°C (41°F) or 8°C (46°F) may be held at a higher temperature but for no longer than 4 hours; it must then be brought back to 5°C (41°F) or 8°C (46°F).
- Displayed foods, e.g. sweet trolley, cheese board, self-service display, 'counter display with assisted service', need not be maintained at the required temperature provided displayed food is kept to a minimum and does not exceed 4 hours.

Exceptions for certain foods from temperature controls

- Sterilised canned foods are exempt, but cans that have only been pasteurised, e.g. large hams, some pâtés should be kept below 5°C (41°F) and the label should specify chilled storage.

- Sandwiches kept for less than 4 hours require no temperature control. Sandwiches containing sirloin, salad, meat or eggs, are subject to relevant control of 5°C (41°F), but may be held at 8°C (46°F) or below so long as they are intended for sale within 24 hours.
- Sausage rolls, cooked pies and pasties encased in pastry which have nothing added after cooking (for example gelatine) must be sold on the day of production.
- Uncut egg, milk and pastry products, e.g. custard tarts must be sold within 24 hours.
- Freshly baked cream cakes, quiches and similar flans may be damaged if put into chiller directly after baking, as moisture could affect the pastry. These items can be cooled slowly up to 2 hours before chilling then cooled quickly.

Foods to be kept at 5°C (41°F) or under

- cut segments of ripened soft cheese;
- hard and soft cheese in a cooked product to be eaten without further heating;
- cooked products containing meat, fish, eggs (or their substitutes such as cheese, cereals, pulses, vegetables);
    intended to be eaten without further heating, e.g. canned meats and poultry once removed from can, cooked vegetable and cereal salads, meat and fish pâté, Scotch eggs, pork pies with gelatine added, quiche, sandwich fillings;
    smoked and cured fish;
    smoked and cured meat;
    salads containing items subject to 5°C (41°F), e.g. rice salad;
    sandwiches and rolls containing ripe soft cheese, smoked or cured fish and meat and cooked products.

Foods to be kept at 8°C (46°F) or under

- uncut whole ripe soft cheese, e.g. Brie, Danish blue, Stilton, Roquefort, Camembert, Dolcelatte and any remaining part of the whole portion from which a segment has been cut;
- hard and soft cheese included in a cooked item intended to be eaten without further heating;
- cooked products where manufacturers' instructions require reheating, e.g. pizzas, ready-made meals;
- dairy-based desserts including milk substitutes, e.g. fromage frais, mousses, cream caramels, whipped cream desserts with a pH value of 4.5 or more;

- vegetable salads that are prepared, e.g. lettuce leaves, coleslaws, cut tomatoes, and those containing fruit;
- uncooked or partly cooked pastry and dough products containing meat or fish or their substitutes, e.g. fresh pasta, with meat or fish filling;
- sandwiches, rolls, etc., containing soft ripe cheese, smoked or canned fish or meat, to be sold within 24 hours;
- cream cakes containing both dairy or non-dairy cream.

An awareness of these regulations is essential, however due to their complexity, if in doubt, err on the side of safety and store at 5°C or below.

Food poisoning

Food poisoning is an illness characterised by stomach pains, diarrhoea and sometimes vomiting, which can develop within 1 to 36 hours after eating affected food.

Prevention

Almost all food poisoning can be prevented by:

- complying with the rules of hygiene;
- taking care and thinking ahead;
- ensuring that high standards of cleanliness are applied to premises and equipment;
- preventing accidents.

More specifically, pay attention to:

- high standards of personal hygiene;
- physical fitness;
- maintaining good working conditions;
- maintaining equipment in good repair and clean condition;
- using separate equipment and knives for cooked and uncooked foods;
- ample provision of cleaning facilities and equipment;
- storing foods at the right temperature;
- safe reheating of foods;
- quick cooking of foods prior to storage;
- protection of foods from vermin and insects;
- hygienic washing-up procedures;
- knowing how food poisoning is caused;
- carrying out procedures to prevent food poisoning.

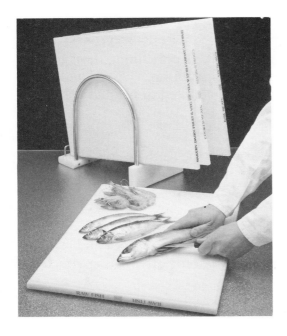

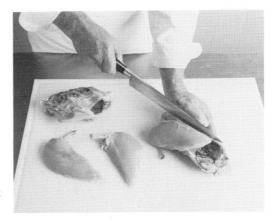

Fig 1.12a–c: Separate chopping boards for different foods will help to prevent cross- contamination

Causes

Causes include *chemicals* having entered food accidentally during the growth, preparation or cooking of the food, and *bacteria* (germs) (see page 46). Chemical food poisoning can occur from:

- arsenic, used in sprays during growth of fruit;
- lead, from using water that has been in contact with lead pipes;
- antimony of zinc, from storing or cooking acid foods in poor-quality enamelled or galvanised containers;

- copper pans, used for storing foods;
- certain plants, such as fungi, rhubarb leaves and parts of potatoes exposed above the soil;
- rat poison.

Chemical food poisoning can be prevented by:

- use of properly maintained utensils;
- obtaining foods from reliable sources;
- taking care in the use of rat poison, etc.

Infestations

Infestations can be caused by:

- inadequate cleaning;
- poor building maintenance;
- suppliers' deliveries.

Rodent infestation can be caused by rats and mice contaminating food. Insect infestation includes flies, cockroaches, beetles and silver fish.

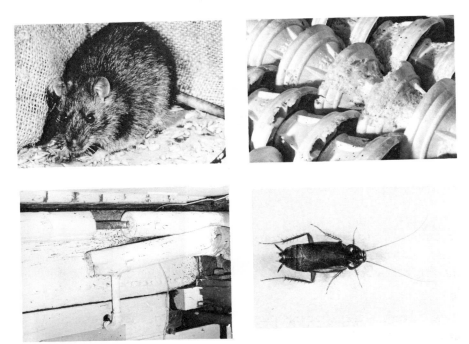

Fig 1.13a–d: Pests and the damage they cause

Prevention

Rats, mice, cockroaches, flies, other insects and birds must be controlled.

- Ensure buildings are sound with no holes or structural defects whereby mice and rats can enter premises.
- Use screens on windows to keep insects and birds out.
- Install ultraviolet electrical fly killers.
- Have no narrow spaces between equipment and fittings and no false bottoms.
- Store all food supplies off the floor.
- Keep all foods in lidded containers where practical.
- Do not allow waste to accumulate in the kitchen or outside.
- Keep all waste bins with lids on.
- Employ a pest control contractor.

Surplus prepared foods or left-overs

Ideally, there should be no foods remaining after the meal service. Over-production should be kept to a minimum as left-over foods can be a source of food poisoning. Therefore, to be safe and to avoid waste, such food must be stored at 5°C (41°F) or below.

Practices to prevent problems with surplus food items include:

- If items have been excessively handled or subjected to high temperature for a long time, they may not be reusable and should be discarded.
- Hot items must be cooled as quickly as possible and when cold kept at 5°C (41°F) or below.
- If food is required to be served hot, reheat to above 70°C (158°F) and keep at above 63°C (145°F) until served; reheat only once, then discard.
- If required, to be served cold, use within 48 hours. Keep at 5°C (41°F) below until required.
- Be extra careful to prevent contamination by practising high standards of food, personal and kitchen hygiene.
- Take extra care with meat, fish, poultry and egg dishes and those dishes containing milk and cream.
- Cover items to be stored and keep fresh foods away from cooked foods to avoid risk of cross-contamination.
- If in doubt, it is wiser to throw it out having checked with the person responsible.

NOTE For further information on storage, please refer to Kinton, Ceserani and Foskett (1995), *The Theory of Catering*, 8th edition, London: Hodder and Stoughton.

2

NUTRITION AND HEALTHY EATING

Nutrition is a key part of the national strategy in the UK of the 'Health of the Nation project'. The overall aim is to encourage people to look after their own health. There is strong evidence that what we eat, together with smoking and lack of exercise, contribute significantly to the high rates of coronary heart disease, other related problems and possibly some cancers. We all need more information about what food does for us and what foods contain. Changing what people eat is a slow process but choice of food has been changing, for example there is a growing number of vegetarians. Caterers need to know enough about nutrition and what changes are needed to enable customers to choose the type of food they like to eat. Whatever we serve we must always remember that the most important aspect of eating is enjoyment. All food must:

- look inviting,
- smell appetising,
- have a good flavour and texture.

— *Elementary nutrition* —

A knowledge of foods and their importance to health is essential to everyone especially those concerned with buying, storing, cooking and serving food in the catering industry.

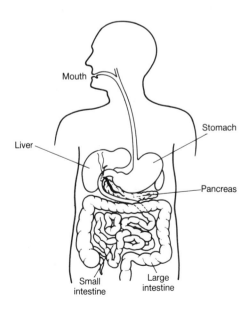

Fig 2.1: The digestive tract

Food is any substance liquid or solid which provides the body with materials:

- for heat and energy;
- for growth and repair;
- to regulate the body processes.

These materials are known as nutrients and the study of them is known as nutrition. Foods containing the various nutrients and their uses in the body are shown in the table below.

NAME	FOOD IN WHICH IT IS FOUND	USE IN BODY
protein	meat, fish, poultry, game, milk, cheese, eggs, pulses, cereals	for building and repairing body tissues; some heat and energy
fat	butter, margarine, cooking fat, oils, cheese, fatty meat, oily fish	provides heat and energy
carbohydrate	flour, flour products and cereals, sugar, syrup, jam, honey, fruit, vegetables	provides heat and energy
vitamin A	oily fish, fish-liver oil, dairy foods, carrots, tomatoes, greens	helps growth, resistance to disease
vitamin B_1 (thiamin)	yeast, pulses, liver, whole grain cereals, meat and yeast extracts	helps growth; strengthens nervous system
vitamin B_2 (riboflavin)	yeast, liver, meat, meat extracts, whole grain cereals	helps growth and helps in the production of energy
nicotinic acid (niacin)	yeast, meat, liver, meat extracts, whole grain cereals	helps growth
vitamin C (ascorbic acid)	fruits such as strawberries, citrus fruits, green vegetables, root vegetables, salad vegetables, potatoes	helps growth; promotes health
vitamin D (sunshine vitamin)	fish-liver oils, oily fish, dairy foods	helps growth; builds bones and teeth
iron	lean meat, offal, egg yolk, wholemeal flour, green vegetables, fish	helps build up the blood
calcium (lime)	milk and milk products, bones of fish, wholemeal bread	helps build bones and teeth, clot the blood, work the muscles
phosphorus	liver and kidney, eggs, cheese, bread	helps build bones and teeth; regulate body processes
sodium (salt)	meat, eggs, fish, bacon, cheese	helps prevent muscular cramp

To enable the body to benefit from the foods, they have to be digested; digestion takes place in the mouth, the stomach and in the small intestine. After the food has been broken down, the product passes through the walls of the digestive tract into the blood stream; this is known as absorbtion.

ENERGY-GIVING FOODS

Sugars, starches and fats provide the body with warmth and energy. Sugars and starches are known as carbohydrates and supply the body with most of its energy and heat. Sources include:

- Sugars: cakes, pastries, jams, honey, sugar, syrup, fresh and dried fruit.
- Starches: potatoes, cereals, bread, flour, pastries.
- Fat: lard, butter, margarine, oil.

BODY-BUILDING FOODS

These foods which help the body to grow are known as proteins and there are two sources:

- Animal protein: meat, fish, eggs, milk, cheese.
- Vegetable protein: peas, beans, lentils, nuts, cereals.

BODY-PROTECTING FOODS

This group of foods assists in keeping the body healthy and consists of mineral elements and vitamins which are found in small quantities in foods. There are 19 mineral elements most of which are required by the body in very small quantities. Vitamins are chemical substances vital for life; if there is deficiency in any vitamins ill health results.

WATER

Water is an essential nutrient; it is responsible for cleansing the body and assists in keeping the body healthy. Sources include:

- drinks of all kinds;
- foods, such as fruits;
- vegetables, meats, eggs.

YOU ARE WHAT YOU EAT

WHITE BREAD ROLLS. It's a good idea to include bread in your daily diet, but choose wholemeal bread whenever possible because it contains more vitamins, minerals and fibre than white bread.

STRAWBERRIES with a yoghurt topping would be far better than with cream because cream contains a lot of saturated fat. Fresh fruit has lots of vitamins and fibre and we should all eat at least one portion a day.

GRILLED OR ROAST CHICKEN with the skin removed is low in fat and therefore good for your heart. Try using chicken as a sandwich filling instead of luncheon meat or cheddar cheese.

FRIED, CRISPY BACON tastes great but so does grilled crispy bacon and this would be much better for your heart. Frying simply coats the bacon with an extra layer of fat. The fat on bacon, like all meat fat, is high in saturated fat and it is best to avoid eating it.

SWEETS AND CHOCOLATES are high in sugar and fat and therefore are not good for your teeth, your appearance or your heart. A piece of fresh fruit such as an apple or tangerine would be a good substitute!

DOUGHNUTS are high in calories and therefore fattening. Deep-fried in oil and then coated in sugar, doughnuts contain very little goodness for all those calories.

TUNA SALAD makes a wonderful filling for a roll or sandwich. Fish is one of the best foods you can eat because it is low in saturated fats and high in protein which helps build healthy growing bodies.

POTATO CRISPS are potatoes with a lot of fat and salt added to them, which is bad for your heart.

COLESLAW is a tasty way of eating vegetables. Try using a low fat mayonnaise or a yoghurt-based dressing on this and other salads.

The British Heart Foundation spends more on heart research than any other charity in Britain. Its aim is to find out what causes heart disease and how it can be prevented.

BRITISH HEART FOUNDATION

MARGARINE has exactly the same amount of fat as butter – it is the type of fat that is different. A soft margarine that claims to be high in polyunsaturated fat will be much better for your heart than butter or hard margarines which usually contain a lot of saturated fat.

SAUSAGES AND PIES contain a lot of fat, especially saturated fat, so it's best not to have them too often. A five ounce pork pie contains nearly eight teaspoons of fat, a large sausage almost four teaspoons of fat.

CHEDDAR CHEESE, like many hard cheeses, is high in calcium (essential for the development of strong bones and teeth). It is, however, also rather high in saturated fat, so try to choose a medium or low fat cheese whenever you can.

FRIED CHIPS contain lots of fat, but large chips have less surface area to absorb fat and so contain less fat than french fries. Oven chips usually have less fat than deep fried chips, but a potato baked in its jacket is the best choice of all.

WHOLEWHEAT BREAKFAST CEREALS contain lots of fibre, vitamins and minerals such as iron. Oats, either as porridge or muesli (preferably unsweetened) are also very nutritious.

COTTAGE CHEESE is one of the best cheeses for your heart because it is low in fat, yet still contains lots of calcium as well as protein.

EGGS contain a lot of essential vitamins, minerals and protein but they are also high in cholesterol so it is probably wise to restrict the number you eat to three or four a week.

BAKED BEANS ON TOAST is a healthy nutritious meal. Beans contain lots of fibre and protein and very little fat which makes them a good heart food.

BEEFBURGERS are best when made of lean meat and grilled rather than fried.

BUTTER is high in saturated fat which tends to increase the cholesterol in your blood. This is bad for your heart.

Plate 2.1: You are what you eat (courtesy of British Heart Foundation)

BALANCED DIET AND HEALTHY EATING

A balanced diet provides adequate amounts of the various nutrients for energy, growth and repair and regulation of body processes.

In order to be healthy the body must have sufficient, but not too much of all the nutrients which are present in foods. Provided the diet provides enough food energy to satisfy the demands for basal metabolism and all other activities and includes a good mixture of foods, all the requirements for the different nutrients will be met.

We all know when we are eating too much food, because we put on weight, and unfortunately this is a very common problem both for the young and old. Carrying too much weight not only looks unattractive, but is also a health hazard as it puts extra strain on the body. An overweight person should cut down on their intake of high energy foods such as butter, fried food, cakes, pastries and also be careful to avoid too many purely energy-providing foods such as sweets and fizzy drinks. In this way energy intake will be reduced, but not at the expense of the important body-building and protective foods.

Many diseases are linked to poor diet; we know, for instance, that too little vitamin C will eventually result in scurvy. Many people in developed countries, such as the UK, tend to have a way of life that includes smoking, a relatively high alcohol intake and a diet which is high in fat, low in dietary fibre (especially that from cereals) and containing too much energy. A better diet would contain less fat (particularly dairy fats), less sugar in sweets, chocolate, puddings and beverages, and more bread and potatoes. Wholemeal bread and cereals are particularly beneficial by increasing the amount of fibre in our diets.

On the whole people in the West eat plenty of protein and could well look to using some vegetable foods, such as peas, beans, nuts and lentils for providing protein as a change from animal protein foods.

—— What changes are needed ——

In 1991 the Department of Health publication (*Dietary Reference Values for the UK, 1991*) gave advice on human energy and nutrient needs and specifically about the intake of fats, NSP (non-starch polysaccharide or what used to be called fibre), sugar and salt. The recommendations give clear guidelines on the eating pattern which we should be adopting, though in a practical situation the figures are not easy to interpret.

Dietary reference values for fat and carbohydrate for adults as a percentage of daily total energy (food energy) are given below. The figures in brackets refer to the percentage without alcohol intake.

FATS AND CARBOHYDRATES	INDIVIDUAL MINIMUM	POPULATION AVERAGE	INDIVIDUAL MAXIMUM
saturated fatty acids		10 (11)	
total fat		33 (35)	
non-milk extrinsic sugars		10 (11)	
intrinsic and milk sugars and starch		37 (39)	
total carbohydrate		47 (50)	
non-starch (fibre) polysaccharide (g/day)	12	18	24

Eight guidelines for a healthy diet have been produced to help us to improve our diet easily. They are:

- Enjoy your food.
- Eat a variety of different foods.
- Eat the right amount to be a healthy weight.
- Eat plenty of foods rich in starch and fibre (or NSP).
- Don't eat too much fat.
- Don't eat sugary foods too often.
- Look after the vitamins and minerals in food.
- If you drink alcohol, keep within sensible limits.

Nutrients are widely distributed among different foods and eating a variety of foods is important to ensure that all of the fifty or so different nutrients required in the diet are obtained. All foods can be divided between a few food groups, the foods in each group having similar nutrients. By eating foods from each food group in the correct proportion we can easily ensure that the balance of the diet is correct.

ARE YOU A HEALTHY WEIGHT?

The right weight for your height can give a rough check on your eating habits. The chart below, taken from the Health Education Authority's *Guide to Healthy*

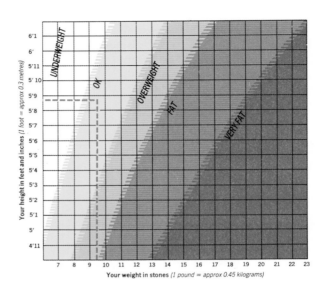

Plate 2.2: Are you a healthy weight?

Eating, shows ranges of weights for a particular height. This accounts for different builds and body frames.

Find out where your height and weight lines cross on the chart opposite and use the guidelines below it to check your weight.

Underweight – Check that you're eating enough.
OK – You're eating the right amount of food, but check that you're eating the right type of food.
Overweight – Your health would benefit if you lost weight.
Fat – For your health you need to lose weight.
Very fat – You urgently need to lose weight. Your doctor might advise you to see a dietician.

WHAT TO EAT

The British Healthy Eating Pyramid shows five groups and the proportion of each that we should choose.

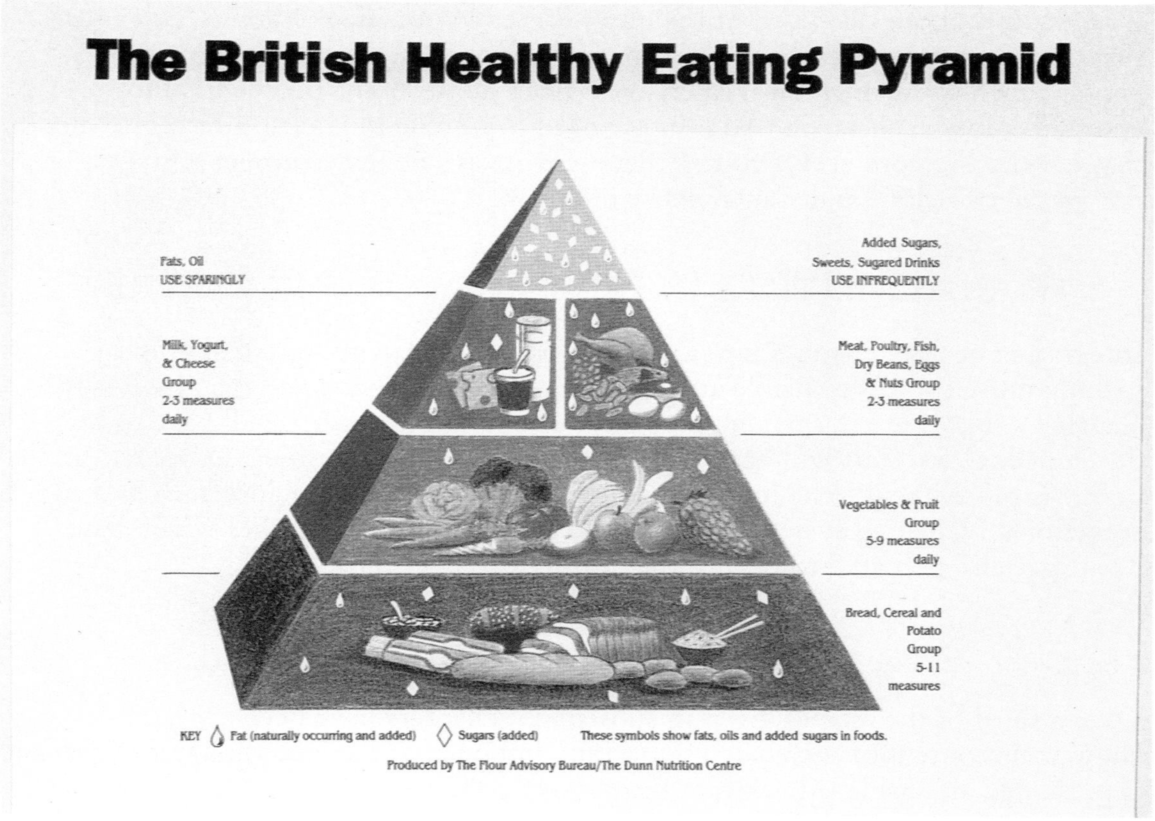

The British Healthy Eating Pyramid

Fats, Oil
USE SPARINGLY

Added Sugars,
Sweets, Sugared Drinks
USE INFREQUENTLY

Milk, Yogurt,
& Cheese
Group
2-3 measures
daily

Meat, Poultry, Fish,
Dry Beans, Eggs
& Nuts Group
2-3 measures
daily

Vegetables & Fruit
Group
5-9 measures
daily

Bread, Cereal and
Potato
Group
5-11
measures

KEY ⬦ Fat (naturally occurring and added)   ◇ Sugars (added)   These symbols show fats, oils and added sugars in foods.

Produced by The Flour Advisory Bureau/The Dunn Nutrition Centre

Plate 2.3: The British Healthy Eating Pyramid (courtesy of The Flour Advisory Bureau and The Dunn Nutrition Unit)

The top of the pyramid is made up of fats and sugar. Fat is present in a lot of the foods already mentioned and we should use as little extra fat as possible while still maintaining palatable food. Customers should be given the choice of low-fat vegetables, such as boiled new potatoes, instead of roast and of having foods served without high-fat sauces or added butter.

Sugar is naturally present in fruit, vegetables and milk and we do not really need to eat any more. Starch is made into sugar in our bodies. Some foods like patisserie will always contain a lot of sugar and, eaten in moderation, these do no harm and add variety and interest to the diet. A regular intake of foods high in sugar adds too much energy to the diet with the addition of very few vitamins and minerals and does your teeth no good.

We need to remember that our customers may not like as much sugar, salt and fat as we do and give them the choice!

In the UK about one third of the meals are eaten outside the home. This means that caterers have a considerable responsibility for what people eat. For many people lunch is the main meal eaten away from home. Some people have to entertain a lot for their job. All of these need to be able to choose a healthier diet if that is what they prefer. Of course there will always be the customer who eats out for special occasions and wants plenty of cream!

HEALTHY EATING IN PRACTICE FOR THE CATERER

Integrating healthy changes into a catering operation can be started simply by making more choices available and altering cooking methods and recipes. For the changes to become a permanent part of your operation a policy will have to be developed. Often staff will have ideas of their own and by gaining co-operation, the policy is more likely to be followed. Customers will need to be informed and sometimes a labelling system is introduced to highlight those dishes which have been specially prepared to fit into the healthy eating criteria.

ANALYSIS OF RECIPES

Over a third of the recipes given in subsequent chapters have been analysed to show their content of the more important components. The nutritional information is presented alongside the relevant recipes using the following format:

1 portion provides:	(states whether analysis is given per portion or per recipe)
1452 kJ/350 kcal	(energy content expressed as kilocalories or kilojoules)
11.7 g fat **(of which 5.2 g saturated)**	(total fat is listed together with its saturated fat – this is most prevalent in animal products)
23.0 g carbohydrate **(of which 2.9 g sugars)**	(the aim is to eat more starchy carbohydrate and less sugar)
7.6 g protein	(intake of protein is not generally a problem in the UK)
1.0 g fibre	(an important part of the foods we eat – found especially in cereals, pulses, vegetables and fruit)

The nutritional analysis for each recipe is based on the ingredients listed in the individual recipe. In other words no garnishes or serving suggestions have been included in the calculations. If the type or quantity of ingredients is altered then the nutritional analysis quoted should not be used. The addition or substitution of different ingredients can change the nutritional value of a recipe enormously. For example, adding prawns to a soup will, amongst other things, increase the protein content; enriching a sauce with cream and egg yolks will increase the fat content, particularly the level of saturated fat.

Nutritional information is presented for all the basic recipes within the text, together with other popular dishes.

What do the analyses tell the caterer?

To the trained eye nutritional data can be a goldmine. An idea of what the information can reveal is shown below:

	Breadcrumbed veal escalope with ham and cheese
1 portion provides:	
2632 kJ/627 kcal	(a male chef may need 10600–11510 kJ/2600–2900 kcal daily)
48.1 g fat **(of which 16.3 g saturated)**	(the maximum recommended amount of fat for the average person is 80–85 g daily. Add a portion of roast potatoes to this dish and you could be eating 56 g fat)
V12.0 g carbohydrate **(of which 1.3 g sugars)**	(the starch and sugar content of this dish is low)
37.1 g protein	(a chef may need about 75 g of protein each day. Most people have no problem achieving this)
0.7 g fibre	(negligible fibre content. This dish contributes little toward the 30 g per day which is recommended for health)

The sample recipe of Breadcrumbed veal escalope with ham and cheese (see page 366) has 48.1 g (nearly 2 oz) of *fat* per portion, which is high, and over one third of this is saturated. The *energy* (calories) supplied per portion is high and about three quarters of this energy is from fat. A glance at the recipe shows where it all comes from: ham and cheese are added to the meat which is then breaded and fried in butter and oil. The dish is served with more butter. It may be possible to make significant reductions in the fat content without forfeiting too much in terms of flavour, texture or appearance of the finished dish.

The recipe is also low in *carbohydrate* and *dietary fibre* because meat has virtually none of these; the amounts from the breadcrumbs and seasoned flour being insignificant. The dish may be eaten with vegetables, like potatoes and broccoli, which would boost the starch and fibre content of the meal and at the same time dilute its fat content.

In general, by adding or augmenting dishes with different accompaniments the nutritional profile of the resulting complete meal can change and may shift towards something more healthy. The aim is to provide proportionately more energy from starchy carbohydrates and fewer from fats and sugars. In food terms this means more potatoes, pasta, rice or bread on the plate, together with greater quantities of vegetables, particularly pulses – a change in meal concept for many people. The addition of a jacket potato and a portion of peas to a recipe can have an important effect: most of the energy will come from the carbohydrate rather than from fat. The analysis of recipes gives total fat and saturated fat. Generally it is agreed that the total quantity of fat in the diet should be reduced, but saturated fat in particular, and that not more than 35% of our energy should come from fat. In practice this means for example:

	AVERAGE ENERGY REQUIREMENT	UPPER LIMIT OF FAT
	(MJ/kcal/day)	(g/day)
15–18-year-old female	8.83/2110	82
19–49-year-old male	10.60/2550	94
19–49-year-old female	8.10/1940	71

Each group of foods, other than sugar, provides important nutrients. By choosing from different groups and ensuring that you have a variety within each group it is easy to choose a healthy diet.

Bread, cereals rice and pasta are the base of the pyramid (see Plate 2.1) and are a major source of NSP (fibre), starch, vitamin B_1 (thiamine) niacin, iron and zinc, and contribute quite a lot of protein to the diet. It is recommended that meals are built around this food group. This is quite a change for caterers who traditionally have thought of the meat as the central part of the meal. It is a good habit to eat bread – without butter! – with meals. Most Europeans already do this! Lots of people still believe that 'starch is fattening'; in excess this is still true, but it is the butter and fat which we put on the 'starch' which is the real culprit.

We depend on fruit and vegetables for most, almost all, of our vitamin C, much of our beta-carotene (vitamin A), vitamin E and dietary fibre. These vitamins are known as antioxidant vitamins and research now being carried out shows that they are very important in helping to prevent some cancers. Everybody needs to eat at least five portions of fruit and vegetables from a wide variety each day; it doesn't matter if some are frozen. We could help as caterers by ensuring that the fruit and vegetables which we serve are always attractive and appetising and by making an interesting variety of salads – with optional dressings – and fresh fruits available.

Meat, fish, eggs and pulses (beans, lentils, etc.) all provide protein and a variety of B vitamins. We all need protein in our diet but the majority of people eat more than they need. To get the best out of this group we need to choose a variety again. Meat (red and white) is a major source of iron, zinc and niacin as well as protein. Oily fish such as sardines or herring contain vitamins D and E and essential polyunsaturated fatty acids. White fish is high in protein and low in fat. Liver contains not only protein and iron but also a wide variety of vitamins. Some of the foods in this group contribute a lot of fat to the overall diet, that is why it is important not to eat too much of this group.

So it is important to consider the 'protein part' of the meal and to ensure that there is plenty of variety, but to pay as much attention to ensuring a variety of rice, pasta, bread or other cereals and plenty of vegetables and fruit is also given.

Milk, cheese and yoghurt are the main providers of calcium and are therefore very important in the diets of the young and pregnant women. The group is also an important source of protein, but may contain a lot of fat. For some people it is advisable to choose the lower fat varieties of this group.

Nutritional analysis of recipes can be used to provide:

- menu labelling schemes, such as the 'traffic light' scheme, which has been used in schools to register the fat and sugar content of foods. This system has been successfully introduced where the colour coding is explained in class and used in the schools meals service;
- recipe cards or handouts for customers which include the nutritional breakdown;
- posters and leaflets detailing nutritional information for customers;
- articles for in-house company magazines, local or national press;
- healthier standard recipes;
- specific marketing initiatives, such as healthy eating days, healthy eating promotion buffets, etc., which help to consolidate healthy catering practice.

NUTRITIONAL GUIDELINES

When compiling menus for institutions, industrial catering, etc., the following guidelines should be considered:

- Spread the calories fairly evenly through the day.
- Provide a dish which is a good source of protein in at least two meals of the day.

- Fruit and vegetables (including potatoes) should be available each day.
- Incorporate high fibre cereals whenever possible, such as brown rice, a proportion of wholemeal flour in pastry, wholemeal bread, wholemeal pastas.
- Use the minimum of salt in cooking.
- Grill rather than fry.
- Let appetite determine the energy-producing food requirements.

—— *Ingredients and ingredient substitutes* ——

Traditional ingredients have been tried and tested in recipes and have given satisfactory results. However, many new ingredients and ingredient substitutes may need to be adopted for reasons such as cost reduction, healthy eating, and problems with sources of supply. When using a new ingredient, the recipe may need to be modified and adapted. This process of modification and adaptation requires skill and knowledge developed through experimentation.

Food manufacturers are constantly launching new products in response to market research, identifying caterers' needs. Such products are often claimed to be better and, in some cases, healthier than existing lines. These may well be technological innovations and could enhance and improve existing recipes, but it will be the chef who will make the final decision on the acceptability of the ingredient. The chef is required to use his/her judgement and creativity, together with his/her skill in experimenting with any new ingredient, based on previous knowledge.

It is important always to follow, where possible, the food manufacturer's recommendations. For example, there are several non-dairy creamers available. Some are produced specifically for pastry work and so, being sweetened, are unsuitable for savoury recipes. However, there are also various unsweetened products that may be used in place of fresh cream for soups, sauces, etc. It is important to determine the heat suitability of these products before use, for example by testing whether or not they will withstand boiling without detriment to the product.

SALT

Chefs often add salt to taste. It is therefore difficult to quantify amounts of salt for each recipe and, as a consequence, no analytical data is given for salt or sodium content. However, a general reduction is recommended and in many dishes, flavour can be enhanced by the use of herbs and spices.

OILS AND FATS

This chart indicates which cooking oils, margarines and fats are healthiest, that is the ones with the smallest percentage of saturated fats.

OIL/FAT	SATURATED %	MONO-UNSATURATED %	POLY-UNSATURATED %
coconut oil	85	7	2
butter	60	32	3
palm oil	45	42	8
lard	43	42	9
beef dripping	40	49	4
margarine, hard (vegetable oil only)	37	47	12
margarine, hard (mixed oils)	37	43	17
margarine, soft	32	42	22
margarine, soft (mixed oils)	30	45	19
low-fat spread	27	38	30
margarine, polyunsaturated	24	22	54
groundnut oil	19	48	28
maize oil	16	29	49
wheatgerm oil	14	11	45
soybean oil	14	24	57
olive oil	14	70	11
sunflower seed oil	13	32	50
safflower seed oil	10	13	72
rape seed oil	7	64	32

—— *Further information* ——

Department of Health (1991) *Dietary reference values for food energy and nutrients for the United Kingdom*, London: HMSO
Health Education Authority (1990) *The Heart Beat Award*, London: HEA
Paul, AA and Southgate, DAT (1991) *McCance and Widdowson's: The Composition of Foods*, 4th edn, London: HMSO
A selection of healthy catering recipes
Department of Health (1989) *Catering for Health, Recipe File*, London: HMSO
Robbins, C (1989) *The Healthy Catering Manual*, London: Dorling Kindersley
Stevenson, D and Scobie, P (1987) *Catering for Health*, London: Hutchinson

3
METHODS OF COOKERY

Methods of cookery

1   Have a knowledge and understanding of the methods or processes of cookery.
2   Be aware of the simple scientific, artistic and commercial implications to be considered regarding food preparation.
3   Be able to state which, why and how foods are cooked by the various methods.
4   Be able to explain why this is so in relation to nutritional, menu and economic factors.
5   Be able to select suitable equipment to use for each process.

The transference of heat to food

(Oven temperature chart page viii.)
   All methods of cooking depend on one or more of the following principles.

RADIATION

Heat passes from its source in direct rays until it falls on an object in its path such as in grilling.

CONDUCTION

This is the transferring of heat through a solid object by contact. Some materials for example, metal used for pans, transfer heat more quickly than, say, wood used for wooden spoons. Conduction is the principle involved in the solid electric ranges.

CONVECTION

This is the movement of heated particles of gases or liquids. On heating, the particles expand, become less dense and rise. The colder particles sink to take their place, thus causing convection currents which distribute heat. This principle is used in heating a gas oven and in the heating of liquids.

The effect of heat on food

PROTEIN

Protein is coagulated by heat. The process is gradual, for example when heat is applied to egg white it thickens, becomes opaque and then firm. Over-heating will harden the protein, making it tough, unpalatable and shrunken. This characteristic coagulation of protein when heated is employed in its use as a coating for deep and shallow fried foods and in the development of crust in bread formed by the protein gluten in wheat.

CARBOHYDRATES

Moist heat on starch causes the starch grains to soften and swell. Near boiling point the cellulose framework bursts, releasing the starch which thickens the liquid.

Dry heat causes the starch to change colour from creamy white to brown and after prolonged heat will carbonise and burn. Water is given off during heating and the starch on the surface is changed to dextrin, a form of sugar, as in toast.

Moist heat causes sugar to dissolve in water – more rapidly in hot water than in cold. On heating it becomes syrup; on further heating it colours then caramelises and will eventually turn to carbon and ash.

Dry heat causes sugar to caramelise quickly and burn.

FATS

Fats melt to oils when heated. Water is given off with a bubbling noise as heating continues. When all the water has been driven off a faint blue haze appears; further heating will result in smoking and burning. The unpleasant smell of burning fat is caused by the presence of fatty acids.

VITAMINS

Vitamin A and *carotene* are insoluble in water so they are not lost by moist methods of cooking, such as boiling and steaming, or by soaking. Therefore boiled vegetables contain the same amount of carotene as raw vegetables.

Vitamin D is not destroyed by heat or lost by solubility.

Thiamine (vitamin B_1) is very soluble in water and about 50% will dissolve in the cooking liquid. High temperatures, e.g. pressure cooking, destroy vitamin B_1 and alkali (baking powder) will cause some destruction.

Riboflavin (vitamin B₂) is soluble in water and will dissolve out in the cooking liquid; some is lost in normal cooking but more losses occur in pressure cooking.

Nicotinic acid (niacin) is soluble in water and dissolves to some extent in the cooking liquid. It is stable in the presence of heat but is easily oxidised, which means that the chemical process of the products is adversely affected by taking in oxygen.

Vitamin C is lost or destroyed very easily in cooking and care must be taken to preserve it as much as possible. It is soluble in water and is easily dissolved in cleaning and cooking water; therefore vegetables containing vitamin C should not be soaked in water and cooking liquid should be made use of. It is best to cook in small quantities and as quickly as possible as vitamin C is destroyed by heat. Raw fruit and vegetables contain most vitamin C.

Vitamin C oxidises (see nicotinic acid) to form a substance which is useless to the body; to minimise oxidation cook with a lid on; also food containing vitamin C should only be stored for short periods and must be used as fresh as possible.

There is an enzyme present with Vitamin C in foods which, once the cells of the plant are damaged by bruising or cutting, begins to destroy the vitamin by oxidising it. The optimum or most favourable condition for destruction of the enzyme is between 65°–88°C (149–190°F) so if the vegetable is put into boiling water the enzyme activity will be quickly destroyed.

—— *Ways of cooking food* ——

- boiling
- poaching
- stewing
- braising
- steaming
- baking
- roasting
- grilling
- frying (shallow and deep)
- paper bag (en papillotte)
- microwave
- pot roasting (*poêlé*)

Included in each method of cookery are examples of food cooked by that method, with the page number. To locate other recipes use the chapter or main index.

Variations in definition and classification of cookery processes occur because certain words used in English may not correspond exactly with French words. For example,

- Boiled or poached turbot in English (*poché* in French).
- Boiled chicken in English (*poché* in French).
- Stewed or poached fruits in English (*compote* in French).

— *Boiling* —

DEFINITION

Boiling is the cooking of prepared foods in a liquid at boiling point. This could be water, court-bouillon, milk or stock.

Plate 3.1: Boiling crab

PURPOSE

The purpose of boiling is to cook food so that it is:

- pleasant to eat with an agreeable flavour;
- of a suitable texture, tender or slightly firm according to the food;
- easy to digest;
- safe to eat.

METHODS

There are two ways of boiling:

- Place the food into boiling liquid, reboil, then reduce the heat for gentle boiling to take place, this is known as simmering.
- Cover food with cold liquid, bring to the boil, then reduce heat to allow food to simmer.

EFFECTS OF BOILING

Gentle boiling helps to break down the tough fibrous structure of certain foods which would be less tender if cooked by other methods. When boiling meats for long periods the soluble meat extracts are dissolved in the cooking liquid. Cooking must be slow in order to give time for the connective tissue in tough meat to be changed into soluble gelatine, so releasing the fibres and making the meat tender. If the connective tissue gelatinises too quickly the meat fibres fall apart and the meat will be tough and stringy. Gentle heat will ensure coagulation of the protein without hardening.

ADVANTAGES OF BOILING

- Older, tougher, cheaper joints of meat and poultry can be made palatable and digestible.
- It is appropriate for large-scale cookery and is economic on fuel.
- Nutritious, well-flavoured stock can be produced.
- Labour saving, as boiling needs little attention.

a) The advantages of food started slowly in cold liquid, brought to the boil and allowed to boil gently:

- helps to tenderise the fibrous structure (meat), extracts starch (vegetable soups) and flavour from certain foods (stocks);
- can avoid damage to foods which would lose their shape if added to boiling liquid, e.g. whole fish.

b) adding food to boiling liquid:

- is suitable for green vegetables as maximum colour and nutritive value are retained, provided boiling is restricted to the minimum time;
- seals in the natural juices as with meat.

TIME AND TEMPERATURE CONTROL

Temperature must be controlled so that the liquid is brought to the boil, or reboil, then adjusted in order that gentle boiling takes place until the food is cooked to the required degree. Stocks, soups and sauces must only simmer, pasta cooked slightly firm (*al dente*), meat and poultry well cooked and tender; vegetables should not be overcooked.

Although approximate cooking times are given for most foods, the age, quality and size of various foods will nevertheless affect the cooking time required.

GENERAL RULES

- Select pans which are neither too small nor too large.
- When cooking in boiling liquid ensure there is sufficient liquid and that it is at boiling point before adding food.
- Frequently skim during the cooking.
- Simmer whenever possible so as to minimise evaporation, maintain volume of liquid and minimise shrinkage.

SAFETY

- Select containers of the right capacity – if they are too small there is danger of boiling liquid splashing over, forming steam and causing scalds.
- Always move pans of boiling liquid on the stove with care.
- Position pan handles so that they do not protrude from stove or become hot over the heat.
- Extra care is required when adding or removing foods from containers of boiling liquid.

—— *Poaching* ——

DEFINITION

Poaching is the cooking of foods in the required amount of liquid at just below boiling point.

PURPOSE

The purpose of poaching food is to cook food so that it is:

- easy to digest;
- a suitable tender texture;
- safe to eat;
- pleasant to eat because, where appropriate, an agreeable sauce is made with the cooking liquid.

METHODS

There are two ways of poaching: shallow and deep.

- *Shallow poaching.* Foods to be cooked by this method, such as cuts of fish and chicken, are cooked in the minimum of liquid, that is, water, stock, milk or wine. The liquid should never be allowed to boil but kept at a temperature as near to boiling point as possible. To prevent the liquid boiling, bring to the boil on top of the stove and complete the cooking in a moderate hot oven, approximately 180°C (356°F).
- *Deep poaching.* Eggs are cooked in approximately 8 cm (3 in) of gently simmering water. (The practice of poaching eggs in individual shallow metal pans over boiling water is cooking by steaming.) The English term boiling is frequently used for what in French is called *poché* (poached). Boiled cod, salmon, turbot and chicken are referred to as boiled in English and poché in French. Whole fish and chicken are covered in cold liquid, brought to the boil and allowed to simmer gently until cooked. Cuts of fish on the bone, such as fish steaks (tronçon and darne) are placed into simmering liquid and cooked gently.

EFFECTS OF POACHING

Poaching helps to tenderise the fibrous structure of the food, and the raw texture of the food becomes edible by chemical action.

TEMPERATURE AND TIME CONTROL

- Temperature must be controlled so that the cooking liquor does not fall below, or exceed, the correct degree required:
  shallow poaching is just below simmering point (and may be carried out in an oven);
  deep poaching is just below gentle simmering.
- Time is important so that the food is neither undercooked, therefore unpalatable, nor overcooked, when it will break up and also lose nutritive value.
- The various types and qualities of food will affect both time and temperature, needed to achieve successful poaching.

SAFETY

- Select suitably sized pans to prevent spillage and possible scalding.
- Move trays, etc., carefully on and off stove, or from the oven, as tilting or jarring may cause spillage.
- Carefully place food in the pan when adding to simmering liquid.
- When a hot container is removed from the oven, sprinkle with a little flour to warn that it is hot.

—— *Stewing* ——

DEFINITION

Stewing is the slow cooking of food cut into pieces and cooked in the minimum amount of liquid (water, stock or sauce); the food and liquid are served together.

PURPOSE

Because stewing is both economical and nutritional, cheaper cuts of meat and poultry, which would be unsuitable for roasting and grilling, can be made tender and palatable. Stewing also produces an acceptable flavour, texture and eating quality.

METHODS OF STEWING

All stews have a thickened consistency achieved by:

- the unpassed ingredients in the stew, such as Irish stew (page 315);
- thickening of the cooking liquor, such as white stew (*blanquette*) (page 315);
- cooking in the sauce, such as brown stew (*navarin*) (page 312).

Stewed foods can be cooked in a covered pan on the stove or in a moderate oven.

EFFECTS OF STEWING

In the slow process of cooking in gentle heat, the connective tissue in meat and poultry is converted into a gelatinous substance so that the fibres fall apart easily and become digestible. The protein is coagulated without being toughened. Unlike boiling, less liquid is used and the cooking temperature is approximately 5°C lower.

See also 'effects of boiling' (page 78) as this also applies to stewing.

ADVANTAGES

- The meat juices which escape from the meat during cooking are retained in the liquid which is part of the stew.
- Correct slow cooking results in very little evaporation.
- Nutrients are conserved.
- Tough goods are tenderised.
- It is economical in labour because foods can be cooked in bulk.

TEMPERATURE AND TIME CONTROL

- Temperature control is essential to the slow cooking required for efficient stewing; therefore, the liquid must barely simmer.
- A tight-fitting lid is used to retain steam which helps maintain temperature and reduce evaporation.
- Time will vary according to the quality of the food used.

- The ideal cooking temperature for stewing on top of the stove is approximately 82°C (180°F) (simmering temperature); or cooking in the oven at 170°C (gas mark 3, 340°F).

CARE AND CLEANLINESS

Thoroughly wash with hot detergent water, rinse with hot water and dry. Moving parts of large-scale equipment should be greased occasionally. Store pans upside-down on clean racks. Check that handles are not loose and that copper pans are completely tinned. Any faults with large equipment should be reported.

GENERAL RULES

- Stews should not be over-thickened. The sauce should be light in consistency; therefore, correct ratios of thickening agents are essential.
- Adjustment to the consistency should be made as required during cooking.
- Overcooking causes: (a) evaporation of liquid; (b) breaking up of the food; (c) discoloration; and (d) spoilage of flavour.

SAFETY

- Select suitably sized pans.
- Care is essential when removing hot pans from the oven.
- When removing lids be careful of escaping steam, which may cause scalds.
- Sprinkle flour on hot pans and lids after removal from the oven as a warning that they are hot.
- Ensure that pan handles are not over the heat or sticking out from the stove.

—— *Braising* ——

DEFINITION

Braising is a method of cooking in the oven; unlike roasting or baking the food is cooked in liquid in a covered pan, casserole or cocotte. It is a combination of stewing and pot roasting.

PURPOSE

The purpose of braising is:

- to give variety to the menu and the diet;
- to make food tender, digestible, palatable and safe to eat;
- to produce and enhance flavour, texture and eating quality.

METHODS OF BRAISING

There are two methods: brown braising, used, for example, for joints and portion-sized cuts of meat; white braising, used, for example, for vegetables and sweetbreads.

Brown braising:
- Joints such as beef and venison, are marinaded and may be larded, then sealed quickly by browning on all sides in a hot oven or in a pan on the stove. Sealing the joints helps retain flavour, nutritive value and gives a good brown colour. Joints are then placed on a bed of root vegetables in a braising pan, with the liquid and other flavourings, covered with a lid and cooked slowly in the oven.
- Cuts (steaks, chops, liver). The brown braising of cuts of meat is similar to that of joints.

White braising (celery, cabbage and sweetbreads). Foods are blanched, refreshed, cooked on a bed of root vegetables with white stock in a covered container in the oven.

Plate 3.2: Preparation for an Irish stew

EFFECTS OF BRAISING

Cooking by braising causes the breakdown of the tissue fibre in the structure of certain foods which softens the texture, thus making it tender and edible. The texture is also improved by being cooked in the braising liquid.

ADVANTAGES

- Tougher, less expensive meats and poultry can be used.
- Maximum flavour and nutritional value are retained.
- Variety of presentation and flavour is given to the menu.

TIME AND TEMPERATURE CONTROL

- Slow cooking is essential for efficient braising; the liquid must barely simmer.
- To reduce evaporation and maintain temperature, use a tight-fitting lid.
- Time needed for braising will vary according to the quality of the food.
- Ideal oven temperature for braising is 160°C (gas mark 3, 320°F).

Plate 3.3: Preparation for braised beef

GENERAL RULES

These are the same as for stewing. However, if the joint is to be served whole, the lid is removed three-quarters of the way through cooking. The joint is then frequently basted to give a glaze for presentation.

SAFETY

- Select a suitably sized pan with a tight-fitting lid and handles.
- Care is required when removing hot pans from the oven and when removing the lid.
- Sprinkle flour on hot pans and lids after removal from the oven as a warning that they are hot.

—— *Steaming* ——

DEFINITION

Steaming is the cooking of prepared foods by steam (moist heat) under varying degrees of pressure.

PURPOSE

The purpose of steaming food is to cook it so that it is:

- easy to digest;
- of an edible texture and pleasant to eat;
- safe to eat;
- as nutritious as possible (steaming minimises nutritive loss).

METHODS OF STEAMING

Atmospheric or low-pressure steaming:

- *direct:* in a steamer or in a pan of boiling water (steak and kidney pudding);
- *indirect:* between two plates over a pan of boiling water.

   High-pressure steaming in purpose-built equipment, which does not allow the steam to escape, therefore enabling steam pressure to build up, thus increasing the temperature and reducing cooking time.

Vacuum cooking in a pouch: this is known as *sous-vide*, a method of cooking in which food contained in vacuum-sealed plastic pouches is cooked by steam. The advantages of *sous-vide* cooking of food are:

- minimal change of texture and weight loss;
- no drying out and very little colour loss;
- dishes can be garnished and decorated before the vacuum packing and cooking process;
- the food cooks in its own natural juices;
- labour saving;
- uniformity of standard.

In this latter method, raw food products (cuts of fish, breast of chicken or duck) are lightly seasoned and any required cut vegetables, herbs, spices, stock or wine added and placed into specially made plastic pouches.

A vacuum packing machine seals the pouch, which is then cooked in a temperature-controlled convection steam cooker. The length of cooking time must be carefully controlled. Once cooked, the pouch is quickly cooled and kept at a temperature of 3°C (37°F).

When required for service the pouches are either placed in boiling water or a steam oven.

EFFECTS OF STEAMING

When food is steamed the structure and texture is changed by chemical action and becomes edible. The texture will vary according to the type of food, type of steamer and degree of heat; sponges and puddings are lighter in texture if steamed rather than baked.

ADVANTAGES OF STEAMING

These include:

- retention of goodness (nutritional value);
- makes some foods lighter and easy to digest, e.g. suitable for invalids;
- low-pressure steaming reduces risk of overcooking protein;
- high-pressure steaming enables food to be cooked or reheated quickly because steam is forced through the food, thus cooking it rapidly;

- labour-saving and suitable for large-scale cookery;
- high-speed steamers used for 'batch' cooking enable the frequent cooking of small quantities of vegetables throughout the service, keeping vegetables freshly cooked, retaining colour, flavour and nutritive value;
- with steamed fish, the natural juices can be retained by serving with the fish or in making the accompanying sauce;
- steaming is economical on fuel as a low heat is needed and a multitiered steamer can be used.

TIME AND TEMPERATURE CONTROL

For high-pressure steaming, foods should be placed in the steamer when the pressure gauge indicates the required degree of pressure. This will ensure that the necessary cooking temperature has been reached.

Cooking times will vary according to the equipment used and the type, size and quality of food to be steamed. Manufacturers' instructions are an essential guide to successful steaming.

CLEANING

The inside of the steamer, trays and runners are washed in hot detergent water,

Plate 3.4: Preparation for a steamed sponge pudding

rinsed and dried. Where applicable the water-generating chamber should be drained, cleaned and refilled. Door controls should be lightly greased occasionally and the door left open slightly to allow air to circulate when the steamer is not in use.

Before use check that the steamer is clean and safe to use. Any fault must be reported immediately.

Metal containers (sleeves and basins), may be thoroughly cleaned with kitchen paper or a clean cloth; other containers must be washed in hot detergent water, rinsed in hot water and dried. Containers are stored in closed cupboards.

SPECIFIC POINTS

Meat and sweet pudding basins must be greased, then after being filled, efficiently covered with greased greaseproof or silicone paper and foil to prevent moisture penetrating and resulting in a soggy pudding.

SAFETY FACTORS

- Where applicable, check that the water in the water well is at the correct level and that the ball-valve arm moves freely.
- Before opening the steamer door, allow the steam pressure to drop.
- Take extra care when opening the door, use it as a shield from escaping steam as a severe scald may result.
- Follow manufacturers' instructions at all times regarding cleaning and operating procedures.

—— *Baking* ——

DEFINITION

Baking is the cooking of food by dry heat in an oven in which the action of the dry convection heat is modified by steam.

PURPOSE

The purpose of baking is:

- to make food digestible, palatable and safe to eat;
- to create eye-appeal through colour and texture and produce an enjoyable eating quality;
- to lend variety to the menu.

METHODS

Note   Ovens must be preheated prior to baking.

- *Dry baking*: when baking, steam arises from the water content of the food; this steam combines with the dry heat of the oven to cook the food (cakes, pastry, baked jacket potatoes).
- *Baking with increased humidity*: when baking certain foods, such as bread, the oven humidity is increased by placing a bowl of water or injection steam into the oven, thus increasing the water content of the food and so improving eating quality.
- *Baking with heat modification*: placing food in a container of water (*bain-marie*), such as baked egg custard, modifies the heat so that the food cooks more slowly, does not over-heat and lessens the possibility of the egg mixture overcooking.

EFFECT OF BAKING

Chemical action caused by the effect of heat on certain ingredients, such as yeast and baking powder, changes the raw structure of many foods to an edible texture (pastry, cakes). However, different ingredients, methods of mixing and types of product required will cause many variations.

ADVANTAGES OF BAKING

- A wide variety of sweet and savoury foods can be produced.
- Bakery products yield appetising goods with eye-appeal and mouth-watering aromas.
- Bulk cooking can be achieved with uniformity of colour and degree of cooking.
- Baking ovens have effective manual or automatic temperature controls.
- There is straightforward access for loading and removal of items.

TIME AND TEMPERATURE CONTROL

- Ovens must always be heated to the required temperature before the food is added.
- In general-purpose ovens, shelves must be placed according to the food being cooked, because the hotter part of the oven is at the top. With convection ovens the heat is evenly distributed.
- Accurate timing and temperature control are essential to baking. The required oven temperature must be reached before each additional batch of goods is placed in the oven. This is known as *recovery time*.

GENERAL RULES

- Always preheat ovens so that the required cooking temperature is immediately applied to the product, otherwise the product will be spoiled.
- Accuracy is essential in weighing, measuring and controlling temperature.
- Trays and moulds must be correctly prepared.
- Minimise the opening of oven doors as draughts may affect the quality of the product, and the oven temperature is reduced.
- Utilise oven space efficiently.
- Avoid jarring of products (fruit cake, sponges, soufflés) before and during baking as the quality may be affected.

SAFETY

- Use thick, dry, sound oven cloths for handling hot trays, etc.
- Jacket sleeves should be rolled down to prevent burns from hot trays and ovens.
- Trays and ovens should not be overloaded.
- Extra care is needed to balance and handle loaded trays in and out of the oven.

—— *Roasting* ——

DEFINITION

Roasting is cooking in dry heat with the aid of fat or oil in an oven or on a spit. Radiant heat is the means of cooking when using a spit; oven roasting is a combination of convection and radiation.

Plate 3.5: Baking pastry blind

PURPOSE

The purpose of roasting is to cook food so that it is tender, easy to digest, safe to eat and palatable. It also gives variety to the menu and the diet.

METHODS

- Placing prepared foods (meat, poultry) on a rotating spit over or in front of fierce radiated heat.
- Placing prepared foods in an oven with either:
    applied dry heat;
    forced air-convected heat;
    convected heat combined with microwave energy.

EFFECTS OF ROASTING

The surface protein of the food is sealed by the initial heat of the oven, thus preventing the escape of too many natural juices. When the food is lightly browned, the oven temperature is reduced to cook the inside of the food without hardening the surface.

ADVANTAGES

- Good quality meat and poultry is tender and succulent when roasted.
- Meat juices issuing from the joint are used for gravy and enhance flavour.

- Both energy and oven temperature can be controlled.
- Ovens with transparent doors enable cooking to be observed.
- Access, adjustment and removal of items is straightforward.
- Minimal fire risk.

Spit roasting

- Skill and techniques can be displayed to the customer.
- Continual basting with the meat juice over the carcass or joint on the revolving spit gives a distinctive flavour, depending on the fuel used (wood, charcoal).

TIME AND TEMPERATURE CONTROL

- Ovens must be preheated.
- Oven temperature and shelf settings in recipes must be followed.
- Shape, size, type, bone proportion and quality of food will affect the cooking time.
- Meat thermometers or probes can be inserted to determine the exact temperature in the centre of the joint.

Plate 3.6: Basting best-end of lamb during roasting

The following table gives approximate cooking times:

	APPROXIMATE COOKING TIMES	DEGREE OF COOKING
beef	15 minutes per $\frac{1}{2}$ kg (1 lb) and 15 minutes over	underdone
lamb	20 minutes per $\frac{1}{2}$ kg (1 lb) and 20 minutes over	cooked through
lamb	15 minutes per $\frac{1}{2}$ kg (1 lb) and 15 minutes over	cooked pink
mutton	20 minutes per $\frac{1}{2}$ kg (1 lb) and 20 minutes over	cooked through
veal	20 minutes per $\frac{1}{2}$ kg (1 lb) and 25 minutes over	cooked through
pork	25 minutes per $\frac{1}{2}$ kg (1 lb) and 25 minutes over	thoroughly cooked

For internal temperature of meat, see page 333.

SAFETY

- Roasting trays should be of a suitable size: if too small, basting becomes difficult and dangerous; if too large, fat in the tray will burn, spoiling the flavour of the meat and gravy.
- Handle hot roasting trays carefully at all times, using a thick, dry cloth.
- Ensure food is securely held before removing from roasting tray.

—— *Pot roasting* ——

DEFINITION

Pot roasting is cooking on a bed of root vegetables in a covered pan. Known as *poêlé*, this method retains maximum flavour of all ingredients.

METHOD

Place the food, e.g. meat or poultry on a bed of roots and herbs, coat generously with butter or oil, cover with a lid and cook in an oven.

GENERAL RULES

- Select pans neither too large nor too small.
- Use the vegetables and herbs with a good stock as a base for the sauce.

—— *Tandoori cooking* ——

DEFINITION

Tandoori cooking is by dry heat in a clay oven called a tandoor. Although the heat source is at the base of the oven the oven heat is evenly distributed because of the clay which radiates heat evenly.

METHOD

Meat (small cuts and small joints), poultry (small cuts and whole chickens) and fish, such as prawns, are usually placed vertically in the oven. No fat or oil is used. The food is cooked quickly and the flavour is similar to that of barbecued food. Oven temperatures reach 375°C (700°F). Depending on the type, foods may be marinaded for 20 minutes to 2 hours before being cooked and in some cases they may be brushed with the marinade during cooking.

Naan, a flat leavened bread, is slapped onto the inside walls of a tandoor and cooks alongside other skewered foods.

If a traditional tandoor is not available, then an oven, grill rôtisserie or barbecue can be used provided the basic rules and principles of tandoori cooking are applied. However, as the spices for a tandoori marinade should be well cooked at a high temperature, then the spices in this case should be briefly cooked over a fierce heat before being added to the marinade.

ADVANTAGES

- The distinctive flavour of tandoori-cooked food comes from both the marinade and the cooking process.
- Marinading tenderises and also adds flavour to foods.
- Colour change may occur depending on the spices used: a red colouring agent is used in some marinades, also onions, garlic, herbs, spices and oil, wine or lemon juice.

— *Grilling* —

DEFINITION

This is a fast method of cooking by radiant heat sometimes known as broiling.

PURPOSE

The purpose of grilling is:

- to make foods digestible, palatable and safe to eat;
- to utilise the speed of the cooking process to produce a distinctive flavour, colour, texture and eating quality;
- to bring variety to the menu and to introduce into the diet simple, uncomplicated dishes.

METHODS OF GRILLING

Grilled foods can be cooked:

- over heat (charcoal, barbecues, gas or electric heated grills);
- under heat (gas or electric salamanders (overfired grills);
- between heat (electrically heated grill bars or plates);
- barbecuing.

Over heat

Grill bars must be preheated and brushed with oil prior to use, otherwise food will stick. The bars should char the food on both sides to give the distinctive appearance and flavour of grilling. Most foods are started on the hottest part of the grill and moved to a cooler part to complete the cooking. The thickness of the food and the heat of the grill determine the cooking time, which is learned by experience.

Under heat (salamander)

This method is also known as broiling.

The salamander should be preheated and the bars greased for cooking on the bars. Steaks, chops and items that are likely to slip between the grill bars may be cooked under the salamander.

Fig 3.1: A traditional tandoor oven

DEGREES OF COOKING GRILLS	APPEARANCE OF JUICE ISSUING FROM THE MEAT WHEN PRESSED
rare	red and bloody
underdone	reddish pink
just done	pink
well done	clear

Plate 3.7: Grilling steak

Food items that are difficult to handle because they may easily break up may be placed in between a well-greased, centre-hinged, *double wire grid* with a handle, making it both easy and swift to cook food such as whole sole, whole plaice.

Tomatoes, mushrooms, bacon, sausages and kidneys may be grilled under a salamander on a flat tray. A rim is required on the tray to prevent spillage of fat and articles of food sliding from the tray.

The salamander can also be used for browning, gratinating and glazing certain dishes such as duchess potato border, macaroni au gratin, fillets of sole bonne femme, and for toasting.

Between heat

This is grilling between electrically heated grill bars or plates and is applied to small cuts of meat.

Barbecuing

This is grilling on preheated, greased bars over a fierce heat (gas, charcoal or wood). When using solid fuel, the flames and smoke must be allowed to die down before placing food on the bars, otherwise the food will be tainted and spoiled. Certain foods, such as brochettes or chicken, may be marinaded before cooking. Other foods (e.g. pork spare ribs) are brushed liberally with a barbecue sauce on both sides during cooking (page 379).

EFFECTS OF GRILLING

Because of the speed of cooking there is maximum retention of nutrients and flavour. Grilling is only suitable for certain cuts of best quality meat; inferior meat would be tough and inedible. The effect of fierce heat on the surface of the meat rapidly coagulates and seals the surface protein, thus helping to retain the meat juices. Grilled meats lose less of their juices than meat cooked by any other method provided they are not pierced with a fork while cooking.

ADVANTAGES

- Speed of grilling enables food to be quickly cooked to order.
- Charring foods gives a distinctive appearance and improves flavour.
- Control of cooking is aided because food is visible whilst being grilled.
- Variety is given to menu and diet.
- Grills may be situated in view of the customer.

GENERAL RULES FOR EFFICIENT GRILLING

- Smaller, thinner items require cooking quickly.
- Seal and colour food on the hot part of the grill then move to a cooler part to complete cooking.
- Slow cooking results in the food drying out.
- Basting of food and oiling of bars prevents dryness.
- Tongs are used for turning and lifting cutlets and steaks. Palette knives and slices are used for turning and lifting tomatoes, mushrooms, whole or cut fish, from trays.

SAFETY

- Take extra care when moving hot salamander and grill bars.
- Trays used for grilling must have raised edges and not be overloaded.
- Never place trays on the top surface of the heated salamander.
- Take care when removing foods from grills and salamanders.

— Shallow frying —

DEFINITION

Shallow frying is the cooking of food in a small quantity of preheated fat or oil in a shallow pan or on a flat surface (griddle plate).

PURPOSE

The purpose of shallow frying is:

- to give variety to the menu and the diet, by making food palatable, digestible and safe to eat;
- to brown food giving it a different colour and an interesting and attractive flavour.

METHODS

There are four methods of frying using a shallow amount of fat or oil: shallow fry; sauté; griddle; stir fry.

Plate 3.8: Preparation for sauté potatoes with onions

Shallow fry

Food is cooked in a small amount of fat or oil in a frying pan or sauté pan. The presentation side of the food should be fried first, as this side will have the better appearance because the fat is clean, then turned so that both sides are cooked and coloured. This applies to small cuts of fish, meat and poultry, also small whole fish (up to 400 g/1 lb). Eggs, pancakes and certain vegetables are cooked by this method. The term *meunière* refers to shallow-fried fish which is passed through seasoned flour, shallow fried and finished with lemon juice, nut-brown butter and chopped parsley.

Sauté

Tender cuts of meat and poultry are cooked in a sauté or frying pan. After the food is cooked on both sides it is removed from the pan, the fat is discarded and the pan deglazed with stock or wine. This then forms an important part of the finished sauce.

Sauté is also used when cooking, for example, potatoes, onions or kidneys, when they are cut into slices or pieces and tossed (*sauter* means to jump or toss) in hot shallow fat or oil in a frying pan until golden brown and cooked.

Griddle

Foods can be cooked on a griddle (a solid metal plate): hamburgers, sausages or sliced onions are placed on a lightly oiled preheated griddle and turned frequently during cooking. Pancakes may be cooked this way but are turned only once.

Stir fry

Vegetables, strips of beef, chicken, etc. can be fast fried in a wok or frying pan in a little fat or oil.

EFFECTS

The high temperature used in shallow frying produces almost instant coagulation of the surface protein of the food and prevents the escape of the natural juices. Some of the frying medium will be absorbed by the food being fried, which will change the nutritional content.

ADVANTAGES

Shallow frying is a quick method of cooking prime cuts of meat and poultry as suitable fats or oils can be raised to a high temperature without burning. As the food is in direct contact with the fat, it cooks rapidly.

TIME AND TEMPERATURE CONTROL

This is particularly important as all shallow-fried foods should have an appetising golden brown colour on both sides. This can only be achieved by careful control of the temperature, which should be initially hot; the heat is then reduced and the food turned when required.

GENERAL RULES

- When shallow frying continuously over a busy period, prepare and cook in a systematic way.
- Pans should be cleaned after every use.
- New pans used for frying (except sauté pans) must be proved before being used.

SAFETY

- Select the correct type and size of pan: not too small, as food, such as fish, will not brown evenly and may break up; not too large, as areas not covered by food will burn and spoil the flavour of the food being cooked.
- Always keep sleeves rolled down as splashing fat may burn the forearm.
- Avoid being splashed by hot fat when placing food in the pan – add it carefully away from you.
- Use a thick, clean, dry cloth when handling pans.
- Move pans carefully in case they jar and tip fat onto the stove.

Deep frying

DEFINITION

This is the cooking of food in preheated deep oil or clarified fat.

PURPOSE

The purpose of deep frying is:

- to cook appetising foods of various kinds thus giving variety to the diet and the menu;
- to produce food with an appetising golden brown colour, crisp, palatable and safe to eat.

METHODS

Conventional deep-fried foods, with the exception of potatoes, are coated with milk and flour, egg and crumbs, batter or pastry to:

- protect the surface of the food from intense heat;
- prevent the escape of moisture and nutrients;
- modify the rapid penetration of the intense heat.

The food is carefully placed into deep preheated oil or fat, fried until cooked and golden brown, well drained and served.

Partial deep-frying is known as *blanching* and may be applied to chipped potatoes. The purpose is to partly cook in advance of service and to complete the cooking to order. With certain types of potatoes this gives an eating quality of a floury inside and crisp exterior to the chips.

EFFECTS OF DEEP FRYING

Deep frying of items coated with milk or egg seals the surface by coagulation of the protein, with the minimum absorption of fat. However, the interior may be raw, as in apple fritters, and will require to be cooked. A cooked interior, as in croquette potatoes, needs only to be heated through. The coating (batter, etc.) does need to be cooked. With uncoated items, such as chipped potatoes, the food absorbs a large amount of fat thus affecting the texture and nutritional content.

The effect of deep drying on the structure of the item being cooked will vary according to the nature of the food.

ADVANTAGES

- Blanching, or partial cooking, enables certain foods to be held for cooking later, which helps during busy service and saves time.
- Coating foods enables a wide variety to be cooked by this method.
- Foods can be cooked quickly and easily handled for service.
- Coated foods are quickly sealed, thus preventing the enclosed food becoming greasy.

TEMPERATURE AND TIME CONTROL

With deep fat frying it is essential for fat temperatures to be maintained at the correct degree. When quantities of food are being continuously fried, after the removal of one batch the temperature of the fat must be allowed to recover before the next batch is cooked. If this is not done the food will be pale and insipid in appearance and soggy to eat.

Timing is important: if thicker pieces of food are being cooked, the temperature must be lowered to allow for sufficient cooking time otherwise the food will be overcoloured and undercooked. The reverse is also true: the smaller the pieces of food the hotter the frying temperature and the shorter the cooking time.

GENERAL RULES

- Systematic preparation and cooking are essential.
- Never overfill fryers with fat or oil or food to be cooked.
- When using free-standing fryers without a thermometer never allow smoke to rise from the fat; this will give a disagreeable taste and smell to food being fried.

Oil temperatures

TYPE	APPROXIMATELY FLASH-POINT (°C)	SMOKE POINT (°C)	RECOMMENDED FRYING TEMP (°C)
finest quality vegetable oils	324	220	180
finest vegetable fat	321	220	180
high-class vegetable oil	324	204	180
pure vegetable fat	318	215	170–182
pure vegetable oil	330	220	
finest quality maize oil	224	215	180
finest fat	321	202	180
finest quality dripping	300	165	170–180
finest natural olive oil	270–273	148–165	175

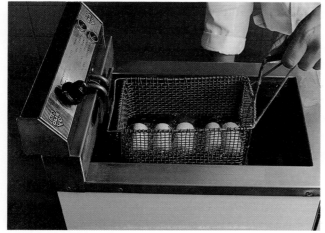

Plate 3.9: Deep frying croquette potatoes

- The normal frying temperature is between 175°C and 195°C (350–380°F), this is indicated by a slight heat haze rising from the fat.
- Do not attempt to fry too much food at one time.
- Allow fat to recover its heat before adding the next batch of food.
- Ensure a correct oil/fat ratio to food. If too much food is cooked in too little fat, even if the initial temperature of the fat is correct, the effect of a large amount of food will reduce the temperature drastically and spoil the food.
- Reduce frying temperatures during slack periods to conserve fuel.
- Restrict holding time to a minimum – fried foods soon lose their crispness.
- Oil and fat should be strained after use, otherwise remaining food particles will burn when the fat is next heated thus spoiling the appearance and flavour of the food.
- Always cover oil or fat when not in use to prevent oxidation.

SAFETY

- Always only half-fill fryers with fat or oil.
- Never overload fryers with food.
- Dry foods, such as potatoes, thoroughly before frying, otherwise they will splutter and cause burns.
- Always place food carefully in the fryer *away* from you. If it is added towards you, hot fat could splash and burn.
- Always have a frying basket and spider to hand in case food is required to be lifted out of the fryer quickly. A combination of the fats being too hot, fat almost ready for discarding and the food being damp can result in the fat boiling over. If it is a free-standing friture on the stove then there is a risk of fire.
- Move free-standing fryers with great care so as not to jar them and spill fat on the stove.
- Ensure that correct fire prevention equipment is to hand and that you are familiar with the fire drill procedure.
- Keep sleeves rolled down at all times when handling fryers.
- Use clean, dry, thick, sound cloths when handling fritures.
- Allow fat to cool before straining.

Paper bag cooking

Known as *en papillotte*, this is method of cookery in which food is tightly sealed in oiled greaseproof paper or foil so that no steam escapes during cooking and maximum natural flavour and nutritive value is retained.

Thick items of food, such as veal chops or red mullet, may be partly and quickly precooked, usually by grilling or shallow frying, then finely cut vegetables, herbs and spices can be added. The bags are tightly sealed, placed on a lightly greased tray and cooked in a hot oven. When cooked, the food is served in the bag and opened by or in front of the customer.

Microwave cooking

DEFINITION

This is a method of cooking and reheating food using electromagnetic waves in a microwave oven powered by electricity. The microwaves are similar to those which carry television signals from the transmitter to the receiver but are at a higher frequency. The microwaves activate the water molecules or particles of food and agitate them, causing heat by friction which cooks or reheats the food.

PURPOSE

- Raw, preprepared or precooked foods are cooked quickly and made palatable and digestible.
- Foods are safer to eat, particularly reheated foods, because the total food is heated at the same time.

APPLICATION

Microwave cooking can be used for cooking raw food, reheating cooked food and defrosting frozen foods.

ADVANTAGES

- A saving of between 50 and 70 per cent over conventional cooking times on certain foods.
- A quick way to cook and reheat foods.
- A fast method of defrosting foods.
- Economical on:
  electricity – less energy required;
  labour – less washing up as foods can be cooked in serving dishes.
- Hot meals can be available 24 hours a day and completely operated on a self-service basis, thereby increasing consumer satisfaction and reducing costs.
- Food is cooked in its own juices so flavour and goodness are retained.
- Minimises food shrinkage and drying-out.
- When used with conventional cooking methods, production can be more flexible.

DISADVANTAGES

- Not suitable for all foods.
- Limited oven space restricts use to small quantities.
- Many microwave ovens do not brown food, although browning elements are available within certain models.
- Not all containers are suitable for use.
- Microwaves can only penetrate 5 cm ($1\frac{1}{2}$ inches) into food (from all sides).

SPECIAL POINTS FOR ATTENTION

- Correct selection of cooking and time controls according to the manufacturer's instructions is essential.
- Certain foods must be removed when underdone to finish cooking, so standing time is important; during this time for example fish turns from opaque to flaky, scrambled eggs turn creamy. Tender, crisp vegetables do not need to stand.
- Baked potatoes and whole unpeeled apples must have the skin pierced in order to release pressure and prevent them bursting.
- Eggs must not be cooked in their shells or they will burst.
- Cover foods when possible to reduce condensation and spluttering.

FACTORS WHICH AFFECT EFFICIENT COOKING

- Only use suitable containers: glass, china, plastic. Only use metal or foil if the particular cooker has been developed to take metal without causing damage. For the best results use straight-sided, round, shallow containers.
- Even-shaped items cook uniformly; arrange uneven-shaped items with the thickest part to the outside of the dish.
- Keep food as level as possible, do not pile into mounds.
- Allow sufficient space to stir or mix.
- Turn items, such as corn on the cob, during cooking because dense items take longer to cook then porous items.
- Foods with a high water content cook faster than those which are drier.
- Most foods should be covered when cooked in a microwave oven. Microwave clingfilm is available to cover food.

SAFETY

- Should the door seal be damaged, do not use the oven. This should be reported to the employer immediately.
- Do not operate the oven when it is empty.
- Remember to pierce foods and cover foods that are likely to burst.
- Regular inspection is essential and manufacturer's instructions must be followed.

4

STOCKS, SOUPS AND SAUCES

Recipe No.			*page no.*
	Stocks		
2	Fish stock	*Fond (or Fumet) de poisson*	114
1	General proportions of stocks		113
3	Vegetable stock, white		114
4	Vegetable stock, brown		115
	Hot Sauces and Gravies		
6	Anchovy sauce	*Sauce anchois*	118
16	Aurore sauce	*Sauce aurore*	120
37	Bread sauce		131
28	Brown onion sauce	*Sauce lyonnaise*	125
20	Brown sauce	*Sauce espagnole*	121
15	Caper sauce	*Sauce au câpres*	120
32	Charcutière sauce	*Sauce charoutière*	127
24	Chasseur sauce	*Sauce chasseur*	123
8	Cheese sauce	*Sauce Mornay*	118
12	Cream sauce	*Sauce crème*	119
34	Curry sauce	*Sauce Kari*	129
22	Demi-glace sauce	*Sauce demi-glace*	122
25	Devilled sauce	*Sauce diable*	124
7	Egg sauce	*Sauce aux œufs*	118
19	Fish velouté	*Poisson velouté*	120
40	Hollandaise sauce	*Sauce hollandaise*	134
27	Italian sauce	*Sauce italienne*	125
18	Ivory sauce	*Sauce ivoire*	120
29	Madeira sauce	*Sauce Madère*	126
39	Melted butter	*Beurre fondu*	133
17	Mushroom sauce	*Sauce aux champignons*	120
13	Mustard sauce	*Sauce moutarde*	119
9	Onion sauce	*Sauce aux oignons*	118
11	Parsley sauce	*Sauce persil*	118
26	Pepper sauce	*Sauce poivrade*	124
30	Piquant sauce	*Sauce piquante*	126
23	Red wine sauce	*Sauce porto*	123
21	Reduced veal stock for sauce		122
33	Reform sauce		128
35	Roast gravy	*Jus rôti*	130
31	Robert sauce		127
10	Soubise sauce	*Sauce Soubise*	118
36	Thickened gravy	*Jus-lié*	131
38	Tomato sauce	*Sauce tomate*	132
14	Velouté sauce	*Velouté*	119
5	White sauce	*Béchamel*	117

110

Soups

64	Asparagus soup	Crème d'asperges	150
66	Autumn vegetable soup		151
62	Basic soup recipe for purées		149
63	Basic soup for creams		150
59	Chicken soup	Crème de volaille/Crème reine	147
53	Chive and potato soup	Vichyssoise	144
41	Clear soup	Consommé	136
49	Cream of green pea soup	Crème St Germain	142
56	Cream of tomato soup	Crème de tomates	146
57	Cream of tomato and potato soup	Crème Solférino	146
61	Cream of vegetable soup	Crème de légumes	148
45	Green pea soup	Purée St Germain	140
46	Haricot bean soup	Purée soissonnaise	141
52	Leek and potato soup	Potage de poireaux et pommes	144
48	Lentil soup	Purée de lentilles	141
67	Minestrone		152
65	Mixed vegetable soup	Potage paysanne	151
58	Mushroom soup	Crème de champignons	146
43	Mutton broth		138
50	Potato soup	Purée Parmentier	143
51	Potato and watercress soup	Purée cressonnière	143
44	Pulse soup		139
42	Royal	Royale	138
54	Tomato soup		145
55	Tomato soup, fresh		146
60	Vegetable soup	Purée de legumes	148
47	Yellow pea soup	Purée egyptienne	141

Sweet sauces are in chapter 14, page 581. More fish sauces can be found in chapter 8, page 240.

Prepare and cook stocks

1. Ensure preparation and cooking areas and equipment are ready for use and satisfy health and hygiene regulations.
2. Plan the work and allocate time appropriately to meet daily schedules.
3. Prepare and cook the ingredients according to the principles of making stock.
4. Store prepared stock in accordance with food hygiene legislation.
5. Clean preparation and cooking areas and equipment after use.
6. Appreciate the value of stock and use it to advantage in the kitchen.
7. Realise that competency implies knowing, understanding and applying, as appropriate, the principles of making and using stock.

Stock is a liquid containing some of the soluble nutrients and flavours of food which are extracted by prolonged and gentle simmering (with the exception of fish stock, which requires only 20 minutes); such liquid is the foundation of soups, sauces and gravies. Stocks are the foundation of many important kitchen preparations; therefore the greatest possible care should be taken in their production.

- Unsound meat or bones and decaying vegetables will give stock an unpleasant flavour and cause it to deteriorate quickly.
- Scum should be removed, otherwise it will boil into the stock and spoil the colour and flavour.
- Fat should be skimmed, otherwise the stock will taste greasy.
- Stock should always simmer gently, for if it is allowed to boil quickly, it will evaporate and go cloudy.
- It should not be allowed to go off the boil, otherwise, in hot weather, there is a danger of its going sour.
- Salt should not be added to stock.
- When making chicken stock, if raw bones are not available, then a boiling fowl can be used.
- If stock is to be kept, strain, reboil, cool quickly and place in the refrigerator.

HEALTH, SAFETY AND HYGIENE

Read the sections in Chapter 1 on 'Maintain a safe and secure working environment' and 'Maintain a professional and hygienic appearance', and also 'Maintain clean food production areas, equipment and utensils; and food hygiene'.

- After stock, sauces, gravies and soups have been rapidly cooled they should be stored in a refrigerator at a temperature below 5°C (41°F).
- If they are to be deep-frozen they should be labelled and dated, and stored below −18°C (0°F).
- When taken from storage they must be boiled for at least 2 minutes before being used.
- They must not be reheated more than once.
- Ideally stocks should be made fresh daily and discarded at the end of the day.
- If stocks are not given the correct care and attention particularly with regard to the soundness of the ingredients used, they can easily become contaminated and a risk to health.
- Never store a stock, sauce, gravy or soup above eye level as this could lead to an accident by someone spilling the contents over themselves.

TYPES OF STOCK

White stocks made from beef, mutton, veal or chicken, can be used in white soups, sauces or stews.

Brown stocks made from beef, mutton, veal, chicken or game, can be used in brown soups, sauces, gravies and stews.

1 – General proportions of ingredients and methods for all stocks except fish stock

	4½ litres	10 litres
raw meaty bones	2 kg (4 lb)	5 kg (10 lb)
water	4½ litres (1 gal)	10 litres (2½ gal)
vegetables (onion, carrot, celery, leek)	400 g (1 lb)	1½ kg (2½ lb)
bouquet garni (thyme, bay leaf, parsley stalks)		
12 peppercorns		

1　Chop up the bones, remove any fat or marrow.
2　Place in a stock pot, add the cold water and bring to the boil.
3　If the scum is dirty then blanch and wash off the bones; cover again with cold water and reboil.
4　Skim, wipe round sides of the pot and simmer gently.
5　Add the washed, peeled, whole vegetables, bouquet garni and peppercorns.
6　Simmer 6–8 hours. Skim and strain.

Note　During the cooking a certain amount of evaporation must take place; therefore add ½ litre (1 pint) cold water just before boiling point is reached. This will also help to throw the scum to the surface and make it easier to skim.

Brown stocks
1　Chop the bones and brown well on all sides either by:
　(a)　placing in a roasting tin in the oven, or
　(b)　carefully browning in a little fat in a frying-pan.
2　Drain off any fat and place the bones in stock pot.
3　Brown any sediment that may be in the bottom of the tray, deglaze (swill out) with ½ litre (1 pint) of boiling water, simmer for a few minutes and add to the bones.

recipe continued ▶

113

4 Add the cold water, bring to the boil and skim.
5 Wash, peel and roughly cut the vegetables, fry in a little fat until brown, strain and add to the bones.
6 Add the bouquet garni and peppercorns.
7 Simmer for 6–8 hours. Skim and strain.

Note For brown stocks a few squashed tomatoes and washed mushroom trimmings can also be added to improve the flavour, as can a calf's foot and/or a knuckle of bacon.

2 – Fish stock

	4½ litres	12 litres
margarine or butter	50 g (2 oz)	125 g (5 oz)
onions	200 g (8 oz)	500 g (1¼ lb)
white fish bones (preferably sole, whiting, or turbot)	2 kg (4 lb)	4 kg (10 lb)
lemon, juice of	½	1½
6 peppercorns		
1 bay leaf		
parsley stalks		
water	4½ litres (1 gal)	12 litres (2½ gal)

> Using hard margarine, this recipe provides for 4½ litres:
>
> 536/kJ/366 kcal
> 40.1 g fat
> (of which 17.6 g saturated)
> 0.2 g carbohydrate
> (of which 0.2 g sugars)
> 0.1 g protein
> 0.0 g fibre

1 Melt the margarine or butter in a thick-bottomed pan.
2 Add the sliced onions, the well-washed fish bones and remainder of the ingredients except the water.
3 Cover with greaseproof paper and a lid and sweat (cook gently without colouring) for 5 minutes.
4 Add the water, bring to the boil, skim and simmer for 20 minutes, then strain. Longer cooking time will spoil the flavour.

3 – White vegetable stock

	4 portions	10 portions
onion	100 g (4 oz)	250 g (10 oz)
carrots	100 g (4 oz)	250 g (10 oz)
celery	100 g (4 oz)	250 g (10 oz)
leek	100 g (4 oz)	250 g (10 oz)
water	1½ litres (3 pt)	3¾ litres (7½ pt)

1   Roughly chop all the vegetables.
2   Place all the ingredients into a saucepan, add the water, bring to the boil.
3   Allow to simmer for approximately 1 hour.
4   Skim if necessary. Strain and use.

4 – Brown vegetable stock

	4 portions	10 portions
onions	100 g (4 oz)	250 g (10 oz)
carrots	100 g (4 oz)	250 g (10 oz)
celery	100 g (4 oz)	250 g (10 oz)
leeks	100 g (4 oz)	250 g (10 oz)
sunflower oil	60 ml ($\frac{1}{8}$ pt)	150 ml (6 fl oz)
tomatoes	50 g (2 oz)	125 g (5 oz)
mushroom trimmings	50 g (2 oz)	125 g (5 oz)
6 peppercorns		
water	1$\frac{1}{2}$ litres (3 pts)	3$\frac{3}{4}$ litres (7 pts)
yeast extract	5 g ($\frac{1}{4}$ oz)	10 g ($\frac{1}{2}$ oz)

1   Roughly chop all the vegetables.
2   Fry the onions, carrots, celery and leeks in the sunflower oil until golden brown.
3   Drain the vegetables, place into a suitable saucepan.
4   Add all the other ingredients except the yeast extract.
5   Cover with the water, bring to the boil.
6   Add the yeast extract, simmer gently for approximately 1 hour.
7   Skim if necessary. Strain and use.

GLAZES

Glazes are made by boiling steadily white or brown beef stock or fish stock and allowing them to reduce to a sticky or gelatinous consistency. They are then stored in jars and when cold kept in the refrigerator for up to one week. If they are to be deep frozen then place into small preserving jars which have been sterilised for 1 hour. The glaze can then be kept for several months.

Glazes are used to improve the flavour of a prepared sauce which may taste bland or be lacking in strength. They may also be used as a base for sauces, such as a fish glaze for fish white wine sauce. Butter and/or cream may be added.

Prepare and cook sauces

1. Ensure preparation and cooking areas and equipment are ready for use and satisfy health and hygiene regulations.
2. Plan the work and allocate time to meet daily schedules.
3. Prepare and cook the ingredients according to the principles of making sauces, with particular regard to consistency.
4. Explain with what sauces are served and state the derivatives of the basic sauces.
5. Store prepared sauces in accordance with food hygiene legislation.
6. Clean the preparation and cooking areas and utensils after use.
7. Realise that competency implies knowing, understanding and as appropriate, applying the principles of making and using sauces.

A sauce is a liquid which has been thickened by

- beurre manié (kneaded butter),
- egg yolks,
- roux,
- cornflour, arrowroot or starch,
- cream, and/or butter added to reduced stock.

All sauces should be smooth, glossy in appearance, definite in taste and light in texture; the thickening medium should be used in moderation.

ROUX

A roux is a combination of fat and flour which are cooked together. There are three degrees to which a roux may be cooked, namely:

- white roux,
- blond roux,
- brown roux.

A boiling liquid should never be added to a hot roux as the result may be lumpy and the person making the sauce may be scalded by the steam produced. If allowed to stand for a time over a moderate heat a sauce made with a roux may become thin due to chemical change (dextrinisation) in the flour.

White roux is used for white (béchamel) sauce and soups. Equal quantities of margarine or butter and flour are cooked together without colouring for a few minutes to a sandy texture.

Alternatively, use polyunsaturated vegetable margarine or make a roux with vegetable oil, using equal quantities of oil to flour. This does give a slack roux but enables the liquid to be easily incorporated.

Blond roux is used for veloutés, tomato sauce and soups. Equal quantities of margarine, butter or vegetable oil and flour are cooked for a little longer than a white roux, but without colouring, to a sandy texture.

Brown roux is used for brown (espagnole) sauce and soups. Use 200 g (8 oz) dripping or vegetable oil to 250 g (10 oz) flour per 4 litres (1 gal) of stock, cooked together slowly to a light-brown colour. Overcooking of brown roux causes the starch to change chemically (dextrinise) and lose some of its thickening property. This will cause the fat to separate from the roux and rise to the surface of the soup or sauce being made. It will also cause too much roux to be used to achieve the required thickness and will give an unpleasant flavour.

OTHER THICKENING AGENTS FOR SAUCES

Cornflower, arrowroot or starch, such as potato starch, is used for thickening gravy and sauces. These are diluted with water, stock or milk, then stirred into the boiling liquid and allowed to reboil for a few minutes and strained. For large-scale cooking and economy, flour may be used.

Beurre manié is used chiefly for fish sauces. Equal quantities of butter or margarine and flour are kneaded to a smooth paste and mixed into a boiling liquid.

Egg yolks are used in mayonnaise, hollandaise and custard sauces. Refer to the appropriate recipe as the yolks are used in a different manner for each sauce.

Vegetables or fruit purées are known as a cullis (*coulis*). No other thickening agent is used.

Blood is used in recipes such as jugged hare.

Reduced stock is now often the basis of brown sauce (see page 121).

BASIC SAUCE RECIPES

5 – White sauce (*béchamel*)
This is a basic white sauce made from milk and a white roux.

	4 portions	10 portions
margarine, oil or butter	100 g (4 oz)	400 g (1 lb)
flour	100 g (4 oz)	400 g (1 lb)
milk	1 litre (1 qt)	4½ litres (1 gal)
1 studded onion		

recipe continued ▶

1 Melt the margarine or butter in a thick-bottomed pan.
2 Add the flour and mix in.
3 Cook for a few minutes over a gentle heat without colouring.
4 Remove from the heat to cool the roux.
5 Gradually add the warmed milk and stir till smooth.
6 Add the onion studded with a clove.
7 Allow to simmer for 30 minutes.
8 Remove the onion, pass the sauce through a conical strainer.
9 Cover with a film of butter or margarine to prevent a skin forming.

Using whole milk/hard margarine, this recipe provides for 1 litre:

7228 kJ/1721 kcal
120.3 g fat
(of which 59.5 g saturated)
124.8 g carbohydrate
(of which 48.6 g sugars)
42.5 g protein
3.6 g fibre

Using skimmed milk/hard margarine, this recipe provides:

5884 kJ/1401 kcal
83.3 g fat
(of which 36.1 g saturated)
127.8 g carbohydrate
(of which 51.6 g sugars)
43.5 g protein
3.6 g fibre

Other sauces made from basic white sauce
(Quantities for $\frac{1}{2}$ litre (1 pint): 8–12 portions)

	SAUCE	SERVED WITH	ADDITIONS PER $\frac{1}{2}$ LITRE (1 PT)
6	anchovy	poached or fried or boiled fish	1 tbsp anchovy essence
7	egg	poached fish or boiled fish	2 hard-boiled eggs, diced
8	cheese or Mornay sauce	fish or vegetables	50 g (2 oz) grated cheese, 1 egg yolk. Mix well in boiling sauce, remove from heat. Strain if necessary but do not allow to reboil
9	onion	roast mutton	100 g (4 oz) chopped or diced onions cooked without colour either by boiling or sweating in butter
10	soubise	roast mutton	as for onion sauce but passed through a strainer
11	parsley	poached or boiled fish and vegetables	1 tbsp chopped parsley

	SAUCE	SERVED WITH	ADDITIONS PER $\frac{1}{2}$ LITRE (I PT)
12	cream	poached fish and boiled vegetables	Add cream, milk, natural yoghurt or fromage blanc to give the consistency of double cream
13	mustard	grilled herrings	Add diluted English or continental mustard to make a fairly hot sauce.

14 – Velouté (chicken, veal, fish, mutton)

This is a basic white sauce made from white stock and a blond roux.

	4 portions	10 portions
margarine, butter or oil	100 g (4 oz)	400 g (1 lb)
flour	100 g (4 oz)	400 g (1 lb)
stock (chicken, veal, fish, mutton) as required	1 litre (1 qt)	4½ litres (1 gal)

> Using hard margarine, this recipe provides for I litre:
>
> 4594 kJ/1094 kcal
> 82.6 g fat
> (of which 35.4 g saturated)
> 79.0 g carbohydrate
> (of which 1.6 g sugars)
> 13.3 g protein
> 3.6 g fibre

1 Melt the fat or oil in a thick-bottomed pan.
2 Add the flour and mix in.
3 Cook out to a sandy texture over gentle heat without colouring it.
4 Allow the roux to cool.
5 Gradually add the boiling stock.
6 Stir until smooth and boiling.
7 Allow to simmer for approximately 1 hour.
8 Pass it through a fine conical strainer.

> Using sunflower oil, this recipe provides for I litre:
>
> 5304 kJ/1263 kcal
> 101.5 g fat
> (of which 13.3 g saturated)
> 78.9 g carbohydrate
> (of which 1.5 g sugars)
> 13.2 g protein
> 3.6 g fibre

Note A velouté sauce for chicken, veal or fish dishes is usually finished with cream and in some cases, also egg yolks.

Sauces made from veloutés
(Quantities for ½ litre (1 pint): 8–12 portions)

	SAUCE	SERVED WITH	ADDITIONS PER ½ LITRE (1 PT)
15	caper	boiled leg of mutton	2 tbsp capers
16	aurore	boiled chicken, poached eggs, chaud-froid sauce	25 g (1 oz) mushroom trimmings, 60 ml (⅛ pt) cream, 1 egg yolk, 2–3 drops lemon juice, 1 tbsp tomato purée
17	mushroom	boiled chicken, sweetbreads	as (16) but substitute for tomato purée, 100 g (4 oz) well-washed, sliced, sweated white button mushrooms after straining velouté, simmer for 10 minutes and add yolk and cream
18	ivory	boiled chicken	as (17) but add a little meat glaze for an ivory colour

19 – Fish velouté

	4 portions	10 portions
margarine or butter	100 g (4 oz)	250 g (5 oz)
flour	100 g (4 oz)	250 g (5 oz)
fish stock	1 litre (1 qt)	2½ litres (2½ pt)

The recipe provides:

4805 kJ/1144 kcal
90.4 g fat
(of which 39.0 g saturated)
77.8 g carbohydrate
(of which 1.6 g sugars)
9.5 g protein
3.6 g fibre

1 Prepare a blond roux using the margarine or butter and flour.
2 Gradually add the stock, stirring continuously until boiling point is reached.
3 Simmer for approximately 1 hour.
4 Pass through a fine conical strainer.

Note This will give a thick sauce which can be thinned down with the cooking liquor from the fish for which the sauce is intended.

20 – Brown sauce (*espagnole*)

	4 portions	10 portions
good dripping or oil	50 g (2 oz)	200 g (8 oz)
flour	60 g (2½ oz)	240 g (10 oz)
tomato purée	25 g (1 oz)	100 g (4 oz)
brown stock	1 litre (1 qt)	4 litres (1 gal)
carrot	100 g (4 oz)	400 g (1 lb)
onion	100 g (4 oz)	400 g (1 lb)
celery	50 g (2 oz)	200 g (8 oz)

Using hard margarine, this recipe provides for 1 litre:

2881 kJ/686 kcal
42.0 g fat
(of which 17.8 g saturated)
67.2 g carbohydrate
(of which 20.2 g sugars)
14.0 g protein
8.6 g fibre

Using sunflower oil, this recipe provides for 1 litre:

3236 kJ/771 kcal
51.5 g fat
(of which 6.8 g saturated)
67.1 g carbohydrate
(of which 20.2 g sugars)
13.9 g protein
8.6 g fibre

1 Heat the dripping or oil in a thick-bottomed pan.
2 Add the flour, cook out slowly to a light brown colour, stirring frequently.
3 Cool and mix in the tomato purée.
4 Gradually mix in the boiling stock. Bring to the boil.
5 Wash, peel and roughly cut the vegetables.
6 Lightly brown in a little fat or oil in a frying-pan.
7 Drain off the fat and add to the sauce.
8 Simmer gently for 4–6 hours. Skim when necessary. Strain.

Note   Care should be taken when making the brown roux not to allow it to cook too quickly, otherwise the starch in the flour (which is the thickening agent) will burn, and its thickening properties weaken. Overbrowning should also be avoided as this tends to make the sauce taste bitter.

Stock-reduced base sauce

Many establishments have discontinued using espagnole and demi-glace as the basis for brown sauces and instead make use of rich, well-flavoured, brown stocks of veal, chicken, etc., reduced until the lightest form of natural thickening from the ingredients is achieved.

No flour is used in the thickening process and consequently a lighter textured sauce is produced. Care needs to be taken when reducing this type of sauce that the end product is not too strong or bitter.

21 ~ Reduced veal stock for sauce

4½ litres (1 gal)

veal bones	4 kg (8 lb)
2 calves feet, split lengthways	
water	4 litres (1 gal)
carrots	400 g (1 lb)
onions	200 g (½ lb)
celery	100 g (¼ lb)
tomatoes	1 kg (2 lb)
mushrooms	200 g (½ lb)
1 large bouquet garni	
4 unpeeled cloves of garlic (optional)	

1 Brown the chopped bones and calves feet (split lengthways) on a roasting tray in the oven.
2 Place the browned bones in a stock pot, cover with cold water and bring to simmering point.
3 Roughly chop the carrots, onions and celery. Using the same roasting tray and the fat from the bones, brown them off.
4 Drain off the fat, add vegetables to the stock and deglaze the tray.
5 Add the quartered tomatoes and chopped mushrooms, simmer gently for 4–5 hours. Skim frequently.
6 Strain the stock into a clean pan and reduce until a light consistency is achieved.

22 ~ Demi-glace sauce

This is a refined espagnole and is made by simmering 1 litre (1 qt) brown sauce and 1 litre (1 qt) brown stock and reducing them by a half. Skim off all impurities as they rise to the surface during cooking. Pass through a fine chinois (conical strainer), reboil and correct the seasoning.

Using sunflower oil, this recipe provides for 1 litre:	Using hard margarine, this recipe provides for 1 litre:
3010 kJ/720 kcal 51.0 g fat (of which 6.6 g saturated) 52.0 g carbohydrate (of which 3.7 g sugars) 15.0 g protein 2.1 g fibre	2634 kJ/630 kcal 42.0 g fats (of which 17.5 g saturated) 52.0 g carbohydrate (of which 3.8 g sugars) 15.0 g protein 2.1 g fibre

Sauces made from demi-glace or stock-reduced base

23 – Red wine sauce

	4 portions	10 portions
chopped shallots	50 g (2 oz)	125 g (5 oz)
red wine	125 ml ($\frac{1}{4}$ pt)	300 ml ($\frac{5}{8}$ pt)
pinch mignonette pepper		
sprig of thyme		
bay leaf		
demi-glace jus-lié or stock-reduced base	250 ml ($\frac{1}{2}$ pt)	600 ml (1$\frac{1}{4}$ pt)

1 Reduce the shallots, red wine, pepper, thyme and bay leaf.
2 Place the reduction in a small sauteuse.
3 Allow to boil until reduced to a quarter.
4 Add the demi-glace. Simmer for 20–30 minutes.
5 Correct the seasoning. Pass through a fine strainer.

Note This sauce traditionally includes poached beef marrow either:

- in dice, poached and added to the sauce;
- cut in slices, poached and placed on meat before being sauced over.

It may be served with fried steaks.

24 – Chasseur sauce

	4 portions	10 portions
butter	25 g (1 oz)	60 g (2$\frac{1}{2}$ oz)
chopped shallots	10 g ($\frac{1}{2}$ oz)	25 g (1$\frac{1}{4}$ oz)
1 clove chopped garlic (optional)		
sliced button mushrooms	50 g (2 oz)	125 g (5 oz)
white wine (dry)	60 ml ($\frac{1}{8}$ pt)	150 ml ($\frac{1}{3}$ pt)
tomatoes, skinned, de-seeded, diced	100 g (4 oz)	250 g (10 oz)
demi-glace jus-lié or reduced stock	250 ml ($\frac{1}{2}$ pt)	600 ml (1$\frac{1}{4}$ pt)
chopped parsley and tarragon		

1 Melt the butter in a small sauteuse.
2 Add the shallots and cook gently for 2–3 minutes without colour.

recipe continued ▶

3 Add the garlic and the mushrooms, cover, and gently cook for 2–3 minutes.
4 Strain off the fat.
5 Add the wine and reduce by half.
6 Add the tomatoes.
7 Add the demi-glace; simmer for 5–10 minutes.
8 Correct the seasoning and add the tarragon and parsley.

Note This may be served with fried steaks, chops, chicken, etc.

25 ~ Devilled sauce

	4 portions	10 portions
shallot or onion, chopped	50 g (2 oz)	125 g (5 oz)
mignonette pepper	5 g ($\frac{1}{4}$ oz)	12 g ($\frac{5}{8}$ oz)
tbsp white wine		
tbsp vinegar		
cayenne pepper		
demi-glace jus-lié or reduced stock	250 ml ($\frac{1}{2}$ pt)	600 ml ($1\frac{1}{4}$ pt)

1 Boil the shallots, pepper, wine and vinegar and reduce by half.
2 Add the demi-glace. Simmer for 5–10 minutes.
3 Season liberally with cayenne.
4 Pass through a fine conical strainer. Correct the seasoning.

Note May be served with grilled or fried fish or meats.

26 ~ Pepper (*Poivrade*) sauce

	4 portions	10 portions
margarine, butter or oil	25 g (1 oz)	60 g ($2\frac{1}{2}$ oz)
onion	50 g (2 oz)	125 g (5 oz)
carrot	50 g (2 oz)	125 g (5 oz)
celery	50 g (2 oz)	125 g (5 oz)
1 bay leaf		
sprig of thyme		
2 tbsp white wine		
2 tbsp vinegar		
mignonette pepper	5 g ($\frac{1}{4}$ oz)	12 g ($\frac{5}{8}$ oz)
demi-glace jus-lié or reduced stock	250 ml ($\frac{1}{2}$ pt)	600 ml ($1\frac{1}{4}$ pt)

1   Melt the fat or oil in a small sauteuse.
2   Add the vegetables and herbs (mirepoix) and allow to brown.
3   Pour off the fat.
4   Add the wine, vinegar and pepper.
5   Reduce by half. Add the demi-glace.
6   Simmer for 20–30 minutes. Correct the seasoning.
7   Pass through a fine conical strainer.

Note   Usually served with joints or cuts of venison.

27 – Italian sauce

	1 portion	10 portions
margarine, oil or butter	25 g (1 oz)	60 g (2½ oz)
shallots, chopped	10 g (½ oz)	25 g (1 oz)
mushrooms, chopped	50 g (2 oz)	125 g (5 oz)
demi-glace jus-lié or reduced stock	250 ml (½ pt)	600 ml (1¼ pt)
chopped lean ham	25 g (1 oz)	60 g (2½ oz)
tomatoes, skinned, de-seeded, diced chopped parsley, chervil and tarragon	100 g (4 oz)	250 g (10 oz)

1   Melt the fat or oil in a small sauteuse.
2   To make a duxelle, add the shallots and gently cook for 2–3 minutes, then the mushrooms and gently cook for a further 2–3 minutes.
3   Add the demi-glace, ham and tomatoes.
4   Simmer for 5–10 minutes. Correct the seasoning.
5   Add the chopped herbs.

Note   Usually served with fried cuts of veal or lamb.

28 – Brown onion sauce (*lyonnaise*)

	4 portions	10 portions
margarine, oil or butter	25 g (1 oz)	60 g (2½ oz)
sliced onions	100 g (4 oz)	250 g (10 oz)
2 tbsp vinegar		
demi-glace jus-lié or reduced stock	250 ml (½ pt)	600 ml (1¼ pt)

recipe continued ▶

1 Melt the fat or oil in a sauteuse.
2 Add the onions, cover with a lid.
3 Cook gently till tender.
4 Remove the lid and colour lightly.
5 Add the vinegar and completely reduce.
6 Add the demi-glace, simmer for 5–10 minutes.
7 Skim and correct the seasoning.

Note May be served with Vienna steaks or fried liver.

29 – Madeira sauce

	4 portions	10 portions
demi-glace jus-lié or reduced stock	250 ml ($\frac{1}{2}$ pt)	600 ml ($1\frac{1}{4}$ pt)
Madeira wine	2 tbsp	5 tbsp
butter	25 g (1 oz)	60 g ($2\frac{1}{2}$ oz)

1 Boil the demi-glace in a small sauteuse.
2 Add the Madeira; reboil. Correct the seasoning.
3 Pass through a fine conical strainer. Gradually mix in the butter.

Note May be served with braised ox tongue. Dry sherry or port wine may be substituted for Madeira and the sauce re-named accordingly.

30 – Piquant sauce

	4 portions	10 portions
vinegar	60 ml ($\frac{1}{8}$ pt)	150 ml ($\frac{1}{3}$ pt)
shallots, chopped	50 g (2 oz)	125 g (5 oz)
demi-glace jus-lié or reduced stock	250 ml ($\frac{1}{2}$ pt)	625 ml ($1\frac{1}{4}$ pt)
gherkins, chopped	25 g (1 oz)	60 g ($2\frac{1}{2}$ oz)
capers, chopped	10 g ($\frac{1}{2}$ oz)	25 g ($1\frac{1}{4}$ oz)
chopped chervil, tarragon and parsley	$\frac{1}{2}$ tbsp	$1\frac{1}{4}$ tbsp

1 Place vinegar and shallots in a small sauteuse and reduce by half.
2 Add demi-glace; simmer for 15–20 minutes.
3 Add the rest of the ingredients.
4 Skim and correct the seasoning.

Note May be served with made-up dishes and grilled meats.

31 – Robert sauce

	4 portions	10 portions
margarine, oil or butter	10 g ($\frac{1}{2}$ oz)	25 g ($1\frac{1}{4}$ oz)
onions, finely chopped	50 g (2 oz)	125 g (5 oz)
vinegar	60 ml ($\frac{1}{8}$ pt)	150 ml ($\frac{1}{3}$ pt)
demi-glace jus-lié or reduced stock	250 ml ($\frac{1}{2}$ pt)	600 ml ($1\frac{1}{4}$ pt)
1 level tbsp English or continental mustard		
$\frac{1}{4}$ level tbsp castor sugar		

1 Melt the fat or oil in a small sauteuse.
2 Add the onion.
3 Cook gently without colour.
4 Add the vinegar and reduce completely.
5 Add the demi-glace; simmer for 5–10 minutes.
6 Remove from the heat and add the mustard diluted with a little water and the sugar, do not boil.
7 Skim and correct the seasoning.

Note May be served with fried pork chop.

32 – Charcutière sauce

Proceed as for sauce Robert and finally add 25 g (1 oz) sliced or julienne gherkins. May also be served with pork chops.

33 – Reform sauce

	4 portions	10 portions
carrot	25 g (1 oz)	60 g (2½ oz)
onion	25 g (1 oz)	60 g (2½ oz)
celery　　mirepoix	10 g (½ oz)	25 g (1¼ oz)
bay leaf	½	2½
sprig of thyme		
margarine or butter	10 g (½ oz)	25 g (1¼ oz)
vinegar	½ tbsp	1 tbsp
redcurrant jelly	½ tbsp	1 tbsp
6 peppercorns		
demi-glace, jus-lié or reduced stock	250 ml (½ pt)	625 ml (1¼ pt)
julienne of cooked beetroot, white of egg, gherkin, mushroom, truffle, tongue	50 g (2 oz)	125 g (5 oz)

1　Fry the vegetables and herbs (mirepoix) in the fat in a sauteuse.
2　Drain off the fat.
3　Add the crushed peppercorns and vinegar and reduce by two-thirds.
4　Add the demi-glace. Simmer for 30 minutes.
5　Skim. Add the redcurrant jelly.
6　Reboil and strain through a chinois.
7　Add the garnish.

Note　May be served with lamb cutlets (see page 308).

MISCELLANEOUS SAUCES

34 ～ Curry sauce

	4 portions	10 portions
onion, chopped	50 g (2 oz)	125 g (5 oz)
clove of garlic	$\frac{1}{4}$	$\frac{1}{2}$
oil, butter or margarine	10 g ($\frac{1}{2}$ oz)	25 g (1$\frac{1}{4}$ oz)
flour	10 g ($\frac{1}{2}$ oz)	25 g (1$\frac{1}{4}$ oz)
curry powder	5 g ($\frac{1}{4}$ oz)	12 g ($\frac{1}{2}$ oz)
tomato purée	5 g ($\frac{1}{4}$ oz)	12 g ($\frac{1}{2}$ oz)
stock	375 ml ($\frac{3}{4}$ pt)	1 litre (2 pt)
apple, chopped	25 g (1 oz)	60 g (2$\frac{1}{2}$ oz)
chutney, chopped	1 tbsp	2 tbsp
desiccated coconut	5 g ($\frac{1}{4}$ oz)	12 g ($\frac{1}{2}$ oz)
sultanas	10 g ($\frac{1}{2}$ oz)	25 g (1$\frac{1}{4}$ oz)
ginger root, *or*	10 g ($\frac{1}{2}$ oz)	25 g (1$\frac{1}{4}$ oz)
ground ginger	5 g ($\frac{1}{4}$ oz)	12 g ($\frac{1}{2}$ oz)
salt		

Using sunflower oil, this recipe provides for 4 portions:

1092 kJ/260 kcal
14.1 g fat
(of which 4.1 g saturated)
30.3 g carbohydrate
(of which 19.9 g sugars)
4.9 g protein
4.1 g fibre

1 Gently cook the onion and garlic in the fat in a small sauteuse without colouring.
2 Mix in the flour and curry powder.
3 Cook gently to a sandy mixture.
4 Mix in the tomato purée, cool.
5 Gradually add the boiling stock and mix to a smooth sauce.
6 Add the remainder of the ingredients; season with salt, and simmer for 30 minutes.
7 Skim and correct the seasoning.

Note This sauce has a wide range of uses with prawns, shrimps, vegetables, eggs, etc.

For poached or soft-boiled eggs it may be strained and for all purposes it may be finished with 2–3 tbsp cream or natural yoghurt.

This is a typical recipe in use today. For a traditional recipe the curry powder would be replaced by either curry paste, or a mixture of freshly ground spices such as turmeric, cumin, allspice, fresh ginger, chilli and clove.

35 – Roast gravy

	4 portions	10 portions
raw bones	200 g (8 oz)	500 g (1¼ lb)
stock or water	250 ml (1 pt)	1¼ litres (2½ pt)
onion	50 g (2 oz)	125 g (5 oz)
celery	25 g (1 oz)	60 g (2½ oz)
carrot	50 g (2 oz)	125 g (5 oz)

> Using sunflower oil, this recipe provides for 4 portions:
>
> 504 kJ/120 kcal
> 10.0 g fat
> (of which 1.3 g saturated)
> 1.8 g carbohydrate
> (of which 0.0 g sugars)
> 5.6 g protein
> 0.0 g fibre

For preference use beef bones for roast beef gravy and the appropriate bones for lamb, veal, mutton and pork.

1. Chop the bones and brown in the oven or brown in a little fat on top of the stove in a frying-pan.
2. Drain off all the fat.
3. Place in saucepan with the stock or water.
4. Bring to the boil, skim and allow to simmer.
5. Add the lightly browned vegetables which may be fried in a little fat in a frying-pan, or added to the bones when partly browned.
6. Simmer for 1½–2 hours.
7. Remove the joint from the roasting tin when cooked.
8. Return the tray to a low heat to allow the sediment to settle.
9. Carefully strain off the fat, leaving the sediment in the tin.
10. Return the joint to the stove and brown carefully; deglaze with the brown stock.
11. Allow to simmer for a few minutes.
12. Correct the colour and seasoning. Strain and skim.

This gravy is illustrated on page 133.

36 – Thickened gravy (*Jus-lié*)

	4 portions	10 portions	
raw veal or chicken bones	200 g (8 oz)	500 g (1¼ lb)	Using sunflower oil, this recipe proves for 4 portions:
celery	25 g (1 oz)	60 g (2½ oz)	
onion	50 g (2 oz)	125 g (5 oz)	189 kcals/793 kJ
carrot	50 g (2 oz)	125 g (5 oz)	10.0 g fat
bay leaf	½	1½	(of which 1.3 saturated)
sprig of thyme	1	3	13.6 g carbohydrate
tomato purée	5 g (¼ oz)	12 g (¼ oz)	(of which 0.6 g sugars)
stock or water	500 ml (1 pt)	1¼ litres (2½ pt)	11.4 g protein
mushroom trimmings	50 g (2 oz)	125 g (5 oz)	0.3 g fibre
arrowroot or cornflour	10 g (½ oz)	25 g (1 g)	

(celery, onion, carrot, bay leaf, sprig of thyme = mirepoix)

1 Chop the bones and brown in the oven or in a little fat in a sauteuse on top of the stove.
2 Add the vegetables and herbs (mirepoix), brown well.
3 Mix in the tomato purée and stock.
4 Simmer for 2 hours. Add mushroom trimmings.
5 Dilute the arrowroot in a little cold water.
6 Pour into the boiling stock, stirring continuously until it reboils.
7 Simmer for 10–15 minutes. Correct the seasoning.
8 Pass through a fine strainer.

37 – Bread sauce

	4 portions	10 portions
milk	375 ml (¾ pt)	1 litre (2 pt)
small onion studded with a clove	1	2
fresh white breadcrumbs	25 g (1 oz)	60 g (2½ oz)
salt, cayenne		
butter	10 g (½ oz)	25 g (1¼ oz)

1 Infuse the simmering milk with the studded onion for 15 minutes.
2 Remove the onion, mix in the crumbs. Simmer for 2–3 minutes.
3 Season, correct the consistency.
4 Add the butter on top of the sauce to prevent a skin forming.
5 Mix well when serving.

Note   Served with roast chicken and turkey. (Illustrated on page 133.)

38 – Tomato sauce

	4 portions	10 portions
margarine or butter	10 g ($\frac{1}{2}$ oz)	25 g (1$\frac{1}{4}$ oz)
onion ⎫	50 g (2 oz)	125 g (5 oz)
carrot ⎪	50 g (2 oz)	125 g (5 oz)
celery ⎬ mirepoix	25 g (1 oz)	60 g (2$\frac{1}{2}$ oz)
bay leaf ⎪	$\frac{1}{2}$	1$\frac{1}{2}$
sprig of thyme ⎭	1	3
bacon scraps	10 g ($\frac{1}{2}$ oz)	25 g (1$\frac{1}{4}$ oz)
flour	10 g ($\frac{1}{2}$ oz)	25 g (1$\frac{1}{4}$ oz)
tomato purée	50 g (2 oz)	125 g (5 oz)
stock	375 ml ($\frac{3}{4}$ pt)	1 litre (2 pt)
clove garlic	$\frac{1}{2}$	1
salt, pepper		

Using hard margarine, this recipe provides for 4 portions:

931 kJ/221 kcal
12.5 g fat
(of which 5.1 g saturated)
20.2 g carbohydrate
(of which 11.5 g sugars)
8.5 g protein
2.9 g fibre

Using butter, this recipe provides for 4 portions:

936 kJ/223 kcal
12.6 g fat
(of which 6.7 g saturated)
20.2 g carbohydrate
(of which 11.5 g sugars)
8.5 g protein
2.9 g fibre

1 Melt the margarine or butter in a small sauteuse.
2 Add the vegetables and herbs (mirepoix) and bacon scraps and brown slightly.
3 Mix in the flour and cook to a sandy texture. Allow to colour slightly.
4 Mix in the tomato purée, allow to cool.
5 Gradually add the boiling stock, stir to the boil.
6 Add the garlic, season. Simmer for 1 hour.
7 Correct the seasoning and cool.
8 Pass through a fine conical strainer.

Note   This sauce has many uses, served with spaghetti, eggs, fish, meats, etc.
   The amount of tomato purée used may need to vary according to its strength. The sauce can be made without using flour by adding 400 g (1 lb) of fresh ripe tomatoes or a tin of tomatoes.

Plate 4.1: Roast gravy (p. 130) and bread sauce (p. 131)

39 – Melted butter

	4 portions	10 portions
butter	200 g (8 oz)	500 g (1¼ lb)
water or white wine	2 tbsp	5 tbsp

Method I
Boil the butter and water gently together until combined, then pass through a fine strainer.

Method II
Melt the butter and carefully strain off the fat leaving the water and sediment in the pan.

Note   Usually served with boiled fish and certain vegetables, for example blue trout, salmon; asparagus and sea kale.

For butter sauce see pages 135 and 254.

40 – Hollandaise sauce

		4 portions	10 portions
crushed peppercorn (optional)	⎱ reduction	6	15
vinegar	⎰	1 tbsp	2½ tbsp
egg yolks		2	5
butter		200 g (8 oz)	500 g (1¼ lb)
salt, cayenne			

> This recipe provides for 4 portions:
>
> 6789 kJ/1616 kcal
> 176.2 g fat
> (of which 107.9 g saturated)
> 0.1 g carbohydrate
> (of which 0.1 g sugars)
> 7.3 g protein
> 0.0 g fibre

1 Place the peppercorns and vinegar in a small sauteuse or stainless steel pan and reduce to one-third.
2 Add 1 tbsp cold water, allow to cool.
3 Mix in the yolks with a whisk.
4 Return to a gentle heat and, whisking continuously, cook to a sabayon (this is the cooking of the yolks to a thickened consistency, like cream, sufficient to show the mark of the whisk).
5 Remove from the heat and cool slightly.
6 Whisk in gradually the melted warm butter until thoroughly combined.
7 Correct the seasoning. If reduction is not used, add a few drops of lemon juice.
8 Pass through a muslin, tammy cloth, or fine conical strainer.
9 The sauce should be kept at only a slightly warm temperature until served.
10 Serve in a slightly warm sauceboat.

Note   The cause of hollandaise sauce curdling is either because the butter has been added too quickly, or because of excess heat which will cause the albumen in the eggs to harden, shrink and separate from the liquid.

Should the sauce curdle, place a teaspoon of boiling water in a clean sauteuse and gradually whisk in the curdled sauce. If this fails to reconstitute the sauce, then place an egg yolk in a clean sauteuse with 1 dessertspoon of water. Whisk lightly over a gentle heat until slightly thickened. Remove from the heat and gradually add the curdled sauce, whisking continuously. To stabilise the sauce during service, 60 ml (⅛ pint) thick béchamel may be added before straining (see page 117).

To reduce the risk of salmonella infection pasteurised egg yolks may be used. Do not keep the sauce for longer than 2 hours, before discarding. This applies to all egg-based sauces.

Served with hot fish (salmon, trout, turbot), and vegetables (asparagus, cauliflower, broccoli).

COMPOUND BUTTER SAUCES

Compound butters are made by mixing the flavouring ingredients into softened butter which can then be shaped into a roll 2 cm (1 inch) in diameter, placed in wet greaseproof paper or foil, hardened in a refrigerator and cut into $\frac{1}{2}$ cm ($\frac{1}{4}$ inch) slices when required.

- *Parsley butter*: chopped parsley and lemon juice.
- *Herb butter*: mixed herbs (chives, tarragon, fennel, dill) and lemon juice.
- *Chive butter*: chopped chives and lemon juice.
- *Garlic butter*: garlic juice and chopped parsley or herbs.
- *Anchovy butter*: few drops anchovy essence.
- *Shrimp butter*: finely chopped or pounded shrimps.
- *Garlic*: mashed to a paste.
- *Mustard*: continental type mustard.
- *Liver pâté*: mashed to a paste.

Compound butters are served with grilled and some fried fish and with grilled meats.

Prepare, and cook soups

1 Ensure preparation and cooking areas and equipment are ready for use and satisfy health and hygiene regulations.
2 Plan the work and allocate time appropriately to meet schedules.
3 Recognise the characteristics of soups are of the type, quality and quantity required.
4 Prepare, cook and finish soups according to customer and dish requirements, paying particular attention to consistency of thick soups and clarity of clear soups.
5 Clean preparation and cooking areas and equipment after use.
6 Realise that competency implies knowing, understanding and applying the principles as appropriate to making soup.

Soups may be served for luncheon, dinner, supper and snack meals. A portion is usually between 200–250 ml ($\frac{1}{3}$–$\frac{1}{2}$ pint), depending on the type of soup and the number of courses to follow.

SOUP CLASSIFICATION	BASE	PASSED OR UNPASSED	FINISH	EXAMPLE
clear	stock	strained	usually garnished	consommé
broth	stock cut vegetables	unpassed	chopped parsley	Scotch broth minestroni
purée	stock fresh vegetables pulses	passed	croûtons	lentil soup potato soup
velouté	blond roux vegetables stock	passed	liaison of yolk and cream	velouté of chicken
cream	stock and vegetables vegetable purée and bechámel velouté	passed	cream, milk or yoghurt	cream of vegetable cream of fresh pea cream of tomato
bisque	shellfish fish stock	passed	cream	lobster soup crab soup
miscellaneous (soups which are not classified under the other headings)				mulligatawny kidney

41 – Clear soup (basic recipe) (*consommé*)

	4 portions	10 portions
chopped or minced beef	200 g (8 oz)	500 g (1¼ lb)
salt		
egg whites	1–2	3–5
cold, white or brown beef stock	1 litre (2 pt)	2½ litres (5 pt)
mixed vegetables (onion, carrot, celery, leek)	100 g (4 oz)	250 g (10 oz)
bouquet garni		
peppercorns	3–4	8–10

I portion provides:

126 kJ/30 kcal
0.0 g fat
(of which 0.0 g saturated)
1.8 g carbohydrate
(of which 0.0 g sugars)
5.6 g protein
0.0 g fibre

Plate 4.2a–b: Ingredients for and clarification of consommé

1 Thoroughly mix the beef, salt, egg white and ¼ litre (½ pint) cold stock in a thick-bottomed pan.
2 Peel, wash and finely chop the vegetables.
3 Add to the beef with the remainder of the stock, the bouquet garni and the peppercorns.
4 Place over a gentle heat and bring slowly to the boil; stirring occasionally.
5 Allow to boil rapidly for 5–10 seconds. Give a final stir.
6 Lower the heat so that the consommé is simmering very gently.
7 Cook for 1½–2 hours without stirring.
8 Strain carefully through a double muslin.
9 Remove all fat, using both sides of 8 cm (3 inch) square pieces of kitchen paper.
10 Correct the seasoning and colour, which should be a delicate amber.
11 Degrease again, if necessary. Bring to the boil and serve.

Note A consommé should be crystal clear. The clarification process is caused by the albumen of the egg white and meat coagulating, rising to the top of the liquid and carrying other solid ingredients. The remaining liquid beneath the coagulated surface should be gently simmering.

Cloudiness is due to some or all of the following:

• poor quality stock;
• greasy stock;
• unstrained stock;
• imperfect coagulation of the clearing agent;

- whisking after boiling point is reached, whereby the impurities mix with the liquid;
- not allowing the soup to settle before straining;
- lack of cleanliness of the pan or cloth;
- any trace of grease or starch.

Consommés are varied in many ways by altering the flavour of the stock (chicken, chicken and beef, game, etc.), also by the addition of numerous garnishes (julienne or brunoise of vegetables – shredded savoury pancakes or pea-sized profiteroles) added at the last moment before serving, or small pasta.

Cold lightly jellied consommés, served in cups, with or without garnish (e.g. diced tomato), may be served in hot weather.

42 – Royal

A royal is a savoury egg custard used for garnishing consommé, it should be firm but tender, the texture smooth, not porous. When cut, no moisture (syneresis) should be apparent; when this happens it is a sign of overcooking.

1 Whisk up 1 egg; season with salt and pepper and add the same amount of stock or milk.
2 Pass through a fine strainer;
3 Pour into a buttered dariole mould, and stand the mould in a pan half full of water.
4 Allow to cook gently in a moderate oven until set, for approximately 15–20 minutes.
5 Remove when cooked; when quite cold turn it out carefully.
6 Trim the edges and cut into neat slices 1 cm ($\frac{1}{2}$ inch) thick, then into squares or diamonds.

43 – Mutton broth

	4 portions	10 portions
scrag end of mutton	200 g (8 oz)	500 g (1$\frac{1}{4}$ lb)
water or mutton or lamb stock	1 litre (2 pt)	2$\frac{1}{2}$ litre (5 pt)
barley	25 g (1 oz)	60 g (2$\frac{1}{2}$ oz)
vegetables (carrot, turnip, leek, celery, onion), chopped	200 g (8 oz)	500 g (1$\frac{1}{4}$ lb)
bouquet garni		
salt, pepper		
chopped parsley		

1 Place the mutton in a saucepan and cover with cold water.
2 Bring to the boil, immediately wash off under running water.
3 Clean the pan, replace the meat, cover with cold water, bring to the boil and skim.
4 Add the washed barley, simmer for 1 hour.
5 Add the vegetables, bouquet garni and season.
6 Skim when necessary; simmer till tender for approximately 30 minutes.
7 Remove the meat, allow to cool and cut from the bone, remove all fat, and cut the meat into neat dice the same size as the vegetables; return to the broth.
8 Correct the seasoning, skim, add the chopped parsley and serve.

44 – Pulse soup basic recipe

Any type of pulse can be made into soup, for example, split green and yellow peas, haricot beans and lentils.

	4 portions	10 portions
pulse (soaked overnight if necessary)	200 g (8 oz)	500 g (1¼ lb)
white stock or water	1½ litres (3 pt)	3¾ litres (7½ pt)
onions, chopped	50 g (2 oz)	125 g (5 oz)
carrots, chopped	50 g (2 oz)	125 g (5 oz)
bouquet garni		
knuckle of ham or bacon (optional)	50 g (2 oz)	125 g (5 oz)
salt, pepper		
Croûtons		
slice stale bread	1	2½
butter	50 g (2 oz)	125 g (5 oz)

1 Pick and wash the pulse (if pre-soaked, change the water).
2 Place in a thick-bottomed pan; add the stock or water, bring to the boil and skim.
3 Add remainder of ingredients, season lightly.
4 Simmer until tender; skim when necessary.
5 Remove bouquet garni and ham.
6 Liquidise and pass through a conical strainer.
7 Return to a clean pan and reboil; correct seasoning and consistency.
8 Serve accompanied by ½ cm (¼ inch) diced bread croûtons shallow fried in butter.

recipe continued ▶

Note   Variations can be made with the addition of:

- Chopped fresh herbs (parsley, chervil, tarragon, etc.).
- Spice/s (garam masala).
- Crisp lardons of bacon.
- Toasted sippets.

45 – Green pea soup (with dried peas)

	4 portions	10 portions
green split peas (soaked overnight if necessary)	200 g (8 oz)	500 g (1¼ lb)
white stock or water	1½ litres (3 pt)	3¾ litres (7 pt)
carrot (whole)	50 g (2 oz)	125 g (5 oz)
bouquet garni		
green of leek	25 g (1 oz)	60 g (2½ oz)
onion	50 g (2 oz)	125 g (5 oz)
knuckle of ham or bacon	50 g (2 oz)	125 g (5 oz)
salt, pepper		
Croûtons		
slice stale bread	1	3
butter	50 g (2 oz)	125 g (5 oz)

I portion provides:

1164 kJ/277 kcal
11.2 g fat
(of which 6.8 g saturated)
33.3 g carbohydrate
(of which 2.3 g sugars)
13.0 g protein
6.7 g fibre

1 Pick and wash the peas.
2 Place in a thick-bottomed pan, cover with cold water or stock; bring to the boil and skim.
3 Add the remainder of the ingredients and season; simmer until tender, skim when necessary.
4 Remove the bouquet garni, carrot and ham.
5 Pass through a sieve or liquidise; then pass through a medium conical strainer.
6 Return to a clean saucepan and reboil; correct the seasoning and consistency. Skim if necessary.
7 Serve accompanied by ½ cm (¼ inch) diced bread croûtons, shallow fried in butter, drained and served in a sauceboat.

46 ~ Haricot bean soup

	4 portions	10 portions
white haricot beans (soaked overnight if necessary)	200 g (8 oz)	500 g (1¼ lb)
white stock or water	1½ litres (3 pt)	3¾ litres (7 pt)
carrot	50 g (2 oz)	125 g (5 oz)
bouquet garni		
onion	50 g (2 oz)	125 g (5 oz)
knuckle of ham or bacon	50 g (2 oz)	125 g (5 oz)
salt, pepper		
Croûtons		
slice stale bread	1	3
butter	50 g (2 oz)	125 g (5 oz)

Method of cooking as for green pea soup (recipe 45).

47 ~ Yellow pea soup (dried peas)

Proceed as for green pea soup (recipe 45), using yellow split peas and omitting the leek. The carrot need not be removed and can be sieved or liquidised with the peas.

48 ~ Lentil soup

	4 portions	10 portions
lentils	200 g (8 oz)	500 g (1¼ lb)
white stock or water	1 litre (2 pt)	2½ litres (5 pt)
carrot	50 g (2 oz)	125 g (5 oz)
bouquet garni		
onion	50 g (2 oz)	125 g (5 oz)
knuckle of ham or bacon (optional)	50 g (2 oz)	125 g (5 oz)
salt, pepper		
tomato purée	1 tsp	3 tsp
Croûtons		
slice stale bread	1	3
butter	50 g (2 oz)	125 g (5 oz)

> 1 portion provides:
>
> 1191 kJ/283 kcal
> 12.4 g fat
> (of which 6.8 g saturated)
> 31.2 g carbohydrate
> (of which 2.2 g sugars)
> 13.7 g protein
> 6.4 g fibre

Method of cooking and serving as for green pea soup (recipe 45).

49 – Cream of green pea soup (fresh or frozen peas)

	4 portions	10 portions
onion	25 g (1 oz)	60 g (2½ oz)
leek	25 g (1 oz)	60 g (2½ oz)
celery	25 g (1 oz)	60 g (2½ oz)
butter	25 g (1 oz)	60 g (2½ oz)
peas (shelled) or frozen	250 ml (½ pt)	600 ml (1½ pt)
water or white stock	500 ml (1 pt)	1¼ litres (2½ pt)
sprig of mint		
bouquet garni		
thin béchamel	500 ml (1 pt)	1¼ litres (2½ pt)
cream	60 ml (⅛ pt)	150 ml (⅓ pt)

> 1 portion provides:
>
> 1356 kJ/323 kcal
> 23.6 g fat
> (of which 12.8 g saturated)
> 19.6 carbohydrate
> (of which 8.0 g sugars)
> 9.3 g protein
> 8.3 g fibre

1 Sweat onion, leak and celery in the butter.
2 Moisten with water or stock and bring to the boil.
3 Add peas, mint and bouquet garni, and allow to boil for approximately 5 minutes.
4 Remove bouquet garni, add béchamel and bring to the boil.
5 Remove from the heat and liquidise or pass through a sieve.
6 Correct seasoning, pass through medium strainer.
7 Finish with cream.

Note Variations can be made with the addition of:

● a garnish of 25 g (1 oz) cooked and washed tapioca added at the same time as the cream;
● a garnish of 25 g (1 oz) cooked and washed vermicelli and julienne of sorrel cooked in butter.

50 – Potato soup

	4 portions	10 portions
butter or margarine	25 g (1 oz)	60 g (2½ oz)
onion	50 g (2 oz)	125 g (5 oz)
white of leek	50 g (2 oz)	125 g (5 oz)
white stock or water	1 litre (2 pt)	2½ litres (5 pt)
peeled potatoes	400 g (1 lb)	1¼ kg (2½ lb)
bouquet garni		
salt, pepper		
chopped parsley		

> Using butter, 1 portion provides:
>
> 1063 kJ/253 kcal
> 15.7 g fat
> (of which 9.8 g saturated)
> 26.1 g carbohydrate
> (of which 2.1 g sugars)
> 3.6 g protein
> 2.9 g fibre

Croûtons

slice stale bread	1	3
butter	50 g (2 oz)	125 g (5 oz)

1. Melt the butter or margarine in a thick-bottomed pan.
2. Add the peeled and washed sliced onion and leek, cook for a few minutes without colour with a lid on.
3. Add the stock and the peeled, washed, sliced potatoes and the bouquet garni and season.
4. Simmer for approximately 30 minutes. Remove the bouquet garni, skim.
5. Liquidise or pass the soup firmly through a sieve then pass through a medium conical strainer.
6. Return to a clean pan, reboil, correct the seasoning and consistency and serve.
7. Sprinkle with chopped parsley. Serve fried or toasted croûtons separately.

51 – Potato and watercress soup

1. Ingredients as for potato soup plus a small bunch of watercress.
2. Pick off 12 neat leaves of watercress, plunge into a small pan of boiling water for 1–2 seconds. Refresh under cold water immediately, these leaves are to garnish the finished soup.
3. Add the remainder of the picked and washed watercress, including the stalks, to the soup at the same time as the potatoes.
4. Finish as for potato soup.

52 – Leek and potato soup

	4 portions	10 portions
leeks, trimmed and washed	400 g (1 lb)	1¼ kg (2½ lb)
butter or margarine	25 g (1 oz)	60 g (2½ oz)
white stock	750 ml (1½ pt)	2 litre (4 pt)
bouquet garni		
potatoes	200 g (8 oz)	½ kg (1¼ lb)
salt, pepper		

> Using butter, I portion provides:
>
> 531 kJ/126 kcal
> 5.3 g fat
> (of which 3.3 g saturated)
> 16.7 g carbohydrate
> (of which 6.3 g sugars)
> 3.9 g protein
> 4.2 g fibre

1　Cut the white and light green of leek into ½ cm (¼ inch) paysanne.
2　Slowly cook in the butter in a pan with a lid on until soft, but without colouring.
3　Add the stock, the bouquet garni, the potatoes cut into ½ cm (¼ inch), paysanne, 2 mm (1/12 inch) thick and season with salt and pepper.
4　Simmer until the leeks and potatoes are cooked, for approximately 15 minutes.

Note　This soup can be enriched by adding 25–50 g (1–2 oz) of butter and 1/16 litre (⅛ pint) of cream and stirring, just before serving.

53 – Chive and potato soup (*Vichyssoise*)

	4 portions	10 portions
butter or margarine	25 g (1 oz)	60 g (2½ oz)
onion, peeled, washed and sliced	50 g (2 oz)	125 g (5 oz)
white of leek, washed and sliced	50 g (2 oz)	125 g (5 oz)
white stock	1 litre (2 pt)	2½ litres (5 pt)
potatoes, peeled, washed and sliced	400 g (1 lb)	1¼ kg (2½ lb)
bouquet garni		
salt, pepper		
cream	125–250 ml (¼–½ pt)	500 ml (1 pt)
chopped chives		

1　Melt the butter or margarine in a thick-bottomed pan.
2　Add the onion and leek, cook for a few minutes without colour with a lid on.
3　Add the stock and the potatoes and the bouquet garni and season.

4   Simmer for approximately 30 minutes. Remove the bouquet garni, skim.
5   Liquidise or pass the soup firmly through a sieve, then through a medium conical strainer.
6   Return to a clean pan and reboil; correct the seasoning and consistency.
7   Finish with cream and garnish with chopped chives, either raw or cooked in a little butter. Usually served chilled.

54 – Tomato soup

	4 portions	10 portions	
butter or margarine	50 g (2 oz)	125 g (5 oz)	Using hard margarine, 1 portion provides:
bacon trimmings, optional	25 g (1 oz)	60 g (2½ oz)	1150 kJ/274 kcal
onion, diced	100 g (4 oz)	250 g (10 oz)	21.3 g fat
carrot, diced	100 g (4 oz)	250 g (10 oz)	(of which 11.2 g saturated)
flour	50 g (2 oz)	125 g (5 oz)	17.1 g carbohydrate
tomato purée	100 g (4 oz)	250 g (10 oz)	(of which 3.7 g sugars)
stock	1¼ litres (2½ pt)	3½ litres (6 pt)	4.6 g protein
bouquet garni			1.0 g fibre
salt, pepper			

Croûtons

slice stale bread	1	3	
butter	50 g (2 oz)	125 g (5 oz)	

1   Melt the butter or margarine in a thick-bottomed pan.
2   Add the bacon, onion and carrot (mirepoix) and brown lightly.
3   Mix in the flour and cook to a sandy texture.
4   Remove from the heat, mix in the tomato purée.
5   Return to heat. Gradually add the hot stock.
6   Stir to the boil. Add the bouquet garni, season lightly.
7   Simmer for approximately 1 hour. Skim when required.
8   Remove the bouquet garni and mirepoix.
9   Liquidise or pass firmly through a sieve, then through a conical strainer.
10   Return to a clean pan, correct the seasoning, and consistency. Bring to the boil.
11   Serve fried or toasted croûtons separately.

Note   If a slight sweet/sour flavour is required, reduce 100 ml ($\frac{3}{16}$ pint) vinegar and 35 g (1½ oz) castor sugar to a light caramel and mix into the completed soup.
    Variations can be made with the addition of:

recipe continued ▶

- juice and lightly grated zest of 1–2 oranges;
- tomato concassé;
- cooked rice;
- chopped fresh coriander, basil or chives;
- 200 g (8 oz) peeled, sliced potatoes with the stock.

55 – Tomato soup (using fresh tomatoes)

1 Prepare the soup as recipe 54, using 1 litre (2 pints) stock.
2 Substitute 1–1½ kg (2–3 lb) fresh ripe tomatoes for the tomato purée.
3 Remove the eyes from the tomatoes, wash them well and squeeze them into the soup after the stock has been added and has come to the boil.
4 If colour is lacking, add a little tomato purée soon after the soup comes to the boil.

56 – Cream of tomato soup

1 Prepare soup as for tomato soup using only 1 litre (2 pints) stock.
2 When finally reboiling the finished soup, add ¼ litre (½ pint) of milk or ⅛ litre (¼ pint) of cream or yoghurt.

57 – Cream of tomato and potato soup

Mix half the cream of tomato and half the potato soup together and garnish with small balls of carrots and potatoes, cooked separately in a little salted water, refreshed and added to the soup just before serving.

58 – Mushroom soup

	4 portions	10 portions
onion, leek and celery	100 g (4 oz)	250 g (10 oz)
margarine or butter	50 g (2 oz)	125 g (5 oz)
flour	50 g (2 oz)	125 g (5 oz)
white stock (preferably chicken)	1 litre (2 pt)	2½ litre (5 pt)
white mushrooms	200 g (8 oz)	500 g (1¼ lb)
bouquet garni		
salt, pepper		
milk (or ⅛ pt cream)	125 ml (¼ pt)	300 ml (⅝ pt)
	or 60 ml	150 ml (⅓ pt)

Using hard margarine, 1 portion provides:

712 kJ/170 kcal
11.8 g fat
(of which 5.2 g saturated)
12.6 g carbohydrate
(of which 3.0 g sugars)
3.8 g protein
1.6 g fibre

1 Gently cook the sliced onions, leek and celery in the margarine or butter in a thick-bottomed pan without colouring.
2 Mix in the flour, cook over a gentle heat to a sandy texture without colouring.
3 Remove from the heat; cool slightly.
4 Gradually mix in the hot stock. Stir to the boil.
5 Add the well-washed, chopped mushrooms, bouquet garni and season.
6 Simmer for 30–45 minutes. Skim when necessary.
7 Remove the bouquet garni. Pass through a sieve or liquidise.
8 Pass through a medium strainer. Return to a clean saucepan.
9 Reboil, correct the seasoning and consistency; add the milk or cream.

Note Natural yoghurt, skimmed milk or non-dairy cream may be used in place of dairy cream.

59 – Chicken soup

	4 portions	10 portions	Using hard margarine, I portion provides:
onion, leek and celery	100 g (4 oz)	250 g (10 oz)	
butter or margarine	50 g (2 oz)	125 g (5 oz)	836 kJ/199 kcal
flour	50 g (2 oz)	125 g (5 oz)	13.6 g fat
chicken stock	1 litre (2 pt)	$2\frac{1}{2}$ litres (5 pt)	(of which 6.2 g saturated)
bouquet garni			14.0 g carbohydrate
salt, pepper			(of which 4.2 g sugars)
milk (or 25 ml ($\frac{1}{4}$ pt) cream)	250 ml ($\frac{1}{2}$ pt)	600 ml ($1\frac{1}{4}$ pt)	5.9 g protein
cooked dice of chicken (garnish)	25 g (1 oz)	60 g ($2\frac{1}{2}$ oz)	1.0 g fibre

1 Gently cook the sliced onions, leek and celery in a thick-bottomed pan, in the butter or margarine without colouring.
2 Mix in the flour; cook over a gentle heat to a sandy texture without colouring.
3 Cool slightly; gradually mix in the hot stock. Stir to the boil.
4 Add the bouquet garni and season.
5 Simmer for 30–45 minutes; skim when necessary.
6 Remove the bouquet garni.
7 Liquidise or pass firmly through a fine strainer.
8 Return to a clean pan, reboil and finish with milk or cream; correct the seasoning.
9 Add the garnish and serve.

recipe continued ▶

Note Natural yoghurt, skimmed milk or non-dairy cream may be used in place of dairy cream.

Add cooked small pasta or sliced mushrooms for variations.

60 – Vegetable soup

	4 portions	10 portions	Using hard margarine, 1 portion provides:
mixed vegetables (onion, carrot, turnip, leek, celery)	300 g (12 oz)	1 kg (2½ lb)	
butter or margarine	50 g (2 oz)	125 g (5 oz)	1105 kJ/263 kcal
flour (white or wholemeal)	25 g (1 oz)	60 g (2½ oz)	20.7 g fat
white stock	1 litre (2 pt)	2½ litres (5 pt)	(of which 11.1 g saturated)
potatoes	100 g (4 oz)	300 g (12 oz)	17.2 g carbohydrate
bouquet garni			(of which 3.7 g sugars)
salt, pepper			3.1 g protein
			2.8 g fibre
Croûtons			
slice stale bread	1	3	
butter	50 g (2 oz)	125 g (5 oz)	

1　Peel, wash and slice all the vegetables (except the potatoes).
2　Cook gently in the butter or margarine in a pan with the lid on, without colouring.
3　Mix in the flour and cook slowly for a few minutes without colouring; cool slightly.
4　Mix in the hot stock.
5　Stir and bring to the boil.
6　Add the sliced potatoes, bouquet garni and season. Simmer for 30–45 minutes; skim when necessary.
7　Remove the bouquet garni.
8　Liquidise or pass through a sieve and then through a medium strainer.
9　Return to a clean pan and reboil; correct the seasoning and the consistency.
10　Serve with croûtons separately.

61 – Cream of vegetable soup

Ingredients and method as for vegetable soup (recipe 60). Either replace ½ litre (1 pint) stock with ½ litre (1 pint) béchamel; or finish with milk or ⅛ litre (¼ pint) cream (see note recipe 58), simmer for 5 minutes and serve as for vegetable soup.

62 ~ Basic soup recipe for purées

	4 portions	10 portions
onions, leek and celery	100 g (4 oz)	250 g (10 oz)
suitable vegetable, sliced	200 g (8 oz)	500 g (1¼ lb)
butter or margarine	50 g (2 oz)	125 g (5 oz)
flour	50 g (2 oz)	125 g (5 oz)
white stock or water	1 litre (2 pt)	2½ litres (5 pt)
bouquet garni		
salt, pepper		

Using hard margarine, 1 portion provides:

601 kJ/143 kcal
10.3 g fat
(of which 4.4 g saturated)
11.4 g carbohydrate
(of which 1.8 g sugars)
1.9 g protein
1.9 g fibre

1 Gently cook all the sliced vegetables, in the fat under a lid, without colour.
2 Mix in the flour and cook slowly for a few minutes without colour. Cool slightly.
3 Gradually mix in the hot stock. Stir to the boil.
4 Add the bouquet garni and season.
5 Simmer for approximately 45 minutes; skim when necessary.
6 Remove the bouquet garni; liquidise or pass firmly through a sieve and then through a medium strainer.
7 Return to a clean pan, reboil and correct the seasoning and consistency.

Note   For cream soups see note to recipe 58.
  Suitable vegetables include artichokes, cauliflower, celery, leeks, onions, parsnips and turnips.

63 – Basic soup for creams

As basic recipe 62 but in place of $\frac{1}{2}$ litre (1 pint) stock use $\frac{1}{2}$ litre (1 pint) thin béchamel or use $\frac{1}{8}$–$\frac{1}{4}$ litre ($\frac{1}{4}$–$\frac{1}{2}$ pint) less stock and finish with $\frac{1}{4}$ litre ($\frac{1}{2}$ pint) milk or $\frac{1}{8}$

Suitable vegetables as for basic soup recipe (62).

Suitable vegetables as for basic soup recipe (62).

> Using hard margarine, 1 portion provides:
>
> 1515 kJ/361 kcal
> 25.3 g fat
> (of which 11.9 g saturated)
> 27.1 g carbohydrate
> (of which 8.1 g sugars)
> 7.7 g protein
> 2.5 g fibre

64 – Asparagus soup

	4 portions	10 portions
onion	50 g (2 oz)	125 g (5 oz)
celery	50 g (2 oz)	125 g (5 oz)
butter or margarine	50 g (2 oz)	125 g (5 oz)
flour	50 g (2 oz)	125 g (5 oz)
white stock (preferably chicken)	1 litre (2 pt)	2½ litres (5 pt)
asparagus stalk trimmings, or	200 g ($\frac{1}{2}$ lb)	500 g ($1\frac{1}{4}$ lb)
tin of asparagus	150 g (6 oz)	3
bouquet garni		
salt, pepper		
milk or cream (see note recipe 58)	250 ml or 125 ml ($\frac{1}{2}$ pt or $\frac{1}{4}$ pt)	600 ml or 300 ml ($1\frac{1}{4}$ pt or $\frac{5}{8}$ pt)

1 Gently sweat the sliced onions and celery, without colouring, in the butter or margarine.
2 Remove from the heat, mix in the flour, return to a low heat and cook out, without colouring, for a few minutes. Cool.
3 Gradually add the hot stock. Stir to the boil.
4 Add the well-washed asparagus trimmings or the tin of asparagus, bouquet garni and season with salt.
5 Simmer for 30–40 minutes. Remove the bouquet garni.

6 Liquidise or pass through a sieve, then a fine chinois, but do not push the asparagus fibres through the mesh.
7 Return to a clean pan, reboil, correct the seasoning and consistency.
8 Add the milk or cream and serve.

65 – Mixed vegetable soup

	4 portions	10 portions
mixed vegetables (onion, leek, carrots, turnips, cabbage, celery)	300 g (12 oz)	750 g (1 lb 14 oz)
butter or margarine	50 g (2 oz)	125 g (5 oz)
white stock or water	750 ml (1½ pr)	2 litres (4½ pt)
bouquet garni		
salt, pepper		
peas	25 g (1 oz)	60 g (2½ oz)
French beans (cut into diamonds)	25 g (1 oz)	60 g (2½ oz)

> Using hard margarine, 1 portion provides:
>
> 472 kJ/112 kcal
> 10.3 fat
> (of which 4.4 g saturated)
> 3.5 g carbohydrate
> (of which 0.0 g sugars)
> 1.7 g protein
> 2.8 g fibre

1 Cut the peeled, washed vegetables into paysanne. Thinly cut into 1 cm-sided (½ inch) triangles, *or* 1 cm-sided (½ inch) squares, *or* small, round pieces.
2 Cook slowly in the butter in a pan, covered, until tender. Do not colour.
3 Add the hot stock, bouquet garni, season and simmer for approximately 20 minutes.
4 Add the peas and beans, simmer until all the vegetables are cooked.
5 Skim off all fat, correct the seasoning and serve.

66 – Autumn vegetable soup

	4 portions	10 portions
courgettes	100 g (4 oz)	250 g (10 oz)
red, green, yellow pepper	100 g (4 oz)	250 g (10 oz)
potato (peeled weight)	100 g (4 oz)	250 g (10 oz)
onion	100 g (4 oz)	250 g (10 oz)
celery	100 g (4 oz)	250 g (10 oz)
butter, margarine or oil	50 g (2 oz)	125 g (5 oz)
vegetable stock or water	¾ litre (1½ pt)	2 litres (4 pt)
bouquet garni		
salt and pepper		

recipe continues ▶

1 Cut the washed vegetables into small dice and sweat them without colour.
2 Add the stock, bouquet garni and seasoning.
3 Bring to the boil and simmer until the vegetables are just tender.
4 Correct the consistency and seasoning, remove the bouquet garni and serve.

Note   Other vegetables may also be used to produce a colourful soup, such as carrots, pumpkin or sweetcorn.

67 – Minestrone

	4 portions	10 portions
mixed vegetables (onion, leek, celery, carrot, turnip, cabbage)	300 g (12 oz)	750 g (30 oz)
butter, margarine or oil	50 g (2 oz)	125 g (5 oz)
white stock or water	$\frac{3}{4}$ litre (1$\frac{1}{2}$ pt)	2 litres (4$\frac{1}{2}$ pt)
bouquet garni		
salt, pepper		
peas	25 g (1 oz)	60 g (2$\frac{1}{2}$ oz)
French beans	25 g (1 oz)	60 g (2$\frac{1}{2}$ oz)
spaghetti	25 g (1 oz)	60 g (2$\frac{1}{2}$ oz)
potatoes	50 g (2 oz)	125 g (5 oz)
tomato purée	1	3
tomatoes, skinned, de-seeded, diced	100 g (4 oz)	250 g (10 oz)
fat bacon	50 g (2 oz)	125 g (5 oz)
chopped parsley		
1 clove garlic		

Using sunflower oil, 1 portion provides:

1115 kJ/265 kcal
22.9 g fat
(of which 5.8 g saturated)
11.9 g carbohydrate
(of which 4.2 g sugars)
3.8 g protein
4.1 g fibre

1 Cut the peeled and washed mixed vegetables into paysanne.
2 Cook slowly without colour in the oil or fat in the pan with a lid on.
3 Add stock, bouquet garni and seasoning; simmer for approximately 20 minutes.
4 Add the peas, beans cut in diamonds and simmer for 10 minutes.
5 Add the spaghetti in 2 cm (1 inch) lengths, the potatoes cut in paysanne, the tomato purée and the tomatoes and simmer gently until all the vegetables are cooked.
6 Meanwhile finely chop the fat bacon, parsley and garlic and form into a paste.
7 Mould the paste into pellets the size of a pea and drop into the boiling soup.
8 Remove the bouquet garni, correct the seasoning.
9 Serve grated Parmesan cheese and thin toasted flutes separately.

~5~
HORS-D'OEUVRE, SALADS, COOKED/CURED/PREPARED FOODS

Recipe No.			page no.
30	Anchovies	Anchois	173
57	Artichokes, Greek-style	Artichauts à la grecque	184
10	Aspic jelly	Gelée d'aspic	165
20	Avocado pear	l'Avocat	168
40	Beetroot	Betterave	178
41	Beetroot salad	Salade de betterave	179
59	Cauliflower, Greek-style	Chou-fleur à la grecque	185
12	Caviar	Caviar	165
48	Celeriac	Céleri-rave	181
62	Celery	Céleri	187
60	Celery, Greek-style	Céleri à la grecque	185
9	Chaud-froid sauce		164
76	Chicken salad	Salade de volaille	194
63	Chicory	Endive belge	187
54	Coleslaw		183
66	Cos lettuce	Laitve romaine	187
42	Cucumber	Concombre	179
43	Cucumber salad	Salade de concombres	179
64	Curled chicory	Endive frisée	187
34	Egg mayonnaise	Oeuf mayonnaise	174
38	Fish salad	Salade de poisson	177
55	Florida salad		184
15	Foie gras	Foie gras	166
49	French bean salad	Salade des haricots verts	182
73	French salad	Salade française	188
21	Fruit cocktail		168
25	Fruit juices		170
18	Grapefruit	Pamplemousse	167
19	Grapefruit cocktail and variations		167
72	Green salad	Salade verte	188
5	Green sauce		162
14	Gulls' eggs	Oeufs de mouettes	166
52	Haricot bean salad	Salade des haricots blancs	183
7	Horseradish sauce	Sauce raifort	163
61	Leeks, Greek-style	Poireaux à la grecque	186
65	Lettuce	Laitve	187
4	Mayonnaise sauce	Sauce mayonnaise	161
39	Meat salad	Salade de viande	178
24	Melon, Charentais	Melon de Charente	170
23	Melon, Chilled	Melon frappé	169
22	Melon cocktail		168
8	Mint sauce		163
71	Mixed salad	Salade panachée	188
67	Mustard and cress		187
50	Niçoise salad	Salade niçoise	182
58	Onions, Greek-style	Oignons à la grecque	185
56	Orange salad	Salade d'orange	184

11	Oysters	*Huîtres*	165
61	Portuguese-style hors d'oeuvre		186
36	Potato salad	*Salade de pomme de terre*	175
17	Potted shrimps		167
68	Radishes	*Radis*	188
77	Raised pork pie		195
47	Rice salad	*Salade de riz*	181
69	Rocket		188
2	Roquefort dressing		160
16	Salami and cooked sausages		167
74	Salmon, boiled		189
75	Salmon mayonnaise		191
31	Sardines	*Sardines à l'huile*	173
27	Shellfish cocktails: crab; lobster; shrimp; prawn	*Cocktail de crabe; homaid; crevettes; crevettes roses*	170
35	Shellfish mayonnaise: shrimp; prawn; crab; lobster		175
29	Smoked mackerel mousse		172
13	Smoked salmon	*Saumon fumé*	166
28	Soused herring or mackerel		172
33	Stuffed eggs	*Oeufs farcis*	174
6	Tartare sauce	*Sauce Tartare*	162
3	Thousand island dressing		160
53	Three-bean salad		183
44	Tomato	*Tomate*	180
46	Tomato and cucumber salad	*Salade de tomate et concombres*	180
26	Tomato juice	*Jus de tomate*	170
45	Tomato salad	*Salade de tomate*	180
32	Tuna fish	*Thon*	173
37	Vegetable salad	*Salade de legume/Salade russe*	177
78	Veal and ham pie		196
1	Vinaigrette		159
51	Waldorf salad		182
70	Watercress	*Cresson*	188

Cold food presentation (hors d'oeuvre, salads, cooked/cured/prepared foods)

1. Ensure preparation and cooking areas are ready for use, satisfy health and hygiene regulations and are cleaned correctly after use.
2. Plan work and allocate time to meet schedules and organise in an efficient manner.
3. Ensure ingredients are of the required type, quality and quantity.
4. Store items in accordance with food hygiene regulations.
5. Appreciate the need for attractive presentation, freshness, colour and variety.
6. Know and understand the principles of making cold dishes.

Cold food is popular in every kind of food service operation for at least three good reasons:

- *Visual appeal*   When the food is attractively displayed, carefully arranged and neatly garnished, the customers can have their appetites stimulated and they can see exactly what is being offered.
- *Efficiency*   Cold food can be prepared in advance allowing a large number of people to be served in a short space of time. Self service is also economic on staff.
- *Adaptability*   If cold food is being served from a buffet, the range of dishes can be simple or large depending on the type of operation.

Cold foods can either be preplated or served from large dishes and bowls. In both cases presentation is important, the food should appear fresh, neatly arranged and not overgarnished.

HEALTH, SAFETY AND HYGIENE

Read Chapter 1 and in addition:

- Where possible use plastic gloves when handling food.
- Keep unprepared and prepared food under refrigeration at a temperature not exceeding 4–5°C (39–41°F). Refrigeration will not kill the bacteria which is present in the foods, but it does help to prevent its growth.
- Whenever possible, the food on display to the public should be kept under refrigeration and the temperature should be checked to ensure that a safe temperature is being maintained.
- Where customers are viewing the food closely, ideally it should be displayed behind a sneeze screen.
- Dishes prepared in advance should be covered with film and refrigerated at 1–3°C (34–37°F) to prevent them drying.
- Personal, food and equipment hygiene of the highest order must be observed with all cold work.

—— *Cold preparations* ——

DEFINITION

The preparation of raw and/or cooked foods into a wide variety of cold items.

PURPOSE

The purpose of these dishes is:

- to add variety to the menu and diet by preparing food that has eye-appeal, is palatable and digestible;
- to produce a variety of flavours and textures and provide food that is particularly suitable for hot weather;
- to prepare food that can be conveniently wrapped for take-aways.

COLD FOOD CHARACTERISTICS

- Appearance must be clean and fresh. Presentation should be eye appealing, neither too colourful or overdecorative, therefore stimulating the appetite.
- Nutritional value is obtained because of the mixture of raw and cooked foods.

TECHNIQUES ASSOCIATED WITH COLD PREPARATION

Peeling

This is the removal of the outer skin of fruit or vegetables using a peeler or small knife, according to the thickness of the skin.

Chopping

This is cutting into very small pieces (parsley, onions).

Cutting

This is using a knife to divide food into required shapes and sizes.

Carving

This means cutting meat or poultry into slices.

Seasoning

This is the addition of salt and pepper.

Dressing

This can either mean an accompanying salad dressing such as vinaigrette, *or* the arrangement of food for presentation on plates, dishes or buffets.

Garnishing

This is the final addition to the dish, such as quarters of tomato added to egg mayonnaise.

Marinade

A richly spiced pickling liquid used to give flavour and to assist in tenderising meats such as venison.

EQUIPMENT

Bowls, basins, whisks, spoons, etc., as well as food processors, mixing machines and blenders are used in cold preparations.

PREPARATION FOR COLD WORK

Well planned organisation is essential to ensure adequate prepreparation (*mise-en-place*), so that foods are assembled with a good work flow and ready on time.

Before, during and after assembling, and before final garnishing, foods must be kept in a cool place, cold room or refrigerator so as to minimise the risk of food contamination. Garnishing and final decoration should take place as close to the serving time as possible.

GENERAL RULES

- Be aware of the texture and flavour of many raw foods that can be mixed together or combined with cooked foods (coleslaw, meat salad).
- Understand what combination of foods, for example salads, are best suited to be served with other foods, such as cold meat or poultry.
- Develop simple artistic skills which require the minimum of time required for preparation and assembly.
- Provide an attractive presentation of food at all times.
- Because of the requirements of food safety, cold foods are often served straight from the refrigerator. This is wrong because at refrigerator temperature, food flavours are not at their best. Individual portions should be removed from refrigeration and allowed to stand at room temperature for 5–10 minutes before being served.

TYPES OF HORS-D'OEUVRE

The choice of a wide variety of foods, combination of foods and recipes is available for preparation and services as hors-d'oeuvre and salads.

Hors-d'oeuvre can be divided into three categories:

- single cold food items (smoked salmon, pâté, melon, etc.);
- a selection of well-seasoned cold dishes;
- well-seasoned hot dishes.

Hors-d'oeuvre may be served for luncheon, dinner or supper and the wide choice, colour appeal and versatility of the dishes makes many items and combinations of items suitable for snacks and salads at any time of day.

Salads may be served as an accompaniment to hot and cold foods and as dishes in their own right. They can be served for lunch, tea, high tea, dinner, supper and snack meals. Salads may be divided in two sections:

- simple, using one ingredient;
- mixed or composite, using more than one ingredient.

Some salads may form part of a composite hors-d'oeuvre.

Accompaniments include dressings and cold sauces.

—— *Dressings and cold sauces* ——

SALAD DRESSINGS

These dressings may be varied by the addition of other ingredients.

1 – Vinaigrette

4–6 portions

olive oil, according to taste	3–6 tbsp
French mustard	1 tsp
vinegar	1 tbsp
salt, mill pepper	

> Using 3 tbsp oil, this recipe provides for 4–6 portions:
>
> 1740 kJ/415 kcal
> 45.5 g fat
> (of which 6.3 g saturated)
> 0.5 carbohydrate
> (of which 0.1 g sugars)
> 0.6 g protein
> 0.0 g fibre

recipe continued ▶

Combine all the ingredients together.

Note Variations to vinaigrette include:

- English mustard in place of French mustard;
- chopped herbs (chives, parsley, tarragon, etc.);
- chopped hard-boiled egg;
- lemon juice in place of vinegar (lemon dressing).

Using 6 tbsp oil, this recipe provides for 4–6 portions:

3439 kJ/819 kcal
90.5 g fat
(of which 12.6 g saturated)
0.5 g carbohydrate
(of which 0.1 g sugars)
0.6 g protein
0.0 g fibre

2 – Roquefort dressing

4–6 portions

Roquefort cheese	50 g (2 oz)
vinaigrette	125 ml ($\frac{1}{4}$ pt)

1 Purée the cheese.
2 Gradually add the vinaigrette mixing continuously.

This recipe provides for 4–6 portions:

2779 kJ/662 kcal
67.7 g fat
of which 16.6 g saturated
0.7 g carbohydrate
of which 0.1 g sugars
12.4 g protein
0.0 g fibre

3 – Thousand island dressing

4–6 portions

salt, pepper	
tabasco	3–4 drops
vinegar	125 ml ($\frac{1}{4}$ pt)
oil	375 ml ($\frac{3}{4}$ pt)
red pimento	50 g (2 oz)
green pimento	50 g (2 oz)
chopped parsley	
hard-boiled eggs	2
tomato ketchup (optional)	2 tbsp

This recipe provides for 4–6 portions:

15 055 kJ/3584 kcal
387.0 g fat
(of which 56.5 g saturated)
10.2 g carbohydrate
(of which 9.8 g sugars)
16.1 g protein
1.8 g fibre

1 Place the salt, pepper, tabasco and vinegar in a basin.
2 Mix well.
3 Mix in the oil.
4 Add the chopped pimentos and parsley.
5 Mix in the sieved hard-boiled eggs.

COLD SAUCES

Plate 5.1: Cold salmon with mayonnaise sauce

4 ~ Mayonnaise sauce

This is a basic cold sauce and has a wide variety of uses, particularly in hors-d'oeuvre dishes. It should always be available on any cold buffet.

	8 portions
egg yolks	2
vinegar	2 tsp
salt, ground white pepper	
English or continental mustard	$\frac{1}{8}$ tsp
olive or other good quality oil	250 ml ($\frac{1}{2}$ pt)
boiling water (approximately)	1 tsp

> This recipe provides for 8 portions:
>
> 10 030 kJ/2388 kcal
> 26.2 g fat
> (of which 38.9 g saturated)
> 0.3 g carbohydrate
> (of which 0.1 g sugars)
> 6.8 g protein
> 0.0 g fibre

1 Place the yolks, vinegar and seasoning in a bowl and whisk well.
2 Gradually pour on the oil very slowly, whisking continuously.
3 Add the boiling water, whisking well.
4 Correct the seasoning.

Note   If during the making of the sauce, it should become too thick, then a little vinegar or water may be added. Mayonnaise will turn or curdle for several reasons:

- if the oil is added too quickly;
- if the oil is too cold;
- if the sauce is insufficiently whisked;
- if the yolk is stale and therefore weak.

The method of rethickening a turned mayonnaise is either:

recipe continued ▶

- by taking a clean basin, adding 1 teaspoon boiling water and gradually whisking in the curdled sauce; or
- by taking another yolk thinned with $\frac{1}{2}$ teaspoon cold water whisked well, then gradually whisking in the curdled sauce.

Many ingredients can be used to vary mayonnaise, such as fresh herbs; garlic juice; parmesan or blue cheese; red pepper purée; chopped sun dried tomatoes.

5 − Green sauce

	8 portions
spinach, tarragon, chervil, chives, watercress	50g (2oz)
mayonnaise	250ml ($\frac{1}{2}$pt)

1 Pick, wash, blanch and refresh the green leaves.
2 Squeeze dry.
3 Pass through a very fine sieve.
4 Mix with the mayonnaise.

Note   May be served with cold salmon or salmon trout.

6 − Tartare sauce

	8 portions
mayonnaise	250ml ($\frac{1}{2}$pt)
capers	25g (1oz)
gherkins	50g (2oz)
sprig of parsley	

1 Chop the capers, gherkins and parsley.
2 Combine all the ingredients together.

Note   This sauce is usually served with deep-fried fish.
A variation is to add 1 teaspoon of anchovy essence (remoulade sauce).

7 – Horseradish sauce

	8 portions
grated horseradish	25 g (1 oz)
vinegar	1 tbsp
salt, pepper	
lightly whipped cream	125 ml (¼ pt)

> This recipe provides for 8 portions:
>
> 1807 kJ/430 kcal
> 43.8 g fat
> (of which 27.8 g saturated)
> 6.0 g carbohydrate
> (of which 5.0 g sugars)
> 3.6 g protein
> 2.1 g fibre

1 Wash, peel and rewash the horseradish.
2 Grate finely.
3 Mix all the ingredients together.

Note Serve with roast beef, smoked trout.

8 – Mint sauce

	8 portions
mint	2–3 tbsp
castor sugar	1 dsp
vinegar	125 ml (¼ pt)

> This recipe provides for 8 portions:
>
> 204 kJ/49 kcal
> 0.0 g fat
> (of which 0.0 g saturated)
> 11.3 g carbohydrate
> (of which 11.3 g sugars)
> 1.5 g protein
> 1.8 g fibre

1 Chop the washed, picked mint and mix with the sugar.
2 Place in a china basin and add the vinegar.
3 If the vinegar is too sharp dilute it with a little water.

Note Serve with roast lamb. A less acid sauce can be produced by dissolving the sugar in 125 ml (¼ pint) boiling water and, when cold, adding the chopped mint and 1–2 tablespoon vinegar to taste.

CHAUD-FROID SAUCES AND ASPIC JELLY

Chaud-froid sauces and aspic jelly are basic larder preparations. Chaud-froid sauces are derived from béchamel (page 117), velouté (page 119) or demi-glace (page 122) to which aspic jelly or gelatine is added so as to help them set when cold. They are used to mask fish, meat, poultry and game, either whole, or cut in pieces, for cold buffets, which are then usually decorated and finally coated with aspic.

Aspic is a savoury jelly which may be used on cold egg, fish, meat, poultry, game and vegetable dishes that are prepared for cold buffets so as to give them an attractive appearance. For meat dishes a beef or veal stock (page 113) is made; for fowl, chicken stock (page 113); and for fish, fish stock (page 114).

9 – Chaud-froid sauce

White

	1 litre
leaf gelatine	50 g (2 oz)
béchamel or velouté	1 litre (1 qt)
cream (if necessary to improve the colour of the sauce)	125 ml ($\frac{1}{4}$ pt)

This recipe provides for 1 litre:

10 285 kJ/2449 kcal
180.6 g fat
(of which 97.7 g saturated)
127.3 g carbohydrate
(of which 51.2 g sugars)
86.6 g protein
3.6 g fibre

1 Soak the gelatine in cold water.
2 Bring the sauce to the boil.
3 Remove from the heat.
4 Add the well-squeezed gelatine and stir until dissolved, and correct the seasoning.
5 Pass through a tammy cloth or fine strainer.
6 When the sauce is half cooled mix in the cream.

Brown

	1 litre
demi-glace	1 litre (1 qt)
leaf gelatine	50 g (2 oz)

Using sunflower oil, this recipe provides for 1 litre:

3624 kJ/863 kcal
51.1 g fat
(of which 6.6 g saturated)
50.7 g carbohydrate
(of which 3.8 g sugars)
53.2 g protein
2.2 g fibre

Proceed as above, omitting the cream.

10 – Aspic jelly

	1 litre
whites of eggs	2–3
strong, fat-free, seasoned stock (as required poultry, meat, game or fish)	1 litre (1 qt)
vinegar	1 tbsp
sprigs tarragon	2
leaf gelatine (approximately 24 leaves)	75 g (3 oz)

> This recipe provides for 1 litre:
>
> 1668 kJ/397 kcal
> 0.0 g fat
> (of which 0.0 g saturated)
> 7.4 g carbohydrate
> (of which 0.1 g sugars)
> 91.3 g protein
> 0.0 g fibre

1   Whisk the egg whites in a thick-bottomed pan with $\frac{1}{4}$ litre ($\frac{1}{2}$ pint) of the cold stock and the vinegar and tarragon.
2   Heat the rest of the stock, add the gelatine (previously soaked for 20 minutes in cold water) and whisk till dissolved.
3   Add the stock and dissolved gelatine into the thick-bottomed pan. Whisk well.
4   Place on the stove and allow to come gently to the boil until clarified.
5   Strain through a muslin.
6   Repeat if necessary, using egg whites only to give a crystal-clear aspic.

—— *Single food hors-d'oeuvre* ——

11 – Oysters

Oysters should be kept in boxes or barrels covered with damp seaweed in a cold room or refrigerator to keep them moist and alive.

The shells should be tightly shut to indicate freshness. The oysters should be carefully opened with a special oyster knife so as to avoid scratching the inside shell, then turned and arranged neatly in the deep shell and served on a bed of crushed ice on a plate. They should not be washed unless gritty and the natural juices should always be left in the deep shell.

Accompaniments include brown bread and butter and lemon. It is usual to serve six oysters as a portion.

12 – Caviar

This is the fresh, salted roe of the sturgeon, a very expensive imported commodity

recipe continued ▶

usually served in its original tin or jar, in a timbale of crushed ice. One spoonful, 25 g (1 oz), represents a portion.

Brown bread and butter should accompany caviar.

13 – Smoked salmon

Before service, a side of smoked salmon must be carefully trimmed to remove the dry outside surface. All bones must be removed; a pair of pliers are found useful for this. The salmon is carved as thinly as possible on the slant and neatly dressed, overlapping, on a plate or dish, decorated with sprigs of parsley 35–50 g (1–2 oz) per portion.

Accompaniments include brown bread and butter and lemon.

(Illustrated as part of a plated hors-d'oeuvre on page 176.)

Other smoked fish served as hors-d'oeuvre include halibut, eel, conger eel, trout, mackerel, herring (buckling), cod's roe, sprats.

1 portion (25 g) provides:
149 kJ/36 kcal
1.1 g fat
(of which 0.3 g saturated)
0.0 g carbohydrate
(of which 0.0 g sugars)
6.4 g protein
0.0 g fibre

1 portion (35 g) provides:
209 kJ/50 kcal
1.6 g fat
(of which 0.4 g saturated)
0.0 g carbohydrate
(of which 0.0 g sugars)
8.9 g protein
0.0 g fibre

14 – Gulls' eggs

These eggs are hard-boiled, then served cold, and may be dressed on a bed of mustard and cress. It is usual to serve two per portion.

Serve brown bread and butter as an accompaniment.

15 – Foie gras

This is a ready-prepared delicacy made from goose liver, and it may be served in its original dish. If tinned, it should be thoroughly chilled, removed from the tin and cut into 1 cm ($\frac{1}{2}$ inch) slices.

Serve garnished with a little chopped aspic jelly.

16 – Salami and assorted cooked or smoked sausages

These are ready-bought sausages usually prepared from pork by specialist butchers. Most countries have their own specialities, and a variety of them are exported. They are thinly sliced and either served individually or an assortment may be offered. Mortadella, garlic sausage and zungenwurst are other examples of this type of sausage.

(Illustrated as part of a plated hors-d'oeuvre on page 176.)

17 – Potted shrimps

Potted shrimps are freshly cooked and peeled shrimps mixed with warmed butter and a little spice, chiefly mace, served in small dishes. Ready prepared commercial potted shrimps are available. Potted shrimps have a better flavour when served warm, accompanied by thin toast or brown bread and butter.

18 – Grapefruit

These are halved, the segments individually cut with a small knife, then chilled. Serve with a maraschino cherry in the centre. The common practice of sprinkling with castor sugar is incorrect, as some customers prefer their grapefruit without sugar. Serve half a grapefruit per portion in a coupe.

19 – Grapefruit cocktail

The fruit should be peeled with a sharp knife in order to remove all the white pith and yellow skin. Cut into segments and remove all the pips. The segments and the juice should then be dressed in a cocktail glass or grapefruit coupe and chilled. A cherry may be added. Allow ½–1 grapefruit per head.
   Variations include:

* *Grapefruit and orange cocktail*, allowing half an orange and half a grapefruit per head.
* *Orange cocktail*, using oranges in place of grapefruit.
* *Florida cocktail*, a mixture of grapefruit, orange and pineapple segments.

20 – Avocado pear

The pears must be ripe (test by pressing gently, the pear should give slightly).

1 Cut it in half length-wise. Remove the stone.
2 Serve garnished with lettuce accompanied by vinaigrette (page 159) or variations on vinaigrette.

Note Avocado pears are sometimes filled with shrimps or crabmeat bound with a shellfish cocktail sauce or other similar fillings, and may be served hot or cold using a variety of fillings and sauces.

Plate 5.2a–d: Preparation and presentation of avocado pear

   Avocado pear may also be halved lengthwise, the stone removed, the skin peeled and the pear sliced and fanned onto a plate. Garnish with a simple or composed salad. Allow half a pear per portion.

21 – Fruit cocktail

This is a mixture of fruits such as apples, pears, pineapples, grapes, cherries, etc., washed, peeled and cut into neat segments or dice and added to a syrup (100 g (4 oz) sugar to $\frac{1}{4}$ litre ($\frac{1}{2}$ pint) water) and the juice of half a lemon. Neatly place in cocktail glasses and chill. Allow $\frac{1}{2}$ kg (1 lb) unprepared fruit for 4 portions, $1\frac{1}{4}$ kg ($2\frac{1}{2}$ lb) for 10.
   Variations include a tropical fruit cocktail which uses a variety of tropical fruits, such as mango, passion fruit, lychees, pineapple, kiwi fruit.

22 – Melon cocktail

The melon, which must be ripe, is peeled, then cut into neat segments or dice or scooped out with a parisienne spoon, dressed in cocktail glasses and chilled. A little liqueur, such as crème de menthe or maraschino, may also be added. Allow approximately half a melon for 4 portions, $1\frac{1}{2}$ for 10.

Plate 5.3: Smoked salmon

Plate 5.4a–c: Preparation of grapefruit, orange and Florida cocktails

Plate 5.5: Clockwise from top-left: half grapefruit; orange cocktail; Florida cocktail; orange cocktail in coupe

23 – Chilled melon

Cut the melon in half, remove the pips and cut it into thick slices. Cut a piece off the skin so that the slice will stand firm and serve on crushed ice. Use castor sugar and ground ginger, as accompaniments. Allow approximately half a honeydew or cantaloup melon for 4 portions.

1 portion provides:
82 kJ/20 kcal
0.0 g fat
(of which 0.0 g saturated)
4.7 g carbohydrate
(of which 4.7 g sugars)
0.6 g protein
0.9 g fibre

24 – Charentais melon

Cut a slice from the top of the melon to form a lid, remove the seeds and replace the lid. Serve chilled. Allow 1 melon per portion.
    Variations:

- Add $\frac{1}{2}$ glass of port to the inside of each melon approximately 15 minutes before service.
- Add 50 g (2 oz) picked and washed raspberries or stawberries.

25 – Fruit juices

These are usually bought ready prepared, but may be made from the fresh fruit. Use pineapple, orange or grapefruit.

26 – Tomato juice

Fresh ripe tomatoes must be used. Wash them, remove the eyes, then liquidise and pass them through a strainer. The juice is then served in cocktail glasses and chilled. Offer Worcester sauce when serving. Use $\frac{1}{2}$ kg (1 lb) tomatoes for 4 portions, $1\frac{1}{4}$ kg ($2\frac{1}{2}$ lb) for 10.

I portion provides:
74 kJ/18 kcal
0.0 g fat
(of which 0.0 g saturated)
3.5 g carbohydrate
(of which 3.5 g sugars)
1.1 g protein
0.0 g fibre

27 – Shellfish cocktails: crab, lobster, shrimp, prawn

	4 portions	10 portions
lettuce	$\frac{1}{2}$	$1\frac{1}{2}$
prepared shellfish	100–150 g (4–6 oz)	250–350 g (10–15 oz)
shellfish cocktail sauce	125 ml ($\frac{1}{4}$ pt)	300 ml ($\frac{5}{8}$ pt)

I portion provides:
966 kJ/230 kcal
21.0 g fat
(of which 3.2 g saturated)
0.6 g carbohydrate
(of which 0.6 g sugars)
9.6 g protein
0.3 g fibre

1 Wash, drain well and finely shred the lettuce, avoiding long strands.
2 Place about 2 cm (1 inch) deep in cocktail glasses or dishes.

3   Add the prepared shellfish:
- crab (shredded white meat only);
- lobster (cut in $\frac{1}{2}$ cm ($\frac{1}{4}$ inch) dice);
- shrimps (peeled and washed);
- prawns (peeled, washed, and if large cut into two or three pieces).

4   Coat with sauce.

5   Decorate with an appropriate piece of the content, such as a prawn with the shell on the tail removed, on the edge of the glass of a prawn cocktail.

Shellfish cocktail sauce
Method I

	4 portions	10 portions
egg yolk	1	3
vinegar	1 dsp	2$\frac{1}{2}$ dsp
salt, pepper, mustard		
olive oil or sunflower oil	5 tbsp	12 tbsp
tomato juice or ketchup to taste	3 tbsp	8 tbsp
Worcester sauce (optional)	2–3 drops	6–8 drops

Make the mayonnaise with the egg yolk, vinegar, seasonings and oil. Combine with the tomato juice and Worcester sauce (if using).

Method II

lightly whipped cream or unsweetened non-dairy cream	5 tbsp	12 tbsp
tomato juice or ketchup to taste	3 tbsp	8 tbsp
salt, pepper		
few drops of lemon juice		

Mix all the ingredients together. Fresh or tinned tomato juice or diluted tomato ketchup may be used for both the above methods, but the use of tinned tomato purée gives an unpleasant flavour.

28 – Soused herring or mackerel

	4 portions	10 portions
herrings or mackerel	2	5
salt, pepper		
button onions	25 g (1 oz)	60 g (2½ oz)
carrots, peeled and fluted	25 g (1 oz)	60 g (2½ oz)
bay leaf	½	1½
peppercorns	6	12
thyme	1 sprig	2 sprigs
vinegar	60 ml (⅛ pt)	150 ml (⅓ pt)

This recipe provides for 4 portions:

2419 kJ/576 kcal
44.5 g fat
(of which 9.4 g saturated)
3.0 g carbohydrate
(of which 3.0 g sugars)
41.0 g protein
1.1 g fibre

1 Clean, scale and fillet the fish.
2 Wash the fillets well and season with salt and pepper.
3 Roll up with the skin outside.
4 Place in an earthenware dish.
5 Peel and wash the onion.
6 Cut the onion and carrot into neat thin rings.
7 Blanch for 2–3 minutes.
8 Add to the fish with the remainder of the ingredients.
9 Cover with greaseproof paper and cook in a moderate oven for 15–20 minutes.
10 Allow to cool, place in a dish with the onion and carrot.
11 Garnish with picked parsley.

29 – Smoked mackerel mousse

	4 portions	10 portions
smoked mackerel, free from bone and skin	200 g (8 oz)	500 g (1¼ lb)
optional seasoning: pepper, chopped parsley, fennel or chervil, 1 tbsp tomato ketchup, two ripe tomatoes free from skin and pips		
double cream (or non-dairy cream)	90 ml (3½ fl oz)	250 ml (½ pt)

1 Ensure that the mackerel is completely free from skin and bones.
2 Liquidise with required seasoning.

3   Three quarter whip the cream.
4   Remove mackerel from liquidiser and fold into the cream. Correct the seasoning.
5   Serve in individual dishes accompanied with hot toast.

Note   This recipe can be used with smoked trout or smoked salmon trimmings. It can also be used for fresh salmon, in which case 50 g (2 oz) of cucumber can be incorporated with the selected seasoning.

—— *Assorted hors-d'oeuvre* ——

The following recipes may be served in four ways unless otherwise indicated:

- as a single hors-d'oeuvre;
- as part of a composite hors-d'oeuvre;
- as a main course when it will be suitably garnished with salad items;
- as an accompaniment to a main course.

30 – Anchovies

As an hors-d'oeuvre only. Remove from the tin and dress in raviers, pour over a little oil and decorate if desired with any of the following: capers, sprigs of parsley, chopped hard-boiled white and yolk of egg.

31 – Sardines

Not as an accompaniment to a main course. Remove carefully from the tin, dress neatly in raviers and add a little oil. The sardines may be decorated with picked parsley and lemon.

32 – Tuna fish

Not as an accompaniment to a main course. Remove from the tin, dress neatly, cut or flaked, in raviers, decorate as desired.

33 – Stuffed eggs

hard-boiled eggs	2
butter	25 g (1 oz)
mayonnaise or natural yoghurt	4 tbsp
salt, pepper	

1 Quarter or halve the eggs.
2 Remove the yolks and pass through a sieve.
3 Mix the yolks with butter and mayonnaise and correct the seasoning.
4 Place in a piping bag with a star tube and pipe neatly back into the egg whites.
5 Dress on a bed of shredded lettuce or lettuce leaves.

Note   For variation add a little tomato ketchup, spinach juice, duxelle or anchovy essence, to the egg yolks.

34 – Egg mayonnaise *(Illustration page 176)*

To cook hard-boiled eggs, place the eggs in boiling water; reboil and simmer for 8–10 minutes. Refresh until cold.

Note   When started in cold water cook for 12 minutes. If the eggs are overcooked, iron in the yolk and sulphur compounds in the white are released to form the blackish ring (ferrous sulphide) around the yolk. This will also occur if the eggs are not refreshed immediately they are cooked.

> 1 portion provides:
>
> 763 kJ/182 kcal
> 15.7 g fat
> (of which 3.4 g saturated)
> 2.4 g carbohydrate
> (of which 2.4 g sugars)
> 8.1 g protein
> 1.6 g fibre

As part of a selection for hors-d'oeuvre
Cut the hard-boiled eggs in quarters or slices, neatly dress in raviers and coat with mayonnaise.

As an individual hors-d'oeuvre
Allow one hard-boiled egg per portion, cut in half and dress on a leaf of lettuce; coat with mayonnaise and garnish with quarters of tomatoes and slices of cucumber.

As a main dish
Allow two hard-boiled eggs per portion, cut in halves and dress on a plate, coat with mayonnaise sauce. Surround with a portion of lettuce, tomato, cucumber, potato salad, beetroot or coleslaw.

35 – Shellfish mayonnaise: shrimp, prawn, crab, lobster

	4 portions	10 portions
lettuce	1	$2\frac{1}{2}$
prepared shellfish	100–150 g (4–6 oz)	250–350 g (10–14 oz)
mayonnaise sauce or natural yoghurt	125 ml ($\frac{1}{4}$ pt)	300 ml ($\frac{5}{8}$ pt)
capers, anchovies		
parsley or fennel for decoration		

1 Shred the lettuce finely and place in a ravier.
2 Add the shellfish cut as for shellfish cocktail.
3 Coat with mayonnaise sauce. Decorate as desired.

Note This may also be served as a fish or a main course, in which case the amount of shellfish is doubled and the other ingredients are slightly increased. As an hors-d'oeuvre allow 25–35 g (1–1$\frac{1}{2}$ oz) prepared shellfish per portion. A variation includes cooked flaked fish in place of shellfish.

36 – Potato salad

	4 portions	10 portions
cooked potatoes	200 g (8 oz)	500 g (1$\frac{1}{2}$ lb)
vinaigrette, salt, pepper	1 tbsp	2$\frac{1}{2}$ tbsp
chopped onion or chive (optional)	10 g ($\frac{1}{2}$ oz)	
mayonnaise or natural yoghurt	60 ml ($\frac{1}{4}$ pt)	300 g ($\frac{5}{8}$ pt)
chopped parsley or mixed fresh herbs		

> Using mayonnaise, this recipe provides for 4 portions:
>
> 2013 kJ/479 kcal
> 34.9 g fat
> (of which 5.1 g saturated)
> 40.0 g carbohydrate
> (of which 1.3 g sugars)
> 4.0 g protein
> 2.6 g fibre

1 Cut the potatoes in $\frac{1}{2}$–1 cm ($\frac{1}{4}$–$\frac{1}{2}$ inch) dice; sprinkle with vinaigrette.
2 Mix with the onion or chive, add the mayonnaise and correct the seasoning. (The onion may be blanched to reduce the harshness.)
3 Dress neatly in a ravier. Sprinkle with chopped parsley.

Note Not usually a single hors-d'oeuvre or main course. Potato salad can also be made by dicing raw peeled or unpeeled potato, cooking them preferably by steaming (to retain shape) and mixing with vinaigrette whilst warm.

recipe continued ▶

Plate 5.6: Various ways of serving egg mayonnaise

Plate 5.7: Selection of plated
hors-d'oeuvre

Plate 5.8: Selection of hors-d'oeuvre
buffet style

Variation includes the addition of 2 chopped hard-boiled eggs, or 100 g (4 oz) of peeled dessert apple mixed with lemon juice.

37 ~ Vegetable salad (Russian salad)

	4 portions	10 portions
carrots	100 g (4 oz)	250 g (10 oz)
turnips	50 g (2 oz)	125 g (5 oz)
French beans	50 g (2 oz)	125 g (5 oz)
peas	50 g (2 oz)	125 g (5 oz)
vinaigrette	1 tbsp	2–3 tbsp
mayonnaise or natural yoghurt	125 ml ($\frac{1}{4}$ pt)	300 ml ($\frac{5}{8}$ pt)
salt, pepper		

> Using mayonnaise, this recipe provides for 4 portions:
>
> 1566 kJ/373 kcal
> 35.0 g fat
> (of which 5.2 g saturated)
> 10.1 g carbohydrate
> (of which 8.2 g sugars)
> 5.0 g protein
> 11.9 g fibre

1 Peel and wash the carrots and turnips, cut into $\frac{1}{2}$ cm ($\frac{1}{4}$ inch) dice or batons.
2 Cook separately in salted water, refresh and drain well.
3 Top and tail the beans, and cut in $\frac{1}{2}$ cm ($\frac{1}{4}$ inch) dice; cook, refresh and drain well.
4 Cook the peas, refresh and drain well.
5 Mix all the well-drained vegetables with vinaigrette and then mayonnaise.
6 Correct the seasoning. Dress neatly in a ravier.

38 ~ Fish salad

	4 portions	10 portions
cooked fish (free from skin and bone)	200 g (8 oz)	500 g (1$\frac{1}{4}$ lb)
hard-boiled egg	1	2–3
cucumber (optional)	50 g (2 oz)	125 g (5 oz)
chopped parsley or fennel		
salt, pepper		
vinaigrette	1 tbsp	2–3 tbsp
lettuce	$\frac{1}{4}$	1

> This recipe provides for 4 portions:
>
> 978 kJ/233 kcal
> 13.5 g fat
> (of which 3.0 g saturated)
> 1.5 g carbohydrate
> (of which 1.4 g sugars)
> 26.4 g protein
> 1.3 g fibre

1 Flake the fish.
2 Cut the egg and cucumber in $\frac{1}{2}$ cm ($\frac{1}{4}$ inch) dice.
3 Finely shred the lettuce.
4 Mix ingredients together, add the parsley.

recipe continued ▶

5   Correct the seasoning. Mix with the vinaigrette.
6   Dress neatly in a ravier.
7   May be decorated with lettuce, anchovies and capers.

Note   Not usually an accompaniment to a main course.

39 ‒ Meat salad

	4 portions	10 portions
cooked lean meat	200 g (8 oz)	500 g (1¼ lb)
gherkins	25 g (1 oz)	60 g (2½ oz)
cooked French beans	50 g (2 oz)	125 g (5 oz)
tomatoes	50 g (2 oz)	125 g (5 oz)
chopped onion or chives (optional)	5 g (¼ oz)	12 g (⅝ oz)
vinaigrette	1 tbsp	2½ tbsp
chopped parsley or mixed fresh herbs		

> This recipe provides for 4 portions:
>
> 1616 kJ/385 kcal
> 15.2 g fat
> (of which 4.8 g saturated)
> 2.7 g carbohydrate
> (of which 2.5 g sugars)
> 59.7 g protein
> 2.7 g fibre

1   Cut the meat, gherkins and beans in ½ cm (¼ inch) dice.
2   Skin tomatoes, de-seed and cut into ½ cm (¼ inch) dice.
3   Mix with remainder of the ingredients, blanching the onions if required.
4   Correct the seasoning.
5   Dress neatly in a ravier.
6   Decorate with lettuce leaves, tomatoes and fans of gherkins.

Note   Well-cooked braised or boiled meat is ideal for this salad.

40 ‒ Beetroot

Wash and cook the beetroot in a steamer or in gently simmering water till tender (test by skinning), cool and peel. Cut into ½ cm (¼ inch) dice or ½ × 1 cm (¼ × ½ inch) batons. Beetroot may be served plain or with vinegar or sprinkled with vinaigrette, not as a main course.

41 — Beetroot salad

	4 portions	10 portions
neatly cut or sliced beetroot	200 g (8 oz)	500 g (1¼ lb)
chopped parsley		
chopped onion or chive (optional)	10 g (½ oz)	25 g (1¼ oz)
vinaigrette	1 tbsp	2½ tbsp

1 Combine all the ingredients, blanching the onion if required.
2 Dress neatly in a ravier. Sprinkle with chopped parsley.

Note Not as a main course. Variations include addition of 60–120 ml ($\frac{1}{8}$–$\frac{1}{4}$ pint) mayonnaise or natural yoghurt in place of vinaigrette (150–200 ml ($\frac{1}{3}$–$\frac{1}{2}$ pint) for 10 portions).

42 — Cucumber

Peel the cucumber if desired; cut into thin slices and dress neatly in a ravier. Not as a single hors-d'oeuvre or main course.

43 — Cucumber salad

	4 portions	10 portions
cucumber	½	1¼
chopped parsley or mixed fresh herbs		
vinaigrette	1 tbsp	2½ tbsp

1 Peel and slice the cucumber.
2 Sprinkle with vinaigrette and parsley.

To remove indigestible juices from the cucumber, slice and lightly sprinkle with salt. Allow the salt to draw out the water for approximately 1 hour, wash well under cold water and drain. This will make the cucumber limp. Not as a main course.

Alternatively, cucumber may be diced ½ cm (¼ inch) and bound with mayonnaise or yoghurt.

44 ‒ Tomato

If of good quality, the tomatoes need not be skinned. Wash, remove the eyes, slice thinly or cut into segments. Dress neatly in a ravier.

45 ‒ Tomato salad

	4 portions	10 portions
tomatoes	200 g (8 oz)	500 g (1¼ lb)
lettuce	¼	½
vinaigrette	1 tbsp	2½ tbsp
chopped onion or chive (optional)	10 g (½ oz)	25 g (1 oz)
chopped parsley or mixed fresh herbs		

This recipe provides for 4 portions:

394 kJ/94 kcal
6.6 g fat
(of which 1.1 g saturated)
6.7 g carbohydrate
(of which 6.6 g sugars)
2.5 g protein
3.9 g fibre

1 Peel tomatoes if required. Slice thinly.
2 Arrange neatly on lettuce leaves.
3 Sprinkle with vinaigrette, onion, blanched if required, and parsley.

46 ‒ Tomato and cucumber salad

	4 portions	10 portions
tomatoes	2	5
cucumber	¼	½
vinaigrette	1 tbsp	2½ tbsp
chopped parsley or mixed fresh herbs		

1 Alternate slices of tomato and cucumber.
2 Sprinkle with vinaigrette and parsley.

47 ~ Rice salad

	4 portions	10 portions
tomatoes	100 g (4 oz)	250 g (10 oz)
cooked rice	100 g (4 oz)	250 g (10 oz)
peas, cooked	50 g (2 oz)	125 g (5 oz)
vinaigrette	1 tbsp	2½ tbsp
salt, pepper		

> This recipe provides for 4 portions:
>
> 906 kJ/216 kcal
> 6.9 g fat
> (of which 1.1 g saturated)
> 34.6 g carbohydrate
> (of which 3.3 g sugars)
> 5.9 g protein
> 8.3 g fibre

1. Skin and de-seed tomatoes; cut in ½ cm (¼ inch) dice.
2. Mix with the rice and peas.
3. Add the vinaigrette and correct the seasoning.
4. Dress neatly in a ravier.

48 ~ Celeriac

	4 portions	10 portions
celeriac	200 g (8 oz)	500 g (1¼ oz)
lemon	½	1
English or continental mustard	1 level tsp	2½ level tsp
salt, pepper		
mayonnaise, cream or natural yoghurt	125 ml (¼ pt)	300 ml (⅝ pt)

1. Wash and peel celeriac. Cut into fine julienne.
2. Combine with lemon juice and remainder of the ingredients.
3. Dress in a ravier.

49 ~ French bean salad

	4 portions	10 portions
cooked French beans	200 g (8 oz)	500 g (1¼ oz)
vinaigrette	1 tbsp	3 tbsp
salt, pepper		

Combine all the ingredients and dress in a ravier.

50 ~ Niçoise salad

	4 portions	10 portions
tomatoes	100 g (4 oz)	250 g (10 oz)
cooked French beans	200 g (8 oz)	500 g (1¼ lb)
cooked diced potatoes	100 g (4 oz)	250 g (10 oz)
salt, pepper		
vinaigrette	1 tbsp	2½ tbsp
anchovy fillets	10 oz (½ oz)	25 g (1¼ oz)
capers	5 g (¼ oz)	12 g (⅝ oz)
stoned olives	10 g (¼ oz)	25 g (1¼ oz)

> This recipe provides for 4 portions:
>
> 867 kJ/207 kcal
> 9.6 g fat
> (of which 1.5 g saturated)
> 25.0 g carbohydrate
> (of which 4.9 g sugars)
> 6.9 g protein
> 9.9 g fibre

1 Peel tomatoes, de-seed and cut into neat segments.
2 Dress the beans, tomatoes and potatoes neatly in a ravier.
3 Season with salt and pepper. Add the vinaigrette.
4 Decorate with anchovies, capers and olives.

51 ~ Waldorf salad

Celery or celeriac and crisp russet apples diced and mixed with shelled and peeled walnuts, bound with a mayonnaise and dressed on quarters or leaves of lettuce. This may also be served in hollowed-out apples.

52 – Haricot bean salad

	4 portions	10 portions
haricot beans, cooked	200 g (8 oz)	500 g (1¼ lb)
vinaigrette	1 tbsp	2½ tbsp
chopped parsley		
chopped onion, blanched if required, or chive (optional)	10 g (½ oz)	25 g (1¼ oz)
salt, pepper		

Combine all the ingredients and dress in a ravier. This recipe can be used for any type of dried bean.

53 – Three-bean salad

Use 200 g (½ lb) (500 g (1¼ lb) for 10 portions) of three different dried beans, (red kidney, black-eyed, flageolet, etc.) Proceed as for recipe 52.

This recipe provides for 4 portions:

1849 kJ/440 kcal
8.7 g fat
(of which 1.1 g saturated)
63.4 g carbohydrate
(of which 6.3 g sugars)
30.9 g protein
36.0 g fibre

54 – Coleslaw

	4 portions	10 portions
mayonnaise, natural yoghurt or fromage frais	125 ml (¼ pt)	300 ml (⅝ pt)
white or Chinese cabbage	200 g (8 oz)	500 g (1¼ lb)
carrot	50 g (2 oz)	125 g (5 oz)
onion (optional)	25 g (1 oz)	60 g (2½ oz)

Using mayonnaise, this recipe provides for 4 portions:

2514 kJ/599 kcal
59.0 g fat
(of which 8.8 g saturated)
11.7 g carbohydrate
(of which 11.4 g sugars)
5.9 g protein
7.2 g fibre

1 Trim off the outside leaves of the cabbage.
2 Cut into quarters. Remove the centre stalk.
3 Wash the cabbage, shred finely and drain well.
4 Mix with a fine julienne of raw carrot and shredded raw onion. To lessen the harshness of raw onion, blanch and refresh.
5 Bind with mayonnaise sauce, natural yoghurt or vinaigrette.

55 ~ Florida salad

1. Remove the orange zest with a peeler.
2. Cut into fine julienne.
3. Blanch for 2–3 minutes and refresh.
4. Peel the oranges and remove all the white skin.
5. Cut into segments between the white pith and remove all the pips.
6. Dress the lettuce in a bowl, keeping it in quarters if possible.
7. Arrange 3 or 4 orange segments in each portion.
8. Sprinkle with a little orange zest.
9. Serve an acidulated cream dressing separately.

Note Allow $\frac{1}{4}$ lettuce and $\frac{1}{2}$ large orange per portion.

56 ~ Orange salad

Segments of orange cut as recipe 55 with a little of the orange juice, neatly dressed in a salad dish.

—— *Greek-style hors-d'oeuvre* ——

All vegetables cooked *à la grecque* are cooked in the following liquid:

	4 portions	10 portions
water	250 ml ($\frac{1}{2}$ pt)	600 ml ($1\frac{1}{4}$ pt)
olive oil	60 ml ($\frac{1}{8}$ pt)	150 ml ($\frac{1}{3}$ pt)
lemon, juice of	1	$1\frac{1}{2}$
bay leaf	$\frac{1}{2}$	1
sprig of thyme		
peppercorns	6	18
coriander seeds	6	18
salt		

57 ~ Artichokes

1. Peel and trim six artichokes for 4 portions (15 for 10).
2. Cut the leaves short. Remove the chokes.

3   Blanch the artichokes in water with a little lemon juice for 10 minutes.
4   Refresh the artichokes. Place in cooking liquid. Simmer for 15–20 minutes.
5   Serve cold in a ravier with a little of the unstrained cooking liquid.

58 – Onions (button)

1   Peel and wash 200 g (8 oz) button onions for 4 portions (500 g (1¼ lb) for 10).
2   Blanch for approximately 5 minutes and refresh.
3   Place onions in the cooking liquor. Simmer till tender.
4   Serve cold with unstrained cooking liquor.

59 – Cauliflower

1   Trim and wash one medium cauliflower for 4 portions (2½ for 10).
2   Break into small sprigs about the size of a cherry.
3   Blanch for approximately 5 minutes and refresh.
4   Simmer in the cooking liquor for 5–10 minutes. Keep the cauliflower slightly undercooked, and crisp.
5   Serve cold with unstrained cooking liquor.

Plate 5.9: Cauliflower à la grecque

60 – Celery

1   Wash and clean two heads of celery for 4 portions (5 heads for 10).
2   Blanch in lemon water for 5 minutes. Refresh. Cut into 2 cm (1 inch) pieces.
3   Place in a shallow pan. Add the cooking liquor, simmer till tender.
4   Serve cold with unstrained cooking liquor.

61 ~ Leeks

1 Trim and clean $\frac{1}{2}$ kg (1 lb) leeks for 4 portions (1$\frac{1}{4}$ kg (2$\frac{1}{2}$ lb) for 10).
2 Tie into a neat bundle.
3 Blanch for approximately 5 minutes and refresh.
4 Cut into 2 cm (1 inch) lengths and place in a shallow pan.
5 Cover with the cooking liquor. Simmer till tender.
6 Serve cold with unstrained cooking liquor.

> This recipe provides for 4 portions:
>
> 2641 kJ/639 kcal
> 60.0 g fat
> (of which 8.4 g saturated)
> 19.3 g carbohydrate
> (of which 19.3 g sugars)
> 7.6 g protein
> 16.4 g fibre

—— *Portuguese-style hors-d'oeuvre* ——

All the vegetables prepared in the Greek-style may also be prepared in the Portuguese-style. They are prepared and blanched in the same way then cooked in the following liquid:

	4 portions	10 portions
onion, chopped	1	2$\frac{1}{2}$
olive oil	1 tbsp	2$\frac{1}{2}$ tbsp
tomatoes	400 g (1 lb)	1$\frac{1}{4}$ kg (2$\frac{1}{2}$ lb)
garlic	1 clove	1$\frac{1}{2}$ cloves
bay leaf	$\frac{1}{2}$	3
chopped parsley		
sprig of thyme		
tomato purée	25 g (1 oz)	60 g (2$\frac{1}{2}$ oz)
salt, pepper		

1 Sweat the onion in the oil.
2 Skin and de-seed the tomatoes. Roughly chop.
3 Add to the onion with the remainder of the ingredients.
4 Correct the seasoning.
5 Add the vegetable and simmer till tender, with the exception of cauliflower which should be left crisp.
6 Serve hot or cold with the unstrained cooking liquor.

— *Salad leaves and vegetables* —

As these are eaten raw it must be borne in mind that they may contain live food-poisoning bacteria and therefore must be thoroughly washed to remove any soil. Watercress as the name suggests is grown in water and as there is always the danger that the water may have been polluted the watercress must also be thoroughly washed in clean water.

62 – Celery

Trim and thoroughly wash the celery. Remove any discoloured outer stalks. Serve stalks whole or cut into strips.

63 – Chicory (Belgian endive)

Trim off the root end. Cut into 1 cm ($\frac{1}{2}$ inch) lengths, wash well and drain.

64 – Curled chicory

Thoroughly wash and trim off the stalk. Drain well.

65 – Lettuce and iceberg lettuce

Trim off the root and remove the outside leaves. Wash thoroughly and drain well. The outer leaves can be pulled off and the hearts cut into quarters.

66 – Cos lettuce

Trim off the root end and remove the outside leaves. Wash thoroughly and drain well. Cut into quarters.

67 – Mustard and cress

Trim off the stalk ends of the cress. Wash well and lift out of the water so as to leave the seed cases behind. Drain well.

68 – Radishes

The green stems should be trimmed to about 2 cm (1 inch) long, the root end cut off. Wash well, drain and dress in a ravier.

69 – Rocket

A small leafed, sharp, peppery tasting salad. Trim, wash well and drain.

70 – Watercress

Trim off the stalk ends, discard any discoloured leaves, thoroughly wash and drain.

71 – Mixed salad

Neatly arrange in a salad bowl. A typical mixed salad would consist of lettuce, tomato, cucumber, watercress, radishes, etc. Almost any kind of salad vegetable can be used. Offer a vinaigrette separately.

Plate 5.10: Mixed salad

72 – Green salad

Any of the green salads, lettuce, cos lettuce, lambs lettuce (also known as corn salad or mâche), curled chicory, or any combination of green salads may be used, and a few leaves of radicchio. Neatly arrange in a salad bowl; serve with vinaigrette separately.

73 – French salad

The usual ingredients are lettuce, tomato and cucumber, but these may be varied with other salad vegetables, in some cases with quarters of egg. A vinaigrette made with French mustard (French dressing) should be offered.

—— *Cooking and presentation of cold fish* ——

74 – Boiled salmon

Salmon may be obtained in varying weights from $3\frac{1}{2}$–15 kg (7–30 lb): $\frac{1}{2}$ kg (1 lb) uncleaned salmon yields 2–3 portions. Size is an important consideration, depending on whether the salmon is to be cooked whole or cut into darnes. A salmon of any size may be cooked whole. When required for darnes, a medium-sized salmon will be more suitable.

*Fish cooking liquid (*Court bouillon*)*

	4 portions	10 portions
water	1 litre (1 qt)	$2\frac{1}{2}$ litres (5 pt)
salt	10 g ($\frac{1}{2}$ oz)	25 g ($1\frac{1}{4}$ oz)
carrots (sliced)	50 g (2 oz)	125 g (5 oz)
bay leaf	1	2
parsley stalks	2–3	5–8
vinegar	60 ml ($\frac{1}{8}$ pt)	150 ml ($\frac{1}{3}$ pt)
peppercorns	6	15
onions (sliced)	50 g (2 oz)	125 g (5 oz)
sprig of thyme		

1 Simmer all the ingredients for 30–40 minutes.
2 Pass through a strainer, use as required.

Cooking of a whole salmon

1 Scrape off all scales with the back of a knife.
2 Remove all gills and clean out the head.
3 Remove the intestines and clear the blood from the backbone.
4 Trim off all fins. Wash well.
5 Place in a salmon kettle, cover with cold court bouillon.
6 Bring slowly to the boil, skim, then simmer gently.
7 Allow the following approximate simmering times:

$3\frac{1}{2}$ kg	(7 lb)	15 minutes
7 kg	(14 lb)	20 minutes
$10\frac{1}{2}$ kg	(21 lb)	25 minutes
14 kg	(28 lb)	30 minutes

Always allow the salmon to remain in the court bouillon until cold. recipe continued ▶

Cold salmon

8–10 portions

cleaned salmon	1¼ kg (2½ lb)
court bouillon (recipe above)	1 litre (1 qt)
cucumber	½
large lettuce	1
tomatoes	200 g (8 oz)
mayonnaise or green sauce	250 ml (½ pt)

> 1 portion provides:
>
> 1794 kJ/427 kcal
> 33.6 g fat
> (of which 6.0 g saturated)
> 1.3 g carbohydrate
> (of which 1.2 g sugars)
> 29.9 g protein
> 0.7 g fibre

1 Cook the salmon in the court bouillon either whole or cut into 4 or 8 darnes.
2 Allow to cool thoroughly in the cooking liquid to keep it moist. Divide a whole salmon into eight even portions; for darnes, remove centre bone and cut each darne in half, if required.
3 Except when whole, remove the centre bone, also the skin and brown surface and dress neatly on a flat dish.
4 Peel and slice the cucumber and neatly arrange a few slices on each portion.
5 Garnish with quarters of lettuce and quarters of tomatoes.
6 Serve the sauce in a sauceboat separately.

Presentation of a whole salmon

If a salmon is to be presented and served cold from the whole fish, the procedure is as follows:

● Carefully remove the skin and the dark layer under the skin (which is cooked blood). The now bared salmon flesh should be perfectly smooth.
● Make sure the salmon is well drained and place it on to the serving dish or board.
● The salmon is now ready for decorating and garnishing. Keep this to the minimum and avoid overcovering the fish and the dish. Neatly overlapping thin slices of cucumber (the skin may be left on or removed), quartered tomatoes (which can be peeled and neatly cut), small pieces of hearts of lettuce can, if artistically set out, give a quick, neat-looking, appetising appearance. Remember time is money and there is no justification for spending a lot of time cutting fiddly little pieces of many different items to form patterns which often look untidy.

75 ~ Salmon mayonnaise

	4 portions	10 portions
lettuce	1	2–3
cooked salmon	300 g (12 oz)	750 g (1¾ lb)
mayonnaise (page 161)	125 ml (¼ pt)	300 ml (⅝ pt)
tomatoes	200 g (8 oz)	500 g (1¼ lb)
hard-boiled egg	1	
cucumber	¼	½
anchovies	5 g (¼ oz)	12 g (⅝ oz)
capers	5 g (¼ oz)	12 g (⅝ oz)
stoned olives	4	
chopped parsley		

1 Shred the washed and drained lettuce, place in a salad bowl.
2 Add the flaked salmon, free from skin and bone.
3 Coat with mayonnaise sauce.
4 Decorate with quarters of tomato, egg, slices of cucumber, thin fillets of anchovies, capers, olives and chopped parsley.

Note Variations include:

- *salmon salad*, serving the mayonnaise separately;
- *cold salmon portions*, mayonnaise sauce separate;
- *lobster mayonnaise*, using 1 kg (2 lb) cooked lobster, cut in escalopes, decorated with lobster head, tail and legs;
- *lobster salad*;
- *cold lobster*, mayonnaise sauce separate.

Plate 5.11: Various presentations of cold salmon

—— *Cold meats* ——

The typical meats or poultry for cold presentation are: roast beef, boiled or honey roast ham or gammon, roast chicken or turkey, and boiled ox tongue. These are available as left-over joints from previous hot meals; cooked specially for cold service; or bought in ready cooked from suppliers. The various ways of presentation and service are:

- sliced from whole joints on the bone in front of the customer (in which case all bones that may hinder carving must be removed first);
- sliced from boned joints, which in some cases may be rolled and stuffed (also in front of the customer);

192

- pre-sliced in the kitchen, in which case the meat or poultry should be cut as close to service time as possible, otherwise it will start to dry and curl up; pre-sliced meats or poultry can be neatly cut, dressed with the slices overlapping each other, placed on to large dishes or individual plates, covered with cling film and kept under refrigeration; when large numbers of plated meals have to be prepared, plate rings can be used and the plates stacked in sensible sized numbers.

When joints of meat, hams, tongue or turkeys are cooked fresh for serving cold, this is usually done the day before. After cooking they are allowed to cool (the hams are left in the cooking liquor), and then kept under refrigeration overnight.

When roast chickens are required for serving cold, ideally they should be cooked 1–2 hours before service, left to cool (not in the refrigerator) and then carved as required. In this way, the meat remains moist and succulent. Chickens can then be cut into eight pieces and the excess bones removed before serving.

When any meats or poultry are required for a cold buffet, the joint can be presented whole with 2–3 slices cut, laid overlapping from the base of the joint, on a suitably sized dish. The two rear sides of the joint can then be garnished (if required) with two small, neatly placed bunches of watercress dressed so that only leaves show. If a little more colour is required, then a tulip-cut tomato or two may be added. It is a mistake to overgarnish any cold dishes.

If the cut surface of any joint begins to look dry, a thin slice should be removed and discarded before cutting any slices for service or presenting the joint on a cold buffet.

Ham should not be confused with gammon. A gammon is the hind leg of a bacon weight pig, and is cut from a side of bacon. A ham is the hind leg of a porker pig, and is cut round from the side of pork with the aitch bone and usually cured by dry salting. Ham is boiled and can be served hot or cold. Certain imported hams, (Parma ham, Bayonne and Ardennes) may be sliced thinly and eaten raw, generally as an hors-d'oeuvre. In order to carve the ham efficiently it is necessary to remove the aitch bone after cooking. Traditional English hams include York and Bradenham.

Pre-prepared pâtés or terrines are available in a wide variety of types and flavourings which include liver (chicken, duck, etc.) poultry and game.

Pâtés are usually cooked enclosed in a thin layer of bacon fat or they may be enclosed in hot water pastry within a special mould.

Pâtés and terrines must be kept under refrigeration at all times and should never be allowed to stand in a warm kitchen or dining room because they are easily contaminated by food poisoning bacteria. For service, the pâté or terrine can be displayed whole with one or two slices cut, or cut in slices and dressed on plates. If in either case these are to be on display to the customer, then the display counter or cabinet must be refrigerated.

Fish and vegetable pâtés and terrines are also available. When serving meat, poultry or game pâtés, a simple garnish of a fan of gherkin and a little salad is sufficient.

The use of plastic gloves when cold foods are being handled will reduce the risk of contamination.

76 – Chicken salad

	4 portions	10 portions
lettuce (washed)	1	2–3
cooked chicken, free from skin and bone	400 g (1 lb)	1¼ kg (2½ lb)
tomatoes	2	5
hard-boiled egg	1	5
anchovies	10 g (½ oz)	25 g (1¼ oz)
olives	4–8	10–20
capers	5 g (¼ oz)	12 g (⅝ oz)
vinaigrette (page 159)	4 tbsp	10 tbsp

1 Remove heart from the lettuce.
2 Shred the remainder.
3 Place in a salad bowl.
4 Cut the chicken in neat pieces and place on the lettuce.
5 Decorate with quarters of tomato, hard-boiled egg, anchovies, olives, quartered heart of the lettuce and capers.
6 Serve accompanied with vinaigrette.

Note   A variation is chicken mayonnaise using 60 ml (¼ pt) mayonnaise instead of vinaigrette. The chicken is dressed on the lettuce, then coated with mayonnaise and the garnish neatly dressed on top.

77 – Raised pork pie

Hot water paste

	4 portions	10 portions
lard or margarine (alternatively use 100 g (4 oz) lard and 25 g (1 oz) butter or margarine)	125 g (5 oz)	300 g (12½ oz)
strong plain flour	250 g (10 oz)	500 g (1½ lb)
water	15 ml (¼ pt)	300 ml (⅝ pt)
salt		

> I portion provides:
>
> 2867 kJ/683 kcal
> 41.8 g fat
> (of which 17.1 g saturated)
> 54.1 g carbohydrate
> (of which 1.5 g sugars)
> 26.1 g protein
> 3.2 g fibre

1 Sift the flour and salt into a basin.
2 Make a well in the centre.
3 Boil the fat with the water and pour immediately into the flour.
4 Mix with a wooden spoon until cool.
5 Mix to a smooth paste and use while still warm.

Main ingredients

shoulder of pork (without bone)	300 g (12 oz)	1 kg (2 lb)
bacon	100 g (4 oz)	250 g (10 oz)
allspice, or mixed spice, and chopped sage	½ tsp	1½ tsp
salt and pepper		
bread soaked in milk	50 g (2 oz)	125 g (5 oz)
stock or water	2 tbsp	5 tbsp

1 Cut the pork and bacon into small even pieces and combine with the rest of the ingredients.
2 Keep one-quarter of the paste warm and covered.
3 Roll out the remaining three-quarters and carefully line a well-greased raised pie mould.
4 Add the filling and press down firmly.
5 Roll out the remaining pastry for the lid, and eggwash the edges of the pie.
6 Add the lid, seal firmly, neaten the edges, cut off any surplus paste; decorate if desired.
7 Make a hole 1 cm (½ inch) in diameter in the centre of the pie; brush all over with eggwash.
8 Bake in a hot oven (230–250°C; Reg. 8–9; 450–500°F) for approximately 20 minutes.

recipe continued ▶

9   Reduce the heat to moderate (150–200°C; Reg. 2–6; 300–400°F) and cook for 1½–2 hours in all.

10   If the pie colours too quickly, cover with greaseproof paper. Remove from the oven and carefully remove tin, eggwash the pie all over and return to the oven for a few minutes.

11   Remove from the oven and fill with approximately 125 ml (¼ pint) of good hot stock in which 5 g (¼ oz) of gelatine has been dissolved.

12   Serve when cold, garnished with picked watercress and offer a suitable salad.

78 – Veal and ham pie

	4 portions	10 portions
ham or bacon	150 g (6 oz)	375 g (15 oz)
salt, pepper		
hard-boiled egg	1	2
lean veal	250 g (10 oz)	600 g (1½ lb)
parsley and thyme	½ tsp	1 tsp
lemon, grated zest of	1	1
stock or water	2 tbsp	5 tbsp
bread soaked in milk	50 g (2 oz)	125 g (5 oz)
hot water paste		

Proceed as for raised pork pie. Place the shelled egg in the centre of the mixture. Serve when cold, garnished with picked watercress and offer a suitable salad.

6

EGGS

Recipe No.			page no.
10	Boiled eggs	*Oeufs à la coque*	204
22	Curried eggs		210
21	Egg croquette	*Croquette d'œuf*	209
7	Eggs in cocotte	*Oeufs en cocotte*	203
8	Eggs in cocotte with creamed chicken	*Oeufs en cocotte à la reine*	203
9	Eggs in cocotte with tomato	*Oeufs en cocotte aux tomates*	209
17	French-style fried eggs	*Oeufs frits à la française*	207
15	Fried eggs	*Oeufs frits*	206
16	Fried eggs and bacon	*Oeufs au lard*	207
12	Hard-boiled eggs	*Oeufs durs*	205
14	Hard-boiled eggs with cheese and tomato sauce	*Oeufs aurore*	206
13	Hard-boiled eggs with mushroom and cheese sauce	*Oeufs chimay*	205
24	Omelets	*Omelettes*	211
18	Poached eggs	*Oeufs pochés*	207
19	Poached eggs with cheese sauce	*Oeufs pochés Mornay*	208
20	Poached eggs with cheese sauce and spinach	*Oeufs pochés florentine*	209
23	Scotch eggs		210
1	Scrambled eggs	*Oeufs brouillés*	201
5	Scrambled eggs with chopped herbs	*Oeufs brouillés aux fines herbes*	202
4	Scrambled eggs with croûtons	*Oeufs brouillés aux croûtons*	202
6	Scrambled eggs with ham	*Oeufs brouillés au jambon*	203
3	Scrambled eggs with mushrooms	*Oeufs brouillés aux champignons*	202
2	Scrambled eggs with tomatoes	*Oeufs brouillés aux tomates*	201
11	Soft-boiled eggs	*Oeufs mollets*	205

Eggs

1 Ensure preparation and cooking areas and equipment satisfy health and hygiene regulations and are cleaned correctly after use.

2 Plan work, allocate, time and organise in an efficient manner.

3 Prepare egg dishes in a variety of ways with suitable garnishes and presented to give consumer satisfaction.

4 Realise that competency implies knowing, understanding and applying the principles of egg cookery.

TYPES

Hens eggs are almost exclusively used for cookery but eggs from turkeys, geese, ducks, guinea fowl, quail and gulls are also edible.

Quails eggs are used in a variety of ways. They can be used as a garnish to many hot and cold dishes or used either as a starter or main course, such as a salad of assorted leaves with hot wild mushrooms and poached quail eggs or tartlet of quail eggs on chopped mushrooms coated with hollandaise sauce.

SIZES

Hens eggs are graded in seven sizes:

- size 1 70 g
- size 2 65 g
- size 3 60 g
- size 4 55 g
- size 5 50 g
- size 6 45 g
- size 7 under 45 g.

PURCHASING AND QUALITY

The size of the eggs does not affect the quality but does affect the price. Eggs are tasted for quality then weighed and graded.

When buying eggs the following points should be noted.

- The eggshell should be clean, well-shaped, strong and slightly rough.
- When eggs are broken there should be a high proportion of thick white to thin white. If an egg is kept, the thick white gradually changes into thin white and water passes from the white into the yolk.
- The yolk should be firm, round (not flattened) and of a good even colour. As eggs are kept the yolk loses strength and begins to flatten, water evaporates from the egg and is replaced by air.

FOOD VALUE

Eggs contain most nutrients and are low in calories (two eggs contain 180 calories). Egg protein is complete and easily digestible; therefore it is useful to balance meals. Eggs are useful as a main dish as they are a protective food and provide energy and material for growth and repair of the body.

SALMONELLA

Hens can pass salmonella bacteria into their eggs and thus cause food poisoning. To reduce this risk, pasteurised eggs may be used where appropriate, e.g. omelets, scrambled eggs.

STORAGE

Store in a cool but not too dry place; 0–5°C (32–41°F) is ideal. The humidity of the air and the amount of carbon dioxide in the air are controlled. Eggs will keep up to nine months under these conditions.

Because eggshells are porous the eggs will absorb any strong odours; therefore, they should not be stored near strong-smelling foods such as onions, fish, cheese, etc.

Pasteurised eggs are washed, sanitised and then broken into sterilised containers. After combining the yolks and whites they are strained, pasteurised, that is heated to 63°C (145°F) for one minute, then rapidly cooled.

HEALTH, SAFETY AND HYGIENE

- Eggs should be stored in a cool place, preferably under refrigeration.
- Eggs should be stored away from possible contaminants, such as raw meat, strong smelling foods.
- Stocks should be rotated: first in, first out.
- Hands should be washed before and after handling eggs.
- Cracked eggs should not be used.
- Preparation surfaces, utensils and containers should be regularly cleaned and always cleaned between preparation of different dishes.
- Egg dishes should be consumed as soon as possible after preparation or if not for immediate use, refrigerated.

VERSATILITY

Fried, scrambled, poached, boiled and omelets are mainly served at breakfast. A variety of dishes may be served for lunch, high teas, supper and snacks.

— *Egg dishes* —

1 – Scrambled eggs (basic recipe)

	4 portions	10 portions
eggs	6–8	15–20
milk (optional)	2 tbsp	5 tbsp
salt, pepper		
butter	50 g (2 oz)	125 g (5 oz)

> Using hard margarine, 1 portion provides:
>
> 1105 kJ/263 kcal
> 22.9 g fat
> (of which 8.7 g saturated)
> 0.5 g carbohydrates
> (of which 0.5 g sugars)
> 13.9 g protein
> 0.0 g fibre

1 Break the eggs in a basin, add milk (if using), lightly season with salt and pepper and thoroughly mix with a whisk.
2 Melt 25 g (1 oz) butter in a thick-bottomed pan, add the eggs and cook over a gentle heat stirring continuously until the eggs are lightly cooked.
3 Remove from the heat, correct the seasoning and mix in the remaining 25 g (1 oz) butter. (A tablespoon of cream may also be added.)
4 Serve in individual egg dishes.

Note If scrambled eggs are cooked too quickly or for too long the protein will toughen, the eggs will discolour because of the iron and sulphur compounds being released and syneresis or separation of water from the eggs will occur. This means that they will be unpleasant to eat. The heat from the pan will continue to cook the eggs after it has been removed from the stove; therefore, the pan should be removed from the heat just before the eggs are cooked.

Scrambled eggs can be served on a slice of freshly-buttered toast with the crust removed.

2 – Scrambled eggs with tomatoes

	4 portions	10 portions
tomatoes	400 g (1 lb)	1¼ lb (2½ lb)
chopped onion or shallot	25 g (1 oz)	60 g (2½ oz)
butter or margarine	25 g (1 oz)	60 g (2½ oz)
chopped parsley		

1 Prepare, cook and serve the eggs as for the basic method.

recipe continued ▶

2 Prepare a cooked tomato concassé (see page 551).
3 To serve, place a spoonful of tomato in the centre of each dish of egg and a little chopped parsley on the top of the tomato.

3 – Scrambled eggs with mushrooms

	4 portions	10 portions
button mushrooms	200 g (8 oz)	500 g (1¼ lb)
butter	25 g (1 oz)	60 g (2½ oz)
chopped parsley		

1 Prepare, cook and serve the eggs as for the basic method.
2 Peel, wash and slice the mushrooms.
3 Toss in the butter in a frying-pan until cooked, drain well.
4 Dress neatly on top of the eggs with a little parsley.

4 – Scrambled eggs with croûtons

	4 portions	10 portions
slices stale bread	2	5
butter	50 g (2 oz)	125 g (5 oz)

1 Prepare, cook and serve the eggs as for the basic recipe.
2 Remove the crusts from the bread and cut into neat ½ cm (¼ inch) dice.
3 Melt the butter in a frying-pan, add the croûtons and fry to a golden brown.
4 Place a spoonful in the centre of each dish of eggs.

5 – Scrambled eggs with chopped herbs

	4 portions	10 portions
chopped parsley	1 tsp	3 tsp
chervil, tarragon and chives		

1 Prepare, cook and serve as for the basic recipe.
2 Add the herbs with the last 25 g (1 oz) of butter.

6 ～ Scrambled eggs with ham

	4 portions	10 portions
thick-sliced lean ham	100 g (4 oz)	250 g (10 oz)

1 Prepare, cook and serve the eggs as for the basic recipe.
2 Trim off all fat from the ham and cut into $\frac{1}{2}$ cm ($\frac{1}{4}$ inch) dice.
3 Add the eggs with the last 25 g (1 oz) butter.

Note There are many other foods served with scrambled eggs: shrimps, cheese, asparagus tips, kidneys, etc.

7 ～ Eggs in cocotte (basic recipe)

	4 portions	10 portions
butter	25 g (1 oz)	60 g (2$\frac{1}{2}$ oz)
salt, pepper		
eggs	4	10

1 portion provides:
534 kJ/127 kcal
11.2 g fat
(of which 5.2 g saturated)
0.0 g carbohydrate
(of which 0.0 g sugars)
6.8 g protein
0.0 g fibre

1 Butter four egg cocottes.
2 Break an egg carefully into each.
3 Place the cocottes in a sauté pan containing 1 cm ($\frac{1}{2}$ inch) water.
4 Cover with a tight-fitting lid, place on a fierce heat so that the water boils rapidly.
5 Cook for 2–3 minutes until the eggs are lightly set and serve.

Note Variations include:

● half a minute before the cooking is completed, adding 1 dessertspoon of cream to each egg and completing the cooking;
● when cooked, adding 1 dessertspoon jus-lié to each egg.

8 ～ Eggs in cocotte with creamed chicken

	4 portions	10 portions
diced cooked chicken	20 g (2 oz)	125 g (5 oz)
sauce suprême (page 408)	125 ml ($\frac{1}{4}$ pt)	300 ml ($\frac{5}{8}$ pt)

recipe continued ▶

1 Combine the chicken with half of the sauce and place in the bottom of the egg cocottes.
2 Break the eggs on top of the chicken and cook as for the basic recipe.
3 When serving, pour over the eggs 1 dessertspoon of the remaining sauce or fresh cream.

9 ~ Eggs in cocotte with tomato

	4 portions	10 portions
tomatoes (cooked concassé) (page 551)	200 g (8 oz)	500 g (1¼ lb)
tomato sauce (page 132)	125 ml (¼ pt)	300 ml (⅝ pt)

1 Place the tomato in the bottom of the egg cocottes.
2 Break the eggs on top and cook as for the basic method.
3 Add 1 dessertspoon of tomato sauce to the eggs before serving.

10 ~ Boiled eggs

Allow 1 or 2 eggs per portion.

Method I
Place the eggs in cold water, bring to the boil, simmer for 2–2½ minutes, remove from the water and serve at once in an egg cup.

Method II
Plunge the eggs in boiling water, reboil, simmer for 3–5 minutes.

Note Boiled eggs are always served in the shell.

Using 1 egg per portion, 1 portion provides:

340 kJ/81 kcal
6.0 g fat
(of which 1.9 g saturated)
0.0 g carbohydrate
(of which 0.0 g sugars)
6.8 g protein
0.0 g fibre

1 portion provides:

1052 kJ/251 kcal
18.9 g fat
(of which 8.7 g saturated)
8.0 g carbohydrate
(of which 3.3 g sugars)
12.5 g protein
1.2 g fibre

11 – Soft-boiled eggs

Plunge the eggs into boiling water, reboil, simmer for $5\frac{1}{2}$ minutes. Refresh immediately. Remove the shells carefully. Reheat when required for 30 seconds in hot salted water.

All the recipes given for poached eggs (recipes 18–20) can be applied to soft-boiled eggs.

12 – Hard-boiled eggs

1 Plunge the eggs into a pan of boiling water.
2 Reboil and simmer for 8–10 minutes.
3 Refresh until cold under running water.

Note If high temperatures or a long cooking time are used to cook eggs, iron in the yolk and sulphur compounds in the white are released to form an unsightly blackish ring around the yolk. Stale eggs will also show a black ring round the yolk.

13 – Hard-boiled eggs with mushroom and cheese sauce

		4 portions	10 portions
hard-boiled eggs		4	
chopped shallots	⎫	10 g ($\frac{1}{2}$ oz)	25 g ($1\frac{1}{4}$ oz)
butter	⎬ duxelle	10 g ($\frac{1}{2}$ oz)	25 g ($1\frac{1}{4}$ oz)
mushrooms	⎭	100 g (4 oz)	250 g (10 oz)
chopped parsley			
salt, pepper			
Mornay sauce, page 118		250 ml ($\frac{1}{2}$ pt)	600 ml ($1\frac{1}{4}$ pt)
grated Parmesan cheese			

Using 2 eggs per portion, 1 portion provides:

679 kJ/162 kcal
12.0 g fat
(of which 3.8 g saturated)
0.0 g carbohydrate
(of which 0.0 g sugars)
13.5 g protein
0.0 g fibre

1 Cut the eggs in halves lengthwise.
2 Remove the yolks and pass them through a sieve.
3 Place the whites in an earthenware serving dish.
4 Prepare the duxelle by cooking the chopped shallot in the butter without colouring, add the well-washed and finely chopped mushroom or mushroom trimmings, cook for 3–4 minutes.
5 Mix the yolks with the duxelle and parsley and correct the seasoning.
6 Spoon or pipe the mixture into the egg white halves.

recipe continued ▶

7 Cover the eggs with Mornay sauce, sprinkle with grated Parmesan cheese and brown slowly under a salamander or in the top of a moderate oven and serve.

14 – Hard-boiled eggs with cheese and tomato sauce

1 Proceed as for recipe 13 using béchamel in place of Mornay sauce.
2 Add a little tomato sauce or tomato purée to the béchamel to give it a pinkish colour.
3 Mask the eggs, sprinkle with grated cheese.
4 Gratinate under the salamander.

15 – Fried eggs

1 Allow 1 or 2 eggs per portion.
2 Melt a little fat in a frying pan. Add the eggs.
3 Cook gently until lightly set. Serve on a plate or flat dish.

Note   To prepare an excellent fried egg it is essential to use a high quality egg, to maintain a controlled low heat and use a high quality fat (butter or oil, such as sunflower oil).

Fried in olive oil, 1 portion provides:	Fried in sunflower oil, 1 portion provides:
536 kJ/128 kcal	1512 kJ/360 kcal
10.7 g fat	31.0 g fat
(of which 2.6 g saturated)	(of which 9.8 g saturated)
0.0 g carbohydrate	0.0 g carbohydrate
(of which 0.0 g sugars)	(of which 0.0 g sugars)
7.6 g protein	20.2 g protein
0.0 g fibre	0.0 g fibre

16 ~ Fried eggs and bacon

1 Allow 2–3 rashers per portion. Remove the rind and bone.
2 Fry in a little fat or grill on a flat tray under the salamander on both sides. Dress neatly around the fried egg.

Note   Fried eggs, may also be served with grilled or fried tomatoes, mushrooms, sauté potatoes, etc., as ordered by the customer.

Fried in butter, I portion provides:

536 kJ/128 kcal
10.7 g fat
(of which 4.1 g saturated)
0.0 g carbohydrate
(of which 0.0 g sugars)
7.6 g protein
0.0 g fibre

17 ~ French-style fried eggs

1 Fry two eggs separately in a frying-pan in a fairly deep hot oil.
2 Shape each egg with a spoon so as to enclose the yolk in crisply fried white.
3 Drain well and serve.

18 ~ Poached eggs

High quality eggs should be used for poaching because they have a large amount of thick white and consequently have less tendency to spread in the simmering water. Low quality eggs are difficult to manage because the large quantity of thin white spreads in the simmering water.

I portion provides:

358 kJ/85 kcal
6.4 g fat
(of which 2.0 g saturated)
0.0 g carbohydrate
(of which 0.0 g sugars)
6.8 g protein
0.0 g fibre

A well-prepared poached egg has a firm tender white surrounding the slightly thickened unbroken yolk. The use of a little vinegar (an acid) helps to set the egg white so preventing it from spreading; it also makes the white more tender and whiter. Too much malt vinegar will discolour and give the eggs a strong vinegar flavour; white vinegar may be used.

1 Carefully break the eggs one by one into a shallow pan containing at least 8 cm (3 inches) gently boiling water to which a little vinegar has been added (1 litre (2 pint) water to 1 tablespoon vinegar).
2 Simmer until lightly set for approximately $2\frac{1}{2}$–3 minutes.
3 Remove carefully with a perforated spoon into a bowl of cold water.

recipe continued ▶

Plate 6.1: Preparation for fried eggs

4   Trim the white of egg if necessary.
5   Reheat, when required, by placing into hot salted water for approximately
    $\frac{1}{2}$–1 minute.
6   Remove carefully from the water using a perforated spoon.
7   Drain on a cloth and use as required.

Plate 6.2a–c: Stages involved in poaching an egg

19 – Poached eggs with cheese sauce or Poached eggs Mornay

	4 portions	10 portions
eggs	4	10
short paste tartlets or	4	10
half slices of buttered toast	4	10
Mornay sauce (page 118)	250 ml ($\frac{1}{2}$ pt)	600 ml ($1\frac{1}{4}$ pt)

1 portion provides:
1177 kJ/280 kcal
19.1 g fat
(of which 8.7 g saturated)
15.2 g carbohydrate
(of which 3.4 g sugars)
12.8 g protein
0.8 g fibre

1   Cook eggs as for poached eggs.
2   Place tartlets or toast in an earthenware dish (the

slices of toast may be halved, cut in rounds with a
cutter, crust removed).

3   Add the hot well-drained eggs.
4   Completely cover with sauce, sprinkle with grated Parmesan cheese, brown
    under the salamander and serve.

20 ～ Poached eggs with cheese sauce and spinach or poached eggs Florentine

	4 portions	10 portions
spinach	$\frac{3}{4}$kg (1 lb 8 oz)	$1\frac{1}{2}$kg (3 lb)
eggs	4	10
Mornay sauce (page 118)	250 ml ($\frac{1}{2}$pt)	600 ml ($1\frac{1}{4}$pt)

1   Remove the stems from the spinach.
2   Wash very carefully in plenty of water several times if necessary.
3   Cook in boiling salted water until tender, for approximately 3–5 minutes.
4   Refresh under cold water, squeeze dry into a ball.
5   When required for service, place into a pan containing 25–50 g (1–2 oz) butter,
    loosen with a fork and reheat quickly without colouring, season lightly.
6   Place in an earthenware dish.
7   Place the eggs on top and finish as for recipe 19.

21 ～ Egg croquettes

	4 portions	10 portions
thick béchamel	250 ml ($\frac{1}{2}$pt)	600 ml ($1\frac{1}{4}$pt)
hard-boiled eggs	4	10
salt, pepper		
egg yolk	1	2–3
flour	25 g (1 oz)	60 g ($2\frac{1}{2}$oz)
beaten egg	1	2–3
white breadcrumbs	50 g (2 oz)	125 g (5 oz)

1 portion provides:

1726 kJ/411 kcal
31.8 g fat
(of which 8.6 g saturated)
18.8 g carbohydrate
(of which 3.5 g sugars)
13.6 g protein
0.9 g fibre

1   Boil the béchamel in a thick-bottomed pan.
2   Add the eggs cut into $\frac{1}{2}$cm ($\frac{1}{4}$inch) dice.
3   Reboil, season, mix in the egg yolk, and remove from the heat.

recipe continued ▶

4   Pour on to a greased tray and leave until cold.
5   Mould into 4 or 8 even-sized croquette shapes.
6   Pass through flour, beaten egg, and crumbs (twice if necessary).
7   Shake off surplus crumbs and reshape with a palette knife.
8   Deep fry to a golden brown in hot fat, drain well.
9   Garnish with fried or sprig parsley and serve with a suitable sauce, such as tomato (page 132).

Note   For variations, add diced mushrooms, sweetcorn, etc.

22 – Curried eggs

	4 portions	10 portions
rice (long grain)	50 g (2 oz)	125 g (5 oz)
hard-boiled eggs	4	10
curry sauce (page 129)	250 ml ($\frac{1}{2}$ pt)	600 ml ($1\frac{1}{4}$ pt)

1   Pick and wash the rice.
2   Add to plenty of boiling, salt water.
3   Stir to the boil and allow to simmer gently until tender, for approximately 12–15 minutes.
4   Wash well under running water, drain and place on a sieve and cover with a cloth.
5   Place on a tray in a moderate oven or on a hot plate until hot.
6   Place the rice in an earthenware dish.
7   Reheat the eggs in hot salt water, cut in halves and dress neatly on the rice.
8   Coat the eggs with sauce and serve.

23 – Scotch eggs

	4 portions	10 portions
hard-boiled eggs	4	10
sausage meat	300 g (12 oz)	1 kg (2 lb)
flour	25 g (1 oz)	60 g ($2\frac{1}{2}$ oz)
beaten egg	1	3
breadcrumbs	50 g (2 oz)	125 g (5 oz)

1 portion provides:
2094 kJ/499 kcal
39.9 g fat
(of which 11.4 g saturated)
18.4 g carbohydrate
(of which 0.6 g sugars)
18.0 g protein
1.0 g fibre

210

1   Completely cover each egg with sausage meat.
2   Pass it through the flour, egg and breadcrumbs.
3   Shake off the surplus crumbs.
4   Deep fry to a golden brown in a moderately hot fat.
5   Drain well, cut in halves and serve hot or cold.
6   *Hot:* garnish with fried or sprig parsley, and a sauceboat of suitable sauce, such as tomato (page 132).
    Cold: garnish with salad in season and a sauceboat of salad dressing (chapter 5).

24 – Omelets (basic recipe)

eggs per portion	2–3
butter	10 g ($\frac{1}{2}$ oz)

1   Allow 2–3 eggs per portion.
2   Break the eggs into a basin, season lightly with salt and pepper.
3   Beat well with a fork or whisk until the yolks and whites are thoroughly combined and no streaks of white can be seen.
4   Heat the omelet pan; wipe thoroughly clean with a dry cloth.
5   Add 10 g ($\frac{1}{2}$ oz) butter; heat until foaming but not brown.
6   Add the eggs and cook quickly, moving the mixture continuously with a fork until lightly set; remove from the heat.
7   Half fold the mixture over at right-angles to the handle.
8   Tap the bottom of the pan to bring up the edge of the omelet.
9   Tilt the pan completely over so as to allow the omelet to fall carefully into the centre of the dish or plate.
10 Neaten the shape if necessary and serve immediately.

Using 2 eggs per portion, 1 portion provides:

990 kJ/236 kcal
20.2 g fat
(of which 9.1 g saturated)
0.0 g carbohydrate
(of which 0.0 g sugars)
13.6 g protein
0.0 g fibre

Using 3 eggs per portion, 1 portion provides:

1330 kJ/317 kcal
26.2 g fat
(of which 11.0 g saturated)
0.0 g carbohydrate
(of which 0.0 g sugars)
20.3 g protein
0.0 g fibre

recipe continued ▶

Plate 6.3a–f: Stages involved in making an omelet

Note   Variations of omelet include:

- *fine herbs* (chopped parsley, chervil and chives);
- *mushroom* (cooked, sliced, wild or cultivated);
- *cheese* (25 g (1 oz) grated cheese added before folding);
- *tomato* (incision made down centre of cooked omelette, filled with hot tomato concassé; served with tomato sauce);
- *chicken livers* (neatly cut chicken livers fried in butter added to a light brown sauce); finished as for tomato omelet);
- *kidney* (made the same as for chicken livers);
- *shrimp* (bound with béchamel sauce, finished as for fine herbs omelet).

Other ingredients which can be used include: ham, bacon, onion, potato, etc.

Spanish omelet has tomato concassé, cooked onions, diced red pimento and parsley added and is cooked and served flat. Many other flat omelets can be served with a variety of ingredients. A flat omelet is made as for a basic omelet up to point 7; sharply tap the pan on the stove to loosen the omelet and toss it over as for a pancake.

7

PASTA AND RICE

Recipe No.			page no.
22	Boiled rice, plain		236
24	Braised rice	*Riz pilaff*	236
27	Braised rice with cheese	*Riz pilaff au fromage*	238
25	Braised rice with mushrooms	*Riz pilaff aux champignons*	237
26	Braised rice with peas and pimento	*Riz à l'orientale*	237
14	Bucatini Amatriciana-style		227
13	Butterfly pasta with crab		226
17	Cannelloni		230
1	Fresh egg pasta dough		218
29	Fried rice		239
19	Gnocchi parisienne		233
21	Gnocchi piemontaise		234
20	Gnocchi romaine		234
12	Green fettuccine with ham and creamy cheese		226
18	Lasagne		231
6	Macaroni cheese	*Macoroni au gratin*	222
7	Noodles	*Nouilles*	222
8	Noodles with butter	*Nouilles au beurre*	223
9	Noodles or spaghetti with eggs and bacon		223
11	Penne and mange-tout		225
16	Ravioli filling		230
15	Ravioli dough		229
28	Risotto		238
10	Spaghetti with bacon and tomatoes		225
5	Spaghetti bolognaise		221
2	Spaghetti with cheese	*Spaghetti italienne*	219
4	Spaghetti milanaise		220
3	Spaghetti with tomato sauce	*Spaghetti napolitaine*	220
23	Steamed rice		236
30	Stir fried rice		239

Pasta and rice

1   Ensure preparation, cooking areas and equipment are ready for use and correctly cleaned after use to comply with health, safety and hygiene regulations.
2   Plan work, allocate time and organise in an efficient manner.
3   Produce a variety of pasta dishes, using fresh and ready prepared pasta to customer satisfaction.
4   Store prepared pasta not for immediate use in accordance with food hygiene regulations.
5   Produce a variety of rice dishes to customer satisfaction.
6   Realise that competency implies knowing, understanding and applying the principles of producing pasta and rice dishes.

Pasta

Pasta is made from a strong wheat flour, known as durum flour, made into a dough by the addition of water, olive oil and egg. There are two main types of pasta, dried and fresh home-made. Dried pasta is available in at least 56 different shapes each of which has a name and which are widely used because of the convenience and the fact that the shelf life is up to 2 years if it is correctly stored. Fresh pasta is more and more readily available in a variety of shapes, colours and flavours from suppliers and there are machines for those who wish to produce their own pasta.

Pasta can be served for lunch, dinner, supper or as a snack meal and also used as an accompaniment or garnish to other dishes. Traditionally pasta is cooked *al dente* which means 'firm to the bite'.

FOOD VALUE

Durum wheat has a 15% protein content which makes it a good alternative to rice and potatoes for vegetarians. Pasta also contains carbohydrates in the form of starch which gives the body energy.

STORAGE

If eggs are used in the making of fresh pasta, the fresher they are the longer the keeping quality of the pasta. When fresh pasta is correctly stored it will keep for up

Plate 7.1: Pasta-making machines

to 3 or 4 weeks. Flat types of fresh pasta, such as noodles, which are dried and transferred to a container or bowl, will keep for up to a month in a cool, dry store. Other shapes can be stored in the freezer. To make fresh egg pasta, see recipe on page 218.

TYPES AND SAUCES

There are basically four types of pasta, each of which may be left plain or flavoured with spinach or tomato.

- dried durum wheat pasta;
- egg pasta;
- semolina pasta;
- wholewheat pasta.

Examples of sauces to go with pasta include:

- tomato sauce;
- cream, butter or béchamel-based;
- rich meat sauce;
- olive oil and garlic;
- soft white or blue cheese.

CHEESES

Examples of cheeses used in pasta include:

- *Parmesan*, the most popular hard cheese, ideal for grating. The flavour is best when it is freshly grated. If bought ready grated, or if it is grated and stored, the flavour deteriorates.
- *Pecorino*, a strong ewe's milk cheese, sometimes studded with peppercorns. Used for strongly flavoured dishes, it can be grated or thinly sliced.
- *Ricotta*, creamy-white in colour, made from the discarded whey of other cheeses. It is widely used in fillings for pasta, such as cannelloni, ravioli, etc. and for sauces.
- *Mozzarella*, traditionally made from the milk of the water buffalo. It is pure white and creamy, with a mild but distinctive flavour, usually round or pear-shaped. It will only keep for a few days in a container half-filled with milk and water.
- *Gorgonzola* or *dolcelatte*, distinctive blue cheeses which can be used in sauces.

INGREDIENTS FOR PASTA DISHES

The following are some examples of ingredients that can be used in pasta dishes. The list is almost endless but can include:

- smoked salmon
- shrimps
- prawns
- mussels
- scallops
- lobster
- tuna fish
- crab
- anchovies
- cockles
- avocado
- mushrooms
- tomatoes
- onions
- courgettes
- peas
- spinach
- chillies
- peppers
- broad beans
- broccoli
- sliced sausage
- salami
- ham
- bacon
- beef
- chicken
- duck
- tongue
- chicken livers
- smoked ham
- mustard and cress
- parsley
- rosemary
- basil
- tarragon
- fennel
- chives
- spring onions
- marjoram
- pine nuts
- walnuts
- stoned olives
- capers
- cooked, dried beans
- eggs
- grated lemon zest
- saffron
- grated nutmeg
- sultanas

COOKING PASTA

- Always cook in plenty of gently boiling salted water.
- Stir to the boil. Do not overcook.
- If not to be used immediately, refresh and reheat carefully in hot salted water when required. Drain well in a colander.
- With most pasta, grated cheese (Parmesan) should be served separately.
- Allow 10 g ($\frac{1}{2}$ oz) pasta per portion as a garnish; allow 25–50 g (1–2 oz) pasta per portion for a main course.

1 – Fresh egg pasta dough

strong flour	400 g (1 lb)
eggs, beaten	4 × size 3
salt	
olive oil as required	

1 Sieve the flour and salt, shape into a well.
2 Pour the beaten eggs into the well.
3 Gradually incorporate the flour and only add oil to adjust to required consistency. The amount of oil will vary according to the type of flour and the size of the eggs.
4 Pull and knead the dough until it is of a smooth, elastic consistency.
5 Cover the dough with a dampened cloth and allow to rest in a cool place for 30 minutes.
6 Roll out the dough and a well floured surface to a thickness of $\frac{1}{2}$ mm ($\frac{1}{8}$ inch) or use a pasta rolling machine.
7 Trim the sides and cut the dough as required using a large knife.

Note   If using a pasta rolling machine, divide the dough into three or four pieces. Pass each section by hand through the machine turning the rollers with the other hand. Repeat this five or six times adjusting the rollers each time to make the pasta thinner.

Fresh egg pasta requires less cooking time than dried pasta. Fresh egg pasta not for immediate use must be stored in a cool dry place. If fresh egg pasta is to be stored, it should be allowed to dry, then kept in a clean, dry container or bowl in a cool dry store. For further storage information, consult *The Theory of Catering* by Kinton, Ceserani and Foskett.

Variations include:

- *Spinach* Add 75–100 g (3–4 oz) finely puréed, dry, cooked spinach to the dough.
- *Tomato* Add 2 tablespoons of tomato purée to the dough.
- Other flavours used include: beetroot, saffron and black ink from squid.
- *Wholewheat pasta* Use half wholewheat and half white flour.

2 ~ Spaghetti with cheese

	4 portions	10 portions
spaghetti	100 g (4 oz)	250 g (10 oz)
butter	25 g (1 oz)	60 g (2½ oz)
grated cheese (preferably Parmesan)	25–50 g (1–2 oz)	60–125 g (2½–5 oz)
salt, mill pepper		

1 Plunge the spaghetti into a saucepan containing plenty of boiling salted water. Allow to boil gently.
2 Stir occasionally with a wooden spoon. Cook for approximately 12–15 minutes.
3 Drain well in a colander. Return to a clean, dry pan.
4 Mix in the butter and cheese. Correct the seasoning and serve.

> Using 28 g/1 oz cheese, this recipe provides:
>
> 2640 kJ/628 kcal
> 30.8 g fat
> (of which 18.4 g saturated)
> 74.2 g carbohydrate
> (of which 3.4 g sugars)
> 18.6 g protein
> 5.2 g fibre

> Using 52 g/2 oz cheese, this recipe provides:
>
> 3066 kJ/730 kcal
> 39.0 g fat
> (of which 23.8 g saturated)
> 74.2 g carbohydrate
> (of which 3.4 g sugars)
> 25.2 g protein
> 5.2 g fibre

3 ~ Spaghetti with tomato sauce

	4 portions	10 portions
spaghetti	100 g (4 oz)	250 g (10 oz)
butter (optional)	25 g (1 oz)	60 g (2½ oz)
tomato sauce (page 132)	250 ml (½ pt)	600 ml (1¼ pt)
salt, mill pepper		
tomato concassé	100 g (4 oz)	250 g (10 oz)

Using hard margarine, this recipe provides:

1672 kJ/400 kcal
17.2 g fat
(of which 9.4 g saturated)
50.0 g carbohydrate
(of which 10.2 g sugars)
11.8 g protein
4.0 g fibre

1 Plunge spaghetti into a saucepan containing boiling salted water. Allow to boil gently.
2 Stir occasionally with a wooden spoon. Cook for approximately 12–15 minutes.
3 Drain well in a colander. Return to a clean, dry pan.
4 Mix in the butter and add the tomato sauce. Correct the seasoning.
5 Add the tomato concassé and serve with grated cheese.

4 ~ Spaghetti milanaise

	4 portions	10 portions
spaghetti	100 g (4 oz)	250 g (10 oz)
butter (optional)	25 g (1 oz)	60 g (2½ oz)
tomato sauce (page 132)	125 ml (¼ pt)	600 ml (1¼ pt)
ham, tongue and cooked mushroom in julienne	25 g (1 oz)	60 g (2½ oz)
salt, mill pepper		

1 Plunge the spaghetti into plenty of boiling salted water.
2 Allow to boil gently. Stir occasionally with a wooden spoon.
3 Cook for approximately 12–15 minutes. Drain well in a colander.
4 Return to a clean pan containing the butter. Add tomato sauce.
5 Correct the seasoning. Add the julienne of ham, tongue, and mushroom and mix in carefully, then serve with grated cheese.

5 – Spaghetti bolognaise

	4 portions	10 portions
butter or oil, optional	25 g (1 oz)	60 g (2½ oz)
chopped onion	50 g (2 oz)	125 g (5 oz)
clove garlic, chopped	1	
lean minced beef or tail end fillet, cut in ⅛ inch dice	100 g (4 oz)	250 g (10 oz)
jus-lié or demi-glace	125 ml (¼ pt)	600 ml (1¼ pt)
tomato purée	1 tbsp	
marjoram or oregano		
diced mushrooms	100 g (4 oz)	250 g (10 oz)
salt, mill pepper		
spaghetti	100 g (4 oz)	250 g (10 oz)

> Using sunflower oil, this recipe provides for 4 portions:
>
> 3188 kJ/760 kcal
> 32.2 g fat
> (of which 5.6 g saturated)
> 83.4 g carbohydrate
> (of which 10.4 g sugars)
> 39.0 g protein
> 9.6 g fibre

1 Place 10 g (½ oz) butter or oil in a sauteuse.
2 Add the chopped onion and garlic and cook for 4–5 minutes without colour.
3 Add the beef and cook, colouring lightly.
4 Add the jus-lié or demi-glace, the tomato purée and the herbs.
5 Simmer till tender.
6 Add the mushrooms and simmer for 5 minutes, then correct the seasoning.
7 Meanwhile cook the spaghetti in plenty of boiling salted water.
8 Allow to boil gently and stir occasionally with a wooden spoon.
9 Cook for approximately 12–15 minutes. Drain well in a colander.
10 Return to a clean pan containing 10 g (½ oz) butter (optional).
11 Correct the seasoning.
12 Serve with the sauce in centre of the spaghetti.
13 Serve grated cheese separately.

Plate 7.2: Spaghetti bolognaise

6 – Macaroni cheese

	4 portions	10 portions
macaroni	100 g (4 oz)	250 g (10 oz)
butter, optional	25 g (1 oz)	60 g (2½ oz)
grated cheese	100 g (4 oz)	250 g (10 oz)
thin béchamel	500 ml (1 pt)	1¼ litre (2½ pt)
diluted English or continental mustard	½ tsp	1½ tsp
salt, mill pepper		

> This recipe provides for 4 portions:
>
> 7596 kJ/1808 kcal
> 116.6 g fat
> (of which 64.2 g saturated)
> 136.6 g carbohydrate
> (of which 26.6 g sugars)
> 60.0 g protein
> 6.8 g fibre

1　Plunge the macaroni into a saucepan containing plenty of boiling salted water.
2　Allow to boil gently and stir occasionally with a wooden spoon.
3　Cook for approximately 15 minutes and drain well in a colander.
4　Return to a clean pan containing the butter.
5　Mix with half the cheese and add the béchamel and mustard.
6　Place in an earthenware dish and sprinkle with the remainder of the cheese.
7　Brown lightly under the salamander and serve.

Note　Macaroni may also be prepared and served as for any of the spaghetti dishes.
　Variations include addition of cooked sliced mushrooms, diced ham, sweet corn, tomato, etc.

7 – Noodles

	4 portions	10 portions
flour	100 g (4 oz)	250 g (10 oz)
salt		
olive or other vegetable oil	1 tsp	3 tsp
egg and egg yolk	1 and 1	3 and 3

> Using white flour and olive oil, this recipe provides for 4 portions:
>
> 2246 kJ/534 kcal
> 18.4 g fat
> (of which 4.8 g saturated)
> 77.8 g carbohydrate
> (of which 1.6 g sugars)
> 19.4 g protein
> 3.6 g fibre

Noodles are usually bought ready prepared but may be made as follows:

1　Sieve the flour and salt. Make a well.
2　Add oil and eggs. Mix to a dough.
3　Knead well until smooth. Leave to rest.
4　Roll out to a thin rectangle 45 × 15 cm (18 × 6 inches).
5　Cut into ½ cm (¼ inch) strips. Leave to dry.

Note For wholemeal noodles use 50 g (2 oz) wholemeal flour and 50 g (2 oz) strong flour.

Semolina is a good dusting agent to use when handling this paste.

The noodles are cooked in the same way as spaghetti and may be served as for any of the spaghetti recipes. The most popular method of serving them is with butter (recipe 8).

> Using wholemeal flour and olive oil, this recipe provides for 4 portions:
>
> 2116 kJ/504 kcal
> 19.2 g fat
> (of which 4.8 g saturated)
> 65.8 g carbohydrate
> (of which 2.2 g sugars)
> 22.6 g protein
> 8.6 g fibre

8 ~ Noodles with butter

	4 portions	10 portions
noodles	100 g (4 oz)	250 g (10 oz)
salt, mill pepper		
a little grated nutmeg		
butter or margarine	50 g (2 oz)	125 g (5 oz)

1. Cook noodles in plenty of gently boiling salted water.
2. Drain well in a colander and return to the pan.
3. Add the seasoning and butter and toss carefully until mixed.
4. Correct the seasoning and serve.

Note Noodles may also be used as a garnish, as with braised beef (see illustration on page 348).

9 ~ Noodles or spaghetti with eggs and bacon

	4 portions	10 portions
noodles or spaghetti	400 g (1 lb)	1 kg (2½ lb)
oil	2 tbsp	5 tbsp
diced streaky bacon	100 g (4 oz)	250 g (10 oz)
crushed clove of garlic, optional	1	2
eggs	3	7
salt and pepper		
grated cheese	50 g (2 oz)	125 g (5 oz)

recipe continued ▶

1 Cook pasta in salted water and drain.
2 Heat the oil and lightly brown the bacon and garlic.
3 Drain off the bacon, discard the garlic.
4 Beat the eggs with salt and pepper.
5 Place the drained pasta back in its pan, mix in the bacon and raw eggs and stir over a low heat for 2–3 minutes. Serve immediately.

Note This recipe can be used with any type of unfilled pasta.
Fettucine and tagliatelle are narrower-cut noodles.

Plate 7.3: Macaroni cheese

10 – Spaghetti with bacon and tomatoes

	4 portions	10 portions
spaghetti	400 g (1 lb)	1 kg (2½ lb)
oil	2 tbsp	5 tbsp
diced bacon	150 g (6 oz)	375 g (15 oz)
finely chopped onion	100 g (4 oz)	250 g (10 oz)
tomatoes, peeled, de-seeded and diced	400 g (1 lb)	1 kg (2½ lb)
marjoram	5 g (¼ oz)	12 g (½ oz)
salt and pepper		
grated cheese	50 g (2 oz)	125 g (5 oz)

I portion provides:

2228 kJ/526 kcal
14.61 g fat
(of which 3.69 g saturated)
24.22 g protein
3.95 g fibre

1   Cook spaghetti in boiling salted water and drain.
2   Heat the oil in a pan and gently cook bacon for 1–2 minutes.
3   Add the onion and continue cooking gently until soft.
4   Add tomatoes, marjoram and salt and pepper, and cook briskly for 10 minutes.

11 – Penne and mange-tout

	6 portions	10 portions
penne or macaroni	400 g (1 lb)	1 kg (2½ lb)
cream cheese	150 g (6 oz)	375 g (15 oz)
gorgonzola	75 g (3 oz)	180 g (7½ oz)
single cream	2–3 tbsp	3–7 tbsp
mange-tout	400 g (1 lb)	1 kg (2½ lb)
butter	50 g (2 oz)	125 g (5 oz)
salt and black mill pepper		

1   Cook the pasta in plenty of boiling salted water.
2   Blend the cream cheese, gorgonzola and cream in a pan over a low heat, to a smooth sauce. If the sauce is too thick, thin with a little water from the pasta.
3   Cook the mange-tout in boiling salted water for 1–2 minutes, keeping them slightly firm.
4   Drain the pasta, add the butter, then the sauce and finally the mange-tout.
5   Finish with freshly ground black pepper. If desired, a few thin red strips of red pepper may be added for decoration.

Note   Macaroni may be used in place of penne.

12 – Green fettuccine with ham and creamy cheese

	4 portions	10 portions
green fettuccine or other pasta	400 g (1 lb)	1¼ kg (2½ lb)
cream cheese, mashed	200 g (½ lb)	500 g (1¼ lb)
single cream	2 tbsp	5 tbsp
grated Parmesan cheese	50 g (2 oz)	125 g (5 oz)
melted butter	50 g (2 oz)	125 g (5 oz)
lean cooked ham, cut in thick julienne	100 g (4 oz)	250 g (10 oz)

1 Cook the fettuccine in plenty of boiling salted water.
2 Mix the cream cheese, cream, Parmesan, salt and pepper.
3 Drain the fettuccine and return to the pan.
4 Mix in butter and cheese.
5 Add ham, toss and serve.

13 – Butterfly pasta with crab

	4 portions	10 portions
pasta	400 g (1 lb)	1 kg (2½ lb)
flaked white crabmeat	200–300 g (8–12 oz)	500–750 g (1½–2 lb)
butter	50 g (2 oz)	125 g (5 oz)
brandy or white wine	2 tbsp	5 tbsp
double cream	125 ml (¼ pt)	300 ml (½ pt)
salt and cayenne pepper		
chopped parsley	25 g (1 oz)	60 g (2½ oz)

1 Cook the pasta in boiling salted water and drain.
2 Gently heat the crabmeat in the butter.
3 Add brandy or wine; raise heat to evaporate the alcohol.
4 Mix in the cream, reheat, correct seasoning, mix in parsley.
5 Serve pasta and coat with the sauce.

Note Any type of unfilled pasta can be used. Any type of shellfish or combination of shellfish can be used.

14 ~ Bucatini Amatriciana-style

	4 portions	10 portions
bucatini or other pasta	400 g (1 lb)	1¼ kg (2½ lb)
thick cut bacon, diced	200 g (½ lb)	500 g (1¼ lb)
olive oil	2 tbsp	5 tbsp
onion, chopped	100 g (4 oz)	250 g (10 oz)
red chilli, seeds removed and chopped	½	1
ripe tomatoes (concassé)	400 g (1 lb)	1¼ kg (2½ lb)
salt and pepper		
grated Parmesan or other cheese	100 g (4 oz)	250 g (10 oz)

1 Fry the bacon in the oil until crisp and remove from the pan.
2 Gently cook the onion and chilli in the same oil until tender.
3 Add the tomatoes, cook for 15 minutes, and season.
4 Cook the pasta in plenty of boiling water and drain.
5 Add the bacon cubes to the sauce.
6 Mix the sauce into the pasta, sprinkle on the cheese and serve.

STUFFED PASTA

Examples of stuffed pasta include the following:

- *Agnolini* are small half-moon shapes usually filled with ham and cheese or minced meat.
- *Cannelloni* are squares of pasta poached, refreshed, dried, stuffed with a variety of fillings (ricotta cheese and spinach), rolled and finished with an appropriate sauce.
- *Cappelletti*, shaped like little hats, are usually filled as agnolini, and are available dried.
- *Ravioli* are usually square with serrated edges. A wide variety of fillings can be used (fish, meat, vegetarian, cheese, etc.).
- *Ravolini* or 'little ravioli' are made half the size of ravioli.
- *Tortellini* a slightly larger version of cappelletti, is also available in dried form.
- *Tortelloni* is a double-sized version of tortellini.

Pasta which is to be stuffed must be rolled as thinly as possible. The stuffing should be pleasant in taste and plentiful in quantity. The edges of the pasta must be thoroughly sealed otherwise the stuffing will seep out during poaching.

All stuffed pasta should be served in or coated with a suitable sauce, and depending on the type of recipe may be finished 'au gratin'.

Stuffings

The examples of stuffing for pasta which follow are for 400 g (1 lb) pasta. The list is almost endless as every district in Italy has its own variations and with thought and experimentation many more can be produced:

- cooked minced chicken — 200 g (8 oz)
  minced ham — 100 g (4 oz)
  butter — 25 g (1 oz)
  2 yolks or 1 egg
  grated cheese — 25 g (1 oz)
  pinch of grated nutmeg
  salt and pepper
  fresh white breadcrumbs — 25 g (1 oz)

- cooked dry spinach, puréed — 200 g (8 oz)
  ricotta cheese — 200 g (8 oz)
  butter — 25 g (1 oz)
  nutmeg, salt and pepper

- cooked minced lean pork — 200 g (8 oz)
  cooked minced lean veal — 200 g (8 oz)
  butter — 25 g (1 oz)
  grated cheese — 25 g (1 oz)
  2 yolks or 1 egg
  fresh white breadcrumbs — 25 g (1 oz)
  salt and pepper
  pinch of chopped marjoram
  ricotta cheese — 150 g (6 oz)
  grated Parmesan — 75 g (3 oz)
  egg — 1
  nutmeg, salt and pepper

- minced cooked meat — 200 g (8 oz)
  spinach, cooked — 100 g (4 oz)
  onion, chopped and cooked — 50 g (2 oz)
  oregano, salt, pepper

- chopped cooked fish — 200 g (8 oz)
  chopped cooked mushroom — 100 g (4 oz)
  chopped parsley, anchovy
    paste

- aubergine, peeled, diced
    and deep fried — 200 g (8 oz)
  walnuts, shelled and chopped — 100 g (4 oz)
  chopped parsley, salt, pepper
  thick white sauce to bind

15 – Ravioli dough

	8 portions	10 portions
flour	200 g (8 oz)	500 g (1¼ lb)
salt		
olive oil	35 ml (1½ fl oz)	150 ml (⅓ pt)
water	105 ml (4 fl oz)	250 ml (½ pt)

1 Sieve the flour and salt. Make a well. Add the liquid.
2 Knead to a smooth dough. Rest for at least 30 minutes in a cool place.
3 Roll out to a very thin oblong 30 cm × 45 cm (12 inches × 18 inches).
4 Cut in half and eggwash.
5 Place the stuffing in a piping bag with a large plain tube.
6 Pipe out the filling in small pieces about the size of a cherry approximately 4 cm (1½ inches) apart onto one-half of the paste.
7 Carefully cover with the other half of the paste, seal, taking care to avoid air pockets.
8 Mark each with the back of a plain cutter.
9 Cut in between each line of filling, down and across with a serrated pastry wheel.
10 Separate on a well-floured tray.
11 Poach in gently boiling salted water for approximately 10 minutes. Drain well.
12 Place in an earthenware serving dish.
13 Cover with 250 ml (½ pt) jus-lié, demi-glace or tomato sauce.
14 Sprinkle with 50 g (2 oz) grated cheese.
15 Brown under the salamander and serve.

Note   For wholemeal ravioli use 100 g (4 oz) wholemeal flour and 100 g (4 oz) strong flour.

16 — Ravioli filling

	4 portions	10 portions
braised or boiled beef or veal	200 g (8 oz)	500 g (1¼ lb)
spinach	400 g (1 lb)	1 kg (2 lb)
chopped onion or shallot	50 g (2 oz)	125 g (5 oz)
clove garlic, chopped	1	
oil or butter	10 g (½ oz)	25 g (1¼ oz)
salt, mill pepper		
marjoram or oregano		
little demi-glace to bind		

1 Mince the beef or veal.
2 Cook and mince the spinach.
3 Cook the onion and garlic in the fat without colouring.
4 Mix the meat, spinach and onion.
5 Season and add a little demi-glace to bind the mixture if necessary, but keep the mixture firm.

17 — Cannelloni
Use the same ingredients as for ravioli dough (recipe 15).

1 Roll out the paste as for ravioli.
2 Cut into squares approximately 6 cm × 6 cm (2½ inches × 2½ inches).
3 Cook in gently boiling salted water for approximately 10 minutes. Refresh in cold water.
4 Drain well and lay out singly on the table.
5 Pipe out the filling across each.
6 Roll up like a sausage-roll.
7 Place in a greased earthenware dish.
8 Add 250 ml (½ pt) demi-glace, jus-lié or tomato sauce.
9 Sprinkle with 25–50 g (1–2 oz) grated cheese.
10 Brown slowly under the salamander or in the oven and serve.

18 – Lasagne

	4 portions	10 portions
lasagne	200 g (8 oz)	500 g (1¼ lb)
oil	1 tbsp	3 tbsp
thin strips of streaky bacon	50 g (2 oz)	125 g (5 oz)
onion, chopped	100 g (4 oz)	250 g (10 oz)
carrot, chopped	50 g (2 oz)	125 g (5 oz)
celery, chopped	50 g (2 oz)	125 g (5 oz)
minced beef	200 g (8 oz)	500 g (1¼ lb)
tomato purée	50 g (2 oz)	125 g (5 oz)
jus-lié or demi-glace	375 ml (¾ pt)	1 litre (2 pt)
clove garlic	1	1½
salt, pepper		
marjoram	½ level tsp	1½
sliced mushrooms	100 g (4 oz)	250 g (10 oz)
béchamel sauce	250 ml (½ pt)	600 ml (1¼ pt)
grated Parmesan or Cheddar cheese	25 g (2 oz)	125 g (5 oz)

> 1 portion provides:
>
> 2416 kJ/575 kcal
> 28.7 g fat
> (of which 11.4 g saturated)
> 56.1 g carbohydrate
> (of which 10.0 g sugars)
> 26.7 g protein
> 5.8 g fibre

1 This recipe can be made using 200 g (8 oz) of ready bought lasagne or preparing it fresh using 200 g (8 oz) flour noodle paste (recipe 7). Wholemeal lasagne can be made using noodle paste made with 100 g (4 oz) wholemeal flour and 100 g (4 oz) strong flour.

2 Prepare the noodle paste and roll out 1 mm (1/16 inch) thick.

3 Cut into 6 cm (2½ inches) squares.

4 Allow to rest in a cool place and dry slightly on a cloth dusted with flour.

5 Whether using fresh or ready bought lasagne, cook in gently simmering salted water for approximately 10 minutes.

6 Refresh in cold water, drain on a cloth.

7 Gently heat the oil in a thick-bottomed pan, add bacon and cook for 2–3 minutes.

8 Add the onion, carrot, celery and cover the pan with a lid and cook for 5 minutes.

9 Add the minced beef, increase the heat and stir until lightly brown.

10 Remove from the heat and mix in the tomato purée.

11 Return to the heat, mix in the jus-lié or demi-glace, stir to boil.

12 Add the garlic, salt, pepper and marjoram and simmer for 15 minutes. Remove the garlic.

recipe continued ▶

Plate 7.4: Moussaka (see p. 320)

13 Mix in the mushrooms, reboil for 2 minutes, remove from the heat.
14 Butter an ovenproof dish and cover the bottom with a layer of the meat sauce.
15 Add layer of lasagne and cover with meat sauce.
16 Add another layer of lasagne and cover with the remainder of the meat sauce.
17 Cover with the béchamel.
18 Sprinkle with cheese, cover with a lid and place in a moderately hot oven at 190°C (Reg. 5; 375°F), for approximately 20 minutes.
19 Remove the lid, cook for a further 15 minutes and serve in the cleaned ovenproof dish.

Note See also vegetarian lasagne, page 509.

19 – Gnocchi parisienne (choux paste)

	4 portions	10 portions
water	125 ml ($\frac{1}{4}$ pt)	300 ml ($\frac{5}{8}$ pt)
margarine or butter	50 g (2 oz)	125 g (5 oz)
salt		
flour, white or wholemeal	60 g (2$\frac{1}{2}$ oz)	150 g (7$\frac{1}{2}$ oz)
eggs	2	5
grated cheese	50 g (2 oz)	125 g (5 oz)
béchamel (thin)	250 ml ($\frac{1}{2}$ pt)	600 ml (1$\frac{1}{4}$ pt)

Using hard margarine, 1 portion provides:

1433 kJ/341 kcal
25.0 g fat
(of which 11.8 g saturated)
19.5 g carbohydrate
(of which 3.3 g sugars)
10.7 g protein
0.8 g fibre

1 Boil water, margarine or butter, and salt in a saucepan.
2 Remove from the heat.
3 Mix in the flour with a wooden spoon. Return to a gentle heat.
4 Stir continuously until the mixture leaves the sides of the pan.
5 Cool slightly. Gradually add the eggs, beating well.
6 Add half the cheese.
7 Place in a piping bag with $\frac{1}{2}$ cm ($\frac{1}{4}$ inch) plain tube.
8 Pipe out in 1 cm ($\frac{1}{2}$ inch) lengths into a shallow pan of gently simmering salted water. Do not allow to boil.
9 Cook for approximately 10 minutes. Drain well in a colander.
10 Combine carefully with béchamel. Correct the seasoning.
11 Pour into an earthenware dish.
12 Sprinkle with the remainder of the cheese.
13 Brown lightly under salamander and serve.

20 ~ Gnocchi romaine (semolina)

	4 portions	10 portions
milk	500 ml (1 pt)	1¼ litre (2½ pt)
semolina	100 g (4 oz)	250 g (10 oz)
salt, pepper		
grated nutmeg		
egg yolk	1	3
grated cheese	25 g (1 oz)	60 g (2½ oz)
butter or margarine	25 g (1 oz)	60 g (2½ oz)
tomato sauce (page 132)	250 ml (½ pt)	600 ml (1¼ pt)

1 Boil the milk in a thick-bottomed pan.
2 Sprinkle in the semolina, stirring continuously.
3 Stir to the boil.
4 Season, simmer until cooked (5–10 minutes).
5 Remove from heat.
6 Mix in egg yolk, cheese and butter.
7 Pour into a buttered tray 1 cm (½ inch) deep.
8 When cold, cut into rounds with a 5 cm (2 inch) round cutter.
9 Place the debris in a buttered earthenware dish.
10 Neatly arrange the rounds on top.
11 Sprinkle with melted butter and cheese.
12 Lightly brown in the oven or under the salamander.
13 Serve with a thread of tomato sauce round the gnocchi.

21 ~ Gnocchi piemontaise (potato)

	4 portions	10 portions
mashed potato	300 g (12 oz)	1 kg (2 lb)
flour, white or wholemeal	100 g (4 oz)	250 g (10 oz)
1 egg and 1 egg yolk		
butter	25 g (1 oz)	60 g (2½ oz)
salt, pepper		
grated nutmeg		
tomato sauce (page 132)	250 ml (½ pt)	600 ml (1¼ pt)

1 Bake or boil the potatoes in their jackets.
2 Remove from skins and mash with a fork or pass through a sieve.

3 Mix with flour, egg, butter and seasoning while hot.
4 Mould into balls the size of a walnut.
5 Dust well with flour and flatten slightly with a fork.
6 Poach in gently boiling water for approximately 5 minutes. Drain carefully.
7 Dress in a buttered earthenware dish, cover with tomato sauce.
8 Sprinkle with grated cheese and brown lightly under the salamander and serve.

—— *Rice* ——

For the cultivation of rice, a hot, wet atmosphere is required and it is grown chiefly in India, the Far East, South America, Italy and in the southern states of the USA. Rice is the food crop for about half the world's population. In order to grow, rice needs more water than any other cereal crop. There are around 250 different varieties of rice. The main types are:

- *Long-grain.* A narrow, pointed grain which has had the full, bran and most of the germ removed so that it is less fibrous than brown rice. Because of its firm structure, which helps to keep the grains separate when cooked it is suitable for plain boiling and savoury dishes such as kedgeree and curry dishes, etc.
- *Brown grain.* Any rice that has had the outer covering removed, but retains its bran and as a result is more nutritious and contains more fibre. It takes longer to cook than long grain rice.
- *Short-grain.* A short, rounded grain with a soft texture suitable for sweet dishes and risotto. *Arborio* is an Italian short grain rice.
- *Basmati.* A narrow long grain rice with a distinctive flavour suitable for serving with Indian dishes. Basmati rice needs to be soaked before being cooked to remove excess starch.
- *Whole grain rice.* The whole unprocessed grain of the rice.
- *Wild rice.* The expensive seed of an aquatic plant related to the rice family.
- *Precooked instant rice.* Par-boiled, ready cooked and boil-in-the-bag rice are similar.
- *Ground rice.* Used for milk puddings (page 618). *Rice flour* can be used for thickening cream soups. *Rice paper* is used for macaroons and nougat.

Cooked rice should not be kept warm for long periods because the spores of *Bacillus cereus* (a bacterium which is found in soil where rice may grow), may revert to bacteria, multiply and produce toxin (poison).

22 ~ Plain boiled rice

	4 portions	10 portions
rice (long-grain)	100 g (4 oz)	250 g (10 oz)
water	1½ litres (3 pt)	3¾ litres (7 pt)
salt		

1 Pick and wash the long-grain rice.
2 Add to plenty of boiling salted water.
3 Stir to the boil and simmer gently till tender, for approximately 12–15 minutes.
4 Wash well under running water, drain and place on a sieve and cover with a cloth.
5 Place on a tray in a moderate oven or in the hot plate until hot.
6 Serve in a vegetable dish separately.

23 ~ Steamed rice

Place the washed rice into a saucepan and add water until the water level is 2.5 cm (1 inch) above the rice. Bring to the boil over a fierce heat until most of the water has evaporated. Turn the heat down as low as possible, cover the pan with a lid and allow the rice to complete cooking in the steam. Once cooked, the rice should be allowed to stand in the covered steamer for 10 minutes.

24 ~ Braised or pilaff rice

	4 portions	10 portions
butter	50 g (2 oz)	125 g (5 oz)
chopped onion	25 g (1 oz)	60 g (2½ oz)
rice (long-grain), white or brown	100 g (4 oz)	250 g (10 oz)
white stock (preferably chicken)	200 ml (approx. ⅜ pt)	500 ml (1¼ pt)
salt, mill pepper		

Using white rice and hard margarine, 1 portion provides:

774 kJ/184 kcal
10.4 g fat
(of which 4.5 g saturated)
22.1 g carbohydrate
(of which 0.3 g sugars)
1.9 g protein
0.6 g fibre

1   Place 25 g (1 oz) butter in a small sauteuse. Add the
    onion.
2   Cook gently without colouring for 2–3 minutes.
    Add the rice.
3   Cook gently without colouring for 2–3 minutes.
4   Add twice the amount of stock to rice.
5   Season, cover with a buttered paper, bring to the
    boil.
6   Place in a hot oven 230–250°C (Reg. 8–9;
    50–500°F) for approximately 15 minutes until
    cooked.
7   Remove immediately into a cool sauteuse.
8   Carefully mix in the remaining butter with a two-pronged fork.
9   Correct the seasoning and serve.

> Using brown rice and hard margarine, I
> portion provides:
>
> 769 kJ/183 kcal
> 10.9 g fat
> (of which 4.6 g saturated)
> 20.7 g carbohydrate
> (of which 0.7 g sugars)
> 1.9 g protein
> 1.0 g fibre

Note   It is usual to use long-grain rice for pilaff because the grains are firm, and
there is less likelihood of them breaking up and becoming mushy. During cooking
the long-grain rice absorbs more liquid, loses less starch and retains its shape as it
swells; the short or medium grains may split at the ends and become less distinct in
outline.

25 – Braised rice with mushrooms

Ingredients as for braised rice with the addition of 50–100 g (2–4 oz) button
mushrooms.

1   Place 25 g (1 oz) butter in a small sauteuse. Add the onion.
2   Cook gently without colour for 2–3 minutes.
3   Add the rice and well-washed sliced mushrooms.
4   Complete as for braised rice from point 4 (recipe 24).

26 – Braised rice with peas and pimento

As for braised rice (recipe 24) plus 25 g (1 oz) cooked peas and 25 g (1 oz) 1 cm
($\frac{1}{2}$ inch) diced pimento carefully mixed in when finishing with butter.

Note   Many other variations of pilaff may be made with the addition of such
ingredients as tomato concassé, diced ham, prawns, etc.

27 – Braised or pilaff rice with cheese

As recipe 24 with 50–100 g (2–4 oz) grated cheese added with the butter, before serving.

28 – Risotto

	4 portions	10 portions
butter or oil	50 g (2 oz)	125 g (5 oz)
chopped onion	25 g (1 oz)	60 g (2½ oz)
rice (short grain or brown)	100 g (4 oz)	250 g (10 oz)
white stock (preferably chicken)	185 ml (approx ⅜ pt)	500 ml (1 pt)
salt, mill pepper		
grated Parmesan cheese	25 g (1 oz)	60 g (2½ oz)

> Using white rice, hard margarine, 1 portion provides:
>
> 881 kJ/210 kcal
> 12.3 g fat
> (of which 5.7 g saturated)
> 22.1 g carbohydrate
> (of which 0.3 g sugars)
> 4.1 g protein
> 0.6 g fibre

> Using brown rice, hard margarine, 1 portion provides:
>
> 881 kJ/210 kcal
> 12.3 g fat
> (of which 5.7 g saturated)
> 22.1 g carbohydrate
> (of which 0.3 g sugars)
> 4.1 g protein
> 1.0 g fibre

1 Melt the butter or oil in a small sauteuse. Add the chopped onion.
2 Cook gently without colour for 2–3 minutes. Add the rice.
3 Cook without colour for 2–3 minutes. Add the stock, season lightly.
4 Cover with a lid. Allow to simmer on the side of the stove.
5 Stir frequently and if necessary add more stock until the rice is cooked.
6 When cooked all the stock should have been absorbed into the rice and evaporated: a risotto should be more moist than a pilaff.
7 Finally mix in the cheese with a two pronged fork, correct the seasoning and serve.

Note   Risotto is a traditional Italian dish for which arborio rice is generally used. Risotto variations include:

- *Saffron or Milanese-style* Soak ¼ teaspoon saffron in a little hot stock and mix in to the risotto near the end of cooking time.
- *Sea food* Add any one or mixture of cooked mussels, shrimp, prawns, etc., just before the rice is cooked. Use also half fish stock, half chicken stock.
- *Mushrooms.*

29 – Fried rice

	4 portions	10 portions
boiled rice (cooked at least 3 hours in advance)	400 g (1 lb)	1 kg (2½ lb)
oil	2 tbsp	5 tbsp
spring onions	2	5
egg	1	2½
oil	2 tsp	5 tsp
a pinch of salt		
thick soy sauce	2 tsp	5 tsp

1 Separate the rice grains as much as possible.
2 Separate the white and green parts of the onions and cut into small rounds.
3 Heat a wok, or thick-bottomed pan over high heat.
4 Add the oil and white spring onions; stir for 30–40 seconds.
5 Beat the egg with oil and salt, and pour into the wok, leave for 6–8 seconds until the egg sets on the bottom, but remains running on top.
6 Add the rice and turn and mix continuously for 3–4 minutes until thoroughly hot.
7 Mix in the soy sauce; if the rice is too hard add a little stock and stir for a few seconds.
8 Add the green spring onion and serve.

30 – Stir fried rice

Stir fried rice dishes consist of a combination of cold precooked rice and ingredients such as cooked meat or poultry, fish, vegetables or egg.

1 Prepare and cook meat or poultry in fine shreds; dice and lightly cook any vegetables. Add bean sprouts just before the egg.
2 Place a wok, or thick-bottomed pan over fierce heat, add some oil and heat until smoking.
3 Add the cold rice and stir-fry for about 1 minute.
4 Add the other ingredients and continue to stir fry over fierce heat for 4–5 minutes.
5 Add the beaten egg and continue cooking for a further 1–2 minutes.
6 Correct the seasoning and serve immediately.

8

FISH AND SHELLFISH

Recipe No.   *page no.*

Fish

22	Brill, boiled	265
2	Butter sauce	254
23	Cod, boiled	265
7	Cod, grilled	258
34	Fish cakes	273
20	Fish fried in batter	264
30	Fish in the shell with cheese sauce	271
6	Fish meunière	257
36	Fish pie	274
14	Frying batters	261
32	Haddock, smoked, poached	272
22	Halibut, boiled	265
8	Herring, grilled	258
31	Kedgeree	271
9	Mackerel, grilled	259
4	Mushroom sauce	255
17	Plaice, fillets fried	263
10	Plaice, fillets, grilled	259
1	Sabayon	254
35	Salmon cutlets	273
13	Salmon, grilled	260
5	Shrimp sauce	256
33	Skate with black butter	272
12	Sole, grilled	260
27	Sole, fillets Bercy	268
24	Sole, fillets Dugléré	266
29	Sole, fillets florentine	270
28	Sole, fillets Mornay	269
26	Sole, fillets Véronique	267
25	Sole, fillets with white wine sauce	267
19	Sole, fried	264
18	Sole, goujons	263
22	Turbot, boiled	265
21	Whitebait	264
3	White wine sauce	255
15	Whiting, fried	263
16	Whiting, fried fillets	263
11	Whiting, grilled	259

Shellfish

37	Lobster, grilled or barbecued	281
38	Lobster Mornay	282
39	Lobster Thermidor	282
40	Scampi, fried	283
41	Seafood in puff pastry (seafood bouchées)	284

Fish

1   Ensure that the preparation and cooking areas are ready for use and cleaned after use to meet the health and safety regulations.
2   Plan work and allocate time, and organise in an efficient manner.
3   Ensure that the fish is of the type, quality and quantity required.
4   Ensure that the fish is correctly prepared, cooked and served according to the dish, customer requirements and food hygiene requirements.
5   Be able to classify fish and list the quality and purchasing points.
6   Know how to store fish.
7   Realise that competency implies knowing, understanding and applying the principles of fish cookery.

Because of health considerations many people choose to eat fish in preference to meat and consequently consumption of fish is and has been steadily increasing.

This popularity has resulted in a far greater selection and due to swift and efficient transport, well over 200 types of fish are on sale throughout the year.

Fish is plentiful in the UK, because we are surrounded by water, although overfishing and pollution are having a detrimental effect on the supplies of certain fish. Most catches are made off Iceland, Scotland, the North Sea, Irish Sea and the English Channel. Salmon are caught in certain English and Scottish rivers, and are also extensively farmed. Frozen fish is imported from Scandinavia, Canada and Japan; the last two countries export frozen salmon to Britain.

Unfortunately the fish supply is not unlimited due to overfishing, so it is now necessary to have fish farms (such as for trout and salmon) to supplement the natural sources. This is not the only problem: due to contamination by man, the seas and rivers are increasingly polluted, thus affecting both the supply and the suitability of fish, particularly shellfish, for human consumption.

Fish are valuable, not only because they are a good source of protein, but because they are suitable for all types of menus and can be cooked and presented in a wide variety of ways. The range of different types of fish of varying textures, taste and appearance is indispensable to the creative chef.

Most fish and shellfish have very little connective tissue which unlike meat makes them naturally tender. Fish must therefore be cooked with great care and overcooking avoided, as this can both dry and toughen the product.

TYPES OR VARIETIES

- *Oily fish* These are round in shape (herring, mackerel, salmon).
- *White fish* Round (cod, whiting, hake) or flat (plaice, sole, turbot).
- *Shellfish* (see page 281).

Fresh fish is bought by the kilogram, by the number of fillets or whole fish of the weight that is required. For example, 30 kg (66 lb) of salmon could be ordered as 2 × 15 kg (33 lb), 3 × 10 kg (22 lb) or 6 × 5 kg (11 lb). Frozen fish can be purchased in 15 kg (33 lb) blocks.

POINTS TO LOOK FOR WHEN BUYING FISH

When buying whole fish the following points should be looked for to ensure freshness.

- Eyes: bright, full and not sunken; no slime or cloudiness.
- Gills: bright red in colour; no bacterial slime.
- Flesh: firm, translucent and resilient so that when pressed the impression goes quickly; the fish must not be limp.
- Scales: flat, moist and plentiful.
- Skin: should be covered with a fresh sea slime, or be smooth and moist, with a good sheen and no abrasions or bruising; there should be no discoloration.
- Smell: pleasant, with no smell of ammonia or sourness.
- Fish should be purchased daily, if possible, direct from the market or supplier.
- The fish should be well iced so that it arrives in good condition.
- Fish may be bought on the bone or filleted. (The approximate loss from boning and waste is 50% for flat fish, 60% for round fish.)
- Medium-sized fish are usually better than large fish, which may be coarse; small fish often lack flavour.

STORAGE

Fresh fish should be stored in a fish box containing ice, or in a separate refrigerator or part of a refrigerator used only for fish at a temperature of 1–2°C (34–35°F).

FOOD VALUE

Fish is as useful a source of animal protein as meat. The oily fish, such as sardines, mackerel, herrings and salmon contain vitamins A and D in their flesh; in white fish, such as halibut and cod, these vitamins are present in the liver.

The bones of sardines, whitebait and tinned salmon, when eaten, provide the body with calcium and phosphorous.

Since all fish contains protein it is a good body-building food and oily fish is useful for energy and as a protective food because of its vitamins.

Owing to its fat content oily fish is not so digestible as white fish and is not suitable in cooking for invalids.

PRESERVATION

Freezing

Fish is either frozen at sea or as soon as possible after reaching port. It should be thawed out before being cooked. Plaice, halibut, turbot, haddock, sole, cod, trout, salmon, herring, whiting, scampi, smoked haddock and kippers are available frozen.

Frozen fish should be checked for:

- no evidence of freezer burn;
- undamaged packaging;
- minimum fluid loss during thawing;
- flesh still feeling firm after thawing;

It should be stored at $-18°C$ (0°F). *Never* refreeze frozen fish once it has thawed as this could be a major health hazard.

Canning

The oily fish are usually canned. Sardines, salmon, anchovies, pilchards, tuna, herring and herring roe are canned in their own juice (as with salmon) or in oil or tomato sauce.

Salting

In this country salting of fish is usually accompanied by a smoking process.

- Cured herrings are packed in salt.
- Caviar, the slightly salted roe of the sturgeon, is sieved, tinned and refrigerated. Imitation caviar is also obtainable.

Plate 8.1: From top:
haddock; cod;
hake (left); codling;
whiting

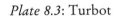

Plate 8.2: From top: lemon sole; plaice; Dover sole

Plate 8.3: Turbot

Pickling

Herrings pickled in vinegar are filleted, rolled and skewered and known as rollmops.

Smoking

Fish to be smoked may be gutted or left whole. It is then soaked in a strong salt solution (brine), and in some cases a dye is added to improve colour. After this, it is drained and hung on racks in a kiln and exposed to smoke for 5 or 6 hours.

Cold smoking takes place at a temperature of no more than 33°C (91°F) (this is to avoid cooking the flesh). Therefore all cold smoked fish is raw and is usually cooked before being eaten, the exception being smoked salmon.

Hot smoking fish is cured at a temperature between 70–80°C (158–176°F) in order to cook the flesh, so does not require further cooking.

Choose fish with a pleasant smoky smell and a bright glossy surface. The flesh should be firm; sticky or soggy flesh means that the fish may have been of low quality or undersmoked.

Storage

Refrigerate before use as the preservative quality of the smoke is only slight. Smoked fish products keep in good condition for a little longer than fresh fish.

- *Arbroath smokies* are small haddocks in Arbroath, Scotland. The fish is hot smoked and can be eaten uncooked or may be brushed with melted butter and grilled.
- *Finnan haddock* (the name deriving from Findon, Scotland) are split, left on the bone, lightly brined without a dye, and cold smoked to give a pale-coloured fish. Usually cooked by poaching in milk.
- *Yellow smoked haddock* is split or filleted, cold smoked and dyed to give a bright yellow colour.
- *Bloaters* are whole herrings, lightly salted and cold smoked. They are traditionally smoked in Yarmouth and on the east coast. They only keep for a few days as they are mildly salted and the gut is not removed so that the body swells and has a gamey flavour. Bloaters are usually gutted and grilled.
- *Buckling* are small, whole, lightly hot-smoked herring served either cold or warmed through.
- *Kippers* are gutted and flattened herring, salted and cold-smoked. High quality kippers come from Loch Fyne, Craister and the Isle of Man. Mass produced varieties are available filleted and vacuum packed. Kippers are at their best between August and April and are cooked by grilling or simmering in water.

- *Red or hard smoked herrings* are whole, heavily brined and smoked until very firm.
- *Smoked cod* is filleted, briefly soaked in brine with bright yellow colouring or dipped into a chemical solution to give colour and a slightly smoky flavour. It should be cooked before eating by poaching, grilling or baking.
- *Smoked eel* is smoked whole or in small fillets; it is usually served cold as a first course.
- *Smoked mackerel* is usually hot smoked so it does not require cooking. Cold smoked mackerel is also available which needs to be cooked, usually by grilling.
- *Smoked salmon* is regarded as the best of the smoked fish and is cured in two ways. The London cure involves light smoking and salting to give the salmon a delicate flavour and moist texture; the Scottish cure is a stronger smoking process giving the fish a more pronounced flavour. It is traditionally served thinly sliced as a first course but is also used in many other dishes.
- *Smoked sprats* are hot smoked and may be eaten cold or grilled.
- *Smoked trout* are hot smoked whole or in fillets and are usually served cold as a first course.
- *Cod's roe* is also smoked and usually served as a first course.

SAFETY ASPECTS

Health and safety aspects of food hygiene are dealt with in Chapter 1. In addition:

- Store fresh fish in containers with ice (changed daily) in a refrigerator at a temperature of 1–2°C (34–36°F).
- To avoid the risk of cross-contamination fish should be stored in a separate refrigerator away from other foods; cooked and raw fish are kept separate.
- Frozen fish should be stored in a deep freezer at −18°C (0°F). When required frozen fish should be defrosted in a refrigerator. If the frozen food is removed from the freezer and left uncovered in the kitchen, there is the danger of contamination.
- Smoked fish should be kept in a refrigerator.
- Use correct colour coded boards for preparing raw fish and different ones for cooked fish. Keep the boards clean with fresh disposable wiping cloths.
- Use equipment reserved for raw fish. If this is not possible wash and sanitise equipment before and immediately after each use.
- Unhygienic equipment, utensils and preparation areas increase the risk of cross-contamination and danger to health.
- Fish offal and bones are a high risk for contamination and must not be mixed, or stored with raw prepared fish.

- Wash equipment, knives and hands regularly using a bactericide detergent, or sanitising agent, to kill germs.
- Dispose of all wiping cloths immediately after use. Reused cloths may cause contamination.

BASIC FISH PREPARATION

Unless otherwise stated, as a guide, allow 100 g (4 oz) fish off the bone and 150 g (6 oz) on the bone for a portion.

- All fish should be washed under running cold water before and after preparation.
- Whole fish are trimmed to remove the scales, fins and head using fish scissors and a knife. If the head is to be left on (as for a salmon for the cold buffet), the gills and the eyes are removed.
- If the fish has to be gutted:

  - Cut from the vent to two thirds along the fish.
  - Draw out the intestines with the fingers or in the case of a large fish use the hook handle of a utensil such as a ladle.
  - Ensure that the blood lying along the main bone is removed then wash and drain thoroughly.
  - If the fish is to be stuffed then it may be gutted by removing the innards through the gill slits, thus leaving the stomach skin intact forming a pouch in which to put the stuffing. When this method is used, care must be taken to ensure that the insides of the fish is clear from all traces of blood.

Filleting of flat fish with the exception of Dover sole

- Using a filleting knife make an incision from the head to tail down the line of the backbone.
- Remove each fillet, holding the knife almost parallel to the work surface and keeping the knife close to the bone.

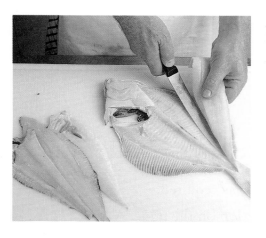

Plate 8.4a–d:
Filleting of
plaice

Plate 8.5:
Skinning of
plaice

Skinning of flat fish fillets with the exception of Dover sole

- Hold the fillet firmly at the tail end.
- Cut the flesh as close to the tail as possible, as far as the skin.
- Keep the knife parallel to the work surface, grip the skin firmly and move the knife from side to side to remove the skin.

Plate 8.6a–d: Preparation of whole Dover sole

Preparation of whole Dover sole

- Hold the tail firmly, then cut and scrape the skin until sufficient is lifted to be gripped.
- Pull the skin away from the tail to the head.
- Both black and white skins may be removed in this way.
- Trim the tail and side fins with fish scissors, remove the eyes and clean and wash the fish thoroughly.

- *After cooking*: Before coating with sauce: place the fish on a flat surface and using a palette knife, remove all the side bones. Carefully fold back two of the fillets and remove approximately 2–5 cm (1–2 inches) of backbone.

Preparation of turbot (see illustration page 252)
- Remove the head with a large chopping knife.
- Cut off the side bones.
- Commencing at the tail end, chop down the centre of the backbone, dividing the fish into two halves.
- Divide each half into steak portions (tronçons) as required.

Note   Allow approximately 300 g (12 oz) per portion on the bone. A $3\frac{1}{2}$ kg (7 lb) fish will yield approximately 10 portions.

Filleting of round fish
- Remove the head and clean thoroughly.
- Remove the first fillet by cutting along the backbone from head to tail.
- Keeping the knife close to the bone, remove the fillet.
- Reverse the fish and remove the second fillet in the same way, this time cutting from tail to head.

METHODS OF COOKING FISH

Boiling
This method is suitable for whole fish such as salmon, turbot, trout, and certain cuts of fish on the bone such as salmon, cod, turbot, halibut, brill, etc. In either case the fish should be completely immersed in the cooking liquid which can be water, water and milk, milk, fish stock (for white fish) or a court bouillon (water, vinegar, thyme, bay leaf, parsley stalks, onion, carrot, peppercorns) for oily fish.

Whole fish are covered with a cold liquid and brought to the boil, cut fish are usually placed in a simmering liquid.

Poaching
This is suitable for small whole fish, cuts or fillets. Barely cover the fish with fish stock, cover with a buttered paper, bring to the boil and cook in the oven without allowing the liquid to boil. The cooking liquor is usually used for the sauce which masks the fish.

Steaming

Any fish which can be poached or boiled may also be cooked by steaming which has a number of advantages.

- It is an easy method of cooking.
- Cooking by steam can be rapid, thus conserving flavour, colour and nutrients.
- It is particularly suitable for large scale operations.

Fish to be steamed is prepared for cooking in the same way as for poaching. The sauce can be prepared separately, but the liquor from the steamed fish should be strained off, reduced and incorporated into the sauce.

Grilling

This method is suitable for small whole fish, cuts and fillets. The fish is passed through seasoned flour, brushed with oil and grilled on both sides. When fish is grilled under the salamander, grill bar marks may be made with a red-hot poker before cooking.

Grilling may also be done on a barbecue, in which case the fish whole, in cuts or in kebabs, may be marinated for a short time then the marinade used to baste the fish whilst cooking. Whole fish can have sprigs of fresh herbs placed in the belly cavity and they can also be wrapped in oiled foil and cooked on a barbecue.

Shallow frying

This method is suitable for small whole fish, cuts and fillets. The fish is passed through seasoned flour, shallow fried on both sides, presentation side first, in clarified fat in a frying-pan. When the fish is placed on a serving dish or plate and masked with nut-brown butter, lemon juice, slice of lemon and chopped parsley, it is termed meunière.

Deep frying

This is suitable for small whole fish, cuts and fillets. The fish can be coated by:

- flour, egg and crumb;
- milk and flour;
- batter.

The coating forms a surface to prevent penetration of the fat into the fish. Deep-fried fish is served with a quarter of lemon and/or a suitable sauce and fried parsley.

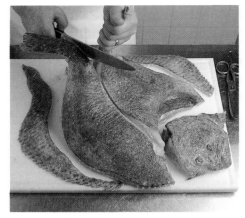

Plate 8.7: Preparation of turbot

Plate 8.8a–b: Filleting of trout

Baking

Many fish whole, portioned or filleted may be baked in an oven. In order to retain the natural moisture it is necessary to protect the fish from the direct heat.

● *Whole fish* (sea bass, bream, mullet, etc.)

- Completely cover in a thick coating of sea-salt and bake.
- Wrap in pastry (puff, brioche or filo) and bake.
- Stuff with a duxelle-based mixture of breadcrumbs, herbs, chopped onion, shallots or garlic, lean minced veal or/and bacon, and brush with oil or butter prior and during cooking.

- *Portions of fish* (cod, haddock, hake, tuna)
- Place in a buttered or oiled dish and bake slowly, basting frequently. Different herbs and suitable finely sliced vegetables can be added to vary flavour.
  - Make a crust of a duxelle base with additional ingredients (tomato, garlic, herbs, spices, lemon juice, breadcrumbs) to cover the fish portions and then bake.

In all cases a suitable sauce can be offered with the fish.

Roasting

Thick cuts of firm fish such as salmon, turbot or monkfish, are suitable for roasting. The fish is usually portioned, lightly covered with oil and roasted in an oven in the usual way (do not overcook). Finely sliced vegetables and sprigs of herbs can be put in the roasting tray and when the fish is cooked and removed the tray can be deglazed with a suitable wine to form the base of an accompanying sauce. Certain fish crusts (half a salmon steak) can have the skin left on both during cooking and for service. Alternatively a crust of breadcrumbs, for example, mixed with chopped fresh herbs, a duxelle-based mixture or a light coating of creamed horseradish, can be used.

CUTS OF FISH

Steaks
- Thick slices of fish on or off the bone.
- Steaks of round fish (salmon, cod) may be called darnes.
- Steaks of flat fish (turbot, halibut) may be called tronçons.

Fillets
- Cuts of fish free from bone: a round fish yields two fillets, a flat fish four fillets.

Suprêmes
- Prime cuts of fish without bone and skin (pieces cut from fillets of salmon, turbot, brill, etc.).

Goujons
- Filleted fish cut into strips approximately 8×0.5 cm ($3 \times \frac{1}{4}$ inch).

Paupiettes

● Fillets of fish (sole, plaice, whiting) spread with a stuffing and rolled.

Plaited

● Also known as *en tresse*; e.g. sole fillets cut into three even pieces lengthwise to within 1 cm ($\frac{1}{2}$inch) of the top, and neatly plaited.

—— *Fish recipes* ——

SAUCES FOR FISH

1 – Sabayon

This is a mixture of egg yolks and a little water whisked to the ribbon stage over gentle heat. The mixture should be the consistency of thick cream. It is added to sauces to assist their glazing.

2 – Butter sauce

	4 portions	10 portions
water	125 ml ($\frac{1}{4}$pt)	300 ml (12 fl oz)
wine vinegar	125 ml ($\frac{1}{4}$pt)	300 ml (12 fl oz)
finely chopped shallot	50 g (2 oz)	125 g (5 oz)
unsalted butter	200 g (8 oz)	500 g (1$\frac{1}{4}$lb)
lemon juice	1 tsp	2$\frac{1}{2}$ tsp
salt and pepper		

1 Reduce the water, vinegar and shallots in a thick-bottomed pan to approximately $\frac{1}{6}$ pint (2 tbsp), and allow to cool slightly.
2 Gradually whisk in the butter in small amounts, whisking continually until the mixture becomes creamy.
3 Whisk in lemon juice, season lightly and keep warm in a bain-marie.

Note The sauce may be strained if desired. Variations include adding freshly shredded sorrel, spinach, blanched fine julienne of lemon or lime.

3 ~ White wine sauce

	4 portions	10 portions
fish velouté	250 ml ($\frac{1}{2}$ pt)	600 ml (1$\frac{1}{4}$ pt)
dry white wine	2 tbsp	5 tbsp
butter	50 g (2 oz)	125 g (5 oz)
cream	2 tbsp	5 tbsp
salt, cayenne		
few drops of lemon juice		

> This recipe provides for 4 portions:
>
> 3255 kJ/775 kcal
> 73.7 g fat
> (of which 42.2 g saturated)
> 21.0 g carbohydrate
> (of which 2.0 g sugars)
> 3.3 g protein
> 1.1 g fibre

1 Boil the fish velouté. Whisk in the wine.
2 Remove from the heat.
3 Gradually add the butter. Stir in the cream.
4 Correct the seasoning and consistency, add the lemon juice.
5 Pass through a tammy cloth or fine strainer.

Note   If the sauce is to be used for a glazed fish dish then 1 egg yolk or 1 tbsp sabayon should be added as soon as the sauce is removed from the heat. (Trade practice sometimes is to whisk in 1 tbsp hollandaise sauce.)

4 ~ Mushroom sauce

	4 portions	10 portions
fish velouté	250 ml ($\frac{1}{2}$ pt)	600 ml (1$\frac{1}{4}$ pt)
fish stock, or cream as necessary		
salt, cayenne		
white button mushrooms	100 g (4 oz)	250 g (10 oz)
butter or margarine	10 g ($\frac{1}{2}$ oz)	25 g (1$\frac{1}{2}$ oz)
lemon juice		

1 Boil the fish velouté.
2 Adjust the consistency with fish stock or cream.
3 Correct the seasoning and strain.
4 Peel, wash and slice the mushrooms.
5 Cook the mushrooms in the butter and lemon juice in a covered pan.
6 Drain well and add to the sauce.

Note   May be served with, for example, boiled halibut.

Plate 8.9: Darne of salmon

Plate 8.10: Tronçon of turbot

Plate 8.11: Suprême of salmon

Plate 8.12: Cuts of fish: (from back) fillet; suprême; délice; paupiette; goujons; goujonettes

5 – Shrimp sauce

	4 portions	10 portions
fish velouté or béchamel	250 ml ($\frac{1}{2}$ pt)	600 ml ($1\frac{1}{4}$ pt)
salt, cayenne		
pickled shrimps	60 ml ($\frac{1}{8}$ pt)	150 ml ($\frac{1}{3}$ pt)

1 Boil the fish velouté or béchamel.
2 Correct the seasoning and consistency using fish stock or cream.
3 Pass through a tammy or fine strainer. Mix in the shrimps.

SHALLOW FRIED FISH

6 – Fish meunière

Many fish, whole or filleted, may be cooked by this method: sole, fillets of plaice, trout, brill, cod, turbot, herring, scampi, etc.

1 Prepare and clean the fish, wash and drain.
2 Pass through seasoned flour, shake off all surplus flour.
3 Shallow fry on both sides, presentation side first, in hot clarified butter, margarine or oil.
4 Dress neatly on an oval flat dish.
5 Peel a lemon, removing the peel, white pith and pips.
6 Cut the lemon into slices and place one slice on each portion.
7 Squeeze some lemon juice on the fish.
8 Allow 10–25 g ($\frac{1}{2}$–1 oz) butter per portion and colour in a clean frying-pan to the nut-brown stage (*beurre noisette*).
9 Pour over the fish.
10 Sprinkle with chopped parsley and serve.

Note   Variations include:

- *Fish meunière with almonds* As for fish meunière (recipe 6) adding 10 g ($\frac{1}{2}$ oz) of almonds cut in short julienne or coarsely chopped to the meunière butter just before it begins to turn brown. This method is usually applied to trout.
- *Fish belle meunière* As for recipe 6 with the addition of a grilled mushroom, a

> 1 portion (125 g white fish) provides:
>
> 1314 kJ/313 kcal
> 24.1 g fat
> (of which 10.3 g saturated)
> 3.1 g carbohydrate
> (of which 0.0 g sugars)
> 21.2 g protein
> 0.1 g fibre

Plate 8.13: Fillets of fish meunière

slice of peeled tomato and a soft herring roe (passed through flour and shallow fried), all neatly dressed on each portion of fish.

- *Fish Doria* As for fish meunière (recipe 6) with a sprinkling of small turned pieces of cucumber carefully cooked in 25 g (1 oz) of butter in a small covered pan, or blanched in boiling salted water.
- *Grenobloise* As for fish meunière (recipe 6), the peeled lemon being cut into segments, neatly dressed on the fish with a few capers sprinkled over.
- *Bretonne* As for fish meunière (recipe 6), with a few picked shrimps and cooked sliced mushroom sprinkled over the fish.

GRILLED FISH

7 – Grilled cod steaks

1 Wash the steaks well and drain.
2 Pass through seasoned flour and brush with melted butter, margarine or oil.
3 Place on a greased baking tray.
4 Cook on both sides under a salamander, brushing occasionally with fat.
5 To test if cooked, carefully remove the centre bone.
6 Serve garnished with a slice or quarter of lemon, picked parsley and a suitable sauce or butter separately.

Fried in sunflower oil, 1 portion provides:

907 kJ/216 kcal
7.3 g fat
(of which 1.1 g saturated)
0.0 g carbohydrate
(of which 0.0 g sugars)
37.4 g protein
0.0 g fibre

8 – Grilled herring

1 Remove the scales from the fish with the back of a knife.
2 Remove the head, clean out the intestines, trim off all fins, take care not to damage the roe, and trim the tail.
3 Wash and drain well.
4 Make three light incisions 2 mm ($\frac{1}{2}$ inch) deep on either side of the fish.
5 Pass through seasoned flour.
6 Brush with melted butter, margarine or oil, place on a greased baking tray.

1 portion provides:

1003 kJ/239 kcal
15.6 g fat
(of which 3.3 g saturated)
0.0 g carbohydrate
(of which 0.0 g sugars)
24.5 g protein
0.0 g fibre

7   Grill on both sides taking care not to burn the tails.
8   Garnish with a slice or quarter of lemon and picked parsley.
9   Serve with a sauceboat of mustard sauce (see page 119).

9 – Grilled mackerel

1   Remove the head and intestines and clean the fish.
2   Cut down both sides of the backbone and remove the bone carefully.
3   Trim off all fins and excess rib bones, trim the tail.
4   Wash well and drain.
5   Pass through seasoned flour, shake off all surplus flour.
6   Place on a greased baking tray, cut side down.
7   Brush with melted butter, margarine or oil.
8   Grill on both sides under salamander.
9   Serve garnished with a slice or quarter of lemon, picked parsley and a suitable sauce separately.

Note   Mackerel may also be grilled whole, like herring.

10 – Fillets of grilled plaice (or sole)

1   Fillet the plaice, remove the black skin.
2   Wash well and drain.
3   Pass through seasoned flour, shake off all surplus flour.
4   Place on a greased baking tray, skinned side down.
5   Brush with melted butter, margarine or oil.
6   Grill on both sides under the salamander.
7   Serve with a slice or quarter of lemon, picked parsley and suitable sauce or butter.

11 – Grilled whiting

Prepare, grill and serve as for mackerel (recipe 9).

12 – Grilled sole (or plaice)

1 Remove the black skin, and scales from soles.
2 Remove the head and side bones, clean well.
3 Wash well and drain.
4 Pass through seasoned flour and shake off surplus flour.
5 Place on a greased baking tray white skin down.
6 Brush with melted butter, margarine or oil.
7 Grill on both sides under salamander.
8 Serve with a slice or quarter of lemon, picked parsley, and a suitable sauce or butter.

Brushed with sunflower oil, 1 portion provides:

703 kJ/167 kcal
6.9 g fat
(of which 0.9 g saturated)
3.9 g carbohydrate
(of which 0.1 g sugars)
22.7 g protein
0.2 g fibre

Plate 8.14: Grilled sole, whole and fillets

13 – Grilled salmon

1 Pass darnes of salmon through seasoned flour, shake off all surplus.
2 Place on a greased baking sheet or grill bars and brush with oil.
3 Grill on both sides, brush frequently with oil, for approximately 10 minutes.
4 Remove the centre bone and garnish with picked parsley.
5 Accompany with sliced cucumber and a suitable sauce.

Brushed with sunflower oil, 1 portion provides:

1178 kJ/280 kcal
19.5 g fat
(of which 3.6 g saturated)
3.9 g carbohydrate
(of which 0.1 g sugars)
22.6 g protein
0.2 g fibre

FRIED FISH

Points on the use of all fats and oils (see also pages 75 and 99–105)

For frying purposes a fat or oil must, when heated, reach a high temperature without smoking. The food being fried will absorb the fat if the fat smokes at a low temperature.

Fats and oils should be free from moisture, otherwise they splutter.

As they are combustible, fats and oils can catch fire. In some fats the margin between smoking and flash point may be narrow. A good frying temperature is 75–180°C (167–356°F).

When fat or oil smokes at about 177°C (350°F), foams, tastes or smells bad, it should be discarded.

14 – Frying batters

Plate 8.15: Fillets of fish coated in breadcrumbs (top); batter (right); milk and flour (left)

Plate 8.16a–c: Preparation of fried fish

Recipe 1

	6–8 portions	10 portions
flour	200 g (8 oz)	500 g (1¼ lb)
salt		
yeast	10 g (⅜ oz)	25 g (1¼ oz)
water or milk	250 ml (½ pt)	600 ml (1¼ pt)

1 Sift the flour and salt into a basin.
2 Dissolve the yeast in a little of the water.
3 Make a well in the flour.
4 Add the yeast and the liquid.
5 Gradually incorporate the flour and beat to a smooth mixture.
6 Allow to rest for at least 1 hour before using.

Recipe 2

	6–8 portions	10 portions
flour	200 g (8 oz)	500 g (1½ lb)
salt		
egg	1	2–3
water or milk	250 ml (½ pt)	600 ml (1¼ pt)
oil	2 tbsp	5 tbsp

1 Sift the flour and salt into a basin.
2 Make a well.
3 Add the egg and the liquid.
4 Gradually incorporate the flour, beat to a smooth mixture.
5 Mix in the oil.
6 Allow to rest before using.

Recipe 3

	6–8 portions	10 portions
flour	200 g (8 oz)	500 g (1¼ lb)
salt		
water or milk	250 ml (½ pt)	600 ml (1¼ pt)
oil	2 tbsp	5 tbsp
egg whites, stiffly beaten	2	5 tbsp

As for recipe 2, but fold in the whites just before using.

15 – Fried whiting

1 Skin the fish and remove the intestines, clean out the head by removing the gills and the eyes.
2 Wash well and drain.
3 Pass through seasoned flour, beaten egg and white breadcrumbs (called pané).
4 Shake off all surplus crumbs.
5 Deep fry to a golden brown in moderately hot fat 175°C (347°F) for approximately 5–6 minutes. Drain well.
6 Serve garnished with fried or picked parsley a quarter of lemon and a suitable sauce.

Fried in peanut oil 1 portion provides:

1453 kJ/346 kcal
18.6 g fat
(of which 3.6 g saturated)
12.6 g carbohydrate
(of which 0.4 g sugars)
32.6 g protein
0.6 g fibre

16 – Fried fillets of whiting

1 Fillet, wash well and drain.
2 Pané, or pass through batter. Deep fry at 185°C (365°F), drain well and serve as for fried whiting with a suitable sauce.

17 – Fried fillets of plaice

1 Fillet the fish, remove the black skin.
2 Wash well and drain.
3 Pass through flour and batter or flour, egg and crumb.
4 Deep fry at 185°C (365°F), drain well and serve as for fried whiting.

18 – Goujons of sole

1 Fillet the sole.
2 Cut each fillet into strips approximately $8 \times \frac{1}{2}$ cm ($3 \times \frac{1}{4}$ inch).
3 Pané, deep fry at 185°C (365°F), drain well and serve as above.

Note All filleted white fish may be prepared, cooked and served by this method.

19 – Fried sole

For fish courses use 200–250 g (8–10 oz) sole per portion, for main course 300–400 g (12–16 oz) sole per portion.

1 Remove the black and white skin. Remove the side fins.
2 Remove the head. Clean well.
3 Wash well and drain. Pané and deep fry at 175°C (347°F).
4 Serve on a dish paper with picked or fried parsley and a quarter of lemon on a flat dish, and with a suitable sauce, such as tartare or anchovy.

20 – Fried fish in batter

This is usually applied to fillets of white fish (plaice, sole, haddock, etc.) or rock fish (a term used for catfish, coley, conger eel, dogfish, etc.) when cleaned and skinned.

1 Pass the fish through seasoned flour and batter.
2 Deep fry at 170°C (338°F), drain well and serve with quarters of lemon and tartare sauce.

Note   Variations include marinading the fillets in a little oil, lemon juice and chopped parsley for a few minutes before frying. Served with a hot tomato sauce, it can be called Fried Fish Orly.

> Fried in peanut oil, 1 portion (200 g plaice) provides:
>
> 2344 kJ/558 kcal
> 36.0 g fat
> (of which 6.6 g saturated)
> 28.8 g carbohydrate
> (of which 1.2 g sugars)
> 31.6 g protein
> 1.2 g fibre

21 – Whitebait

1 Pick over the whitebait.
2 Wash carefully and drain well.
3 Pass through milk and seasoned flour.
4 Shake off all surplus flour in a wide mesh sieve and place the fish into a frying-basket.
5 Plunge into very hot fat, just smoking (195°C/383°F).
6 Cook till brown and crisp, approximately 1 minute.
7 Drain well.
8 Season lightly with salt and cayenne pepper.
9 Serve garnished with fried or pickled parsley and quarters of lemon.

Note   Allow 100 g (4 oz) per portion.

BOILED FISH

22 – Boiled turbot, brill or halibut

1 Place the prepared turbot into a shallow pan of simmering salted water, containing lemon juice. The citric acid in the lemon juice helps to make the fish firm and white.
2 Allow to simmer gently until cooked, the time depends very much on the thickness of the fish.
3 Remove with a fish slice from the pan.
4 Remove the black skin, drain and serve.
5 When served in an earthenware dish add a little of the cooking liquor.
6 Garnish with picked parsley and a plain boiled potato.
7 Serve with a suitable sauce separately, such as hollandaise sauce.

1 portion provides:

990 kJ/236 kcal
7.2 g fat
(of which 0.8 g saturated)
0.0 g carbohydrate
(of which 0.0 g sugars)
42.8 g protein
0.0 g fibre

23 – Boiled cod

1 When using whole cod cut into 1–2 cm ($\frac{1}{2}$–1 inch) slices on the bone (darne). Where required, tie with string.
2 Cook as for turbot (recipe 22) and serve in the same way.
3 Remove the centre bone and string before serving.
4 A suitable sauce should be served separately, such as parsley, egg or anchovy.

POACHED FISH

Although recipes 24–29 are given for fillets of sole, any white fish may be prepared and served in the following manner. Always place a little sauce under the fish before masking; this is to keep the fish moist, to prevent it overcooking and sticking to the dish, thus facilitating the service. If shallots are used, they must be finely chopped and may need to be sweated in a little butter beforehand to soften them.

24 – Fillets of sole Dugléré

	4 portions	10 portions
2 soles	500–600 g (1–1¼ lb)	5 soles
finely chopped shallot	10 g (½ oz)	25 g (1¼ oz)
tomatoes concassé	200 g (8 oz)	500 g (1¼ oz)
pinch chopped parsley		
salt, pepper		
fish stock	60 ml (⅛ pt)	150 ml (⅓ pt)
dry white wine	60 ml (⅛ pt)	150 ml (⅓ pt)
lemon, juice of	¼	½
fish velouté	250 ml (½ pt)	600 ml (1¼ pt)
butter	50 g (2 oz)	125 g (5 oz)

> 1 portion provides:
>
> 699 kJ/167 kcal
> 11.6 g fat
> (of which 6.8 g saturated)
> 1.9 g carbohydrate
> (of which 1.9 g sugars)
> 11.5 g protein
> 0.9 g fibre

1 Remove the black and white skins and fillet the soles.
2 Wash and drain well.
3 Butter and season an earthenware dish or sauté pan.
4 Sprinkle in the sweated chopped shallots.
5 Add the fillets which may be folded in two, add the tomatoes and chopped parsley.
6 Season with salt and pepper.
7 Add the fish stock, wine and the lemon juice.
8 Cover with a buttered greaseproof paper.
9 Poach gently in a moderate oven at 150–200°C (Reg. 2–6; 300–400°F) for 5–10 minutes.
10 Remove the fillets and the garnish, place on a flat dish, or in a clean earthenware dish, keep warm.
11 Pass and reduce the cooking liquor in a small sauteuse, add the fish velouté, pass through a fine strainer, then incorporate the butter.
12 Correct the seasoning and consistency.
13 Coat the fillets with the sauce and serve.

25 ~ Fillets of sole with white wine sauce

	4 portions	10 portions
2 soles	500–600 g (1–1¼ lb)	5 soles
finely chopped shallot	10 g (½ oz)	25 g (1¼ oz)
fish stock	60 ml (⅛ pt)	150 ml (⅓ pt)
dry white wine	60 ml (⅛ pt)	150 ml (⅓ pt)
lemon, juice of	¼	½
fish velouté	250 ml (½ pt)	600 ml (1¼ pt)
butter	50 g (2 oz)	125 g (5 oz)
cream, lightly whipped	2 tbsp	5 tbsp

1 Skin and fillet the soles, trim and wash.
2 Butter and season and earthenware dish.
3 Sprinkle with the sweated chopped shallot and add the fillets of sole.
4 Season, add the fish stock, wine and lemon juice.
5 Cover with a buttered greaseproof paper.
6 Poach in a moderate oven at 150–200°C (Reg. 2–6; 300–400°F) for 5–10 minutes.
7 Drain the fish well; dress neatly on a flat dish or earthenware dish.
8 Bring the cooking liquor to the boil with the velouté.
9 Correct the seasoning and consistency and pass through a tammy cloth or a fine strainer.
10 Mix in the butter, finally add the cream.
11 Coat the fillets with the sauce. Garnish with fleurons (puff paste crescents).

26 ~ Fillets of sole Véronique

	4 portions	10 portions
2 soles	500–600 g (1–1¼ lb)	5 soles
salt, pepper		
fish stock	60 ml (⅛ pt)	150 ml (⅓ pt)
dry white wine	60 ml (⅛ pt)	150 ml (⅓ pt)
lemon, juice of	¼	½
fish velouté	250 ml (½ pt)	600 ml (1¼ pt)
butter	50 g (2 oz)	125 g (5 oz)
cream, lightly whipped	2 tbsp	5 tbsp
white grapes (blanched, skinned and pipped)	50 g (2 oz)	125 g (5 oz)

> 1 portion provides:
>
> 1077 kJ/256 kcal
> 19.3 g fat
> (of which 10.7 g saturated)
> 6.9 g carbohydrate
> (of which 2.1 g sugars)
> 11.8 g protein
> 0.4 g fibre

recipe continued ▶

Plate 8.17: Fillets of sole Dugléré

Plate 8.18: Sole Véronique

1 Prepare and cook as for recipe 25, adding an egg yolk or spoonful of sabayon to the sauce.
2 Glaze under the salamander.
3 Arrange the grapes neatly on the dish.

27 – Fillets of sole Bercy

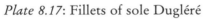

	4 portions	10 portions
2 soles	500–600 g (1–1¼ lb)	5 soles
chopped shallot	25 g (1 oz)	60 g (2½ oz)
chopped parsley		
fish stock	60 ml (⅛ pt)	150 ml (⅓ pt)
dry white wine	60 ml (⅛ pt)	150 ml (⅓ pt)
lemon, juice of	¼	½
fish velouté	250 ml (½ pt)	600 ml (1¼ pt)
butter	50 g (2 oz)	125 g (5 oz)
cream, lightly whipped	2 tbsp	5 tbsp
egg yolk or sabayon	1	2

1   Skin, fillet, trim and wash the fish.
2   Season and butter an earthenware dish.
3   Sprinkle with sweated, chopped shallots and chopped parsley.
4   Add the fillets of sole, season.
5   Add the stock, wine and lemon juice.
6   Cover with a buttered paper.
7   Poach in a moderate oven at 150–200°C (Reg. 2–6; 300–400°F) for approximately 5–10 minutes.
8   Remove the fillets, place in a clean earthenware or flat dish. Keep warm.
9   Place the cooking liquor and velouté in a small sauteuse.
10 Correct the consistency and seasoning and pass through a strainer.
11 Finish with the butter and then the cream and sabayon.
12 Mask the fish and glaze under the salamander.

Note   Variations include:

- *Fillets of sole bonne femme* As for fillets of sole Bercy with the addition of 100 g (4 oz) sliced button mushrooms which are placed in the earthenware dish with raw fish. Finish as for Bercy (recipe 27).
- *Fillets of sole Bréval or d'Antin* As for bonne femme with the addition of 100 g (4 oz) for 4 portions (250 g/10 oz for 10) tomatoes which are added with the mushrooms. The tomatoes are cut concassé. Finish as for Bercy (recipe 27).
- *Fillets of sole Marguery* As for fillets of sole Bercy (recipe 27). Garnish the fillets of sole with 75 g (3 oz) for 4 portions (180 g/7½ oz for 10) cooked prawns and 12 cooked mussels before coating with the sauce. Finish the dish by glazing under the salamander and garnish with fleurons.

28 – Fillets of sole Mornay

	4 portions	10 portions
2 soles	500–600 g (1–1½ lb)	5 soles
fish stock	125 ml (¼ pt)	300 ml (⅝ pt)
béchamel sauce	250 ml (½ pt)	600 ml (1¼ pt)
egg yolk or sabayon	1	3
grated cheese, preferably Gruyère or Parmesan	50 g (2 oz)	125 g (5 oz)
salt, cayenne		
butter	25 g (1 oz)	60 g (2½ oz)
cream, lightly whipped	2 tbsp	5 tbsp

recipe continued ▶

1 Prepare the fillets; place in a buttered, seasoned earthenware dish or shallow pan, such as a sauté pan.
2 Add the fish stock, cover with a buttered paper.
3 Cook in a moderate oven at 150–200°C (Reg. 2–6; 300–400°F) for approximately 5–10 minutes.
4 Drain the fish well, place in a clean earthenware or flat dish.
5 Bring the béchamel to the boil, add the reduced cooking liquor, whisk in the yolk and remove from the heat. Add the cheese and correct the consistency. Do not reboil, otherwise the egg will curdle.
6 Correct the seasoning and pass through a fine strainer.
7 Mix in the butter and cream, check the consistency.
8 Mask the fish, sprinkle with grated cheese and gratinate under the salamander.

Note   A variation includes:

- *Fillets of sole Walewska* Place a slice of cooked lobster on each fish fillet before coating with the sauce. After the dish is browned decorate each fillet with a slice of truffle.

29 – Fillets of sole florentine

	4 portions	10 portions
Ingredients as for Fillet of sole Mornay, recipe 28		
leaf spinach	$\frac{1}{2}$ kg (1 lb)	$1\frac{1}{4}$ kg ($2\frac{1}{2}$ lb)

1 Remove the stems from the spinach.
2 Wash very carefully in plenty of water several times if necessary.
3 Cook in boiling salted water until tender for approximately 3–5 minutes.
4 Refresh under cold water, squeeze dry into a ball.
5 When required for service, place into a pan containing 25–50 g (1–2 oz) butter, loosen with a fork and reheat quickly without colouring; season lightly with salt and mill pepper.
6 Place in the serving dish.
7 Proceed as for fillet of sole Mornay.
8 Dress the fillets on the spinach. Coat with Mornay sauce, sprinkle with grated cheese and gratinate under the salamander.

30 – Fish in the shell with cheese sauce

The fish to be used should be named.

1 Prepare ½ kg (1 lb) duchess potato mixture (page 566) for 4 portions (1¼ kg/2½ lb for 10).
2 Using a piping bag and a large star tube, pipe a neat border around the serving shells or dishes.
3 Dry in the oven or under the salamander for 2 or 3 minutes.
4 Brush with eggwash.
5 Prepare and cook the fish and sauce as for fillets of sole Mornay (recipe 28).
6 Place a little sauce in the bottom of each serving shell or dish.
7 Add the well-drained fish, which is usually flaked.
8 Coat with sauce, taking care not to splash the potato.
9 Sprinkle with grated cheese, brown under the salamander and serve.

31 – Fish kedgeree

	4 portions	10 portions
fish (usually smoked haddock or fresh salmon)	400 g (1 lb)	1¼ kg (2½ lb)
rice pilaff (page 236)	200 g (8 oz)	500 g (1¼ lb)
hard-boiled eggs	2	5
butter	50 g (2 oz)	125 g (5 oz)
curry sauce (page 129)	250 ml (½ pt)	600 ml (1¼ pt)

The fish to be used should be named.

1 Poach the fish. Remove all skin and bone. Flake.
2 Cook the rice pilaff. Cut the eggs in dice.
3 Combine the eggs, fish, rice and heat in the butter. Correct the seasoning.
4 Serve hot with a sauceboat of curry sauce.

Note Traditionally served for breakfast, lunch or supper.

32 – Poached smoked haddock

	4 portions	10 portions
smoked haddock	400–600 g (1–1½ lb)	¼ kg (2½ lb)
milk	250 ml (½ pt)	600 ml (1¼ pt)
water	250 ml (½ pt)	600 ml (1¼ pt)

1 Trim off all fins from the fish. Cut into 4 (or 10) even pieces.
2 Simmer gently in the milk and water.
3 When cooked, the backbone should be easy to remove.
4 Remove the backbone and serve.

Note   A variation includes:

● *Haddock Monte Carlo* As for poached haddock, garnished with slices of peeled tomato or tomato concassé, poached egg and cream or cream sauce.

33 – Skate with black butter

	4 portions	10 portions
skate wings	400–600 g (1–1½ lb)	1¼ kg (2½ lb)
court bouillon		
butter	50 g (2 oz)	125 g (5 oz)
vinegar	1 tsp	2½ tsp
chopped parsley		
capers	10 g (½ oz)	25 g (1¼ oz)

1 Cut the skate into 4 (or 10) even pieces.
2 Simmer in a court bouillon (page 250) until cooked, approximately 10 minutes.
3 Drain well, place on a serving dish or plates.
4 Heat the butter in a frying-pan until well browned, almost black; add the vinegar, pour over the fish, sprinkle with chopped parsley and a few capers and serve.

34 ～ Fish cakes

	4 portions	10 portions
cooked fish (free from skin and bone)	200 g (8 oz)	500 g (1¼ lb)
mashed potatoes	200 g (8 oz)	500 g (1¼ lb)
salt, pepper		
flour	25 g (1 oz)	60 g (2½ oz)
egg	1	3
breadcrumbs	50 g (2 oz)	125 g (5 oz)

1 Combine the fish, potatoes and egg and season.
2 Divide into 4 (or 10) pieces. Mould into balls.
3 Pass through the coating of flour, egg and breadcrumbs.
4 Flatten slightly, neaten with a palette knife.
5 Deep fry in hot fat (185°C/365°F) for 2–3 minutes.
6 Serve with fried or picked parsley.
7 Serve with a suitable sauce, such as tomato sauce (page 132).

35 ～ Salmon cutlets

Method I

Prepare a fish-cake mixture using cooked salmon. Shape into cutlets, insert a piece of macaroni, deep fry and serve as for fish cakes.

Method II

	4 portions	10 portions
béchamel	¼ litre (½ pt)	¾ litre (1½ pt)
cooked flaked salmon	300 g (12 oz)	750 g (2 lb)
seasoning		
egg yolks	1–2	4–5

1 Boil the thick béchamel (page 117).
2 Add the salmon free from skin and bone.
3 Season, add egg yolks, mix in and remove from the heat. Place on a greased tray.
4 When cold mould into 4 (or 10) even-sized cutlet-shaped pieces. Flour, egg and crumb and insert a piece of macaroni into each.
5 Deep fry (185°C/365°F) and serve with fried or picked parsley. Serve a suitable sauce separately, such as anchovy sauce (page 118).

36 – Fish pie

	4 portions	10 portions
béchamel (thin) (page 117)	250 ml ($\frac{1}{2}$ pt)	600 ml ($1\frac{1}{4}$ pt)
fish cooked free from skin and bone	200 g (8 oz)	500 g ($1\frac{1}{4}$ lb)
cooked diced mushrooms	50 g (2 oz)	125 g (5 oz)
chopped hard-boiled egg	1	3
chopped parsley		
salt, pepper		
mashed or duchess potatoes	200 g (8 oz)	500 g ($1\frac{1}{4}$ lb)

> 1 portion provides:
>
> 879 kJ/209 kcal
> 12.0 g fat
> (of which 5.3 g saturated)
> 11.9 g carbohydrate
> (of which 3.2 g sugars)
> 14.1 g protein
> 0.9 g fibre

1 Bring the béchamel to the boil.
2 Add the fish, mushrooms, egg and parsley. Correct the seasoning.
3 Place in a buttered pie-dish.
4 Place or pipe the potato on top. Brush with eggwash or milk.
5 Brown in a hot oven or under the salamander and serve.

Note Many variations can be made to this recipe with the addition of a) prawns or shrimps; b) herbs such as dill, tarragon or fennel; or c) raw fish, poached in white wine, the cooking liquor strained off, double cream added and reduced to a light consistency.

Shellfish

1 Ensure that the preparation and cooking areas are ready for use and cleaned after use to meet health and safety regulations.
2 Plan the work, allocate time and organise in an efficient manner.
3 Ensure that the shellfish is of the type, quality and quantity required. Particular attention must be paid to freshness of shellfish and that, where appropriate, it is alive. Know how to purchase and store shellfish.
4 Prepare, cook and serve shellfish correctly according to dish, customer requirements and food hygiene requirements.
5 Realise that competency implies knowing, understanding and applying the principles of shellfish cookery.

Shellfish are divided into two main groups:

- *Crustacea* (lobster, crab, crawfish, crayfish, prawns and shrimps);
- *Mollusca* (oysters, mussels, scallops); these are also known as bivalves.

Shellfish is a good body-building food. As the flesh is coarse and therefore indigestible, a little vinegar may be used in cooking to soften the fibres.

SAFETY ASPECTS

Health and safety aspects of food hygiene are dealt with in Chapter 1.

QUALITY, PURCHASING POINTS AND STORAGE

- Whenever possible, all shellfish should be purchased live so as to ensure freshness.
- Shellfish should be kept in suitable containers, covered with damp seaweed or damp cloths and stored in a cold room or refrigerator.
- Shellfish should be cooked as soon as possible after purchasing.

SHRIMPS AND PRAWNS

These are often bought cooked either in the shells or peeled. Smell is the best guide to freshness. Shrimps and prawns can be used for garnishes, decorating fish dishes, cocktails, sauces, salads, hors-d'oeuvre omelets and snack and savoury dishes. They can also be used for a variety of hot dishes: stir-fry, risotto, curries, etc. Potted shrimps are also a popular dish. Freshly cooked prawns in the shells may also be served cold accompanied by a mayonnaise-based sauce, such as garlic mayonnaise.

King prawns are a larger variety which can also be used in any of the above ways.

Raw and cooked shrimps and prawns are prepared by having the head, carapace (upper shell), legs, tail section and the dark intestinal vein running down the back removed.

(For shellfish cocktails, see pages 170–171.)

SCAMPI, SALT WATER CRAYFISH AND DUBLIN BAY PRAWNS

These are also known as Norway lobster or langoustine and are sold fresh, frozen, raw or cooked. Their tails are prepared like shrimps and they are used in a variety of ways: salads, rice dishes, stir-fried, deep fried, poached and served with a number of different sauces. They are also used as garnishes to hot and cold fish dishes.

Freshwater crayfish are also known as écrevisse. These are small fresh water crustaceans with claws, found in lakes and lowland streams. They are prepared and cooked like shrimps and prawns and used in many dishes including soup. They are often used whole to garnish hot and cold fish dishes.

LOBSTER

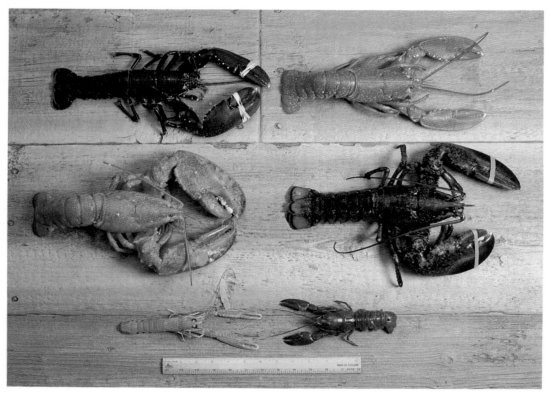

Plate 8.19: From top: Scottish lobster (raw and cooked); Canadian lobster (cooked and raw); crayfish; langoustine

Purchasing points

- Purchase alive, with both claws attached, to ensure freshness.
- Lobsters should be heavy in proportion to their size.
- The coral of the hen lobster is necessary to give the required colour for certain soups, sauces and lobster dishes.
- Hen lobsters are distinguished from cock lobsters by a broader tail.

Cooking of lobster

1 Wash, plunge them into a pan of boiling salted water containing 60 ml ($\frac{1}{8}$ pint) vinegar to 1 litre (2 pints) water.
2 Cover with a lid, reboil, then allow to simmer for 15–20 minutes according to size.
3 Overcooking can cause the tail flesh to toughen and the claw meat to become hard and fibrous.
4 Allow to cool in the cooking liquid when possible.

Cleaning of cooked lobster

- Remove the claws and remove the pincers from the claws.
- Crack the claws and joints and remove the meat.
- Cut the lobster in half by inserting the point of a large knife 2 cm (1 inch) above the tail on the natural central line.
- Cut through the tail firmly.
- Turn the lobster around and cut through the upper shell (carapace).
- Remove the halves of the sac (which contains grit) from each half. This is situated at the top near the head.
- Using a small knife remove the intestinal trace from the tail and wash if necessary.

Uses

Lobsters are served cold in cocktails (page 170), hors-d'oeuvre, salads, sandwiches and in halves on cold buffets.

They are used hot in soups, sauces, rice dishes, stir-fry dishes and in numerous ways served in the half shell with various sauces. They are also used to garnish fish dishes.

CRAWFISH

These are sometimes referred to as spring lobsters but unlike lobsters they have no claws and the meat is solely in the tail. Crawfish vary considerably in size from 1–3 kg (2–6 lb); they are cooked as for lobsters and the tail meat can be used in any of the lobster recipes. Because of their impressive appearance crawfish dressed whole are sometimes used on special cold buffets. They are very expensive and are also available frozen.

CRAB

Purchasing points

- Buy alive to ensure freshness.
- Ensure that both claws are attached.
- Crabs should be heavy in relation to size.

Cooking

1 Place the crabs in boiling salted water with a little vinegar added.
2 Reboil, then simmer for 15–30 minutes according to size. These times apply to crabs weighing from $\frac{1}{2}$–$2\frac{1}{2}$ kg (1–5 lb).
3 Allow the crabs to cool in the cooking liquor.

Removing the meat from the shell

- Remove large claws and sever at the joints.
- Remove the flexible pincers from the claws.
- Crack the claws and joints carefully and remove all the flesh (the white meat).
- Carefully remove the soft under shell from the main shell by pressing firmly with both thumbs.
- Discard the gills and the gravel sac behind the eyes from the inside of the carapace.
- Scrape out all the inside of the shell and pass through a sieve; this is the brown meat.
- Further white meat is obtained by cutting the soft under shell into two or three pieces and carefully picking out the white flesh using a small knife.

Uses of crab meat

Crab meat can be used cold for hors-d'oeuvre, cocktails, salads, sandwiches and dressed crab. Used hot, it can be covered with a suitable sauce and served with rice, in bouchées or pancakes, or made into crab fish cakes.

COCKLES

Cockles are enclosed in small, attractive, cream-coloured shells. As they live in sand it is essential to purge them by washing well under running cold water and leaving them in cold salted water (changed frequently) until no traces of sand remain.

Cockles can be cooked either by steaming; boiling in unsalted water; on a preheated griddle, or as for any mussel recipe.

Cockles should only be cooked until the shells open.

They can be used in soups, sauces, salads, stir-fry and rice dishes and as garnish for fish dishes.

MUSSELS

Mussels are extensively cultivated on wooden hurdles in the sea, producing tender, delicately flavoured plump fish. Mussels are produced in Britain and imported from France, Holland and Belgium. French mussels are small, Dutch and Belgian are plumper. The quality tends to vary from season to season.

Purchasing points

- The shells must be tightly closed indicating they are alive.
- Mussels should be of good size.
- There should not be an excessive number of barnacles attached.
- Mussels should smell fresh.

Storage

Mussels should be kept in containers, covered with damp seaweed or cloths and stored in a cold room or refrigerator.

Use

Mussels can be used for soups, sauces, salads, and cooked in a wide variety of hot dishes.

Cooking

1 Scrape the shells to remove any barnacles, etc. Wash well and drain in a colander.
2 In a thick-bottomed pan with a tight-fitting lid, place 25 g (1 oz) chopped shallot or onion for 1 litre (1 qt) mussels.
3 Add the mussels, cover with a lid and cook on a fierce heat for 4–5 minutes until the shells open completely.
4 Remove the mussels from the shells, checking carefully for sand, weed, etc.
5 Retain the liquid for the sauce.

Plate 8.20:
Spidercrab (top left);
crab; crawfish

SCALLOPS

There are a number of varieties:

- Great scallops are up to 15 cm (6 inches) in size.
- Bay scallops are up to 8 cm (3 inches).
- Queen scallops also known as Queenies are small cockle-sized scallops.

Scallops are found on the seabed and are therefore dirty, so it is advisable to purchase them ready cleaned. If scallops are bought in the shells, the shells should be tightly shut which indicates they are alive and fresh. The roe (orange in colour) should be bright and moist. Scallops in the shells should be covered with damp seaweed or cloths and kept in a cold room or refrigerator.

To remove from the shells, place the shells on top of the stove or in an oven for a few seconds, when they will open and the flesh can then be removed with a knife.

Scallops should then be well washed; remove the trail leaving only the white scallop and orange roe.

Cooking
Scallops should be only lightly cooked.

Plate 8.21: From top: scallops; large clams; small clams; mussels

- Poach gently for 2–3 minutes in dry white wine with a little onion, carrot, thyme, bayleaf and parsley. Serve with a suitable sauce (white wine, mornay, etc).
- Lightly fry on both sides (if the scallops are very thick they can be cut in halves sideways) and serve with a suitable garnish (sliced wild or cultivated mushrooms or a fine brunoise of vegetables and tomato) and a liquid which need not be thickened (white wine and fish stock, or cream- or butter-mounted sauce). Fried scallops can also be served hot on a plate of salad leaves.
- Deep fry, either egg and crumbed or passed through a light batter and served with segments of lemon and a suitable sauce (tartare).
- Wrap in thin streaky bacon, place on skewers for grilling or barbecuing.

SHELLFISH RECIPES

37 – Grilled or barbecued lobster

1. Three-quarter boil the lobsters and remove from the cooking liquid.
2. Split in halves, remove the gravel sac and intestinal tract.
3. Sprinkle with melted butter and cook for a short time under or on a hot grill.

Note Lobsters can be split and grilled without preboiling but there is a tendency for them to become tough and chewy.

38 – Lobster Mornay

	4 portions	10 portions
cooked lobsters (400 g 1 lb)	2	5
butter	25 g (1 oz)	60 g (2½ oz)
salt, cayenne		
Mornay sauce	250 ml (½ pt)	625 ml (1¼ pt)
grated cheese (Parmesan)		

1 Remove the lobsters' claws and legs.
2 Cut the lobsters carefully in half lengthwise.
3 Remove all the meat. Discard the sac and trail.
4 Wash, shell and drain on a baking sheet upside down.
5 Cut the lobster meat into escalopes.
6 Heat the butter in a thick-bottomed pan, add the lobster and season.
7 Turn two or three times; overcooking will toughen the meat.
8 Meanwhile, finish the Mornay sauce.
9 Place a little sauce in the bottom of each shell.
10 Add the lobster, press down to make a flat surface.
11 Mask completely with sauce, sprinkle with grated cheese, and brown under the salamander and serve garnished with pickled parsley.

39 – Lobster Thermidor

	4 portions	10 portions
cooked lobsters	2	5
butter	25 g (1 oz)	60 g (2½ oz)
finely chopped shallot	12 g (½ oz)	30 g (1¼ oz)
dry white wine	60 ml (⅛ pt)	150 ml (⅓ pt)
diluted English mustard	½ tsp	1 tsp
chopped parsley		
Mornay sauce	¼ litre (½ pt)	⅝ litre (1¼ pt)
grated Parmesan cheese	25 g (1 oz)	60 g (2½ oz)

1   Remove the lobsters' claws and legs.
2   Cut the lobsters carefully in halves lengthwise. Remove the meat.
3   Discard the sac and remove the trail from the tail.
4   Wash the halves of shell and drain on a baking sheet.
5   Cut the lobster meat into thick escalopes.
6   Melt the butter in a sauteuse, add the chopped shallot and cook until tender without colour.
7   Add the white wine to the shallot and allow to reduce to a quarter of its original volume.
8   Mix in the mustard and chopped parsley.
9   Add the lobster slices, season lightly with salt, mix carefully and allow to heat slowly for 2–3 minutes. If this part of the process is overdone the lobster will become tough and chewy.
10 Meanwhile spoon a little of the warm Mornay sauce into the bottom of each lobster half shell.
11 Neatly add the warmed lobster pieces and the juice in which they were reheated. If there should be an excess of liquid it should be reduced and incorporated into the Mornay sauce.
12 Coat the half lobsters with the remaining Mornay sauce, sprinkle with Parmesan cheese and place under a salamander until a golden brown, and serve garnished with picked parsley.

40 ~ Fried scampi

	4 portions	10 portions
shelled scampi	375–500 g ($\frac{3}{4}$–1 lb)	1$\frac{1}{4}$ kg (2$\frac{1}{2}$ lb)
flour	50 g (2 oz)	125 g (5 oz)
egg	1	3
fresh white breadcrumbs	50 g (2 oz)	125 g (5 oz)
lemon	1	2
parsley		

> Fried in peanut oil, 1 portion provides:
>
> 1327 kJ/316 kcal
> 17.6 g fat
> (of which 3.1 g saturated)
> 28.9 g carbohydrate
> (of which 1.1 g sugars)
> 12.2 g protein
> 1.2 g fibre

1   Pass the scampi through the flour and eggwash and roll in fresh white breadcrumbs.
2   Shake off all surplus crumbs and lightly roll each piece of scampi to firm the surface.
3   Deep fry at 185°C (365°F).

recipe continued ▶

4   Drain well and serve.
5   Garnish with quarters of lemon and sprigs of fried or fresh parsley.
6   Accompany with a suitable sauce, such as sauce tartare.

41 ‑ Seafood in puff pastry (seafood bouchées)

	4 portions	10 portions
button mushrooms	50 g (2 oz)	125 g (5 oz)
butter	25 g (1 oz)	60 g (2½ oz)
lemon, juice of	¼	½
cooked lobster, prawns, shrimps, mussels, scallops	200 g (8 oz)	500 g (1¼ lb)
white wine sauce (page 255)	125 ml (¼ pt)	300 ml (⅝ pt)
chopped parsley		
bouchée cases (page 684)	4	10

1   Peel and wash the mushrooms, cut in neat dice.
2   Cook in butter with the lemon juice.
3   Add the shellfish (mussels, prawns, shrimps left whole, the scallops and lobster cut in dice).
4   Cover the pan with a lid and heat through slowly for 3–4 minutes.
5   Add the white wine sauce, chopped parsley and season.
6   Meanwhile warm the bouchées in the oven or hot plate.
7   Fill the bouchées with the mixture and place the lids on top.
8   Serve garnished with picked parsley.

Note   Vol-au-vents can be prepared and cooked as puff pastry cases (page 684). The filling is prepared as above and dressed similarly.

9
MEAT AND POULTRY

Recipe No.   *page no.*

Lamb and mutton recipes

4	Best-end of lamb boulanger	*Carré d'agneau boulanger*	306
3	Best-end of lamb with breadcrumbs and parsley	*Carré d'agneau persillé*	306
16	Brown lamb stew	*Navarin d'agneau*	312
12	Chump chops, braised		310
11	Chump chops, grilled		309
20	Cornish pasties		316
17	Curried lamb	*Kari d'agneau*	313
8	Cutlets, breadcrumbed	*Côtelettes d'agneau panées*	307
7	Cutlets, fried		307
5	Cutlets, grilled	*Côtelettes d'agneau grillées*	306
9	Cutlets, Reform		308
14	Fillet of lamb, sauté	*Filet mignon sauté*	311
21	Hot-pot		317
18	Irish stew		315
10	Kebabs		308
12	Loin chops, braised		310
13	Loin chops, Champvallon	*Chop Champvallon*	311
11	Loin chops, grilled		309
23	Minced lamb or mutton	*Hachis d'agneau ou mouton*	319
6	Mixed grill		307
24	Moussaka		320
16	Mutton stew		312
11	Noisettes of lamb, grilled	*Noisettes d'agneau grillées*	309
23	Noisettes of lamb, sauté	*Noisettes d'agneau sautées*	311
1	Roast lamb or mutton		303
1	Roast leg of lamb or mutton	*Gigot d'agneau rôti*	303
22	Shepherd's pie or cottage pie		318
10	Shish kebab		308
2	Stuffing for lamb		305
15	Valentine of lamb		312
19	White lamb stew	*Blanquette d'agneau*	315

Lamb offal

27	Braised lambs' hearts	*Cœurs d'agneau braisés*	322
29	Fried liver and bacon	*Foie d'agneau au lard*	323
25	Grilled lambs' kidneys	*Rognons d'agneau grillés*	321
26	Kidney sauté	*Rognons sautés*	321
28	Stuffed braised hearts	*Cœurs d'agneau braisés farcis*	323

Beef

36	Beef Burgundy style	*Bœuf Bourguignonne*	336
51	Beef olives	*Paupiettes de bœuf*	349
44	Beef Stroganoff	*Sauté de bœuf Stroganoff*	342

35	Boiled beef, French style	*Bœuf bouille à la française*	334
34	Boiled silverside, carrots and dumplings		333
49	Braised beef	*Bœuf braisé*	347
57	Braised ox liver and onions	*Foie de bœuf lyonnaise*	353
56	Braised ox tongue, Madeira sauce	*Langue de bœuf braisée au Madère*	353
50	Braised steak and dumplings		348
48	Braised steaks		346
30	Brine		327
36	Brown beef stew	*Ragoût de bœuf*	335
47	Carbonnade of beef	*Carbonnade de bœuf*	345
41	Curried beef	*Kari de bœuf*	340
45	Goulash		343
37	Grilled beef		337
53	Hamburger American style		351
52	Hamburg or Vienna steak	*Bitok*	351
31	Horseradish sauce	*Sauce raifort*	331
55	Ox tongue	*Langue de bœuf*	353
33	Roast beef	*Bœuf rôti*	332
43	Sauté of beef		342
39	Sirloin steak with red wine sauce	*Entrecôte bordelaise*	339
38	Sirloin steak chasseur	*Entrecôte chasseur*	338
46	Steak pie		346
42	Steak pudding		341
58	Stewed oxtail	*Ragoût de queue de boeuf*	354
40	Tournedos		340
54	Tripe and onions		352
32	Yorkshire pudding		332

Veal

77	Braised shin of veal	*Osso buco*	371
66	Braised stuffed shoulder of veal	*Epauk de veau farcie*	364
79	Braised sweetbreads	*Ris de veau braisé*	372
62	Braised veal	*Noix de veau braisées*	362
59	Brown veal stew	*Ragoût de veau*	360
78	Calf's liver and bacon	*Foie de veau au lard*	372
68	Escalope of veal and variations	*Escalope de veau*	365
69	Escalope, breadcrumbed with ham and cheese		366
71	Escalope with cream and mushrooms	*Escalope de veau à la crème et champignons*	367
70	Escalope with Madeira	*Escalope de veau Madère*	367
72	Escalopes with Parma ham and Mozzarella cheese		368
61	Fricassée of veal	*Fricassée de veau*	361
65	Fried veal cutlet	*Côte de veau sautée*	364
76	Grenadin of veal	*Grenadin de veau*	370
64	Grilled veal cutlet	*Côte lette de veau grillée*	364

74	Roast stuffed breast of veal	370
73	Stuffing	369
80	Sweetbread escalope	373
81	Sweetbread escalope, crumbed	374
60	White stew of veal	360

Pork

88	Barbecued spare ribs	379
85	Boiled leg of pork	378
93	Forcemeat	382
89	Grilled pork chop	380
86	Pork chop charcutière	378
87	Pork chop flamande	378
90	Pork escalopes	380
91	Pork escalopes with Calvados sauce	381
83	Roast pork	377
84	Sage and onion stuffing	378
92	Sausage toad in the hole	382
94	Sweet and sour pork	383

Bacon

99	Bacon chops, honey and orange sauce	387
98	Baked bacon and pineapple	387
95	Boiled bacon	386
97	Fried bacon	387
96	Grilled back or streaky rashers	386
101	Grilled gammon rashers	389
100	Sauerkraut with frankfurters and garlic sausage	388

Chicken and turkey

113	Boiled or poached chicken with rice and suprême sauce	408
120	Braised rice and chicken livers	415
114	Chicken à la king	409
121	Chicken in red wine	415
116	Chicken pancakes	411
118	Chicken pie	413
106	Chicken sauté chasseur	402
105	Chicken sauté with mushrooms	401
110	Chicken sauté with potatoes	406
107	Chicken spatchcock	403
115	Chicken vol-au-vent	410
112	Crumbed breast of chicken with asparagus	407
119	Curried chicken	414
117	Fricassée of chicken	412
111	Fried chicken	406
108	Grilled chicken	403
103	Roast chicken	399

102	Roast turkey	398
104	Sauté of chicken	400
109	Suprême of chicken in cream sauce	404
	Duck	
125	Duckling, orange sauce	418
126	Duckling with cherries	419
122	Roast duck	416
124	Roast duckling, orange salad	417
123	Stuffing for duck	417

Meats and poultry

1 Prepare areas and equipment for use and correctly clean after use, according to health, safety and hygiene regulations.
2 Plan the work, allocate time and organise in an efficient way.
3 Identify the quality cuts of beef, lamb, pork or veal and the various cuts and uses.
4 Identify poultry types and cuts, and prepare correctly.
5 Cook and present dishes to satisfy consumer requirements.
6 Ensure storage is correct, with correct thawing and thorough cooking if necessary, particularly of poultry.
7 Realise that competency implies knowledge, understanding and applying the principles of meat and poultry cookery.

Meats

STRUCTURE

To cook meat properly it is important to understand the structure of meat. Lean flesh is composed of muscles, which are numerous bundles of fibres held together by connective tissues. The size of these fibres is extremely small especially in tender cuts or cuts from young animals and only the coarsest fibres may be distinguished by the naked eye. The size of the fibres varies in length, depth and thickness and this variation will affect the grain and the texture of the meat.

The quantity of connective tissue binding the fibres together will have much to do with the tenderness and eating quality. There are two kinds of connective tissue, elastic which is yellow in colour and collagen which is white. The thick yellow strip that runs along the neck and back of animals is an example of elastic. Elastin is found in the muscles, especially of older animals or those muscles receiving considerable exercise. Elastin will not cook and must therefore be removed before the meat is cooked or broken up mechanically by pounding or mincing. Collagen can be cooked as it decomposes in moist heat to form gelatine.

The quantity of fat and its condition are important factors in determining eating quality. Fat is found on the exterior and interior of the carcass and in the flesh itself. Fat deposited between muscles or between the bundles of fibres is called marbling. If marbling is present in the flesh of meat, the meat is likely to be tender, of better flavour and moist. Much of the flavour of meat is given by fats found in lean or fatty tissues of the meat. Animals absorb flavour from the food they are given, therefore the type of feed is important in the final eating quality of the meat.

Extractives in meat are also responsible for flavour. Muscles that receive a good deal of exercise have a higher proportion of flavour extractives than those receiving less exercise. Shin, shank, neck and other parts receiving exercise will yield richer stocks and gravies and meat with more flavour than the tender cuts.

Tenderness, flavour and moistness are increased if meat is hung after slaughter. The hanging process is essential as animals muscles stiffen (rigor mortis) shortly after death but after a time chemical action caused by enzymes and increasing acidity relaxes the muscles and softens or tenderises the meat. As meat continues to hang in storage, rigor mortis is lost and tenderness, flavour and moistness increase. Pork, lamb and veal are obtained from young animals so that toughness is not a significant factor and 3–7 days hanging should be sufficient according to the temperature.

Meat having a high protein content is valuable for the growth and repair of the body and as a source of energy.

STORAGE

- Fresh meat must be hung to allow it to become tender.
- The ideal storage temperature is usually between 1°C and 5°C. Under hygienic conditions, safe storage times at these temperatures are:

  - *beef* up to 3 weeks
  - *veal* 1–3 weeks
  - *lamb* 10–15 days
  - *pork* 7–14 days.

- Meat should be suspended on hooks.

OFFAL AND OTHER EDIBLE PARTS OF THE CARCASS

Offal is the name given to the edible parts taken from the inside of a carcass of meat: liver, kidneys, heart and sweetbreads. Tripe, brains, tongue, head, oxtail are also sometimes included under this term.

Fresh offal (unfrozen) should be purchased as required and can be refrigerated under hygienic conditions at a temperature of −1°C (30°F), at a relative humidity of 90% for up to 7 days. Frozen offal must be kept in a deep freeze and defrosted in a refrigerator as required.

Liver

Calf's liver is considered the best in terms of tenderness and flavour. It is also the most expensive.

Lambs's liver is mild in flavour, light in colour and tender. Sheep's liver, being from an older animal is firmer in substance, deeper in colour and has a stronger flavour.

Ox or *beef liver* is the cheapest and if taken from an older animal can be coarse in texture and strong in flavour. It is usually braised.

Pig's liver has a strong full flavour and is mainly used for pâté recipes.

Quality points
- Liver should look fresh, moist, smooth with a pleasant colour and no unpleasant smell.
- Liver should not be dry or contain an excessive number of tubes.

Food value
Liver is valuable as a protective food. It consists mainly of protein and contains useful amounts of vitamin A and iron.

Kidneys

Lamb's kidneys are light in colour, delicate in flavour and are ideal for grilling and frying.

Sheep's kidneys are darker in colour and stronger in flavour.

Calf's kidneys are light in colour, delicate in flavour and are used in a variety of dishes.

Ox kidney is dark in colour, strong in flavour and is either braised, or used in pies and puddings (mixed with beef).

Pig's kidneys are smooth, long and flat and have a strong flavour.

Quality points

- Suet, which is the fat in which kidneys are encased should be left on otherwise the kidneys will dry out. The suet should be removed when kidneys are being prepared for cooking.
- Both suet and kidneys should be moist and have no unpleasant smell.

Food value

This is similar to that of liver.

Hearts

Lamb's hearts are small and light and normally served whole.

Sheep's hearts are dark and solid and can be dry and tough unless carefully cooked.

Ox or *beef hearts* are dark coloured, solid and tend to be dry and tough.

Calf's hearts, coming from a younger animal, are lighter in colour and more tender. Most hearts need slow braising to tenderise them.

Quality points

Hearts should not be too fatty and should not contain too many tubes. When cut they should be moist, not sticky and with no unpleasant smell.

Food value

Hearts have a high protein content and are valuable for growth and repair of the body.

Sweetbreads

These and the pancreas and thymus glands known as neck and heart breads. The heart bread is round, plump and of better quality than the neck bread which is long and uneven in shape. Calf's heart breads considered the best weigh up to 600 g (1½ lb), lamb's heart bread up to 100 g (4 oz).

Quality points
- Heart and neck breads should be fleshly and of good size.
- They should be creamy white in colour and have no unpleasant smell.

Food value
Sweetbreads are easily digested and are useful for building body tissues which makes them valuable for invalid diets.

Tripe

Tripe is the stomach lining or white muscle of the ox consisting of the ruman or paunch and the honeycomb tripe (considered the best); sheep tripe, darker in colour is obtainable in some areas.

Quality points
Tripe should be fresh, with no signs of stickiness or unpleasant smell.

Food value
Tripe contains protein, is low in fat and high in calcium.

Brains

Calf's brains are those normally used. They must be fresh and have no unpleasant smell. They are a good source of protein with trace elements.

Tongues

Ox tongues and lamb and sheep tongues are those most used in cooking. Ox tongues are usually salted then soaked before being cooked. Lamb tongues are cooked fresh.

Quality points
- Tongues must be fresh and have no unpleasant smell.
- There should not be an excess of waste at the root end.

Head

Sheep's heads can be used for stock, pig's head for brawn (a cold meat preparation) and calf's head for speciality dishes (calf's head vinaigrette). Heads should be fresh, not sticky, well fleshed and free from any unpleasant smell.

Oxtail

Oxtails weigh usually 1½–1¾ kg (3–5 lb); they should be lean with not too much fat. There should be no sign of stickiness and no unpleasant smell.

Suet

Beef suet should be creamy white, brittle and dry. Other meat fat should be fresh, not sticky, and with no unpleasant smell.

Marrow

Marrow is obtained from the bones of the leg of beef. It should be of good size, firm, creamy white and odourless. Sliced, poached marrow may be used as a garnish for some meat dishes and savouries.

Bones

Bones must be fresh, not sticky, with no unpleasant smell and preferably meaty as they are used for stock, the foundation for so many preparations.

PRESERVATION OF MEAT

Salting

Meat can be pickled in brine, and this method of preservation may be applied to silverside, brisket and ox tongues. Salting is also used in the production of bacon, before the sides of pork are smoked, and for hams.

Chilling

This means that meat is kept at a temperature just above freezing-point in a controlled atmosphere. Chilled meat cannot be kept in the usual type of cold room for more than a few days, and this is sufficient time for the meat to hang, enabling it to become tender.

Freezing

Small carcasses, such as lamb and mutton, can be frozen and the quality is not affected by freezing. They can be kept frozen until required and then thawed out before being used. Some beef is frozen, but it is inferior in quality to chilled beef.

Canning

Large quantities of meat are canned and corned beef is of importance since it has a very high protein content. Pork is used for tinned luncheon meat.

TEXTURED VEGETABLE PROTEIN (TVP)

This is a meat substitute manufactured from protein derived from wheat, oats, cotton-seed, soyabean and other sources. The main source of TVP is the soyabean; this is due to its high protein content.

TVP is used chiefly as a meat extender, varying from 10–60% replacement of fresh meat. Some caterers on very tight budgets make use of it, but is main use is in food manufacturing.

By partially replacing the meat in certain dishes, such as casseroles, stews, pies, pasties, sausage rolls, hamburgers, meat loaf, and pâté, it is possible to reduce costs, provide nutrition and serve food acceptable in appearance.

MYCO-PROTEIN

A meat substitute e.g. quorn is produced from a plant which is a distant relative of the mushroom. This myco-protein contains protein and fibre and is the result of a fermentation process similar to the way yoghurt is made. It may be used as an alternative to chicken or beef or in vegetarian dishes.

HEALTH, SAFETY AND HYGIENE

Health, safety and hygiene guidelines are given in Chapter 1. In addition, to reduce the risk of cross-contamination:

- When preparing uncooked meat or poultry, and then cooked food, or changing from one type of meat or poultry to another, equipment, working areas and utensils must be thoroughly cleaned, or changed.
- If colour-coded boards are used, it is essential to always use the correct colour-coded boards for preparation of foods and different ones for cooked foods.
- Store uncooked meat and poultry on trays to prevent dripping, in separate refrigerators at a temperature of 3–5°C (37–41°F), but preferably at the lower

temperature. If separate refrigerators are not available then separate areas within the one refrigerator.

- Wash all work surfaces with a bactericidal detergent to kill bacteria. This is particularly important when handling poultry and pork.
- When using boning knives a safety apron acts as a protection; if a great deal of boning is being done then protective gloves are also available.

—— *Lamb and mutton* ——

As a guide when ordering, allow approximately 100 g (4 oz) meat off the bone per portion, and 150 g (6 oz) on the bone per portion. It must be clearly understood that the weights given can only be approximate. They must vary according to the quality of the meat and also for the purpose for which the meat is being butchered. For example, a chef will often cut differently from a shop butcher, i.e. a chef frequently needs to consider the presentation of the particular joint whilst the butcher is more often concerned with economical cutting. We have given simple orders of dissection for each carcass. In general, bones need to be removed only when preparing joints, so as to facilitate carving. The bones are used for stock and the excess fat can be rendered down for second-class dripping.

CLARIFICATION OF FAT

All fat trimmings can be chopped or minced and placed in a pan with a little water, then allowed to cook until there is no movement, and the fat is golden in colour. When cool, pass through a clean cloth, then use as required.

JOINTS, USES AND WEIGHTS

		APPROXIMATE WEIGHT	
JOINT	USES	LAMB KG (LB)	MUTTON KG (LB)
whole carcass		16 (32)	25 (50)
(1) shoulder (two)	roasting, stewing	3 (6)	$4\frac{1}{2}$ (9)
(2) leg (two)	roasting (mutton boiled)	$3\frac{1}{2}$ (7)	$5\frac{1}{2}$ (11)
(3) breast (two)	roasting, stewing	$1\frac{1}{2}$ (3)	$2\frac{1}{2}$ (5)
(4) middle neck	stewing	2 (4)	3 (6)
(5) scrag end	stewing, broth	$\frac{1}{2}$ (1)	1 (2)
(6) best-end (two)	roasting, grilling, frying	2 (4)	3 (6)
(7) saddle	roasting, grilling, frying	$3\frac{1}{2}$ (7)	$5\frac{1}{2}$ (11)
kidneys	grilling, sauté		
heart	braising		
liver	frying		
sweetbreads	braising, frying		
tongue	braising, boiling		

QUALITY OF LAMB (SHEEP UNDER 1 YEAR OLD) AND MUTTON

- A good quality animal should be compact and evenly fleshed.
- The lean flesh should be firm, of a pleasing dull red colour and of a fine texture or grain.
- There should be an even distribution of surface fat which should be hard, brittle and flaky in structure and a clear white colour.
- In a young animal the bones should be pink and porous, so that, when cut, a degree of blood is shown in their structure. As age progresses the bones become hard, dense, white and inclined to splinter when chopped.

ORDER OF DISSECTION OF A CARCASS

- Remove the shoulders.
- Remove the breasts.
- Remove the middle neck and scrag.
- Remove the legs.
- Divide the saddle from the best-end.

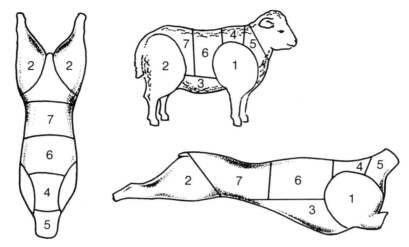

Fig 9.1: Joints of lamb

PREPARATION OF JOINTS AND CUTS

Shoulder

- *Roasting* Clean and trim the knucklebone so as to leave approximately 3 cm (1½ inch) of clean bone.
- *Boning* Remove the blade bone and upper arm bone (see below), tie with string. The shoulder may be stuffed (page 305) before tying.
- *Cutting for stews* Bone out, cut into even 25–50 g (1–2 oz) pieces.
- *Roasting* Remove the pelvic or aitchbone. Trim the knuckle cleaning 3 cm (1½ inch) of bone. Trim off excess fat and tie with string if necessary.

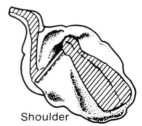

Shoulder

Fig 9.2: Shoulder of lamb

Breasts

- Remove excess fat and skin.
- *Roasting* Bone, stuff and roll, tie with string.
- *Stewing* Cut into even 25–50 g (1–2 oz) pieces.

Middle neck

- *Stewing* Remove excess fat, excess bone and the gristle. Cut into even 50 g (2 oz) pieces. This joint, when correctly butchered, can give good uncovered second-class cutlets.

Scrag-end

- *Stewing* This can be chopped down the centre, the excess bone, fat and gristle removed; cut into even 50 g (2 oz) pieces, or bone out and cut into pieces.

Saddle

- A full saddle is illustrated in Figure 9.3 including the chumps and the tail.
- For large banquets it is sometimes found better to remove the chumps and use short saddles.
- Saddles may also be boned and stuffed.

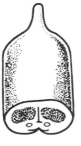

Fig 9.3: Saddle of lamb

Saddle	roasting, pot roasting (poêlé)
Loin	roasting
Fillet	grilling, frying
Loin chop	grilling, frying, stewing, braising
Chump chop	grilling, frying, stewing, braising
Kidney	grilling, sauté

The saddle may be divided as follows: remove the skin, starting from head to tail and from breast to back, split down the centre of the backbone to produce two loins; each loin can be roasted whole, boned and stuffed, or cut into loin and chump chops.

Saddle for roasting
- Skin and remove the kidney.
- Trim the excess fat and sinew.
- Cut off the flaps leaving about 15 cm (6 inches) each side so as to meet in the middle under the saddle.
- Remove the aitch or pelvic bone.

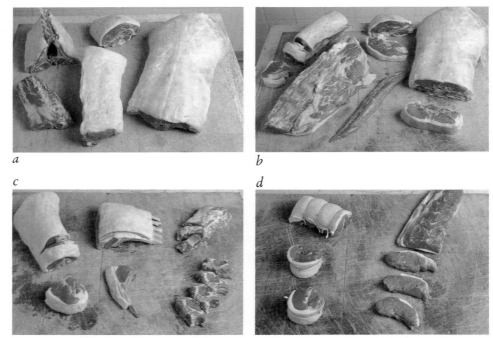

Plate 9.1: *a* Clockwise from top left: pair of best-ends; chump; full saddle; loin; middle neck.
b: Clockwise from top left: loin chop; chump chop; Barnsley chop; fillet, loin – fillet removed.
c: Left to right: loin chop; cutlet; uncovered cutlets. *d*: From left: rosettes; noisettes

- Score neatly and tie with string.
- For presentation the tail may be left on, protected with paper and tied back.
- The saddle can also be completely boned, stuffed and tied.

Loin for roasting
- Skin, remove excess fat and sinew, remove the pelvic bone, tie with string.

Loin boned and stuffed
- Remove the skin, excess fat and sinew. Bone out, replace the fillet and tie with string. When stuffed, bone out, season, stuff and tie.

Chops

Loin chops
- Skin the loin, remove the excess fat and sinew, then cut into chops approximately 100–150 g (4–6 oz) in weight.
- A first-class loin chop should have a piece of kidney skewered in the centre.

300

Double loin chop (also known as a Barnsley chop)

- These are cut approximately 2 cm (1 inch) across a saddle on the bone.
- When trimmed they are secured with a skewer and may include a piece of kidney in the centre of each chop.

Chump chops

- These are cut from the chump end of the loin.
- Cut into approximately 150 g (6 oz) chops, trim where necessary.

Noisette

- This is a cut from a boned-out loin.
- Cut slantwise into approximately 2 cm (1 inch) thick slices, bat out slightly, trim into a cutlet shape.

Rosette

- This is a cut from a boned out loin approximately 2 cm (1 inch) thick. It is shaped round and tied with string.

Best-end

Best-end preparation

- Remove the skin from head to tail and from breast to back.

Plate 9.2a–f: Preparation of best-end

301

- Remove the sinew and the tip of the blade bone.
- Complete the preparation of the rib bones as indicated in the diagram.
- Clean the sinew from between the rib bones and trim the bones.
- Score the fat neatly to approximately 2 mm ($\frac{1}{12}$ inch) deep.
- The overall length of the rib bones to be trimmed to two and a half times the length of the nut of meat.
- *Roasting* Prepare as above.
- *Cutlets* Prepare as for roasting, excluding the scoring and divide evenly between the bones, or the cutlets can be cut from the best-end and prepared separately. A double cutlet consists of two bones; therefore a 6 bone best-end yields 6 single or 3 double cutlets.

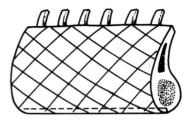

Fig 9.4: Best-end of lamb

PREPARATION OF OFFAL

Kidney

- *Grilling* Skin and split three-quarters the way through lengthwise; cut out and discard the gristle, and skewer.
- *Sauté* Skin and remove the gristle. Cut slantways into 6–8 pieces.

Hearts

- *Braising* Remove the tubes and excess fat.

Liver

- Remove skin, gristle and tubes and cut into thin slices on the slant.

Sweetbreads

- Wash well, blanch and trim.
- Soak in salted water for 2–3 hours to remove any traces of blood.

Tongue

- Remove the bone and gristle from the throat end.
- Soak in cold water for 2–4 hours. If salted, soak for 3–4 hours.

LAMB RECIPES

1 – Roasting of lamb and mutton

Allow approximately 150 g (6 oz) meat on the bone per portion (legs, shoulders, saddle or loin, best-end and breast).

1   Season the joints lightly with salt and place on a trivet, or bones, in a roasting tray.
2   Place a little vegetable oil or dripping on top and cook in a hot oven at 230–250°C (Reg. 8–9; 450–500°F).
3   Baste frequently and reduce the heat gradually when necessary, as for example in the case of large joints.
4   Roast for approximately 20 minutes per $\frac{1}{2}$ kilo (1 lb) and 20 minutes over.
5   To test if cooked, place on a tray and press firmly in order to see if the juices released contain any blood.
6   In general, all joints should be cooked through. If joints are required pink, reduce the cooking time by a quarter. For internal temperatures, see page 333.
7   Allow to stand for approximately 10–15 minutes before carving; if this is not done the meat will tend to shrink and curl.

> Using leg of lamb, 1 portion (113 g/4 oz lamb) provides:
>
> 1262 kJ/301 kcal
> 20.2 g fat
> (of which 10.5 g saturated)
> 0.0 g carbohydrate
> (of which 0.0 g sugars)
> 29.5 g protein
> 0.0 g fibre

Note   Variations include: several peeled cloves of garlic inserted into the flesh of joints before roasting; a little rosemary sprinkled into boned joints before tying.

– *Roast gravy*

This can be made at the end of roasting (see also page 130).

1   Place the roasting tray on the stove over a gentle heat to allow the sediment to settle.
2   Carefully strain off the fat, leaving the sediment in the tray.
3   Return to the stove and brown carefully, deglaze with brown stock.
4   Allow to simmer for a few minutes.
5   Correct the seasoning and colour, then strain and skim.

Note   In some establishments the gravy served with stuffed joints and also pork and veal is slightly thickened with diluted cornflour, fécule or arrowroot.

CARVING

Roast leg

Holding the bone, carve with a sharp knife at an angle of 45° and take off each slice as it is cut. Continue in this manner along the joint, turning it from side to side as the slices get wider.

Shoulder

To obtain reasonable sized slices of meat, carve the flesh side not the skin side of the joint. Having obtained the slices, carve round the bones. Due to the awkward shape of the bone structure, the shoulder may be boned out, rolled and tied before cooking to facilitate carving.

Roast saddle

- *Carving on the bone* There are two usual ways of carving the saddle, one is by carving lengthways either side of the backbone, the other by making a deep cut lengthwise either side of the backbone and then slicing across each loin. It is usual to carve the saddle in thick slices.
- *Carving off the bone* For economical kitchen carving it is often found best to bone the loins out whole, carve into slices, then re-form on the saddle bone.
- The fillets may be left on the saddle or removed; in either case they are carved and served with the rest of the meat.

Roast loin

- *On the bone* Proceed as for the saddle.
- *Boned-out* Cut in slices across the joint; when stuffed, the slices are cut slightly thicker.

Roast best-end or racks of lamb

Divide into cutlets by cutting between bones.

SERVICE

All roast joints are served garnished with watercress and a sauceboat of roast gravy separately.

When carved, serve a little gravy over the slices as well as a sauceboat of gravy. Mint sauce should be served with roast lamb and redcurrant jelly should be available. For roast mutton, redcurrant jelly and/or onion sauce should be served, with mint sauce available.

2 – Stuffing for lamb

This is used for stuffing joints, e.g. loin, shoulder, breast.

	For 1 joint
chopped suet	50 g (2 oz)
chopped onions cooked in a little butter or margarine without colour	50 g (2 oz)
egg yolk or small egg	1
white breadcrumbs	100 g (4 oz)
pinch powdered thyme	
pinch chopped parsley	
salt, pepper	
grated zest of lemon	

Combine all the ingredients together.

Note   Variations can be found on page 398. For mint sauce see page 163.

Plate 9.3: Irish stew (see recipe 18)

3 ~ Best-end of lamb with breadcrumbs and parsley

Roast the best-end; 10 minutes before cooking is completed cover the fat surface of the meat with a mixture of 25–50 g (1–2 oz) of fresh white breadcrumbs mixed with plenty of chopped parsley, an egg and 25–50 g (1–2 oz) melted butter or margarine. Return to the oven to complete the cooking, browning carefully.

Note   Variations include:

- mixed fresh herbs used in addition to parsley;
- finely chopped garlic added.

4 ~ Best-end of lamb boulanger

Any roast lamb joint may be served in this manner.

1   Prepare a dish of savoury potatoes (page 574).
2   Roast the joint.
3   Remove from the tray 15 minutes before completion of cooking.
4   Place on top of the cooked potatoes.
5   Return to the oven to complete the cooking.
6   Serve the joint whole or carved as required on the potatoes.
7   Garnish with watercress and serve with a sauceboat of gravy separately.

5 ~ Grilled cutlets

1   Season the cutlets lightly with salt and mill pepper.
2   Brush with oil or fat.
3   When cooked on the bars of the grill, place the prepared cutlet on the preheated bars which have been greased.
4   Cook for approximately 5 minutes, turn and complete the cooking.
5   When cooked under the salamander place on a greased tray, cook for approximately 5 minutes, turn and complete the cooking.
6   Serve dressed garnished with a deep-fried potato and watercress. A compound butter (parsley, herb or garlic) may also be served.
7   Each cutlet bone may be capped with a cutlet frill.

6 – Mixed grill (*Illustration page 317*)

	4 portions	10 portions
sausages	4	10
cutlets	4	10
kidneys	4	10
tomatoes	4	10
mushrooms	4	10
rashers streaky bacon	4	10
watercress		
straw potatoes		
parsley butter (page 135)		

I portion (2 cutlets) provides:

2050 kJ/488 kcal
40.8 g fat
(of which 19.3 g saturated)
0.0 g carbohydrate
(of which 0.0 g sugars)
30.4 g protein
0.0 g fibre

With straw potatoes, parsley, watercress, I portion provides:

3050 kJ/726 kcal
59.2 g fat
(of which 26.6 g saturated)
20.2 g carbohydrate
(of which 2.5 g sugars)
29.5 g protein
4.9 g fibre

These are the usually accepted items for a mixed grill, but it will be found that there are many variations to this list. Steaks, liver, a Welsh rarebit and fried egg may also be used.

1 Grill in the order given.
2 Dress neatly on an oval flat dish or plates.
3 Garnish with deep-fried potato, watercress and a slice of compound butter on each kidney.

7 – Fried cutlets

Season and carefully cook in a sauté pan. Garnish as required.

8 – Breadcrumbed cutlets

1 Pass the prepared cutlets through seasoned flour, eggwash and fresh white breadcrumbs. Pat firmly, then shake off surplus crumbs.
2 Shallow fry in hot clarified fat for the first few minutes; then allow to cook gently.
3 Turn, and continue cooking until a golden brown, for approximately 5 minutes each side.
4 To test if cooked, press firmly, no signs of blood should appear.

Note These may be served with a garnish of pasta, such as spaghetti, noodles.

Plate 9.4: Roast best-end of lamb

Plate 9.5: Preparation of mixed grill

9 ‒ Lamb cutlets Reform

1 Pass the prepared cutlets through seasoned flour, eggwash and breadcrumbs containing chopped ham and chopped parsley.
2 Cook as for crumbed cutlet.
3 Serve garnished with Reform sauce (page 128) and a sauceboat of Reform sauce separately.

10 ‒ Lamb kebabs (shish kebab)

Kebabs, a dish of Turkish origin, are pieces of food impaled and cooked on skewers over a grill or barbecue. There are many variations and different flavours can be added by marinating the kebabs in oil, wine, vinegar or lemon juice with spices and herbs for 1–2 hours before cooking. Kebabs can be made using tender cuts, or mince of lamb and beef, pork, liver, kidney, bacon, ham, sausage and chicken, using either the meats individually, or combining two or three. Vegetables and fruit can also be added (onion, apple, pineapple, peppers, tomatoes, aubergine). Kebabs can be made using vegetables exclusively (peppers, onion, aubergine, tomatoes, etc.). Kebabs are usually served with a pilaff rice (page 236).

The ideal cuts of lamb are the nut of the lean meat of the loin, best-end or boned-out meat from a young shoulder of lamb.

1 Cut the meat into squares and place them on skewers with squares of green pepper, tomato, onion and bay leaves in between.
2 Sprinkle with powdered thyme and cook over a hot grill.
3 Serve with pilaff rice, or with chick peas and finely sliced raw onion.

Note Variations include:

- Miniature kebabs (one mouthful) can be made, impaled on cocktail sticks, grilled and served as a hot snack at receptions.
- Fish kebabs can be made using a firm fish, such as monkfish, and marinating in olive oil, lemon or lime juice, chopped fennel or dill, garlic and a dash of tabasco or Worcester sauce.

11 ~ Grilled loin or chump chops or noisettes of lamb

1 Season the chops or noisettes with salt and pepper mill.
2 Brush with fat and place on hot greased grill bars or place on a greased baking tray.
3 Cook quickly for the first 2–3 minutes on each side, in order to seal the pores of the meat.
4 Continue cooking steadily, allowing approximately 12–15 minutes in all.

Note A compound butter may also be served and deep fried potatoes. Variations include sprigs of rosemary or other herbs laid on the chops during the last few minutes of grilling to impart flavour.

12 – Braised loin or chump chops

	4 portions	10 portions
chops	4	10
dripping or oil	25 g (1 oz)	60 g (2½ oz)
onion	100 g (4 oz)	250 g (10 oz)
carrot	100 g (4 oz)	250 g (10 oz)
flour, white or wholemeal	25 g (1 oz)	60 g (2½ oz)
tomato purée	1 level tsp	2½ level tsp
brown stock	500 ml (1 pt)	1¼ litre (2½ pt)
bouquet garni		
clove garlic, optional	1	2
seasoning		
chopped parsley		

1 Fry the seasoned chops in a sauté pan quickly on both sides in hot fat.
2 When turning the chops, add the mirepoix.
3 Draw aside, drain off the surplus fat.
4 Add the flour and mix in, singe in the oven or on top of the stove. (Alternatively, use flour which has been browned in the oven.)
5 Add the tomato purée and the hot stock.
6 Stir with a wooden spoon until thoroughly mixed.
7 Add the bouquet garni and garlic, season, skim and allow to simmer; cover with a lid.
8 Cook preferably in the oven, skimming off all fat and scum.
9 When cooked transfer the chops to a clean pan.
10 Correct the seasoning and consistency of the sauce.
11 Skim off any fat and pass the sauce through a fine strainer over the chops.
12 Serve, sprinkled with chopped parsley.

Note Variations includes additions after the sauce has been strained:

- cooked pulse beans (haricot, butter, flageolet);
- cooked neatly cut vegetables (carrots, turnips, swede, green beans, peas).

13 ‑ Chops Champvallon

	4 portions	10 portions
chops	4	10
flour	25 g (1 oz)	60 g (2½ oz)
dripping or oil	25 g (1 oz)	60 g (2½ oz)
onions	100 g (4 oz)	250 g (10 oz)
clove garlic (optional)	1	2
brown stock	250 ml (½ pt)	600 ml (1¼ pt)
potatoes	400 g (1 lb)	1¼ kg (2½ lb)

1 Pass the chops through seasoned flour.
2 Fry quickly on both sides in hot fat or oil.
3 Shred the onions finely and toss lightly in butter, with garlic if using, and place in a shallow earthenware dish.
4 Place the chops on top, cover with brown stock.
5 Add ¼ cm (⅛ inch) sliced potatoes neatly arranged with a knob or two of good dripping on top or brush with oil.
6 Cook in a hot oven at 230–250°C (Reg. 8–9; 450–500°F) until the potatoes are cooked and a golden brown, approximately 1½–2 hours.
7 Serve sprinkled with chopped parsley, in the cleaned earthenware dish.

14 ‑ Noisettes of lamb or fillet of lamb sauté

Season and shallow fry on both sides in a sauté pan and serve with the appropriate garnish and sauce. Unless specifically stated a jus-lié or demi-glace should be served. Fillet of lamb should be trimmed of fat and sinew before cooking.

Suitable garnishes

- Tomatoes filled with jardinère of vegetables and château potatoes.
- Balls of cauliflower Mornay and château potatoes.
- Artichoke bottoms filled with carrot balls and noisette potatoes.
- Artichoke bottoms filled with asparagus heads and noisette potatoes.
- Braised lettuce and parisienne potatoes.
- Artichoke bottoms filled with peas and cocotte potatoes.

15 ~ Valentine of lamb

1 Prepare a short saddle with all the bones, kidneys and internal fat removed.
2 Split into two loins.
3 Trim off excess fat and sinew.
4 Cut across the muscle grain into thick boneless chops.
5 Slice three parts through the lean meat and open to give a double-sized cut surface (butterfly cut).
6 Valentines are cooked in the same way as noisettes and rosettes. They may also be grilled or braised.

Note Best-end may be used in place of the loin.

16 ~ Brown lamb or mutton stew (*Navarin of lamb*)

	4 portions	10 portions
stewing lamb	500 g (1¼ lb)	1½ kg (3 lb)
oil	2 tbsp	5 tbsp
salt, pepper		
onion	100 g (4 oz)	250 g (10 oz)
carrot	100 g (4 oz)	250 g (10 oz)
clove garlic (if desired)	1	3
flour, white or wholemeal	25 g (1 oz)	60 g (2½ oz)
tomato purée	1 level tbsp	2½ level tbsp
brown stock (mutton stock or water)	500 g (1 pt)	1¼ litre (2½ pt)
bouquet garni		

Using sunflower oil, 1 portion provides:

1320 kJ/314 kcal
18.7 g fat
(of which 6.2 g saturated)
9.4 g carbohydrate
(of which 3.2 g sugars)
27.9 g protein
1.3 g fibre

1 Trim the meat and cut into even pieces.
2 Partly fry off the seasoned meat, then add the carrot, onion and garlic and continue frying.
3 Drain off the surplus fat, add the flour and mix.
4 Singe in the oven or brown on top of the stove for a few minutes or add previously browned flour.
5 Add the tomato purée and stir with a wooden spoon.
6 Add the stock and season.
7 Add the bouquet garni, bring to the boil, skim and cover with a lid.
8 Simmer gently until cooked, preferably in the oven, for approximately 1–2 hours.

9   When cooked, place the meat in a clean pan.
10   Correct the sauce and pass the sauce on to the meat.
11   Serve sprinkled with chopped parsley.

Note   A variation includes a garnish of vegetables (turned glazed carrots and turnips, glazed button onions, potatoes, peas and diamonds of French beans) which may be cooked separately or in the stew (glazed vegetables, see page 335).

17 – Curried lamb

	4 portions	10 portions
stewing lamb	500 g (1¼ lb)	1½ kg (3 lb)
oil	3 tbsp	8 tbsp
onions	200 g (8 oz)	500 g (1¼ lb)
clove garlic	1	2½
curry powder	10 g (½ oz)	25 g (1¼ oz)
flour, white or wholemeal	10 g (½ oz)	25 g (1¼ oz)
tomato purée	10 g (½ oz)	25 g (1¼ oz)
stock of water	½ litre (1 pt)	1¼ litre (2½ pt)
chopped chutney	25 g (1 oz)	60 g (2½ oz)
desiccated coconut	25 g (1 oz)	60 g (2½ oz)
sultanas	25 g (1 oz)	60 g (2½ oz)
chopped apple	50 g (2 oz)	125 g (5 oz)
grated root ginger		

Using sunflower oil, 1 portion provides:

1699 kJ/405 kcal
26.6 g fat
(of which 10.0 g saturated)
14.8 g carbohydrate
(of which 11.6 g sugars)
27.7 g protein
3.2 g fibre

1   Trim the meat and cut into even pieces.
2   Season and quickly colour in hot oil.
3   Add the chopped onion and chopped garlic, cover with a lid and sweat for a few minutes. Drain off the surplus fat.
4   Add the curry powder and flour, mix in and cook out.
5   Mix in the tomato purée and gradually add the hot stock; stir thoroughly; bring to the boil and season with salt and skim.
6   Allow to simmer and add the rest of the ingredients.
7   Cover with a lid and simmer in the oven or on top of the stove until cooked.
8   Correct the seasoning and consistency; skim off all fat. At this stage a little cream or yoghurt may be added.
9   Serve accompanied with rice which may be plain boiled, pilaff or pilaff with saffron.

recipe continued ▶

Note   This is a typical recipe in use. For a traditional recipe the curry powder would be replaced by either curry paste or a mixture of freshly ground spices, such as turmeric, cumin, allspice, fresh ginger, chilli and clove.

– *Plain boiled rice*

	4 portions	10 portions
rice (long-grain or basmati)	100 g (4 oz)	250 g (10 oz)
water	1½ litre (3 pt)	3 litre (6 pt)
salt		

1   Pick and wash the long-grain rice.
2   Add to plenty of boiling salted water.
3   Stir to the boil and simmer gently until tender, approximately 12–15 minutes.
4   Wash well under running water, drain and place on a sieve and cover with a cloth.
5   Place on a tray in a moderate oven or in the hot plate until hot.
6   Serve in vegetable dish separately.

Other accompaniments to curry
There are many other accompaniments to curry, for example, grilled Bombay duck (dried fish fillets) and poppadums (thin vegetable wafers) which are grilled or deep fried. Also:

chopped chutney	chow-chow
sultanas	quarters of orange
desiccated coconut	sliced banana
slices of lemon	chopped onions
chopped apple	diced cucumber in natural yoghurt
segments of lime	mint in natural yoghurt

See also pages 442–4.

18 ~ Irish stew

	4 portions	10 portions
stewing lamb	500 g (1¼ lb)	1½ kg (3 lb)
bouquet garni		
potatoes	400 g (1 lb)	1 kg (2½ lb)
onions	100 g (4 oz)	250 g (10 oz)
celery	100 g (4 oz)	250 g (10 oz)
Savoy cabbage	100 g (4 oz)	250 g (10 oz)
leeks	100 g (4 oz)	250 g (10 oz)
button onions	100 g (4 oz)	250 g (10 oz)
chopped parsley		

> 1 portion provides:
>
> 1339 kJ/319 kcal
> 11.2 g fat
> (of which 5.2 g saturated)
> 26.1 g carbohydrate
> (of which 5.7 g sugars)
> 30.2 g protein
> 5.0 g fibre

1 Trim the meat and cut into even pieces. Blanch and refresh.
2 Place in a shallow saucepan, cover with water, bring to the boil, season with salt and skim. If tough meat is being used, allow ½–1 hour stewing before adding any vegetables.
3 Add the bouquet garni. Turn the potatoes into barrel shapes.
4 Cut the potato trimmings, onions, celery, cabbage and leeks into small neat pieces and add to the meat; simmer for 30 minutes.
5 Add the button onions and simmer for a further 30 minutes.
6 Add the potatoes and simmer gently, with a lid on the pan until cooked.
7 Correct the seasoning and skim off all fat.
8 Serve sprinkled with chopped parsley.

Note   Optional accompaniments include Worcester sauce or pickled red cabbage.

19 ~ White lamb stew (*Blanquette of lamb*)

	4 portions	10 portions
stewing lamb	500 g (1¼ lb)	1½ kg (3 lb)
white stock	750 ml (1½ pt)	1½ litre (3 pt)
studded onion	50 g (2 oz)	125 g (5 oz)
carrot	50 g (2 oz)	125 g (5 oz)
bouquet garni		
butter or margarine	25 g (1 oz)	60 g (2½ oz)
flour	25 g (1 oz)	60 g (2½ oz)
cream, yoghurt or quark	2–3 tbsp	5 tbsp
chopped parsley		

recipe continued ▶

315

1 Trim the meat and cut into even pieces. Blanch and refresh.
2 Place in a saucepan and cover with cold water.
3 Bring to the boil then place under running cold water until all the scum has been washed away.
4 Drain and place in a clean saucepan and cover with stock, bring to the boil and skim.
5 Add whole onion and carrot, bouquet garni, season lightly with salt and simmer until tender, approximately 1–1½ hours.
6 Meanwhile prepare a blond roux with the butter and flour and make into a velouté with the cooking liquor. Cook out for approximately 20 minutes.
7 Correct the seasoning and consistency and pass through a fine strainer on to the meat, which has been placed in a clean pan.
8 Reheat, mix in the cream and serve, finished with chopped parsley.
9 To enrich this dish a liaison of yolks and cream is sometimes added at the last moment to the boiling sauce, which must not be allowed to reboil, otherwise the eggs will scramble.

20 – Cornish pasties

	4 portions	10 portions	
			1 portion provides:
short paste	200 g (½ lb)	500 g (1¼ lb)	1217 kJ/290 kcal
finely diced potato (raw)	100 g (4 oz)	250 g (10 oz)	16.2 g fat
raw lamb or beef (cut in thin pieces)	100 g (4 oz)	250 g (10 oz)	(of which 6.0 g saturated) 29.3 g carbohydrate
chopped onion	50 g (2 oz)	125 g (5 oz)	(of which 1.2 g sugars) 8.7 g protein
finely diced swede (raw) (optional)	50 g (2 oz)	125 g (5 oz)	1.8 g fibre

1 Roll out the short paste 3 mm (⅛ inch) thick and cut into rounds 12 cm (5 inches) diameter.
2 Mix the remaining ingredients together, moisten with a little water and place in the rounds in piles. Eggwash the edges.
3 Fold in half and seal, flute the edge and brush with eggwash.
4 Cook in a moderate oven at 150–200°C (Reg. 2–6; 300–400°F) for ¾–1 hour.
5 Serve with a suitable sauce, such as demi-glace.
6 A variety of cooked fillings and seasonings may be used.

Plate 9.6: Service of mixed grill

21 ～ Hot pot of lamb or mutton

	4 portions	10 portions
stewing lamb	500 g (1¼ lb)	1½ kg (3 lb)
salt and pepper		
onions	100 g (4 oz)	250 g (10 oz)
potatoes	400 g (1 lb)	1¼ kg (2½ lb)
brown stock	1 litre (2 pt)	2½ litre (5 pt)
dripping or oil	25 g (1 oz)	60 g (2½ oz)
chopped parsley		

Using sunflower oil, 1 portion provides:

1505 kJ/360 kcal
17.0 g fat
(of which 6.4 g saturated)
22.0 g carbohydrate
(of which 1.8 g sugars)
29.0 g protein
2.5 g fibre

recipe continued ▶

1   Trim the meat and cut into even pieces.
2   Place in a deep earthenware dish. Season with salt and pepper.
3   Mix the shredded onion and thinly sliced potatoes together.
4   Season and place on top of the meat; three parts cover with stock.
5   Neatly arrange an overlapping layer of 2 mm thick ($\frac{1}{12}$ inch) sliced potatoes on top.
6   Add the dripping in small pieces.
7   Thoroughly clean the edges of the dish and place to cook in a hot oven at 230–250°C (Reg. 8–9; 450–500°F) until lightly coloured.
9   Reduce the heat and simmer gently until cooked, approximately $1\frac{1}{2}$–2 hours.
10 Press the potatoes down occasionally during cooking.
11 Serve with the potatoes brushed with butter or margarine and sprinkle with chopped parsley.

Note   Variations include:

● Use leek in place of onion.
● Add 200 g ($\frac{1}{2}$ lb) lambs' kidneys.
● Quickly fry off the meat before putting in the pot.
● Add 100–200 g (4–8 oz) sliced mushrooms.
● Add a small tin of baked beans, or a layer of thickly sliced tomatoes before adding the potatoes.
● Use sausages in place of lamb.

22 – Shepherd's pie (cottage pie)

	4 portions	10 portions
chopped onion	100 g (4 oz)	250 g (10 oz)
fat or oil	35 g ($1\frac{1}{2}$ oz)	100 g (4 oz)
cooked lamb or mutton (minced)	400 g (1 lb)	$1\frac{1}{4}$ kg ($2\frac{1}{2}$ lb)
salt and pepper		
Worcester sauce	2–3 drops	5 drops
jus-lié or demi-glace	125–250 ml ($\frac{1}{4}$–$\frac{1}{2}$ pt)	300–600 ml ($\frac{3}{4}$–$1\frac{1}{2}$ pt)
cooked potato	400 g (1 lb)	$1\frac{1}{4}$ kg ($2\frac{1}{2}$ lb)
butter or margarine	25 g (1 oz)	60 g ($2\frac{1}{2}$ oz)
milk		

Using sunflower oil with hard margarine in topping, 1 portion provides:

1744 kJ/415 kcal
25.3 g fat
(of which 9.1 g saturated)
22.1 g carbohydrate
(of which 2.5 g sugars)
26.3 g protein
1.6 g fibre

1 Cook the onion in the fat or oil without colouring.
2 Add the cooked meat from which all fat and gristle has been removed.
3 Season, add Worcester sauce and add sufficient sauce to bind.
4 Bring to the boil; simmer for 10–15 minutes.
5 Place in a pie or earthenware dish.
6 Prepare the mashed potatoes and pipe or arrange neatly on top.
7 Brush with milk or eggwash.
8 Colour lightly under salamander or in a hot oven.
9 Serve accompanied with a sauceboat of jus-lié.

Note   This dish prepared with cooked beef is known as cottage pie. When using reheated meats, care must be taken to heat thoroughly and quickly.
   Variations include:

- Add 100–200 g (4–8 oz) sliced mushrooms.
- Add a layer of thickly sliced tomatoes (sprinkle with rosemary).
- Mix a tin of baked beans in with the meat.
- Sprinkle with grated cheese and brown.
- Vary the flavour of the mince by adding herbs or spices.
- The potato topping can also be varied by mixing in grated cheese, chopped spring onions or herbs, or by using duchess potato mixture.
- A meatless recipe (using TVP) will be found on page 501.

23 – Minced lamb or mutton

Prepare the meat for shepherd's pie (recipe 22). Then place on a dish which has been previously piped with a border of duchess potatoes dried for a few minutes in the oven, eggwashed and lightly browned.
   Variations include the addition of sliced mushrooms, sweetcorn, or cooked small pasta.

24 ~ Moussaka

This is a dish of Greek origin.

	4 portions	10 portions
onions	50 g (2 oz)	125 g (5 oz)
small clove garlic	1	2
butter, margarine or oil	25 g (1 oz)	60 g (2½ oz)
tomato purée	25 g (1 oz)	60 g (2½ oz)
cooked mutton, diced or minced	400–600 g (1–1½ lb)	1½ kg (3 lb)
demi-glace	125 ml (¼ pt)	600 ml (⅝ pt)
aubergine	200 g (½ lb)	500 g (1¼ lb)
tomatoes	200 g (½ lb)	500 g (1¼ lb)
flour, white or wholemeal		
oil	60 ml (⅛ pt)	150 ml (⅓ pt)
breadcrumbs	25 g (1 oz)	60 g (2½ oz)
grated Parmesan cheese	25 g (1 oz)	60 g (2½ oz)
melted butter, margarine or oil, as necessary		

> Using hard margarine and sunflower oil,
> 1 portion provides:
>
> 1909 kJ/455 kcal
> 33.3 g fat
> (of which 11.1 g saturated)
> 10.5 g carbohydrate
> (of which 5.1 g sugars)
> 28.9 g protein
> 2.8 g fibre

1 Finely chop the onions and garlic.
2 Cook in the butter, margarine or oil without colour.
3 Mix in the tomato purée and the cooked mutton.
4 Add the demi-glace and bring to the boil.
5 Correct the seasoning and allow to simmer for 10–15 minutes. The mixture should be fairly dry.
6 Peel the aubergines and cut into ½ cm (¼ inch) slices.
7 Pass the slices of aubergine through the flour.
8 Fry the slices of aubergine in shallow hot oil on both sides and drain.
9 Peel the tomatoes and cut into ½ cm (¼ inch) slices.
10 Place the mixture of mutton into an earthenware dish.
11 Cover the mixture with the slices of tomato, and then neatly with the slices of aubergine.
12 Season with salt and pepper.
13 Sprinkle with breadcrumbs, cheese and melted butter.
14 Gratinate in a hot oven at 230–250°C (Reg. 8–9; 450–500°F).
15 Sprinkle with chopped parsley and serve.

Note Variations include:

● Minced beef may be used in place of mutton.

- It may be seasoned with a little cinnamon and oregano.
- It may be finished by masking the dish, when all the ingredients have been added, with 250 ml (½ pint) (600 ml (½ pint) for 10 portions) of thin béchamel sauce to which 2 beaten eggs have been added. If this method is being adopted, then the breadcrumbs, cheese and melted butter should be added after the béchamel.
- A vegetarian recipe for Moussaka is on page 510.

25 – Grilled lambs' kidneys

1   Season the prepared skewered kidneys.
2   Brush with melted butter, margarine or oil.
3   Place on preheated greased grill bars or on a greased baking tray.
4   Grill fairly quickly on both sides, approximately 5–10 minutes depending on size.
5   Serve with parsley butter, pickled watercress and straw potatoes.

Note   Devilled kidneys are brushed with a flavoured mustard mixture during cooking.

26 – Kidney sauté

	4 portions	10 portions
sheep's kidneys	8	20
butter, fat or oil	50 g (2 oz)	125 g (5 oz)
demi-glace	250 ml (½ pt)	600 ml (1¼ pt)

Using sunflower oil, I portion provides:

1 680 kJ/400 kcal
28.3 g fat
(of which 4.3 g saturated)
15.5 g carbohydrate
(of which 3.7 g sugars)
21.8 g protein
1.8 g fibre

1   Skin and halve the kidneys.
2   Remove the sinews.
3   Cut each half into 3 or 5 pieces and season.
4   Fry quickly in a frying-pan using the butter for approximately 4–5 minutes.
5   Place in a colander to drain and discard the drained liquid.
6   Deglaze pan with demi-glace, correct the seasoning and add the kidneys.
7   Do not reboil before serving as kidneys will toughen.
8   After draining the kidneys, the pan may be deglazed with white wine, sherry or port.

recipe continued ▶

9   As an alternative, a sauce suprême (page 408) may be used in place of demi-glace.

Note   A variation includes Kidney sauté Turbigo. Cook as for kidney sauté then add 100 g (4 oz) small button mushrooms cooked in a little butter, margarine or oil, and 8 small 2-cm (1-inch) long grilled or fried chipolatas. Serve with the kidneys in an entrée dish, garnished with heart-shaped croûtons (double these amounts for 10 portions).

27 – Braised lambs' hearts

	4 portions	10 portions	Using sunflower oil, 1 portion provides:
lambs' hearts	4	10	1489 kJ/354 kcal
salt and pepper			19.0 g fat
fat or oil	25 g (1 oz)	60 g (2½ oz)	(of which 5.6 g saturated)
onions	100 g (4 oz)	250 g (10 oz)	5.0 g carbohydrate
carrots	100 g (4 oz)	250 g (10 oz)	(of which 4.3 g sugars)
brown stock	500 ml (1 pt)	1¼ litre (2½ pt)	41.2 g protein
bouquet garni			1.7 g fibre
tomato purée	10 g (½ oz)	25 g (1¼ oz)	
espagnole or demi-glace	250 ml (½ pt)	600 ml (1¼ pt)	

1   Remove tubes and excess fat from the hearts.
2   Season and colour quickly on all sides in hot fat to seal the pores.
3   Place into a small braising pan (any pan with a tight-fitting lid which may be placed in the oven) or in a casserole.
4   Place the hearts on the lightly fried, sliced vegetables.
5   Add the stock, which should be two-thirds of the way up the meat; season lightly.
6   Add the bouquet garni and tomato purée and if available add a few mushroom trimmings.
7   Bring to the boil, skim and cover with a lid and cook in a moderate oven at 150–200°C (Reg. 2–6; 300–400°F).
8   After 1½ hours add the espagnole, reboil, skim and strain.
9   Continue cooking until tender.
10 Remove the hearts and correct the seasoning, colour and consistency of the sauce.
11 Pass the sauce on to the sliced hearts and serve.

28 ～ Stuffed braised lambs' hearts

	4 portions	10 portions
lambs' hearts	4	10
salt and pepper		
chopped suet	50 g (2 oz)	125 g (5 oz)
chopped onions cooked in a little fat without colour	50 g (2 oz)	125 g (5 oz)
egg yolk or small egg	1	2
white breadcrumbs	100 g (4 oz)	250 g (10 oz)
pinch powdered thyme		
pinch chopped parsley		
selection of root vegetables		

1 Combine all the ingredients together for the stuffing.
2 Prepare as for braised hearts, then after removing the tubes fill the hearts with the stuffing.
3 Place on a lightly fried bed of root vegetables and continue as for braised hearts.
4 Cut in halves, coat with the corrected sauce and serve.

29 ～ Fried lambs' liver and bacon

	4 portions	10 portions
liver	300 g (12 oz)	1 kg (2 lb)
fat for frying	50 g (2 oz)	125 g (5 oz)
streaky bacon (4 rashers)	50 g (2 oz)	125 g (5 oz)
jus-lié	125 ml ($\frac{1}{4}$ pt)	300 ml ($\frac{5}{8}$ pt)

1 Skin the liver and remove the gristle.
2 Cut in thin slices on the slant.
3 Pass the slices of liver through seasoned flour.
4 Shake off the excess flour.
5 Quickly fry on both sides in hot fat.
6 Remove the rind and bone from the bacon and grill on both sides.
7 Serve the liver and bacon with a cordon of jus-lié and a sauceboat of jus-lié.

Lamb sweetbreads See recipes for veal sweetbreads, pages 372–374

— *Beef* —

BUTCHERY

Side of beef (approximate weight 180 kg/360 lb)

A whole side is divided between the wing ribs and the fore ribs.

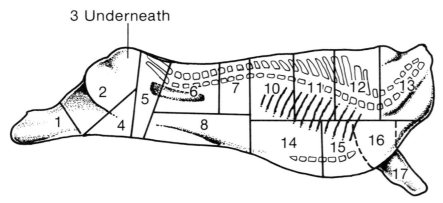

Fig 9.5: Side of beef

Hindquarter of beef

Dissection of the hindquarter

- Remove the rump suet and kidney.
- Remove the thin flank.
- Divide the loin and rump from the leg (topside, silverside, thick flank and shin).
- Remove the fillet.
- Divide rump from the sirloin.
- Remove the wing ribs.
- Remove the shin.
- Bone-out the aitchbone.
- Divide the leg into the three remaining joints (silverside, topside and thick flank).

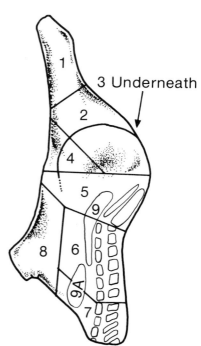

Fig 9.6: Hindquarter of beef

Joints, uses and weights of hindquarter

JOINT	USES	APPROXIMATE WEIGHT	
		(KG)	(LB)
(1) shin	consommé, beef tea, stewing	7	14
(2) topside	braising, stewing, second-class roasting	10	20
(3) silverside	pickled in brine then boiled	14	28
(4) thick flank	braising and stewing	12	24
(5) rump	grilling and frying as steaks, braised in the piece	10	20
(6) sirloin	roasting, grilling and frying in steaks	9	18
(7) wing ribs	roasting, grilling and frying in steaks	5	10
(8) thin flank	stewing, boiling, sausages	10	20
(9) fillet	roasting, grilling and frying in steaks	3	6
fat and kidney		10	20
	total weight	90	180

Preparation of joints and cuts of hindquarter

- *Shin* Bone-out, remove excess sinew. Cut or chop as required.
- *Topside*
  roasting: remove excess fat, cut into joints and tie with string;
  braising: as for roasting;
  stewing: cut into dice or steaks as required.
- *Silverside* Remove the thigh bone. This joint is usually kept whole and pickled in brine prior to boning.
- *Thick flank* As for topside.
- *Rump* Bone-out. Cut off the first outside slice for pies and puddings. Cut into approximately 1½cm (¾inch) slices for steaks. The point steak, considered the tenderest, is cut from the pointed end of the slice.

Forequarter of beef

Dissection of the forequarter
- Remove the shank.
- Divide in half down the centre.
- Take off the fore ribs.
- Divide into joints.

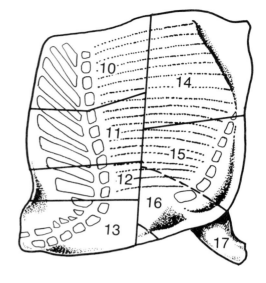

Fig 9.7: Forequarter of beef

Joints, uses and weights of forequarter

JOINT	USES	APPROXIMATE WEIGHT	
		(KG)	(LB)
(10) fore rib	roasting and braising	8	16
(11) middle rib	roasting and braising	10	20
(12) chuck rib	stewing and braising	15	30
(13) sticking piece	stewing and sausages	9	18
(14) plate	stewing and sausages	10	20
(15) brisket	pickled in brine and boiled, pressed beef	19	38
(16) leg of mutton cut	braising and stewing	11	22
(17) shank	consommé, beef tea	6	12
	total weight	88	176

Beef offal

OFFAL	USES
tongue	pickled in brine, boiling, braising
heart	braising
liver	braising, frying
kidney	stewing, soup
sweetbread	braising, frying
tripe	boiling, braising
tail	braising, soup
suet	suet paste and stuffing or rendered down for first-class dripping
bones	beef stocks
marrow	savouries and sauces

QUALITY OF BEEF

- The lean meat should be bright red, with small flecks of white fat (marbled).
- The fat should be firm, brittle in texture, creamy white in colour and odourless. Older animals and dairy breeds have fat which is usually a deeper yellow colour.

30 – Brine

cold water	$2\frac{1}{2}$ litres (8 pt)
saltpetre	15 g ($\frac{3}{4}$ oz)
salt	$\frac{1}{2}$–1 kg (1–2 lb)
bayleaf	1
juniper berries	6
brown sugar	50 g (2 oz)
peppercorns	6

recipe continued ▶

327

1 Boil the ingredients together for 10 minutes, skimming frequently.
2 Strain into a china, wooden or earthenware container.
3 When the brine is cold, add the meat.
4 Immerse the meat for up to 10 days under refrigeration.

PREPARATION OF JOINTS AND CUTS

Sirloin

● *Roasting*

Method I: whole on the bone
Saw through the chine bone, lift back the covering fat in one piece for approximately 10 cm (4 inches). Trim off the sinew and replace the covering fat. String if necessary. Ensure that the fillet has been removed.

Method II: boned-out
The fillet is removed and the sirloin boned-out and the sinew is removed as before. Remove the excess fat and sinew from the boned side. This joint may be roasted open, or rolled and tied with string.

● *Grilling and frying* Prepare as for Method II above and cut into steaks as required.

Minute steaks Cut into 1 cm ($\frac{1}{2}$ inch) slices, flatten with a cutlet bat dipped in water, making as thin as possible, then trim.

Plate 9.7: Left to right: minute steak; sirloin steak; double sirloin steak

Plate 9.8: T-bone steak; rump cut into steaks

Sirloin steaks (Entrecôte) Cut into 1 cm (½ inch) slices and trim (approximate weight 150 g, 6 oz).

Double sirloin steaks Cut into 2 cm (1 inch) thick slices and trim (approximate weight 250–300 g, 10–12 oz).

Porterhouse and T-bone steak Porterhouse steaks are cut including the bone from the rib end of the sirloin; T-bone steaks are cut from the rump end of the sirloin, including the bone and fillet.

Fillet

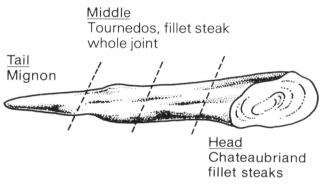

Fig 9.8: Cuts of beef

Plate 9.9: Left to right: slice of rump; whole fillet; piece of sirloin

Plate 9.10: Top: fillet chain, joint; left to right: chateaubriand, fillet steak, tournedos, tail, tail cut for stroganoff

As a fillet of beef can vary from 2½–4½ kg (5–9 lb) it follows that there must be considerable variation in the number of steaks obtained from it. A typical breakdown of a 3 kg (6 lb) fillet would be as above.

- *Chateaubriand* Double fillet steak 3–10 cm (1½–4 inches) thick, 2–4 portions. Average weight 300 g–1 kg (¾–2 lb). Cut from the head of the fillet, trim off all the nerve and leave a little fat on the steak.
- *Fillet steaks* Approximately 4 steaks of 100–150 g (4–6 oz) each 1½–2 cm (¾–1 inch) thick. These are cut as shown in the diagram and trimmed as for chateaubriand.
- *Tournedos* Approximately 6–8 at 100 g (4 oz) each, 2–4 cm (1–1½ inches) thick. Continue cutting down the fillet. Remove all the nerve and all the fat and tie each tournedos with string.
- *Tail of fillet* Approximately ½ kg (1 lb). Remove all fat and sinew and slice or mince as required.
- *Whole fillet* Preparation for roasting and pot roasting (poêlé): remove the head and tail of the fillet leaving an even centre piece from which all the nerve and fat is removed. This may be larded by inserting pieces of fat bacon cut into long strips, with a larding needle.

Wing rib

This joint usually consists of the last three rib bones which, because of their curved shape, act as a natural trivet and because of its prime quality make it a first-class roasting joint, for hot or cold, particularly when it is to be carved in front of the customer.

To prepare, cut seven-eighths of the way through the spine or chine bone, remove the nerve, saw through the rib bones on the underside 5–10 cm (2–4 inches) from the end. Tie firmly with string. When the joint is cooked the chine bone is removed to facilitate carving.

- *Thin flank* Trim off excessive fat and cut or roll as required.

Forequarter

Fore ribs and middle ribs – prepare as for wing ribs.

Chuck ribs
Sticking piece
Brisket ⎤ bone-out, remove excess fat and sinew,
Plate ⎟ use as required.
Leg of mutton cut
Shank

Beef offal

Tongue	Remove bone and gristle from the throat end.
Hearts	Remove arterial tubes and excess fat.
Liver	Skin, remove the gristle and cut in thin slices on the slant.
Kidney	Skin, remove the gristle and cut as required.
Sweetbreads	Soak in salted water for 2–3 hours to remove any traces of blood. Wash well, trim, blanch and refresh.
Tripe	Wash well and soak in cold water, then cut into even pieces.
Tail	Cut between the natural joints, trim off excess fat. The large pieces may be split in two.

BEEF RECIPES

31 ‑ Horseradish sauce

	4–6 portions	10 portions
grated horseradish	25–30 g (1–1½ oz)	60–85 g (2½–4 oz)
lightly whipped cream	120 ml (¼ pt)	300 ml (⅝ pt)
vinegar	1 tbsp	2½ tbsp
pepper, salt		

1 Wash, peel and rewash the horseradish.
2 Grate finely and mix all the ingredients together.

32 – Yorkshire pudding

	4–6 portions	10 portions
flour	100 g (4 oz)	250 g (10 oz)
salt		
egg	1	2–3
milk or milk and water	250 ml ($\frac{1}{2}$ pt)	600 ml ($1\frac{1}{4}$ pt)
dripping or oil	25 g (1 oz)	60 g ($2\frac{1}{2}$ oz)

1 Sieve the flour and salt into a basin and make a well in the centre.
2 Break in the egg, add half the liquid and whisk to a smooth mixture, gradually adding the rest of the liquid and allow to rest.
3 Select a shallow pan 15 cm (6 inches) in diameter (preferably a sauté pan).
4 Add dripping from the joint and heat in the oven.
5 Pour in the mixture and cook in a hot oven at 230–250°C (Reg. 8–9; 450–500°F) for approximately 15 minutes.

33 – Roasting of beef

Suitable joints
First class – sirloin (on the bone and boned), wing ribs, fore ribs, fillet.
Second class – topside, middle ribs.

1 Season joints with salt, place on a trivet, or bones, in a roasting tray.
2 Place a little dripping or oil on top and cook in a hot oven at 230–250°C (Reg. 8–9; 450–500°F).
3 Baste frequently and reduce the heat gradually when necessary, as for example in the case of large joints.
4 Roasting time is approximately 15 minutes per $\frac{1}{2}$ kg (1 lb) and 15 minutes over.
5 To test if cooked, place on a tray and press firmly in order to see if the juices released contain any blood.
6 Beef is normally cooked underdone and a little blood should show in the juice.
7 On removing the joint from the oven, rest for 15 minutes to allow the meat to set and facilitate carving, then carve against the grain.

Note Serve the slices moistened with a little gravy. Garnish with Yorkshire

1 portion provides:

911 kJ/217 kcal
10.3 g fat
(of which 4.7 g saturated)
0.0 g carbohydrate
(of which 0.0 g sugars)
31.2 g protein
0.0 g fibre

pudding (recipe 32) (allowing 25 g (1 oz) flour per portion) and watercress. Serve separately sauceboats of gravy and horseradish sauce.

Some roughly chopped onion, carrot, celery can be added to the roasting tray approximately 30 minutes before the joint is cooked to give additional flavour.

Roast gravy

This can be made when the joint is cooked and removed from the roasting tray (see page 303).

TESTING FOR COOKING OF MEAT JOINTS

Using a temperature probe

When using a temperature probe, insert it into the thickest part of the joint before placing the food in the oven. The internal temperature reached should be:

Rare meat	55–60°C (130–140°F)
Medium done	66–71°C (150–160°F)
Just done	78–80°C (172–176°F)

Without using a temperature probe:

- Remove the joint from the oven and place onto a plate or dish.
- Firmly press the surface of the meat so that some juice issues.
- Check the colour of the juice:

> *red* indicates the meat is underdone;
> *pink* indicates the meat is medium done;
> *clear* indicates the meat is cooked through.

34 – Boiled silverside, carrots and dumplings

	4 portions	10 portions
silverside	400 g (1 lb)	1¼ kg (2½ lb)
onions	200 g (8 oz)	500 g (1¼ lb)
carrots	200 g (8 oz)	500 g (1¼ lb)
suet paste (page 666)	100 g (4 oz)	250 g (10 oz)

1 portion provides:

1068 kJ/254 kcal
10.1 g fat
(of which 4.6 g saturated)
15.5 g carbohydrate
(of which 5.5 g sugars)
26.3 g protein
2.6 g fibre

1 Soak the meat in cold water to remove excess brine for 1–2 hours.

recipe continued ▶

2 Place in a saucepan and cover with cold water,
   bring to the boil, skim and simmer for 45 minutes.
3 Add the whole prepared onions and carrots and simmer until cooked.
4 Divide the suet paste into even pieces, lightly mould into balls.
5 Add the dumplings and simmer for a further 15–20 minutes.
6 Serve by carving the meat across the grain, garnish with carrots, onions and
   dumplings and moisten with a little of the cooking liquor.

Note   It is usual to cook a large joint of silverside (approximately 6 kg [12 lb]), in
which case soak it overnight and allow 25 minutes per ½ kg (1 lb) plus 25 minutes.

35 – Boiled beef – French style

	4 portions	10 portions
thin flank or brisket	600 g (1½ lb)	1½ kg (3½ lb)
salt, pepper		
head celery	1	2½
leek	200 g (8 oz)	500 g (1¼ lb)
small cabbage	1	2–3
onions	200 g (8 oz)	500 g (1¼ lb)
turnips	100 g (4 oz)	250 g (10 oz)
carrots	200 g (8 oz)	500 g (1¼ lb)

This recipe provides for 4 portions:

4178 kJ/995 kcal
28.3 g fat
(of which 12.5 g saturated)
50.4 g carbohydrate
(of which 49.9 g sugars)
137.1 g protein
29.6 g fibre

1 Blanch and refresh the meat.
2 Place in a clean pan and cover with cold water.
3 Bring to the boil and skim, season and allow to simmer.
4 Prepare all the vegetables by tying the celery and leek into bundles and by tying
   the cabbage to keep it in one piece; leave the rest of the vegetables whole.
5 After the meat has simmered for 30 minutes, add the celery, onions and carrots
   and continue cooking for 30 minutes.
6 Add the leek, cabbage and turnips and continue cooking until everything is
   tender, approximately 2–2½ hours.
7 Serve by carving the meat in slices against the grain, garnish with the vegetables
   and a little liquor over the meat.

Note   This dish may be accompanied by pickled gherkins and coarse salt.

36 – Brown beef stew (*Ragoût of beef*)

	4 portions	10 portions
prepared stewing beef	400 g (1 lb)	1¼ kg (2½ lb)
dripping or oil	25 g (1 oz)	60 g (2½ oz)
onions	75 g (3 oz)	180 g (7½ oz)
carrots	75 g (3 oz)	180 g (7½ oz)
flour, white or wholemeal	25 g (1 oz)	60 g (2½ oz)
tomato purée	1 tbsp	2½ tbsp
brown stock	750 ml (1½ pt)	2¼ litre (4½ pt)
bouquet garni		
clove of garlic (if desired)	1	2
seasoning		

> Using sunflower oil 1 portion provides:
>
> 907 kJ/216 kcal
> 11.0 g fat
> (of which 2.9 g saturated)
> 7.7 g carbohydrate
> (of which 2.5 g sugars)
> 21.9 g protein
> 1.0 g fibre

1 Remove excess sinew and fat from the beef.
2 Cut into 2 cm (1 inch) pieces.
3 Fry quickly in hot fat until lightly browned.
4 Add roughly cut onion and carrot and continue frying to a golden colour.
5 Add the flour and mix in; singe in the oven or brown on top of the stove for a few minutes, or use previously browned flour.
6 Add the tomato purée and stir in with a wooden spoon.
7 Mix in the stock, bring to the boil and skim.
8 Add the bouquet garni and garlic, season and cover with a lid; simmer gently until cooked, preferably in the oven, approximately 1½–2 hours.
9 When cooked place the meat into a clean pan.
10 Correct the sauce and pass on to the meat.
11 Serve with chopped parsley sprinkled on top of the meat.

Note Variations include:

● Add a cooked pulse bean (butter, haricot, flageolet).
● Add lightly sautéed mushrooms, wild or cultivated, once sauce is strained.
● Glazed vegetables can be added as a garnish.

– Glazed vegetables

Glazed carrots, turnips and button onions, peas and diamonds of French beans, and mushrooms may be used. The vegetables are cooked separately and they may be mixed in, arranged in groups or sprinkled on top of the stew.

recipe continued ▶

Plate 9.11a–c: Right: (background) boiled beef French-style;
(foreground) boiled silverside with carrots, onions and dumplings
Left: (top) ingredients for boiled beef French-style; (bottom) boiled silverside ingredients

1   To cook glazed carrots and turnips, turn or cut into even shapes.
2   Barely cover with water in separate thick-bottomed pans and add 25–50 g
    (1–2 oz) butter or margarine per $\frac{1}{2}$ kg (1 lb) of vegetables.
3   Season very lightly and allow to cook fairly quickly so as to evaporate the
    water.
4   Check that the vegetables are cooked, if not add a little more water; then toss
    over a quick fire to give a glossy appearance and a little colour.
5   Care should be taken with turnips as they may break up easily.
6   Button mushrooms, if of good quality, need not be peeled, but a slice should be
    removed from the base of the stalk. Wash well, then use whole, halved,
    quartered or turned, depending on their size. They may be coloured first in the
    oil, butter or margarine, then cooked in a little stock and butter and seasoned
    lightly; cover with a lid and cook for a few minutes only.

●   Beef Bourguignonne is a brown beef stew using red wine in place of stock and garnishing with glazed button onions, sautéed button mushrooms and lardons of bacon and heart-shaped croûtons.

Plate 9.12: Beef Bourguignonne (p. 336)

37 – Grilled beef

Approximate weight per portion 100–150 g (4–6 oz); in many establishments these weights will be exceeded.

Rump steak
Point steak
Double fillet steak (chateaubriand)
Fillet steak
Tournedos
Porterhouse or T-bone steak
Sirloin steak (entrecôte)
Double sirloin steak
Minute steak

I portion (100 g cooked weight) provides:

706 kJ/168 kcal
6.0 g fat
(of which 2.7 g saturated)
0.0 g carbohydrate
(of which 0.0 g sugars)
28.6 g protein
0.0 g fibre

All steaks may be lightly seasoned with salt and pepper and brushed on both sides with oil. Place on hot preheated greased grill bars. Turn half-way through the cooking and brush occasionally with oil. Cook to the degree ordered by the customer.

Serve garnished with watercress, deep-fried potato, and offer a suitable sauce, such as compound butter or sauce béarnaise.

DEGREES OF COOKING GRILLED MEATS

Rare   Just done
Underdone   Well done

Using a temperature probe

Rare   45–50°C (115–125°F)
Under done   55–60°C (130–140°F)
Just done   75–77°C (167–172°F)

Without a temperature probe

Test with finger pressure and the springiness or resilience of the meat together with the amount of blood issuing from the meat indicates the degree to which the steak is cooked. This calls for experience, but if the meat is placed on a plate and tested, then the more underdone the steak the greater the springiness and the more blood will be shown on the plate.

38 – Sirloin steak with mushroom, tomato, tarragon and white wine sauce (*Steak chasseur*)

	4 portions	10 portions
butter or oil	50 g (2 oz)	125 g (5 oz)
sirloin steaks 150–200 g (6–8 oz)	4	10
dry white wine	60 ml ($\frac{1}{8}$ pt)	150 ml ($\frac{1}{3}$ pt)
chasseur sauce (page 123)	$\frac{1}{4}$ litre ($\frac{1}{2}$ pt)	600 ml ($1\frac{1}{4}$ pt)
chopped parsley		

1 Heat the butter in a sauté pan.
2 Lightly Season the steaks on both sides with salt and pepper.
3 Fry the steaks quickly on both sides, keep them underdone.
4 Dress the steaks on a serving dish.

5   Pour off the fat from the pan.
6   Deglaze with the white wine. Reduce by half and strain.
7   Add the chasseur sauce, reboil, correct the seasoning.
8   Coat the steaks with the sauce.
9   Sprinkle with chopped parsley and serve.

39 ~ Sirloin steak with red wine sauce

	4 portions	10 portions
butter or oil	50 g (2 oz)	125 g (5 oz)
sirloin steaks 150–200 g (6–8 oz)	4	10
red wine	60 ml ($\frac{1}{8}$ pt)	150 ml ($\frac{1}{3}$ pt)
red wine sauce (page 123)	$\frac{1}{4}$ litre ($\frac{1}{2}$ pt)	$\frac{1}{2}$ litre (1 pt)
beef bone marrow	100 g (4 oz)	250 g (10 oz)
chopped parsley		

Using sunflower oil, I portion (150 g/60 oz raw steak) provides:

3013 kJ/717 kcal
62.2 g fat
(of which 21.6 g saturated)
6.0 g carbohydrate
(of which 3.0 g sugars)
26.1 g protein
1.4 g fibre

Using sunflower oil, I portion (200 g/8 oz raw steak) provides:

3584 kJ/853 kcal
73.6 g fat
(of which 26.2 g saturated)
6.0 g carbohydrate
(of which 3.0 g sugars)
34.4 g protein
1.4 g fibre

1   Heat the butter in a sauté pan.
2   Lightly season the steaks on both sides with salt and pepper.
3   Fry the steaks quickly on both sides, keep them underdone.
4   Dress the steaks on a serving dish.
5   Pour off the fat from the pan.
6   Deglaze with the red wine. Reduce by a half and strain.
7   Add the bordelaise sauce, reboil and correct seasoning.
8   Cut the marrow into $\frac{1}{2}$ cm ($\frac{1}{4}$ inch) slices.
9   Poach the marrow in a little stock for 1–2 minutes.
10 Dress two slices of marrow on each steak.
11 Coat the steaks with the sauce.
12 Sprinkle with chopped parsley and serve.

Plate 9.13a–c: Stages involved in grilling steak

40 ‑ Tournedos

Lightly season and shallow fry on both sides in a sauté pan and serve with the appropriate garnish or sauce. It is usual to serve the tournedos cooked underdone on a round croûte of bread fried in butter.

Tournedos can be served with a variety of sauces such as chasseur, red wine, mushroom, etc. and numerous garnishes (diced cubed potatoes, wild or cultivated mushroom, etc.).

41 ‑ Curried beef

Proceed as for Curried lamb on page 313 using 500 g (1¼ lb) stewing beef.

Plate 9.14: Grilled T-bone steak

Plate 9.15: Fried sirloin steak with French fried onions, sauté potatoes and French beans; uncooked and cooked stir-fry

42 – Steak pudding

	4 portions	10 portions
suet paste (page 666)	200 g (8 oz)	500 g (1¼ lb)
prepared stewing beef (chuck rib)	400 g (1 lb)	1¼ kg (2½ lb)
Worcester sauce		
chopped parsley	1 tsp	2½ tsp
salt, pepper		
onion (optional)	50–100 g (2–4 oz)	200 g (8 oz)
water (approximately)	125 ml (¼ pt)	300 ml (⅝ pt)

> 1 portion provides:
>
> 1369 kJ/326 kcal
> 17.3 g fat
> (of which 7.8 g saturated)
> 20.6 g carbohydrate
> (of which 1.0 g sugars)
> 23.0 g protein
> 1.1 g fibre

1   Line a greased ¾ litre (1½ pint) basin with three-quarters of the used paste and retain one-quarter for the top.

recipe continued ▶

2   Mix all the other ingredients together.
3   Place in the basin with the water to within 1 cm ($\frac{1}{2}$ inch) of the top.
4   Moisten the edge of the suet paste, cover with the top and seal firmly.
5   Cover with greased greaseproof paper and also, if possible, foil or a pudding cloth securely tied with string.
6   Cook in a steamer for at least 3$\frac{1}{2}$ hours.
7   Serve with the paper and cloth removed, clean the basin, place on a round flat dish and fasten a serviette round the basin.

Note   Extra gravy should be served separately. If the gravy in the pudding is to be thickened, the meat can be lightly floured.
   Variations include:

● Add 50–100 g (2–4 oz) ox or sheep's kidneys cut in pieces with skin and gristle removed.
● Add 50–100 g (2–4 oz) sliced or quartered mushrooms.

   This may also be made with a cooked filling, in which case simmer the meat until cooked in brown stock with onions, parsley, Worcester sauce and seasoning. Cool quickly and proceed as before, steaming for 1–1$\frac{1}{2}$ hours.

43 – Sauté of beef

This term is often applied to a brown beef stew, and it will be found that the word 'sauté' in this case is used instead of the word 'ragoût'. Alternatively, a sauté may be made using first-quality meat, e.g. fillet. The meat is then sautéed quickly (see page 100) and served in a finished sauce; this would be a typical à la carte dish.

44 – Beef Stroganoff

	4 portions	10 portions
fillet of beef (tail end)	400 g (1 lb)	1$\frac{1}{4}$ kg (2$\frac{1}{2}$ lb)
butter, margarine or oil	50 g (2 oz)	125 g (5 oz)
finely chopped shallots	25 g (1 oz)	60 g (2$\frac{1}{2}$ oz)
dry white wine	125 ml ($\frac{1}{4}$ pt)	300 ml ($\frac{5}{8}$ pt)
cream	125 ml ($\frac{1}{4}$ pt)	300 ml ($\frac{5}{8}$ pt)
lemon, juice of	$\frac{1}{4}$	$\frac{1}{2}$
chopped parsley		

Using sunflower oil, 1 portion provides:

1364 kJ/325 kcal
23.7 g fat
(of which 7.9 g saturated)
1.7 g carbohydrate
(of which 1.7 g sugars)
21.2 g protein
0.3 g fibre

1 Cut the meat into strips approximately $1 \times 5\,cm$ ($\frac{1}{2} \times 2$ inches).
2 Place the butter in a sauteuse over a fierce heat.
3 Add the beef strips, lightly season with salt and pepper and allow to cook rapidly for a few seconds. The beef should be brown but underdone.
4 Drain the beef into a colander.
5 Pour the butter back into the pan.
6 Add the shallots, cover with a lid and allow to cook gently until tender.
7 Drain off the fat, add the wine and reduce to one-third.
8 Add the cream and reduce by a quarter.
9 Add the lemon juice and the beef strips; do not reboil.
10 Correct the seasoning.
11 Serve lightly sprinkled with chopped parsley.
12 Accompany with rice pilaff.

45 – Goulash

	4 portions	10 portions
prepared stewing beef	400 g (1 lb)	1¼ kg (2½ lb)
lard or oil	35 g (1½ oz)	100 g (4 oz)
onions, chopped	100 g (4 oz)	250 g (10 oz)
flour	25 g (1 oz)	60 g (2½ oz)
paprika	10–25 g (½–1 oz)	25–60 g (1¼–2½ oz)
tomato purée	25 g (1 oz)	60 g (2½ oz)
stock or water (approximately)	750 ml (1½ pt)	2 litre (4 pt)
turned potatoes or small new potatoes	8	20
choux paste	125 ml (¼ pt)	300 ml (1 pt)

1 Remove excess fat from the beef.
2 Cut into 2 cm (1 inch) square pieces.
3 Season and fry in the hot fat until slightly coloured.
4 Add the chopped onion.
5 Cover with a lid and sweat gently for 3 or 4 minutes.
6 Add the flour and paprika and mix in with a wooden spoon.
7 Cook out in the oven or on top of the stove.
8 Add the tomato purée, mix in.
9 Gradually add the stock, stir to the boil, skim, season and cover.
10 Allow to simmer, preferably in the oven, for approximately 1½–2 hours until the meat is tender.

recipe continued ▶

11 Add the potatoes and check that they are covered with the sauce. (Add more stock if required.)
12 Re-cover with the lid and cook gently until the potatoes are cooked.
13 Skim and correct the seasoning and consistency. A little cream or yoghurt may be added at the last moment.
14 Serve sprinkled with a few gnocchis, reheated in hot salted water or lightly tossed in butter or margarine.

Note In Hungary this traditional dish is called *gulyas*.

– *Choux paste for gnocchi* (as a garnish, sufficient for 8 portions)

1 Prepare the choux paste following the recipe on page 666 omitting the sugar.
2 Place the mixture into a piping bag with a $\frac{1}{2}$cm ($\frac{1}{4}$inch) or 1 cm ($\frac{1}{2}$inch) plain tube.
3 Pipe into a shallow pan of gently simmering salted water, cutting the mixture into 2 cm (1 inch) lengths with a small knife, dipping the knife into the water frequently to prevent sticking.
4 Poach very gently for approximately 10 minutes. If not required at once lift out carefully into cold water and when required reheat in hot salted water.

46 – Steak pie

	4 portions	10 portions
prepared stewing beef (chuck rib)	400 g (1 lb)	1$\frac{1}{2}$kg (2$\frac{1}{2}$lb)
oil or fat	50 ml (2 fl oz)	125 ml (5 fl oz)
onion, chopped (optional)	100 g (4 oz)	250 g (10 oz)
water, stock, red wine or dark beer	125 ml ($\frac{1}{4}$pt)	300 ml ($\frac{5}{8}$pt)
salt, pepper		
few drops Worcester sauce		
chopped parsley	1 tsp	3 tsp
cornflour	10 g ($\frac{1}{2}$oz)	25 g (1$\frac{1}{2}$oz)
short, puff or rough puff pastry (pages 661, 662, 664)	100 g (4 oz)	250 g (10 oz)

1 Cut the meat into 2 cm (1 inch) strips then cut into squares.
2 Heat the oil in a frying pan until smoking, add the meat and quickly brown on all sides.
3 Drain the meat off in a colander.

4 Lightly fry the onion.
5 Place the meat, onion, Worcester sauce, parsley and the liquid in a pan, season lightly with salt and pepper.
6 Bring to the boil, skim, then allow to simmer gently until the meat is tender.
7 Dilute the cornflour with a little water, stir into the simmering mixture, reboil and correct seasoning.
8 Place the mixture into a pie dish and allow to cool.
9 Cover with pastry, eggwash and bake at 200°C (Reg. 6; 400°F) for approximately 30–45 minutes.

Note 25–50% wholemeal flour may be used in place of plain flour.
  Variations include:

- Adding 50–100 g (2–4 oz) ox or sheep's kidneys with skin and gristle removed and cut into neat pieces.
- Adding 50–100 g (2–4 oz) sliced or quartered mushrooms.
- Adding 1 heaped teaspoon tomato purée and some mixed herbs.

47 – Carbonnade of beef

	4 portions	10 portions
lean beef (topside)	400 g (1 lb)	1¼ kg (2½ lb)
flour, white or wholemeal	25 g (1 oz)	60 g (2½ oz)
dripping or oil	25 g (1 oz)	60 g (2½ oz)
sliced onions	200 g (8 oz)	500 g (1¼ lb)
beer	250 ml (½ pt)	600 ml (1¼ pt)
castor sugar	10 g (½ oz)	25 g (1¼ oz)
tomato purée	25 g (1 oz)	60 g (2½ oz)
brown stock	500 ml (1 pt)	1¼ kg (2½ pt)

1 Cut the meat into thin slices.
2 Season with salt and pepper and pass through the flour.
3 Quickly colour on both sides in hot fat and place in a casserole.
4 Fry the onions to a light brown colour. Add to the meat.
5 Add the beer, sugar and tomato purée and sufficient brown stock to cover the meat.

recipe continued ▶

6 Cover with a tight-fitting lid and simmer gently in a moderate oven at 150–200°C (Reg. 2–6; 300–400°F) until the meat is tender, for approximately 2 hours.
7 Skim, correct the seasoning and serve.

Note This is a traditional Flemish (Belgian) dish.

48 – Braised steaks

	4 portions	10 portions
stewing beef	400 g (1 lb)	1¼ kg (2½ lb)
fat or oil	25 g (1 oz)	60 g (2½ oz)
onions	75 g (3 oz)	180 g (7½ oz)
carrots	75 g (3 oz)	180 g (7½ oz)
flour, browned in the oven	25 g (1 oz)	60 g (2½ oz)
tomato purée	25 g (1 oz)	60 g (2½ oz)
brown stock	750 ml (1½ pt)	2 litre (4 pt)
bouquet garni		
clove of garlic (if desired)	1	2–3
seasoning		

1 Remove excess sinew and fat from the beef.
2 Cut into ½–1 cm (¼–½ inch) thick steaks.
3 Fry quickly in hot fat until lightly browned.
4 Add the roughly cut onion and carrot and continue frying to a golden colour. Mix in the flour.
5 Add the tomato purée and stir in with a wooden spoon.
6 Mix in the stock, bring to the boil and skim.
7 Add the bouquet garni and garlic, season and cover with a lid and simmer gently until cooked, preferably in the oven, approximately 1½–2 hours.
8 When cooked place the meat into a clean pan.
9 Correct the sauce and pass on to the meat.
10 Serve lightly sprinkled with chopped parsley.

Note Braised steaks may be garnished with vegetables (turned or cut in neat, even pieces), or a pasta, e.g., noodles.

49 ~ Braised beef

	4 portions	10 portions
lean beef (topside or thick flank)	400 g (1 lb)	1¼ kg (2½ lb)
fat or oil	25 g (1 oz)	60 g (2½ oz)
onions	100 g (4 oz)	250 g (10 oz)
carrots	100 g (4 oz)	250 g (10 oz)
brown stock	500 ml (1 pt)	1¼ litre (2½ pt)
bouquet garni		
tomato purée	25 g (1 oz)	60 g (2½ oz)
demi-glace or jus-lié	250 ml (½ pt)	600 ml (1¼ pt)

Using sunflower oil, 1 portion provides:

1380 kJ/329 kcal
14.3 g fat
(of which 3.3 g saturated)
26.8 g carbohydrate
(of which 4.7 g sugars)
24.7 g protein
2.4 g fibre

Method I

1 Trim and tie the joint securely.
2 Season and colour quickly on all sides in hot fat to seal the pores.
3 Place into a small braising pan (any pan with a tight-fitting lid which may be placed in the oven) or in a casserole.
4 Place the joint on the lightly fried, sliced vegetables.
5 Add the stock, which should be two-thirds of the way up the meat, season lightly.
6 Add the bouquet garni and tomato purée and if available add a few mushroom trimmings.
7 Bring to the boil, skim and cover with a lid and cook in a moderate oven at 150–200°C (Reg. 2–6; 300–400°F).
8 After approximately 1½ hours cooking, remove the meat.
9 Add the demi-glace or jus lié, reboil, skim and strain.
10 Replace the meat, do not cover, but baste frequently and continue cooking for approximately 2–2½ hours in all. Braised beef should be well cooked (approximately 35 minutes per ½ kg (1 lb) plus 35 minutes. To test if cooked, pierce with a trussing needle, which should penetrate the meat easily and there should be no sign of blood.
11 Remove the joint and correct the colour, seasoning and consistency of the sauce.
12 To serve: remove the string and carve slices across the grain. Pour some of the sauce over the slices and serve the remainder of the sauce in a sauceboat.

Note Suitable garnishes include spring vegetables (see page 533), or pasta, e.g., noodles (page 222).

Red wine may be used in place of stock.

recipe continued ▶

Plate 9.16: Ingredients for braised beef

Plate 9.17: Larding in preparation for braising

Plate 9.18: Plated service of braised beef with noodles (p. 223) and courgettes; top: ratatouille (p. 527) and joint of braised beef

Method II

As for Method I, but use for cooking liquor either:

- jus-lié;
- half brown stock or red wine and half demi-glace.

Method III

As for Method I, but when the joint and vegetables are browned, sprinkle with 25 g (1 oz) (60 g, 2½ oz for 10 portions) flour and singe in the oven, add the tomato purée, stock and bouquet garni; season and complete the recipe.

50 – Braised steak and dumplings

1   Cut the beef into ½–1 cm (¼–½ inch) thick steaks and proceed as for brown beef stew (recipe 36).

2 Prepare 100 g (4 oz) suet paste (page 666) and make 8 dumplings (increase the amount for 10 portions).

3 After the meat has cooked for 1½ hours, pick out the meat and place into a clean pan.

4 Strain the sauce on to the meat.

5 Reboil and correct the seasoning and consistency, which should be fairly thin. Add sufficient to cover the dumplings.

6 Cover with a lid.

7 Complete cooking, preferably in the oven for ¾–1 hour at 150–200°C (Reg. 2–6; 300–400°F). Alternatively, the dumplings can be cooked gently in simmering salted water, for approximately 20 minutes, drained and served with the braised steak.

8 Skim off all the fat and serve.

51 – Beef olives

	4 portions	10 portions
stuffing	50 g (2 oz)	125 g (5 oz)
lean beef	400 g (1 lb)	1¼ kg (2½ lb)
fat or oil	35 g (1½ oz)	85 g (4 oz)
carrot	100 g (4 oz)	250 g (10 oz)
onion	100 g (4 oz)	250 g (10 oz)
flour (browned in the oven)	25 g (1 oz)	60 g (2½ oz)
tomato purée	25 g (1 oz)	60 g (2½ oz)
brown stock	500–750 ml (1–1½ pt)	1¼–1½ litre (2½–3 pt)
bouquet garni		

1 Prepare the stuffing (below).

2 Cut the meat into thin slices across the grain and bat out.

3 Trim to approximately 10 × 8 cm (4 × 3 inches), chop the trimmings finely and add to the stuffing.

4 Season the slices of meat lightly with salt and pepper and spread a quarter of the stuffing down the centre of each slice.

5 Roll up neatly and secure with string.

6 Fry off the meat to a light brown colour add the vegetables and continue cooking to a golden colour.

7 Drain off the fat into a clean pan and make up to 25 g (1 oz) fat if there is not enough (increase the amount for 10 portions). Mix in the flour.

recipe continued ▶

8   Mix in the tomato purée, cool, and mix in the boiling stock.
9   Bring to the boil, skim, season and pour on to the meat.
10   Add the bouquet garni.
11   Cover and simmer gently, preferably in the oven, for approximately $1\frac{1}{2}$–2 hours.
12   Remove the string from the meat.
13   Skim and correct the sauce and pass on to the meat.

– Stuffing

	4 portions	10 portions
white or wholemeal breadcrumbs	50 g (2 oz)	125 g (5 oz)
chopped parsley	1 tsp	3 tsp
pinch of thyme		
egg to bind	approximately $\frac{1}{2}$	1
prepared chopped suet	5 g ($\frac{1}{4}$ oz)	25 g (1 oz)
sweated onion, finely chopped	25 g (1 oz)	60 g ($2\frac{1}{2}$ oz)
salt, pepper		

Mix all the ingredients together with the chopped meat trimmings. Other stuffings may be used, for example sausage meat, various herbs, duxelle, etc.

52 – Hamburg or Vienna steak

	4 portions	10 portions
finely chopped onion	25 g (1 oz)	60 g (2½ oz)
butter, margarine or oil	10 g (½ oz)	25 g (1¼ oz)
leaned minced beef	200 g (½ lb)	500 g (1¼ lb)
small egg	1	2–3
breadcrumbs	100 g (4 oz)	250 g (10 oz)
cold water or milk (approximately)	2 tbsp	60 ml (⅛ pt)
salt and pepper		

> 1 portion provides:
>
> 681 kJ/162 kcal
> 6.7 g fat
> (of which 1.9 g saturated)
> 12.7 g carbohydrate
> (of which 1.0 g sugars)
> 13.8 g protein
> 1.0 g fibre

1 Cook the onion in the fat without colour, then allow to cool.
2 Add to the rest of the ingredients and mix in well.
3 Divide into even pieces and using a little flour make into balls, flatten and shape round.
4 Shallow fry in hot fat on both sides, reducing the heat after the first few minutes, making certain they are cooked right through.
5 Serve with a light sauce, such as sauce piquante (page 126).

Note The steaks may be garnished with French fried onions (page 545) and sometimes with a fried egg.

53 – Hamburger, American style

Hamburgers now more commonly known as burgers, were originally made using 200 g (8 oz) of minced beef per portion. The meat should be pure beef with 20–25% beef fat by weight. Less fat than this will cause a tough, dry hamburger. If more fat is used the hamburgers will be unpalatable, nutritionally undesirable and will shrink considerably during cooking.

The meat should be passed twice through a mincer which helps to make for a more tender product. The minced meat should be lightly mixed and moulded into patties. Overmixing the beef can cause toughness.

Hamburgers should not be pricked whilst cooking as the juices will seep out leaving a dry product.

recipe continued ▶

Variations in seasonings and ingredients can be added to the minced beef, but traditionally the sauces and garnishes offered are sufficient. These can include: ketchup, mustard, mayonnaise, chilli sauce, horseradish, cheese, raw onion rings, lettuce, avocado slices, bacon and various pickles and relishes; freshly fried chips and/or cut pieces of raw vegetables (carrot, celery, spring onions, etc.) can be added. The bun may be plain or seeded (sesame seeds).

Alternative fillings can include:

- *cheese*: either on its own, or added to the beef;
- *egg*: a freshly fried egg, or added to the beef;
- *chicken*: a freshly grilled portion of chicken either minced, or in the piece;
- *fish*: a freshly grilled portion of a whole fish (cod or haddock);
- *vegetables*: a selection of freshly grilled, or fried vegetables (onions, peppers, aubergines, mushrooms, etc.).

Note Mini burgers (one mouthful) can be served as hot snacks at receptions.

54 – Tripe and onions

	4 portions	10 portions
tripe	400 g (1 lb)	$1\frac{1}{4}$ kg ($2\frac{1}{2}$ lb)
milk and water	500 ml (1 pt)	$1\frac{1}{4}$ litre ($2\frac{1}{2}$ pt)
onions	200 g (8 oz)	500 g ($1\frac{1}{4}$ lb)
salt, pepper		
flour or cornflour	25 g (1 oz)	60 g ($2\frac{1}{2}$ oz)

1 Wash the tripe well. Cut into neat 5 cm (2 inches) squares.
2 Blanch and refresh.
3 Cook the tripe in the milk and water with the sliced onions.
4 Season and simmer for $1\frac{1}{2}$–2 hours.
5 Gradually add the diluted flour or cornflour, stir with a wooden spoon to the boil.
6 Simmer for 5–10 minutes correct the seasoning and serve.

Note An alternative thickening is 125 ml ($\frac{1}{4}$ pt) (310 ml, $\frac{5}{8}$ pt for 10 portions) of béchamel in place of the cornflour and milk.

55 ~ Ox tongue

Ox tongues are usually pickled in brine. Wash and place in cold water, bring to the boil, skim and simmer for 3–4 hours. Cool slightly and peel off the skin and trim off the root. Secure into a neat shape either on a board or in a wooden frame. Unsalted ox tongues may also be braised whole.

56 ~ Braised ox tongue with Madeira sauce

Cut the cooked tongue in 3-mm ($\frac{1}{8}$-inch) thick slices and arrange neatly in an entrée dish. Sauce over with Madeira sauce (page 126) and allow to heat through slowly and thoroughly.

57 ~ Braised ox liver and onions

	4 portions	10 portions
liver	300 g (12 oz)	1 kg (2 lb)
flour, white or wholemeal	25 g (1 oz)	60 g (2$\frac{1}{2}$ oz)
fat or oil	50 g (2 oz)	125 g (5 oz)
onions, sliced	200 g ($\frac{1}{2}$ lb)	500 g (1$\frac{1}{4}$ lb)
brown stock	500 ml (1 pt)	1$\frac{1}{4}$ litre (2$\frac{1}{2}$ pt)
tomato purée	25 g (1 oz)	60 g (2$\frac{1}{2}$ oz)
bouquet garni		
clove garlic	1	2

1 Prepare the liver by removing the skin and tubes then cut into slices.
2 Pass the sliced liver through seasoned flour.
3 Fry on both sides in hot fat.
4 Place in a braising pan or casserole.
5 Fry the onion to a golden brown, drain and add to the liver.
6 Just cover with the stock and add the tomato purée, bouquet garni and garlic.
7 Lightly season and cover with a lid.
8 Simmer gently in the oven until tender for approximately 1$\frac{1}{2}$–2 hours.
9 Correct the sauce and serve.

58 – Stewed oxtail

	4 portions	10 portions
oxtail	1 kg (2 lb)	2½ kg (5 lb)
fat or oil	50 g (2 oz)	125 g (5 oz)
onion	100 g (4 oz)	250 g (10 oz)
carrot	100 g (4 oz)	250 g (10 oz)
flour, browned in the oven	35 g (1½ oz)	100 g (4 oz)
tomato purée	25 g (1 oz)	60 g (2½ oz)
brown stock	1 litre (2 pt)	2½ litre (5 pt)
bouquet garni		
clove garlic	1	2
salt and pepper		

1   Cut the oxtail into sections. Remove the excess fat.
2   Fry on all sides in hot fat.
3   Place in a braising pan or casserole.
4   Add the fried roughly cut onion and carrot.
5   Mix in the flour.
6   Add tomato purée, brown stock, bouquet garni, garlic and season lightly.
7   Bring to the boil, skim.
8   Cover with a lid and simmer in the oven until tender, approximately 3 hours.
9   Remove the meat from the sauce, place in a clean pan.
10   Correct the sauce and pass on to the meat and reboil.
11   Serve sprinkled with chopped parsley.

Note   This dish, also known as braised oxtail, is usually garnished with glazed turned or neatly cut carrots and turnips, button onions, peas and diamonds of beans. Oxtail must be very well cooked so that the meat comes away easily from the bone.

Haricot oxtail can be made as for the previous recipe with the addition of 100 g (4 oz) (250 g, 10 oz for 10 portions) cooked haricot beans, added approximately ½ hour before the oxtail has completed cooking.

— Veal —

Veal is obtained from good quality carcasses weighing around 100 kg (200 lb). This quality of veal is required for first-class cookery and is produced from calves slaughtered at between 12–24 weeks.

BUTCHERY

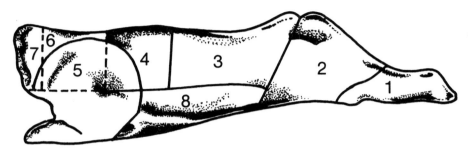

Fig 9.9: Side of veal

1	Knuckle
2	Leg
3	Loin
4	Best-end
5	Shoulder
6	Neck-end
7	Scrag
8	Breast

Joints, uses and weights

JOINT	USES	APPROXIMATE WEIGHT (KG)	(LB)
(1) knuckle	osso buco, sauté, stock	2	4
(2) leg	roasting, braising, escalopes, sauté	5	10
(3) loin	roasting, frying, grilling	$3\frac{1}{2}$	7
(4) best-end	roasting, frying, grilling	3	6
(5) shoulder	braising, stewing	5	10
(6) neck-end	stewing, sauté	$2\frac{1}{2}$	5
(7) scrag	stewing stock	$1\frac{1}{2}$	3
(8) breast	stewing, roasting	$2\frac{1}{2}$	5
kidneys	stewing (pies and puddings), sauté	—	—
liver	frying	—	—
sweetbreads	braising, frying	—	—
head	boiling, soup	4	8
brains	boiling, frying	—	—
bones	used for stock	—	—

Joints of the leg
Average weight of English or Dutch milk-fed veal calves is 18 kg (36 lb).

CUTS (ENGLISH)	WEIGHT	PROPORTION OF LEG	USES
cushion or nut	2.75 kg (5½ lb)	15%	escalopes, roasting, braising, sauté
undercushion or under nut	3 kg (6 lb)	17%	escalopes, roasting, braising, sauté
thick flank	2.5 kg (5 lb)	14%	escalopes, roasting, braising, sauté
knuckle (whole)	2.5 kg (5 lb)	14%	osso buco, sauté
bones (thigh and aitch)	2.5 kg (5 lb)	14%	stock, jus-lié, sauces
usable trimmings	2 kg (4 lb)	11%	pies, stewing
skin and fat	2.75 kg (5½ lb)	15%	

Corresponding joints in beef
- Cushion = topside
- Undercushion = silverside
- Thick flank = thick flank

Dissection of a leg of veal
1 Remove the knuckle by dividing the knee joint (A) and cut through the meat away from the cushion-line A–B.
2 Remove aitch bone (C) at thick end of the leg separating it at the ball and socket joint.
3 Remove all the outside skin and fat thus exposing the natural seams. It will now be seen that the thigh bone divides the meat into two-thirds and one-third (thick flank).
4 Stand the leg on the thick flank with point D uppermost. Divide the cushion from the undercushion, following the natural seam, using the hand and the point of a knife. Having reached the thigh bone, remove it completely.
5 When the boned leg falls open, the three joints can easily be seen joined only by membrane. Separate and trim the cushion removing the loose flap of meat.
6 Trim the undercushion removing the layer of thick gristle. Separate into three small joints through the natural seams. It will be seen that one of these will correspond with the round in silverside of beef.

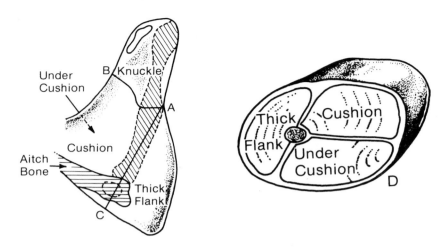

Fig 9.10: Dissection of leg of veal

7 Trim the thick flank by laying it on its round side and making a cut along the length about 2.5 cm (1 inch) deep. A seam is reached and the two trimmings can be removed.

The anticipated yield of escalopes from this size leg would be 62.5 kg (13¾ lb), that is 55 kg × 100 g (4 oz) or 73 kg × 80 g (3 oz).

Order of dissection

- Remove the shoulders.
- Remove the breast.
- Take off the leg.
- Divide the loin and best-end from the scrag and neck-end.
- Divide the loin from the best-end.

Preparation of the joints and cuts of veal

Shin

- *Stewing (on the bone) (osso buco)* Cut and saw into 2–4 cm (1–1½ inches) thick slices through the knuckle.
- *Sauté* Bone-out and trim and cut into even 25 g (1 oz) pieces.

Leg

- *Braising or roasting whole* Remove the aitch bone, clean and trim 4 cm (1½ inch) off the knuckle bone. Trim off the excess sinew.

- *Braising or roasting the nut* Remove all the sinew and if there is insufficient fat on the joint then bard thinly and secure with string.
- *Escalopes* Remove all the sinew and cut into large 50–75 g (2–3 oz) slices against the grain and bat out thinly.
- *Sauté* Remove all the sinew and cut into 25 g (1 oz) pieces.

Loin and Best-end
- *Roasting* Bone-out and trim the flap, roll out and secure with string. This joint may be stuffed before rolling.
- *Frying* Trim and cut into cutlets.

Shoulder
- *Braising* Boned-out as for lamb and usually stuffed (page 369).
- *Stewing* Bone-out, remove all the sinew and cut into 25 g (1 oz) pieces.

Neck-end and Scrag
- *Stewing and sauté* Bone-out and remove all the sinew and cut into approximately 25 g (1 oz) pieces.

Breast
- *Stewing* As for neck-end.
- *Roasting* Bone-out, season, stuff and roll up then tie with string.

Kidneys
Remove the fat and skin and cut down the middle lengthwise. Remove the sinew and cut into thin slices or neat dice.

Liver
Skin if possible, remove the gristle and cut into thin slices on the slant.

Sweetbreads
Soak in several changes of cold salted water to remove blood which would darken the sweetbreads during cooking. Blanch and refresh and peel off membranes and corrective tissues. The sweetbreads can then be pressed between two trays with a weight on top and refrigerated.

Head
- Bone-out by making a deep incision down the middle of the head to the nostrils.
- Follow the bone carefully and remove all the flesh in one piece.
- Lastly remove the tongue.

- Wash the flesh well and keep covered in acidulated water.
- Wash off, blanch and refresh.
- Cut into 2–5 cm (1–2 inch) squares.
- Cut off the ears and trim the inside of the cheek.

Brains

Using a chopper or saw, remove the top of the skull, making certain that the opening is large enough to remove the brain undamaged. Soak the brains in running cold water, then remove the membrane, or skin and wash well to remove all blood. Keep in cold salted water until required.

QUALITY OF VEAL

- Veal is available all the year round.
- The flesh should be pale pink in colour.
- The flesh should be firm in structure, not soft or flabby.
- Cut surfaces should be slightly moist, not dry.
- Bones, in young animals, should be pinkish white, porous and with a degree of blood in their structure.
- The fat should be firm and pinkish white.
- The kidney should be firm and well covered with fat.

VEAL RECIPES

59 – Brown veal stew

Proceed as for Brown beef stew recipe (page 335) using veal in place of beef and allowing 1–1½ hours cooking time.

60 – White stew or blanquette of veal

Proceed as for White lamb stew recipe (page 315) using 400 g (1 lb) of prepared stewing veal.

61 – Fricassée of veal

	4 portions	10 portions	Using butter, 1 portion provides:
boned stewing veal (shoulder or breast)	400 g (1 lb)	1¼ kg (2½ lb)	992 kJ/236 kcal
margarine or butter	35 g (1½ oz)	100 g (4 oz)	13.6 g fat (of which 7.5 g saturated)
flour	25 g (1 oz)	60 g (2½ oz)	5.3 g carbohydrate
white veal stock	500 ml (1 pt)	1¼ litre (2½ pt)	(of which 0.4 g sugars)
salt, pepper			23.3 g protein
egg yolk	1	2–3	0.2 g fibre
cream (dairy or vegetable)	2–3 tbsp	5–7 tbsp	
few drops of lemon juice			

1　Trim the meat. Cut into even 25 g (1 oz) pieces.
2　Set the meat gently in the butter without colour in a sauté pan.
3　Mix in the flour with a wooden spoon and cook out without colour.
4　Allow to cool.
5　Gradually add boiling stock just to cover the meat, stir until smooth.
6　Season, bring to the boil, skim.
7　Cover and simmer gently on the stove until tender, 1½–2 hours.
8　Pick out the meat into a clean pan.
9　Correct the sauce.
10　Pass on to the meat and reboil.
11　Mix the yolk and cream in a basin.
12　Add a little of the boiling sauce, mix in and pour back on to the meat, shaking the pan until thoroughly mixed; do not reboil.
13　Add the lemon juice.
14　Serve, finished with chopped parsley and heart-shaped croûtons fried in butter or oil.

Note　A variation is to add mushrooms and button onions. Proceed as in recipe 61; after 1 hour's cooking pick out the meat, strain the sauce back on to the meat and add 8 small button onions. Simmer for 15 minutes, add 8 small white button mushrooms, washed and peeled if necessary, then complete the cooking. Finish and serve as in recipe 61.

62 – Braised veal

	4 portions	10 portions
carrots	100 g (4 oz)	250 g (10 oz)
onions	100 g (4 oz)	250 g (10 oz)
fat or oil	25 g (1 oz)	60 g ($2\frac{1}{2}$ oz)
cushion or nut of veal	400 g (1 lb)	$1\frac{1}{4}$ kg ($2\frac{1}{2}$ lb)
tomato purée	25 g (1 oz)	60 g ($2\frac{1}{2}$ oz)
bouquet garni		
brown veal stock	250 ml ($\frac{1}{2}$ pt)	600 ml ($1\frac{1}{4}$ pt)
jus-lié	250 ml ($\frac{1}{2}$ pt)	600 ml ($1\frac{1}{4}$ pt)

1 Slice the carrots and onions thickly.
2 Fry lightly and place in a braising pan.
3 Trim and tie the joint with string and fry quickly on all sides.
4 Place on the bed of roots.
5 Add the tomato purée, bouquet garni, stock, jus-lié, mushroom trimmings if available. Season lightly.
6 Bring to the boil, skim, cover with a lid and cook gently in a moderate oven at 150–200°C (Reg. 2–6; 300–400°F) for 1 hour.
7 Remove the lid and continue cooking with the lid off for a further 30 minutes basting frequently.
8 Remove the joint from the sauce, take off the strings.
9 Correct the colour, consistency and seasoning of the sauce.
10 Pass through a fine conical strainer.
11 Carve in slices against the grain.
12 Pour some of the sauce over the slices and serve a sauceboat of sauce separately.

Note For larger joints allow 30–35 minutes per $\frac{1}{2}$ kg (1 lb) plus 35 minutes (approximately) cooking time; 125 ml ($\frac{1}{4}$ pint) red wine may replace the same amount of jus-lié. Noodles are often served with this dish.

63 – Hot veal and ham pie

	4 portions	10 portions
bacon rashers	100 g (4 oz)	250 g (10 oz)
stewing veal without bone	400 g (1 lb)	1¼ kg (2½ lb)
chopped or quartered hard-boiled egg	1	2
chopped parsley	1 tsp	2 tsp
chopped onion	50 g (2 oz)	125 g (5 oz)
salt, pepper		
stock (white)	250 ml (½ pt)	600 ml (1¼ pt)
rough puff or puff paste (page 664/662)	100 g (4 oz)	250 g (10 oz)

I portion provides:

1394 kJ/332 kcal
20.7 g fat
(of which 8.1 g saturated)
8.9 g carbohydrate
(of which 0.8 g sugars)
27.9 g protein
0.7 g fibre

1 Bat out the bacon thinly and line the bottom and sides of a ½ litre (1 pint) pie dish, leaving two or three pieces for the top.
2 Trim the veal, cut into small pieces and mix with the egg, parsley and onion. Season and place in the pie dish.
3 Just cover with stock. Add the rest of the bacon.
4 Roll out the pastry, eggwash the rim of the pie dish and line with a strip of pastry 1 cm (½ inch) wide. Press this down firmly and eggwash.
5 Without stretching the pastry, cover the pie and seal firmly.
6 Trim off excess pastry with a sharp knife, notch the edge neatly, eggwash and decorate.
7 Allow to rest in the refrigerator or a cool place.
8 Place on a baking sheet in a hot oven at 200°C (Reg. 7; 425°F) for 10–15 minutes until the paste has set and is lightly coloured.
9 Remove the pie from oven, cover with foil and return to the oven reducing the heat to 190°C (Reg. 5; 375°F) for 15 minutes, then to 160°C (Reg. 3; 325°F) for a further 15 minutes, then to 140°C (Reg. 1; 275°F).
10 Complete the cooking at this temperature ensuring that the liquid is gently simmering.

Note Variations include rabbit, pork or chicken in place of veal.

64 ~ Grilled veal cutlet

1 Season the prepared chop with salt and mill pepper.
2 Brush with oil. Place on previously heated grill bars.
3 Cook on both sides for 8–10 minutes in all.
4 Brush occasionally to prevent the meat from drying.
5 Serve with watercress, a deep-fried potato and a suitable sauce or butter, such as béarnaise or compound butter.

> Using sunflower oil, 1 portion provides:
>
> 990 kJ/236 kcal
> 9.7 g fat
> (of which 2.6 g saturated)
> 0.0 g carbohydrate
> (of which 0.0 g sugars)
> 36.9 g protein
> 0.0 g fibre

65 ~ Fried veal cutlet

Season and cook in a sauté pan, in clarified butter or oil and butter, on both sides for 8–10 minutes in all. Chops must be started in hot fat, the heat reduced to allow the meat to cook through.

Serve with a suitable garnish (jardinière of vegetables or braised celery) and finish with a cordon of jus-lié.

Note Crumbed veal cutlet can be made as an alternative: cook as for the previous recipe and finish with nut brown butter, a cordon of jus-lié and a suitable garnish.

66 ~ Braised stuffed shoulder of veal

	4 portions	10 portions
onion	100 g (4 oz)	250 g (10 oz)
carrot	100 g (4 oz)	250 g (10 oz)
fat or oil	25 g (1 oz)	60 g (2½ oz)
shoulder of veal (boned)	400 g (1 lb)	1¼ kg (2½ lb)
tomato purée	50 g (2 oz)	125 g (5 oz)
brown veal stock	250 ml (½ pt)	600 ml (1¼ pt)
bouquet garni		
jus-lié or demi-glace	250 ml (½ pt)	600 ml (1¼ pt)
clove garlic, crushed	1	2

> Using sunflower oil, 1 portion provides:
>
> 824 kJ/196 kcal
> 9.0 g fat
> (of which 1.9 g saturated)
> 5.0 g carbohydrate
> (of which 4.1 g sugars)
> 24.0 g protein
> 1.1 g fibre

1 Bone-out the shoulder, season, stuff (recipe 73) and secure with string. Cook and serve as for braised veal (recipe 62).

2   For larger joints allow 30–35 minutes per $\frac{1}{2}$ kg (1 lb) plus 35 minutes (approximately) cooking time.

Note   A whole shoulder may serve from 8 portions depending on its size. Breast of veal can be prepared and cooked in the same way.

67 – Roast leg of veal

Use a whole leg or joints. In order to increase the flavour it is usual to roast on a bed of root vegetables with a sprig of thyme or rosemary. Baste frequently and allow approximately 25 minutes per $\frac{1}{2}$ kg (1 lb) plus 25 minutes over. There should be no sign of blood when cooked. Prepare the roast gravy from the sediment and thicken slightly with a little arrowroot or cornflour diluted with water.

   Serve the slices, carved against the grain, dress neatly with thin slices of ham and veal stuffing (recipe 73). Lightly cover with gravy and garnish with watercress and a sauceboat of gravy separately.

68 – Escalope of veal

	4 portions	10 portions
nut or cushion of veal	400 g (1 lb)	1¼ kg (2½ lb)
seasoned flour	25 g (1 oz)	60 g (2½ oz)
egg	1	2
breadcrumbs	50 g (2 oz)	125 g (5 oz)
oil ⎫ for frying	50 g (2 oz)	125 g (5 oz)
butter ⎭	50 g (2 oz)	125 g (5 oz)
beurre noisette	50 g (2 oz)	125 g (5 oz)
butter for finishing (optional)		

Fried in sunflower oil, butter to finish, 1 portion provides:

2079 kJ/495 kcal
39.8 g fat
(of which 11.4 g saturated)
10.3 g carbohydrate
(of which 0.5 g sugars)
24.7 g protein
1.0 g fibre

1   Trim and remove all sinew from the veal.
2   Cut into four even slices and bat out thinly using a little water.
3   Flour, egg and crumb. Shake off surplus crumbs.
4   Mark with a palette knife.
5   Place the escalopes into shallow hot fat and cook quickly for a few minutes on each side.
6   Dress on a serving dish or plate.

recipe continued ▶

7   An optional finish is to pour over 50 g (2 oz) beurre noisette (nut-brown butter), and finish with a cordon of jus-lié (page 131).

Note   Variations include:

- *Escalope of veal viennoise* As recipe 68, but garnish the dish with chopped yolk, white of egg and chopped parsley. On top of each escalope place a slice of peeled lemon decorated with chopped egg yolk, egg white and parsley, an anchovy fillet and a stoned olive. Finish with a little lemon juice and nut brown butter.
- *Veal escalope Holstein* Prepare and cook the escalopes as for recipe 68. Add an egg fried in butter or oil, and place two neat fillets of anchovy criss-crossed on each egg. Serve.
- *Escalope of veal with spaghetti and tomato sauce* Cook and serve the escalopes as for recipe 68, and garnish with spaghetti with tomato sauce (page 220) allowing 10 g ($\frac{1}{2}$ oz) spaghetti per portion. (Wholemeal spaghetti may be used.)

69 – Breadcrumbed veal escalope with ham and cheese

	4 portions	10 portions
nut or cushion of veal	400 g (1 lb)	1$\frac{1}{4}$ kg (2$\frac{1}{2}$ lb)
slices of cooked ham	4	10
slices of Gruyère cheese	4	10
seasoned flour	25 g (1 oz)	60 g (2$\frac{1}{2}$ oz)
egg	1	2
breadcrumbs	50 g (2 oz)	125 g (5 oz)
oil	50 g (2 oz)	125 g (5 oz)
butter	100 g (4 oz)	250 g (10 oz)
jus-lié (page 131)	60 ml ($\frac{1}{8}$ pt)	150 ml ($\frac{1}{3}$ pt)

Fried in sunflower oil, butter to finish, 1 portion provides:

2632 kJ/627 kcal
48.1 g fat
(of which 16.3 g saturated)
12.0 g carbohydrate
(of which 1.3 g sugars)
37.1 g protein
0.7 g fibre

1   Trim and remove all sinew from the veal.
2   Cut into 8 (20 for 10 portions) even slices and bat out thinly using a little water.
3   Place a slice of ham and a slice of cheese on to 4 (10 for 10 portions) of the veal slices, cover with the remaining slices and press firmly together.
4   Flour, egg and crumb. Shake off all surplus crumbs.
5   Mark on one side with a palette knife.
6   Place the escalopes marked side down into the hot fat and cook quickly for a few minutes on each side, until golden brown.

7   An optional finish is to serve coated with 50 g (2 oz) (125 g, 5 oz for 10 portions) nut-brown butter (beurre noisette) and a cordon of jus-lié.

Note   Veal escalopes may be cooked plain (not crumbed) in which case they are only slightly batted.

70 – Veal escalope with Madeira

	4 portions	10 portions
butter or margarine	50 g (2 oz)	125 g (5 oz)
seasoned flour	25 g (1 oz)	60 g (2½ oz)
veal escalopes (slightly battened)	4	10
Madeira	30 ml ($\frac{1}{16}$ pt)	75 ml ($\frac{1}{8}$ pt)
demi-glace	125 ml ($\frac{1}{4}$ pt)	300 ml ($\frac{5}{8}$ pt)

1   Heat the butter in a sauté pan.
2   Lightly flour the escalopes. Fry to a light brown colour on both sides.
3   Drain off the fat from the pan. Deglaze with the Madeira.
4   Add the demi-glace and bring to the boil.
5   Correct the seasoning and consistency.
6   Pass through a fine strainer onto the escalopes and serve.

Note   In place of Madeira, sherry or Marsala may be used.

71 – Veal escalope with cream and mushrooms

	4 portions	10 portions
butter or margarine	50 g (2 oz)	125 g (5 oz)
seasoned flour	25 g (1 oz)	60 g (2½ oz)
veal escalopes (slightly battened)	4	10
button mushrooms	100 g (4 oz)	250 g (10 oz)
sherry or white wine	30 ml ($\frac{1}{16}$ pt)	125 ml ($\frac{1}{4}$ pt)
double cream	125 ml ($\frac{1}{4}$ pt)	300 ml ($\frac{5}{8}$ pt)
salt, cayenne		

1   Heat the butter in a sauté pan.
2   Lightly flour the escalopes.

recipe continued ▶

3   Cook the escalopes on both sides with the minimum of colour. They should be a delicate light brown.
4   Place the escalopes in a serving dish, cover and keep warm.
5   Peel, wash and slice the mushrooms.
6   Gently sauté the mushrooms in the same butter and pan as the escalopes and add them to the escalopes.
7   Drain off all the fat from the pan.
8   Deglaze the pan with the sherry.
9   Add the cream bring to the boil and season.
10 Reduce to a lightly thickened consistency. Correct the seasoning.
11 Pass through a fine strainer over the escalopes and mushrooms.

Note   An alternative method of preparing the sauce is to use half the amount of cream and an equal amount of chicken velouté (page 119).

72 ~ Veal escalopes with Parma ham and Mozzarella cheese

	4 portions	10 portions
small, thin veal escalopes	(8 in total) 400 g (1 lb)	(20 in total) 1¼ kg (2¼ lb)
Parma ham thinly sliced	100 g (4 oz)	250 g (10 oz)
Mozzarella cheese, thinly sliced	200 g (8 oz)	500 g (1¼ lb)
fresh leaves of sage or	8	20
dried sage	1 tsp	2½ tsp
seasoning		
butter, margarine or oil	50 g (2 oz)	125 g (5 oz)
grated Parmesan cheese		

1   Sprinkle each slice of veal lightly with flour and flatten.
2   Place a slice of Parma ham on each escalope.
3   Add several slices of Mozzarella cheese to each.
4   Add a sage leaf or a light sprinkling of dried sage.
5   Season, roll up each escalope and secure with a toothpick or cocktail stick.
6   Melt the butter in a sauté pan, add the escalopes and brown on all sides.
7   Transfer the escalopes and butter to a suitably sized ovenproof dish.
8   Sprinkle generously with grated Parmesan cheese and bake in a moderately hot oven at 190°C (Reg. 5; 375°F) for 10 minutes.
9   Clean the edges of the dish and serve.

73 – Veal stuffing

	4 portions	10 portions
white or wholemeal breadcrumbs	100 g (4 oz)	250 g (10 oz)
onion cooked in oil, butter or margarine without colour	50 g (2 oz)	125 g (5 oz)
pinch of chopped parsley		
chopped suet	50 g (2 oz)	125 g (5 oz)
good pinch of powdered thyme or rosemary		
grated zest and juice of lemon	$\frac{1}{2}$	1
salt, pepper		

1 Combine all the ingredients.
2 This may be used for stuffing joints or may be cooked separately in buttered paper or in a basin in the steamer for approximately 1 hour.

Note The stuffing for veal joints may be varied by using:

● orange in place of lemon;
● addition of duxelle;
● leeks in place of onion;
● various herbs;
● adding a little spice (ginger, nutmeg, allspice).

Plate 9.19a–b: Two methods of serving escalopes of veal viennoise

74 – Roast stuffed breast of veal

Bone, trim, season and stuff (page 369). Tie with string and cook and serve as for roast leg of veal.

75 – Pojarski of veal

	4 portions	10 portions
trimmed veal	200 g (8 oz)	500 g (1¼ lb)
white or wholemeal breadcrumbs soaked in milk	40 g (1½ oz)	100 g (4 oz)
single cream or non-dairy unsweetened creamer	60 ml (⅛ pt)	150 ml (⅓ pt)
egg	1	2
seasoning		

1 Mince the veal finely twice or chop finely in a food processor.
2 Remove into a clean basin, add the breadcrumbs, cream and egg.
3 Season thoroughly and mix.
4 Form into cutlet shapes and breadcrumb with white or wholemeal breadcrumbs.
5 Shallow fry in hot butter, margarine or oil gently on both sides, presentation side down first, until cooked and golden brown.
6 Serve with a cordon of jus-lié and a sauceboat of jus-lié.

76 – Grenadin of veal

1 Prepare slices of veal, cutting a little thicker than for escalopes.
2 Lard with fat bacon strips. Sauté in oil and butter.
3 Serve with a suitable garnish.

77 – Braised shin of veal (*Osso buco*)

	4 portions	10 portions
meaty knuckle of veal	1½ kg (3 lb)	3¾ kg (7½ lb)
flour	25 g (1 oz)	60 g (2½ oz)
butter or margarine	50 g (2 oz)	125 g (5 oz)
oil	60 ml (⅛ pt)	150 ml (⅓ pt)
onion	50 g (2 oz)	125 g (5 oz)
small clove garlic	1	2–3
carrot	50 g (2 oz)	125 g (5 oz)
leek	25 g (1 oz)	60 g (2½ oz)
celery	25 g (1 oz)	60 g (2½ oz)
dry white wine	60 ml (⅛ pt)	150 ml (⅓ pt)
white stock	60 ml (⅛ pt)	150 ml (⅓ pt)
tomato purée	25 g (1 oz)	60 g (2½ oz)
bouquet garni		
tomatoes	200 g (½ lb)	500 g (1¼ lb)
grated zest and juice of lemon or orange	½	1
chopped parsley and basil		

> Using hard margarine and sunflower oil,
> 1 portion provides:
>
> 1748 kJ/416 kcal
> 28.6 g fat
> (of which 7.8 g saturated)
> 9.3 g carbohydrate
> (of which 4.1 g sugars)
> 28.5 g protein
> 1.9 g fibre

1　Prepare the veal knuckle by cutting and sawing through the bone in 5-cm (2-inches) thick pieces.
2　Season the veal pieces with salt and pepper and pass through flour on both sides.
3　Melt the butter and oil in a sauté pan.
4　Add the veal slices and cook on both sides, colouring slightly.
5　Add the finely chopped onion and garlic, cover with a lid and allow to sweat gently for 2–3 minutes.
6　Add the carrot, leek and celery cut in brunoise, cover with a lid and allow to sweat for 3–4 minutes. Pour off the fat.
7　Deglaze with the white wine and stock. Add the tomato purée.
8　Add the bouquet garni, replace the lid and allow the dish to simmer gently, preferably in an oven, for 1 hour.
9　Add the concasséd tomatoes, correct the seasoning.
10　Replace the lid, return to the oven and allow to continue simmering until the meat is so tender that it can be pulled away from the bone easily with a fork.

recipe continued ▶

11 Remove the bouquet garni, add the lemon juice, correct seasoning and serve sprinkled with a mixture of chopped fresh basil, parsley and grated orange and lemon zest.

Note A risotto with saffron may be served separately. *Osso buco* is an Italian regional dish which has many variations.

78 – Calf's liver and bacon

	4 portions	10 portions
calf's liver	300 g (12 oz)	1 kg (2 lb)
oil for frying	50 g (2 oz)	125 g (5 oz)
streaky bacon	50 g (2 oz)	125 g (5 oz)
jus-lié	125 ml ($\frac{1}{4}$ pt)	300 ml ($\frac{5}{8}$ pt)

I portion provides:

998 kJ/238 kcal
13.4 g fat
(of which 5.0 g saturated)
2.8 g carbohydrate
(of which 2.7 g sugars)
26.9 g protein
1.1 g fibre

1 Skin the liver and remove the gristle.
2 Cut in slices on the slant.
3 Pass the slices of liver through seasoned flour.
4 Shake off the excess flour.
5 Quickly fry on both sides in hot fat.
6 Remove the rind and bone from the bacon and grill on both sides.
7 Serve the liver and bacon with a cordon of jus-lié and a sauceboat of jus-lié separately.

Note Variations include:

- Fry in butter and sprinkle with powdered sage.
- Fry in butter, remove the liver, deglaze the pan with raspberry vinegar and powdered thyme.
- When cooked, sprinkle with chopped parsley and a few drops of lemon juice.

79 – Braised veal sweetbreads (white)

Sweetbreads are glands, and two types are used for cooking. The thymus glands (throat) are usually long in shape and are of inferior quality. The pancreatic glands (stomach) are heart-shaped and of superior quality.

	4 portions	10 portions
heart-shaped sweetbreads	8	20
salt, pepper		
onion	100 g (4 oz)	250 g (10 oz)
carrot	100 g (4 oz)	250 g (10 oz)
bouquet garni		
veal stock	250 ml ($\frac{1}{2}$ pt)	600 ml ($1\frac{1}{4}$ pt)

Using hard margarine and sunflower oil,
1 portion provides:

1103 kJ/263 kcal
20.7 g fat
(of which 4.4 g saturated)
1.7 g carbohydrate
(of which 0.0 g sugars)
17.6 g protein
0.0 g fibre

1 Wash, blanch, refresh and trim the sweetbreads (see page 359).
2 Season and place in a casserole or sauté pan on a bed of roots.
3 Add the bouquet garni and stock.
4 Cover with buttered greaseproof paper and a lid.
5 Cook in a moderate oven at 150–200°C (Reg. 2–6; 300–400°F) for approximately 45 minutes.
6 Remove the lid, baste occasionally with cooking liquor to glaze.
7 Serve with some of the cooking liquor, thickened with diluted arrowroot if necessary, and passed on to the sweetbreads.

Note   Variations include:

- *Braised veal sweetbreads (brown).* Prepare as in the recipe above and place on a lightly browned bed of roots. Barely cover with brown veal stock, or half-brown veal stock and half jus-lié. Cook in a moderate oven at 150–200°C (Reg. 2–6; 300–400°F) without a lid, basting frequently (approximately 1 hour). Cover with the corrected, strained sauce to serve. (If veal stock is used, thicken with arrowroot.)
- *Braised veal sweetbreads with vegetables.* Braise white with a julienne of vegetables in place of the bed of roots, the julienne served in the sauce.

80 – Sweetbread escalope

Braise the sweetbreads white, press slightly between two trays and allow to cool. Cut into thick slices, $\frac{1}{2}$–1 cm ($\frac{1}{4}$–$\frac{1}{2}$ inch) thick and shallow fry.

Serve with the garnish and sauce as indicated on a bed of leaf spinach; coat with Mornay sauce and glaze.

81 – Sweetbread escalope (crumbed)

Braise the sweetbreads white, press slightly and allow to cool. Cut into thick slices. Then flour, egg and crumb and shallow fry. Serve with a suitable garnish (asparagus tips) and a cordon of jus-lié. Finish with nut-brown butter.

82 – Grilled veal sweetbreads

Blanch, braise, cool and press the sweetbreads. Cut in halves crosswise, pass through melted butter and grill gently on both sides. Serve with a sauce and garnish as indicated.

In some recipes they may be passed through butter and crumbs before being grilled, garnished with noisette potatoes, buttered carrots, purée of peas and béarnaise sauce.

—— *Pork* ——

Approximately 95% of pork used in Britain is home-produced. The keeping quality of pork is less than that of other meat, therefore it must be handled, prepared and cooked with great care. Pork must always be well cooked.

BUTCHERY

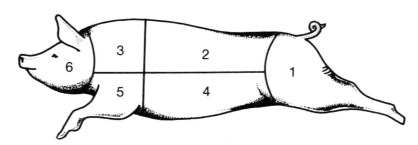

Fig 9.11: Pig carcass dissection

Cuts, uses and weights

ENGLISH	USES	APPROXIMATE WEIGHT	
		(KG)	(LB)
(1) leg	roasting and boiling	5	10
(2) loin	roasting, frying, grilling	6	12
(3) spare rib	roasting, pies	$1\frac{1}{2}$	3
(4) belly	pickling, boiling, stuffed, rolled and roasted	2	4
(5) shoulder	roasting, sausages, pies	3	6
(6) head (whole)	brawn	4	8
(7) trotters	grilling, boiling		
kidneys	sauté, grilling		
liver	frying, pâté		

When 5–6 weeks old a piglet is known as a suckling or suckling pig. The weight is then between 5–10 kg (10–20 lb).

Order of dissection

- Remove the head.
- Remove the trotters.
- Remove the leg.
- Remove the shoulder.
- Remove the spare ribs.
- Divide the loin from the belly.

Preparation of joints and cuts

Leg

- *Roasting* Remove the pelvic or aitch bone, trim and score the rind neatly; that is, with a sharp-pointed knife, make a series of 3 mm ($\frac{1}{8}$ inch) deep incisions

375

approximately 2 cm (1 inch) apart all over the skin of the joint. Trim and clean the knuckle bone.

- *Boiling* It is usual to pickle the joint either by rubbing dry salt and saltpetre into the meat or by soaking in a brine solution (page 327). Then remove the pelvic bone, trim and secure with string if necessary.

Loin

- *Roasting (on the bone)* Saw down the chine bone in order to facilitate carving; trim the excess fat and sinew and score the rind in the direction that the joint will be carved. Season and secure with string.
- *Roasting (boned-out)* Remove the fillets and bone-out carefully. Trim off the excess fat and sinew, score the rind and neaten the flap, season, replace the filet mignon, roll up and secure the string. This joint is sometimes stuffed (page 378).
- *Grilling or frying chops* Remove the skin, excess fat and sinew, then cut and saw or chop through the loin in approximately 1 cm ($\frac{1}{2}$ inch) slices; remove the excess bone and trim neatly.

Spare rib

- *Roasting* Remove the excess fat, bone and sinew and trim neatly.
- *Pies* Remove the excess fat and sinew, bone-out and cut as required.

Belly

Remove all the small rib bones, season with salt, pepper and chopped sage, roll and secure with string. This joint may be stuffed.

Shoulder

- *Roasting* The shoulder is usually boned-out, the excess fat and sinew removed, seasoned, scored and rolled with string. It may be stuffed and can also be divided into two smaller joints.
- *Sausages and pies* Skin, bone-out and remove the excess fat and sinew and cut into even pieces or mince.

Head

Brawn Bone-out as for the calf's head (page 359) and keep in acidulated water until required. Or split down the centre and remove the brain and tongue.

Trotters

Boil in water for a few minutes, scrape with the back of a knife to remove the hairs, wash off in cold water and split in half.

Kidneys

Remove the fat and skin, cut down the middle lengthwise. Remove the sinew and cut into slices or neat dice.

Liver

Skin if possible, remove the gristle and cut into thin slices on the slant.

SIGNS OF QUALITY

- Lean flesh should be pale pink, firm and of a fine texture.
- The fat should be white, firm, smooth and not excessive.
- Bones should be small, fine and pinkish.
- The skin or rind should be smooth.

PORK RECIPES

83 – Roast leg of pork

1 Season the prepared leg of pork.
2 Lightly brush the skin with oil in order to make the crackling crisp.
3 Place on a trivet in a roasting tin with a little oil or dripping on top.
4 Start to cook in a hot oven at 230–250°C (Reg. 7–9; 450–500°F) basting frequently.
5 Gradually reduce the heat, allowing approximately 25 minutes per $\frac{1}{2}$kg (1 lb) and 25 minutes over. Pork must always be well cooked. If using a probe, the minimum temperature should be 80°C (176°F).
6 When cooked remove from the pan and prepare a roast gravy from the sediment (see page 303).
7 Serve the joint garnished with picked watercress and accompanied by roast gravy, apple sauce and sage and onion stuffing. If to be carved, proceed as for roast lamb (page 304).

Note Other joints can also be used for roasting (loin, shoulder and spare rib).

> 4 oz (113 g) portion (with lean, fat), 1 portion provides:
>
> 1357 kJ/323 kcal
> 22.4 g fat
> (of which 8.9 g saturated)
> 0.0 g carbohydrate
> (of which 0.0 g sugars)
> 30.4 g protein
> 0.0 g fibre

84 ~ Sage and onion stuffing for pork

	4 portions	10 portions
white breadcrumbs	100 g (4 oz)	250 g (10 oz)
pork dripping	50 g (2 oz)	125 g (5 oz)
pinch chopped parsley		
chopped onion	50 g (2 oz)	125 g (5 oz)
good pinch powdered sage		
salt, pepper		

1   Cook the onion in the dripping without colour.
2   Combine all the ingredients. Stuffing is usually served separately.

85 ~ Boiled leg of pork

1   Place the leg in cold water. Bring to the boil and skim.
2   Add bouquet garni and a garnish of vegetables as for boiled beef (page 333), onions, carrots, leeks and celery.
3   Simmer gently for approximately 25 minutes per $\frac{1}{2}$ kg (1 lb) and 25 minutes over.
4   Serve garnished with the vegetables.
5   A sauceboat of cooking liquor and a dish of pease pudding (purée of peas) may be served separately (page 553).

86 ~ Pork chop charcutière

1   Season the chop on both sides with salt and mill pepper.
2   Brush with melted fat and either grill on both sides with moderate heat for approximately 10 minutes or cook in a little fat in a plat à sauté.
3   Serve accompanied by a sharp sauce, e.g., of charcutière (page 127).

87 ~ Pork chop flamande

	4 portions	10 portions
pork chops	4	10
dessert apples	300 g (12 oz)	750 g (2 lb 14 oz)

1 Season the chops with salt and mill pepper.
2 Half cook on both sides in a little fat or oil in a sauté pan.
3 Peel, core and slice the apples and place in an earthenware dish.
4 Put the chops on the apples. Sprinkle with a little fat.
5 Complete the cooking in a moderate oven at 180–200°C (Reg. 4–6; 350–400°F) for approximately 10–15 minutes. Clean the dish and serve.

88 ~ Barbecued spare ribs of pork

	4 portions	10 portions
finely chopped onion	100 g (4 oz)	250 g (10 oz)
clove of garlic (chopped)	1	2
oil	60 ml ($\frac{1}{8}$ pt)	150 ml ($\frac{3}{8}$ pt)
vinegar	60 ml ($\frac{1}{8}$ pt)	150 ml ($\frac{3}{8}$ pt)
tomato purée	150 g (6 oz)	375 g (15 oz)
honey	60 ml ($\frac{1}{8}$ pt)	150 ml ($\frac{3}{8}$ pt)
brown stock	250 ml ($\frac{1}{2}$ pt)	625 ml ($1\frac{1}{4}$ pt)
Worcester sauce	4 tbsp	10 tbsp
dry mustard	1 tsp	2 tsp
pinch thyme		
salt		
spare ribs of pork	2 kg (4 lb)	5 kg (10 lb)

Using sunflower oil, 1 portion provides:

6151 kJ/1465 kcal
126 g fat
(of which 37.3 g saturated)
20.3 g carbohydrate
(of which 17.1 g sugars)
63.5 g protein
0.3 g fibre

1 Sweat the onion and garlic in the oil without colour.
2 Mix in the vinegar, tomato purée, honey, stock, Worcester sauce, mustard, thyme and season with salt.
3 Allow the barbecue sauce to simmer for 10–15 minutes.
4 Place the prepared spare ribs fat side up on a trivet in a roasting tin.
5 Brush the spare ribs liberally with the barbecue sauce.
6 Place in a moderately hot oven at 180–200°C (Reg. 4–6; 350–400°F).
7 Cook for $\frac{3}{4}$–1 hour.
8 Baste generously with the barbecue sauce every 10–15 minutes.
9 The cooked spare ribs should be brown and crisp.
10 Cut the spare ribs into individual portions and serve.

89 – Grilled pork chop

Season and grill in the usual way and serve with picked watercress and a deep fried potato; offer a suitable sauce separately (apple sauce, page 672).

Using 150g chop (with bone, lean, fat), 1 portion provides:

1625 kJ/387 kcal
28.2 g fat
(of which 11.3 g saturated)
0.0 g carbohydrate
(of which 0.0 g sugars)
33.3 g protein
0.0 g fibre

90 – Pork escalopes

Plate 9.20a–d: Pork escalope with spaghetti milanaise

Pork escalopes are usually cut from the prime cuts of meat in the leg and can be dealt with in the same way as a leg of veal. They may be cut into 75–100 g (3–4 oz) slices, flattened with a meat bat. They may be used plain or crumbed and served with vegetables or a pasta (noodles) or as with veal escalope recipes (pages 365–368).

91 ‒ Pork escalopes with Calvados sauce

	4 portions	10 portions
4 pork escalopes (recipe 90)	4 × 100 g (4 oz)	10 × 100 g (4 oz)
shallot or onion finely chopped	50 g (2 oz)	125 g (5 oz)
butter, margarine or oil	50 g (2 oz)	125 g (5 oz)
Calvados	30 ml ($\frac{1}{16}$ pt)	75 ml ($\frac{1}{6}$ pt)
double cream or natural yoghurt	125 ml ($\frac{1}{4}$ pt)	300 ml ($\frac{5}{8}$ pt)
chopped basil, sage or rosemary		
salt, cayenne pepper		
crisp eating apples (e.g. russet)	2	5
cinnamon		
lemon juice		
brown sugar		
butter, melted		

1 Core and peel the apples.
2 Cut into $\frac{1}{2}$ cm ($\frac{1}{4}$ inch) thick rings and sprinkle with a little cinnamon and a few drops of lemon juice.
3 Place onto a baking sheet, sprinkle with brown sugar, a little melted butter and caramelise under the salamander or in the top of a hot oven.
4 Lightly sauté the escalopes on both sides in the butter.
5 Remove from the pan and keep warm.
6 Add the chopped shallots to the same pan, cover with a lid and cook gently without colouring (use a little more butter if necessary).
7 Strain off the fat leaving the shallots in the pan and deglaze with the Calvados.
8 Reduce by a half, add the cream or yoghurt, seasoning and herbs.
9 Reboil, correct the seasoning and consistency and pass through a fine strainer onto the meat.
10 Garnish with slices of caramelised apples.

Note Calvados can be replaced with twice the amount of cider and reduced by three quarters as an alternative. Add a crushed clove of garlic and 1 tablespoon of continental mustard (2–3 cloves and $2\frac{1}{2}$ tablespoons for 10 portions).

92 – Sausage toad in the hole

	4 portions	10 portions
sausages	8	20
Yorkshire pudding (page 332)		

1 Place the sausages in a roasting tray or ovenproof dish with a little oil.
2 Place in a hot oven at 230–250°C (Reg. 8–9; 450–500°F) for 5–10 minutes.
3 Remove, add the Yorkshire pudding and return to the hot oven until the sausages and Yorkshire pudding are cooked, approximately 15–20 minutes.
4 Cut into portions and serve with a thickened gravy or sauce.

Note Other meats may be cooked and served this way: chops, steak, corned beef, etc.

93 – Forcemeat

This is a term given to numerous mixtures of meats (usually veal and pork); meat and poultry; poultry; game; fish; vegetables and bread.

Forcemeats range from a simple sausagemeat to the finer mixtures used in the making of hot mousses (ham, chicken, fish) and soufflés. Also included are mixtures of bread, vegetables and herbs which alternatively are referred to as stuffings.

Forcemeats are used for galantines, raised pies, terrines, meat balls and a wide variety of other dishes.

94 ~ Sweet and sour pork

	4 portions	10 portions
loin of pork	250 g (10 oz)	600 g (1½ lb)
sugar	12 g (½ oz)	30 g (1¼ oz)
dry sherry	70 ml (⅛ pt)	180 ml (⅓ pt)
soy sauce	70 ml (⅛ pt)	180 ml (⅓ pt)
vegetable oil	70 ml (⅛ pt)	180 ml (⅓ pt)
cornflour	50 g (2 oz)	125 g (5 oz)
oil	2 tbsp	5 tbsp
clove garlic	1	2
fresh root ginger	50 g (2 oz)	125 g (5 oz)
onion, chopped	75 g (3 oz)	180 g (7½ oz)
green pepper in 1 cm (½ inch) dice	1	2½
chillies, chopped	2	5
sweet and sour sauce	210 ml (⅜ pt)	500 ml (1 pt)
pineapple rings (fresh or canned)	2	5
spring onions	2	5

> Using sunflower oil, I portion provides:
>
> 3067 kJ/730 kcal
> 43.9 g fat
> (of which 9.2 g saturated)
> 69.7 g carbohydrate
> (of which 54.7 g sugars)
> 13.4 g protein
> 1.6 g fibre

1 Cut the boned loin of pork into 2 cm (¼ inch) pieces.
2 Marinade the pork for 30 minutes in the sugar, sherry and soy sauce.
3 Pass the pork through cornflour, pressing the cornflour in well.
4 Deep fry the pork pieces in oil at 190°C (375°F) until golden brown, drain. Add the tablespoons of oil to a sauté pan.
5 Add the garlic and ginger, fry until fragrant.
6 Add the onion, pepper and chillies, sauté for a few minutes.
7 Stir in sweet and sour sauce, bring to boil.
8 Add the pineapple cut into small chunks, thicken slightly with diluted cornflour. Simmer for 2 minutes.
9 Deep fry the pork again until crisp. Drain, mix into vegetables and sauce or serve separately.
10 Serve garnished with rings of spring onions or button onions.

recipe continued ▶

— *Sweet and sour sauce*

	4 portions	10 portions
white vinegar	375 ml ($\frac{3}{4}$ pt)	1 litre (2 pt)
brown sugar	150 g (6 oz)	375 g (15 oz)
tomato ketchup	125 ml ($\frac{1}{4}$ pt)	300 ml ($\frac{5}{8}$ pt)
Worcester sauce	1 tbsp	2$\frac{1}{2}$ tbsp
seasoning		

1 Boil the vinegar and sugar in a suitable pan.
2 Add the tomato ketchup, Worcester sauce and seasoning.
3 Simmer for a few minutes then use as required. This sauce may also be lightly thickened with cornflour.

—— *Bacon* ——

Bacon is the cured flesh of a bacon weight pig which is specifically reared for bacon because its shape and size yields economic bacon joints. Bacon is cured either by dry salting and then smoking or by soaking in brine followed by smoking. Green

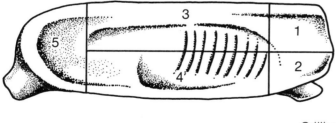

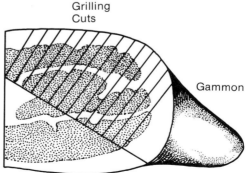

Fig 9.12: Pig carcass dissection for bacon

384

bacon is brine-cured but not smoked; it has a milder flavour but does not keep as long as smoked bacon.

Depending on the degree of salting during the curing process bacon joints may or may not require soaking in cold water for a few hours before being cooked.

BUTCHERY

Cuts, uses and weights

SIDE OF BACON	USES	APPROXIMATE WEIGHT	
		(KG)	(LB)
(1) collar	boiling, grilling	$4\frac{1}{2}$	9
(2) hock	boiling, grilling	$4\frac{1}{2}$	9
(3) back	grilling, frying	9	18
(4) streaky	grilling, frying	$4\frac{1}{2}$	9
(5) gammon	boiling, grilling, frying	$7\frac{1}{2}$	15

Preparation of joints and cuts

Collar
- *Boiling* Remove bone (if any) and tie with string.
- *Grilling* Remove the rind and trim off the outside surface and cut into thin slices (rashers), across the joint.

Hock
- *Boiling* Leave whole or bone-out and secure with string.

Back
- *Grilling* Remove all bones and rind and cut into thin rashers.
- *Frying* Remove the rind, trim off the outside surface and cut into rashers or chops of the required thickness.

Streaky
As for back.

Gammon

- *Grilling* Fairly thick slices are cut from the middle of the gammon. They are then trimmed and the rind removed.
- *Frying* As for grilling.

QUALITY

- There should be no sign of stickiness.
- There should be a pleasant smell.
- The rind should be thin, smooth and free from wrinkles.
- The fat should be white, smooth and not excessive in proportion to the lean.
- The lean should be a deep pink colour and firm.

Note Do not confuse ham with gammon.

BACON RECIPES

95 – Boiled bacon (hock, collar or gammon)

1 Soak the bacon in cold water for 24 hours before cooking.
2 Change the water.
3 Bring to the boil, skim and simmer gently, approximately 25 minutes per ½ kg (1 lb) and 25 minutes over. Allow to cool in the liquid.
4 Remove the rind and brown skin and carve.
5 Serve with a little of the cooking liquor.

> Using 4 oz (113 g) per portion, 1 portion provides:
>
> 1543 kJ/367 kcal
> 30.5 g fat
> (of which 12.2 g saturated)
> 0.0 g carbohydrate
> (of which 0.0 g sugars)
> 23.1 g protein
> 0.0 g fibre

Note Boiled bacon may be served with hot pease pudding (page 553) and a suitable sauce such as parsley sauce (page 118) or cold with salad.

96 – Grilled back or streaky rashers

Arrange on a baking tray and grill on both sides under the salamander.

97 ~ Fried bacon

Fry on both sides in a frying-pan in very little fat.

> Using sunflower oil, I portion (50 g) provides:
>
> 977 kJ/233 kcal
> 20.3 g fat
> (of which 7.2 g saturated)
> 0.0 g carbohydrate
> (of which 0.0 g sugars)
> 12.5 g protein
> 0.0 g fibre

98 ~ Bacon with pineapple

1 Hock, collar or gammon may be used.
2 Soak the bacon joint in cold water for approximately 24 hours (if necessary).
3 Change the water.
4 Cover with water, bring to the boil and skim; simmer gently for half the required cooking time (30 minutes per ½ kg (per pound) and 30 minutes over).
5 Allow to cool. Remove rind and brown skin.
6 Cover the fat surface of the joints with demerara sugar and press well into surface. Stud with 12–24 cloves.
7 Arrange a layer of tinned pineapple rings down the centre of the joint (secure with cocktail sticks if necessary).
8 Place joint in a baking tin for second half of the cooking time.
9 Bake in a moderate oven at 200°C (Reg. 6; 400°F) basting frequently with pineapple juice until well cooked.
10 Remove the cloves and pineapple.
11 Carve in thickish slices and serve garnished with the pineapple.

99 ~ Bacon chops with honey and orange sauce

	4 portions	10 portions
4 bacon chops (trimmed weight)	4 × 100 g (4 oz)	10 × 100 g (4 oz)
butter, margarine or oil	50 g (2 oz)	125 g (5 oz)
oranges	2	5
honey	1 dsp	2½ dsp
lemon, juice of	½	1½
arrowroot		

recipe continued ▶

1 Ensure that the chops are well trimmed of fat.
2 Lightly fry the chops on both sides in the butter, margarine or oil without colouring.
3 Remove from the pan and keep warm.
4 Thinly remove the zest from one orange so that no white pith remains; cut into very fine julienne; blanch and refresh.
5 Peel and segment both oranges ensuring that all the white pith and pips are removed. Retain all the juice.
6 Boil the orange and lemon juice and honey and lightly thicken with diluted arrowroot.
7 Strain the sauce, add the julienne of orange and pour over the chops.
8 Garnish with the segments of orange.

Note Variations include:

● using 1 orange and 1 pink grapefruit instead of 2 oranges;
● using a small tin of peaches or apricots or pineapple in place of the oranges.

100 – Sauerkraut with frankfurters and garlic sausage

	4 portions	10 portions
lard or margarine	50 g (2 oz)	125 g (5 oz)
sauerkraut	400 g (1 lb)	1¼ kg (2½ lb)
streaky bacon	300 g (12 oz)	1 kg (2 lb)
whole peeled carrots	2	5
onion studded	1	3
bouquet garni		
juniper berries	10	25
peppercorns	5	12
seasoning		
white wine	125 ml (¼ pt)	300 ml (⅝ pt)
bacon rind	100 g (4 oz)	250 g (10 oz)
garlic sausage	200 g (8 oz)	500 g (1¼ lb)
frankfurter sausages	8	20
boiled potatoes	8	20

1 Well grease a braising pan with the lard or margarine.
2 Place a layer of sauerkraut in the bottom of the pan.
3 Place the piece of streaky bacon on top with the carrots, onion and bouquet garni; add juniper berries and peppercorns tied in a muslin bag.

4 Cover with the remainder of the sauerkraut, season and add white wine.
5 Cover with bacon rind and a tight-fitting lid.
6 Place in a moderate oven at 180°C (Reg. 4; 350°F) and braise gently for 1 hour.
7 Remove the streaky bacon and replace with the garlic sausage. Continue braising for another hour until the sauerkraut is tender.
8 Reheat the frankfurters if canned or poach in water if fresh.
9 Remove the sauerkraut from the oven and discard the bacon rind.
10 Slice the streaky bacon, garlic sausage, carrots and frankfurters.
11 Dress the sauerkraut in an earthenware dish with the sliced items.
12 Serve plain boiled potatoes separately.

Note Sauerkraut is a pickled white cabbage and a traditional German dish (see page 534).

101 ⁓ Grilled gammon rashers

Brush the rashers with fat on both sides and cook on greased, preheated grill bars on both sides for approximately 5–10 minutes in all. Serve with watercress and any other food as indicated, such as tomatoes, mushrooms, eggs. If a sauce is required, serve any sharp demi-glace sauce.

Using 100 g per portion, 1 portion provides:

958 kJ/228 kcal
12.2 g fat
(of which 4.8 g saturated)
0.0 g carbohydrate
(of which 0.0 g sugars)
29.5 g protein
0.0 g fibre

—— *Poultry – Chicken* ——

The term in its general sense is applied to all domestic fowl bred for food and means turkeys, geese, ducks, fowls and pigeons.

Originally fowl were classified according to size and feeding by specific names as follows:

	WEIGHT		NUMBER OF PORTIONS
	(KG)	(LB)	
single baby chicken	$\frac{3}{10}-\frac{1}{2}$	$\frac{3}{4}-1$	1
double baby chicken	$\frac{1}{2}-\frac{3}{4}$	$1-1\frac{1}{2}$	2
small roasting chicken	$\frac{3}{4}-1$	$1\frac{1}{2}-2$	3–4
medium roasting chicken	1–2	2–4	4–6
large roasting or boiling chicken	2–3	4–6	6–8
capon	$3-4\frac{1}{2}$	6–9	8–12
old boiling fowl	$2\frac{1}{2}-4$	5–8	

There is approximately 15–20% bone in poultry.

TYPES

- *Spring chickens* 4–6 weeks old used for roasting and grilling.
- *Small roasting chickens* 3–4 months old used for roasting, grilling, casserole.
- *Medium roasting chickens* Fully grown, tender prime birds are used for roasting, grilling, sauté, casserole, suprêmes and pies.
- *Large roasting or boiling chickens* used for roasting, boiling, casserole, galantine.
- *Capons* Specially bred, fattened cock birds used for roasting.
- *Old hens* Used for stocks and soups.

FOOD VALUE

The flesh of poultry is more easily digested than that of butchers' meat. It contains protein and is therefore useful for building and repairing body tissues and providing heat and energy. The fat content is low and contains a high percentage of unsaturated acids.

STORAGE

Fresh undrawn poultry must be hung by the legs in a well ventilated room for at least 24 hours, otherwise it will not be tender. The innards are not removed until the bird is required. Oven-ready birds are eviscerated and should be stored in a refrigerator. Frozen birds must be kept in deep freeze until required but must be completely thawed, preferably in a refrigerator, before being cooked. This procedure is essential to reduce the risk of food poisoning: chickens are potential carriers of salmonella and if birds are cooked from the frozen state there is the risk of the required degree of heat to kill off salmonella not reaching the centre of the birds.

Frozen poultry should be checked that:

- the packaging is undamaged;
- there are no signs of freezer burns which are indicated by white patches on the skin.

Frozen birds should be defrosted by removing them from the freezer to a refrigerator.

SIGNS OF QUALITY

- Plump breast.
- Pliable breast bone.
- Flesh firm.
- Skin white, unbroken and with a faint bluish tint.
- Smooth legs with small scales and spurs.

Old birds have coarse scales and large spurs on the legs and long hairs on the skin.

CLEANING

- Pick out any pens or down, using a small knife.
- Singe in order to remove any hairs, take care not to scorch the skin.
- Split the neck skin by gripping firmly and making a lengthwise incision on the underside; cut off the neck as close to the body as possible.
- Cut off the head.
- Remove the crop and loosen the intestines and lungs with a forefinger.
- Cut out the vent and wipe clean.
- Loosen the intestines with a forefinger.
- Draw out the innards being careful not to break the gall bladder, because the green liquid (bile) is bitter and will contaminate the bird.

- Wipe the vent end if necessary.
- Split and clean the gizzard.
- Cut off the gall bladder from the liver and discard.
- Keep the neck and heart for stock.

TRUSSING

Roasting

- Clean the legs by dipping in boiling water for a few seconds then remove the scales with a cloth.
- Cut off the outside claws leaving the centre ones, trim these to half their length.
- To facilitate carving remove the wish-bone.
- Place the bird on its back.
- Hold the legs back firmly.
- Insert the trussing needle through the bird, midway between the leg joints.
- Turn on to its side.
- Pierce the winglet, the skin of the neck, the skin of the carcass and the other winglet.
- Tie the ends of string securely.
- Secure the legs by inserting the needle through the carcass and over the legs, take care not to pierce the breast.

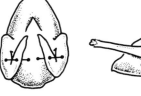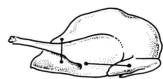

Fig 9.13: Trussing a chicken for roasting

Boiling and pot roasting

- Proceed as for roasting.
- Cut the leg sinew just below the joint.
- Bend back the legs so that they lie parallel to the breast and secure when trussing, *or*
- Insert the legs through incisions made in the skin at the rear end of the bird and secure when trussing.

Fig 9.14: Trussing a chicken for boiling

CUTS OF CHICKEN

The pieces of cut chicken are named as follows:

Leg $\begin{cases} \text{(4) drumstick} \\ \text{(3) thigh} \end{cases}$

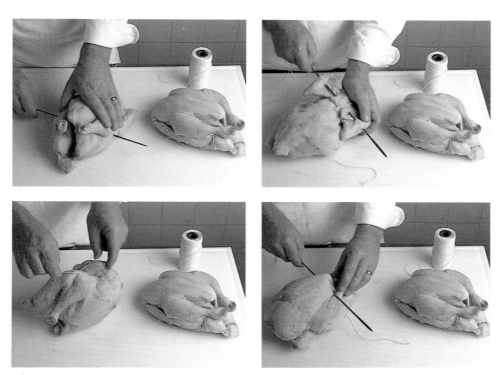

Plate 9.21a–f: Trussing of chicken for roasting

(1) Wing
(2) Breast
(5) Winglet
(6) Carcass

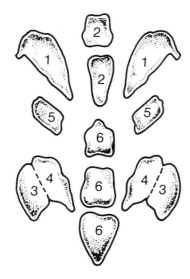

Fig 9.15: Cuts of chicken

CUTTING FOR SAUTÉ, FRICASSÉE, PIES, ETC.
(illustrated on page 396)

- Remove the feet at the first joint.
- Remove the legs from the carcass.
- Cut each leg in two at the joint.
- Remove the wish-bone. Remove the winglets and trim.
- Remove the wings carefully, leaving two equal portions on the breast.
- Remove the breast and cut in two.
- Trim the carcass and cut into three pieces.

PREPARATION FOR GRILLING

- Remove the wish-bone.
- Cut off the claws at the first joint.
- Place the bird on its back.
- Insert a large knife through the neck-end and out of the vent.
- Cut through the backbone and open out.
- Remove back and rib bones.

PREPARATION FOR SUPRÊMES (illustrated on page 396)

A suprême is the wing and half the breast of a chicken with the trimmed wing bone attached; the white meat of one chicken yields two suprêmes.

- Use a chicken weighing $1\frac{1}{4}$–$1\frac{1}{2}$ kg ($2\frac{1}{2}$–3 lb).
- Cut off both the legs from the chicken.
- Remove the skin from the breasts.
- Remove the wish-bone.
- Scrape the wing bone bare adjoining the breasts.
- Cut off the winglets near the joints leaving $1\frac{1}{2}$–2 cm ($\frac{1}{2}$–$\frac{3}{4}$ inch) of bare bone attached to the breasts.
- Cut the breasts close to the breastbone and follow the bone down to the wing joint.
- Cut through the joint.
- Lay the chicken on its side and pull the suprêmes off assisting with the knife.
- Lift the fillets from the suprêmes and remove the sinew from each.
- Make an incision lengthways, along the thick side of the suprêmes, open and place the fillets inside.
- Close, lightly flatten with a bat moistened with water and trim if necessary.

PREPARATION FOR BALLOTTINES

A ballottine is a boned stuffed leg of bird.

- Using a small sharp knife remove the thigh bone.
- Scrape the flesh off the bone of the drumstick towards the claw joint.
- Sever the drumstick bone leaving approximately 2–3 cm ($\frac{3}{4}$–1 inch) at the claw joint end.
- Fill the cavities in both the drumstick and thigh with a savoury stuffing.
- Neaten the shape and secure with string using a trussing needle.

Ballottines of chicken may be cooked and served using any of the recipes for chicken sauté.

CUTTING OF COOKED CHICKEN (ROASTED OR BOILED)

- Remove the legs and cut in two (drumstick and thigh).
- Remove the wings.
- Separate the breast from the carcass and divide in two.
- Serve a drumstick with a wing and the thigh with the breast.

—— *Poultry – Turkey* ——

Turkeys can vary in weight from 3$\frac{1}{2}$–20 kg (7–40 lb). They are cleaned and trussed in the same way as chicken. The wish-bone should always be removed before trussing. The sinews should be drawn out of the legs. Allow 200 g ($\frac{1}{2}$ lb) per portion raw weight.

When cooking a large turkey the legs may be removed, boned, rolled, tied and roasted separately from the remainder of the bird. This will reduce the cooking time and enable the legs and breast to cook more evenly.

Stuffings may be rolled in foil, steamed or baked and thickly sliced. If a firmer stuffing is required, mix in one or two raw eggs before cooking.

SIGNS OF QUALITY

- Large full breast with undamaged skin and no signs of stickiness.
- Legs smooth with supple feet and a short spur.

As birds age the legs turn scaly and the feet harden.

Plate 9.22a–b: Preparing chicken for sauté

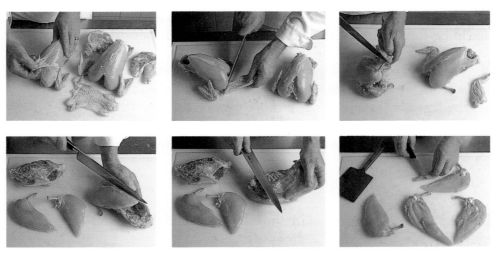

Plate 9.23: Preparation of chicken for suprêmes

Poultry – Duck, Duckling, Goose, Gosling

SIZES (APPROXIMATE)

- *Duck* 3–4 kg (4–6 lb)
- *Duckling* 1½–2 kg (3–4 lb)
- *Goose* 6 kg (12 lb)
- *Gosling* 3 kg (6 lb)

SIGNS OF QUALITY

- Plump breasts.
- Lower back bends easily.
- Webbed feet tear easily.
- Feet and bill should be yellow.

PREPARATION FOR ROASTING

This is the same as for chicken (page 392). The gizzard is not split but trimmed off with a knife. Roast goose is cooked and served as for roast duck.

Game

For information and recipes for game, please refer to *Advanced Practical Cookery* by Kinton, Ceserani and Foskett.

CHICKEN AND TURKEY RECIPES

102 – Roast turkey

	10 portions	25 portions
chestnut stuffing		
chestnuts	200 g (½ lb)	500 g (1¼ lb)
sausage meat	600 g (1½ lb)	2¼ kg (4½ lb)
chopped onion	50 g (2 oz)	125 g (5 oz)
parsley and thyme stuffing		
chopped onion	50 g (2 oz)	125 g (5 oz)
oil, butter or margarine	100 g (4 oz)	250 g (10 oz)
salt, pepper		
white or wholemeal breadcrumbs	100 g (4 oz)	250 g (10 oz)
pinch powdered thyme		
pinch chopped parsley		
chopped turkey liver (raw)		
turkey	5 kg (10 lb)	12 kg (25 lb)
fat bacon	100 g (4 oz)	250 g (10 oz)
brown stock	375 ml (¾ pt)	1 litre (2 pt)
bread sauce (page 131)		

No accompaniments, I portion (200 g raw with skin, bone):

836 kJ/200 kcal
11.75 g fat
(of which 4.0 g saturated)
0.0 g carbohydrate
(of which 0.0 g sugars)
29.0 g protein
0.0 g fibre

With stuffing, roast gravy, bread sauce, I portion (200 g raw, with skin, bone):

1589 kJ/380 kcal
24.0 g fat
(of which 8.4 g saturated)
8.6 g carbohydrate
(of which 1.6 g sugars)
34.0 g protein
0.9 g fibre

1 Slit the chestnuts on both sides using a small knife.
2 Boil the chestnuts in water for 5–10 minutes.
3 Drain and remove the outer and inner skins whilst warm.
4 Cook the chestnuts in a little stock for 5 minutes.
5 When cold, dice and mix into the sausage meat and cooked onion.
6 For the parsley and thyme stuffing, cook the onion in oil, butter or margarine without colour.
7 Remove from the heat, add the seasoning, crumbs and herbs.
8 Mix in the raw chopped liver (optional) from the bird.
9 Truss the bird firmly (removing the wish-bone first).
10 Season with salt and pepper.
11 Cover the breast with fat bacon.
12 Place the bird in a roasting tray on its side and coat with 200 g (4 oz) dripping or oil.

13 Roast in a moderate oven at 200–230°C (Reg. 6–8; 400–450°F).
14 Allow to cook on both legs and complete the cooking with the breast upright for the last 30 minutes.
15 Baste frequently and allow 15–20 minutes per lb. If using a temperature probe, insert in the thickest part of the leg for a reading of 75°C (167°F).
16 Bake the two stuffings separately in greased trays until well cooked.
17 Prepare the gravy from the sediment and the brown stock. Correct the seasoning and remove the fat.
18 Remove the string and serve with stuffings, roast gravy, bread sauce and/or hot cranberry sauce.
19 The turkey may be garnished with chipolata sausages and bacon rolls.

103 – Roast chicken

	4 portions	10 portions
chicken 1¼–1½ kg (2½–3 lb)	1	2½
oil, butter or margarine	50 g (2 oz)	125 g (5 oz)
brown stock	125 ml (¼ pt)	300 ml (⅝ pt)
game chips	25 g (1 oz)	60 g (2½ oz)
bunch watercress	1	2
bread sauce (page 131)	125 ml (¼ pt)	300 ml (⅝ pt)

Without accompaniments, 1 portion (200 g raw with skin, bone):

1134 kJ/270 kcal
16.0 g fat
(of which 5.3 g saturated)
0.0 g carbohydrate
(of which 0.0 g sugars)
28.3 g protein
0.0 g fibre

1 Season the chicken inside and out with salt.
2 Place on its side in a roasting tin.
3 Cover with the oil, butter or margarine.
4 Place in hot oven for approximately 20–25 minutes.
5 Turn on to the other leg.
6 Cook for a further 20–25 minutes approximately. Baste frequently.

With game chips, bread sauce, 1 portion (200 g raw with skin, bone):

2513 kJ/598 kcal
46.8 g fat
(of which 17.3 g saturated)
6.9 g carbohydrate
(of which 2.4 g sugars)
37.8 g protein
1.1 g fibre

recipe continued ▶

399

Plate 9.24: Portioning of roast chicken
(white and dark meat for one portion) with bacon

7 To test if cooked pierce with a fork between the drumstick and thigh and hold over a plate. The juice issuing from the chicken should not show any sign of blood. If using a temperature probe, proceed as for turkey (recipe 102).
8 Make roast gravy with the stock and sediment in the roasting tray.
9 Serve on a flat dish with game chips in front and the watercress at the back of the bird.

Note Roast gravy and bread sauce are served separately. Always remove the trussing string from the bird before serving.

104 ‒ Sauté of chicken

	4 portions	10 portions
chicken $1\frac{1}{4}$–$1\frac{1}{2}$ kg ($2\frac{1}{2}$–3 lb)	1	$2\frac{1}{2}$
butter, margarine or oil	50 g (2 oz)	125 g (5 oz)
salt, pepper		
jus-lié or demi-glace	250 ml ($\frac{1}{2}$ pt)	600 ml ($1\frac{1}{4}$ pt)
chopped parsley		

1   Prepare the chicken for sauté (page 394).
2   Place the butter, margarine or oil in a sauté pan on a fairly hot stove.
3   Season the pieces of chicken and place in the pan in the following order: drumsticks, thighs, carcass, wings, winglets and breast (tougher pieces first as they take longer to cook).
4   Cook to a golden brown on both sides.
5   Cover with a lid and cook on the stove or in the oven until tender.
6   Dress the chicken pieces neatly in an entrée dish.
7   Drain off all fat from the sauté pan.
8   Return to the heat and add the jus-lié or demi-glace, and simmer for 3–4 minutes.
9   Correct the seasoning and skim.
10 Pass through a fine strainer on to the chicken.
11 Sprinkle with chopped parsley and serve.

Note   The chicken giblets may be used in the making of the sauce.

105 – Chicken sauté with mushrooms

	4 portions	10 portions
butter, margarine or oil	50 g (2 oz)	125 g (5 oz)
chicken cut for sauté 1¼–1½ kg (2½–3 lb)	1	2½
chopped shallot	10 g (½ oz)	25 g (1¼ oz)
button mushrooms	100 g (4 oz)	250 g (10 oz)
dry white wine	60 ml (⅛ pt)	150 ml (⅓ pt)
demi-glace or jus-lié	250 ml (½ pt)	600 ml (1¼ pt)
salt, pepper		
chopped parsley		

1   Prepare chicken for sauté (page 394).
2   Pour off the fat, add the white wine and reduce by half.
3   Add the demi-glace, simmer for 5 minutes and correct the seasoning.
4   Pour over the pieces of chicken, sprinkle with chopped parsley.

106 – Chicken sauté chasseur

	4 portions	10 portions
butter, margarine or oil	50 g (2 oz)	125 g (5 oz)
chicken cut for sauté 1¼–1½ kg (2½–3 lb)	1	2½
chopped shallots	10 g (½ oz)	25 g (1¼ oz)
button mushrooms	100 g (4 oz)	250 g (10 oz)
dry white wine	3 tbsp	8 tbsp
jus-lié or demi-glace	250 ml (½ pt)	600 ml (1¼ pt)
tomatoes	200 g (8 oz)	500 g (1¼ lb)
chopped parsley and tarragon		

Using butter, 1 portion provides:

2430 kJ/579 kcal
45.8 g fat
(of which 20.7 g saturated)
2.1 g carbohydrate
(of which 1.6 g sugars)
37.6 g protein
1.5 g fibre

1 Place the butter, margarine or oil in a sauté pan on a fairly hot stove.
2 Season the pieces of chicken and place in the pan in the following order: drumsticks, thighs, carcass, wings, winglets and breast.
3 Cook to a golden brown on both sides.
4 Cover with a lid and cook on the stove or in the oven until tender. Dress neatly in a suitable dish.
5 Add the shallot to the sauté pan, cover with a lid, cook on a gentle heat for 1–2 minutes without colour.
6 Add the washed sliced mushrooms and cover with a lid; cook gently 3–4 minutes without colour.
7 Drain off the fat.
8 Add the white wine and reduce by half.
9 Add the sauce.
10 Add the tomate concassé; simmer for 5 minutes.
11 Correct the seasoning and pour over the chicken.
12 Sprinkle with chopped parsley and tarragon and serve.

107 – Chicken spatchcock *(Illustration page 405)*

	4 portions	10 portions
chicken $1\frac{1}{4}$–$1\frac{1}{2}$ kg ($2\frac{1}{2}$–3 lb)	1	$2\frac{1}{2}$

> **1 portion provides:**
>
> 1560 kJ/372 kcal
> 24.1 g fat
> (of which 8.0 g saturated)
> 0.0 g carbohydrate
> (of which 0.0 g sugars)
> 38.9 g protein
> 0.0 g fibre

1　Truss the chicken as for boiling (page 392), but do not tie with string.
2　Cut horizontally from below the point of the breast over the top of the legs down to the wing joints without removing the breasts. Fold back the breasts.
3　Snap and reverse the backbone into the opposite direction so that the point of the breast now extends forward to resemble the nose and face of a toad.
4　Flatten slightly. Remove any small bones.
5　Skewer the wings and legs in position.
6　Season with salt and mill pepper.
7　Brush with oil or melted butter.
8　Place on preheated grill bars or on a flat tray under a salamander.
9　Brush frequently with melted fat or oil during cooking and allow approximately 15–20 minutes on each side.
10　Test if cooked by piercing the drumstick with a needle or skewer – there should be no sign of blood.
11　When serving, two eyes for the 'toad' may be made from slices of hard boiled white of egg with a pupil of truffle or gherkin.
12　Serve garnished with picked watercress and offer a suitable sauce separately (devilled sauce, compound butter).

108 – Grilled chicken

1　Season the chicken prepared for grilling (see page 394) with salt and mill pepper.
2　Brush with oil or melted butter or margarine and place on preheated greased grill bars or on a barbecue or on a flat baking tray under a salamander.
3　Brush frequently with melted fat during cooking and allow approximately 15–20 minutes each side.
4　Test if cooked by piercing the drumstick with a skewer or trussing needle; there should be no sign of blood issuing from the leg.
5　Serve garnished with picked watercress and offer a suitable sauce separately.

Note Grilled chicken is frequently served garnished with streaky bacon, tomatoes and mushrooms.

The chicken may be marinaded for 2–3 hours before grilling, in a mixture of oil, lemon juice, spices, herbs, freshly grated ginger, finely chopped garlic, salt and pepper. Chicken or turkey portions can also be grilled and previously marinaded if wished (breasts or boned-out lightly battered thighs of chicken).

Plate 9.25a–b Ballottines of chicken chasseur

109 – Suprême of chicken in cream sauce

	4 portions	10 portions
butter or margarine	50 g (2 oz)	125 g (5 oz)
seasoned flour	25 g (1 oz)	60 g (2½ oz)
suprêmes of chicken (page 394)	4	10
sherry or white wine	30 ml ($\frac{1}{16}$ pt)	125 ml ($\frac{1}{4}$ pt)
double cream or non-dairy cream	125 ml ($\frac{1}{4}$ pt)	300 ml ($\frac{5}{8}$ pt)
salt, cayenne		

Plate 9.26a–c: Preparation and presentation of chicken spatchcock

1   Heat the butter or margarine in a sauté pan.
2   Lightly flour the suprêmes.
3   Cook the suprêmes gently on both sides (7–9 minutes) with the minimum of colour.
4   Place the suprêmes in an earthenware serving dish, cover to keep warm.
5   Drain off the fat from the pan.
6   Deglaze the pan with the sherry or white wine.
7   Add the cream, bring to the boil and season.
8   Allow to reduce to a lightly thickened consistency. Correct the seasoning.
9   Pass through a fine strainer on to the suprêmes and serve.

Note   An alternative method of preparing the sauce is to use half the amount of cream (fresh or non-dairy) and an equal amount of chicken velouté (page 119).

Plate 9.27: Preparation and presentation of grilled chicken

110 – Chicken sauté with potatoes

	4 portions	10 portions
chicken cut for sauté $1\frac{1}{4}$–$1\frac{1}{2}$kg ($2\frac{1}{2}$–3 lb) (page 394)	1	$2\frac{1}{2}$
butter, margarine or oil	50 g (2 oz)	125 g (5 oz)
dry white wine	3–4 tbsp	8–10 tbsp
demi-glace or jus-lié	250 ml ($\frac{1}{2}$ pt)	600 ml ($1\frac{1}{4}$ pt)
potatoes	200 g (8 oz)	500 g ($1\frac{1}{4}$ lb)
salt, pepper		
chopped parsley		

1   Cook and dress chicken as for sauté. Pour off the fat.
2   Add wine and reduce by half. Add the sauce.
3   Simmer for 5 minutes.
4   Pass through a fine strainer over the chicken.
5   Meanwhile peel and wash the potatoes.
6   Cut into 1 cm ($\frac{1}{2}$ inch) dice.
7   Wash well, drain and shallow fry to a golden brown in hot fat in a frying-pan.
8   Drain, season and sprinkle over the chicken.
9   Sprinkle with chopped parsley and serve.

111 – Fried chicken (deep fried)

Cut the chicken as for sauté or suprêmes and coat with either flour, egg and crumbs (pané) or pass through a light batter (page 261) to which herbs can be added or an incision made, stuffed with a compound butter, flour, egg and crumbed and deep-fried such as in Chicken Kiev.

112 – Crumbed breast of chicken with asparagus

	4 portions	10 portions
suprêmes of chicken (page 394)	4	10
seasoned flour	25 g (1 oz)	60 g (2½ oz)
egg	1	2
breadcrumbs, white or wholemeal	50 g (2 oz)	125 g (5 oz)
oil ⎱ for frying	50 g (2 oz)	125 g (5 oz)
butter or margarine ⎰	50 g (2 oz)	125 g (5 oz)
butter	50 g (2 oz)	125 g (5 oz)
jus-lié	60 ml (⅛ pt)	150 ml (⅓ pt)
asparagus	200 g (½ lb)	500 g (1¼ lb)

1 Pané the chicken suprêmes. Shake off all surplus crumbs.
2 Neaten and mark on one side with a palette knife.
3 Heat the oil and fat in a sauté pan.
4 Gently fry the suprêmes to a golden brown on both sides (6–8 minutes).
5 Dress the suprêmes on a flat dish and keep warm.
6 Mask the suprêmes with the remaining butter cooked to the nut-brown stage.
7 Surround the suprêmes with a cordon of jus-lié.
8 Garnish each suprême with a neat bundle of asparagus points (previously cooked, refreshed and reheated with a little butter).
9 Place a cutlet frill on to each wing bone and serve.

Note A slice or two of truffle or mushroom can be used as garnish.

Plate 9.29: Chicken suprêmes with asparagus and truffle

Plate 9.28: Chicken sauté with potatoes

113 – Boiled or poached chicken with rice and suprême sauce

	4 portions	10 portions	
boiling fowl 2–2½ kg (4–5 lb)	1	2–3	Using hard margarine, 1 portion provides:
studded onion	50 g (2 oz)	125 g (5 oz)	
bouquet garni			5259 kJ/1252 kcal
carrot	50 g (2 oz)	125 g (5 oz)	86.0 g fat
celery	50 g (2 oz)	125 g (5 oz)	(of which 35.7 g saturated)
peppercorns	6	12	59.6 g carbohydrate
Pilaff			(of which 1.5 g sugars)
chopped onion	50 g (2 oz)	125 g (5 oz)	63.3 g protein
butter, margarine or oil	50 g (2 oz)	125 g (5 oz)	1.9 g fibre
rice (long grain)	200 g (8 oz)	500 g (1¼ oz)	
chicken stock	500 ml (1 pt)	1¼ litre (2½ pt)	
Sauce			
butter or margarine	75 g (3 oz)	180 g (7½ oz)	
flour (white or wholemeal)	75 g (3 oz)	180 g (7½ oz)	
chicken stock	1 litre (2 pt)	2½ litre (5 pt)	
cream (non-dairy cream)	4 tbsp	10 tbsp	
few drops of lemon juice			

1   Place the chicken in cold water. Bring to the boil and skim.
2   Add peeled, whole vegetables, bouquet garni, peppercorns and salt.
3   Simmer until cooked. To test, remove the chicken from the stock and hold over a plate to catch the juices from the inside of the bird. There should be no sign of blood. Also test the drumstick with a trussing needle, which should penetrate easily to the bone.
4   Prepare $\frac{1}{2}$ litre (1 pint) }($1\frac{1}{2}$ litre ($2\frac{1}{2}$ pint) for 10 portions) of velouté from the cooking liquor, cook out, correct the seasoning and pass through a fine strainer.
5   Finish with cream. Prepare a pilaff of rice.
6   To serve, cut into portions. Dress the rice neatly in an entrée dish, arrange the portions of chicken on top and coat with sauce.

114 – Chicken à la king

	4 portions	10 portions
button mushrooms	100 g (4 oz)	250 g (10 oz)
butter or margarine	25 g (1 oz)	60 g ($2\frac{1}{2}$ oz)
red pimento (skinned)	50 g (2 oz)	125 g (5 oz)
cooked boiled chicken	400 g (1 lb)	$1\frac{1}{4}$ kg ($2\frac{1}{2}$ lb)
sherry	30 ml ($\frac{1}{6}$ pt)	75 ml ($\frac{1}{4}$ pt)
chicken velouté	125 ml ($\frac{1}{4}$ pt)	150 ml ($\frac{1}{3}$ pt)
cream or non-dairy cream	30 ml ($\frac{1}{16}$ pt)	75 ml ($\frac{1}{4}$ pt)

Using butter, hard margarine, 1 portion provides:

1226 kJ/292 kcal
16.7 g fat
(of which 7.8 g saturated)
3.2 g carbohydrate
(of which 0.8 g sugars)
30.4 g protein
0.9 g fibre

1   Wash, peel and slice the mushrooms.
2   Cook them without colour in the butter or margarine.
3   If using raw pimento, discard the seeds, cut the pimento in dice and cook with the mushrooms.
4   Cut the chicken in small, neat slices.
5   Add the chicken to the mushrooms and pimento.
6   Drain off the fat. Add the sherry.
7   Add the velouté, bring to the boil.
8   Finish with the cream and correct the seasoning.
9   Place into a serving dish and decorate with small strips of cooked pimento.

Note   1 or 2 egg yolks may be used to form a liaison with the cream mixed into the boiling mixture at the last possible moment and immediately removed from the heat. Chicken à la king may be served in a border of golden brown duchesse potato or a pilaff of rice may be offered as an accompaniment. It is suitable for hot buffet dish.

115 – Chicken vol-au-vent

8 portions

puff paste (page 662)	400 g (1 lb)
boiling chicken 2 kg (4 lb)	1
chicken velouté	½ litre (1 pt)
cream	4 tbsp

> Using hard margarine, I portion provides:
>
> 2754 kJ/656 kcal
> 50.7 g fat
> (of which 21.2 g saturated)
> 20.0 g carbohydrate
> (of which 0.6 g sugars)
> 31.0 g protein
> 0.9 g fibre

1 Prepare the puff pastry using ½ kg (1 lb) flour and ½ kg (1 lb) margarine and ¼ litre (½ pint) water.
2 Roll out sufficient to cut eight rounds 8 cm (3 inch) diameter.
3 Turn upside down on a lightly greased, damped baking sheet.
4 Using a smaller plain cutter dipped in hot oil, make incisions half-way through each leaving approximately ½ cm (¼ inch) border.
5 Eggwash, rest for 20 minutes and bake in a hot oven at 230–250°C (Reg. 8–9; 450–500°F) for approximately 15–20 minutes.
6 When cool remove the lids carefully with a small knife.
7 Empty out the raw pastry from the centre.
8 Cook the chicken as for boiled chicken (page 392).
9 Make a velouté and cook out, correct the seasoning and pass through a fine strainer; finish with cream.
10 Remove all skin and bone from the chicken.
11 Cut into neat pieces, mix with the sauce.
12 Fill the warm vol-au-vent to overflowing.
13 Add the lids, garnish with picked parsley and serve.

Note Chicken and mushroom vol-au-vent can be made with the addition of 100 g (4 oz) of washed button mushrooms cut into quarters and cooked in a little stock with a few drops of lemon juice and 5 g (¼ oz) butter.

116 – Chicken pancakes

	4 portions	10 portions
Pancake		
flour, white or wholemeal	100 g (4 oz)	250 g (10 oz)
egg	1	2–3
salt, pepper		
chopped parsley		
milk, whole or skimmed	$\frac{1}{4}$ litre ($\frac{1}{2}$ pt)	600 ml ($1\frac{1}{4}$ pt)
melted butter or margarine	10 g ($\frac{1}{2}$ oz)	25 g ($1\frac{1}{4}$ oz)
Filling		
thick béchamel or chicken velouté	125 ml ($\frac{1}{4}$ pt)	300 ml ($\frac{5}{8}$ pt)
cooked chicken free from bone and skin	200 g ($\frac{1}{2}$ lb)	500 ml ($1\frac{1}{4}$ pt)
salt, pepper		

1 portion provides:

1423 kJ/339 kcal
18.9 g fat
(of which 6.3 g saturated)
24.7 g carbohydrate
(of which 3.4 g sugars)
19.0 g protein
1.1 g fibre

1 Sieve the flour into a bowl and make a well in the centre.
2 Add the egg, salt, pepper, parsley and milk.
3 Gradually incorporate the flour from the sides of the bowl and whisk to a smooth batter.
4 Mix in the melted butter.
5 Heat the pancake pan, clean thoroughly.
6 Add 5 g ($\frac{1}{4}$ oz) lard or oil and heat until smoking.
7 Add sufficient mixture to thinly cover the bottom of the pan.
8 Cook for a few seconds until lightly brown.
9 Turn and cook on the other side. Turn onto a plate.
10 Wipe the pan clean and make a total of 8 small or 4 large pancakes (20 or 10 pancakes for 10 portions).
11 Meanwhile prepare the filling by boiling the sauce.
12 Cut the chicken in neat small pieces and add to the sauce.
13 Mix in and correct the seasoning.
14 Divide the mixture between the pancakes, roll up each one and place in an earthenware dish.
15 Reheat in a hot oven and serve.

Note Additions to the pancake filling can include mushrooms, ham, sweetcorn, etc., and the pancakes can be finished with a sauce such as Mornay, chasseur, etc.

117 – Fricassée of chicken

	4 portions	10 portions
chicken 1¼–1½ kg (2½–3 lb)	1	2–3
butter or margarine	50 g (2 oz)	125 g (5 oz)
flour	35 g (1½ oz)	100 g (4 oz)
chicken stock	½ litre (1 pt)	1¼ litre (2½ pt)
yolks of eggs	1–2	5
cream or non-dairy cream	4 tbsp	10 tbsp
chopped parsley		

Using butter, 1 portion provides:

2699 kJ/643 kcal
51.3 g fat
(of which 23.3 g saturated)
7.4 g carbohydrate
(of which 0.6 g sugars)
38.2 g protein
0.4 g fibre

1 Cut the chicken as for sauté and season with salt and pepper.
2 Place the butter in a sauté pan. Heat gently.
3 Add pieces of chicken. Cover with a lid.
4 Cook gently on both sides without colouring. Mix in the flour.
5 Cook out carefully without colouring. Gradually mix in the stock.
6 Bring to the boil and skim.
7 Allow to simmer gently until cooked.
8 Mix the yolks and cream in a basin (liaison).
9 Pick out the chicken into a clean pan.
10 Pour a little boiling sauce on to the yolks and cream and mix well.
11 Pour all back into the sauce, combine thoroughly but do not reboil.
12 Correct the seasoning and pass through a fine strainer.
13 Pour over the chicken, reheat without boiling.
14 Serve sprinkled with chopped parsley.
15 May be garnished with heart-shaped croûtons, fried in butter.

Note A fricassée of chicken with button onions and mushrooms can be made similarly with the addition of 50–100 g (2–4 oz) button onions and 50–100 g (2–4 oz) button mushrooms. They are peeled and the mushrooms left whole, turned or quartered depending on size and quality. The onions are added to the chicken as soon as it comes to the boil and the mushrooms 15 minutes later. Heart-shaped croûtons may be used to garnish.

118 – Chicken pie

	4 portions	10 portions
chicken $1\frac{1}{4}$–$1\frac{1}{2}$ kg ($2\frac{1}{2}$–3 lb)	1	2–3
salt, pepper		
streaky bacon	100 g (4 oz)	250 g (10 oz)
button mushrooms	100 g (4 oz)	250 g (10 oz)
chopped onion	1	$2\frac{1}{2}$
chicken stock	$\frac{1}{4}$ litre ($\frac{1}{2}$ pt)	600 ml ($1\frac{1}{4}$ pt)
pinch of chopped parsley		
hard-boiled egg (chopped)	1	2
puff paste (page 392)	200 g (8 oz)	500 g ($1\frac{1}{4}$ lb)

> Using hard margarine in pastry, 1 portion provides:
>
> 3357 kJ/799 kcal
> 62.6 g fat
> (of which 25.1 g saturated)
> 16.4 g carbohydrate
> (of which 1.9 g sugars)
> 43.3 g protein
> 1.8 g fibre

1 Cut the chicken as for sauté or bone-out completely and cut into pieces 4×1 cm ($1\frac{1}{2}$ × $\frac{1}{2}$ inch).
2 Season with salt and pepper.
3 Wrap each piece in very thin streaky bacon. Place in a pie dish.
4 Add the washed sliced mushrooms and remainder of the ingredients.
5 Add sufficient cold stock to barely cover the chicken.
6 Cover and cook as for steak pie (page 346), allowing approximately 1–$1\frac{1}{2}$ hours cooking.
7 Serve. If pie is served whole use a pie collar.

119 – Curried chicken

	4 portions	10 portions
chicken ($1\frac{1}{4}$–$1\frac{1}{2}$ kg ($2\frac{1}{2}$–3 lb)	1	2–3
oil	50 g (2 oz)	125 g (5 oz)
onion	200 g (8 oz)	500 g ($1\frac{1}{4}$ lb)
clove garlic	1	2
flour	10 g ($\frac{1}{2}$ oz)	25 g ($1\frac{1}{4}$ oz)
curry powder	10 g ($\frac{1}{2}$ oz)	25 g ($1\frac{1}{4}$ oz)
tomato purée	25 g (1 oz)	60 g ($2\frac{1}{2}$ oz)
chicken stock	$\frac{1}{2}$ litre (1 pt)	$1\frac{1}{4}$ litre ($2\frac{1}{2}$ pt)
sultanas	25 g (1 oz)	60 g ($2\frac{1}{2}$ oz)
chopped chutney	25 g (1 oz)	60 g ($2\frac{1}{2}$ oz)
desiccated coconut	10 g ($\frac{1}{2}$ oz)	25 g ($1\frac{1}{4}$ oz)
chopped apple	50 g (2 oz)	125 g (5 oz)
grated root ginger	10 g ($\frac{1}{2}$ oz)	25 g ($1\frac{1}{4}$ oz)
or		
ground ginger	5 g ($\frac{1}{4}$ oz)	12 g ($\frac{5}{8}$ oz)

Using sunflower oil, 1 portion provides:

2755 kJ/656 kcal
49.9 g fat
(of which 17.1 g saturated)
15.1 g carbohydrate
(of which 11.8 g sugars)
37.4 g protein
2.3 g fibre

1 Cut the chicken as for sauté, season with salt.
2 Heat the oil in a sauté pan, add the chicken.
3 Lightly brown on both sides.
4 Add the chopped onion, garlic and curry powder.
5 Cover with lid; cook gently for 3–4 minutes.
6 Mix in the flour.
7 Mix in the tomato purée. Moisten with stock.
8 Bring to the boil, skim.
9 Add the remainder of the ingredients. Simmer until cooked.
10 The sauce may be finished with 2 tablespoons cream or yoghurt.

Note Accompany with 100 g (4 oz) plain boiled rice, grilled poppadum and Bombay duck; see also page 314 for extra accompaniments.

This is a typical recipe in use today. For a traditional recipe the curry powder would be replaced by either curry paste or a mixture of freshly ground spices (turmeric, cumin, allspice, fresh ginger, chilli and clove). (See also the chapter on ethnic cooking.)

120 ~ Braised rice with chicken livers

	4 portions	10 portions
chicken livers	100 g (4 oz)	250 g (10 oz)
salt, mill pepper		
butter or margarine	25 g (1 oz)	60 g (2½ oz)
demi-glace or jus-lié	60 ml (⅛ pt)	150 ml (⅓ pt)
braised rice (page 236)	200 g (½ lb)	500 g (1¼ lb)

> Using hard margarine, I portion provides:
>
> 1115 kJ/265 kcal
> 17.0 g fat
> (of which 7.2 g saturated)
> 22.4 g carbohydrate
> (of which 0.3 g sugars)
> 7.0 g protein
> 0.6 g fibre

1 Trim the livers, cut into 1 cm (½ inch) pieces.
2 Season lightly with salt and pepper.
3 Fry quickly in the butter in a frying-pan. Drain well.
4 Mix with the demi-glace or the jus-lié; do not reboil.
5 Correct the seasoning.
6 Make a well with the riz pilaff on the dish.
7 Serve the livers in the centre of the rice.

121 ~ Chicken in red wine

	4 portions	10 portions
roasting chicken 1½ kg (3 lb)	1	2–3
lardons	50 g (2 oz)	125 g (5 oz)
small chipolatas	4	10
button mushrooms	50 g (2 oz)	125 g (5 oz)
sunflower oil	3 tbsp	7 tbsp
butter or margarine	50 g (2 oz)	125 g (5 oz)
small button onions	12	30
red wine	125 ml (¼ pt)	300 ml (⅝ pt)
brown stock	375 ml (¾ pt)	1 litre (2 pt)
or		
red wine	500 ml (1 pt)	900 ml (1½ pt)
butter or margarine	25 g (1 oz)	60 g (2½ oz)
flour	25 g (1 oz)	60 g (2½ oz)
heart-shaped croûtons	4	10
chopped parsley		

> Using sunflower oil, hard margarine, I portion provides:
>
> 4794 kJ/1141 kcal
> 95.7 g fat
> (of which 32.9 g saturated)
> 16.6 g carbohydrate
> (of which 2.3 g sugars)
> 49.0 g protein
> 1.7 g fibre

1 Cut the chicken as for sauté.
2 Blanch the lardons.

recipe continued ▶

3   If the chipolatas are large divide into two.

4   Wash and cut the mushrooms in quarters.

5   Sauté the lardons, mushrooms and chipolatas in a mixture of butter/margarine and oil. Remove when cooked.

6   Season the pieces of chicken and place in the pan in the correct order with button onions. Sauté until almost cooked. Drain off fat.

7   Just cover with red wine and brown stock, cover with a lid and finish cooking.

8   Remove chicken and onions, place into a clean pan.

9   Lightly thicken the liquor with a beurre manié from the 25 g (1 oz) butter/margarine and 25 g (1 oz) flour.

10   Pass sauce over the chicken and onions, add mushrooms, chipolatas and lardons. Correct seasoning and reheat.

11   Serve garnished with heart-shaped croûtons with the points dipped in chopped parsley.

DUCK RECIPES

122 – Roast duck or duckling

	4 portions	10 portions
duck	1	2–3
oil		
salt		
brown stock	$\frac{1}{4}$ litre ($\frac{1}{2}$pt)	600 ml ($1\frac{1}{4}$pt)
bunch watercress	1	2
apple sauce (page 672)	125 ml ($\frac{1}{4}$pt)	300 ml ($\frac{5}{8}$pt)

> With apple sauce, watercress, 1 portion provides:
>
> 3083 kJ/734 kcal
> 60.5 g fat
> (of which 16.9 g saturated)
> 8.2 g carbohydrate
> (of which 7.8 g sugars)
> 40.0 g protein
> 1.4 g fibre

1   Lightly season the duck inside and out with salt.

2   Truss and brush lightly with oil.

3   Place on its side in a roasting tin, with a few drops of water.

4   Place in a hot oven for 20–25 minutes.

5   Turn on to the other side.

6   Cook for a further 20–25 minutes. Baste frequently.

7   To test if cooked, pierce with a fork between the drumstick and thigh and hold over a plate. The juice issuing from the duck should not show any signs of blood. If using a probe, the temperature should be 80°C (176°F).

8 Prepare the roast gravy with the stock and the sediment in the roasting tray. Correct the seasoning, remove the surface fat.

9 Serve garnished with picked watercress.

10 Accompany with a sauceboat of hot apple sauce and a sauceboat of gravy and game chips. Also serve a sauceboat of sage and onion stuffing as prepared in the following recipe.

123 – Stuffing for duck

	4 portions	10 portions
chopped onion	100 g (4 oz)	250 g (10 oz)
duck dripping or butter	100 g (4 oz)	250 g (10 oz)
powdered sage	50 g (2 oz)	125 g (5 oz)
chopped parsley		
salt, pepper		
white or wholemeal breadcrumbs		
chopped duck liver (optional)	50 g (2 oz)	125 g (5 oz)

1 Gently cook the onion in the dripping without colour.

2 Add the herbs and seasoning. Mix in the crumbs and liver. Stuff the neck end and cook the remaining stuffing separately. Cook and serve as for roast duck.

124 – Roast duckling and orange salad

Proceed as for roast duck and serve separately in a bowl 4 hearts of lettuce or good leaves of lettuce and on each heart place 3 segments of orange, free from pips and skin, and a little blanched fine julienne of orange zest sprinkled over.

Accompany with a sauceboat of cream lightly acidulated with lemon juice.

125 – Duckling with orange sauce

		4 portions	10 portions
duckling 2 kg (4 lb)		1	2–3
butter		50 g (2 oz)	125 g (5 oz)
carrots		50 g (2 oz)	125 g (5 oz)
onions		50 g (2 oz)	125 g (5 oz)
celery	mirepoix	25 g (1 oz)	60 g (2½ oz)
bayleaf		1	2–3
small sprig thyme		1	2–3
brown stock		250 ml (½ pt)	600 ml (1¼ pt)
arrowroot		10 g (½ pt)	25 g (1¼ oz)
oranges		2	5
lemon		1	2
vinegar		2 tbsp	5 tbsp
sugar		25 g (1 oz)	60 g (2½ oz)

Using butter, 1 portion proves:

744 kcas/3125 kJ
60.1 fat
(of which 17.1 g saturated)
11.8 g carbohydrate
(of which 9.3 g sugars)
39.9 g protein
0.1 g fibre

1 Clean and truss the duck. Use a fifth of the butter to grease a deep pan. Add the mirepoix (vegetables and herbs).
2 Season the duck. Place the duck on the mirepoix.
3 Coat the duck with the remaining butter.
4 Cover the pan with a tight fitting lid.
5 Place the pan in oven at 200–230°C (Reg. 6–8; 400–450°F).
6 Baste occasionally; cook for approximately 1 hour.
7 Remove the lid and continue cooking the duck basting frequently until tender (about a further 30 minutes).
8 Remove the duck, cut out the string and keep the duck in a warm place. Drain off all the fat from the pan.
9 Deglaze with the stock, bring to the boil and allow to simmer for a few minutes.
10 Thicken by adding the arrowroot diluted in a little cold water.
11 Reboil, correct the seasoning, degrease and pass through a fine strainer.
12 Thinly remove the zest from one orange and the lemon and cut into fine julienne.
13 Blanch the julienne of zest for 3–4 minutes and refresh.
14 Place the vinegar and sugar in a small sauteuse and cook to a light caramel stage.
15 Add the juice of the oranges and the lemon.
16 Add the sauce and bring to the boil.
17 Correct the seasoning and pass through a fine strainer.

18 Add the julienne to the sauce, keep warm.
19 Remove the legs from the duck, bone out and cut in thin slices.
20 Carve the duck breasts into thin slices and neatly dress.
21 Coat with the sauce and serve.

Note An alternative method of service is to cut the duck into eight pieces which may then be either left on the bone or the bones removed.

126 – Duckling with cherries

	4 portions	10 portions
duckling 2 kg (4 lb)	1	2–3
butter	50 g (2 oz)	125 g (5 oz)
carrots	50 g (2 oz)	125 g (5 oz)
onions	50 g (2 oz)	125 g (5 oz)
celery	25 g (1 oz)	60 g (2½ oz)
bayleaf	1	2–3
small sprig thyme	1	2–3
sherry or Madeira	2 tbsp	5 tbsp
brown stock	250 ml (½ pt)	600 ml (1¼ pt)
arrowroot	10 g (½ oz)	25 g (1¼ oz)
stoned cherries	24	60

1 Cook the duck as in recipe 125.
2 Deglaze the pan with the sherry.
3 Add the stock, bring to the boil and simmer for 4–5 minutes.
4 Thicken by gradually adding the arrowroot diluted in a little cold water.
5 Reboil, correct the seasoning, degrease and pass through a fine strainer.
6 Add the stoned cherries to the sauce and simmer gently for 3–4 minutes.
7 Remove the legs from the duck, bone out and cut into thin slices.
8 Cut the duck breasts into thin slices and neatly dress.
9 Coat with the sauce and cherries and serve.

Note An alternative method is to cut the duck into eight pieces which may then either be left on the bone or have the bones removed.

10

ETHNIC DISHES

Recipe No.		*Page No.*
	Caribbean	
2	Almond chicken	426
1	Metagee (saltfish with coconut and plantains)	425
	China	
6	Chinese vegetables and noodles	430
8	Chop suey	431
9	Chow mein	432
4	Fried noodles with shredded pork	428
7	Pork, ham and bamboo shoot soup	430
5	Sole with mushrooms and bamboo shoots	429
3	Walnut chicken	427
	Greece	
11	Avgolemono soup (egg and lemon soup)	434
14	Baklavas (filo pastry with nuts and sugar)	438
13	Dolmades (stuffed vine leaves)	437
12	Kalamarakia yemista (stuffed squid)	435
10	Taramasalata (paste of smoked cod's roe)	434
	India and Pakistan	
27	Alu-Chole vegetarian curry	451
20	Beef do-piazza	445
21	Beef Madras	446
32	Chapatis	456
15	Chemmeen kari	440
24	Chicken palak (chicken fried with spinach and spices)	448
25	Chicken tikka	449
26	Dahl	450
19	Kashmira lamb	444
22	Keema Matar (medium spiced mince and peas)	446
18	Lamb pasanda	443
29	Onion bhajias	452
30	Pakora (batter-fried vegetables or shrimps)	453
17	Palak lamb	442
28	Pepper bhajee	452
31	Samosas	453
23	Tandoori chicken	447
16	Tandoori prawns (grilled spiced prawns)	441
	Indonesia	
33	Gado gado (vegetable salad with peanut dressing)	457
35	Nasi goreng (rice with bacon, chicken and soy sauce)	459
34	Rendang (Indonesian beef curry)	458

Japan

43	Bara sushi (vinegared rice with fish and beans)	465
36	Hotate gai shoyu yaki (scallops grilled with soy sauce)	460
40	Sashimi	463
41	Sushi	464
42	Sushi rice (vinegared rice)	464
38	Tempura (vegetable and shrimp fritters)	462
39	Teppanyaki	463
37	Tonkatsu (deep-fried pork cutlet)	460
39	Yakitori	463

Mexico

46	Burritos (Mexican pancakes)	468
45	Picadillo	467
44	Tortillas	466

Middle East and Israel

50	Couscous	471
47	Hummus (chick pea and sesame seed paste)	469
51	Khoshaf (dried fruit with nuts, perfumed with rose and orange water)	474
49	Kibbeh bil sanieh (spiced lamb with cracked wheat)	470
48	Tabbouleh (cracked wheat salad)	470

Israeli kosher foods

56	Blitz kuchen (baked fluffy batter with nuts and cinnamon)	478
57	Carrot kugel	479
54	Chollo bread	477
53	Koenigsberger klops (meat balls)	476
55	Matzo fritters	478
52	Potato latkes	475

Spain

59	Cocido madrileno (pork with chick peas)	482
58	Paella (savoury rice with chicken, fish, vegetables and spices)	480

Thailand

60	Thai mussaman curry	483

United States of America

61	Chilli con carne (beef with beans in chilli sauce)	484
65	Chocolate brownies	487
63	Clam chowder	486
62	Hash brown potatoes	486
66	Pecan pie	487
64	Succotash (butter beans, sweetcorn and bacon in cream sauce)	487

Ethnic cookery

1   Be aware of the various ethnic influences on cookery such as religious, geographical, tourism, etc.
2   Produce dishes prepared, cooked and presented in accordance with traditional and/ or consumer requirements.
3   Ensure that work complies with food hygiene, safety and health legislation.
4   Comply with any taboos, restrictions or specifications applicable to particular customers.

Ethnic means a group of people with common national or cultural traditions. Many ethnic groups move and settle from country to country and as our multi-ethnic society continues to grow it becomes increasingly important to have a basic understanding of the commodities available, the styles of cooking and some of the more popular dishes. Many countries such as China, Japan and India and those in the Middle East have long established cookery traditions with a wide range of foods dating back two or three thousand years.

In many groups religious influences affect what people eat. Muslims are traditionally forbidden alcohol and pork and only meat that has been prepared by a halal butcher is permitted. Most Hindus do not eat meat and none eat beef as the cow is a sacred animal to them (strict Hindus are vegetarians). Many Sikhs also are vegetarians as are strict Buddhists. The Jewish religion has strict dietary laws. Shellfish, pork and birds of prey are forbidden. Strict Jews eat only meat that has been specially slaughtered known as Kosher meat. Milk and meat must neither be used together in cooking nor served at the same meal and three hours should elapse between eating food containing milk and food containing meat.

Ethnic cookery also varies within specific countries, Great Britain subdivides into England, Scotland, Wales and Northern Ireland. The once subcontinent of India subsequently became India, Pakistan and Bangladesh. In terms of cookery styles and dishes there is often further divisions within these and most other countries according to area or region.

Asian, Middle Eastern and Far-Eastern cookery makes considerable use of a range of spices and herbs. Ideally spices are freshly ground (in some dishes there may be up to five or six spices) and then carefully fried at the beginning of recipes to extract the maximum flavour. Inevitably to save time and labour a variety of different strengths and blends of ready-prepared mixes of spices are available (curry powder or paste) which may be hot, medium or mild or may be named after the area of the country in which it is traditionally used. Garam masala, five spice powder are two other mixes. Many ready-prepared sauces are also available.

It would be impossible within a chapter and even within a book to give a comprehensive study of total ethnic cookery but the recipes which follow are examples from a number of countries.

—— *Caribbean cooking* ——

The history of the West Indies shows the many cultural influences brought to the islands over the centuries which makes it difficult to generalise or to standardise the various types of cuisine that still exist. The Dutch, English, French and Spanish have left their individual traditions and African, Chinese and Creole immigrants have brought their styles to add to the culture and gastronomy.

In the Caribbean there is an abundance of exotic fruits and vegetables, fresh fish and shellfish, pork as the main source of meat, plenty of poultry and dried pulses and cereals, all cooked in interesting combinations with simplicity but with an emphasis on the intense aroma of spices to make it more significant.

1 – Metagee (saltfish with coconut and plantains)

	4 portions	10 portions
saltfish pieces	200 g (8 oz)	500 g (1¼ lb)
green plantains	400 g (1 lb)	1 kg (2½ lb)
yam	100 g (4 oz)	250 g (10 oz)
sweet potato	100 g (4 oz)	250 g (10 oz)
shredded onion	100 g (4 oz)	250 g (10 oz)
tomato, skinned de-seeded, diced	100 g (4 oz)	250 g (10 oz)
sprig of thyme		
desiccated coconut	100 g (4 oz)	250 g (10 oz)
white stock	250 ml (½ pt)	600 ml (1¼ pt)
okra	4	10

1 Soak the saltfish in cold water for 30 minutes.
2 Dice the plantain, yam and sweet potato into 1 cm (½ inch) cubes and place in a pan with the onion and tomato.
3 Sprinkle with thyme. Arrange pieces of saltfish on top. Sprinkle with desiccated coconut. Cover with white stock.
4 Top and tail the okra. Do not cut, otherwise the starchy substance will be released. Place the okra in with the fish and vegetables.
5 Bring to the boil and simmer gently until the vegetables and fish are cooked.
6 Serve hot in a suitable dish, decorated with the okra on top.

Note   When possible it is preferable to use coconut milk in place of white stock and desiccated coconut.

425

2 – Almond chicken

	4 portions	10 portions
peanut oil	60 ml ($\frac{1}{8}$ pt)	150 ml ($\frac{1}{3}$ pt)
suprêmes of chicken, thinly sliced	4	10
onion, finely chopped	100 g (4 oz)	250 g (10 oz)
chopped chives	25 g (1 oz)	60 g (2$\frac{1}{2}$ oz)
cucumber } cut in paysanne	100 g (4 oz)	250 g (10 oz)
carrot	100 g (4 oz)	250 g (10 oz)
water chestnuts, sliced	200 g (8 oz)	500 g (1$\frac{1}{4}$ lb)
bamboo shoots, sliced	50 g (2 oz)	125 g (5 oz)
mushrooms, finely sliced	100 g (4 oz)	250 g (10 oz)
soy sauce	60 ml ($\frac{1}{8}$ pt)	150 ml ($\frac{1}{3}$ pt)
whole blanched almonds	100 g (4 oz)	250 g (10 oz)
butter, margarine or oil	50 g (2 oz)	125 g (5 oz)

1 Heat the peanut oil in a sauté pan or wok, season and stir-fry the chicken over a fierce heat for 2–3 minutes.
2 Add the onion, chives, cucumber, carrot, water chestnuts, bamboo shoots and mushrooms, and season.
3 Continue to stir-fry over a fierce heat for 5 minutes.
4 Add the soy sauce and cook for 1 minute.
5 Meanwhile sauté the almonds in a little butter, margarine or oil until golden brown.
6 Place the chicken and vegetables into a suitable dish for serving and garnish with the almonds.
7 Serve with a braised or pilaff rice.

—— *Chinese cooking* ——

The People's Republic of China has twenty-eight provinces, five major religions, eight dialects with Mandarin as the common speech and more than one thousand million inhabitants. There are however, only four main styles of cookery these being the Canton, Peking, Shanghai and Szechwan styles which correspond to the southern, northern, eastern and western regions respectively.

The gastronomy of China is recognised as one of the world's greatest. A certain depth of knowledge is necessary to understand the fundamentals of Chinese cookery and service which are, however, based on meagre peasant diets and long traditions which ensured that everything was used, no food thrown away and a few ingredients stretched inventively with accent on taste, flavour and aroma. The repertoire is extensive even though the staple ingredient is rice and almost everything is cooked in a wok or a steamer. The sequence of courses as we know it is not followed in a Chinese meal as several dishes are laid on the table at once, although there is a progress from light to heavy and back to light. The use of chopsticks means that everything is cut small before it is cooked and the chefs use only a chopper for all work, even for the very realistic carvings in vegetables and fruit for which they are famous.

A resumé of the four regions shows Cantonese as being the best – where rice is most widely used and sweet and sour dishes are favoured and duck and other foods are given a glossy finish and a lot of the dishes are cooked by steaming. Peking cookery features noodles rather than rice and there are other farinaceous items such as steamed dumplings and pancake dishes. The dishes are more substantial and the cookery is more cosmopolitan than elsewhere in the country; more foods are deep-fried and generally there is more crispness of texture. Shanghai cookery is more robust with more use of flour and oil, greater emphasis on garlic, ginger and other spices, and a more peppery result. Here also it is the tradition to serve noodles instead of rice. The cookery of the western region of Szechwan bordering on India and Myanmar is noted for its hot spiciness, including the use of chillies.

3 – Walnut chicken

This recipe yields 20 bite-sized pieces, served as an appetiser.

suprêmes of chicken	2
walnuts, coarsely chopped	100 g (4 oz)
egg whites	2
dry sherry	1 tbsp
sesame seed oil	1 tsp
plain flour	50 g (2 oz)
water	60 ml ($\frac{1}{8}$ pt)
seasoning	

1   Remove the wing bones from the suprêmes. Remove the fillets and take out the nerve from each fillet.
2   Open each suprême out by cutting almost in half horizontally. Open and lay flat. Bat out the suprêmes and each fillet.

recipe continued ▶

3 Mix in a basin the egg whites, sherry, water, sesame seed oil and seasoning. Gradually stir in the sieved flour.
4 Heat sufficient oil in a frying pan to cover the bottom.
5 Dip the four pieces of chicken in the flour, coating both sides. Then coat with the chopped walnuts.
6 Gently fry in the hot oil, taking care that the walnuts do not burn. Turn over and cook the other side.
7 When cooked and dried, cut into bite-sized pieces and serve on dish paper.

4 – Fried noodles with shredded pork

	4 portions	10 portions
pork fillet, cut into batons	100 g (4 oz)	250 g (10 oz)
dark soy sauce	1½ tsp	4–5 tsp
granulated sugar	1 tsp	2–3 tsp
cornflour	10 g (½ oz)	25 g (1 oz)
water	60 ml (⅛ pt)	150 ml (⅓ pt)
vegetable oil	60 ml (⅛ pt)	150 ml (⅓ pt)
Chinese egg noodles	150 g (6 oz)	375 g (15 oz)
bean sprouts	150 g (6 oz)	375 g (15 oz)
Chinese dried mushrooms	2	5
dry sherry	1 tsp	2–3 tsp
chicken stock	125 ml (¼ pt)	300 ml (½ pt)
1 light soy sauce	1 tsp	2–3 tsp
sesame oil	½ tsp	1 tsp
spring onions for garnish	2 tsp	5 tsp

1 Marinade the pork in half the dark soy sauce, and half the sugar and cornflour, seasoning, half the water and half the oil. Allow to stand for 15 minutes.
2 Blanch the noodles in boiling salted water for 1 minute, refresh and drain.
3 In a suitable pan, heat sufficient oil to deep fry the noodles. Drain on kitchen paper or in a cloth.
4 Heat the remainder of the oil in a wok. Add the bean sprouts. Cook quickly and remove.
5 Add the pork and cook until lightly browned.
6 Add the bean sprouts to the pork and add the mushrooms.
7 Blend the remaining cornflour with the rest of the water and add all the remaining ingredients. Stir this into the pork and simmer until thickened.

8   Place the noodles in a suitable serving dish, place the pork in the centre and garnish with chopped spring onions.

5 – Sole with mushrooms and bamboo shoots

	4 portions	10 portions
fillet of lemon or Dover sole, cut into goujons	200 g (8 oz)	500 g ($1\frac{1}{4}$ lb)
sherry	2 tbsp	5 tbsp
soy sauce	2 tbsp	5 tbsp
cornflour	10 g ($\frac{1}{2}$ oz)	25 g (1 oz)
egg white, lightly beaten	1	2
fresh ginger (grated)	10 g ($\frac{1}{2}$ oz)	25 g (1 oz)
finely chopped onion	25 g (1 oz)	60 g ($2\frac{1}{2}$ oz)
mushrooms, sliced	50 g (2 oz)	125 g (5 oz)
bamboo shoots, sliced	50 g (2 oz)	125 g (5 oz)
pinch of monosodium glutamate (MSG), optional		
white stock	30 ml ($\frac{1}{16}$ pt)	75 ml ($\frac{1}{4}$ pt)

1   Place the goujons of fish into a small basin, add half the sherry and half the soy sauce.
2   Season, mix in half the cornflour and stir in the egg white.
3   Carefully take out the goujons and deep fry until golden brown. Drain.
4   Heat a little oil in a frying pan or wok, add the grated ginger and chopped onion; fry for 1 minute.
5   Add the mushrooms and bamboo shoots; fry for 1 minute.
6   Blend the remaining sherry and cornflour together, add the monosodium glutamate and stock. Pour into the wok and cook, stirring, for 1–2 minutes.
7   Place the sole into a suitable serving dish, mask with the mushroom and bamboo shoot sauce and serve.

6 – Chinese vegetables and noodles (illustrated on page 432 with prawns)

	4 portions	10 portions
Chinese noodles	400 g (1 lb)	1¼ kg (2½ lb)
oil	60 ml (⅛ pt)	150 ml (⅓ pt)
celery ⎫	100 g (4 oz)	250 g (10 oz)
carrot ⎬ cut in paysanne	100 g (4 oz)	250 g (10 oz)
bamboo shoots ⎭	50 g (2 oz)	125 g (5 oz)
mushrooms, finely sliced	75 g (3 oz)	180 g (7½ oz)
Chinese cabbage, shredded	75 g (3 oz)	180 g (7½ oz)
bean sprouts	100 g (4 oz)	250 g (10 oz)
soy sauce	30 ml (1/16 pt)	75 ml (¼ pt)
garnish: spring onions, sliced lengthways and quickly stir-fried	4	10

1   Cook the noodles in boiling salted water for about 5–6 minutes until *al dente*. Refresh and drain.
2   Heat the oil in a wok and stir fry all the vegetables except the bean sprouts, for 1 minute. Then add the bean sprouts and cook for a further 1 minute.
3   Add the drained noodles, stirring well; allow to reheat through.
4   Correct the seasoning.
5   Serve in a suitable dish, garnished with the spring onions.

7 – Pork, ham and bamboo shoot soup

	4 portions	10 portions
pork fillet	100 g (4 oz)	250 g (10 oz)
soy sauce	30 ml (1/16 pt)	125 ml (¼ pt)
brown stock or consommé	500 ml (1 pt)	1¼ litres (2½ pt)
cooked ham	100 g (4 oz)	250 g (10 oz)
bamboo shoots	100 g (4 oz)	250 g (10 oz)
dry sherry	30 ml (1/16 pt)	75 ml (¼ pt)
seasoning		

1   Place the pork fillet into a basin and mix with the soy sauce.
2   Bring the brown stock or consommé to the boil.

3 Add the pork, ham and bamboo shoots cut into julienne, to the brown stock or consommé.

4 Bring back to the boil, correct the seasoning, add the sherry and serve.

Note This soup may also be lightly thickened with arrowroot or cornflour.

8 – Chop suey (illustrated on page 433)

	4 portions	10 portions
pork fillet	400 g (1 lb)	1 kg (2½ lb)
or		
suprêmes of chicken	4	10
or		
entrecote steak	400 g (1 lb)	1 kg (2½ lb)
soy sauce	60 ml (⅛ pt)	150 ml (⅓ pt)
sherry	30 ml (1/16 pt)	75 ml (¼ pt)
cornflour	10 g (½ oz)	25 g (1 oz)
ginger root	5 g (¼ oz)	12 g (½ oz)
green pepper	200 g (8 oz)	500 g (1¼ lb)
broccoli florets or cauliflower	100 g (4 oz)	250 g (10 oz)
carrot	50 g (2 oz)	125 g (5 oz)
French beans	50 g (2 oz)	125 g (5 oz)
vegetable oil	60 ml (⅛ pt)	150 ml (⅓ pt)
spring onions	4	10
bean sprouts	200 g (8 oz)	500 g (1¼ lb)
tomato, skinned, de-seeded, diced	100 g (4 oz)	250 g (10 oz)
seasoning		
sugar	10 g (½ oz)	25 g (1 oz)
white stock	60 ml (⅛ pt)	150 ml (⅓ pt)

1 Cut the meat into scallops or large julienne. Place into a basin with the soy sauce, sherry and cornflour and mix well.

2 Cut the ginger into 1 cm (½ inch) lengths and finely slice.

3 Cut the green pepper into 1 cm (½ inch) dice, the broccoli or cauliflower into small florets, the carrots into large julienne and the French beans into lozenges.

4 Stir fry the meat in half the oil for approximately 1 minute. Remove and drain.

5 Add the rest of the oil, the ginger, the spring onions and the remainder of the vegetables. Season and add a pinch of sugar. Stir well.

6 Add the meat and mix well, moisten with a little stock if necessary. Serve in a suitable dish immediately.

Plate 10.1: Chinese vegetables and noodles with prawns

9 – Chow mein

	4 portions	10 portions
egg noodles	400 g (1 lb)	1 kg (2½ lb)
pork fillet	250 g (10 oz)	600 g (1½ lb)
cornflour	10 g (½ oz)	25 g (1¼ oz)
bamboo shoots	100 g (4 oz)	250 g (10 oz)
cucumber	100 g (4 oz)	250 g (10 oz)
spinach leaves	100 g (4 oz)	250 g (10 oz)
oil	60 ml (⅛ pt)	150 ml (⅓ pt)

Sauce

	4 portions	10 portions
soy sauce	30 ml (1/16)	75 ml (¼ pt)
dry sherry	30 ml (1/16 pt)	75 ml (¼ pt)
cornflour	10 g (½ oz)	25 g (1 oz)
sesame seed oil	30 ml (1/16 pt)	75 ml (¼ pt)
pinch salt		
pinch sugar		

1 Cook the noodles in boiling salted water until *al dente*, refresh and drain.
2 Cut the pork into large julienne, place in a basin, add the cornflour and mix well.

432

3   Cut the bamboo shoots and peeled cucumber into julienne. Cut the spinach into chiffonade.

4   Heat half the oil in a wok. Reheat the noodles in the oil for 2–3 minutes. Season, then drain and place in a serving dish.

5   Heat the remaining oil in a wok, stir fry the pork for approximately 1–2 minutes, add the bamboo shoots, cucumber and spinach.

6   Mix all the sauce ingredients in a basin, add to the wok. Cook for a further 2 minutes.

7   Carefully arrange the sauce in a serving dish with the noodles. Serve immediately.

Plate 10.2: Chop suey

—— *Greek cookery* ——

Greek cooking offers very fresh ingredients, well flavoured with herbs and a hint of spiciness and cooked as simply as possible, that is, stewed, grilled or roasted with an emphasis on the use of olive oil, olives, yoghurt and lemon juice to enhance the products. Fish is used in great variety, including salt cod, baby squid, octopus, sea urchins and fresh sardines. Lamb is very popular, also veal and poultry.

10 – Taramasalata (paste of smoked cod's roe) (illustrated on page 437)

Served as an hors-d'oeuvre or appetiser. Tarama is the salted roe of the grey mullet, tuna fish or smoked cod's roe.

	4 portions	10 portions
white bread, without crusts	150 g (6 oz)	375 g (15 oz)
milk	125 ml ($\frac{1}{4}$ pt)	300 ml ($\frac{5}{8}$ pt)
smoked cod's roe, skinned	150 g (6 oz)	375 g (15 oz)
finely chopped onion, optional	50 g (2 oz)	125 g (5 oz)
clove garlic, optional	1	2–3
olive or vegetable oil	250 ml ($\frac{1}{2}$ pt)	600 ml (1$\frac{1}{4}$ pt)
seasoning		
stoned olives, lemon, to serve		

1 Soak the bread in the milk for 2–3 minutes. Squeeze dry.
2 Place all the ingredients except the oil in a food processor, liquidise and gradually add the oil to make a smooth paste.
3 Place into individual ramekin dishes, decorate with stoned olives, garnish with lemon. Serve with hot breakfast toast, or hot pitta bread.

11 – Avgolemono soup (egg and lemon soup)

	4 portions	10 portions
chicken stock	750 ml (1$\frac{1}{2}$ pt)	2$\frac{1}{4}$ litres (4$\frac{1}{2}$ pt)
patna rice	35 g (1$\frac{1}{2}$ oz)	100 g (4 oz)
seasoning		
yolks plus egg (the egg is optional)	2 plus 1	5 plus 2
lemon, juice of	$\frac{1}{2}$	1

1 Bring the stock to the boil, add the rice and stir well.
2 Season and cook for 12–15 minutes, remove from heat.
3 In a basin thoroughly mix the yolks, egg and lemon juice.
4 Add 1 tablespoon of the stock a little at a time to the egg and lemon mixture, beating continuously.
5 Add a further 6 tablespoons, mixing continuously. If added too quickly the mixture will curdle.

6   Return the mixture to the stock and heat gently, mixing all the time to cook the egg and to thicken before serving.

12 – Kalamarakia yemista (stuffed squid)

	4 portions	10 portions
medium-sized squid	4	10
onion, finely chopped	50 g (2 oz)	125 g (5 oz)
clove garlic, crushed and chopped	1	2–3
oil	60 ml ($\frac{1}{8}$ pt)	150 ml ($\frac{1}{3}$ pt)
wholegrain rice	100 g (4 oz)	250 g (10 oz)
fish stock	250 ml ($\frac{1}{2}$ pt)	725 ml ($1\frac{1}{4}$ pt)
pine kernels	50 g (2 oz)	125 g (5 oz)
raisins	100 g (4 oz)	250 g (10 oz)
chopped parsley		
seasoning		
dry white wine	125 ml ($\frac{1}{4}$ pt)	250 ml ($\frac{1}{2}$ pt)
tomatoes, skinned, de-seeded, diced	200 g (8 oz)	500 g ($1\frac{1}{4}$ lb)

1   Prepare the squid: pull the body and head apart, remove the transparent pen from the bag and any soft remaining part. Rinse under cold water. Pull off the thin purple membrane on the outside.
2   Remove the tentacles and cut into pieces. Remove the ink sac. Reserve the ink to finish the sauce.
3   Sweat the onion and garlic in the oil.
4   Add the rice and moisten with half the fish stock. Stir and add the chopped tentacles, nuts, raisins and chopped parsley. Season. Stir well and allow to simmer for 5–8 minutes so that the rice is partly cooked.
5   Stuff the squid loosely with this mixture. Seal the end by covering with aluminium foil.
6   Lay the squid into a sauté pan with the remaining fish stock, white wine and tomatoes.
7   Cover with a lid and cook in a moderate oven at 180°C (Reg. 4; 350°F) for 30–40 minutes turning the squid gently during the cooking. Cook very gently or the squid will burst.
8   When cooked, remove the squid and place into a suitable serving dish.

recipe continued ▶

9   Reboil the cooking liquor and reduce by one-third. Strain the ink into the sauce, boil and reduce for 5 minutes. Check the seasoning.

10 Mask the squid with the sauce and finish with chopped parsley to serve.

13 – Dolmades (stuffed vine leaves)

The word *dolmades* comes from a Turkish verb meaning 'to stuff'.

	4 portions	10 portions
vine leaves	8	20
Filling		
onion, finely chopped	50 g (2 oz)	125 g (5 oz)
clove garlic, crushed and chopped	1	2–3
olive oil	60 ml ($\frac{1}{8}$ pt)	150 ml ($\frac{1}{3}$ pt)
brown rice	100 g (4 oz)	250 g (10 oz)
tomato purée	25 g (1 oz)	50 g (2 oz)
white stock (approximately)	60 ml ($\frac{1}{8}$ pt)	150 ml ($\frac{1}{3}$ pt)
seasoning		
pine kernels	25 g (1 oz)	50 g (2 oz)
fresh chopped mint		
fresh chopped dillweed		
currants	25 g (1 oz)	50 g (2 oz)
clove garlic, crushed and chopped	1	2–3
lemon, juice of	$\frac{1}{2}$	1
pinch of sugar		
olive oil		

Plate 10.3: Taramasalata

1 Blanch the fresh vine leaves in boiling salted water for 1 minute, refresh and drain.
2 To make the filling: sweat the onion and garlic in the oil without colour.
3 Add the brown rice and tomato purée and moisten with the stock. Stir in the nuts, herbs and currants. Simmer on top of the stove, or cover with a lid and place in the oven, until half cooked.
4 Correct the seasoning. Stuff each vine leaf with the rice mixture and roll up, making sure that the ends are closed.
5 In a sauté pan add the other clove of garlic and the lemon juice and sprinkle with sugar and oil.
6 Lay the stuffed vine leaves in the sauté pan and sprinkle with more lemon juice.
7 Add 125 ml (¼ pint) water or white stock and season. Cover with aluminium foil.
8 Bring to the boil, draw to the side of the stove, gently cook until tender. Alternatively, place in a moderate oven at 180°C (Reg. 4; 350°F) covered with a lid for about 30 minutes until tender.
9 When cooked, serve in a suitable earthenware dish in their cooking liquor, which has been thickened with egg yolks and finished with lemon juice. This is avgolemono sauce (see below).

recipe continued ▶

– *Avgolemono sauce*

	4 portions	10 portions
egg yolks	2	5
lemon, juice of	½	1
stock (cooking liquor)	250 ml (½ pt)	625 ml (1¼ pt)

1 Beat egg yolks and lemon juice over a bain-marie until light.
2 Add the stock gradually and return to the saucepan.
3 Cook over a low heat until the sauce thickens but does not boil.

Note Dolmades may also be eaten cold, served with a lemon vinaigrette dressing, and as part of an assorted hors-d'oeuvre.

14 – Baklavas (filo pastry with nuts and sugar)

	4 portions	10 portions
filo pastry, sheets of	12	30
clarified butter or ghee	200 g (8 oz)	500 g (1¼ lb)
hazelnuts, flaked	100 g (4 oz)	250 g (10 oz)
almonds, nibbed	100 g (4 oz)	250 g (10 oz)
castor sugar	100 g (4 oz)	250 g (10 oz)
cinnamon	10 g (½ oz)	25 g (1¼ oz)
grated nutmeg		

Syrup

unrefined sugar or castor sugar	200 g (8 oz)	500 g (1¼ lb)
lemons, grated zest and juice of	2	5
water	60 ml (⅛ pt)	150 ml (⅓ pt)
orange, grated zest and juice of	1	2
cinnamon stick	1	2
rose water		

1 Prepare a shallow tray slightly smaller than the sheets of filo pastry by brushing with melted clarified butter or ghee.

2　Place on sheets of filo pastry, brushing each with the fat.
3　Now prepare the filling by mixing the nuts, sugar and spices together, and place into the prepared tray, layered alternatively with filo pastry. Brush each layer with the clarified fat so that there is at least 2–3 layers of filling separated by filo pastry.
4　Cover completely with filo pastry and brush with the clarified fat.
5　Mark the pastry into diamonds, sprinkle with water and bake in a moderately hot oven at 190°C (Reg. 5; 375°F) for approximately 40 minutes.
6　Meanwhile make the syrup: place all the ingredients in a saucepan and bring to the boil. Simmer for 5 minutes, pass through a fine strainer and finish with 2–3 drops of rose water.
7　When the baklavas are baked, cut into diamonds, place on a suitable serving dish and mask with the syrup.

– Filo pastry

	4 portions	10 portions
strong flour	1 kg (2 lb)	2½ kg (5 lb)
water	250–375 ml (½–¾ pt)	¾ litre (1½ pt)
vinegar	1 tbsp	2–3 tbsp
salt	2 tsp	5 tsp
olive oil	4 tbsp	10 tbsp

1　Sift the flour in a bowl.
2　Add water, vinegar and salt to the bowl and mix ingredients to a thick paste.
3　Add the oil, very slowly, while working the mixture.
4　Mix until the dough becomes smooth and elastic. Cover for 30 minutes.
5　Split the paste into suitable pieces.
6　First roll out with an ordinary rolling pin, then use a very thin rolling pin or pasta machine, to make the paste wafer thin.
7　The pastry is now ready for use. It must be covered with a damp or oiled cloth when not being rolled out or before use.

Note　Always cover filo pastry with a damp cloth or polythene when not using, otherwise it dries quickly and is difficult to handle. Filo pastry is usually purchased ready made.

Indian cookery

There are 25 States in this subcontinent each with its own capital and India is the second most populous country in the world with the majority being Hindus. Religion plays an important part in the choice of food and the method of cookery.

The northern part of India and Pakistan use what is called the Mogul style of cooking, the Mogul dynasty of the Shahs having installed itself as long ago as 1526 at the capital Delhi. They were hearty meat-eaters and used wheat more than rice. Tandoori cooking is done here and there is greater emphasis on presentation than elsewhere in the subcontinent. Apart from this there is not very much difference from the other countries of this region.

15 – Chemmeen kari

A prawn curry from the South of India.

	4 portions	10 portions
large king size prawns, raw (preferably) or cooked	400 g (1 lb)	1 kg (2½ lb)
malt vinegar	4 tsp	10 tsp
onion, finely chopped	50 g (2 oz)	125 g (5 oz)
vegetable oil	4 tsp	10 tsp
red chillies	4	10
desiccated coconut	100 g (4 oz)	250 g (10 oz)
mustard seeds	1 tsp	2½ tsp
curry leaves	10	25
fresh ginger, finely chopped	25 g (1 oz)	62 g (2½ oz)
cloves garlic, crushed and chopped	2	5
ground turmeric	1 tsp	2½ tsp
ground coriander	12 g (½ oz)	30 g (1¼ oz)
tomato flesh, de-seeded and chopped	100 g (4 oz)	250 g (10 oz)
hot water	125 ml (¼ pt)	312 ml (⅜ pt)

1 Shell the prawns and de vein them by slitting the back.
2 Rub the prawns with salt and half the teaspoons of vinegar and keep aside.
3 Sweat the onions in a little of the oil until a very little golden brown colour. Remove from heat, add the chillies, coconut and mustard seeds. Place in the

oven stirring occasionally for approximately 8 minutes, or continue to sweat on top of the stove to extract the flavours. Remove from heat, place in a food processor and blend to a fine paste. This is the masala.

4   Heat the oil in a wok on other suitable pan and fry the curry leaves for 1 minute. Add the ginger and garlic and fry for a further 1 minute. Now add the turmeric, ground coriander and chilli powder and the masala. Stir-fry for 1–2 minutes.

5   Add the tomatoes, salt to taste and the hot water. Bring to the boil, simmer for 5 minutes.

6   Drain the prawns. Add them to the pan. Mix well, continue to cook until the prawns are tender (if you are using raw prawns this usually takes 8–10 minutes). They will curl and turn a pinky/orange colour. Add the remaining vinegar. Do not overcook the prawns otherwise they will become hard and dry.

7   Serve immediately garnished with coriander leaves.

16 ~ Tandoori prawns (grilled spiced prawns)

	4 portions	10 portions
king size prawns	12	30
unsalted butter	100 g (4 oz)	250 g (10 oz)
fresh ginger, grated	1 tsp	2½ tsp
clove garlic, crushed and chopped	1	2–3
chilli powder	1 tsp	2½ tsp
ground cumin	1 tsp	2½ tsp
ground coriander	1 tsp	2½ tsp
fresh coriander leaves		
seasoning		
Garnish		
lettuce leaves		
onion rings		
chillies, chopped	2	5
lemon, cut into wedges	1	2

1   Shell and wash the prawns, leaving the head attached. Place in a shallow tray.
2   Melt the butter and add all the spices, including the coriander leaves.
3   Pour this melted butter mixture over the prawns.

recipe continued ▶

4   Gently grill on both sides under the salamander for 5–6 minutes.
5   Serve on a bed of lettuce, garnished with onion, chillies and lemon.

Note   This dish should be prepared using live prawns, but if unobtainable cooked prawns may be used, in which case the prawns should be reheated for 2–3 minutes. Tandoori prawns may be served as a first or fish course.

17 – Palak lamb

A medium spiced dish from the Punjab.

	4 portions	10 portions
vegetable ghee or oil	62 ml ($\frac{1}{8}$ pt)	155 ml ($\frac{3}{8}$ pt)
cumin seeds	1 tsp	$2\frac{1}{2}$ tsp
onion, finely chopped	50 g (2 oz)	125 g (5 oz)
fresh ginger, finely chopped	12 g ($\frac{1}{2}$ oz)	30 g ($1\frac{1}{4}$ oz)
clove garlic, crushed and chopped	1	3
shoulder loin or leg of lamb	400 g (1 lb)	1 kg ($2\frac{1}{2}$ lb)
hot curry paste	2 tsp	5 tsp
natural yoghurt	125 ml ($\frac{1}{4}$ pt)	312 ml ($\frac{5}{8}$ pt)
tomato purée	25 g (1 oz)	625 g ($2\frac{1}{2}$ oz)
spinach, chopped	200 g (8 oz)	500 g ($1\frac{1}{4}$ lb)
salt to taste		
coriander and lemon for garnish		

1   Heat the ghee or oil in a frying pan.
2   Add the cumin seeds; fry for 1 minute.
3   Add the onion; fry until golden brown.
4   Add the ginger and garlic; stir-fry until all is brown.
5   Add the lamb cut in 2 cm (1 inch) dice; simmer for 15–20 minutes.
6   Add the curry paste, yoghurt and salt.
7   Cook for 5 minutes; add water if necessary to prevent sticking.
8   Stir in the tomato purée and spinach. Cover and simmer for 10–15 minutes until lamb is tender.
9   Serve garnished with lemon quarter(s) and coriander leaves.

18 – Lamb pasanda

	4 portions	10 portions
ghee or unsalted butter	32 g ($1\frac{1}{2}$ oz)	80 g ($3\frac{3}{4}$ oz)
onion, finely chopped	150 g (6 oz)	375 g (15 oz)
shoulder, leg of loin of lamb, diced	400 g (1 lb)	1 kg ($2\frac{1}{2}$ lb)
clove garlic, crushed and chopped	2	$4\frac{1}{2}$
fresh ginger, finely chopped	12 g ($\frac{1}{2}$ oz)	30 g ($1\frac{1}{4}$ oz)
natural yoghurt	125 ml ($\frac{1}{4}$ pt)	312 ml ($\frac{5}{8}$ pt)
ground turmeric	$2\frac{1}{4}$ g ($\frac{1}{2}$ tsp)	$5\frac{1}{2}$ g ($1\frac{1}{4}$ tsp)
ground coriander	10 g (2 tsp)	25 g (5 tsp)
ground cumin	5 g (1 tsp)	$12\frac{1}{2}$ g ($2\frac{1}{2}$ tsp)
ground nutmeg	$2\frac{1}{2}$ g ($\frac{1}{2}$ tsp)	$6\frac{1}{4}$ g ($1\frac{1}{4}$ tsp)
pinch of cayenne pepper		
single cream	125 ml ($\frac{1}{4}$ pt)	312 ml ($\frac{5}{8}$ pt)
ground almonds	25 g (1 oz)	$62\frac{1}{2}$ g ($2\frac{1}{2}$ oz)
salt	$2\frac{1}{4}$ g ($\frac{1}{2}$ tsp)	$5\frac{1}{2}$ g ($1\frac{1}{2}$ tsp)
garam masala	5 g (1 tsp)	$12\frac{1}{2}$ g ($2\frac{1}{2}$ tsp)

1 Melt the butter in a frying pan. Sweat the onions until just lightly brown.
2 Add the lamb and cook until sealed.
3 Add the garlic, ginger, yoghurt, turmeric, coriander, cumin, nutmeg and cayenne pepper. Just cover with water and bring to the boil.
4 Cover with a suitable lid; simmer for 30–45 minutes or until the meat is tender.
5 Stir in the cream, ground almonds, salt and garam masala.
6 Bring back to the boil. Simmer for a further 5 minutes.
7 Serve garnished with toasted almonds.

19 – Kashmira lamb

A medium spiced dish from North India.

	4 portions	10 portions
tikka paste	100 g (4 oz)	250 g (10 oz)
natural yoghurt	125 ml ($\frac{1}{4}$ pt)	312 ml ($\frac{5}{8}$ pt)
shoulder loin or leg of lamb	400 g (1 lb)	1 kg (2$\frac{1}{2}$ lb)
ghee or oil	62 ml ($\frac{1}{8}$ pt)	155 ml ($\frac{3}{8}$ pt)
cumin seeds	1 tsp	2$\frac{1}{2}$ tsp
cardamom pods	4	10
cloves	4	10
cinnamon sticks	4	10
onions, finely chopped	100 g (4 oz)	250 g (10 oz)
clove garlic, crushed and chopped	1	1$\frac{1}{2}$
fresh ginger, finely chopped	12 g ($\frac{1}{2}$ oz)	30 g (1$\frac{1}{4}$ oz)
ground chilli	$\frac{1}{2}$ tsp	1$\frac{1}{4}$ tsp
salt to taste		
fresh coriander and roasted almonds		

1 Mix together tikka paste and yoghurt in a suitable bowl.
2 Dice the lamb into 2 cm (1 inch) cubes and marinate in the yoghurt mixture for a minimum of 1 hour.
3 Heat the ghee or oil in a suitable frying pan.
4 Add the cumin seeds, cardamom, cloves and cinnamon; fry for 1 minute.
5 Add the onion, garlic and ginger. Fry for 5 minutes or until golden brown.
6 Add the lamb; fry together for 10–15 minutes. Add a little water if necessary to prevent sticking.
7 Add salt and chilli. Cover and simmer for a further 15 minutes or until the lamb is tender.
8 Serve garnished with coriander leaves and roasted almonds.

20 – Beef do-piazza

A medium spiced dish from the Punjab.

	4 portions	10 portions
topside or chuck steak, cubed	400 g (1 lb)	1 kg (2½ lb)
vegetable ghee or oil	62 ml (⅛ pt)	155 ml (⅜ pt)
onion, finely chopped	100 g (4 oz)	250 g (10 oz)
fresh ginger, finely chopped	12 g (½ oz)	30 g (1¼ oz)
clove garlic, crushed and chopped	1	3
medium curry powder	3 tsp	7½ tsp
natural yoghurt	125 ml (¼ pt)	312 ml (⅝ pt)
lemon, juice of	½	1¼
salt to taste		
julienne of lemon rind		
large onion, cut into rings	1	2

1 Fry the beef in the oil until brown.
2 Add the onions and continue to fry until brown.
3 Drain off the excess oil.
4 Add the ginger, garlic and curry powder; fry for a further 5 minutes.
5 Remove from heat; add the yoghurt and lemon juice.
6 Simmer for 1–1½ hours, adding small amounts of water or stock during the cooking to prevent sticking.
7 Fry the onion rings in oil until golden brown. Keep some for the garnish, add the remainder to the beef.
8 Season with the salt.
9 Serve garnished with the onion rings and the julienne of lemon rind.

21 – Beef Madras

A hot curry from the South of India.

	4 portions	10 portions
topside or chunk steak, cubed	400 g (1 lb)	1 kg (2½ lb)
onion, finely chopped	100 g (4 oz)	250 g (10 oz)
clove garlic, crushed and chopped	2	5
vegetable ghee or oil	68 ml (⅛ pt)	155 ml (⅜ pt)
hot Madras curry paste	3 tsp	7½ tsp
brown beef stock	500 ml (1 pt)	1¼ litre (2½ pt)
tomato purée	50 g (2 oz)	125 g (5 oz)
mango chutney, chopped	5 g (2 oz)	125 g (5 oz)
lemon, juice of	½	1½
season to taste		
coriander leaves for garnish		

1 Fry the beef in the oil until sealed and brown, add the onion and garlic, continue to fry for a further 5 minutes.
2 Add the curry paste and mix well; cook for a further 2 minutes.
3 Add the remaining ingredients, cover with brown stock and bring to the boil. Simmer for 1–1½ hours, or until tender.
4 Correct the seasoning and consistency.
5 Garnish with coriander leaves and serve with pilaff rice.

22 – Keema Matar (medium spiced mince and peas)

	4 portions	10 portions
minced beef	400 g (1 lb)	1 kg (2½ lb)
vegetable ghee or oil	62 ml (⅛ pt)	155 ml (⅜ pt)
onion, finely chopped	100 g (4 oz)	250 g (10 oz)
clove garlic, crushed and chopped	1	3
fresh ginger, finely chopped	12 g (½ oz)	30 g (1¼ oz)
medium curry paste	4 tsp	10 tsp
brown stock or water	250 ml (½ pt)	625 ml (1¼ pt)
frozen peas	100 g (4 oz)	250 g (10 oz)
chopped fresh coriander	4 tsp	10 tsp
lemon, juice of	½	1¼

1　Fry the beef in the oil until brown.
2　Add the onions and garlic. Fry for a further 5 minutes.
3　Add the ginger, curry paste; cook for a further 8 minutes, adding spoonfuls of water or stock to prevent burning.
4　Add the rest of the water or stock, peas, chopped coriander and lemon juice.
5　Simmer for 20 minutes or until cooked. Serve.

Note　This recipe is suitable for low-cost catering.

23 – Tandoori chicken (illustrated on page 448)

chicken cut as for sauté	$1\frac{1}{4}$–$1\frac{1}{2}$ kg ($2\frac{1}{2}$–3 lb)
salt	1 tsp
lemon, juice of	1
plain yoghurt	12 fl oz
small onion, chopped	1
clove garlic, peeled	1
ginger, piece of, peeled and quartered	5 cm (2 inch)
fresh hot green chilli, sliced	$\frac{1}{2}$
garam masala	2 tsp
ground cumin	1 tsp
few drops each red and yellow colouring	

1　Cut slits bone deep in the chicken pieces.
2　Sprinkle the salt and lemon juice on both sides of the pieces, lightly rubbing into the slits; leave for 20 minutes.
3　Combine the remaining ingredients in a blender or food processor.
4　Brush the chicken pieces on both sides ensuring the marinade goes into the slits. Cover and refrigerate for 6–24 hours.
5　Preheat the oven to the maximum temperature.
6　Shake off as much of the marinade as possible from the chicken pieces, place on skewers and bake for 15–20 minutes or until cooked.
7　Serve with red onion rings and lime or lemon wedges.

Plate 10.4: Tandoori chicken

24 – Chicken palak (chicken fried with spinach and spices)

	4 portions	10 portions
chicken, cut for sauté	$1 \times 1\frac{1}{2}$ kg (3 lb)	$2 \times 1\frac{1}{2}$ kg (6 lb)
ghee or butter, margarine or oil	50 g (2 oz)	125 g (5 oz)
onion, finely chopped	50 g (2 oz)	125 g (5 oz)
clove garlic, crushed and chopped	1	2–3
fresh ginger	25 g (1 oz)	60 g ($2\frac{1}{2}$ oz)
green chilli	1	2
ground cumin	1 tsp	$2\frac{1}{2}$ tsp
ground coriander	1 tsp	$2\frac{1}{2}$ tsp
spinach, washed and finely chopped	250 g (10 oz)	625 g ($1\frac{1}{2}$ lb)
tomatoes, skinned, de-seeded, diced	200 g (8 oz)	500 g ($1\frac{1}{4}$ lb)
chicken stock	250 ml ($\frac{1}{2}$ pt)	625 ml ($1\frac{1}{4}$ pt)

1 Gently fry the chicken in the fat until golden brown.
2 Remove the chicken and fry the onion and garlic until lightly browned. Add the spices and sweat for 3 minutes.
3 Stir in the spinach, add the tomatoes and season. Add the chicken pieces.
4 Add the chicken stock, bring to the boil.
5 Cover with a lid and cook in a moderate oven at 180°C (Reg. 4; 350°F) for 30 minutes or until the chicken is tender. Stir occasionally, adding more stock if necessary.
6 Serve in a suitable dish with rice, chapatis (see page 456) and dhal (see page 450).

25 – Chicken tikka

	4 portions	10 portions
chicken, cut for sauté	1 × 1½ kg (3 lb)	2 × 1½ kg (6 lb)
natural yoghurt	125 ml (¼ pt)	250 ml (½ pt)
grated ginger	1 tsp	2½ tsp
ground coriander	1 tsp	2½ tsp
ground cumin	1 tsp	2½ tsp
chilli powder	1 tsp	2½ tsp
clove garlic, crushed and chopped	1	2–3
lemon, juice of	½	1
tomato purée	50 g (2 oz)	125 g (5 oz)
onion, finely chopped	50 g (2 oz)	125 g (5 oz)
oil	60 ml (⅛ pt)	150 ml (⅓ pt)
lemon, wedges of	4	10
seasoning		

1 Place the chicken pieces into a suitable dish.
2 Mix together the yoghurt, seasoning, spices, garlic, lemon juice and tomato purée.
3 Pour this over the chicken, mix well and leave to marinade for at least 3 hours.
4 In a suitable shallow tray, add the chopped onion and half the oil.
5 Lay the chicken pieces on top and grill under the salamander, turning the pieces over once or gently cook in a moderate oven at 180°C (Reg. 4; 350°F) for 20–30 minutes.
6 Baste with the remaining oil.
7 Serve on a bed of lettuce garnished with wedges of lemon.

26 – Dahl

Dahl is made from lentils and is an important part of the basic diet for many Indians. It can also be made using yellow split peas.

	4 portions	10 portions
lentils	200 g (8 oz)	500 g ($1\frac{1}{4}$ lb)
turmeric	1 tsp	$2\frac{1}{2}$ tsp
ghee, butter or oil	50 g (2 oz)	125 g (5 oz)
onion, finely chopped	50 g (2 oz)	125 g (5 oz)
garlic clove of, crushed and chopped	1	2–3
green chilli, finely chopped, optional	1	2–3
cumin seeds	1 tsp	$2\frac{1}{2}$ tsp

1 Place the lentils in a saucepan and cover with water. Add the turmeric, bring to the boil and gently simmer until cooked. Stir occasionally.
2 In a suitable pan, heat the fat and sweat the onion, garlic, chilli (if using) and cumin seeds. Stir into the lentils and season.
3 Serve hot to accompany other dishes. The consistency should be fairly thick but spoonable.

27 ~ Alu-Chole (vegetarian curry)

A dish from North India.

	4 portions	10 portions
vegetable ghee or oil	45 ml (3 tsp)	112 ml (7$\frac{1}{2}$ tsp)
small cinnamon sticks	4	10
bayleaves	4	10
cumin seeds	15 g (1 tsp)	12$\frac{1}{2}$ g (2$\frac{1}{2}$ tsp)
onion, finely chopped	100 g (4 oz)	250 g (10 oz)
cloves garlic, finely chopped and crushed	2	5
plum tomatoes, canned, chopped	400 g (1 lb)	1 kg (2$\frac{1}{2}$ lb)
hot curry paste	45 ml (3 tsp)	112 g (7$\frac{1}{2}$ tsp)
salt to taste		
chick peas, canned drained	400 g (1 lb)	1 kg (2$\frac{1}{2}$ lb)
potato in 1 cm ($\frac{1}{2}$ inch) dice	100 g (4 oz)	250 g (10 oz)
water	125 ml ($\frac{1}{4}$ pt)	312 ml ($\frac{5}{8}$ pt)
tamarind sauce or lemon juice	30 g (2 tsp)	75 g (5 tsp)
chopped coriander leaves	50 g (2 oz)	125 g (5 oz)

1   Heat the ghee in a suitable pan.
2   Add the cinnamon, bayleaves and cumin seeds; fry for 1 minute.
3   Add the onion and garlic. Fry until golden brown.
4   Add the chopped tomatoes, curry paste and salt and fry for a further 2–3 minutes.
5   Stir in the potatoes and water. Bring to the boil. Cover and simmer until the potatoes are cooked.
6   Add the chick peas; allow to heat through.
7   Stir in the coriander and lemon juice. Serve immediately.

28 – Pepper bhajee

	4 portions	10 portions
oil	45 ml (3 tsp)	112 ml (7½ tsp)
onion, finely chopped	100 g (4 oz)	250 g (10 oz)
black mustard seeds	5 g (1 tsp)	12½ g (2½ tsp)
hot curry powder	30 ml (2 tsp)	75 ml (5 tsp)
plum, tomatoes canned, chopped	100 g (4 oz)	250 g (10 oz)
potatoes cut in 1 cm (½ inch) cubes	200 g (8 oz)	500 g (1¼ lb)
mixed red and green peppers, cut in half, de-seeded and finely shredded	600 g (½ lb)	1½ kg (3¼ lb)
salt to taste		

1 Heat oil in a suitable pan.
2 Fry the mustard seeds for 1 minute.
3 Add the onions and fry until golden brown in colour.
4 Stir in the curry powder. Cook for 1 minute.
5 Add the tomatoes.
6 Add the potatoes, red and green peppers. Mix well.
7 Add a little water to prevent sticking occurring. Cover the pan and cook for 15 minutes. Season and serve.

29 – Onion bhajias

	6 portions	10 portions
bessan or gram flour	45 g (3 tsp)	112 g (7½ tsp)
hot curry powder	15 g (1 tsp)	37½ g (2½ tsp)
salt		
water	75 ml (5 tsp)	187 ml (12½ tsp)
onion, finely shredded	100 g (4 oz)	250 g (10 oz)

1 Mix together the flour, curry powder and salt.
2 Blend in the water carefully to form a smooth, thick batter.
3 Stir in the onion, stir well.
4 Drop the mixture off a tablespoon into deep oil at 200°C (400°F). Fry for 5–10 minutes until golden brown.
5 Drain well and serve as a snack with mango chutney as a dip.

30 – Pakora (batter-fried vegetables and shrimps)

A reception or bar snack or as a main course.

	4 portions	10 portions
Batter		
bessan (chick-pea flour)	125 g (5 oz)	250 g (10 oz)
water	375 ml ($\frac{3}{4}$ pt)	750 ml (1$\frac{1}{2}$ pt)
turmeric	$\frac{1}{4}$ tsp	$\frac{1}{2}$ tsp
ground coriander	1 tsp	2 tsp
cayenne	$\frac{1}{4}$ tsp	$\frac{1}{2}$ tsp
salt		

Vegetables such as: batons of carrot, florets of cauliflower, florets of broccoli, sliced aubergines, batons of celery, slices of par-boiled peeled or unpeeled potato, batons of parsnip, large cooked shrimps or prawns (peeled and seasoned with salt and curry powder)

1 Sieve the flour and slowly add the water, whisking continuously.
2 Pass through a strainer.
3 Add the turmeric, coriander and cayenne pepper, season with salt. Allow to stand for 15 minutes.
4 Dip the vegetables and shrimps or prawns into the batter, coating well.
5 Deep fry in hot oil at 190°C (375°F) until a light saffron colour.
6 Drain well and serve with chutney.

Note Unlike plain wheat flour, batter made with bessan produces a non-porous surface and no fat will penetrate to the food inside.

31 – Samosas

	40–60 pasties	100–150 pasties
short pastry made from ghee fat and fairly strong flour as the dough should be fairly elastic	400 g (1 lb)	1 kg (2$\frac{1}{2}$ lb)

Brush the pastry with ghee or vegetable after rolling into a smooth ball.

recipe continued ▶

~ *Potato filling*

peeled potatoes	200 g (8 oz)	500 g (1¼ lb)
vegetable oil	1½ tsp	3¾ tsp
black mustard seeds	½ tsp	1¼ tsp
onions, finely chopped	50 g (2 oz)	125 g (5 oz)
fresh ginger, finely chopped	12 g (½ oz)	30 g (1¼ oz)
fennel seeds	1 tsp	2½ tsp
cumin seeds	¼ tsp	1 tsp
turmeric	¼ tsp	1 tsp
frozen peas	75 g (3 oz)	187 g (7½ oz)
salt to taste		
water	2½ tsp	6¼ tsp
fresh coriander, finely chopped	1 tsp	2½ tsp
garam masala	½ tsp	2½ tsp
pinch of cayenne pepper		

1 Cut the potatoes into ½ cm (¼ inch); cook in water until only just cooked.
2 Heat the oil in a suitable pan, add the mustard seeds and cook until they pop.
3 Add the onions and ginger. Fry for 7–8 minutes, stirring continuously until golden brown.
4 Stir in the fennel, cumin and turmeric, add the potatoes, peas, salt and water.
5 Reduce to a low heat, cover the pan and cook for 5 minutes.
6 Stir in the coriander; cook for a further 5 minutes.
7 Remove from the heat, stir in the garam masala and the cayenne seasoning.
8 Remove from the pan, place into a suitable bowl to cool before using.

~ *Lamb filling*

saffron	½ tsp	1¼ tsp
boiling water	2½ tsp	6¼ tsp
vegetable oil	3 tsp	7½ tsp
fresh ginger, finely chopped	12 g (½ oz)	30 g (1¼ oz)
cloves garlic, crushed and chopped	2	5
onions, finely chopped	50 g (2 oz)	125 g (5 oz)
salt to taste		
lean minced lamb	400 g (1 lb)	1 kg (2½ lb)
pinch of cayenne pepper		
garam masala	1 tsp	2½ tsp

1   Infuse the saffron in the boiling water; allow to stand for 10 minutes.
2   Heat the vegetable oil in a suitable pan. Add the ginger, garlic, onions and salt, stirring continuously. Fry for 7–8 minutes, until the onions are soft and golden brown.
3   Stir in the lamb, add the saffron with the water. Cook stirring the lamb until it is cooked.
4   Add the cayenne, garam masala, reduce the heat, and allow to cook gently for a further 10 minutes.
5   The mixture should be fairly tight with very little moisture.
6   Transfer to a bowl and allow to cool before using.

– *To fill the samosas*

1   Take a small piece of dough, roll into a ball 2 cm (1 inch) in diameter. Keep the rest of the dough covered with either a wet cloth, cling film or plastic, otherwise a skin will form on the dough.
2   Roll the ball into a circle about 9 cm ($3\frac{1}{2}$ inches) round on a lightly floured surface. Cut the circle in half.
3   Moisten the straight edge with eggwash or water.
4   Shape the semicircle into a cone. Fill the cone with approximately $1\frac{1}{2}$ teaspoons of filling, moisten the top edges and press them well together.
5   The samosas may be made in advance, covered with cling film or plastic and refrigerated before being deep fried.
6   Deep fry at 180°C (375°F) until golden brown; remove from fryer and drain well.
7   Serve on a suitable dish garnished with coriander leaves. Serve a suitable chutney separately.

32 – Chapatis

Chapatis are cooked on a *tawa* or frying pan. They are made fresh for each meal, and are dipped into sauces and used to scoop up food.

	4 portions	10 portions
wholewheat flour	200 g (8 oz)	500 g (1¼ lb)
pinch of salt		
water	125 ml (¼ pt)	250 ml (1½ pt)
vegetable oil		

1 Sieve the flour and salt, add the water and knead to a firm dough.
2 Knead on a floured table until smooth and elastic.
3 Cover with a damp cloth or polythene and allow to relax for 30–40 minutes.
4 Divide into 10 pieces (25 pieces for 10 portions), flatten each and roll into a circle 12–15 cm (5–6 inches) in diameter.
5 Lightly grease a frying pan with oil, add the chapati and cook as for a pancake. Traditionally chapatis are allowed to puff by placing them over an open flame.
6 Just before serving reheat the chapatis under the salamander.

—— *Indonesian cooking* ——

Indonesia includes Bali, Borneo, Java and Sumatra and was previously known as the East Indies; it is an agricultural economy which produces rice as its staple food and many kinds of spice, mainly for export. The first two cultural and religious influences were the arrival of Buddhists and Hindus from India who were followed by Portuguese settlers, then a hundred years later by the Dutch. Immigrants came in large numbers from China who had a great deal of influence on the islands' cookery.

Plate 10.5: Gado gado

33 ~ Gado gado (vegetable salad with peanut dressing)

This dish is popular throughout Indonesia. It may be served as a starter or with a main meal and rice.

	4 portions	10 portions
white cabbage, finely shredded and washed	200 g (8 oz)	500 g (1¼ lb)
bean sprouts, washed	100 g (4 oz)	250 g (10 oz)
cooked potato, cut in 1 cm (½ inch) dice	200 g (8 oz)	500 g (1¼ lb)
tomato, skinned, de-seeded, diced	50 g (2 oz)	125 g (5 oz)
eggs, hard-boiled	2	5
vegetable oil	60 ml (⅛ pt)	150 ml (⅓ pt)
Dressing		
onion, finely chopped	50 g (2 oz)	125 g (5 oz)
clove garlic, crushed and chopped	1	2–3
green chilli, finely chopped	1	2–3
crunchy peanut butter	50 g (2 oz)	125 g (5 oz)
malt vinegar	2 tsp	5 tsp
coconut milk	125 ml (¼ pt)	250 ml (½ pt)

1   Drain the cabbage and bean sprouts and mix together.
2   Add the potato and the tomato, lightly season.

recipe continued ▶

3   Arrange neatly into individual dishes just prior to service and decorate with quarters of hard-boiled egg.
4   Prepare the dressing: heat the oil in a sauteuse and stir fry the onion, garlic and chilli for 2 minutes.
5   Stir in the peanut butter, vinegar and coconut milk, simmer for a further 2–3 minutes.
6   Pour the hot sauce over the salad or serve separately.

34 – Rendang (Indonesian beef curry)

	4 portions	10 portions
cooking oil	45 ml (3 tsp)	112 ml (7½ tsp)
onion, finely chopped	100 g (4 oz)	250 g (10 oz)
cloves garlic, crushed and chopped	2	5
fresh ginger, finely chopped	12 g (½ oz)	30 g (1¼ oz)
hot Thai curry blend	30 g (2 tsp)	75 g (5 tsp)
ground lemon grass	5 g (1 tsp)	12½ g (2½ tsp)
desiccated coconut	100 g (4 oz)	250 g (10 oz)
rump or sirloin cut into thin strips	400 g (1 lb)	1 kg (2½ lb)
creamed coconut	100 g (4 oz)	250 g (10 oz)
hot water	250 ml (½ pt)	625 ml (1¼ pt)
salt to taste		

1   Heat the oil in a suitable pan. Fry the onions, garlic and ginger until lightly coloured.
2   Add the curry blend and lemon grass; continue to fry for a further 2 minutes.
3   Add the desiccated coconut; fry for a further 1 minute.
4   In a separate pan, quickly fry the beef, to seal. Drain off the excess oil and place the beef in a clean saucepan. Season.
5   Blend the coconut and hot water to make coconut milk and add to beef.
6   Add the other ingredients which have been prepared.
7   Bring to boil, simmer until the beef is tender and the liquid has evaporated; stir occasionally. The curry should be quite dry.
8   Serve with prawn crackers.

35 ~ Nasi goreng (rice with bacon, chicken and soy sauce)

	4 portions	10 portions
vegetable oil	60 ml (⅛ pt)	150 ml (⅓ pt)
onion, finely chopped	100 g (4 oz)	250 g (10 oz)
clove garlic, crushed and chopped	1	2–3
red chilli, finely chopped	1	2–3
small lardons of bacon	200 g (8 oz)	500 g (1¼ lb)
cooked chicken, cut into 2 cm (1 inch) slices	100 g (4 oz)	250 g (10 oz)
soy sauce	2 tbsp	5 tbsp
rice cooked as pilaff, dry and fluffy	250 g (10 oz)	625 g (1½ lb)
Garnish		
eggs, beaten and seasoned	2	5
finely sliced cucumber	50 g (2 oz)	125 g (5 oz)

1 Heat a little oil in a wok, add the onion, garlic and chilli and stir-fry. Add the lardons of bacon and cook quickly.
2 Add the cooked chicken and cook for a further 2–3 minutes.
3 Add the soy sauce and cooked rice. Reheat the rice thoroughly. Stir occasionally.
4 For the garnish, heat a little oil in a small frying pan. Beat the egg well with seasoning. Pour this into the frying pan, cook one side, turn over and cook the other. Turn out onto a board. Cut into thin strips.
5 Serve in a suitable dish, garnished with strips of the cooked egg and slices of cucumber.

Note Prawns are sometimes added to this dish.

—— *Japanese cooking* ——

In Japan, the emphasis is not so much on taste as on preparation which is always expected to be perfect, thus showing the cook's skills, imagination and creativity. The main methods of cooking can be carried out using only a steamer and a wok with tempura work being done in the wok. Meals are small, the ingredients are few and simple, made sharper to the taste with soy and other seasoning and there is no order of course so that the entire meal can be served together and can be hot, tepid or cold or a mixture of these. The Japanese method of precise presentation was adopted by the founders of nouvelle cuisine.

The contents of a dinner could be soup, rice, marinated raw fish known as *sashimi* served with soy sauce and very hot horseradish relish and vegetables. *Sushi* are small thin circles or rectangles of rice and seaweed made like canapés with coverings of omelet, mushrooms or fish. *Tempura* is the deep frying of items in batter; *yakitori* are brochettes of marinated meat and vegetables; *sukiyaki* is the way that guests cook small pieces of food in hot oil at their table; *teriyaki* is the cooking of pieces of marinated fish, meat and poultry on a charcoal grill. Much use is made of *dashi* (soup stock made from *kombo* which is the dried seaweed, kelp); *katsoubishi* (flavouring of dried bonito flakes); *agi-no-moto* (monosodium glutamate), *ako miso* (red bean paste, used for thickening soups, etc.); *shichimi-togarashi* (mixture of spices, poppy and sesame seeds, hemp, rape plus tangerine peel and pepper leaf).

36 − Hotate gai shoyu yaki (scallops grilled with soy sauce)

	4 portions	10 portions
scallops	8	20
sake	30 ml ($\frac{1}{16}$ pt)	75 ml ($\frac{1}{8}$ pt)
soy sauce	30 ml ($\frac{1}{16}$ pt)	75 ml ($\frac{1}{8}$ pt)
lemon wedges	4	10
parsley		

1 Wash the scallops well.
2 Place the scallops shells over a fierce heat to brown.
3 Carefully remove the meat from the shells.
4 Mix the soy sauce and sake together in a basin.
5 Divide the cleaned scallops into four china scallop shells and pour the soy sauce and sake over each of the scallops.
6 Place in a suitable tray and grill under the salamander until just cooked.
7 Serve the scallops hot, in the shells, garnished with lemon wedge and parsley.

37 – Tonkatsu (deep-fried pork cutlet)

Tonkatsu is a half-Japanese and half-fragmented English word. *Ton* is a pig or pork and *katsu* is the Japanisation of 'cutlet'. The dish itself is of European origin. It is a popular fast food in Tokyo and other Japanese cities.

	4 portions	10 portions
slices of loin of pork, cut 1 cm ($\frac{1}{2}$ inch) thick	4	10
salt and black pepper		
eggs, beaten	2	5
flour		
dried breadcrumbs	100 g (4 oz)	250 g (10 oz)
vegetable oil		
white cabbage	150 g (6 oz)	425 g (15 oz)
tomato ketchup	60 ml ($\frac{1}{8}$ pt)	150 ml ($\frac{1}{3}$ pt)
lemon	$\frac{1}{2}$	1
Worcester sauce	3–4 drops	7–10 drops
dark soy sauce	3–4 drops	7–10 drops
English mustard	1 tsp	$2\frac{1}{2}$ tsp
sake	30 ml ($\frac{1}{16}$ pt)	75 ml ($\frac{1}{8}$ pt)

1 Score the edges of the pork. Season, pass through the egg, flour and breadcrumbs.
2 Deep fry the cutlets in oil at 180°C (350°F) for 5 to 7 minutes.
3 Remove, drain the cutlets and slice diagonally into 1 cm ($\frac{1}{2}$ inch) strips.
4 Shred the cabbage finely. Divide onto four plates.
5 Arrange the cutlet pieces on the cabbage and garnish with a lemon wedge. (Cucumber and tomato may also be used.)
6 Mix the tomato ketchup, Worcester sauce, soy sauce, mustard and sake to a paste and place into individual bowls so that the cutlets may be dipped into the sauce.

38 – Tempura (vegetable and shrimp fritters)

	4 portions	10 portions
mange-tout, topped and tailed	12	30
white button mushrooms, halved	100 g (4 oz)	250 g (10 oz)
carrot, cut in matchstick pieces	100 g (4 oz)	250 g (10 oz)
sweet potato, peeled and thinly sliced	100 g (4 oz)	250 g (10 oz)
shrimps, shelled, cleaned, tails left attached	150 g (6 oz)	425 g (15 oz)
flour	150 g (6 oz)	425 g (15 oz)
Frying batter		
flour	200 g (8 oz)	500 g (1¼ lb)
baking powder	10 g (½ oz)	25 g (1 oz)
egg yolk	1	2
iced water (approximately)	175 ml (⅓ pt)	350 ml (⅔ pt)

1 Heat the friture to 175°C (350°F).
2 Ensure all the vegetables are dry.
3 Flour the vegetables and shrimps one at a time, shake off the surplus, pass through batter, shake off the surplus and deep fry for 2–3 minutes.
4 Drain the vegetables well and keep warm.
5 Increase the temperature of the friture to 180°C (360°F) and fry the shrimps, drain well.
6 Serve the vegetables and shrimps on dish paper, to ensure they are dry, and accompany with dipping sauce (see below).

– *Dipping sauce for vegetables, meat, poultry*

	4 portions	10 portions
fish stock	125 ml (¼ pt)	250 ml (½ pt)
soy sauce	1 tbsp	2 tbsp
rice wine or sweet sherry	½ tbsp	1 tbsp
rice vinegar or white vinegar	½ tbsp	1 tbsp

Combine all the ingredients and serve in individual bowls.

39 – Yakitori and teppanyaki

Yakitori and *teppanyaki* are Japanese styles of grilling poultry or meat. Grilled fish is known as *shioyaki*. Restaurants that specialise in serving grilled foods are known as *teppanyaki* restaurants and in most cases the food is cooked on a table-top grill in front of the diner.

For *yakitori*, small pieces of chicken, duck or other small birds are marinated for 30–45 minutes in a mixture of soy sauce and sake (rice wine) or sherry, pierced on skewers and grilled over charcoal.

For *teppanyaki*, the best quality steaks or pork fillets or chops are marinated for 45 minutes to 1 hour. They are then dried well and grilled on flat metal plates or domed grills or perforated metal.

– Marinade

	4 portions	10 portions
soy sauce	3 tbsp	7 tbsp
sweet sherry	3 tbsp	7 tbsp
sesame oil	1 tbsp	2 tbsp
white vinegar	1 tbsp	2 tbsp
sugar	1 tbsp	2 tbsp

Mix all the ingredients together.

Yakitori and *teppanyaki* dishes would usually be accompanied by a dish of lightly stir-fried vegetables, e.g. shredded Chinese or ordinary cabbage, mushrooms, sweet peppers, broccoli florets, bean sprouts, asparagus tips, etc. Bowls of dipping sauce would also be served.

40 – Sashimi (illustrated on page 465)

This is a style of serving raw fish, which must therefore be absolutely fresh. Bream, salmon, trout, etc. may be used, either individually or as a mixture of different fish. The thoroughly washed fillets are very thinly sliced with a sharp knife and the slices arranged neatly on the plate. A delicate garnish, such as a decorative leaf, curl of carrot or chopped spring onion may be used.

Sashimi is served with dipping sauce and *wasabi* paste. This is pungent, like horseradish sauce. It is obtained in powdered form and made up with a little water, as if using dried mustard.

41 ~ Sushi

Sushi (zushi) is a style of serving a variety of foods. The main ingredient is
vinegared rice, which is served cold with raw fish, shrimps, prawns, vegetables, etc.
The proportion of rice to water will vary according to the rice used, and the
cooking time may also need to be adjusted. Firm short or long grain rice may be
used, but not soft pudding rice or brown rice. When cooked the rice will be white
and the grains will cohere. An example of using sushi is *bara sushi* (recipe 43).

42 ~ Sushi rice (vinegared rice)

	4 portions	10 portions
rice	150 g (6 oz)	375 g (15 oz)
water	375 ml ($\frac{3}{4}$ pt)	750 ml (1$\frac{1}{2}$ pt)
salt		
Dressing		
few drops of oil		
rice vinegar	3 tbsp	7 tbsp
sugar	1$\frac{1}{2}$ tbsp	3–4 tbsp
salt	1 tsp	2$\frac{1}{2}$ tsp
mirin (sweet sake) or dry sherry	1 tbsp	2$\frac{1}{2}$ tbsp

1 Thoroughly wash the rice.
2 Place the rice, water, salt and oil in a heavy-based pan.
3 Bring to the boil, cover with a tight-fitting lid and reduce the heat.
4 Allow to simmer for 20 minutes.
5 Remove from the heat and stand with the lid on for 15 minutes.
6 Meanwhile place the dressing ingredients in a pan and bring to the boil.
7 Sprinkle the rice with the dressing whilst both are still warm, and mix
   thoroughly but lightly.

Plate 10.6: Sashimi

43 ~ Bara sushi (vinegared rice with fish and beans)

	4 portions	10 portions
sushi rice (as recipe 49)	150 g (6 oz)	375 g (15 oz)
mackerel or shrimps	400 g (1 lb)	1 kg (2½ lb)
vinegar	6 tbsp	15 tbsp
sugar	3 tbsp	7 tbsp
salt	2 tbsp	5 tbsp
slices of ginger, optional	2	5
French or runner beans, cooked	100 g (4 oz)	250 g (10 oz)
sesame seeds, toasted and chopped	1 tbsp	2½ tbsp

1   Prepare and cook the rice and dressing as in recipe 42.

recipe continued ▶

2   Fillet the fish, sprinkle lightly with salt and leave for 15 minutes.
3   Wash and soak the fish in seasoned vinegar for 10 minutes.
4   Remove the skin and slice thinly.
5   If using shrimps, soak the cooked shelled shrimps in the vinegar.
6   Slice the ginger, sprinkle with salt and soak in vinegar.
7   Mix the rice, fish, ginger and sliced beans together, and sprinkle with the sesame seeds to serve.

Note   The fish must be very fresh. If rice vinegar is not available a light wine vinegar can be used.

—— *Mexican cooking* ——

The food of this Spanish-speaking nation has become very popular in many countries. Mexico has an old established cuisine which stems from the native Indians to the Aztecs and then from the Spanish who arrived there in 1519 along with some French influence which came with the installation of Emperor Maximilian. It is based on an abundance of native ingredients made extremely hot by the use of chillies, cooked simply without roasting or baking, supported by accompaniments made of maize which plays a much larger part in the diet than wheat.

44 ~ Tortillas

Tortillas are served with all Mexican meals. Although in Mexico a special flour is used, tortillas may be produced using cornmeal and wholemeal flour.

	4 portions	10 portions
wholemeal flour	100 g (4 oz)	250 g (10 oz)
cornmeal flour	100 g (4 oz)	250 g (10 oz)
water	250 ml ($\frac{1}{2}$ pt)	625 ml ($1\frac{1}{4}$ pt)

1   Sieve the flours together into a bowl, add a pinch of salt and sufficient water to make a smooth dough.
2   Knead well until elastic. Divide into 12 or 16 pieces (30 or 40 for 10 portions), depending on the size of the tortilla required.
3   Place a ball of dough between two pieces of well oiled greaseproof paper (or use silicone paper). Roll the dough into a circle, diameter 10–15 cm (4–6 inches).
4   Lightly oil a frying pan. Peel off the top layer of paper and place the tortilla in

the pan. Cook for 2 minutes. Remove the top paper, turn over and cook the other side for 2 minutes. Both sides should be quite pale and dry.

5   Keep the tortillas warm for service, stacking between pieces of dry greaseproof paper.

Notes   The tortilla can be served in different ways. When crisp and golden it is called a *tostada*. These are served with red kidney beans, cheese and a chilli sauce.

Tacos are tortillas curled into a shell shape and fried, usually filled with picadillo (see following recipe) and served with salad and chilli sauce.

Tortillas that are rolled and filled, then served with a sauce, are called *enchiladas*.

Chilli sauce is usually purchased as a commercial product, but it can be made by mixing together tomato ketchup and tabasco sauce or by making a fresh tomato coulis (page 741), strengthened with tomato purée and finished with tabasco.

Tortillas may be made lighter by adding 1 teaspoon ($2\frac{1}{2}$ teaspoons for 10 portions) baking powder.

45 ~ Picadillo

Used as a filling for tacos.

	4 portions	10 portions
oil	60 ml ($\frac{1}{8}$ pt)	150 ml ($\frac{1}{3}$ pt)
minced lean beef	400 g (1 lb)	1 kg ($2\frac{1}{2}$ lb)
onion, finely chopped	100 g (4 oz)	250 g (10 oz)
clove garlic, crushed and chopped	1	2–3
chilli, finely chopped	1	2–3
tomatoes, skinned, de-seeded, diced	100 g (4 oz)	250 g (10 oz)
tomato purée	50 g (2 oz)	125 g (5 oz)
cumin seed	$\frac{1}{4}$ tsp	$\frac{1}{2}$ tsp
raisins	50 g (2 oz)	125 g (5 oz)
brown stock or water	250 ml ($\frac{1}{2}$ pt)	625 ml ($1\frac{1}{4}$ pt)
cornflour	18 g ($\frac{3}{4}$ oz)	36 g ($1\frac{1}{2}$ oz)
green olives, chopped	25 g (1 oz)	60 g ($2\frac{1}{2}$ oz)
capers, chopped	25 g (1 oz)	60 g ($2\frac{1}{2}$ oz)
flaked almonds, roasted	50 g (2 oz)	125 g (5 oz)

1   Heat the oil in a frying pan, add the minced beef and brown quickly.

recipe continued ▶

2 Add the onion, garlic, and the chopped chilli pepper. Season and cook for a further 3 minutes.
3 Pour off the excess oil and place the meat into a suitable saucepan.
4 Add to the saucepan the tomatoes, tomato purée, cumin seed and raisins.
5 Barely cover with brown stock or water and gently simmer for 30 minutes.
6 Lightly thicken with a little diluted cornflour and stir in the olives and capers.
7 Correct the seasoning and consistency. Finish by adding the roasted flaked almonds.

46 – Burritos (Mexican pancakes)

The pancakes are filled with meat and served with a cheese sauce.

	4 portions	10 portions
pancake batter (see below)	250 ml (½ pt)	625 ml (1¼ pt)
portions chilli con carne, page 484	4	10
Mornay sauce flavoured with Dijon-type mustard	500 ml (1 pt)	1¼ litre (2½ pt)
grated cheese, Parmesan or cheddar		

1 Make the pancakes in the normal way (see below).
2 Fill the pancakes with chilli con carne. Place in a suitable earthenware dish.
3 Mask with Mornay sauce and sprinkle with grated cheese.
4 Glaze under the salamander or in a hot oven and serve.

– Pancake batter

	4 portions	10 portions
flour, white or wholemeal	100 g (4 oz)	250 g (10 oz)
pinch of salt		
egg	1	2
milk, whole or skimmed	250 ml (½ pt)	625 ml (1¼ pt)
melted butter, margarine or oil	10 g (½ oz)	25 g (1 oz)
oil for frying		

1 Sieve the flour and salt into a bowl, make a well in the centre.

2   Add the egg and milk, gradually incorporating the flour from the sides; whisk to a smooth batter.
3   Mix in the melted butter.
4   Heat the pancake pan, clean thoroughly.
5   Add a little oil, heat until smoking.
6   Add enough mixture to just cover the bottom of the pan thinly.
7   Cook for a few seconds until brown.
8   Turn and cook on the other side. Turn on to a plate.
9   Repeat until all the batter is used up.

—— *Middle Eastern cookery* ——

The countries of the middle east have shared their past and this has been given unity in the kitchen. The spread of Islam has played a significant role in the development of the traditional cuisine. The death of the prophet Muhammad in the year AD 632 was followed by victorious wars waged by the followers of his faith. The establishment of an Islamic empire, stretching across Asia, North Africa, Spain and Sicily, brought together cooking styles and refinements in eating habits. Great value is attached to food as a means of offering hospitality. Regional differences do not have much to do with national boundaries but depend more on geography, history and local produce.

47 – Hummus (chick pea and sesame seed paste)
Served with pitta bread as a starter or an accompaniment to main dishes.

	4 portions	10 portions
soaked chick peas	300 g (12 oz)	750 g (1 lb 14 oz)
seasoning		
sesame seed paste (tahini)	75 g (3 oz)	187 g (7½ oz)
clove garlic, crushed and chopped	1	2–3
onion, finely chopped	50 g (2 oz)	125 g (5 oz)
lemon, juice of	1	2
paprika	5 g (¼ oz)	10 g (½ oz)

1   Cook the chick peas in simmering water for 2 hours. Drain well.

recipe continued ▶

2 Purée the peas in a food processor, add seasoning, sesame seed paste, garlic and onion. Finish with lemon juice.
3 Place into a suitable serving dish decorated with a line of paprika.

48 ‑ Tabbouleh (cracked wheat salad)

Serve with hummus or kebabs.

	4 portions	10 portions
cracked wheat (burghul)	75 g (3 oz)	187 g (7½ oz)
onion, finely chopped	25 g (1 oz)	60 g (2½ oz)
diced cucumber	50 g (2 oz)	125 g (5 oz)
tomato, peeled, de-seeded, diced	50 g (2 oz)	125 g (5 oz)
salt, pepper		
vegetable oil	30 ml ($\frac{1}{16}$ pt)	75 ml ($\frac{1}{4}$ pt)
lemon, juice of	½	1
chopped fresh parsley and mint		

1 Cover the cracked wheat with cold water and leave to soak for 10 minutes. Drain well, place into a suitable basin.
2 Add the onion, cucumber and tomato, season with salt and pepper.
3 Mix in the oil and lemon juice, stir in the chopped parsley and chopped mint.
4 Serve on individual side plates, dressed in lettuce leaves.

49 ‑ Kibbeh bil sanieh (spiced lamb with cracked wheat)

Eaten with salad, pitta bread, hummus and yoghurt. Served hot or cold.

	4 portions	10 portions
burghul (cracked wheat)	200 g (8 oz)	500 g (1¼ lb)
leg or shoulder of lamb, boned and diced	400 g (1 lb)	1 kg (2½ lb)
onion, finely chopped	50 g (2 oz)	125 g (5 oz)
cinnamon	1 tsp	2½ tsp
seasoning		
cold water	2 tbsp	5 tbsp

Filling

onion, finely chopped	50 g (2 oz)	125 g (5 oz)
clove garlic, crushed and chopped	1	2
oil	60 ml ($\frac{1}{8}$ pt)	150 ml ($\frac{1}{3}$ pt)
minced lamb	200 g (8 oz)	500 g (1$\frac{1}{4}$ lb)
allspice	$\frac{1}{2}$ tsp	1 tsp
pine kernels	50 g (2 oz)	125 g (5 oz)
chopped raisins	50 g (2 oz)	125 g (5 oz)
melted butter or margarine	50 g (2 oz)	125 g (5 oz)

1 Cover the cracked wheat with cold water and allow to stand for 5 minutes. Drain well.
2 Place the lamb in a food processor with the finely chopped onion, cinnamon and seasoning, and blend to a smooth paste. Add the cold water, mix well.
6 Add the well drained cracked wheat. Blend in a processor until a smooth paste is formed.
4 For the filling: first, sweat the onion and garlic together in the oil. Add the minced lamb, allow to brown quickly.
5 Mix in the allspice, pine kernels and raisins.
6 In a suitable dish, spread half of the lamb and wheat mixture on the bottom (the kibbeh). Cover with the filling. Finish by topping with the rest of the kibbeh.
7 Cut diagonal lines over the top to make diamond shapes and brush the melted fat over the top.
8 Bake in a moderately hot oven, 190°C (Reg. 5; 375°F) for approximately 45 minutes. The surface should be brown and crisp. Baste occasionally with a few tablespoons of stock, so that the interior is moist.

50 – Couscous

This is the national dish of the Maghreb, the North African countries of Morocco, Tunisia and Algeria of Berber origin. A couscous has been adopted by other Arab countries who call it Maghebia which is different from the North African dish. Couscous itself is a type of fine semolina.

The basic process for the preparation of couscous is the steaming of the grain over a stew or broth. This is generally made with lamb or chicken and a variety of vegetables. Chick peas are usually added and sometimes raisins. The broth is often coloured red with tomato purée or yellow with saffron.

recipe continued ▶

The actual process of cooking the couscous is very simple, but calls for careful handling of the grain. The aim is to make it swell and become extremely light, each grain soft, delicate and separate. The grain must never cook in the broth or sauce, but only in the steam. The couscousier, the pot traditionally used, is in two parts: the bottom part is the round pan in which the stew is cooked; the top consists of a sieve which holds the couscous.

The treatment of the grain is always the same, whatever the sauce. This recipe is for a basic Moroccan couscous.

	4 portions	10 portions
couscous	200 g (8 oz)	500 g (1¼ lb)
lean stewing lamb	400 g (1 lb)	1 kg (2½ lb)
or		
stewing lamb and	200 g (8 oz)	500 g (1¼ lb)
stewing beef	200 g (8 oz)	500 g (1¼ lb)
or		
chicken, cut for sauté	1 × 1½ kg (3 lb)	2 × 1½ kg (7 lb)
olive oil	2 tbsp	5 tbsp
onion, finely chopped	50 g (2 oz)	125 g (5 oz)
clove garlic, crushed and chopped	1	2–3
celery	100 g (4 oz)	250 g (10 oz)
leek	100 g (4 oz)	250 g (10 oz)
carrot	100 g (4 oz)	250 g (10 oz)
chick peas	25 g (1 oz)	60 g (2½ oz)
ground ginger (optional)	¼ tsp	½ tsp
saffron (optional)	¼ tsp	½ tsp
raisins	50 g (2 oz)	125 g (5 oz)
courgettes	100 g (4 oz)	250 g (10 oz)
tomatoes, skinned, de-seeded, diced	50 g (2 oz)	125 g (5 oz)
chopped parsley		
tomato purée	50 g (2 oz)	125 g (5 oz)
cayenne pepper		
paprika	½ tsp	1 tsp
butter or margarine	50 g (2 oz)	125 g (5 oz)

1 Soak the couscous in warm water for 10 minutes.
2 Fry the meat in the oil until browned and sealed. Remove quickly, fry the onions and garlic.
3 Drain, place the meat, onions and garlic into a saucepan.

Plate 10.7: Couscous

4 Add the celery, leeks, carrots cut into 1 cm ($\frac{1}{2}$ inch) dice. Add the chick peas, cover with water, season.

5 Add the ginger and saffron. Bring to the boil and simmer for about 1 hour.

6 Drain the couscous, place in the top part of the couscousier and steam for 30 minutes. Alternatively, place the couscous in a metal colander lined with muslin. Fit into the top of the saucepan, making sure that the liquid from the stew does not touch the steamer as the couscous will become lumpy. Stir occasionally.

7 Add to the stew the raisins and courgettes, the tomato, chopped parsley and tomato purée. Cook for a further 30 minutes.

8 Remove approximately 250 ml ($\frac{1}{2}$ pint) sauce from the stew and stir in the cayenne pepper, enough to make it strong and fiery. Finish with paprika.

9 To serve pile the couscous into a suitable serving dish, preferably earthenware, add knobs of butter or margarine and work into the grains with a fork.

10 Carefully arrange the meat and vegetables over the couscous and pour the broth over. Serve the hot peppery sauce separately.

11 Alternatively, the couscous, meat and vegetables, the broth and the peppery sauce can be served in separate bowls.

Note A precooked couscous is also available.

51 – Khoshaf (dried fruit with nuts, perfumed with rose and orange water)

During Ramadan, Muslims fast all day and only eat after sunset. This is one of the dishes enjoyed during Ramadan. It is served hot or cold.

	4 portions	10 portions
dried apricots	100 g (4 oz)	250 g (10 oz)
prunes	100 g (4 oz)	250 g (10 oz)
dried figs	100 g (4 oz)	250 g (10 oz)
raisins	100 g (4 oz)	250 g (10 oz)
rose water	1 tbsp	2½ tbsp
orange blossom water	1 tbsp	2½ tbsp
blanched almonds (halved)	50 g (2 oz)	125 g (5 oz)
pine kernels	50 g (2 oz)	125 g (5 oz)

1 Wash the fruit if necessary, soak overnight.
2 Drain, place fruit in a large saucepan, cover with water and bring to boil. Simmer for 10 minutes.
3 Add the rose water and the orange blossom water.
4 Place into a serving dish sprinkled with nuts.

—— *Israeli kosher cooking* ——

Israel, although a Middle Eastern country, is like a European state set down in Asia. It is populated by a total of some 4 million Jewish and Arab people. The Jewish people in Israel are mainly immigrants from Europe who have come from Germany, Poland and Russia; there are also immigrants from Spain and Portugal and more recently the Jewish minorities from North African countries including Ethiopia, Syria and Iran have made their homes in Israel. No matter where they originated from, Jewish people still carry out the cooking traditions of the time when Israel was their God-given homeland and in accordance with the food laws as written in the Torah which is comprised of the first five books of the Old Testament. *Kosher* is a Jewish word meaning 'pure' or 'clean'. This lists the fish, birds and animals which orthodox Jews are allowed to eat, how they must be slaughtered, and how the meat must be koshered; milk and meat may not be cooked together nor eaten at the same meal and separate cooking and serving utensils must be kept specifically for each. After eating any form of meat it is not permitted to consume any milk foods, including cheese, for 3 hours. Products bearing the seal of the Beth Din – the authority appointed and approved by the

Chief Rabbi – should be used. Shellfish, game birds and pork products are forbidden.

The laws also govern the way certain foods are stored, the kitchen and its equipment and the cook's personal knives. Knives in use for general catering may not be used for kosher catering.

Many interesting dishes are made for the many Jewish festivals in the calendar and only unleavened bread called *matzos* may be eaten during the Feast of the Passover which commemorates the night when a destroying angel smote the first-born of the Egyptians but spared those in the houses where the doorposts and lintels had been daubed with blood.

52 – Potato latkes

	4 portions	10 portions
potatoes, washed, peeled and grated	400 g (1 lb)	1 kg (2½ lb)
onion, finely chopped	50 g (2 oz)	125 g (5 oz)
salt and pepper		
egg	1	2
plain flour or breadcrumbs	1 tbsp	2½ tbsp

1 Wash the grated potatoes, drain well and mix in a basin with the finely chopped onion.
2 Season with salt and pepper and add the beaten egg, flour or breadcrumbs and season.
3 Heat a little oil in a shallow pan and place potato mixture in 50 g (2 oz) pieces in the pan.
4 Cook on both sides for 3–4 minutes until golden brown; serve immediately.

Note A little grated carrot or courgette may be added to the potato.

53 – Koenigsberger klops (meat balls)

A reception snack *or* main course.

	4 portions	10 portions
bread, white or wholemeal	75 g (3 oz)	187 g (7½ oz)
egg	1	2
minced beef	200 g (8 oz)	500 g (1¼ lb)
minced veal	200 g (8 oz)	500 g (1¼ lb)
onion, chopped	50 g (2 oz)	125 g (5 oz)
salt and pepper		
chopped parsley		
paprika	¼ tsp	½ tsp
grated lemon rind	½ tsp	1 tsp
lemon, juice of	½	1
Worcester sauce	1 tsp	2½ tsp
brown vegetable stock	1 litre (2 pt)	2½ litre (5 pt)
cornflour or arrowroot		
tomato purée		
capers	25 g (1 oz)	60 g (2½ oz)
gherkins	25 g (1 oz)	60 g (2½ oz)

1 Remove the crusts from the bread and soak the bread in water.
2 Mix together the beaten egg and meat.
3 Sweat the chopped onion in a little oil until soft, then allow to cool and add to the meat.
4 Season with salt and pepper and add the chopped parsley.
5 Squeeze out excess water from the bread, add to the meat.
6 Add the paprika, lemon rind and juice, and Worcester sauce, and mix well.
7 Form into 18 g (¾ oz) balls for a reception snack or 75 g (3 oz) balls for a main course (2 per portion).
8 Cook in boiling vegetable stock, cover and simmer until cooked. Remove when cooked and keep warm.
9 Boil the remaining stock, lightly thicken with arrowroot or cornflour and colour slightly by adding a little tomato purée.
10 Season with salt and pepper and add the chopped capers and gherkins.
11 Reheat the meat balls in the gravy. Serve the small balls with cocktail sticks.

54 – Chollo bread

2 loaves

butter or margarine	56 g ($2\frac{1}{4}$ oz)
strong flour	500 g ($1\frac{1}{4}$ lb)
castor sugar	18 g ($\frac{3}{4}$ oz)
salt	1 tsp
egg	63 g ($2\frac{1}{2}$ oz)
yeast	25 g (1 oz)
tepid water (26°C; 80°F)	185 ml (8 fl oz)

1 Rub the butter or margarine into the sieved flour in a suitable basin.
2 Mix the sugar, salt and egg together.
3 Disperse the yeast in the water.
4 Add all these ingredients to the sieved flour and mix well to develop the dough. Cover with a damp cloth or plastic and allow it to ferment for about 45 minutes.
5 Divide into 125–150 g (5–6 oz) strands and begin to plait.

For 4-strand plait	*5-strand plait*
2 over 3	2 over 3
4 over 2	5 over 2
1 over 3	1 over 3

6 After moulding place on a lightly greased baking sheet and eggwash lightly.
7 Prove in a little steam until double in size. Eggwash again lightly and decorate with maw seeds.
8 Bake in a hot oven, at 220°C (Reg. 7; 425°F) for 25–30 minutes.

55 – Matzo fritters

	4 portions	10 portions
matzos (wafers of unleavened bread)	3	7
milk	250 ml ($\frac{1}{2}$ pt)	600 ml ($1\frac{1}{4}$ pt)
eggs, separated	2	5
matzo meal	150 g (6 oz)	375 g (15 oz)
brown sugar	100 g (4 oz)	250 g (10 oz)
salt		
cinnamon		
vegetable oil	60 ml ($\frac{1}{8}$ pt)	150 ml ($\frac{1}{3}$ pt)

1 Sprinkle warm water over the matzos. Place on a baking sheet and dry in a hot oven for 1 minute.
2 In a suitable basin beat the milk and egg yolks together, add the matzo meal, sugar, salt and cinnamon.
3 Fold in the stiffly beaten egg whites.
4 Spread this mixture on one side of each matzo. Fry in hot oil on the batter side until brown.
5 Spread batter on other side and fry again until brown.
6 Serve hot, sprinkled with sugar.

56 – Blitz kuchen (baked fluffy batter with nuts and cinnamon)

	4 portions	10 portions
cake flour	200 g (8 oz)	500 g ($1\frac{1}{4}$ lb)
baking powder	10 g ($\frac{1}{2}$ oz)	25 g (1 oz)
butter or margarine	100 g (4 oz)	250 g (10 oz)
castor sugar	100 g (4 oz)	250 g (10 oz)
eggs, separated	4	10
lemon, grated rind of		
milk	60 ml $\frac{1}{8}$ pt	150 ml ($\frac{1}{3}$ pt)
egg white	1	2–3
water	1 tbsp	2–3 tbsp
chopped mixed nuts	100 g (4 oz)	250 g (10 oz)
cinnamon		

1 Sieve the flour and baking powder into a suitable bowl.
2 Cream the butter and sugar together until light and white.
3 Gradually add the egg yolks to the butter and sugar, beating continuously. Add the lemon rind.
4 Gradually add the flour, beating well, then add the milk. Cream well. (Add a little more milk if necessary.)
5 Beat 4 egg whites until full peak.
6 Gently fold the egg whites into the batter.
7 Heat a lightly oiled 20 cm (8 inch) frying pan, suitable for placing in the oven. Pour in sufficient batter to cover the surface and spread with diluted egg white.
8 Sprinkle liberally with castor sugar, cinnamon and chopped mixed nuts.
9 Bake in a moderate oven at 190°C (Reg. 5; 375°F) for about 20 minutes. Serve hot or cold.

57 ‑ Carrot kugel

	4 portions	10 portions
eggs, separated	4	10
castor sugar	75 g (3 oz)	180 g (7½ oz)
carrots, finely grated	225 g (9 oz)	550 g (1 lb 6 oz)
cooking apple, finely grated	75 g (3 oz)	187 g (7½ oz)
orange, grated rind and juice of	1	2–3
lemon juice	1 tsp	2–3 tsp
potato flour or cornflour	50 g (2 oz)	125 g (5 oz)
butter or margarine	25 g (1 oz)	60 g (2½ oz)

1 Place the egg yolks into a suitable basin and beat with sugar until ribbon stage.
2 Squeeze out excess liquid from the carrots and apple.
3 Add this to the egg yolks and sugar with the orange rind and juice, then add the lemon juice, potato flour or cornflour and mix well.
4 Beat the egg whites until full peak and fold into the carrot mixture.
5 Use butter or margarine to well grease a 4-portion soufflé dish and fill it with the kugel mixture.
6 Bake in an oven at 190°C (Reg. 5; 375°F) for 30 minutes or until golden brown. Serve immediately.

Spanish cooking

The flavours of Spain like much else of its culture are strangely influenced by the Moors who, for seven centuries, ruled a large part of the country. Its closeness to North Africa and the almost tropical culture of its southern and eastern coastal strip, have done much to preserve a culinary tradition reliant on almonds, saffron, chick peas, egg yolk, honey and quince, as well as onion, garlic, olive oil, tomato and lamb common to Mediterranean countries. The cooking can be rich and distinctive. Many of its popular dishes are mixtures of fish, shellfish, meat, poultry, game with an assortment of vegetables and cereals.

58 ~ Paella (savoury rice with chicken, fish, vegetables and spices)

	4 portions	10 portions
cooked lobster	1 × 400 g (1 lb)	2½ × 400 g (2½ lb)
squid	200 g (8 oz)	500 g (1¼ lb)
gambas (Mediterranean prawns), cooked	400 g (1 lb)	1 kg (2½ lb)
mussels	400 g (1 lb)	1 kg (2½ lb)
white stock	1 litre (2 pt)	2½ litre (5 pt)
pinch of saffron		
onion, finely chopped	50 g (2 oz)	125 g (5 oz)
clove garlic, finely chopped	1	2–3
red pepper, diced	50 g (2 oz)	125 g (5 oz)
green pepper, diced	50 g (2 oz)	125 g (5 oz)
roasting chicken, cut for sauté	1½ kg (3 lb)	2 × 1½ kg (3 lb)
olive oil	60 ml ($\frac{1}{8}$ pt)	150 ml ($\frac{1}{3}$ pt)
short grain rice	200 g (8 oz)	500 g (1¼ lb)
thyme, bayleaf and seasoning		
tomatoes, skinned, de-seeded, diced	200 g (8 oz)	500 g (1¼ lb)

1　Prepare the lobster: cut it in half, remove the claws and legs, discard the sac and trail. Remove meat from the claws and cut the tail into 3–4 pieces, leaving the meat in the shell.
2　Clean the squid, pull the body and head apart. Extract the transparent 'pen' from the body. Rinse well, pulling off the thin purple membrane on the outside. Remove the ink sac. Cut the body into rings and tentacles into 1 cm ($\frac{1}{2}$ inch) lengths.

Plate 10.8: Paella

3 Prepare the gambas by shelling the body.
4 Shell the mussels and retain the cooking liquid.
5 Boil the white stock and mussel liquor together, infused with saffron. Simmer for 5–10 minutes.
6 Sweat the finely chopped onion in a suitable pan, without colour. Add the garlic and the peppers.
7 Sauté the chicken in olive oil until cooked and golden brown, then drain.
8 Add the rice to the onions and garlic and sweat for 2 minutes.
9 Add about 200 ml ($\frac{3}{8}$ pint) white stock and mussel liquor.
10 Add the thyme, bayleaf and seasoning. Bring to the boil, then cover with a lightly oiled greaseproof paper and lid. Cook for 5–8 minutes, in a moderately hot oven at 180°C (Reg. 4; 350°F).
11 Add the squid and cook for another 5 minutes.
12 Add the tomatoes, chicken and lobster pieces, mussels and gambas. Stir gently, cover with a lid and reheat the rice in the oven.
13 Correct the consistency of the rice if necessary by adding more stock, so that it looks sufficiently moist without being too wet. Correct the seasoning.

recipe continued ▶

14 When all is reheated and cooked, place in a suitable serving dish, decorate with 4 gambas and 4 mussels halved and shelled. Finish with wedges of lemon.

Note For a traditional paella a raw lobster may be used, which should be prepared as follows. Remove the legs and claws and crack the claws. Cut the lobster in half crosswise, between the tail and the carapace. Cut the carapace in two lengthwise. Discard the sac. Cut across the tail in thick slices through the shell. Remove the trail, wash the lobster pieces and cook with the rice.

59 – Cocido madrileno (pork with chick peas)

	4 portions	10 portions
garlic sausage or Spanish chorizo	100 g (4 oz)	250 g (10 oz)
loin of pork, boned	400 g (1 lb)	1 kg (2½ lb)
smoked bacon	50 g (2 oz)	125 g (5 oz)
chick peas (dried)	100 g (4 oz)	250 g (10 oz)
potato	100 g (4 oz)	250 g (10 oz)
carrot	100 g (4 oz)	250 g (10 oz)
onion, finely chopped	100 g (4 oz)	250 g (10 oz)
seasoning		

1 Cut the sausage and the pork into 1 cm (½ inch) dice, the bacon into lardons.
2 Place the sausage, bacon and pork into a large saucepan, cover with water or white stock, and add the chick peas. Bring to the boil and skim.
3 Simmer gently for 30 minutes, then add the vegetables. Add more water or white stock if necessary, season well and simmer for another hour until the meat is very tender.
4 Traditionally the broth is served first, then the vegetables and meat.

—— *Thai cooking* ——

Among the South-East Asian cuisines Thai owes the least to any European influences and could be described as a cross between Chinese and Indian, sharing similarities with Malaysian and Indonesian. Rice is the staple food, as in other Asian countries, and is eaten at all meals. Presentation of carved fruit and vegetables is important. The four predominant elements are hot, salty, sweet and sour. These are supplied by chillies, garlic, ginger, galangal (a relation of ginger), soya sauce, coconut, basil and lemon grass. Hampla (a sauce of fermented figs) and coriander also play a major part in the flavouring components.

60 – Thai mussaman curry

	4 portions	10 portions
Curry paste		
cayenne pepper	¾ tsp	2 tsp
ground coriander	1 tbsp	2½ tbsp
ground cumin	½ tsp	1½ tsp
ground cinnamon	½ tsp	1½ tsp
whole green cardamoms	2	4½
lemon, grated rind	½	1½
vegetable oil	1 tbsp	2½ tbsp
onion, finely chopped	75 g (3 oz)	187 g (7½ oz)
cloves garlic, crushed and chopped	3	7
dried shrimp paste	¼ tsp	¾ tsp

1 Place all spices and lemon rind together in a suitable bowl.
2 Lightly fry the onion and garlic in the oil until cooked but not coloured.
3 Add the shrimp paste and stir well.
4 Place in a liquidiser with the spices and 3 tablespoons cold water. Blend until smooth.

shoulder or loin of lamb, diced	400 g (1 lb)	1 kg (2½ lb)
diced potatoes	200 g (8 oz)	500 g (1¼ lb)
creamed coconut	175 g (7 oz)	400 g (1 lb)
hot water	500 ml (1 pt)	1½ litre (2½ pt)
fish glaze	1 tbsp	2 tbsp
whole green cardamoms	8	20
cinnamon stick	½	1¼
tamarind liquid	5 tsp	12 tsp
lemon, juice of	½	1
castor sugar	12 g (½ oz)	30 g (1¼ oz)
roasted peanuts	50 g (2 oz)	125 g (5 oz)

1 Fry the lamb quickly in vegetable oil to a golden brown colour.

recipe continued ▶

2 Place the lamb in a saucepan with the potatoes, coconut milk, fish glaze, cardamoms and cinnamon and bring slowly to the boil, stirring continuously.
3 Allow to simmer for one hour.
4 Stir in the curry paste, tamarind liquid, lemon juice and sugar. Simmer for a further 5 minutes.
5 Serve garnished with roasted peanuts.

—— *USA cooking* ——

It is not easy to encompass all that can be classed as American cookery, as it is an amalgam of the waves of immigrants who went there seeking a better way of life than that of their mother country. These people had to adopt their styles of cooking to the conditions which prevailed where they settled but kept to the basis that it is still possible to find communities with what are now regional specialities but which were originally alien.

The major influences may have been Dutch, French, English and native Indian but almost every other nationality in the world is now represented in the USA and in addition to Creole and Cajun in the deep south there is Spanish, Mexican, Jewish, German, Swiss, Scandinavian, Chinese, Japanese and many other forms of cookery included in the basic American mode of living, but very much more noticeable in the places where these people live.

America is the world's greatest producer of foods thus allowing of a very interesting and widely varied menu and many good dishes are accepted as international favourites.

Indigenous cooking has grown up in which dishes developed from forgotten cultures is simply inspired by local ingredients have developed. The style of cooking sometimes referred to as Tex Mex using beans, chilli pepper and corn pancakes, and corn chips with avocado pear as basic ingredients, is typical of this development.

61 – Chilli con carne (beef with beans in chilli sauce)

Originally from Texas and Mexico, chilli con carne is now eaten throughout the United States.

	4 portions	10 portions
dried kidney beans or pinto beans	200 g (8 oz)	500 g (1¼ lb)
lean topside of beef	400 g (1 lb)	1 kg (2½ lb)
sunflower oil	60 ml (⅛ pt)	150 ml (⅓ pt)
onions, finely chopped	100 g (4 oz)	250 g (10 oz)
cloves garlic, crushed and chopped	2	5
chilli powder	2 tsp	5 tsp
oregano	1 tsp	2–3 tsp
ground cumin	½ tsp	1 tsp
tomato purée	50 g (2 oz)	125 g (5 oz)
tomatoes, skinned, de-seeded, diced	200 g (8 oz)	500 g (1¼ lb)
white or brown stock	500 ml (1 pt)	1¼ litre (2½ pt)

1 Soak the beans in cold water for 24 hours. Drain, cover with cold water and bring to the boil. Boil for 10 minutes then gently simmer until tender.
2 Prepare the beef by removing all the excess fat and cutting into batons 5 cm (2 inches) long ×½ cm (¼ inch) wide or mincing.
3 Heat a little of the oil in a frying pan and quickly fry the beef until golden brown.
4 Drain the beef, place in a suitable saucepan.
5 Add a little more oil to the frying pan, add the onions and garlic and quickly fry until a light golden colour.
6 Stir in the chilli powder, oregano and cumin and cook for a further 3 minutes. Add to the beef.
7 Stir in the tomato purée, tomatoes and seasoning, and cover with white or brown stock.
8 Gently cook by simmering on the stove or cover and cook in a moderate oven at 180°C (Reg. 4; 350°F) for 1½–2 hours.
9 Check constantly to make sure that the meat does not become too dry. Add a little more stock or water if necessary.
10 Drain the cooked beans and add to the cooked beef.
11 Serve in an earthenware dish sprinkled with chopped parsley.

Note   This dish must be quite moist, the consistency of a stew. Chilli powders and chilli seasonings vary in strength, therefore the amount used may be varied.

62 – Hash brown potatoes

	4 portions	10 portions
potatoes	600 g (1½ lb)	2 kg (4 lb)
butter or margarine	25 g (1 oz)	60 g (2½ oz)
lardons of bacon	100 g (4 oz)	250 g (10 oz)
seasoning		

1　Wash, peel and rewash the potatoes.
2　Coarsely grate the potatoes, rewash quickly and then drain well.
3　Melt the butter in a suitable frying pan. Add the lardons of bacon, fry until crisp and brown, remove from the pan and drain.
4　Pour the fat back into the frying pan, add the grated potato and season.
5　Press down well, allow 2 cm (1 inch) thickness, and cook over a heat for 10–15 minutes or in a moderate oven at 190°C (Reg. 5; 190°C) until a brown crust forms on the bottom.
6　Turn out onto a suitable serving dish and sprinkle with the lardons of bacon and chopped parsley.

63 – Clam chowder

A chowder is usually an unpassed shellfish soup. It originated in the USA where there are many regional variations. Clams, oysters, scallops and fresh or frozen crabs may be used.

	4 portions	10 portions
belly of pork, chopped	100 g (4 oz)	250 g (10 oz)
potatoes	150 g (6 oz)	375 g (15 oz)
leek	50 g (2 oz)	125 g (5 oz)
celery	50 g (2 oz)	125 g (5 oz)
butter or margarine	50 g (2 oz)	125 g (5 oz)
fish stock (or chicken stock)	1 litre (2 pt)	2½ litre (5 pt)
diced clams, fresh or frozen	200 g (8 oz)	500 g (1¼ lb)
salt, pepper		
bouquet garni		
tomatoes, skinned, de-seeded, diced	100 g (4 oz)	250 g (10 oz)
cream	125 ml (¼ pt)	300 ml (⅝ pt)
chopped parsley		
cracker biscuits	4	10

1 Sweat the pork, potatoes, leek and celery in the butter without colour.
2 Add the stock and clams, season, add the bouquet garni, bring to the boil and simmer for 45 minutes.
3 Add the tomatoes and simmer for a few minutes.
4 Correct the seasoning, add the cream and chopped parsley. Crushed cracker biscuits may be added just before serving or served separately.

Note Garlic, bayleaf and thyme may also be added and small pieces of crisply fried bacon served separately.

64 ~ Succotash (butter beans, sweetcorn and bacon in cream sauce)

	4 portions	10 portions
lardons of bacon	50 g (2 oz)	125 g (5 oz)
butter or margarine	25 g (1 oz)	60 g (2½ oz)
butter beans, cooked	350 g (14 oz)	1 kg (2 lb)
sweetcorn, cooked	150 g (6 oz)	375 g (15 oz)
cream sauce	125 ml (¼ pt)	300 ml (⅝ pt)
seasoning		
single cream (or yoghurt)	60 ml (⅛ pt)	150 ml (⅓ pt)

1 Quickly fry the lardons of bacon in the fat.
2 Add the drained butter beans and sweetcorn.
3 Bind with cream sauce, correct the seasoning and finish with cream.
4 Serve in a suitable dish sprinkled with chopped parsley.

65 ~ Chocolate brownies

	25 pieces approx.
butter or margarine	100 g (4 oz)
cocoa powder	50 g (2 oz)
eggs	2
castor sugar	200 g (8 oz)
self-raising flour	50 g (2 oz)
vanilla essence	
chopped walnuts	100 g (4 oz)
raisins	50 g (2 oz)

recipe continued ▶

1 Melt the butter or margarine, stir in the cocoa powder and remove from heat.
2 Beat the eggs and sugar together until light and white and add the butter and cocoa powder mixture.
3 Add the sieved flour and mix well.
4 Add the vanilla essence, walnuts and raisins.
5 Place this mixture into a greased and lined 20 cm (8 inch) square shallow cake tin. Bake at 180°C (Reg. 4; 350°F) for about 30 minutes.
6 Remove from oven and allow to cool. Cut into 2 cm (1 inch) squares to serve.

66 – Pecan pie

	4 portions	10 portions
sweet pastry	150 g (6 oz)	375 g (15 oz)
eggs	3	7–8
soft brown sugar	200 g (8 oz)	500 g (1¼ lb)
vanilla essence		
pinch of salt		
melted butter or margarine	75 g (3 oz)	180 g (7½ oz)
treacle syrup	6 tbsp	15 tbsp
coarsely chopped pecan nuts	200 g (8 oz)	500 g (1¼ lb)

1 Line an 18–20 cm (7–8 inch) flan ring with the sweet pastry and partly bake blind.
2 Prepare the filling from the remaining ingredients. Lightly heat the eggs and sugar together with the vanilla essence and salt.
3 Stir in the melted butter or margarine and syrup, and add the chopped pecan nuts.
4 Pour this mixture into the flan case and decorate with pecan halves.
5 Bake in a moderately hot oven at 180°C (Reg. 4; 350°F) for 30–35 minutes until the filling is set. Cover with aluminium foil if the pastry starts to get too dark.
6 Serve with cream, ice-cream or yoghurt.

11

VEGETARIAN DISHES

Recipe No.		page no.
7	Bean goulash	497
2	Bean and nut burgers	492
11	Bread and butter pudding, light savoury	500
6	Bread dough, wholemeal	496
8	Broccoli sauce	498
4	Caribbean fruit curry	494
3	Chinese-style stir-fry vegetables	493
5	Cornish vegetable feast bake pie	495
9	Gougère	498
20	Kedgeree, vegetarian	508
21	Lasagne, vegetarian	509
10	Lentil and cider loaf	499
14	Mexican bean pot	502
22	Moussaka, vegetarian	510
12	Mushroom sauce, piquant	500
1	Mushroom, wine and mustard sauce	491
26	Pizza, wholemeal vegetarian	514
15	Potato and nut cutlets	502
16	Ratatouille wholemeal pancakes with a cheese sauce	504
13	Shepherd's pie, meatless	501
25	Strudel, vegetarian	513
18	Tomato savarin filled with cucumber, apple and walnut dressing	506
23	Vegetable biryani	511
19	Vegetable crumble	507
17	Vegetable curry with wholegrain rice pilaff	505
24	Vegetable and nut Stroganoff	512

Vegetarian

I	Be aware of a variety of vegetarian dishes and appreciate the concept of vegetarian cookery in society.
2	Produce dishes to the satisfaction of vegetarians and others, and provide for their nutritional needs.
3	Work methodically, clearly and safely so as to comply with legislation.

The professional chef today has to cater for a much wider, discerning clientele. This includes being able to produce exciting, well balanced vegetarian dishes for a growing vegetarian market. Vegetarian cookery can, with imagination and creativity, be as interesting in ingredient usage and presentation as many of the other styles of cookery.

1 – Mushroom, wine and mustard sauce

	4 portions	10 portions
firm white button mushrooms	100 g (4 oz)	250 g (10 oz)
margarine	25 g (1 oz)	60 g (2½ oz)
lemon, juice of	½	1
velouté made with vegetable stock	250 ml (1 pt)	1¼ litre (2½ pt)
English or continental mustard	12 g (½ oz)	25 g (1¼ oz)
white wine (dry)	60 ml (⅛ pt)	150 ml (⅓ pt)
single cream or unsweetened vegetable creamer	60 ml (⅛ pt)	150 ml (⅓ pt)

1   Sweat the sliced mushroom in margarine and lemon juice for 1–2 minutes.
2   Add the boiled and passed velouté.
3   Stir in the English mustard diluted in the wine.
4   Finish with cream.

2 – Bean and nut burgers

	4 portions	10 portions
aduki beans	200 g (8 oz)	500 g (1¼ lb)
sunflower oil	60 ml (⅛ pt)	150 ml (⅓ pt)
finely chopped onion	50 g (2 oz)	125 g (5 oz)
clove of garlic	1	2
dried rosemary	3 g (⅛ oz)	10 g (½ oz)
button mushrooms	100 g (4 oz)	250 g (10 oz)
small carrots (grated)	2	5
chopped walnuts and hazelnuts	100 g (4 oz)	250 g (10 oz)
tomato purée	50 g (2 oz)	125 g (5 oz)
seasoning		
eggs	1–2	2–3
flour		
rolled oats	100 g (4 oz)	250 g (10 oz)
parsley		

> 1 portion provides:
>
> 2343 kJ/556 kcal
> 32.1 g fat
> (of which 4.4 g saturated)
> 48.8 g carbohydrate
> (of which 5.6 g sugars)
> 21.4 g protein
> 17.3 g fibre

1 Soak the beans in cold water for 24 hours, drain. Cover with cold water in a saucepan, bring to the boil, simmer gently until tender. Drain, purée in a food processor.
2 Heat the oil and sweat the onion and crushed garlic without colouring for 2 minutes, add the rosemary and sweat for a further 2 minutes.
3 Add the washed and finely chopped mushrooms, grated carrot and nuts.
4 Cook for 2–3 minutes. Drain off any surplus liquid. Remove from heat.
5 Mix in the bean purée. Add the tomato purée. Season, bind with beaten egg.
6 Shape into burgers, pass through flour, beaten egg and rolled oats.
7 Place on a greased baking sheet, brush with oil. Bake in a preheated oven 180°C (Reg. 4; 350°F) for 10–15 minutes, turning over at the half-way stage.
8 Alternatively, carefully shallow fry burgers in hot sunflower oil, taking special care that they do not break up.
9 Serve garnished with picked parsley and a suitable sauce, (tomato sauce) made with vegetable stock and no bacon flavouring.

3 – Chinese-style stir fry vegetables

	4 portions	10 portions
beansprouts	100 g (4 oz)	250 g (10 oz)
button mushrooms	100 g (4 oz)	250 g (10 oz)
carrots	100 g (4 oz)	250 g (10 oz)
celery	100 g (4 oz)	250 g (10 oz)
cauliflower	100 g (4 oz)	250 g (10 oz)
broccoli	100 g (4 oz)	250 g (10 oz)
baby sweetcorn	50 g (2 oz)	125 g (5 oz)
French beans	50 g (2 oz)	125 g (5 oz)
red peppers	50 g (2 oz)	125 g (5 oz)
green peppers	50 g (2 oz)	125 g (5 oz)
sunflower oil	125 ml ($\frac{1}{4}$ pt)	300 ml ($\frac{5}{8}$ pt)
grated root ginger	5 g ($\frac{1}{4}$ oz)	12 g ($\frac{5}{8}$ oz)
soy sauce	60 ml ($\frac{1}{8}$ pt)	150 ml ($\frac{1}{3}$ pt)
ground white or mill pepper to season		

> 1 portion provides:
>
> 1429 kJ/340 kcal
> 31.9 g fat
> (of which 4.2 g saturated)
> 9.1 g carbohydrate
> (of which 4.2 g sugars)
> 4.7 g protein
> 4.5 g fibre

1 Wash the beansprouts, wash and slice the mushrooms. Peel the carrots, cut into large batons. Trim the celery, cut into large batons. Wash the cauliflower and broccoli and cut into florets. Top and tail the French beans, cut in halves. Wash and slice the peppers. The green vegetables may be quickly blanched and refreshed to retain colour.

2 Heat the sunflower oil in a wok or frying pan and add all the vegetables. Fry and continuously stir for approximately 3 minutes.

3 Add the grated ginger, cook for 1 minute. Add the soy sauce, stir well.

4 Correct the seasoning, serve immediately.

Plate 11.1: Preparation of Chinese-style stir fry vegetables

4 ~ Caribbean fruit curry

	4 portions	10 portions
pineapple	1 small	1 large
small dessert pears	2	5
dessert apples	2	5
mangoes	2	5
bananas	2	5
paw paw	1	2–3
guava	1	2–3
grated rind and juice of lime	1	2–3
onion, chopped	50 g (2 oz)	125 g (5 oz)
sunflower margarine	25 g (1 oz)	60 g (2½ oz)
sunflower oil	60 ml (⅛ pt)	150 ml (⅓ pt)
Madras curry powder	50 g (2 oz)	125 g (5 oz)
wholemeal flour	25 g (1 oz)	60 g (2½ oz)
fresh grated ginger	10 g (½ oz)	25 g (1¼ oz)
desiccated coconut	50 g (2 oz)	125 g (5 oz)
tomato, skinned, de-seeded and diced	100 g (4 oz)	250 g (10 oz)
tomato purée	25 g (1 oz)	60 g (2½ oz)
sultanas	50 g (2 oz)	125 g (5 oz)
fruit juice	½ litre (1 pt)	1¼ litre (2½ pt)
yeast extract	5 g (¼ oz)	12 g (⅝ oz)
cashew nuts	50 g (2 oz)	125 g (5 oz)
single cream or smetana (page 744)	60 ml (⅛ pt)	150 ml (⅓ pt)

Using single cream, 1 portion provides:

1729 kJ/412 kcal
19.6 g fat
(of which 6.1 g saturated)
57.2 g carbohydrate
(of which 51.6 g sugars)
5.4 g protein
8.3 g fibre

1　Skin, cut the pineapple in half, remove the tough centre. Cut in 1 cm (½ inch) chunks. Peel the apples and pears, remove the cores, cut into 1 cm (½ inch) pieces. Peel and slice the mangoes. Skin and cut the bananas into 1 cm (½ inch) pieces. Cut the guavas and paw paws in half, remove the seeds, peel, dice into 1 cm (½ inch) pieces. Marinade the fruit in lime juice.

2　Fry the onion in the sunflower margarine and oil until lightly brown, add the curry powder, sweat together, add the wholemeal flour and cook for 2 minutes.

3　Add the ginger, coconut, tomato concassé, tomato purée and sultanas.

4　Gradually add sufficient boiling fruit juice to make a light sauce.

5　Add yeast extract, stir well. Simmer for 10 minutes.

6　Add the fruit and cashew nuts, stir carefully, allow to heat through.

7 Finish with cream or smetana.
8 Serve in a suitable dish; separately serve poppadoms, wholegrain pilaff rice and a green salad.

5 – Cornish vegetable feast bake pie

	4 portions	10 portions	I portion provides:
wholemeal bread dough (recipe 6)	200 g (8 oz)	500 g (1¼ lb)	1832 kJ/436 kcal 26.4 g fat (of which 3.9 g saturated) 37.7 g carbohydrate (of which 0.0 g sugars) 15.0 g protein 11.3 g fibre
steamed or boiled jacket potatoes	200 g (8 oz)	500 g (1¼ lb)	
French beans	150 g (6 oz)	375 g (15 oz)	
sunflower oil	60 ml (⅛ pt)	150 ml (⅓ pt)	
onion, finely chopped	50 g (2 oz)	125 g (5 oz)	
button mushrooms	50 g (2 oz)	125 g (5 oz)	
cooked leaf spinach	400 g (1 lb)	1¼ kg (2½ lb)	
béchamel made with wholemeal flour and skimmed milk	250 ml (½ pt)	1¼ litre (2½ pt)	
English or continental mustard	10 g (½ oz)	25 g (1¼ oz)	
seasoning, ground nutmeg			

1 Make the wholemeal bread dough (see next recipe).
2 Peel and cut the potatoes into 1 cm (½ inch) dice.
3 Top and tail the French beans, cut in halves, blanch and refresh.
4 Heat the sunflower oil and gently fry the onion without colour.
5 Add the sliced button mushrooms, cook for 2–3 minutes.
6 Add the potatoes, French beans and spinach, mix and heat through.
7 Boil the béchamel, mix in the English mustard.
8 Add to the vegetables, stir, season and add the grated nutmeg.
9 Line a deep 18 cm (7 inch) flan ring using two-thirds of the dough.
10 Fill with vegetable and béchamel mixture.
11 Eggwash the edges, cover with the remaining dough.
12 Bake in a preheated oven 180–190°C (Reg. 4–5; 350–375°F) for 20–25 minutes.
13 Serve with tomato sauce made with vegetable stock and no bacon.

6 ~ Wholemeal bread dough

skimmed milk	75 ml (3 fl oz)
fresh yeast	10 g ($\frac{1}{2}$ oz)
wholemeal flour	150 g (6 oz)
sunflower margarine	25 g (1 oz)
pinch salt	
pinch sugar	
ascorbic acid powder	3 g ($\frac{1}{8}$ oz)
egg	1

1 Warm the skimmed milk to 36°C (90°F).
2 Disperse the yeast in milk and add sufficient of the sieved flour to make a light batter. Sprinkle a little flour over the top, cover with a damp cloth, allow to prove until the ferment breaks through the flour.
3 Place the remainder of the sieved flour into a mixing bowl, add the ferment, melted sunflower margarine, salt, sugar, acid and beaten egg.
4 Mix well together to form a smooth dough, if the dough is too tight add a little warm water or skimmed milk.
5 Place back into the basin, allow to prove until double in size, cover with a damp cloth.
6 Knock back to equalise the dough and bring the yeast back into contact with the dough. Then use as required.

7 – Bean goulash

	4 portions	10 portions
red kidney beans or haricot beans	200 g (8 oz)	500 g (1¼ lb)
sunflower oil	60 ml (⅛ pt)	150 ml (⅓ pt)
onion, finely chopped	50 g (2 oz)	125 g (5 oz)
clove garlic, crushed	1	2–3
paprika	25 g (1 oz)	60 g (2½ oz)
red peppers	2	5
green pepper	1	2–3
yellow pepper	1	2–3
sliced button mushrooms	200 g (8 oz)	500 g (1¼ lb)
tomato purée	50 g (2 oz)	125 g (5 oz)
vegetable stock	750 ml (1½ pt)	2 litre (4¼ pt)
bouquet garni		
seasoning		
small turned potatoes (cooked)	8	20

> I portion provides:
>
> 1728 kJ/411 kcal
> 17.9 g fat
> (of which 2.7 g saturated)
> 50.0 g carbohydrate
> (of which 7.3 g sugars)
> 17.3 g protein
> 18.5 g fibre

1 Soak the beans for 24 hours in cold water. Drain, place into a saucepan. Cover with cold water, bring to the boil and simmer until tender.
2 Heat the oil in a sauté pan, sweat the onion and garlic without colour for 2–3 minutes and add the paprika; sweat for a further 2–3 minutes.
3 Add the peppers, cut in halves, seeds removed and cut into 1 cm (½ inch) dice. Add the button mushrooms; sweat for a further 2 minutes.
4 Add the tomato purée, vegetable stock and bouquet garni. Bring to the boil and simmer until the pepper and mushrooms are cooked.
5 Remove the bouquet garni. Add the drained cooked beans, correct seasoning and stir.
6 Garnish with potatoes and chopped parsley.
7 Serve wholegrain pilaff or wholemeal noodles separately.

Plate 11.2: Bean goulash

8 – Broccoli sauce

	4 portions	10 portions
cooked broccoli	200 g (8 oz)	500 g (1¼ lb)
sunflower seeds	40 g (1½ oz)	100 g (4 oz)
smetana or silken tofu (pages 744, 745)	125 ml (¼ pt)	300 ml (⅝ pt)
lemon, juice of	½	1–1½
seasoning		

1 Place the broccoli, sunflower seeds and approximately 500 ml (½ pint) of water into a liquidiser with the smetana and lemon juice. Liquidise until smooth.
2 Strain through a coarse strainer into a small saucepan. Correct the seasoning and consistency.
3 Heat *very* gently before serving. *Do not boil.*

9 – Gougère

Choux pastry (page 666)

	4 portions	10 portions
water	250 ml (½ pt)	600 ml (1¼ pt)
sunflower margarine	100 g (4 oz)	250 g (10 oz)
strong flour	125 g (5 oz)	300 g (12½ oz)
eggs (size 3)	4	10
Gruyère cheese, diced	75 g (3 oz)	180 g (7½ oz)
seasoning		

1 Make the choux pastry, cool and add the finely diced Gruyère cheese.
2 With a 1 cm (½ inch) plain tube, pipe individual rings approximately 8 cm (3 inches) diameter on to a very lightly greased baking sheet.
3 Brush lightly with eggwash and relax for approximately 15 minutes.
4 Bake in a preheated oven at 190°C (Reg. 5; 375°F) for 20 to 30 minutes.
5 When cooked place on individual plates. Fill the centre with a suitable filling:

- ratatouille
- stir-fry vegetables
- cauliflower cheese
- button mushrooms in a tomato and garlic sauce
- leaf spinach with chopped onions in a béchamel sauce
- button mushrooms and sweetcorn in a béchamel yoghurt sauce.

10 – Lentil and cider loaf

	4 portions	10 portions
red split lentils	150 g (6 oz)	375 g (15 oz)
dry cider	250 ml ($\frac{1}{2}$ pt)	600 ml ($1\frac{1}{4}$ pt)
sunflower margarine	100 g (4 oz)	250 g (10 oz)
dried breadcrumbs	50 g (2 oz)	125 g (5 oz)
onion, chopped	100 g (4 oz)	250 g (10 oz)
carrots	100 g (4 oz)	250 g (10 oz)
stick of celery	1	2–3
clove garlic, chopped	1	2–3
dried thyme	3 g ($\frac{1}{8}$ oz)	7 g ($\frac{5}{8}$ oz)
ground roasted hazelnuts	50 g (2 oz)	125 g (5 oz)
grated Parmesan cheese	50 g (2 oz)	125 g (5 oz)
chopped parsley		
egg	1	2–3
seasoning		

> I portion provides:
>
> 2086 kJ/497 kcal
> 30.6 g fat
> (of which 6.7 g saturated)
> 35.3 g carbohydrate
> (of which 6.3 g sugars)
> 18.0 g protein
> 7.2 g fibre

1 Place the lentils in a saucepan with the cider and sufficient water to cover. Bring to the boil and allow to cook until almost tender and all the liquid has been absorbed.
2 Line a 400 g (1 lb) loaf tin with silicone paper, brush with melted sunflower margarine and sprinkle with the breadcrumbs.
3 With the rest of the margarine cook the onions, the carrots and celery cut into large brunoise. Cook until soft and lightly brown.
4 Add the garlic and vegetables to the lentils, mix well.
5 Add the thyme, nuts, cheese, parsley and egg. Season.
6 Place into prepared tin, cover with greased aluminium foil. Bake in a preheated oven at 180°C (Reg. 4; 350°F) for approximately 1 hour.
7 Remove the foil 10 minutes before completion of cooking to brown top.
8 To serve turn out on to a warm dish. Portion as required. Garnish with picked parsley and serve a suitable sauce separately such as broccoli sauce (recipe 11).

11 – Light savoury bread and butter pudding

	4 portions	10 portions
slices of wholemeal bread spread with sunflower margarine	2	5
grated Cheddar cheese	150 g (6 oz)	375 g (15 oz)
skimmed milk (or half milk and half vegetable stock)	500 ml (1 pt)	$1\frac{1}{4}$ litre ($2\frac{1}{2}$ pt)
eggs (size 3)	3	8
seasoning		
tomatoes	150 g (6 oz)	375 g (15 oz)

> 1 portion provides:
>
> 1349 kJ/321 kcal
> 17.9 g fat
> (of which 9.0 g saturated)
> 16.7 g carbohydrate
> (of which 7.7 g sugars)
> 24.4 g protein
> 2.2 g fibre

1 Grease a pie dish with sunflower margarine.
2 Remove the crusts from the bread and cut in half diagonally.
3 Arrange the slices of bread neatly in the pie dish.
4 Sprinkle in the grated cheese.
5 Warm the milk to blood heat, mix the eggs together with the seasoning, whisk in the milk and strain through a fine strainer.
6 Pour this mixture onto the bread and cheese.
7 Arrange slices of blanched peeled tomato on top.
8 Stand the pie dish in a tray of warm water, bake in a preheated oven 160°C (Reg. 3; 325°F) for approximately 40–45 minutes until set and serve.

12 – Piquant mushroom sauce

	4 portions	10 portions
sunflower oil	4 tbsp	10 tbsp
onions, finely chopped	50 g (2 oz)	125 g (5 oz)
button mushrooms, sliced	200 g (8 oz)	500 g ($1\frac{1}{4}$ oz)
apple juice	125 ml ($\frac{1}{4}$ pt)	300 ml ($\frac{5}{8}$ pt)
red wine vinegar	4 tbsp	10 tbsp
yeast extract	10 g ($\frac{1}{2}$ oz)	25 g ($1\frac{1}{4}$ oz)
dried mixed herbs	3 g ($\frac{1}{4}$ oz)	12 g ($\frac{5}{8}$ oz)
arrowroot	5 g ($\frac{1}{4}$ oz)	12 g ($\frac{5}{8}$ oz)

1 Heat the sunflower oil in suitable pan and fry the onions lightly for 5 minutes until brown. Add the mushrooms and sweat for 2 minutes.
2 Stir in the remaining ingredients, except the arrowroot, mix well.

3 Bring to the boil, simmer for 15 minutes. Correct the seasoning.
4 Dilute the arrowroot with a little water, stir into the sauce, mix well.
5 Simmer for 2 minutes, use as required.

13 ~ Meatless shepherd's pie

	4 portions	10 portions
lentils	100 g (4 oz)	250 g (10 oz)
vegetable stock	500 ml (1 pt)	1¼ litre (2½ pt)
textured vegetable protein (TVP) mince, natural flavour	100 g (4 oz)	250 g (10 oz)
onions, finely chopped	100 g (4 oz)	250 g (10 oz)
dried mixed herbs	3 g (⅛ oz)	8 g (⅜ oz)
sunflower margarine	50 g (2 oz)	125 g (5 oz)
wholemeal flour	25 g (1 oz)	60 g (2½ oz)
tomato purée	50 g (2 oz)	125 g (5 oz)
yeast extract	10 g (½ oz)	25 g (1¼ oz)
seasoning		
drops Worcester sauce	2–3	5–6
duchess potatoes (page 566)	500 g (1 lb)	1¼ kg (2½ lb)
grated Cheddar cheese	50 g (2 oz)	125 g (5 oz)

> 1 portion provides:
>
> 2198 kJ/523 kcal
> 22.3 g fat
> (of which 6.0 g saturated)
> 54.3 g carbohydrate
> (of which 4.9 g sugars)
> 29.9 g protein
> 7.5 g fibre

1 Cook the lentils in the vegetable stock.
2 Reconstitute the TVP by soaking in cold water for the recommended time according to the manufacturer's instructions.
3 Sweat the onion and mixed herbs in the margarine without colour.
4 Stir in the wholemeal flour and cook out for 1–2 minutes.
5 Add the TVP and vegetable stock from the lentils, simmer for 10 minutes.
6 Mix in the lentils, tomato purée and yeast extract.
7 Correct the seasoning and consistency, add 2–3 drops of Worcester sauce to taste.
8 Place this mixture into a pie dish; allow to cool.
9 Pipe the duchess potato on top using a star tube.
10 Sprinkle with the grated Cheddar cheese.
11 Bake in a preheated oven at 180°C (Reg. 4; 350°F) for approximately 20 minutes until golden brown.

Note   In place of the TVP a selection of freshly diced blanched vegetables may be used or twice the amount of lentils.

14 – Mexican bean pot

	4 portions	10 portions
dry red beans or haricot beans	300 g (12 oz)	1 kg (2 lb)
onions, finely chopped	100 g (4 oz)	250 g (10 oz)
carrots, sliced	100 g (4 oz)	250 g (10 oz)
tomato, skinned, de-seeded and diced	200 g (8 oz)	500 g (1¼ lb)
cloves garlic, crushed and chopped	2	5
paprika	10 g (½ oz)	25 g (2½ oz)
dried marjoram	3 g (⅛ oz)	9 g (⅜ oz)
small fresh chilli, finely chopped	1	2–3
small red pepper, finely diced	1	2–3
yeast extract	5 g (¼ oz)	12 g (⅝ oz)
chopped chives		
seasoning		

> 1 portion provides:
>
> 672 kJ/161 kcal
> 1.2 g fat
> (of which 0.2 g saturated)
> 27.0 g carbohydrate
> (of which 4.6 g sugars)
> 12.3 g protein
> 14.0 g fibre

1 Soak the beans in cold water for 24 hours, drain. Place into a saucepan cover with cold water, bring to the boil and simmer gently.
2 When three-quarters cooked, add all the other ingredients except the chopped chives.
3 Continue to simmer until all is completely cooked.
4 Serve sprinkled with chopped chives.

15 – Potato and nut cutlets

	4 portions	10 portions
onion, finely chopped	50 g (2 oz)	125 g (5 oz)
sunflower oil	60 ml (⅛ pt)	150 ml (⅓ pt)
duchess potato	300 g (12 oz)	750 g (2 lb)
ground walnuts	100 g (4 oz)	250 g (10 oz)
ground cashew nuts	50 g (2 oz)	125 g (5 oz)
yeast extract	3 g (⅛ oz)	9 g (⅜ oz)
pinch of dried mixed herbs		
flour		
beaten egg		
wholemeal breadcrumbs		

> 1 portion provides:
>
> 2616 kJ/623 kcal
> 53.0 g fat
> (of which 6.8 g saturated)
> 28.7 g carbohydrate
> (of which 2.1 g sugars)
> 9.7 g protein
> 4.3 g fibre

1 Cook the onion in the sunflower oil without colouring.
2 Mix the duchess potato with the nuts, yeast extract and mixed herbs.

3   Season and add the onion.
4   Place onto a floured board, divide and shape into cutlets.
5   Flour, egg and crumb the cutlets.
6   Shallow or deep fry in hot oil (190°C; 375°F) until golden brown.
7   Drain on kitchen paper and serve with a suitable sauce such as asparagus.

Asparagus sauce

	4 portions	10 portions
cooked asparagus	300 g (12 oz)	1 kg (2 lb)
vegetable stock	250 ml ($\frac{1}{2}$ pt)	600 ml (1$\frac{1}{4}$ pt)
white wine	125 ml ($\frac{1}{4}$ pt)	300 ml ($\frac{5}{8}$ pt)
smetana or double cream	4 tbsp	10 tbsp
seasoning		

1   Liquidise the asparagus, stock and wine until a smooth sauce is obtained.
2   Gently bring to the boil.
3   Strain through a coarse strainer into a clean saucepan. Season and reheat.
4   Add the smetana or double cream. *Do not boil.*
5   Correct the seasoning and consistency, use as required.

16 – Ratatouille wholemeal pancakes with a cheese sauce

	4 portions	10 portions
Pancake batter (see page 611)		
wholemeal flour	100 g (4 oz)	250 g (10 oz)
skimmed milk	250 ml ($\frac{1}{2}$ pt)	600 ml ($1\frac{1}{4}$ pt)
egg	1	2–3
pinch of salt		
melted sunflower margarine	10 g ($\frac{1}{2}$ oz)	25 g ($1\frac{1}{4}$ oz)
Ratatouille (see page 527)		
courgettes	200 g (8 oz)	500 g ($1\frac{1}{4}$ lb)
aubergines	200 g (8 oz)	500 g ($1\frac{1}{4}$ lb)
red pepper	1	2–3
green pepper	1	2–3
tomatoes	100 g (4 oz)	250 g (10 oz)
yellow pepper	1	2–3
onion, chopped	50 g (2 oz)	125 g (5 oz)
clove garlic, chopped	1	2
sunflower oil	4 tbsp	10 tbsp
tin plum tomatoes	1 × 400 g	$1\frac{1}{4}$ kg ($2\frac{1}{2}$ lb)
tomato purée	50 g (2 oz)	125 g (5 oz)
Cheese sauce (page 118)		
skimmed milk	500 ml (1 pt)	$1\frac{1}{4}$ litre ($2\frac{1}{2}$ pt)
sunflower oil	50 g (2 oz)	125 g (5 oz)
flour	50 g (2 oz)	125 g (5 oz)
onion studded with clove	1	2–3
grated Parmesan	25 g (1 oz)	60 g ($2\frac{1}{2}$ oz)
egg yolk	1	2–3
seasoning		

> 1 portion provides:
>
> 2398 kJ/571 kcal
> 35.8 g fat
> (of which 6.5 g saturated)
> 46.1 g carbohydrate
> (of which 19.0 g sugars)
> 19.6 g protein
> 6.5 g fibre

1 Prepare and make the pancakes.
2 Prepare the ratatouille and cheese sauce.
3 Season with salt and cayenne pepper.
4 Fill the pancakes with the ratatouille, roll up and serve on individual plates or on a service dish, coated with cheese sauce, sprinkled with grated Parmesan cheese and finished by gratinating under the salamander.

17 – Vegetable curry with wholegrain rice pilaff

	4 portions	10 portions
mixed vegetables (cauliflower, broccoli, peppers, carrots, courgettes, mushrooms, aubergines)	600 g (1½ lb)	2¼ kg (4¼ lb)
sunflower margarine	100 g (4 oz)	250 g (10 oz)
onions, chopped finely	150 g (6 oz)	375 g (15 oz)
garam masala	25 g (1 oz)	60 g (2½ oz)
creamed coconut or 2 oz (50 g) desiccated coconut	25 g (1 oz)	60 g (2½ oz)
curry sauce made from vegetable stock (pages 114–115)	500 ml (1 pt)	1¼ litre (2½ pt)

> 1 portion provides:
>
> 1814 kJ/432 kcal
> 35.5 g fat
> (of which 7.4 g saturated)
> 23.5 g carbohydrate
> (of which 16.3 g sugars)
> 6.4 g protein
> 6.7 g fibre

1 Prepare the vegetables: cut the cauliflower and broccoli into small florets, blanch and refresh; cut the peppers into half, remove the seeds, cut into 1 cm (½ inch) dice; cut the carrots into large dice, blanch and refresh; and the courgettes into 1 cm (½ inch) dice; leave the mushrooms whole; cut the aubergines into 1 cm (½ inch) dice.
2 Heat the margarine and sweat the onion.
3 Add the garam masala; sweat for approximately 2 minutes and add the coconut.
4 Add all the vegetables; sweat together for approximately 5 minutes.
5 Add the curry sauce, bring to the boil and gently simmer until all the vegetables are cooked but crunchy in texture.
6 Serve in a suitable dish with a wholegrain rice pilaff garnished with flaked almonds, poppadoms and a curry tray with mango chutney.

Note To the basic recipe of wholegrain rice pilaff (page 236) using 100 g (4 oz) rice, add 50 g (2 oz) roasted flaked almonds after cooking (increase the quantities by 2½ for 10 portions).

18 – Tomato savarin filled with cucumber, apple and walnut dressing

	4 portions	10 portions
can of plum tomatoes	1 × 400 g (1 lb)	1¼ kg (2½ lb)
tomato purée	25 g (1 oz)	60 g (2½ oz)
agar-agar (gelatine substitute) (page 739)	25 g (1 oz)	60 g (2½ oz)
mayonnaise	125 ml (¼ pt)	300 ml (⅝ pt)
lemon, juice of	½	1
green pepper	½	1
yellow pepper	½	1
sticks of celery	3	7
egg whites	2	5
whipping cream or natural yoghurt	125 ml (¼ pt)	300 ml (⅝ pt)
seasoning		

> I portion provides:
>
> 1215 kJ/289 kcal
> 25.8 g fat
> (of which 9.2 g saturated)
> 4.8 g carbohydrate
> (of which 4.7 g sugars)
> 9.8 g protein
> 1.8 g fibre

1 Purée the tomatoes with their juice to measure 500 ml (1 pint).
2 Bring to the boil, and whisk in tomato purée.
3 Dissolve the agar-agar in hot water, add to the tomatoes and vegetables, cut in large dice.
4 Place the mixture in a basin on a bowl of ice, stir until cool.
5 Season, whisk in the mayonnaise and lemon juice.
6 Continue to cool until setting point is reached, carefully fold in stiffly beaten egg whites and whipping cream.
7 Pour into an 18–19 cm (7–8 inch) savarin mould and set in refrigerator.
8 Unmould onto a suitable serving dish, fill the centre with cucumber, apple and walnut dressing. Decorate with tomato and mint leaves.

Note soaked leaf gelatine may be used to replace the agar-agar, although gelatine is not a vegetarian but an animal product. It is advisable to use pasteurised egg whites.

― Cucumber, apple and walnut dressing

	4 portions	10 portions
small cucumber	1	2–3
dessert apples	3	8
lime, juice of	1	2–3
crushed walnuts	75 g (3 oz)	180 g (7½ oz)
natural yoghurt	250 ml (½ pt)	600 ml (1¼ pt)

1 Peel the cucumber and cut into ½ cm (¼ inch) dice.
2 Peel and cut the dessert apples into 2 cm (¾ inch) dice, sprinkle with the lime juice.
3 Place the cucumber and apple into a basin, add the walnuts and bind with the natural yoghurt.
4 Use this mixture to fill the centre of the tomato savarin and serve with a green salad of mixed lettuce.

19 ― Vegetable crumble

	4 portions	10 portions
Crumble topping		
100% wholemeal flour	150 g (6 oz)	375 g (15 oz)
butter or margarine	100 g (4 oz)	250 g (10 oz)
grated Cheddar cheese	100 g (4 oz)	250 g (10 oz)
chopped mixed nuts	50 g (2 oz)	125 g (5 oz)
sesame seeds	25 g (1 oz)	60 g (2½ oz)
mixed vegetables (swede, turnips, parsnips, potatoes, carrots, etc.)	600 g (1½ lb)	2¼ kg (3¾ lb)
onion, finely chopped	100 g (4 oz)	250 g (10 oz)
butter or margarine	50 g (2 oz)	125 g (5 oz)
100% wholemeal flour	25 g (1 oz)	60 g (2½ oz)
fresh tomatoes	200 g (8 oz)	500 g (1¼ lb)
vegetable stock	250 ml (½ pt)	600 ml (1¼ pt)
milk	125 ml (¼ pt)	300 ml (⅝ pt)
chopped parsley		
seasoning		

> Using hard margarine, 1 portion provides:
>
> 2931 kJ/698 kcal
> 49.0 g fat
> (of which 20.3 g saturated)
> 50.4 g carbohydrate
> (of which 12.4 g sugars)
> 18.5 g protein
> 10.5 g fibre

recipe continued ▶

1 Make crumble by sieving flour and rubbing in butter or margarine.
2 Add grated Cheddar cheese, nuts and sesame seeds.
3 Wash, peel and rewash the vegetables, cut into macedoine.
4 Sweat the onion in the butter or margarine without colour.
5 Add the rest of the vegetables and continue to sweat for 10 minutes.
6 Stir in the flour, add the other ingredients, including the liquid which should be added slowly stirring well between each addition.
7 Bring to the boil, reduce the heat, cover and simmer for about 15 minutes, until the vegetables are just tender.
8 Transfer to a pie dish. Press the crumble topping over the vegetables and bake in a preheated oven at 190°C (Reg. 5; 375°F) for 30 minutes or until golden brown, and serve.

20 – Vegetarian kedgeree

	4 portions	10 portions	1 portion provides:
cauliflower	100 g (4 oz)	250 g (10 oz)	2367 kJ/563 kcal
French beans	100 g (4 oz)	250 g (10 oz)	39.6 g fat
courgettes	100 g (4 oz)	250 g (10 oz)	(of which 6.3 g saturated)
mange-tout	100 g (4 oz)	250 g (10 oz)	46.4 g carbohydrate
sunflower oil	125 ml ($\frac{1}{4}$ pt)	300 ml ($\frac{5}{8}$ pt)	(of which 11.7 g sugars)
onion, finely chopped	50 g (2 oz)	125 g (5 oz)	8.7 g protein
clove garlic, crushed and chopped	1	2–3	8.9 g fibre
curry powder	25 g (1 oz)	60 g (2$\frac{1}{2}$ oz)	
grated root ginger	10 g ($\frac{1}{2}$ oz)	25 g (1$\frac{1}{4}$ oz)	
ground cardamom	3 g ($\frac{1}{8}$ oz)	9 g ($\frac{3}{8}$ oz)	
turmeric	3 g ($\frac{1}{8}$ oz)	9 g ($\frac{3}{8}$ oz)	
Basmati rice	100 g (4 oz)	250 g (10 oz)	
vegetable stock	180 ml ($\frac{3}{8}$ pt)	500 ml (1 pt)	
cooked green lentils	75 g (3 oz)	180 g (7$\frac{1}{2}$ oz)	
curry sauce (page 129) using vegetable stock	500 ml (1 pt)	1$\frac{1}{4}$ litre (2$\frac{1}{2}$ pt)	

1 Prepare the vegetables in the following way: cut the cauliflower into small florets, cook in boiling salted water; top and tail French beans, cut in half and cook in boiling salted water; remove the ends from the courgettes, peel carefully, cut into 1 cm ($\frac{1}{2}$ inch) lengths, blanch in boiled salted water; top and tail the mange-tout, leave whole, blanch in boiling salted water for 30 seconds. Refresh and drain all the vegetables.

2 Heat half the oil in a sauté pan, add the chopped onion and garlic, sweat without colour.

3 Add the curry powder, ginger, cardamom and turmeric; sweat for 1 minute.

4 Add the Basmati rice, stir well. Add the boiling vegetable stock, cover with a greased greaseproof paper and lid. Cook in a moderately hot oven, 200–230°C (Reg. 6–8; 400–450°F) until the rice is tender but retains a bite.

5 When cooked remove from the oven and stir in the cooked lentils.

6 Reheat the vegetables by lightly frying them in the remaining oil, keeping all the vegetables crisp.

7 Drain the vegetables, stir into the rice and serve, with the curry sauce.

21 – Vegetarian lasagne

	4 portions	10 portions
pieces of wholemeal lasagne	10	30
sunflower oil	125 ml ($\frac{1}{4}$ pt)	300 ml ($\frac{5}{8}$ pt)
finely chopped onion	100 g (4 oz)	250 g (10 oz)
garlic cloves, chopped	2	5
mushrooms, sliced	200 g (8 oz)	500 g ($1\frac{1}{4}$ lb)
seasoning		
medium-sized courgettes	2	5
oregano	3 g ($\frac{1}{8}$ oz)	9 g ($\frac{3}{8}$ oz)
tomato skinned, de-seeded and diced	200 g (8 oz)	500 g ($1\frac{1}{4}$ lb)
tomato purée	50 g (2 oz)	125 g (5 oz)
broccoli (small florets)	300 g (12 oz)	750 g (2 lb)
carrots	100 g (4 oz)	250 g (10 oz)
pine kernels	25 g (1 oz)	60 g ($2\frac{1}{2}$ oz)
béchamel	250 ml ($\frac{1}{2}$ pt)	600 ml ($1\frac{1}{4}$ pt)
grated Parmesan cheese	50 g (2 oz)	125 g (5 oz)
natural yoghurt	250 ml ($\frac{1}{2}$ pt)	600 ml ($1\frac{1}{4}$ pt)

I portion provides:

2993 kJ/713 kcal
46.2 g fat
(of which 8.5 g saturated)
54.6 g carbohydrate
(of which 16.5 g sugars)
22.9 g protein
11.8 g fibre

1 Cook the lasagne sheets in boiling salted water until *al dente*, refresh and drain.

2 Heat half the oil and sweat the onion and garlic.

3 Add the mushrooms and continue to cook without colour. Season.

4 Heat the remaining oil in a sauteuse, add the courgettes, cut in 1 cm ($\frac{1}{2}$ inch) dice, and lightly fry; sprinkle with the oregano. Cook until crisp, add the tomato concassé and tomato purée.

recipe continued ▶

5 Add the broccoli florets and carrots (cut in ½cm (¼inch) dice), previously blanched and refreshed. Mix together with the pine kernels.

6 Make a cheese sauce using the béchamel and half the grated cheese, finish with the natural yoghurt.

7 Well grease a suitable ovenproof dish with the sunflower oil and place a layer of lasagne in the bottom.

8 Cover with a layer of mushrooms, then a layer of lasagne, then the broccoli and tomato mixture, then lasagne, then cheese sauce. Continue to do this finishing with a layer of cheese sauce on the top.

9 Sprinkle with remaining grated Parmesan cheese.

10 Bake in a preheated oven at 180°C (Reg. 4; 350°F) for 20–25 minutes.

22 ~ Vegetarian moussaka

	4 portions	10 portions
finely chopped onion	50 g (2 oz)	125 g (5 oz)
clove garlic, chopped	1	2–3
sunflower oil	4 tbsp	10 tbsp
TVP mince (natural flavour), soaked in cold water 2–3 hours	100 g (4 oz)	250 g (10 oz)
tomato skinned, de-seeded and diced	200 g (8 oz)	500 g (1¼ lb)
tomato purée	50 g (2 oz)	125 g (5 oz)
pinch oregano		
seasoning		
vegetable stock	500 ml (1 pt)	1¼ litre (2½ pt)
yeast extract	5 g (¼ oz)	12 g (⅝ oz)
arrowroot	10 g (½ oz)	25 g (1¼ oz)
potatoes	400 g (1 lb)	1¼ kg (2½ lb)
large aubergines	2	5

Cheese sauce

	4 portions	10 portions
sunflower margarine	25 g (1 oz)	60 g (2½ oz)
wholemeal flour	25 g (1 oz)	60 g (2½ oz)
skimmed milk	250 ml (½ pt)	600 ml (1¼ pt)
Parmesan cheese	25 g (1 oz)	60 g (2½ oz)
egg yolk	1	2–3
natural yoghurt	2 tbsp	5 tbsp
grated Parmesan cheese	50 g (2 oz)	125 g (5 oz)

I portion provides:

2249 kJ/536 kcal
29.1 g fat
(of which 7.0 g saturated)
46.2 g carbohydrate
(of which 11.4 g sugars)
25.5 g protein
6.4 g fibre

1 Cook the onion and garlic in the sunflower oil until lightly coloured.
2 Add the drained TVP.
3 Add the tomato concassé, tomato purée, oregano and seasoning.
4 Add the vegetable stock to cover. Bring to the boil; simmer for 5 minutes.
5 Add the yeast extract, stir well.
6 Dilute the arrowroot with a little water and gradually stir into the TVP.
7 Bring back to the boil. Simmer for 2 minutes.
8 Cook the potatoes with the skins on, by steaming or boiling. Peel and slice into $\frac{1}{2}$ cm ($\frac{1}{4}$ inch) slices.
9 Slice the aubergines into $\frac{1}{2}$ cm ($\frac{1}{4}$ inch) slices, pass through the wholemeal flour, shallow fry in the sunflower oil on both sides, until golden brown. Drain on kitchen paper.
10 In a suitable ovenproof dish arrange layers of TVP mixture and overlapping slices of potato and aubergines.
11 Make the cheese sauce (page 118) and pour on top, sprinkle with the grated Parmesan cheese.
12 Bake in a preheated oven at 190°C (Reg. 5; 375°F) for approximately 30 minutes.

23 – Vegetable biryani

	4 portions	10 portions
Basmati rice	400 g (1 lb)	1$\frac{1}{4}$ kg (2$\frac{1}{2}$ lb)
oil	2 tbsp	5 tbsp
cinnamon stick	$\frac{1}{2}$	1
cardamom pods	4	10
cloves	4	10
sliced onions	100 g (4 oz)	250 g (10 oz)
clove garlic	1	2–3
green chilli, finely chopped	1	2–3
grated root ginger	1 tbsp	2–3 tbsp
mixed vegetables (carrots, celery, broccoli, cauliflower, French beans)	600 g (1$\frac{1}{2}$ lb)	2 kg (3$\frac{3}{4}$ lb)
tomatoes, blanched, de-seeded and chopped or canned plum tomatoes	400 g (1 lb)	1$\frac{1}{4}$ kg (2$\frac{1}{2}$ lb)
tomato purée	25 g (1 oz)	60 g (2$\frac{1}{2}$ oz)
chopped coriander leaves		

recipe continued ▶

1   Wash, soak and drain the rice.
2   Partly cook the rice in boiling salted water for 3 minutes. Refresh and drain well.
3   Heat the oil in a suitably sized pan. Add the crushed cinnamon, cardamom and cloves and sweat for 2 minutes.
4   Add the sliced onions, garlic, chilli and ginger. Continue to sweat until soft.
5   Prepare the vegetables: cut the carrots and celery into batons, the cauliflower and broccoli into florets and the French beans into 2.5 cm (1 inch) lengths.
6   Add the vegetables and fry for 2–3 minutes.
7   Add the tomatoes and tomato purée. Season.
8   Make sure there is sufficient moisture in the pan to cook the vegetables. Usually a little water needs to be added. Ideally the vegetables should cook in their own juices combined with the tomatoes.
9   When the vegetables are partly cooked, layer them in a casserole or suitable pan with the rice. (Make sure that there is sufficient liquid to cook the rice.)
10 Cover the casserole, finish cooking in a moderate oven at 180°C (Reg. 4; 350°F) for about 20 minutes, or until the rice is tender.
11 Sprinkle with chopped coriander leaves and serve.

24 – Vegetable and nut Stroganoff

	4 portions	10 portions
sunflower oil	4 tbsp	10 tbsp
onions, finely chopped	50 g (2 oz)	125 g (5 oz)
Chinese leaves, shredded	300 g (12 oz)	1 kg (2 lb)
sticks celery, cut in paysanne	6	15
button mushrooms, sliced	300 g (12 oz)	1 kg (2 lb)
mixed nuts (peanuts, cashews, hazelnuts)	200 g (8 oz)	500 g (1¼ lb)
paprika	1 tsp	2–3 tsp
English or continental mustard	1 tsp	2–3 tsp
white wine	125 ml (¼ pt)	300 ml (⅝ pt)
unsweetened vegetable creamer or smetana	125 ml (¼ pt)	300 ml (⅝ pt)
seasoning		

I portion provides:

2098 kJ/500 kcal
41.5 g fat
(of which 7.0 g saturated)
12.0 g carbohydrate
(of which 7.0 g sugars)
15.7 g protein
6.4 g fibre

1   Heat the oil and sweat the onions for 2–3 minutes.
2   Add the Chinese leaves, celery and mushrooms. Cook for 5 minutes.
3   Add the nuts whole. Stir in the paprika and diluted mustard.

4   Add the white wine, bring to the boil and simmer for 5 minutes.
5   Season. Cool slightly, add heat-stable unsweetened vegetable creamer or smetana. Serve with a dish of plain-boiled wholewheat noodles tossed in sunflower margarine or wholegrain pilaff rice.

25 – Vegetarian strudel

	4 portions	10 portions
Strudel dough		
wholemeal flour	125 g (5 oz)	300 g (12½ oz)
strong flour	75 g (3 oz)	180 g (7½ oz)
pinch of salt		
sunflower oil	25 g (1 oz)	60 g (2½ oz)
egg	1	2–3
water at 37°C (100°F)	83 ml ($\frac{1}{6}$ pt)	125 ml ($\frac{1}{4}$ pt)
large cabbage leaves	200 g (8 oz)	500 g (1¼ lb)
sunflower oil	4 tbsp	10 tbsp
finely chopped onion	50 g (2 oz)	125 g (5 oz)
cloves garlic, chopped	2	5
courgettes	400 g (1 lb)	1¼ kg (2½ lb)
carrots	200 g (8 oz)	500 g (1¼ lb)
turnips	100 g (4 oz)	250 g (10 oz)
tomato skinned, de-seeded and diced	300 g (12 oz)	750 g (30 oz)
tomato purée	25 g (1 oz)	60 g (2½ oz)
toasted sesame seeds	25 g (1 oz)	60 g (2½ oz)
wholemeal breadcrumbs	50 g (2 oz)	125 g (5 oz)
fresh chopped basil	3 g ($\frac{1}{8}$ oz)	9 g ($\frac{3}{8}$ oz)
seasoning		

> 1 portion provides:
>
> 2117 kJ/504 kcal
> 27.6 g fat
> (of which 4.0 g saturated)
> 54.1 g carbohydrate
> (of which 10.5 g sugars)
> 14.3 g protein
> 9.7 g fibre

1   Make strudel paste by sieving the flour with the salt, make a well.
2   Add the oil, egg and water, gradually incorporate the flour to make a smooth dough and knead well.
3   Place in a basin, cover with a damp cloth; relax for 3 minutes.
4   Meanwhile prepare the filling: take the large cabbage leaves, wash and discard the tough centre stalks, blanch in boiling salted water for 2 minutes, until limp. Refresh and drain well in a clean cloth.
5   Heat the oil in a sauté pan, gently fry the onion and garlic until soft.
6   Peel and chop the courgettes into ½ cm (¼ inch) dice, blanch and refresh. Peel and dice the carrots and turnips, blanch and refresh.

recipe continued ▶

7 Place the well drained courgettes, carrots and turnips into a basin, add the tomato concassé, tomato purée, sesame seeds, breadcrumbs, chopped basil. Mix well, season.

8 Roll out strudel dough to a thin rectangle, place on a clean cloth and stretch until extremely thin.

9 Lay the drained cabbage leaves on the stretched strudel dough, leaving approximately 1 cm ($\frac{1}{2}$ inch) gap from the edge.

10 Place the filling in the centre. Eggwash the edges.

11 Fold in the longer side edges to meet in the middle. Roll up.

12 Transfer to a lightly oiled baking sheet. Brush with the sunflower oil.

13 Bake for 40 minutes in a preheated oven at 180–200°C (Reg. 4–6; 350–400°F).

14 When cooked serve hot, sliced on individual plates with a cordon of tomato sauce made with vegetable stock and without bacon.

26 ～ Wholemeal vegetarian pizza

	4 portions	10 portions
Pizza dough		
wholemeal flour	300 g (12 oz)	750 g (30 oz)
soya flour	10 g ($\frac{1}{2}$ oz)	25 g ($1\frac{1}{4}$ oz)
pinch of salt		
warm water at 32°C/90°F	180 ml ($\frac{3}{8}$ pt)	500 ml (1 pt)
fresh yeast	10 g ($\frac{1}{2}$ oz)	25 g ($1\frac{1}{4}$ oz)
ascorbic acid	5 g ($\frac{1}{4}$ oz)	12 g ($\frac{5}{8}$ oz)
onions, finely chopped	200 g (8 oz)	500 g ($1\frac{1}{4}$ lb)
cloves of garlic, crushed	2	5
sunflower oil	4 tbsp	10 tbsp
tomatoes, skinned, de-seeded and diced	400 g (1 lb)	$1\frac{1}{4}$ kg ($2\frac{1}{2}$ lb)
tomato purée	50 g (2 oz)	125 g (5 oz)
fresh parsley	10 g ($\frac{1}{2}$ oz)	25 g ($1\frac{1}{4}$ oz)
fresh chopped basil	10 g ($\frac{1}{2}$ oz)	25 g ($1\frac{1}{4}$ oz)
cooked artichoke bottoms	2	5
pine kernels	25 g (1 oz)	60 g ($2\frac{1}{2}$ oz)
sesame seeds	10 g ($\frac{1}{2}$ oz)	25 g ($1\frac{1}{4}$ oz)
capers	10 g ($\frac{1}{2}$ oz)	25 g ($1\frac{1}{4}$ oz)
green olives	8	20
black olives	8	20
sultanas	25 g (1 oz)	60 g ($2\frac{1}{2}$ oz)
Mozzarella cheese	50 g (2 oz)	125 g (5 oz)

I portion provides:

2272 kJ/541 kcal
26.6 g fat
(of which 4.8 g saturated)
64.0 g carbohydrate
(of which 13.7 g sugars)
17.0 g protein
10.4 g fibre

1   Sieve the flour, soya flour and a pinch of salt into a basin.
2   Warm the water, place in a separate basin with the yeast, disperse the yeast in the warm water, allow sufficient flour to make a light batter, sprinkle a little flour over the ferment, cover with a damp cloth and allow the ferment to break through the flour.
3   When the ferment is ready pour into the rest of the flour.
4   Add the ascorbic acid, incorporate the flour until a smooth elastic dough is obtained.
5   Turn out onto a floured surface and continue to knead the dough until smooth.
6   Return to the basin, cover with a damp cloth and allow to prove in a warm place until double in size.
7   Knock back the dough to bring the yeast back into contact with the dough and to equalise the dough.
8   Roll out the dough into 15 cm (6 inch) rounds or in a rectangle, and cover a lightly greased swiss roll tin.
9   Allow to prove for 10 minutes in a warm atmosphere.
10 Bake for 4–5 minutes in a preheated oven at 200°C (Reg. 5–6; 400°F).
11 Sweat the onions and garlic in the oil.
12 Add the tomato concassé and purée. Stir well.
13 Add the chopped parsley and basil. Cook out the tomatoes for about 15 minutes. Season.
14 Spread this tomato mixture on the pizza base.
15 Arrange neatly on top the artichoke bottoms into small pieces, sprinkle on the pine kernels, sesame seeds, capers, stoned olives and sultanas.
16 Finally sprinkle with grated Mozzarella cheese.
17 Bake in oven for about 15 minutes at 200°C (Reg. 6; 400°F). Serve very hot.

Note   Alternatively a ratatouille mixture, or a variation of it, may be used as a pizza topping with grated cheese.

12

VEGETABLES AND PULSES

Recipe No.		*page nos.*
2	Artichoke bottoms	524
1	Artichokes, globe	523
5	Artichokes, Jerusalem, in cream sauce	525
4	Artichokes, Jerusalem, purée of	525
6	Asparagus	526
7	Asparagus points or tips	526
8	Aubergine, fried	527
10	Aubergine, stuffed	528
43	Beans, dried	541
60	Beetroot	551
3	Blanc	525
42	Broad beans	541
11	Broccoli	529
25	Brussels sprouts	535
26	Brussels sprouts fried in butter	536
19	Cabbage	532
22	Cabbage, braised	533
24	Cabbage, red, braised	535
21	Cabbage, stir-fry, with mushrooms and beansprouts	533
12	Carrots, buttered	529
15	Carrots, cream sauce	530
13	Carrots, purée	529
14	Carrots Vichy	530
27	Cauliflower	536
28	Cauliflower Mornay	537
29	Cauliflower polonaise	537
17	Celery, braised	531
38	Chicory, braised	540
39	Chicory, shallow-fried	540
47	Corn on the cob	544
35	Courgette	539
37	Courgettes, deep-fried	539
36	Courgettes, shallow-fried	539
66	Fennel	554
44	French beans	542
68	Ladies fingers (okra) in cream sauce	555
62	Leeks, braised	552
46	Lettuce, braised	543
58	Mangetout (sugar peas)	546
32	Marrow	538
35	Marrow, baby	539
34	Marrow, provençale	538
33	Marrow, stuffed	538
18	Mushrooms, grilled	532
16	Mushrooms, stuffed	530
52	Onions, braised	546

517

51	Onions, French-fried	*Oignons frits à la française*	545
50	Onions, fried	*Oignons sautés ou lyonnaise*	545
63	Parsnips	*Panais*	552
53	Peas	*Petits pois*	546
54	Peas, French-style	*Petits pois à la française*	547
64	Pease pudding		553
55	Pimento, stuffed	*Piment farci*	547
9	Ratatouille	*Ratatouille*	527
45	Runner beans		543
56	Salsify	*Salsifis*	548
23	Sauerkraut	*Choucroûte*	534
30	Sea-kale	*Chou de mer*	537
31	Sea-kale Mornay	*Chou de mer Mornay*	537
40	Spinach leaf	*Epinards en branches*	540
41	Spinach purée	*Epinards en purée*	541
20	Spring greens	*Choux de printemps*	533
61	Tomato, basic preparation	*Tomate concassée*	551
58	Tomatoes, grilled	*Tomates grillées*	549
59	Tomatoes, stuffed	*Tomates farcies*	550
48	Turnips or swedes, buttered	*Navets ou rutabaga au beurre*	544
49	Turnips or swedes, purée	*Purée de navets ou rutabaga*	545
57	Vegetables, grilled		549
65	Vegetables, mixed	*Macédoine ou Jardinière de légumes*	553
67	Vegetables, mixed fried in batter	*Légumes en fritot*	554
69	Vegetable moulds		555

Prepare and cook vegetable dishes

1 Ensure that the preparation and cooking areas and equipment are ready for use and that they satisfy the health, safety and food hygiene regulations.
2 Know which vegetables are of the type, quality and quantity required.
3 Prepare vegetables correctly and combine with other ingredients so that they are cooked, finished and presented according to the dish and customer requirements.
4 Ensure that prepared and finished vegetables not for immediate consumption are stored in accordance with the laid down procedures.
5 Clean preparation and cooking areas and equipment after use.
6 Realise that competency implies knowledge, understanding and apply as appropriate the principles of cooking vegetables.

Fresh vegetables are important foods both from an economic and nutritional point of view. Vegetables are an important part of our diet therefore the recognition of quality, purchasing, storage and efficient preparation and cooking is essential if the nutritional content of vegetables is to be conserved. Potatoes are discussed separately in Chapter 13.

PURCHASING

The purchasing of vegetables is affected by:

- the perishable nature of the products;
- varying availability owing to seasonal fluctuations and supply and demand;
- the effects of preservation, e.g. freezing, drying, canning vegetables.

The high perishability of vegetables causes problems not encountered in other markets. Fresh vegetables are living organisms and will lose quality quickly if not properly stored and handled. Automation in harvesting and packaging speeds the handling process and helps retain quality.

The EEC vegetable quality grading system is:

- *Extra class* Produce of the highest quality.
- *Class 1* Produce of good quality.
- *Class 2* Produce of reasonably good quality.
- *Class 3* Produce of low market quality.

FOOD VALUE

Root vegetables contain starch or sugar for energy, a small, but valuable amount of protein, some mineral salts and vitamins. They are also useful sources of cellulose and water. Green vegetables are rich in mineral salts and vitamins, particularly vitamin C and carotene. The greener the leaf the larger the quantity of vitamins present. The chief mineral salts are calcium and iron.

QUALITY AND PURCHASING POINTS

Root vegetables must be:

- clean, free from soil;
- firm, not soft or spongy;
- sound;

- free from blemishes;
- of an even size;
- of an even shape.

Green vegetables must be absolutely fresh and have leaves bright in colour, crisp and not wilted. In addition:

- Cabbage and Brussels sprouts should be compact and firm.
- Cauliflowers should have closely grown flowers, a firm white head and not too much stalk, or too many outer leaves.
- Peas and beans should be crisp and of medium size. Pea pods should be full and beans not stringy.
- Blanched stems must be firm, white, crisp and free from soil.

STORAGE

- Store all vegetables in a cool, dry, well ventilated room at an even temperature of 4–8°C (39–46°F) which will help to minimise spoilage. Check vegetables daily and discard any that are unsound.
- Remove root vegetables from their sacks and store in bins, or racks.
- Store green vegetables on well ventilated racks.
- Store salad vegetables in a cool place and leave in their containers.
- Store frozen vegetables at −18°C (0°F) or below. Keep a check on use-by dates, damaged packages and any signs of freezer burn.
- The fresher the vegetables the better the flavour so that ideally they should not be stored at all. However, as in many cases storage is necessary, then it should be for the shortest time possible.
- Green vegetables lose vitamin C quickly if they are bruised, damaged, stored for too long, or overcooked.

HEALTH, SAFETY AND HYGIENE

Chapter 1 contains information on these aspects. In addition:

- If vegetables are stored at the incorrect temperature micro-organisms may develop.
- If vegetables are stored in damp conditions moulds may develop.
- To prevent bacteria from raw vegetable passing on to cooked vegetables, store them in separate areas.
- Thaw out frozen vegetables correctly and *never* refreeze them once they have thawed out.

Plate 12.1: Winter vegetables

TYPES

Vegetables are sometimes classified under the following headings:

- Beetroot, carrots, celeriac, horseradish, mooli, parsnips, radish, salsify, scorzonera, swede, turnips.
- *Tubers* Potatoes, sweet potatoes, Jerusalem artichokes, yams.
- *Bulbs* Garlic, leeks, onion, shallots.
- *Leafy* Chicory, Chinese leaves, corn salad, lettuce, mustard and cress, radishes, sorrel, spinach, Swiss chard, watercress.
- *Brassicas* Broccoli, Brussels sprouts, cabbage, calabrese, cauliflower, curly kale, spring greens.
- *Pods and seeds* Broad beans, butter beans, runner beans, mangetout, okra, peas, sweetcorn.
- *Fruiting* Aubergine, avocado, courgette, cucumber, marrow, peppers, pumpkin, squash, tomatoes.
- *Stem and shoots* Asparagus, cardoon, celery, endive, globe artichokes, kohlrabi, sea-kale.
- *Mushroom and fungi* Mushrooms, ceps, horns of plenty, morels, oyster mushrooms, shitake, girolle (also known as chanterelle).

521

COOKING

Approximate times are given for the cooking of vegetables as quality, age, freshness and size all affect the length of cooking time required. Young, freshly picked vegetables will cook for a shorter time than vegetables allowed to grow older and which may have been stored after picking.

As a general rule all root vegetables are started to cook in cold salted water, with the exception of new potatoes: those vegetables which grow above the ground are started in boiling salted water. This is so that they may be cooked as quickly as possible for the *minimum* period of time so that *maximum* flavour, food value and colour are retained.

All vegetables cooked by boiling may also be cooked by steaming. The vegetables are prepared in exactly the same way as for boiling, placed into steamer trays, lightly seasoned with salt and steamed under pressure for the minimum period of time in order to conserve maximum food value and retain colour. High speed steam cookers are ideal for this purpose and also because of the speed of cooking; batch cooking (cooking in small quantities throughout the service) can be practised instead of cooking large quantities prior to service, refreshing and reheating.

Many vegetables are cooked from raw by the stir-fry method, a quick and nutritious method of cooking.

CUTS OF VEGETABLES

The size to which the vegetables are cut may vary according to their use; however, the shape does not change.

- **Julienne** (strips)
  - Cut the vegetables into 2 cm (1 inch) lengths.
  - Cut the lengths into thin slices.
  - Cut the slices into thin strips.
- **Brunoise** (small dice)
  - Cut the vegetables into convenient-sized lengths.
  - Cut the lengths into 2 mm ($\frac{1}{12}$ inch) slices.
  - Cut the slices into 2 mm ($\frac{1}{12}$ inch) strips.
  - Cut the strips into 2 mm ($\frac{1}{12}$ inch) squares.
- **Macédoine** ($\frac{1}{2}$ cm ($\frac{1}{4}$ inch) dice)
  - Cut the vegetables into convenient lengths.
  - Cut the lengths into $\frac{1}{2}$ cm ($\frac{1}{4}$ inch) slices.
  - Cut the slices into $\frac{1}{2}$ cm ($\frac{1}{4}$ inch) strips.
  - Cut the strips into $\frac{1}{2}$ cm ($\frac{1}{4}$ inch) squares.

- **Jardinière** (batons)
  - Cut the vegetables into $1\frac{1}{2}$ cm ($\frac{3}{4}$ inch) lengths.
  - Cut the lengths into 3 mm ($\frac{1}{4}$ inch) slices.
  - Cut the slices into batons ($3 \times 3 \times 18$ mm ($\frac{1}{8} \times \frac{1}{8} \times \frac{3}{4}$ inch)).
- **Paysanne**
  There are at least four accepted methods of cutting paysanne. In order to cut economically, the shape of the vegetables should decide which method to choose. All are cut thinly.
  - 1 cm sided ($\frac{1}{2}$ inch) triangles.
  - 1 cm sided ($\frac{1}{2}$ inch) squares.
  - 1 cm diameter ($\frac{1}{2}$ inch) rounds.
  - 1 cm diameter ($\frac{1}{2}$ inch) rough-sided rounds.

—— *Vegetable recipes* ——

1 ~ Globe artichokes

1. Allow 1 artichoke per portion.
2. Cut off the stems close to the leaves.
3. Cut off about 2 cm (1 inch) across the tops of the leaves.
4. Trim the remainder of the leaves with scissors or a small knife.
5. Place a slice of lemon at the bottom of each artichoke.
6. Secure with string.
7. Simmer in gently boiling lightly salted water (to which a little ascorbic acid – one vitamin C tablet – may be added) until the bottom is tender (20–30 minutes).
8. Refresh under running water until cold.
9. Remove the centre of the artichoke carefully.
10. Scrape away all the furry inside and leave clean.
11. Replace the centre, upside down.
12. Reheat by placing in a pan of boiling salted water for 3–4 minutes.
13. Drain and serve accompanied by a suitable sauce.

> Not including sauce, I portion provides:
>
> 32 kJ/8 kcal
> 0.0 g fat
> (of which 0.0 g saturated)
> 1.4 g carbohydrate
> (of which 1.4 g sugars)
> 0.6 g protein
> 0.0 g fibre

recipe continued ▶

Plate 12.2: Ingredients for and service of stir-fry vegetables

Note   Artichokes may also be served cold with vinaigrette sauce.

Do not cook artichokes in an iron or aluminium pan because these metals cause a chemical reaction which will discolour the artichokes.

2 ~ Artichoke bottoms

1   Cut off the stalk and pull out all the underneath leaves.
2   With a large knife cut through the artichoke leaving only $1\frac{1}{2}$ cm ($\frac{3}{4}$ inch) at the bottom of the vegetable.
3   With a small sharp knife, whilst holding the artichoke upside down, peel carefully removing all the leaf and any green part, keeping the bottom as smooth as possible. If necessary smooth with a peeler.
4   Rub immediately with lemon and keep in lemon water or ascorbic acid solution.
5   Using a spoon or the thumb, remove the centre furry part which is called the choke. The choke is sometimes removed after cooking.
6   Artichoke bottoms should always be cooked in a blanc (see below).

Note   Artichoke bases may be served as a vegetable; they are sometimes filled with another vegetable, (peas, spinach, etc.). When they are served ungarnished they are usually cut into quarters.

3 ~ Blanc

	4 portions	10 portions
cold water	$\frac{1}{2}$ litre (1 pt)	1 litre (2 pt)
flour	10 g ($\frac{1}{4}$ oz)	12 g ($\frac{5}{8}$ oz)
lemon, juice of	$\frac{1}{2}$	1
salt		

1 Mix the flour and water together.
2 Add the salt and lemon juice. Pass through a strainer.
3 Place in a pan, bring to the boil, stirring continuously.

Note Alternatively artichokes may be cooked in $\frac{1}{2}$ litre (1 pint) water, 2 vitamin C tablets (ascorbic acid) and 30 ml ($\frac{1}{16}$ pt) oil and salt (increase the quantities $2\frac{1}{2}$ times for 10 portions).

4 ~ Purée of Jerusalem artichokes

	4 portions	10 portions
Jerusalem artichokes	600 g (1$\frac{1}{2}$ lb)	1$\frac{1}{2}$ kg (3 lb)
butter	25 g (1 oz)	60 g (2$\frac{1}{2}$ oz)
salt, pepper		

1 Wash, peel and rewash the artichokes.
2 Cut in pieces if necessary. Barely cover with water; add a little salt.
3 Simmer gently until tender. Drain well.
4 Pass through a sieve, mouli or liquidise.
5 Return to the pan, reheat and mix in the butter and correct the seasoning and serve.

> 1 portion provides:
>
> 291 kJ/69 kcal
> 5.1 g fat
> (of which 3.3 g saturated)
> 4.1 g carbohydrate
> (of which 0.0 g sugars)
> 2.1 g protein
> 0.0 g fibre

Note 125 ml ($\frac{1}{4}$ pint) (300 ml, $\frac{5}{8}$ pint for 10 portions) cream or natural yoghurt may be mixed in before serving.

5 – Jerusalem artichokes in cream sauce

1 Wash and peel the artichokes and rewash. Cut to an even size.
2 Barely cover with water, add a little salt and simmer until tender; do not overcook.
3 Drain well and add 250 ml ($\frac{1}{2}$ pint) (600 ml, $1\frac{1}{4}$ pint for 10 portions) cream sauce (page 118).

Note Cream sauce may be made with wholemeal flour, skimmed milk and natural yoghurt.

6 – Asparagus

Allow 6–8 good-sized pieces per portion. An average bundle will yield 3–4 portions.

1 Using the back of a small knife, carefully remove the tips of the leaves.
2 Scrape the stem, either with the blade of a small knife or a peeler.
3 Wash well. Tie into bundles of about 12 heads.
4 Cut off the excess stem.
5 Cook in boiling lightly salted water for approximately 15 minutes.
6 Test if cooked by gently pressing the green part of the stem, which should be tender; do not overcook.
7 Lift carefully out of the water. Remove the string, drain well and serve.

1 portion provides:
580 kJ/138 kcal
12.3 g fat
(of which 7.8 g saturated)
1.7 g carbohydrate
(of which 1.7 g sugars)
5.2 g protein
2.3 g fibre

Note Serve a suitable sauce separately (hollandaise or melted butter). Asparagus are usually served as a separate course. They may also be served cold, in which case they should be immediately refreshed when cooked in order to retain the green colour. Serve with vinaigrette or mayonnaise.

7 – Asparagus points or tips

Young thin asparagus, 50 pieces to the bundle, is known as sprew or sprue.
  They are prepared in the same way as asparagus except that when they are very thin removing of the leaf tips is dispensed with. They may be served as a vegetable.
  They are also used in numerous garnishes for soups, egg dishes, fish, meat and poultry dishes, cold dishes, salad, etc.

8 ~ Fried aubergine

1 Allow $\frac{1}{2}$ aubergine per portion.
2 Remove alternate strips with a peeler.
3 Cut into $\frac{1}{2}$ cm ($\frac{1}{4}$ inch) slices on the slant.
4 Pass through seasoned flour or milk and flour.
5 Shake off all surplus flour.
6 Deep fry in hot fat at 185°C (365°F). Drain well and serve.

Note Aubergines may also be shallow fried.

> 1 portion provides:
>
> 994 kJ/225 kcal
> 20.0 g fat
> (of which 3.8 g saturated)
> 10.1 g carbohydrate
> (of which 5.9 g sugars)
> 1.9 g protein
> 5.2 g fibre

9 ~ Ratatouille

	4 portions	10 portions
baby marrow	200 g (8 oz)	500 g (1¼ lb)
aubergines	200 g (8 oz)	500 g (1¼ lb)
tomatoes	200 g (8 oz)	500 g (1¼ lb)
oil	50 ml ($\frac{1}{8}$ pt)	150 ml ($\frac{1}{3}$ pt)
onion, finely sliced	50 g (2 oz)	125 g (5 oz)
clove garlic, peeled and chopped	1	2
red peppers, diced	50 g (2 oz)	125 g (5 oz)
green peppers, diced	50 g (2 oz)	125 g (5 oz)
salt, pepper		
chopped parsley	1 tsp	2–3 tsp

> 1 portion provides:
>
> 579 kJ/138 kcal
> 12.6 g fat
> (of which 1.7 g saturated)
> 5.2 g carbohydrate
> (of which 4.6 g sugars)
> 1.3 g protein
> 2.4 g fibre

1 Trim off both ends of the marrow and aubergines.
2 Remove the skin using a peeler.
3 Cut into 3 mm ($\frac{1}{8}$ inch) slices.
4 Concassé the tomatoes (peel, remove seeds, roughly chop).
5 Place the oil in a thick-bottomed pan and add the onions.
6 Cover with a lid and allow to cook gently 5–7 minutes without colouring.
7 Add the garlic, the marrow and aubergine slices and the peppers.
8 Season lightly with salt and mill pepper.
9 Allow to cook gently for 4–5 minutes, toss occasionally and keep covered.
10 Add the tomato and continue cooking for 20–30 minutes or until tender.
11 Mix in the parsley, correct the seasoning and serve.

Plate 12.3: Ingredients of ratatouille

10 – Stuffed aubergine

	4 portions	10 portions
aubergines	2	5
shallots, chopped	10 g ($\frac{1}{2}$oz)	25 g (1$\frac{1}{4}$oz)
mushrooms	100 g (4 oz)	250 g (10 oz)
chopped parsley		
tomato concassé	100 g (4 oz)	250 g (10 oz)
salt, pepper		
demi-glace	125 ml ($\frac{1}{4}$pt)	300 ml ($\frac{5}{8}$pt)

1   Cut the aubergines in two lengthwise.
2   With the point of a small knife make a cut round the halves approximately $\frac{1}{2}$cm ($\frac{1}{4}$ inch) from the edge, then make several cuts $\frac{1}{2}$cm ($\frac{1}{4}$ inch) deep in the centre.
3   Deep fry in hot fat at 185°C (365°F) for 2–3 minutes; drain well.
4   Scoop out the centre pulp and finely chop it.
5   Cook the shallots in a little oil or fat without colouring.
6   Add the well-washed mushrooms.
7   Cook gently for a few minutes.
8   Mix in the pulp, parsley and tomato; season.
9   Replace in the aubergine skins.
10   Sprinkle with breadcrumbs and melted butter.
11   Brown under the salamander.
12   Serve with a cordon of demi-glace or jus-lié.

11 – Broccoli

Cook and serve as for any of the cauliflower recipes
(page 537). Green and purple broccoli, because of their
size, need less cooking time than cauliflower.

> I portion provides:
>
> 76 kJ/18 kcal
> 0.0 g fat
> (of which 0.0 g saturated)
> 1.6 g carbohydrate
> (of which 1.5 g sugars)
> 3.1 g protein
> 4.1 g fibre

12 – Buttered carrots

	4 portions	10 portions
carrots	400 g (1 lb)	1¼ kg (2½ lb)
salt, pepper		
butter	25 g (1 oz)	60 g (2½ oz)
chopped parsley		

> I portion provides:
>
> 297 kJ/71 kcal
> 5.1 g fat
> (of which 3.3 g saturated)
> 5.8 g carbohydrate
> (of which 5.8 g sugars)
> 0.7 g protein
> 2.8 g fibre

1 Peel and wash the carrots.
2 Cut into neat even pieces or turn barrel shape.
3 Place in a pan with a little salt, a pinch of sugar and
   butter. Barely cover with water.
4 Cover with a buttered paper and allow to boil steadily in order to evaporate all
   the water.
5 When the water has completely evaporated check that the carrots are cooked; if
   not, add a little more water and continue cooking. Do not overcook.
6 Toss the carrots over a fierce heat for 1–2 minutes in order to give them a glaze.
7 Serve sprinkled with chopped parsley.

13 – Purée of carrots

	4 portions	10 portions
carrots	600 g (1½ lb)	1½ kg (3¾ lb)
butter or margarine	25 g (1 oz)	60 g (2½ oz)
salt, pepper		

recipe continued ▶

1   Wash, peel and rewash the carrots. Cut in pieces.
2   Barely cover with water, add a little salt. Simmer gently or steam until tender.
3   Drain well. Pass through a sieve or mouli.
4   Return to the pan, reheat and mix in the butter, correct the seasoning, and serve.

14 – Vichy carrots

1   Allow the same ingredients as for buttered carrots, substitute Vichy water for the liquid.
2   Peel and wash the carrots (which should not be larger than 2 cm (1 inch) in diameter).
3   Cut into 2 mm ($\frac{1}{12}$ inch) thin slices on the mandolin.
4   Cook and serve as for buttered carrots.

15 – Carrots in cream sauce

	4 portions	10 portions
carrots	400 g (1 lb)	1 kg (2$\frac{1}{2}$ lb)
cream sauce (page 118)	$\frac{1}{4}$ litre ($\frac{1}{2}$ pt)	600 ml (1$\frac{1}{4}$ pt)
butter or margarine	10 g ($\frac{1}{2}$ oz)	25 g (1$\frac{1}{4}$ oz)
salt, pepper		

Prepare and cook carrots as for buttered carrots. Mix with the sauce, correct the seasoning and serve.

Note   The cream sauce may be made with wholemeal flour, skimmed milk and natural yoghurt.

16 – Stuffed mushrooms

	4 portions	10 portions
grilling mushrooms	300 g (12 oz)	1 kg (2 lb)
shallots, chopped	10 g ($\frac{1}{2}$ oz)	25 g (1$\frac{1}{4}$ oz)
butter, margarine or oil	50 g (2 oz)	125 g (5 oz)
breadcrumbs	25 g (1 oz)	60 g (2$\frac{1}{2}$ oz)

Using sunflower oil, 1 portion provides:

577 kJ/137 kcal
13.1 g fat
(of which 1.8 g saturated)
3.2 g carbohydrate
(of which 0.3 g sugars)
1.9 g protein
2.1 g fibre

1   Peel, remove the stalk and wash well.
2   Retain 8 or 12 of the best mushrooms. Finely chop

the remainder with the well washed peelings and stalks.

3 Cook the shallots, without colour, in a little fat.
4 Add the chopped mushrooms and cook for 3–4 minutes (duxelle).
5 Grill as in the recipe 18.
6 Place the duxelle in the centre of each mushroom.
7 Sprinkle with a few breadcrumbs and melted butter.
8 Reheat in the oven or under the salamander and serve.

17 − Braised celery (illustrated on page 532)

	4 portions	10 portions
heads of celery	2	5
carrots, sliced	100 g (4 oz)	250 g (10 oz)
onion, sliced	100 g (4 oz)	250 g (10 oz)
bouquet garni		
white stock	$\frac{1}{4}$ litre ($\frac{1}{2}$ pt)	600 ml ($1\frac{1}{4}$ pt)
salt, pepper		
fat bacon or suet	50 g (2 oz)	125 g (5 oz)
crusts of bread	2	5

> I portion provides:
>
> 505 kJ/120 kcal
> 10.2 g fat
> (of which 4.1 g saturated)
> 4.8 g carbohydrate
> (of which 4.5 g sugars)
> 2.8 g protein
> 3.8 g fibre

1 Trim the celery heads and the root, cut off the outside discoloured stalks and cut the heads to approximately 15 cm (6 inch) lengths.
2 Wash well under running cold water.
3 Place in a pan of boiling water. Simmer for about 20 minutes until limp. Refresh and rewash.
4 Place the sliced vegetables in a sauté pan, sauteuse or casserole.
5 Add the celery heads whole or cut them in halves lengthwise, fold over and place on the bed of roots.
6 Add the bouquet garni, barely cover with stock and season.
7 Add the fat bacon or suet, the crusts of bread, cover with a buttered greaseproof paper and a tight lid and cook gently in a moderate oven at 150–200°C (Reg. 2–6; 300–400°F) for 2 hours or until tender.
8 Remove the celery from the pan, drain well and dress neatly.
9 Add the cooking liquor to an equal amount of jus-lié or demi-glace, reduce and correct the seasoning and consistency.
10 Mask the celery, finish with chopped parsley, and serve.

Plate 12.4: Braised celery

18 – Grilled mushrooms

	4 portions	10 portions
grilling mushrooms	200 g (8 oz)	500 g (1¼ lb)
salt, pepper		
butter, margarine or oil	50 g (2 oz)	125 g (5 oz)

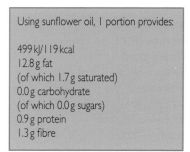

Using sunflower oil, I portion provides:

499 kJ/119 kcal
12.8 g fat
(of which 1.7 g saturated)
0.0 g carbohydrate
(of which 0.0 g sugars)
0.9 g protein
1.3 g fibre

1 Peel the mushrooms, remove the stalks and wash and drain well.
2 Place on a tray and season lightly with salt and pepper.
3 Brush with melted fat or oil and grill on both sides for 3–4 minutes. Serve with picked parsley.

19 – Cabbage

½ kg (1 lb) will serve 3–4 portions (1¼ kg, 2½ lb will serve 8–10 portions).

I portion provides:

38 kJ/9 kcal
0.0 g fat
(of which 0.0 g saturated)
1.1 g carbohydrate
(of which 1.1 g sugars)
1.3 g protein
2.5 g fibre

1 Cut cabbage in quarters.
2 Remove the centre stalk and outside leaves.
3 Shred and wash well.
4 Place into boiling lightly salted water.
5 Boil steadily or steam until cooked, 10–15 minutes, according to the age and type. Do not overcook.
6 Drain immediately in a colander and serve.

Note Overcooking will lessen the vitamin content and also spoil the colour. This is also true when cooking any green vegetable.

20 ~ Spring greens

Prepare and cook as for cabbage for 10–15 minutes according to the age and type. Do not overcook. ½ kg (1 lb) will serve 3–4 portions (1¼ kg, 2½ lb will serve 8–10 portions).

21 ~ Stir-fry cabbage with mushrooms and beansprouts

	4 portions	10 portions
sunflower oil	2 tbsp	5 tbsp
spring cabbage, shredded	400 g (1 lb)	1 kg (2½ lb)
soy sauce	2 tbsp	5 tbsp
mushrooms	200 g (8 oz)	500 g (1¼ lb)
beansprouts	100 g (4 oz)	250 g (10 oz)
freshly ground pepper		

1   Heat the oil in a suitable pan (wok).
2   Add the cabbage and stir for 2 minutes.
3   Add the soy sauce, stir well. Cook for a further 1 minute.
4   Add the mushrooms cut into slices and cook for a further 2 minutes.
5   Stir in the beansprouts and cook for 1–2 minutes.
6   Stir well. Season with freshly ground pepper and serve.

Note   This recipe can be prepared without the mushrooms and/or beansprouts if desired.

22 ~ Braised cabbage

	4 portions	10 portions
cabbage	½ kg (1 lb)	1¼ kg (2½ lb)
carrot	100 g (4 oz)	250 g (10 oz)
onion	100 g (4 oz)	250 g (10 oz)
white stock	250 ml (½ pt)	600 ml (1¼ pt)
salt, pepper		
bouquet garni		
jus-lié	125 ml (¼ pt)	300 ml (⅝ pt)

1   Quarter the cabbage, remove the centre stalk and wash.

recipe continued ▶

2   Retain four light green leaves, shred the remainder.
3   Blanch the leaves and shredded cabbage for 2–3 minutes; refresh.
4   Lay the four blanched leaves flat on the table.
5   Place the remainder of the cabbage on the centre of each and season.
6   Wrap each portion of cabbage in a tea-cloth and shape into a fairly firm ball.
7   Remove from the tea-cloth. Place on a bed of roots.
8   Add the stock half way up cabbage, season and add bouquet garni.
9   Bring to the boil, cover with a lid and cook in the oven for 1 hour.
10   Dress the cabbage in a serving dish.
11   Add the cooking liquor to the jus-lié, correct the seasoning and consistency and strain.
12   Pour over the cabbage and serve.

Note   Braised stuffed cabbage can be made with the addition of 25–50 g (1–2 oz) (60–125 g, 2½–5 oz for 10 portions) sausage meat placed in the centre before shaping into a ball. This recipe can be prepared using Chinese leaves.

23 − Sauerkraut (pickled white cabbage)

	4 portions	10 portions
sauerkraut	400 g (1 lb)	1¼ kg (2½ lb)
studded onion	50 g (2 oz)	125 g (5 oz)
carrot	50 g (2 oz)	125 g (5 oz)
bouquet garni		
peppercorns	6	15
juniper berries	6	15
white stock	250 ml (½ pt)	600 ml (1¼ pt)

1   Season the sauerkraut and place in a casserole or pan, suitable for placing in the oven.
2   Add the whole onion and carrot, the bouquet garni and the peppercorns and berries.
3   Barely cover with good white stock.
4   Cook with a buttered paper and lid.
5   Cook slowly in a moderate oven for 3–4 hours.
6   Remove the bouquet garni and onion. Cut the onion in slices.
7   Serve the sauerkraut garnished with slices of carrot.

Note   Garnished sauerkraut can be served as a main course (see page **388**).

24 ‒ Braised red cabbage

	4 portions	10 portions
red cabbage	300 g (12 oz)	1 kg (2 lb)
salt, pepper		
butter	50 g (2 oz)	125 g (5 oz)
vinegar or red wine	125 ml ($\frac{1}{4}$ pt)	300 ml ($\frac{5}{8}$ pt)
bacon trimmings (optional)	50 g (2 oz)	125 g (5 oz)
cooking apples	100 g (4 oz)	250 g (10 oz)
castor sugar	10 g ($\frac{1}{2}$ oz)	25 g ($1\frac{1}{4}$ oz)

> 1 portion provides:
>
> 754 kJ/180 kcal
> 15.2 g fat
> (of which 8.4 g saturated)
> 7.8 g carbohydrate
> (of which 7.7 g sugars)
> 3.4 g protein
> 3.2 g fibre

1 Quarter, trim and shred the cabbage. Wash well and drain.
2 Season lightly with salt and pepper.
3 Place in a well-buttered casserole or pan suitable for placing in the oven (not aluminium or iron because these metals will cause a chemical reaction which will discolour the cabbage).
4 Add the vinegar and bacon (if using), cover with a buttered paper and lid.
5 Cook in a moderate oven at 150–200°C (Reg. 2–6; 300–400°F) for 1$\frac{1}{2}$ hours.
6 Add the peeled and cored apples cut into 1 cm ($\frac{1}{2}$ inch) dice and sugar. Re-cover with the lid and continue cooking for 2 hours until tender. If a little more cooking liquor is needed use stock.
7 Remove the bacon (if used) and serve.

25 ‒ Brussels sprouts

$\frac{1}{2}$ kg (1 lb) will yield 3–4 portions (1$\frac{1}{4}$ kg, 2$\frac{1}{2}$ lb will serve 8–10 portions).

> 1 portion proves:
>
> 82 kJ/20 kcals
> 0.0 g fat
> (of which 0.0 g saturated)
> 1.9 g carbohydrate
> (of which 1.8 g sugars)
> 3.1 g protein
> 3.2 g fibre

1 Using a small knife trim the stems and cut a cross 2 mm ($\frac{1}{12}$ inch) deep and remove any discoloured leaves. Wash well.
2 Cook in boiling lightly salted water or steam for 10–15 minutes according to size. Do not overcook.
3 Drain well in a colander and serve.

Note Brussels sprouts with butter are cooked and served as in previous recipe, but brushed with 25–50 g (1–2 oz) melted butter (60–125 g, 2$\frac{1}{2}$–5 oz for 10 portions).
   Brussels sprouts with chestnuts. To every 400 g (1 lb) sprouts add 100 g (4 oz) cooked peeled chestnuts.

26 – Brussels sprouts fried in butter

1. Cook and drain.
2. Melt 25–50 g (1–2 oz) (60–125 g, 2½–5 oz for 10 portions) butter in a frying-pan.
3. When foaming, add the sprouts and toss lightly, browning slightly.

27 – Cauliflower

Allow 1 medium-sized cauliflower for 4 portions.

1. Trim the stem and remove the outer leaves.
2. Hollow out the stem with a peeler. Wash.
3. Cook in boiling lightly salted water or steam for approximately 20 minutes. Do not overcook.
4. Drain well and serve cut into 4 even portions.

Note Buttered cauliflower is brushed with 25–50 g (1–2 oz) melted butter before serving and can be sprinkled with chopped parsley.

Other variations include:

- *Cauliflower fried in butter*
    1. Cut the cooked cauliflower in 4 portions.
    2. Lightly colour on all sides in 25–50 g (1–2 oz) butter.
- *Cauliflower, cream sauce*
    1. Cook and serve as for cauliflower.
    2. Accompany with ¼ litre (½ pint) cream sauce in a sauceboat.
- *Cauliflower, melted butter*
    As for cauliflower, with a sauceboat of 100 g (4 oz) melted butter (see page 133).
- *Cauliflower, hollandaise sauce*
    As for cauliflower, accompanied by a sauceboat of ⅛ litre (¼ pint) hollandaise sauce (see page 134).

Note Increase the above quantities 2½ times for 10 portions.

28 – Cauliflower au gratin or Cauliflower Mornay

1 Cut the cooked cauliflower into four.
2 Reheat in a pan of hot salted water (chauffant), or reheat in butter in a suitable pan.
3 Place in vegetable dish or on greased tray.
4 Coat with $\frac{1}{4}$ litre ($\frac{1}{2}$ pint) Mornay sauce (see page 118).
5 Sprinkle with grated cheese.
6 Brown under the salamander and serve.

> 1 portion (au gratin) provides:
>
> 632 kJ/150 kcal
> 10.4 g fat
> (of which 3.9 g saturated)
> 8.6 g carbohydrate
> (of which 3.8 g sugars)
> 6.3 g protein
> 2.0 g fibre

29 – Cauliflower polonaise

1 Cut the cooked cauliflower into four, reheat in a chauffant or in butter in a suitable pan.
2 Heat 50 g (2 oz) butter, add 10 g ($\frac{1}{2}$ oz) white or wholemeal breadcrumbs in a frying-pan and lightly brown. Pour over the cauliflower, sprinkle with sieved hard-boiled egg and chopped parsley.

30 – Sea-kale

$\frac{1}{2}$ kg (1 lb) will yield about 3 portions.

1 Trim the roots, remove any discoloured leaves.
2 Wash well and tie into a neat bundle.
3 Cook in boiling lightly salted water for 15–20 minutes. Do not overcook.
4 Drain well, serve accompanied with a suitable sauce (melted butter, hollandaise, etc.).

31 – Sea-kale Mornay or Sea-kale au gratin

1 Prepare and cook as for sea-kale (recipe 30).
2 Reheat and cut into 5 cm (2 inch) lengths; place in a vegetable dish.
3 Coat with $\frac{1}{4}$ litre ($\frac{1}{2}$ pint) Mornay sauce (page 118) and sprinkle with grated cheese.
4 Brown under the salamander and serve.

> 1 portion provides:
>
> 628 kJ/157 kcal
> 10.4 g fat
> (of which 3.9 g saturated)
> 8.4 g carbohydrate
> (of which 3.6 g sugars)
> 6.1 g protein
> 1.4 g fibre

32 ‒ Marrow

1 Peel the marrow with a peeler or small knife.
2 Cut in half lengthwise.
3 Remove the seeds with a spoon.
4 Cut into even pieces approximately 5 cm (2 inches) square.
5 Cook in boiling lightly salted water or steam for 10–15 minutes. Do not overcook.
6 *Drain well* and serve.

Note All the variations for cauliflower may be used with marrow.

> 1 portion provides:
>
> 44 kJ/11 kcal
> 0.0 g fat
> (of which 0.0 g saturated)
> 2.1 g carbohydrate
> (of which 2.0 g sugars)
> 0.6 g protein
> 0.9 g fibre

33 ‒ Stuffed marrow

1 Peel the marrow and cut in half lengthwise.
2 Remove the seeds with a spoon.
3 Season and add the stuffing. Replace the two halves.
4 Cook as for braised celery (page 531) allowing about 1 hour.
5 To serve, cut into thick slices and dress neatly in a vegetable dish. Baby marrows are ideal for this.

Note Various stuffings may be used: 100 g (4 oz) sausage meat or 100 g (4 oz) rice for 4 portions: cooked rice with chopped cooked meat, seasoned with salt, pepper and herbs; well-seasoned cooked rice with sliced mushroom, tomatoes, etc.

34 ‒ Marrow provençale

	4 portions	10 portions
marrow	400 g (1 lb)	1 kg (2½ lb)
chopped onion	50 g (2 oz)	125 g (5 oz)
clove garlic, chopped	1	2–3
oil or butter	50 g (2 oz)	125 g (5 oz)
salt, pepper		
tomatoes, skinned, de-seeded and diced	400 g (1 lb)	1 kg (2½ lb)
chopped parsley		

1 Peel the marrow, remove the seeds and cut into 2 cm (1 inch) dice.
2 Cook the onion and garlic in the oil in a pan for 2–3 minutes without colouring.
3 Add the marrow, season with salt and pepper.
4 Add the tomato concassé.
5 Cover with a lid, cook gently in the oven or on the side of the stove for 1 hour or until tender.
6 Sprinkle with chopped parsley and serve.

Note Baby marrows may be served, similarly, but reduce the cooking time to 5–10 minutes.

35 ~ Baby marrow (courgette)

$\frac{3}{4}$ kg (1$\frac{1}{2}$ lb) yields about 4 portions (2 kg, 4 lb yields about 10 portions). Because they are tender, courgettes are not peeled or de-seeded.

1 Wash. Top and tail and cut into round slices 3–6 cm ($\frac{1}{8}$–$\frac{1}{4}$ inch) thick.
2 Gently boil in lightly salted water or steam for 2 or 3 minutes. Do not overcook.
3 Drain well and serve either plain or brushed with melted butter or margarine and/or sprinkled with chopped parsley.

1 portion provides:
113 kJ/27 kcal
0.1 g fat
(of which 0.0 g saturated)
5.9 g carbohydrate
(of which 0.4 g sugars)
1.0 g protein
0.8 g fibre

36 ~ Shallow-fried courgettes

1 Prepare as recipe 35.
2 Gently fry in hot oil or butter for 2 or 3 minutes, drain and serve.

37 ~ Deep-fried courgettes

1 Prepare as recipe 35.
2 Pass through flour, or milk and flour, or batter and deep fry in hot fat at 185°C (365°F). Drain well and serve.

38 – Braised chicory

½ kg (1 lb) will yield 3 portions.

1 Trim the stem, remove any discoloured leaves, wash.
2 Place in a well-buttered casserole or pan suitable to place in the oven.
3 Season lightly with salt and a little sugar if desired (to counteract the bitterness).
4 Add the juice of half a lemon to prevent discoloration.
5 Add 25–50 g (1–2 oz) butter per ½ kg (1 lb) and a few drops of water.
6 Cover with a buttered paper and lid.
7 Cook gently in a moderate oven at 150–200°C (Reg. 2–6; 300–400°F) for 1 hour.
8 Dress and serve.

Using 25 g butter per ½ kg, 1 portion provides:

304 kJ/73 kcal
6.8 g fat
(of which 4.3 g saturated)
1.8 g carbohydrate
(of which 0.0 g sugars)
1.0 g protein
1.0 g fibre

39 – Shallow-fried chicory

Cook the chicory as in the previous recipe. Drain, shallow fry in a little butter, and colour lightly on both sides. Serve with 10 g (½ oz) per portion nut-brown butter, lemon juice and chopped parsley.

40 – Leaf spinach

½ kg (1 lb) will yield 2 portions.

1 Remove the stems and discard them.
2 Wash the leaves very carefully in plenty of water several times if necessary.
3 Cook in boiling lightly salted water for 3–5 minutes; do not overcook.
4 Refresh under cold water, squeeze dry into a ball.
5 When required for service, either reheat and serve plain or place into a pan containing 25–50 g (1–2 oz) butter, loosen with a fork and reheat quickly without colouring; season lightly with salt and mill pepper and serve.

Using 25 g butter per ½ kg, 1 portion provides:

515 kJ/123 kcal
10.8 g fat
(of which 6.6 g saturated)
1.4 g carbohydrate
(of which 1.2 g sugars)
5.2 g protein
6.3 g fibre

41 ⁓ Spinach purée

1 Cook, refresh and drain the spinach as above.
2 Pass through a sieve or mouli, or use a food processor.
3 Reheat in 25–50 g (1–2 oz) butter, mix with a wooden spoon, correct the seasoning and serve.

Note Creamed spinach purée can be made by mixing in 30 ml ($\frac{1}{8}$ pint) cream, 60 ml ($\frac{1}{4}$ pint) béchamel or natural yoghurt before serving. Serve with a border of cream. An addition would be 1 cm ($\frac{1}{2}$ inch) triangle-shaped croûtons fried in butter. Spinach may also be served with toasted pine kernels or finely chopped garlic.

42 ⁓ Broad beans

$\frac{1}{2}$ kg (1 lb) will yield about 2 portions.

1 Shell the beans and cook in boiling salted water for 10–15 minutes until tender. Do not overcook.
2 If the inner shells are tough they should also be removed before serving.

Note Variations include:

- Brushing with butter.
- Brushing with butter, then sprinkling with chopped parsley.
- Binding with $\frac{1}{4}$ litre ($\frac{1}{2}$ pint) cream sauce or fresh cream.

I portion provides:
142 kJ/34 kcals
0.4 g fat
(of which 0.1 g saturated)
5.0 g carbohydrate
(of which 0.4 g sugars)
2.9 g protein
3.0 g fibre

43 ⁓ Dried beans

$\frac{1}{2}$ kg (1 lb) will yield 8 portions. Black-eyed, borlotti, butter, haricot, kidney, flageolet beans only require soaking if they have been stored for a long time.

1 If necessary soak in cold water overnight in a cool place.
2 Change the water, refresh.
3 Cover with cold water. Do not add salt (as salt toughens the skin and lengthens the cooking time). Bring to the boil.

I portion provides:
29 kJ/7 kcals
0.0 g fat
(of which 0.0 g saturated)
1.1 g carbohydrate
(of which 0.8 g sugars)
0.8 g protein
3.2 g fibre

recipe continued ▶

4   Skim when necessary.
5   Add 50 g (2 oz) carrot, 50 g (2 oz) studded onion, 50 g (2 oz) bacon bone or
    trimmings (optional) and bouquet garni.
6   Simmer until tender. Season lightly with salt.
7   Drain and serve.

Note   Pulse beans can be served sprinkled with chopped parsley, mixed fresh herbs
or chives. They can also be lightly dressed with a good quality oil (natural or
flavoured) and/or a suitably flavoured warm vinaigrette.

   Puy lentils are a popular, green-coloured lentil which do not require soaking and
hold their shape when cooked. They require only about 30 minutes cooking and
they can be braised in a little stock, vegetables, herbs, wine, etc. Usually cooked *al
dente*, they are a suitable accompaniment for many meat, game and poultry dishes.

44 ~ French beans

½ kg (1 lb) will yield 3–4 portions.

1   Top and tail the beans, carefully and economically.
2   Using a large sharp knife cut the beans into strips
    5 cm × 3 mm (2 × ⅛ inch).
3   Wash.
4   Cook in boiling lightly salted water or steam for
    10–15 minutes, until tender.
5   Do not overcook. Drain well and serve.

> 1 portion provides:
>
> 646 kJ/154 kcals
> 2.9 g fat
> (of which 0.5 g saturated)
> 28.5 g carbohydrate
> (of which 2.1 g sugars)
> 5.1 g protein
> 5.9 g fibre

Note   Variations include:

● Brushing the beans with butter.
● Gently tossing the cooked beans in butter over heat without colouring.
● Adding to 400 g (1 lb) cooked French beans, 50 g (2 oz) shallow-fried onions.
● Combining 400 g (1 lb) cooked French beans with 100 g (4 oz) cooked flageolet
   beans.

45 – Runner beans

Wash and string the beans with a small knife, then cut them into thin strips approximately 4–6 cm (2–3 inches) long. Cook in boiling lightly salted water or steam for 10 minutes. Drain well and serve. Do not overcook.

1 portion provides:
80 kJ/19 kcal
0.2 g fat
(of which 0.0 g saturated)
2.7 g carbohydrate
(of which 1.3 g sugars)
1.9 g protein
3.4 g fibre

46 – Braised lettuce

	4 portions	10 portions
large lettuce	2	5
carrots, sliced	50 g (2 oz)	125 g (5 oz)
onions, sliced	50 g (2 oz)	125 g (5 oz)
salt, pepper		
bouquet garni		
white stock approximately	125 ml ($\frac{1}{4}$ pt)	300 ml ($\frac{5}{8}$ pt)
fat bacon (optional)	50 g (2 oz)	125 g (5 oz)
slices stale bread	2	5
butter or margarine	50 g (2 oz)	125 g (5 oz)
jus-lié or demi-glace	60 ml ($\frac{1}{8}$ pt)	150 ml ($\frac{1}{3}$ pt)
chopped parsley		

Using hard margarine, 1 portion provides:
1023 kJ/243 kcal
20.9 g fat
(of which 8.7 g saturated)
11.0 g carbohydrate
(of which 2.7 g sugars)
3.6 g protein
2.4 g fibre

1 Wash the lettuce, keeping whole.
2 Place in boiling lightly salted water and cook for 5 minutes; refresh.
3 Squeeze carefully.
4 Arrange the sliced vegetables in a pan or casserole suitable for placing in the oven.
5 Season lightly, add the bouquet garni and stock to come half-way up the lettuce, add the bacon (if used).
6 Cover with a buttered greaseproof paper and a lid.
7 Cook in a moderate oven at 150–200°C (Reg. 2–6; 300–400°F) for 1 hour.
8 Remove the lettuce, cut in halves lengthwise, flatten slightly and fold each in half.

recipe continued ▶

9   Meanwhile cut 4 neat heart-shaped croûtons from the bread and fry in butter or margarine to a golden brown.

10   Reduce the cooking liquor from the lettuce with the jus-lié or demi-glace, keeping the sauce thin.

11   Serve the lettuce masked with the thin sauce.

12   Dip the points of the croûtons in the sauce and then into chopped parsley and arrange neatly on or by the lettuce.

47 – Corn on the cob

Allow 1 cob per portion.

1   Trim the stem.
2   Cook in boiling lightly salted water for 10–20 minutes or until the corn is tender. Do not overcook.
3   Remove the outer leaves and fibres.
4   Serve with a sauceboat of melted butter.

I portion provides:

646 kJ/154 kcal
2.9 g fat
(of which 0.5 g saturated)
28.5 g carbohydrate
(of which 2.1 g sugars)
5.1 g protein
5.9 g fibre

Note   Creamed sweetcorn can be made by removing the corn from the cooked cobs, draining well, and lightly binding with cream, fresh or non-dairy, béchamel or yoghurt.

48 – Buttered turnips or swedes

	4 portions	10 portions
turnips or swedes	400 g (1 lb)	1 kg (2½ lb)
salt, sugar		
butter	25 g (1 oz)	60 g (2½ oz)
chopped parsley		

I portion provides:

253 kJ/60 kcal
5.4 g fat
(of which 3.3 g saturated)
2.5 g carbohydrate
(of which 2.5 g sugars)
0.7 g protein
1.9 g fibre

1   Peel and wash the vegetables.
2   Cut into neat pieces or turn barrel shape.
3   Place in a pan with a little salt, a pinch of sugar and butter. Barely cover with water.
4   Cover with a buttered paper and allow to boil steadily in order to evaporate all the water.

5 When the water has completely evaporated check that the vegetables are cooked, if not, add a little more water and continue cooking. Do not overcook.
6 Toss the vegetables over a fierce heat for 1–2 minutes in order to glaze.
7 Drain well, and serve.

49 – Purée of turnips or swedes

	4 portions	10 portions
turnips or swedes	600 g (1½ lb)	1½ kg (3 lb)
salt, pepper		
butter	25 g (1 oz)	60 g (2½ oz)

1 Wash, peel and rewash the vegetables. Cut in pieces if necessary.
2 Barely cover with water; add a little salt.
3 Simmer gently until tender or steam. Drain well.
4 Pass through a sieve or mouli, or use a food processor.
5 Return to the pan, reheat and mix in the butter, correct the seasoning and serve.

50 – Fried onions

½ kg (1 lb) will yield approximately 2 portions.

1 Peel and wash the onions, cut in halves, slice finely.
2 Cook slowly in 25–50 g (1–2 oz) fat in a frying-pan, turning frequently until tender and nicely browned; season lightly with salt.

Using peanut oil, 1 portion provides:

681 kJ/162 kcal
12.9 g fat
(of which 2.4 g saturated)
10.4 g carbohydrate
(of which 10.4 g sugars)
1.8 g protein
2.6 g fibre

51 – French-fried onions (illustrated on page 548)

1 Peel and wash the onions.
2 Cut in 2 mm (1/12 inch) thick slices, against the grain. Separate into rings.
3 Pass through milk and seasoned flour.
4 Shake off the surplus. Deep fry in hot fat at 185°C (365°F).
5 Drain well, season lightly with salt and serve.

52 – Braised onions

1 Select medium even-sized onions, allow 2–3 portions per $\frac{1}{2}$ kg (1 lb).
2 Peel, wash and cook in boiling lightly salted water for 30 minutes or steam.
3 Drain and place in a pan or casserole suitable for placing in the oven.
4 Add a bouquet garni, half-cover with stock and a lid and braise gently at 180–200°C (Reg. 4–6; 350–400°F) in the oven until tender.
5 Drain well and dress neatly in a vegetable dish.
6 Reduce the cooking liquor with an equal amount of jus-lié or demi-glace. Correct the seasoning and consistency and pass. Mask the onions and sprinkle with chopped parsley.

> 1 portion provides:
>
> 245 kJ/58 kcal
> 0.4 g fat
> (of which 0.1 g saturated)
> 10.9 g carbohydrate
> (of which 10.4 g sugars)
> 3.4 g protein
> 2.8 g fibre

53 – Peas

Fresh peas 1 kg (2 lb) will yield about 4 portions.

1 Shell and wash the peas.
2 Cook in boiling lightly salted water or steam with a sprig of mint for 10–15 minutes until tender. Do not overcook. Drain in a colander.
3 Add 25 g (1 oz) butter and $\frac{1}{2}$ teaspoon castor sugar, toss gently.
4 Serve with blanched, refreshed mint leaves.

> 1 portion provides:
>
> 62 kJ/260 kcal
> 0.4 g fat
> (of which 0.1 g saturated)
> 9.8 g carbohydrate
> (of which 3.7 g sugars)
> 5.4 g protein
> 4.8 g fibre

Frozen peas $\frac{1}{4}$ kg ($\frac{1}{2}$ lb) will yield about 4 portions.

1 Cook in boiling lightly salted water for 5 minutes or until tender. Drain in a colander.
2 Add 25 g (1 oz) butter and $\frac{1}{2}$ teaspoon castor sugar; toss gently.
3 Serve with blanched refreshed mint leaves.

Mange-tout $\frac{1}{2}$ kg (1 lb) will yield 4–6 portions

1 Top and tail, wash and drain.
2 Cook in boiling salted water for 5 minutes, until *al dente*.
3 Serve whole, brushed with butter.

54 – Peas French-style

	4 portions	10 portions
peas (in the pod)	1 kg (2 lb)	2½ kg (5 lb)
spring or button onions	12	40
small lettuce	1	2–3
butter	25 g (1 oz)	60 g (2½ oz)
salt		
castor sugar	½ tsp	1 tsp
flour	5 g (¼ oz)	12 g (⅝ oz)

> 1 portion provides:
>
> 515 kJ/123 kcal
> 5.6 g fat
> (of which 3.4 g saturated)
> 12.9 g carbohydrate
> (of which 5.8 g sugars)
> 5.9 g protein
> 5.7 g fibre

1 Shell and wash the peas and place in a sauteuse.
2 Peel and wash the onions, shred the lettuce and add to the peas with half the butter, a little salt and the sugar.
3 Barely cover with water. Cover with a lid and cook steadily, preferably in the oven, until tender.
4 Correct the seasoning.
5 Mix the remaining butter with the flour and shake into the boiling peas until thoroughly mixed, and serve.

Note When using frozen peas, allow the onions to almost cook before adding the peas.

55 – Stuffed pimento

	4 portions	10 portions
medium-sized red pimentos	4	10
Pilaff		
rice (long grain)	200 g (8 oz)	500 g (1¼ lb)
onion, chopped	50 g (2 oz)	125 g (5 oz)
butter	50 g (2 oz)	125 g (5 oz)
salt, pepper		
carrots, sliced	50 g (2 oz)	125 g (5 oz)
onions, sliced	50 g (2 oz)	125 g (5 oz)
bouquet garni		
white stock	½ litre (1 pt)	1¼ litre (2½ pt)

> 1 portion provides:
>
> 1291 kJ/308 kcal
> 11.4 g fat
> (of which 6.7 g saturated)
> 48.8 g carbohydrate
> (of which 5.3 g sugars)
> 5.4 g protein
> 3.1 g fibre

recipe continued ▶

1 Place the pimentos on a tray in the oven or under the salamander for a few minutes or deep fry in hot oil at 180°C (365°F), until the skin blisters.
2 Remove the skin and stalk carefully and empty out all the seeds.
3 Stuff with a well-seasoned pilaff of rice which may be varied by the addition of mushrooms, tomatoes, ham, etc.
4 Replace the stem.
5 Place the pimentos on the sliced carrot and onion in a pan suitable for the oven; add the bouquet garni, stock and seasoning. Cover with a buttered paper and lid.
6 Cook in a moderate oven at 180–200°C (Reg. 4–6; 350–400°F) for 1 hour or until tender.
7 Serve garnished with picked parsley.

56 – Salsify

½ kg (1 lb) will yield 2–3 portions.

1 Wash, peel and rewash the salsify.
2 Cut into 5 cm (2 inch) lengths.
3 Cook in a blanc as for artichokes (recipe 3). Do not overcook.
4 They may then be served as for any of the cauliflower recipes, page 537.
5 Salsify may also be passed through batter and deep fried.

1 portion provides:
76 kJ/18 kcal
0.0 g fat
(of which 0.0 g saturated)
2.8 g carbohydrate
(of which 2.8 g sugars)
1.9 g protein
0.0 g fibre

Plate 12.5a–b: Preparation and cooking of French fried onions

57 ‒ Grilled vegetables

Root vegetables (carrots, turnips, parsnips, swedes) can be peeled, cut into thick slices, par-boiled until half cooked, well drained, dried, brushed with a good quality oil and grilled on both sides.

For aubergines, courgettes and red or yellow peppers:

- Slice the aubergines lengthwise 1 cm ($\frac{1}{2}$ inch) thick.
- Slice the courgettes into thick oblique slices.
- Quarter and de-seed the peppers.
- Cook on a well oiled grill, brush with oil and cook over a medium heat, turning them over when necessary until the vegetables are tender and a good colour.
- Peel the peppers before serving.

Note   Sprinkle with chopped herbs (coriander, chives or/and chopped garlic) for variety.

58 ‒ Grilled tomatoes

Allow 1 or 2 per portion according to size; $\frac{1}{2}$ kg (1 lb) will yield 3–4 portions.

1   Wash the tomatoes, and remove the eyes with a small knife.
2   Place on a greased, seasoned baking tray.
3   Make an incision 2 mm ($\frac{1}{12}$ inch) cross-shape on the opposite side to the eye and peel back the four corners.
4   Brush with melted fat or oil and season lightly with salt and pepper.
5   Grill under a moderately hot salamander. Serve garnished with picked parsley.

Using sunflower oil, 1 portion provides:

121 kJ/29 kcal
1.3 g fat
(of which 0.3 g saturated)
3.5 g carbohydrate
(of which 3.5 g sugars)
1.1 g protein
1.9 g fibre

59 – Stuffed tomatoes

	4 portions	10 portions
medium-sized tomatoes	8	20

Duxelle

	4 portions	10 portions
shallots, chopped	10 g ($\frac{1}{2}$ oz)	25 g ($1\frac{1}{4}$ oz)
butter or oil	25 g (1 oz)	60 g ($2\frac{1}{2}$ oz)
mushrooms	150 g (6 oz)	375 g (15 oz)
salt, pepper		
clove garlic, crushed (optional)	1	2–3
white or wholemeal breadcrumbs	25 g (1 oz)	60 g ($2\frac{1}{2}$ oz)
chopped parsley		

1 Wash the tomatoes, remove the eyes.
2 Remove $\frac{1}{4}$ of the tomato with a sharp knife.
3 Carefully empty out the seeds without damaging the flesh.
4 Place on a greased baking tray.
5 Cook the shallots in a little oil or butter or margarine without colouring.
6 Add the washed chopped mushrooms, season with salt and pepper; add the garlic if using and cook for 2–3 minutes.
7 Add a little of the strained tomato juice, the breadcrumbs and the parsley; mix to a piping consistency. Correct the seasoning. At this stage several additions may be made: chopped ham, cooked rice, etc.
8 Place the mixture in a piping bag with a large star tube and pipe into the tomato shells.
9 Replace the tops.
10 Brush with melted fat, season lightly with salt and pepper.
11 Cook in a moderate oven at 180–200°C (Reg. 4–6; 350–400°F) for 4–5 minutes.
12 Serve garnished with picked parsley.

60 ~ Beetroot

Select medium-sized or small beetroots, carefully twist off the green leaves (do not cut). Well wash in cold water, cover with water and simmer gently until the skin is easily removed by rubbing between the fingers. Do *not* cut or prick with knife as the beetroots will 'bleed' and turn pale. Beetroots may also be cooked in a steamer.

1 portion provides:
92 kJ/22 kcal
0.0 g fat
(of which 0.0 g saturated)
5.0 g carbohydrate
(of which 5.0 g sugars)
0.9 g protein
1.3 g fibre

61 ~ Basic tomato preparation (tomate concassé)

This is a cooked preparation which is usually included in the normal *mise en place* of a kitchen as it is used in a great number of dishes.

	4 portions	10 portions
tomatoes	400 g (1 lb)	$1\frac{1}{4}$ kg ($2\frac{1}{2}$ lb)
shallots or onions, chopped	25 g (1 oz)	60 g ($2\frac{1}{2}$ oz)
butter, margarine or oil	25 g (1 oz)	60 g ($2\frac{1}{2}$ oz)
salt, pepper		

1 Plunge the tomatoes into *boiling* water for 5–10 seconds, the riper the tomatoes the less time required. Refresh *immediately*.
2 Remove the skins, cut in halves across the tomato and remove all the seeds.
3 Roughly chop the flesh of the tomatoes.
4 Meanwhile cook the chopped onion or shallot without colouring in the butter or margarine.
5 Add the tomatoes and season.
6 Simmer gently on the side of the stove until the moisture is evaporated.

62 ~ Braised leeks

½ kg (1 lb) of leeks will yield 2 portions.

1 Cut the roots from the leek, remove any discoloured outside leaves and trim the green.
2 Cut through lengthwise and wash well under running water.
3 Tie into a neat bundle.
4 Place in boiling lightly salted water for 5 minutes or steam.
5 Place on a bed of root vegetables.
6 Barely cover with stock, add the bouquet garni and season.
7 Cover with a lid and cook for ½–1 hour or until tender.
8 Remove the leeks from the pan and fold neatly; arrange in a vegetable dish.
9 Meanwhile add jus-lié to the cooking liquor and correct the seasoning and consistency.
10 Pour the sauce over the leeks.

> I portion provides:
>
> 130 kJ/31 kcal
> 0.0 g fat
> (of which 0.0 g saturated)
> 5.6 g carbohydrate
> (of which 5.4 g sugars)
> 2.3 g protein
> 2.8 g fibre

Note Boiled leeks are prepared as above, cooking for 10–15 minutes. Drain well, cut the string and serve plain, or brushed with melted butter. Leeks may also be served coated with cream or parsley sauce.

63 ~ Parsnips

Wash well. Peel the parsnips and again wash well. Cut into quarters lengthwise, remove the centre root if tough. Cut into neat pieces and cook in lightly salted water until tender or steam. Drain and serve with melted butter or in a cream sauce. Parsnips may be roasted in the oven in a little fat or in with a joint and can be cooked and prepared as a purée.

> I portion provides:
>
> 235 kJ/56 kcal
> 0.0 g fat
> (of which 0.0 g saturated)
> 13.5 g carbohydrate
> (of which 2.7 g sugars)
> 1.3 g protein
> 2.5 g fibre

64 – Pease pudding

	4 portions	10 portions
yellow split peas, soaked	200 g (8 oz)	500 g (1¼ lb)
water	½ litre (1 pt)	1¼ litre (2½ pt)
studded onion	50 g (2 oz)	125 g (5 oz)
carrot	50 g (2 oz)	125 g (5 oz)
bacon trimmings	50 g (2 oz)	125 g (5 oz)
butter or margarine	50 g (2 oz)	125 g (5 oz)
salt, pepper		

Using hard margarine, 1 portion provides:

1277 kJ/304 kcal
15.6 g fat
(of which 6.5 g saturated)
29.6 g carbohydrate
(of which 2.3 g sugars)
13.1 g protein
6.5 g fibre

1 Place all the ingredients, except the butter and margarine, in a saucepan with a tight-fitting lid.
2 Bring to the boil, cook in a moderate oven at 180–200°C (Reg. 4–6; 350–400°] for 2 hours.
3 Remove the onion, carrot and bacon and pass the peas through a sieve or use a food processor.
4 Return to a clean pan, mix in the butter or margarine, correct the seasoning and consistency (this should be firm).

65 – Mixed vegetables

	4 portions	10 portions
carrots	100 g (4 oz)	250 g (10 oz)
turnips	50 g (2 oz)	125 g (5 oz)
salt		
French beans	50 g (2 oz)	125 g (5 oz)
peas	50 g (2 oz)	125 g (5 oz)

1 portion provides:

58 kJ/14 kcal
0.1 g fat
(of which 0.0 g saturated)
2.5 g carbohydrate
(of which 1.7 g sugars)
1.0 g protein
2.1 g fibre

1 Peel and wash the carrots and turnips; cut into ½ cm (¼ inch) dice (macédoine) or batons (jardinière); cook separately in salted water, do not overcook. Refresh.
2 Top and tail the beans; cut into ½ cm (¼ inch) dice, cook and refresh, do not overcook.
3 Cook the peas and refresh.
4 Mix the vegetables and when required reheat in hot salted water.
5 Drain well, serve brushed with melted butter.

66 ~ Fennel

The foliage of this plant is a herb of distinctive flavour used in fish cookery and salads. One good-sized bulb will serve 2–4 portions.

1   Trim the bulb, remove the stalks and leaves and wash well.
2   Cook in boiling lightly salted water for 15–20 minutes. Do not overcook.
3   Drain well, cut into portions and serve as for any of the cauliflower recipes on page 537.

Note   Fennel may also be braised as for celery, page 531.

1 portion provides:
21 kJ/5 kcal
0.0 g fat
(of which 0.0 g saturated)
0.7 g carbohydrate
(of which 0.7 g sugars)
0.6 g protein
2.2 g fibre

67 ~ Mixed fried vegetables in batter

The vegetables are prepared in small pieces and may be served individually.

cauliflower	fennel
broccoli	parsnips
celery	salsify
French beans	courgettes

Fried in peanut oil, 1 portion provides:
1062 kJ/253 kcal
16.5 g fat
(of which 3.6 g saturated)
22.7 g carbohydrate
(of which 2.7 g sugars)
4.9 g protein
3.1 g fibre

1   Boil or steam the vegetables (except the courgettes) keeping them slightly firm.
2   Marinade in oil, lemon juice and chopped parsley.
3   Dip in batter (see page 261).
4   Deep fry in hot fat 180°C (356°F) until golden brown.
5   Drain and serve.

68 ~ Ladies fingers (okra) in cream sauce

	4 portions	10 portions
ladies fingers	400 g (1 lb)	1¼ kg (2½ lb)
butter or margarine	50 g (2 oz)	125 g (5 oz)
cream sauce	¼ litre (½ pt)	600 ml (1¼ pt)

> Using hard margarine, 1 portion provides:
>
> 928 kJ/221 kcal
> 20.2 g fat
> (of which 9.8 g saturated)
> 5.7 g carbohydrate
> (of which 5.7 g sugars)
> 4.4 g protein
> 3.2 g fibre

1 Top and tail the ladies fingers.
2 Blanch in boiling lightly salted water, or steam; drain.
3 Sweat in the margarine or butter for 5–10 minutes, or until tender.
4 Carefully add the cream sauce.
5 Bring to the boil, correct seasoning and serve in a suitable dish.

Note   Okra may also be served brushed with butter or sprinkled with chopped parsley.

69 ~ Vegetable moulds (mousse)

Many vegetables are suitable for making into moulds (usually dariole or small timbale moulds): asparagus, broccoli, carrot, cauliflower, egg plant, fennel, spinach, etc.

	4 portions	10 portions
seasoned vegetable purée	400 g (1 lb)	1 kg (2½ lb)
eggs	3–4	7–10
double cream	2 tbsp	5 tbsp

1 Thoroughly mix the eggs without overbeating.
2 Pass them through a fine strainer on to the cold vegetable purée; add the cream and combine thoroughly.
3 Three quarter fill the buttered moulds (this allows for expansion during cooking).
4 Place the moulds in a bain-marie of hot water and bake at 190°C (Reg. 5; 375°F) until set.
5 Remove from oven and allow to stand for 10 minutes before turning out.

recipe continued ▶

Note   Variations include:

- Béchamel sauce can be used in place of cream.
- Extra ingredients, spices or herbs, may be added to the various moulds (chopped garlic with aubergine; toasted pine nuts in spinach; chopped coriander in carrot; grated Parmesan cheese with broccoli, etc.).
- Vegetable moulds can be served as vegetables, as a garnish or as a light course in which case they would be served with a suitable sauce (asparagus mousse, mushroom sauce page 120).
- Vegetable soufflé uses the same basic recipe; keep the purée stiff. Separate the eggs, mix the yolks into the purée then fold in the stiffly beaten whites. Place the mixture into buttered and floured soufflé moulds and bake in a hot oven 220°C (Reg. 7; 425°F) until set.

Pulse dishes

1. Ensure that preparation, cooking areas and utensils are ready for and cleaned after use and satisfy health, safety and hygiene regulations.
2. Plan work, allocate time and organise efficiently.
3. Ensure that the ingredients are of the type, quality and quantity required.
4. Prepare, cook and present dishes according to dish and customer requirements.
5. Realise that competency implies knowing, understanding and applying the principles of cooking pulses.

Pulses are the dried seeds of plants which form pods and they fall into three types: peas, beans and lentils.

There are numerous varieties of pulses and as the majority are grown in warm temperate climates most of those used in the UK are imported. Pulses are available in three forms: fresh, dried and tinned. Fresh pulses can be cooked for any of the recipes in the vegetable section pages.

FOOD VALUE

Pulses are a good source of protein and carbohydrate and therefore help to provide the body with energy. They also contain iron and vitamin B, are high in fibre and, with the exception of the soy bean, contain no fat.

STORAGE

Chapter 1 contains details of stock rotation procedures. In addition:

- Store fresh pulses in a refrigerator at a temperature below 5°C (41°F).
- Store frozen pulses in a freezer at a temperature below −18°C (0°F).
- Store dried pulses in clean airtight containers off the floor in the dry store.
- Unpack tinned pulses and check that the tins are sound and undamaged.

HEALTH AND HYGIENE

Chapter 1 contains details of health and food safety. In addition:

- Always check pulses for food pests (flour moths) and any foreign matter (stones, etc.).
- When storing cooked pulses, keep them covered and in a refrigerator at a temperature below 5°C (41°F).
- To prevent risk of cross-contamination, store cooked pulses away from any raw foods.

Plate 12.6: Pulses and rice

TYPES OF PULSES

Beans

- *Aduki* Small, round, deep red, shiny, nutty and sweet (the flavour used in oriental confectionery).
- *Black* Glistening black skins, creamy flesh.
- *Black-eyed* White beans with a black blotch, savoury flavour.
- *Broad* Also known as java beans, strongly flavoured.
- *Borlotti* Pink blotched, mottled, kidney-shaped with pleasant flavour.
- *Butter* Also known as Lima beans, available large or small.
- *Cannellini* Italian haricot, slightly larger than the English.
- *Dutch brown* Light brown in colour.
- *Flageolet* Pale green, kidney-shaped with delicate flavour.
- *Ful medames* Also known as Egyptian brown beans, small, brown and knobbly, known as the field bean in England.
- *Haricot* White, smooth, oval, used for baked beans.
- *Pinto* Pink, blotched, mottled colour.
- *Red kidney* Used in chilli con carne. They contain an enzyme which must be destroyed by presoaking, washing off, then boiling and ensuring that the beans are well cooked. Failure to do this may cause chemical food poisoning.
- *Soissons* Finest haricot beans.
- *Soy* Soy beans are very high in nutrients, especially protein and they contain all the essential amino acids. They are processed into many forms: soy flour, TVP (meat substitute), tofu (curd), oils, margarines, soy milk and soy sauce.
- *Mung beans* Small, olive green in colour, good flavour, available split, whole and skinless. Widely used by being sprouted for their shoots.

Peas

- *Blue* Also known as marrowfat peas, pleasant flavour, floury texture, retains shape when cooked.
- *Chick* Available whole and split skinless. Whole chick peas look like the kernel of a hazelnut. They have a nutty taste.
- *Split green* A sweeter variety than the blue pea; cook to a purée easily.
- *Split yellow* Cook to a purée easily.

Both yellow and green split peas are used for vegetable purées and soups.

Lentils

- *Orange* Several types which vary in size and shade and may be sold whole or split.
- *Green or continental* Retain shape after cooking, available in small or large varieties.
- *Yellow* Of Asian origin, often used as an dhal accompaniment to curry dishes.
- *Red* Purée easily, used for soups and stews etc.
- *Indian brown* Red lentils from which the seed coat has not been removed; they purée easily.
- *Puy* Dark French lentils, varied in size, retain their shape when cooked and are considered the best of their type.
- *Dhal* The Hindi word for dried peas and beans.

USE OF PULSES

Pulses are one of the most versatile commodities. They can be used extensively in a wide range of dishes. Imaginative and experimental use of different herbs, spices, flavourings and vegetables, can give individual variation to the pulse recipes.

There are several recipes given in this book:

- Haricot bean and three bean salads (page 183).
- Pulse soups (page 139).
- Pease pudding (page 553).
- Bean goulash (page 497).
- Bean and nut burgers (page 492).
- Lentil and cider loaf (page 499).
- Meatless shepherd's pie (lentils) (page 501).
- Mexican bean pot (page 502).
- Moussaka (TVP) (page 510).
- Vegetable recipes (chapter 12).

COOKING

Some pulses require presoaking in cold water before cooking; the soaking time will vary according to the type and quality and the length of time they have been stored.

For soaking, pulses should be amply covered with cold water (they will expand gradually) and kept in a cold place. In some cases this may be for a few hours, in others it may be overnight, in which case they should be stored in the refrigerator at a temperature below 5°C (41°F). After soaking, salt should not be added before or during the cooking as this causes the pulses to toughen. Salt, however, may be added if required towards the end of the cookery process.

13

POTATOES

Recipe No.			*page nos.*
9	Almond potatoes	*Pommes amandines*	567
11	Baked jacket potatoes	*Pomme au four*	567
12	Baked jacket potatoes with cheese	*Pommes gratinées*	568
1	Boiled potatoes	*Pommes nature*	564
8	Brioche potatoes	*Pommes brioche*	566
27	Byron potatoes	*Pommes Byron*	575
30	Château potatoes	*Pommes château*	577
22	Chips	*Pommes frites*	571
32	Cocotte potatoes	*Pommes cocottes*	577
18	Crisps (game chips)		570
6	Croquette potatoes	*Pommes croquettes*	566
23	Deep fried potato wedges in butter		572
36	Delmonico potatoes		578
5	Duchess potatoes	*Pommes duchesse*	565
28	Fondant potatoes	*Pommes fondantes*	576
24	Fried diced potatoes		573
26	Macaire potatoes	*Pomme Macaire*	575
10	Marquis potatoes	*Pomme marquise*	567
4	Mashed potatoes	*Pommes purées*	565
20	Matchstick potatoes	*Pommes allumettes*	570
37	New potatoes	*Pommes nouvelles*	579
38	New rissolée potatoes	*Pommes nouvelles rissolées*	579
33	Noisette potatoes	*Pommes noisette*	577
34	Parisienne potatoes	*Pommes parisienne*	578
39	Parmentier potatoes	*Pommes Parmentier*	580
2	Parsley potatoes	*Pommes persillées*	564
7	Potato cakes		566
35	Potatoes with bacon and onions	*Pommes au lard*	578
3	Riced potatoes	*Pommes à la neige*	564
31	Rissolée potatoes	*Pommes rissolées*	577
29	Roast potatoes	*Pommes rôties*	576
15	Sauté potatoes	*Pommes sautées*	569
17	Sauté potatoes with onions	*Pommes lyonnaise*	570
25	Savoury potatoes	*Pommes boulangère*	574
16	Shallow fried potatoes	*Pommes sautées à cru*	569
3	Snow potatoes	*Pommes à la neige*	564
13	Steamed potatoes	*Pommes vapeur*	569
14	Steamed jacket potatoes	*Pommes en robe de chambre*	569
21	Straw potatoes	*Pommes pailles*	571
19	Wafer potatoes	*Pommes gavfrettes*	570

Several named varieties of potatoes are grown in Britain and these will be available according to the season. The different varieties have differing characteristics and some are more suitable for certain methods of cooking than others; eg:

- *Maris Piper* Suitable for boiling, mashing, baking, roasting, frying.
- *Desirée, Wilja Cara* Excellent for chips.
- *King Edwards* Excellent for most purposes.

Potatoes are also imported from Cyprus, Egypt, Spain, France, Greece, Italy, the Canary Islands, The Netherlands and Belgium.

PURCHASING

Potatoes should be of even shape, free from dirt, blemishes (possible disease), green patches, mechanical damage and any growth shoots.

STORAGE

Store in paper sacks or on vegetable racks in a cool, dry dark, airy store. If kept near warmth they will start to turn green and sprout; if kept in damp conditions they will quickly deteriorate. These are signs that the potatoes are producing poisonous alkaloids which can be a potential health hazard.

FOOD VALUE

Potatoes are a source of vitamin C and they also contain iron, calcium, thiamin, nicotine acid, protein and fibre.

YIELD

$\frac{1}{2}$ kg (1 lb) old potatoes will yield approximately 3 portions. $\frac{1}{2}$ kg (1 lb) new potatoes will yield approximately 4 portions. $1\frac{1}{2}$ kg (3 lb) old potatoes will yield approximately 10 portions. $1\frac{1}{4}$ kg ($2\frac{1}{2}$ lb) new potatoes will yield approximately 10 portions.

READY PACKED

Potatoes are obtainable in many convenience forms: peeled, turned, cut into various shapes for frying, or scooped into balls (Parisienne) or olive shape.

Chips are available fresh, frozen, chilled or vacuum packed.

Frozen potatoes are available as croquettes, hash browns, sauté and roast. Mashed potato powder is also used.

1 – Plain boiled potatoes

1 Wash, peel and wash the potatoes.
2 Cut or turn into even-sized pieces allowing 2–3 pieces per portion.
3 Cook carefully in lightly salted water for approximately 20 minutes.
4 Drain well and serve.

> Using old potatoes, I portion provides:
>
> 487 kJ/116 kcal
> 0.1 g fat
> (of which 0.0 g saturated)
> 28.6 g carbohydrate
> (of which 0.6 g sugars)
> 2.0 g protein
> 1.5 g fibre

2 – Parsley potatoes

1 Prepare and cook the potatoes as for plain boiled.
2 Brush with melted butter and sprinkle with chopped parsley.

> Using 10 g butter per portion old potatoes, I portion provides:
>
> 798 kJ/190 kcal
> 8.3 g fat
> (of which 5.2 g saturated)
> 28.6 g carbohydrate
> (of which 0.6 g sugars)
> 2.1 g protein
> 1.5 g fibre

3 – Riced or snow potatoes

1 Wash, peel and rewash the potatoes. Cut to an even size.
2 Cook in lightly salted water or steam.
3 Drain off the water, cover and return to a low heat to dry out the potatoes.
4 Pass through a medium sieve or a special potato masher. Serve without further handling.

> Using old potatoes, I portion provides:
>
> 116 kJ/487 kcal
> 0.1 g fat
> (of which 0.0 g saturated)
> 28.6 g carbohydrate
> (of which 0.6 g sugars)
> 2.0 g protein
> 1.5 g fibre

4 – Mashed potatoes

1. Wash, peel and rewash the potatoes. Cut to an even size.
2. Cook in lightly salted water or steam.
3. Drain off the water, cover and return to a low heat to dry out the potatoes.
4. Pass through a medium sieve of a special potato masher.
5. Return the potatoes to a clean pan.
6. Add 25 g (1 oz) butter per ½ kg (1 lb) and mix in with a wooden spoon.
7. Gradually add warm milk 30 ml (⅛ pint) stirring continuously until a smooth creamy consistency is reached.
8. Correct the seasoning and serve.

> Using old potatoes, butter and whole milk, 1 portion provides:
>
> 763 kJ/182 kcal
> 7.1 g fat
> (of which 4.4 g saturated)
> 29.0 g carbohydrate
> (of which 1.1 g sugars)
> 2.4 g protein
> 1.5 g fibre

Note   Variations of mashed potatoes can be achieved by:

- dressing in a serving dish and surrounding with a cordon of fresh cream;
- placing in a serving dish, sprinkling with grated cheese, melted butter and browning under a salamander;
- adding 50 g (2 oz) diced cooked lean ham, 25 g (1 oz) diced red pepper and chopped parsley;
- adding chopped spring onions (this dish is known as champ);
- adding a good quality olive oil in place of butter.

Plate 13.1: Brioche (p. 567), marquis (p. 567) and duchess potatoes (p. 566)

5 — Duchess potatoes (basic recipe)

1 Wash, peel and rewash the potatoes. Cut to an even size.
2 Cook in lightly salted water.
3 Drain off the water, cover and return to a low heat to dry out the potatoes.
4 Pass through a medium sieve or a special potato masher or mouli.
5 Place the potatoes in a clean pan.
6 Add 1 egg yolk per $\frac{1}{2}$kg (1 lb) and stir in vigorously with a wooden spoon.
7 Mix in 25 g (1 oz) butter or margarine per $\frac{1}{2}$kg (1 lb). Correct the seasoning.
8 Place in a piping bag with a large star tube and pipe out into neat spirals about 2 cm (1 inch) diameter and 5 cm (2 inches) high on to a lightly greased baking sheet.
10 Place in a hot oven at 230°C (Reg. 8; 450°F) for 2–3 minutes in order to slightly firm the edges.
11 Remove from the oven and brush with eggwash.
12 Brown lightly in a hot oven or under the salamander.

> Using old potatoes, whole milk, hard margarine, I portion provides:
>
> 819 kJ/195 kcal
> 8.2 g fat
> (of which 3.3 g saturated)
> 28.6 g carbohydrate
> (of which 0.6 g sugars)
> 3.5 g protein
> 1.5 g fibre

6 — Croquette potatoes

1 Use a duchess mixture moulded cylinder shape 5 × 2 cm (2 × 1 inches).
2 Pass through flour, eggwash and breadcrumbs.
3 Reshape with a palette knife and deep fry in hot deep fat (185°C/365°F) in a frying-basket (see illustration p. 568).
4 When the potatoes are a golden colour, drain well and serve.

> Using hard margarine and frying in peanut oil, I portion provides:
>
> 1699 kJ/405 kcal
> 25.4 g fat
> (of which 6.6 g saturated)
> 40.8 g carbohydrate
> (of which 1.1 g sugars)
> 6.0 g protein
> 2.2 g fibre

7 — Potato cakes

Use a duchess mixture moulded into flat cakes, 3 cm (1$\frac{1}{2}$inches) diameter, 1 cm ($\frac{1}{2}$inch) thick. Shallow fry as for Macaire potatoes (recipe 26).

8 — Brioche potatoes

Use a duchess mixture in small brioche or cottage loaf shape, a 2 cm (1 inch) diameter ball with a ½ cm (½ inch) diameter ball on top pierced completely through with a small knife. Place in a hot oven to firm the surface. Brush with eggwash and brown lightly in a hot oven or under a salamander and serve.

(This dish is illustrated on page 565).

9 — Almond potatoes

Prepare and cook and serve as for croquette potatoes (recipe 6), using nibbed almonds in place of breadcrumbs.

10 —Marquis potatoes

1 Pipe duchess mixture in the shape of an oval nest, 5 × 2 cm (2 × 1 inches).
2 Cook and glaze as for duchess potatoes (recipe 5).
3 Place a spoonful of cooked tomato concassé (page 551) in the centre, sprinkle with a little chopped parsley and serve.

Using 200 g potato per portion, 1 portion provides:

643 kJ/153 kcal
0.2 g fat
(of which 0.0 g saturated)
36.5 g carbohydrate
(of which 0.8 g sugars)
3.8 g protein
3.6 g fibre

11 — Baked jacket potatoes

1 Select good-sized potatoes and allow one potato per portion.
2 Scrub well, make a 2 mm ($\frac{1}{12}$ inch) deep incision round the potato.
3 Place on a bed of salt on a tray in a hot oven at 230–250°C (Reg. 8–9; 450–500°F) for about 1 hour. Turn the potatoes over after 30 minutes.
4 Test by holding the potato in a cloth and squeezing gently; if cooked it should feel soft.

Note   If the potatoes are being cooked by microwave, prick the skins first.

12 – Baked jacket potatoes and cheese

	4 portions	10 portions
large potatoes	4	10
butter	75 g (3 oz)	180 g ($7\frac{1}{2}$ oz)
grated Parmesan	25 g (1 oz)	60 g ($2\frac{1}{2}$ oz)

1 Bake the potatoes as for recipe 11.
2 Cut the potatoes in halves, lengthwise.
3 Remove the potato from the skin using a spoon.
4 Place the potato in a basin.
5 Add 50 g (2 oz) butter, season lightly with salt and pepper.
6 Mix lightly with a fork.
7 Refill the potato skin with the mixture.
8 Place on a baking sheet.
9 Sprinkle with grated cheese and the remaining 25 g (1 oz) melted butter.
10 Place in the oven at 200°C (Reg. 6; 400°F) until golden brown and serve.

Note   Variations include: split and filled with cheese, baked beans, minced beef, chilli con carne, creamed cheese and chives, mushrooms, bacon, ratatouille, prawns in mayonnaise or coleslaw. Baked jacket potatoes are popular as snacks and may be accompanied by salads.

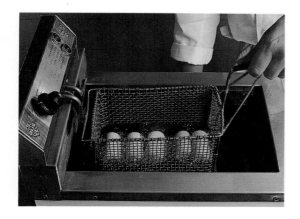

Plate 13.2: Deep frying croquette potatoes

13 ‒ Steamed potatoes

1 Prepare the potatoes as for plain boiled (recipe 1); season lightly with salt.
2 Cook in a steamer and serve.

Using old potatoes, 1 portion provides:

487 kJ/116 kcal
0.1 g fat
(of which 0.0 g saturated)
28.6 g carbohydrate
(of which 0.6 g sugars)
2.0 g protein
2.9 g fibre

14 ‒ Steamed jacket potatoes

1 Select small even-sized potatoes and scrub well.
2 Cook in a steamer or boil in lightly salted water and serve unpeeled.

Note This method is frequently used with small new potatoes.

Using old potatoes, 1 portion provides:

487 kJ/116 kcal
0.1 g fat
(of which 0.0 g saturated)
28.6 g carbohydrate
(of which 0.6 g sugars)
2.0 g protein
1.5 g fibre

15 ‒ Sauté potatoes

1 Select medium even-sized potatoes. Scrub well.
2 Plain boil or cook in the steamer. Cool slightly and peel.
3 Cut into 3 mm ($\frac{1}{8}$ inch) slices.
4 Toss in hot shallow fat in a frying-pan until lightly coloured; season lightly with salt.
5 Serve sprinkled with chopped parsley.

(See page 573 for an example of service of this dish.)

Using old potatoes and sunflower oil, 1 portion provides:

1249 kJ/297 kcal
11.4 g fat
(of which 1.3 g saturated)
46.8 g carbohydrate
(of which 0.4 g sugars)
4.9 g protein
1.7 g fibre

16 ‒ Shallow fried potatoes

1 Select medium sized potatoes, wash, peel and rewash.
2 Cut into 3 mm ($\frac{1}{8}$ inch) slices. Wash and dry.
3 Shallow fry in hot fat in a frying pan until cooked and lightly coloured.
4 Drain, season, toss lightly in butter or margarine.
5 Serve sprinkled with chopped parsley.

17 – Sauté potatoes with onions (illustrated on page 573)

1 Allow $\frac{1}{4}$ kg (8 oz) onion to $\frac{1}{2}$ kg (1 lb) potatoes.
2 Cook the onions as for fried onions (page 545).
3 Prepare sauté potatoes as for the previous recipe.
4 Combine the two and toss together.
5 Serve as for sauté potatoes.

18 – Crisps (game chips)

1 Wash, peel and rewash the potatoes.
2 Cut in thin slices on the mandolin.
3 Wash well and dry in a cloth.
4 Cook in hot deep fat (185°C/365°F) until golden brown and crisp.
5 Drain well and season lightly with salt.

Note   Crisps are not usually served as a potato by themselves, but are used as a garnish and are also served with drinks and for snacks.

> Using old potatoes and peanut oil, 1 portion (25 g) provides:
>
> 424 kJ/101 kcal
> 9.0 g fat
> (of which 1.7 g saturated)
> 4.9 g carbohydrate
> (of which 0.1 g sugars)
> 0.4 g protein
> 0.3 g fibre

19 – Wafer potatoes

1 Wash, peel and rewash the potatoes.
2 Using a corrugated mandolin blade, cut in slices, giving a half turn in between each cut in order to obtain a wafer or trellis pattern.
3 Cook and serve as for crisps.

20 – Matchstick potatoes

1 Select medium even-sized potatoes.
2 Wash, peel and rewash.
3 Trim on all sides to give straight edges.
4 Cut into slices 5 cm × 3 mm (2 × $\frac{1}{8}$ inch).
5 Cut the slices into 5 cm × 3 mm × 3 mm (2 × $\frac{1}{8}$ × $\frac{1}{8}$ inch) strips.
6 Wash well and dry in a cloth.

7 Fry in hot deep fat (185°C/365°F) until golden brown and crisp. Drain

8 Season lightly with salt and serve.

Note   These may also be blanched as for fried potatoes (recipe 22).

21 – Straw potatoes

1 Wash, peel and rewash the potatoes.

2 Cut into fine julienne.

3 Wash well and drain in a cloth.

4 Cook in hot deep fat (185°C/365°F) until golden brown and crisp.

5 Drain well and season lightly with salt.

Note   This potato is used as a garnish, usually for grills of meat.

> Using old potatoes and peanut oil, I portion (25 g) provides:
>
> 424 kJ/101 kcal
> 9.0 g fat
> (of which 1.7 g saturated)
> 4.9 g carbohydrate
> (of which 0.1 g sugars)
> 0.4 g protein
> 0.3 g fibre

22 – Fried or chipped potatoes

1 Prepare and wash the potatoes.

2 Cut into slices 1 cm (½ inch) thick and 5 cm (2 inches) long.

3 Cut the slices into strips 5 × 1 × 1 cm (2 × ½ × ½ inch).

4 Wash well and dry in a cloth.

5 Cook in a frying-basket without colour in moderately hot fat (165°C/330°F).

6 Drain and place on kitchen paper on trays until required.

7 When required, place in a frying-pan and cook in hot fat (185°C/365°F) until crisp and golden.

8 Drain well, season lightly with salt and serve.

> Using old potatoes and peanut oil, I portion provides:
>
> 1541 kJ/367 kcal
> 15.8 g fat
> (of which 2.8 g saturated)
> 54.1 g carbohydrate
> (of which 0.0 g sugars)
> 5.5 g protein
> 1.5 g fibre

Note   Because chips are so popular, the following advice from the Potato Marketing Board is useful:

● Cook chips in small quantities which will allow the oil to regain its temperature more quickly; the chips cook faster and absorb less fat.

recipe continued ▶

- Do not let the temperature of the oil exceed 199°C (390°F) as this will accelerate the fat breakdown.
- Use oils high in polyunsaturates for a healthier chip.
- Ideally use a separate fryer for chips and ensure that it has the capacity to raise the fat temperature rapidly to the correct degree when frying chilled or frozen chips.
- Although the majority of chipped potatoes are purchased frozen, the Board recommends the following potatoes for those who prefer to make their own chips:

  - Maris Piper
  - King Edward

  - Pentland Squire
  - Pentland Dell

  - Cara
  - Desirée

23 – Deep fried potato wedges in batter

This is a Potato Marketing Board recipe.

	4 portions	10 portions
medium sized potatoes, unpeeled, but well scrubbed	4	10
flour (self-raising) made into a batter (page 261)	200 g (8 oz)	500 g (20 oz)
grated peeled potato, washed and pressed dry	150 g (6 oz)	375 g (15 oz)

1 Cut each potato into 8 even-sized wedges.
2 Steam the wedges until cooked, but still firm.
3 Add the grated potato to the batter.
4 Dip the wedge into the batter and deep fry in hot fat or oil (185°C/365°F).

Note Potato wedges can be used as snacks, used with dips and served with main courses.

Plate 13.3a–b: Ingredients for and service of sauté potatoes with onions

24 – Fried diced potatoes

1 Select large even-sized potatoes.
2 Wash, peel and rewash.
3 Cut into 1 cm (½ inch) slices.
4 Cut the slices into 1 cm (½ inch) strips.
5 Cut the strips into 1 cm (½ inch) dice.
6 Wash and dry on a cloth.
7 Cook as for fried potatoes (recipe 22).

Plate 13.4: Deep fried potatoes: background, clockwise from left: fried, matchstick, croquette, bataille; foreground, left to right: straw, game chips, wafer

25 – Savoury potatoes

	4 portions	10 portions
potatoes	400 g (1 lb)	1¼ kg (2½ lb)
onions	100 g (4 oz)	250 g (10 oz)
salt, pepper		
white stock	¼ litre (½ pt)	600 ml (1¼ pt)
butter, margarine or oil	25–50 g (1–2 oz)	60–100 g (4–5 oz)
chopped parsley		

Using 25 g hard margarine, 1 portion provides:

595 kJ/142 kcal
5.3 g fat
(of which 2.2 g saturated)
22.3 g carbohydrate
(of which 1.8 g sugars)
2.8 g protein
2.4 g fibre

Using 50 g hard margarine, 1 portion provides:

787 kJ/187 kcal
10.3 g fat
(of which 4.4 g saturated)
22.3 g carbohydrate
(of which 1.8 g sugars)
2.8 g protein
2.4 g fibre

1   Cut the potatoes into 2 mm (½ inch) slices on a mandolin. Keep the best slices for the top.
2   Peel, halve and finely slice the onions.
3   Mix the onions and potatoes together and season lightly with pepper and salt.
4   Place in a well-buttered shallow earthenware dish or roasting tin.
5   Barely cover with stock.
6   Neatly arrange overlapping slices of potato on top.
7   Add a few knobs of butter or a little oil.
8   Place in a hot oven at 230–250°C (Reg. 8–9; 450–500°F) for 20 minutes until lightly coloured.
9   Reduce the heat and allow to cook steadily, pressing down firmly from time to time with a flat-bottomed pan.
10 When ready all the stock should be cooked into the potato. Allow 1½ hours cooking time in all.
11 Serve sprinkled with chopped parsley. If cooked in an earthenware dish, clean the edges of the dish with a cloth dipped in salt, and serve in the dish.

Note   Leeks can be used in place of onions for variety.

26 – Macaire potatoes (*potato cakes*)
(illustrated on page 577)

1 ½ kg (1 lb) will yield 2–3 portions.
2 Prepare and cook as for baked jacket potatoes (recipe 11).
3 Cut in halves, remove the centre with a spoon, and place in a basin.
4 Add 25 g (1 oz) butter per ½ kg (1 lb), a little salt and milled pepper.
5 Mash and mix as lightly as possible with a fork.
6 Using a little flour, mould into a roll, then divide into pieces, allowing one or two per portion.
7 Mould into 2 cm (1 inch) round cakes, flour lightly.
8 Shallow fry on both sides in very hot oil and serve.

> Using hard margarine and sunflower oil, this recipe provides:
>
> 4392 kJ/1047 kcal
> 65.7 g fat
> (of which 14.7 g saturated)
> 109.8 g carbohydrate
> (of which 2.7 g sugars)
> 11.4 g protein
> 10.8 g fibre

Note   Additions to potato cakes can include:

- chopped parsley or fresh herbs or chives;
- duxelle;
- cooked chopped onion;
- grated cheese.

27 – Byron potatoes

1 Prepare and cook as for Macaire potatoes.
2 Using the back of a dessertspoon make a shallow impression on each potato.
3 Carefully sprinkle the centres with grated cheese. Make sure no cheese is on the edge of the potato.
4 Cover the cheese with cream.
5 Brown lightly under the salamander and serve.

28 – Fondant potatoes

1 Select small or even-sized medium potatoes.
2 Wash, peel and rewash.
3 Turn into eight-sided barrel shapes, allowing 2–3 per portion, about 5 cm (2 inches) long, end diameter $1\frac{1}{2}$ cm ($\frac{3}{4}$ inch), centre diameter $2\frac{1}{2}$ cm ($1\frac{1}{4}$ inches).
4 Brush with melted butter, margarine or oil.
5 Place in a pan suitable for the oven.
6 Half cover with white stock, season with salt and pepper.
7 Cook in a hot oven at 230–250°C (Reg. 8–9; 450–500°F), brushing the potatoes frequently with melted butter, margarine or oil.
8 When cooked the stock should be completely absorbed by the potatoes.
9 Brush with melted butter, margarine or oil and serve.

Using old potatoes and hard margarine, 1 portion (125 g raw potato) provides:

956 kJ/228 kcal
7.0 g fat
(of which 2.1 g saturated)
39.6 g carbohydrate
(of which 0.9 g sugars)
4.1 g protein
1.5 g fibre

Note   Fondant potatoes can be lightly sprinkled with:

- thyme or rosemary or oregano;
- grated cheese (Gruyère and Parmesan or Cheddar).

29 – Roast potatoes

1 Wash, peel and rewash the potatoes.
2 Cut into even-sized pieces, allow 3–4 pieces per portion.
3 Heat a good measure of oil or dripping in a roasting tray.
4 Add the well-dried potatoes and lightly brown on all sides.
5 Season lightly with salt and cook for about 1 hour in a hot oven at 230–250°C (Reg. 8–9; 450–500°F).
6 Turn the potatoes over after 30 minutes.
7 Cook to a golden brown. Drain and serve.

Using old potatoes and peanut oil, 1 portion (125 g raw potato) provides:

956 kJ/228 kcal
7.0 g fat
(of which 1.1 g saturated)
39.6 g carbohydrate
(of which 0.9 g sugars)
4.1 g protein
1.5 g fibre

Note   Roast potatoes can be part-boiled for 10 minutes, refreshed and well dried before roasting. This will cut down on the cooking time and can also give a crisper potato.

Plate 13.5: Macaire potatoes

30 – Château potatoes

1 Select small even-sized potatoes and wash.
2 If they are of fairly even size, they need not be peeled, but can be turned into barrel-shaped pieces approximately the size of fondant potatoes.
3 Place in a saucepan of boiling water for 2–3 minutes, refresh immediately. Drain in a colander.
4 Finish as for roast potatoes (recipe 29).

31 – Rissolée potatoes

Proceed as for château potatoes, with the potatoes half the size. Cooked potatoes may also be used, in which case they are browned in shallow fat in a frying-pan.

32 – Cocotte potatoes

Proceed as for château potatoes, but with the potatoes a quarter the size, cooking them in a sauté pan or frying-pan.

33 – Noisette potatoes

$\frac{1}{2}$ kg (1 lb) will yield 2 portions.

1 Wash, peel and rewash the potatoes.
2 Scoop out balls with a noisette spoon.
3 Cook in a little fat in a sauté pan or frying-pan. Colour on top of the stove and finish cooking in the oven at 230–250°C (Reg. 8–9; 450–500°F).

34 ‒ Parisienne potatoes

1 Prepare and cook as for noisette potatoes.
2 Just before serving, for each ½ kg (1 lb) potatoes melt 1 tablespoon of meat glaze in a pan, add the cooked potatoes, roll them round so as to give a light overall coating and serve.

35 ‒ Potatoes with bacon and onions

	4 portions	10 portions
peeled potatoes	400 g (1 lb)	1¼ kg (2½ lb)
streaky bacon (lardons)	100 g (4 oz)	250 g (10 oz)
button onions	100 g (4 oz)	250 g (10 oz)
white stock	¼ litre (½ pt)	600 ml (1¼ pt)
salt and pepper		
chopped parsley		

Using old potatoes, I portion provides:

836 kJ/199 kcal
10.1 g fat
(of which 3.8 g saturated)
22.2 g carbohydrate
(of which 1.8 g sugars)
6.4 g protein
2.5 g fibre

1 Cut the potatoes in 1 cm (½ inch) dice.
2 Cut the bacon into ½ cm (¼ inch) lardons, lightly fry in a little fat together with the onions and brown lightly.
3 Add the potatoes, half cover with stock, season lightly with salt and pepper. Cover with a lid and cook steadily in the oven at 230–250°C (Reg. 8–9; 450–500°F) for approximately 30 minutes.
4 Correct the seasoning, serve in a vegetable dish and sprinkle with chopped parsley.

36 ‒ Delmonico potatoes

1 Wash, peel and rewash the potatoes.
2 Cut into 6 mm (¼ inch) dice.
3 Barely cover with milk, season lightly with salt and pepper and allow to cook for 30–40 minutes.
4 Place in an earthenware dish, sprinkle with crumbs and melted butter, brown in the oven or under the salamander and serve.

Using old potatoes, whole milk, I portion provides:

900 kJ/214 kcal
6.3 g fat
(of which 3.7 g saturated)
37.5 g carbohydrate
(of which 2.7 g sugars)
4.4 g protein
2.0 g fibre

37 – New potatoes

Method I

1 Wash the potatoes and boil or steam in their jackets until cooked.
2 Cool slightly, peel while warm and place in a pan of cold water.
3 When required for service add a little salt and a bunch of mint to the potatoes and heat through slowly.
4 Drain well, serve brushed with melted butter and sprinkle with chopped mint or decorate with blanched refreshed mint leaves.

> 1 portion provides:
>
> 383 kJ/91 kcal
> 0.1 g fat
> (of which 0.0 g saturated)
> 22.0 g carbohydrate
> (of which 0.8 g sugars)
> 1.9 g protein
> 2.4 g fibre

Method II

1 Scrape the potatoes and wash well.
2 Place in a pan of lightly salted boiling water with a bunch of mint and boil gently until cooked for about 20 minutes. Serve as above.

Note The starch cells of new potatoes are immature; to help break down these cells new potatoes are started to cook in boiling water.

38 – New rissolée potatoes

New potatoes are cooked, drained and fried to a golden brown in oil or butter.

> Using peanut oil, 1 portion provides:
>
> 610 kJ/145 kcal
> 6.1 g fat
> (of which 1.1 g saturated)
> 22.0 g carbohydrate
> (of which 0.8 g sugars)
> 1.9 g protein
> 2.4 g fibre

39 – Parmentier potatoes

$\frac{1}{2}$kg (1 lb) will yield 2–3 portions.

Using peanut oil, 1 portion provides:

1819 kJ/433 kcal
33.5 g fat
(of which 6.3 g saturated)
32.8 g carbohydrate
(of which 0.7 g sugars)
2.3 g protein
1.7 g fibre

1   Select medium to large size potatoes.
2   Wash, peel and rewash.
3   Trim on three sides and cut into 1 cm ($\frac{1}{2}$inch) slices.
4   Cut the slices into 1 cm ($\frac{1}{2}$inch) strips.
5   Cut the strips into 1 cm ($\frac{1}{2}$inch) dice.
6   Wash well and dry in a cloth.
7   Cook in hot shallow fat in a frying-pan until golden brown.
8   Drain, season lightly and serve sprinkled with chopped parsley.

14

PASTRY

Recipe No.   *page nos.*

Desserts

45	Almond sauce		623
57	Apple, baked	*Pommes bonne femme*	629
53	Apple charlotte	*Charlotte aux pommes*	627
54	Apple fritters	*Beignets aux pommes*	627
41	Apricot sauce	*Sauce abricot*	622
63	Avocado mousse		634
31	Baked Alaska	*Omelette soufflée surprise*	616
55	Banana fritters	*Beignets aux bananes*	628
7	Bavarois	*Bavarois*	599
3	Bread and butter pudding		595
38	Bread pudding		620
51	Butter cream		626
50	Butter cream, boiled		625
5	Cabinet pudding		597
49	Chocolate sauce	*Sauce au chocolat*	624
23	Christmas pudding		610
18	Cold lemon soufflé	*Soufflé milanaise*	607
67	Coupe Jacques	*Coupe Jacques*	636
6	Cream caramel	*Crème caramel*	598
19	Currant roll, steamed		608
44	Custard sauce		623
20	Dried fruit pudding, steamed		608
4	Egg custard, baked		596
15	Egg custard sauce, fresh	*Sauce à l'anglaise*	605
36	Empress rice	*Riz à l'impératrice*	619
58	Fresh fruit salad	*Salade de fruits*	629
60	Fruit, poached		631
59	Fruit fool		630
64	Fruit Melba		635
68	Glazed fruits		636
21	Golden syrup pudding		609
32	Jam omelet	*Omelette à la confiture*	617
40	Jam sauce		621
37	Junket		620
10	Lemon sorbet	*Sorbet au citron*	602
48	Melba sauce		624
27	Meringue	*Meringue*	614
29	Meringue with ice-cream	*Meringue glacée Chantilly*	615
28	Meringue with whipped cream	*Meringue Chantilly*	614
42	Orange, lemon or lime sauce		622
11	Orange sorbet	*Sorbet à l'orange*	603
26	Pancakes with apple	*Crêpes normandes*	613
25	Pancakes with jam	*Crêpes au confiture*	613
24	Pancakes with lemon or orange	*Crêpes au citron ou à l'orange*	611

582

16	Pastry cream	Crème patissière	605
66	Peach cardinal	Pêche cardinal	636
65	Pear Belle Hélène	Poire Belle Hélène	636
61	Pear condé	Poire condé	633
62	Pears in red wine	Poires au vin rouge	634
56	Pineapple fritters	Beignets aux ananas	628
52	Praline	Praline	626
1	Queen of puddings		594
8	Raspberry bavarois	Bavarois aux framboises	600
12	Raspberry sorbet	Sorbet à la framboise	603
34	Rice pudding		618
33	Rice pudding, baked		618
47	Rum or brandy butter		623
46	Rum or brandy cream		623
13	Sabayon sauce		604
14	Sabayon with Marsala	Zabaglione	604
35	Semolina pudding		619
17	Soufflé pudding, basic recipe	Soufflé	606
22	Sponge pudding, steamed, basic recipe		609
8	Strawberry bavarois	Bavarois aux fraises	600
43	Syrup sauce		622
21	Treacle pudding		609
2	Trifle		594
30	Vacherin with strawberries and cream		615
9	Vanilla ice-cream	Glace vanille	602
39	White chocolate mousse		621

Dough products

73	Bath buns		645
69	Bread rolls		642
70	Bun dough, basic recipe		643
74	Chelsea buns		645
76	Doughnuts		647
71	Fruit buns		644
72	Hot cross buns		645
81	Marignans Chantilly		650
77	Rum baba		647
79	Savarin paste (basic recipe)		649
80	Savarin with fruit		649
75	Swiss buns		645
78	Syrup for baba, savarin and marignans		648

Pastry dishes

98	Apple dumpling		674
93	Apple flan	Flan aux pommes	671
95	Apple meringue flan	Flan aux pommes meringuées	671
113	Apple turnover	Chausson aux pommes	683

101	Apricot flan	676
94	Apricot glaze	671
106	Banana flan	678
115	Bouchées	684
92	Cherry flan	670
122	Chocolate éclairs	689
87	Choux paste	666
127	Choux paste fritters with apricot sauce	691
123	Coffee éclairs	689
125	Cream buns	690
108	Cream horns	679
112	Cream slice (mille-feuilles)	682
99	Dutch apple tart	675
109	Eccles cakes	680
91	Flans	670
105	Fruit barquettes	678
88	Fruit pies	667
128	Fruit puddings, steamed	691
120	Fruit slice	687
104	Fruit tarts	678
117	Gâteau Pithiviers	686
116	Jalousie	685
111	Jam puffs	682
97	Jam roll, baked	674
129	Jam roll, steamed	691
89	Jam tart	668
110	Jam turnovers	680
121	Kiwi slice	688
96	Lemon meringue pie	673
118	Mince pies	686
107	Mincemeat tart	678
114	Palmiers	683
101	Plum flan	676
124	Profiteroles	689
126	Profiteroles with chocolate sauce	690
83	Puff pastry	662
115	Puff pastry cases (vol-au-vent)	684
103	Raspberry flan	677
100	Rhubarb flan	676
84	Rough puff pastry	664
119	Sausage rolls	687
82	Short pastry	661
102	Soft fruit flans	677
103	Strawberry flan	677
86	Suet paste	666
85	Sugar paste	665
90	Syrup tart	669

102	Tinned fruit flans	677
90	Treacle tart	669
115	Vol-au-vent	684

Cakes and biscuits

152	Almond biscuits	719
143	Bakewell tart	716
145	Cats' tongues (langues de chat)	718
141	Chocolate gâteau	712
140	Chocolate genoese	712
133	Christmas cake	708
142	Coffee gâteau	713
150	Cornets	718
148	Frangipane	717
132	Fruit cake, large	707
139	Genoese sponge	711
134	Marzipan (almond paste)	709
136	Mincemeat	710
151	Piped biscuits	719
137	Rock cakes	711
135	Royal icing	709
130	Scones	705
145	Shortbread biscuits	714
131	Small cakes, basic recipe	706
146	Sponge fingers	716
143	Stock syrup	713
144	Swiss roll	714
138	Victoria sandwich	711

Prepare and cook desserts

1. Ensure that preparation cooking areas and equipment are ready for use and satisfy health and hygiene regulations.
2. Plan the work and allocate your time appropriately to meet daily schedules.
3. Ensure that the ingredients are of the type, quality and quantity required.
4. Prepare and cook the ingredients according to customer and dish requirements.
5. Clean preparation and cooking areas and equipment after use.
6. Understand that finished desserts not for immediate consumption are stored in accordance with laid-down procedures.

Egg custard-based dessert

Egg custard mixture provides the chef with a versatile basic set of ingredients which cover a wide range of sweets. Often the mixture is referred to as crème renversée. Some examples of sweets produced from this mixture are:

- Cream caramel
- Bread and butter pudding
- Diplomat pudding
- Cabinet pudding
- Queen of puddings
- Crème beau rivage
- Baked egg custard

Savoury egg custard is used to make:

- Quiches
- Tartlettes
- Flans

When a starch such as flour is added to the ingredients for an egg custard mix, this changes the characteristic of the end product.

Pastry cream (also known as confectioner's custard) is a filling which is used for many sweets, gâteaux, flans, tartlettes and as a basis for soufflé mixes. *Sauce anglaise* is used as a base for some ice-creams. It is also used in its own right as a sauce to accompany a range of sweets.

Basic egg custard sets by coagulation of the egg protein. Egg white coagulates at approximately 60°C (140°F), egg yolks at 70°C (158°F). Whites and yolks mixed will give a coagulation at 66°C (151°F). If the egg protein is overheated or overcooked, it will shrink and water will be lost from the mixture causing undesirable bubbles in the custard. This loss of water is called syneresis.

INGREDIENTS FOR EGG CUSTARDS

Eggs

Eggs have a high nutritional value. The egg yolks contain a phospholipid called lecithin which acts as an emulsifier. An emulsifier is a substance which will hold fat and water together.

Milk

Full cream, skimmed or semi-skimmed can be used for these desserts.

Cream

Cream is often added to egg custard desserts to enrich and to improve the oral 'feel' of the final product. Fat contents of various types are listed in the table on page 655.

Whipping and double cream may be whipped to make them lighter and to increase volume.

All cream products must be kept in the refrigerator for health and safety reasons, but also cream will whip easier if it is kept at refrigeration temperature. All dairy products must be kept in the refrigerator as these present the perfect medium for the growth of micro-organisms. Handle these products with care and remember that they will also absorb odour. Never store near onions or other strong-smelling foods.

Traditional custard made from custard powder

Custard powder is used to make custard sauce. Custard powder is made from vanilla-flavoured cornflour with yellow colouring and is a substitute for eggs.

ICE-CREAM

Traditional ice-cream is made from a basic egg custard sauce. The sauce is cooled and mixed with fresh cream. It is then frozen by a rotating machine where the water content forms ice crystals.

Ice-cream should be served at −5°C to −6°C (21°F–23°F). This is the correct eating temperature, otherwise it is too hard. Long-term storage should be at −18°C to −20°C (−0.4°F to −4°F).

The manufacture of ice-cream is governed by the Food and Drugs Act 1962 and the Food Standard Regulations 1970.

MERINGUES

Egg white forms a foam which is used for aerating sweets and many other desserts.

POINTS TO REMEMBER

Egg custard-based desserts

- Always work in a clean and tidy way, complying with food hygiene regulations.
- Prevent cross-contamination occurring by not allowing any foreign substances to come into contact with the mixture.
- Always heat the egg yolks or egg to 70°C otherwise use pasteurised egg yolks or eggs.
- Follow the recipe carefully.
- Ensure that all heating and cooling temperatures are followed.
- Always store the end-product carefully at the right temperature.
- Check all weighing scales.
- Check all raw materials for correct use by dates.
- Always wash your hands when handling fresh eggs or dairy products and other pastry ingredients.
- Never use cream to decorate a product that is still warm.
- Always remember to follow the Food Hygiene (Amendments) Regulations 1993.
- *Check at all times the temperature of the refrigerators and freezers* that they comply with the current regulations.

Fresh cream

- Piping is a skill; like all other skills it takes practice to become proficient. The finished item should look attractive, the piping being neat, simple, clean and tidy.
- All piping bags should be sterilised after each use as these may well be a source of contamination.
- Make sure that all the equipment you need for this operation is hygienically cleaned before and after use to avoid cross-contamination.

Egg whites

- To avert danger of salmonella, if the egg white is not going to be cooked or will not reach a temperature of 70°C (158°F), use pasteurised egg whites. Egg white is available chilled, frozen or dried.
- Equipment must be scrupulously clean, free from any traces of fat as these prevent the whites from whipping. Fat or grease presents the albumen strands from bonding and trapping the air bubbles.

- Take care that there are no traces of yolk in the white, as yolk contains fat.
- A little acid (cream of tartar or lemon juice) strengthens the egg white, extends the foam and produces more meringue. The acid also has the effect of stabilising the meringue.
- If the foam is overwhipped, the albumen strands, which hold the water molecules with the sugar suspended on the outside of the bubble, are overstretched. The water and sugar make contact and the sugar dissolves making the meringue heavy and wet. This sometimes can be rescued by further whisking until it foams up but very often you will find that you may have to discard the mixture and start again.

—— *Fruit dishes* ——

For culinary purposes fruit can be divided into the following groups:

STONE FRUITS	HARD FRUITS	SOFT FRUITS	CITRUS FRUITS	TROPICAL/ MEDITERRANEAN FRUITS	OTHER FRUITS
apricots	apples	bilberries	clementines	bananas	cranberries
cherries	crab apples	blackberries	grapefruit	cape gooseberries	grapes
damsons	pears	blackcurrants	kumquats	carambola	melons
greengages		blueberries	lemons	dates	rhubarb
nectarines		gooseberries	limes	figs	
peaches		loganberries	mandarins	granadillas	
plums		raspberries	oranges	guavas	
		redcurrants	pomeloes	kiwi fruit	
		strawberries	tangerines	lychees	
			tangelos	mangosteens	
			(uglis)	mangoes	
				passion fruit	
				papayas	
				pawpaws	
				persimmons	
				pineapples	
				sharon fruits	

SEASONS

The chief citrus fruits (oranges, lemons and grapefruit) are available all the year round. Mandarins, clementines, satsumas and tangerines are available in the winter.

Rhubarb is in season in the spring, and the soft and stone fruits become available from June in the following order: gooseberries, strawberries, raspberries, cherries, currants, damsons, plums.

Imported apples and pears are available all the year round; home-grown mainly from August to April. Many varieties of fruits are imported from all over the world and speedy air transport cargo services enable some fruits such as strawberries to be in season virtually the whole year round.

QUALITY REQUIREMENTS AND PURCHASING POINTS

Fresh fruit should be:

- whole and of fresh appearance (for maximum flavour the fruit must be ripe but not overripe);
- firm according to the type and variety;
- clean, free from traces of pesticides and fungicides;
- free from external moisture;
- free from an unpleasant foreign smell or taste;
- free from pests or disease;
- sufficiently mature; it must be capable of being handled and travelling without damage;
- free of any defects characteristic of the variety in shape, size and colour;
- free of bruising and any other damage due to weather conditions.

Soft fruits deteriorate quickly, especially if not sound. Care must be taken to see that they are not damaged or over-ripe when purchased. Soft fruits should look fresh; there should be no signs of wilting, shrinking or mould. The colour of certain soft fruits is an indication of ripeness (the pinkness of strawberries or dessert gooseberries).

FOOD VALUE

The nutritive value of fruit depends on its vitamin content, especially vitamin C; it is therefore valuable as a protective food. The cellulose of fruit is useful as roughage.

STORAGE

Hard fruits, such as apples, are left in boxes and kept in a cool store.

Soft fruits, such as raspberries and strawberries, should be left in their punnets or baskets in a cold room.

Stone fruits are best placed in trays so that any damaged fruit can be seen and discarded.

Peaches and citrus fruits are left in their delivery trays or boxes.

Bananas should not be stored in too cold a place because the skins turn black.

USES

With the exception of certain fruits (lemon, rhubarb, cranberries), fruit can be eaten as a dessert or in its raw state. Some fruits have dessert and cooking varieties (apples, pears, cherries and gooseberries).

Stone fruits

Damsons, plums, greengages, cherries, apricots, peaches and nectarines are used as a dessert; stewed (compote) for jam, pies, puddings and in various sweet dishes. Peaches are also used to garnish certain meat dishes.

Hard fruits

Apples: the popular English dessert varieties include Beauty of Bath, Discovery, Spartan, Worcester Pearmain, Cox's Orange Pippin, Blenheim Orange, Laxton's Superb and James Grieve. Imported applies include Golden Delicious, Granny Smith, McIntosh, Starking, Sturmers, Red Delicious and Yellow Delicious. The Bramley is the most popular cooking apple.

Pears: the William, Conference and Doyenne du Comice are among the best known pears.

Apples and pears are used in many pastry dishes. Apples are also used for garnishing meat dishes and for sauce which is served with roast pork and duck.

Soft fruits

Raspberries, strawberries, loganberries and gooseberries are used as a dessert. Gooseberries, black and red currants and blackberries are stewed, used in pies and puddings. They are used for jam and flavourings.

Citrus fruits

Oranges, lemons and grapefruit are not usually cooked, except for marmalade. Lemons and limes are used for flavouring and garnishing, particularly fish dishes. Oranges are used mainly for flavouring, and in fruit salads, also to garnish certain poultry dishes. Grapefruit are served at breakfast and as a first course generally for luncheon. Mandarins, clementines and satsumas are eaten as a dessert or used in sweet dishes. Kumquats look and taste like tiny oranges and are eaten with the skin on. Tangelos are a cross between tangerines and grapefruit, and are sometimes called uglis. Pomelos are the largest of the citrus fruits, predominantly round but with a slightly flattened base and pointed top.

Tropical and other fruits

- Bananas: as well as being used as a dessert, bananas are grilled for a fish garnish, fried as fritters and served as a garnish to poultry, they are used in fruit salad and other sweet dishes.
- Cape gooseberries: a sharp, pleasant-flavoured small round fruit dipped in fondant and served as a type of sweetmeat.
- Carambola: also known as starfruit, has a yellowish-green skin with a waxy sheen; the fruit is long and narrow and has a delicate lemon flavour.
- Cranberries: these hard red berries are used for cranberry sauce, which is served with roast turkey.
- Dates: whole dates are served as a dessert; stoned dates are used in various sweet dishes and petits fours.
- Figs: fresh figs may be served as a first course or dessert; dried figs may be used for fig puddings, and other sweet dishes.
- Granadillos: these are like an orange in shape and colour, are light in weight and similar to a passion fruit in flavour.
- Grapes: black and white grapes are used as a dessert, in fruit salad, as a sweet meat and also as a fish garnish.
- Guavas: size varies between that of a walnut to an apple; ripe guavas have a sweet pink flesh; they can be eaten with cream or mixed with other fruits.
- Kiwi fruit: have a brown furry skin; the flesh is green with edible black seeds which when thinly sliced gives a pleasant decorative appearance.
- Lychees: a Chinese fruit with a delicate flavour; obtainable tinned in syrup and also fresh.
- Mangoes: can be as large as a melon or as small as an apple; ripe mangoes have smooth pinky-golden flesh with a pleasing flavour; they may be served in

halves sprinkled with lemon juice, sugar, rum, or ginger; mangoes can also be used in fruit salads and for sorbets.

- Mangostines: are apple-shaped with a tough reddish-brown skin which turns purple as the fruit ripens; they have juicy creamy flesh.
- Passion fruit: the name comes from the flower of the plant which is meant to represent the Passion of Christ; size and shape of an egg with crinkled purple-brown skin when ripe; flesh and seeds are all edible.
- Pawpaw (papaya): green to golden skin, orangey flesh with a sweet subtle flavour and black seeds; eaten raw sprinkled with lime or lemon juice.
- Persimmon: a round orange-red fruit with a tough skin which can be cut when the fruit is ripe; when under-ripe they have an unpleasant acid-like taste of tannin.
- Pineapple: served as a dessert; it is also used in many sweet dishes and as a garnish to certain meat dishes.
- Sharon fruit: a seedless persimmon tasting like a sweet exotic peach.
- Rhubarb: forced or early rhubarb is obtainable from January; the natural rhubarb from April–June.

Melon

There are several types of melon. The most popular are:

- Honeydew: these are long, oval-shaped melons with dark green skins; the flesh is white with a greenish tinge.
- Charentais: small and round with a mottled green and yellow skin; the flesh is orange coloured.
- Cantaloup: large round melons with regular indentations; the rough skin is mottled orange and yellow and the flesh is light orange in colour.
- Ogen: small round mottled green skins suitable for one portion (depending on size); mainly used as a dessert, for hors-d'oeuvre and sweet dishes.

Care must be taken when buying as melons should not be over- or under-ripe. This can be assessed by carefully pressing the top or bottom of the fruit. There should be a slight degree of softness to the cantaloup and charentais melons. The stalk should be attached, otherwise the melon deteriorates quickly.

Egg custard-based dessert recipes

1 ~ Queen of puddings

	4 portions	10 portions
milk, whole or skimmed	$\frac{1}{2}$ litre (1 pt)	$1\frac{1}{4}$ litre ($2\frac{1}{2}$ pt)
eggs	3	8
castor or unrefined sugar	50 g (2 oz)	125 g (5 oz)
vanilla essence		
cake or breadcrumbs	75 g (3 oz)	180 g ($7\frac{1}{2}$ oz)
butter or margarine	25 g (1 oz)	60 g ($2\frac{1}{2}$ oz)
castor sugar for meringue	50 g (2 oz)	125 g (5 oz)
jam	50 g (2 oz)	125 g (5 oz)

I portion provides:

1522 kJ/362 kcal
14.7 g fat
(of which 6.8 g saturated)
50.0 g carbohydrate
(of which 41.2 g sugars)
10.9 g protein
0.9 g fibre

1 Boil the milk.
2 Pour on to 2 yolks, 1 egg (5 yolks, 2 eggs for 10 portions), sugar and vanilla essence, whisk well.
3 Place the crumbs in a buttered pie dish.
4 Strain the custard on to the crumbs.
5 Bake in a moderate oven in a bain-marie for 30 minutes or until set.
6 Allow to cool.
7 Stiffly beat the egg whites; fold in the castor sugar.
8 Spread the warmed jam over the baked mixture.
9 Using a large star tube, pipe the meringue to cover the jam.
10 Brown in a hot oven at 220°C (Reg. 7; 425°F) and serve.

2 ~ Trifle

	6–8 portions
sponge (3 eggs)	1
jam	25 g (1 oz)
tin fruit (pears, peaches, pineapple)	1
Custard	
custard powder	35 g ($1\frac{1}{2}$ oz)
milk, whole or skimmed	375 ml ($\frac{3}{4}$ pt)
castor sugar	50 g (2 oz)

Using whole milk and whipping cream, I portion provides:

2280 kJ/543 kcal
29.1 g fat
(of which 17.1 g saturated)
66.2 g carbohydrate
(of which 51.3 g sugars)
8.2 g protein
1.9 g fibre

cream (¾ whipped) or non-dairy cream	125 ml (¼ pt)
whipped sweetened cream or non-dairy cream	¼ litre (½ pt)
angelica	25 g (1 oz)
glacé cherries	25 g (1 oz)

1 Cut the sponge in half, sideways, and spread with jam.
2 Place in a glass bowl and soak with fruit syrup; a few drops of sherry may be added.
3 Cut the fruit into small pieces and add to the sponge.
4 Dilute the custard powder in a basin with some of the milk, add the sugar.
5 Boil the remainder of the milk, pour a little on the custard powder, mix well, return to the saucepan and over a low heat stir to the boil. Allow to cool, stirring occasionally to prevent a skin forming; fold in the three-quarters whipped 125 ml (¼ pint) cream.
6 Pour on to the sponge. Leave to cool.
7 Decorate with whipped cream, angelica and cherries.

Note Other flavourings or liqueurs may be used in place of sherry: whisky, rum, brandy, Tia Maria.

3 ~ Bread and butter pudding (illustrated on page 596)

	4 portions	10 portions
sultanas	25 g (1 oz)	60 g (2½ oz)
slices of white or wholemeal bread, spread with butter or margarine	2	5
eggs	3	7
sugar, castor or unrefined	50 g (2 oz)	125 g (5 oz)
vanilla essence or a vanilla pod	2–3 drops	5 drops
milk, whole or skimmed	½ litre (1 pt)	1¼ (2½ pt)

> Using white bread and butter, 1 portion provides:
>
> 1093 kJ/260 kcal
> 11.6 g fat
> (of which 5.9 g saturated)
> 30.4 g carbohydrate
> (of which 23.4 g sugars)
> 10.6 g protein
> 1.0 g fibre

1 Wash the sultanas and place in a pie dish.
2 Remove the crusts from the bread and cut each slice into four triangles, neatly arrange overlapping in the pie dish.
3 Prepare an egg custard as in recipe 4.
4 Strain on to the bread, dust lightly with sugar.
5 Cook and serve as for baked egg custard.

Plate 14.1: Bread and butter pudding

4 ‒ Baked egg custard

	4 portions	10 portions
small eggs	3	7
sugar, castor or unrefined	50 g (2 oz)	125 g (5 oz)
vanilla essence	2–3 drops	5 drops
milk, whole or skimmed	½ litre (1 pt)	1¼ litre (2½ pt)
grated nutmeg		

Using whole milk, 1 portion provides:

780 kJ/186 kcal
8.4 g fat
(of which 4.3 g saturated)
19.0 g carbohydrate
(of which 19.0 g sugars)
8.7 g protein
0.0 g fibre

1   Whisk the eggs, sugar and essence.

2 Pour on the warmed milk, whisking continuously.
3 Pass through a fine strainer into a pie dish.
4 Add a little grated nutmeg. Wipe the edge of the pie dish clean.
5 Stand in a roasting tray half full of water and cook slowly in a moderate oven at 160°C (Reg. 3; 325°F) for 45 minutes to 1 hour.
6 Clean the edges of the pie dish and serve.

5 – Cabinet pudding

	4 portions	10 portions
plain sponge cake	100 g (4 oz)	250 g (10 oz)
glacé cherries	25 g (1 oz)	60 g (2½ oz)
currants and sultanas	25 g (1 oz)	60 g (2½ oz)
angelica	10 g (½ oz)	25 g (1¼ oz)
milk, whole or skimmed	½ litre (1 pt)	1¼ litres (2½ pt)
eggs	3–4	8–10
castor or unrefined sugar	50 g (2 oz)	125 g (5 oz)
vanilla essence or a vanilla pod	2–3 drops	7 drops

Using whole milk and 3 eggs, 1 portion provides:

1427 kJ/340 kcal
15.8 g fat
(of which 7.2 g saturated)
40.9 g carbohydrate
(of which 35.5 g sugars)
11.0 g protein
0.7 g fibre

Using whole milk and 4 eggs, 1 portion provides:

1512 kJ/360 kcal
17.3 g fat
(of which 7.7 g saturated)
40.9 g carbohydrate
(of which 35.5 g sugars)
12.7 g protein
0.7 g fibre

1 Cut the cake into ½ cm (¼ inch) dice.
2 Mix with the chopped cherries and fruits (which can be soaked in rum).
3 Place in a greased, sugared charlotte mould or four dariole moulds. Do not fill more than half-way.
4 Warm the milk and whisk on to the eggs, sugar and essence (or vanilla pod).
5 Strain on to the mould.
6 Place in a roasting tin, half full of water; allow to stand for 5–10 minutes.
7 Cook in a moderate oven at 150–160°C (Reg. 2–3; 300–325°F) for 30–45 minutes.
8 Leave to set for a few minutes before turning out.
9 Serve a fresh egg custard or hot apricot sauce separately.

Note Diplomat pudding is made as for cabinet pudding, but served cold with redcurrant, raspberry, apricot or vanilla sauce.

6 — **Cream caramel** (illustrated on page 601)

	6 portions	10 portions
sugar, granulated or cube	100 g (4 oz)	200 g (8 oz)
water	125 ml (¼ pt)	250 ml (½ pt)
milk, whole or skimmed	½ litre (1 pt)	1 litre (2 pt)
eggs	4	8
sugar, castor or unrefined	50 g (2 oz)	100 g (4 oz)
vanilla essence or a vanilla pod	3–4 drops	6–8 drops

> Using whole milk, I portion provides:
>
> 868 kJ/207 kcal
> 7.2 g fat
> (of which 3.3 g saturated)
> 30.2 g carbohydrate
> (of which 30.2 g sugars)
> 7.3 g protein
> 0.0 g fibre

1 Prepare the caramel by placing three-quarters of the water in a thick-based pan, adding the sugar and allowing to boil gently, without shaking or stirring the pan.
2 When the sugar has cooked to a golden brown caramel colour, add the remaining quarter of the water, reboil until the sugar and water mix, then pour into the bottom of six dariole moulds.
3 Prepare the cream by warming the milk and whisking on to the beaten eggs, sugar and essence (or vanilla pod).
4 Strain and pour into the prepared moulds.
5 Place in a roasting tin half full of water.
6 Cook in a moderate oven at 150–160°C (Reg. 2–3; 300–325°F) for 30–40 minutes.
7 When thoroughly cold, loosen the edges of the cream caramel with the fingers, shake firmly to loosen and turn out on to a flat dish or plates.
8 Pour any caramel remaining in the mould around the creams.

Note Cream caramels may be served with whipped cream or a fruit sauce such as passion fruit.

7 – Bavarois (basic recipe)

	6–8 portions
gelatine	10 g ($\frac{1}{2}$ oz)
eggs, separated	2
castor sugar	50 g (2 oz)
milk, whole or skimmed	$\frac{1}{4}$ litre ($\frac{1}{2}$ pt)
whipping or double cream or non-dairy cream	125 ml ($\frac{1}{4}$ pt)

> Using whole milk and whipping cream, 1 portion provides:
>
> 970 kJ/231 kcal
> 18.2 g fat
> (of which 10.9 g saturated)
> 11.8 g carbohydrate
> (of which 11.8 g sugars)
> 5.8 g protein
> 0.0 g fibre

1   If using leaf gelatine, soak in cold water.
2   Cream the yolks and sugar in a bowl until almost white.
3   Whisk on the milk which has been brought to the boil; mix well.
4   Clean the milk saucepan which should be a thick based one, and return the mixture to it.
5   Return to a low heat and stir continuously with a wooden spoon until the mixture coats the back of the spoon. The mixture must not boil.
6   Remove from the heat; add the gelatine and stir until dissolved.
7   Pass through a fine strainer into a clean bowl, leave in a cool place, stirring occasionally until almost setting point.
8   Fold in the lightly beaten cream.
9   Fold in the stiffly beaten whites.
10 Pour the mixture into a mould (may be very lightly greased with oil).
11 Allow to set in the refrigerator.
12 Shake and turn out on to a flat dish.

Note   Bavarois may be decorated with sweetened, flavoured whipped cream. Variations include:

- *Chocolate bavarois* Dissolve 50 g (2 oz) chocolate couverture in the milk. Decorate with whipped cream and grated chocolate.
- *Coffee bavarois* Proceed as for bavarois with the addition of coffee essence to taste.
- *Lemon bavarois* As orange bavarois using lemons in place of oranges.
- *Lime bavarois* As orange bavarois using limes in place of oranges.
- *Orange bavarois* Add grated zest and juice of 2 oranges and 1 or 2 drops orange colour to the mixture, and increase the gelatine by 2 leaves. Decorate with blanched, fine julienne of orange zest, orange segments and whipped cream.

recipe continued ▶

- *Vanilla bavarois* Add a vanilla pod or a few drops of vanilla essence to the milk. Decorate with vanilla-flavoured cream.

Plate 14.2: Orange bavarois

8 – Strawberry or raspberry bavarois

	4 portions	10 portions
fruit (picked, washed and sieved)	200 g ($\frac{1}{2}$ lb)	500 g (1$\frac{1}{4}$ lb)
eggs	2	5
gelatine	10 g ($\frac{1}{2}$ oz)	25 g (1$\frac{1}{4}$ oz)
milk, whole or skimmed	180 ml ($\frac{3}{8}$ pt)	500 ml (1 pt)
sugar, castor or unrefined	50 g (2 oz)	125 g (5 oz)
whipping or double cream or non-dairy cream	125 ml ($\frac{1}{4}$ pt)	300 ml ($\frac{5}{8}$ pt)

Prepare as for the basic recipe (recipe 7). When the custard is almost cool add the fruit purée. Decorate with whole fruit and whipped cream.

Plate 14.3: Cream caramels (with copper sugar boiler and dariole moulds)

—— *Ice-creams and sorbets* ——

The Ice-Cream Regulations 1959 and 1963 require ice-cream to be pasteurised by heating to:

- 65°C (150°F) for 30 minutes or
- 71°C (160°F) for 10 minutes or
- 80°C (175°F) for 15 seconds or
- 149°C (300°F) for 2 seconds (sterilised).

After heat treatment the mixture is reduced to 7.1°C (45°F) within 1½ hours and kept at this temperature until the freezing process begins. Ice-cream needs this treatment so as to kill harmful bacteria. Freezing without correct heat treatment does not kill bacteria, it allows them to remain dormant. The storage temperature for ice-cream should not exceed −2°C. All establishments making ice-cream for sale must be licensed by the local authority Environmental Health Officer.

9 ~ Vanilla ice-cream

	8–10 portions
egg yolks	4
castor or unrefined sugar	100 g (4 oz)
vanilla pod or essence	
milk, whole or skimmed	375 ml ($\frac{3}{4}$ pt)
cream or non-dairy cream	125 ml ($\frac{1}{4}$ pt)

Using whole milk and single cream, I portion provides:

616 kJ/147 kcal
8.1 g fat
(of which 4.2 g saturated)
15.8 g carbohydrate
(of which 15.8 g sugars)
3.5 g protein
0.0 g fibre

1 Whisk the yolks and sugar in a bowl until almost white.
2 Boil the milk with the vanilla pod or essence in a thick-based pan.
3 Whisk on to the eggs and sugar; mix well.
4 Return to the cleaned saucepan, place on a low heat.
5 Stir continuously with a wooden spoon until the mixture coats the back of the spoon.
6 Pass through a fine strainer into a bowl.
7 Freeze in an ice-cream machine, gradually adding the cream.

Note Variations include:

- *Coffee ice-cream* Add coffee essence to taste to the custard after it is cooked.
- *Chocolate ice-cream* Add 50–100 g (2–4 oz) of chopped couverture to the milk before boiling.
- *Strawberry ice-cream* Add 125 ml ($\frac{1}{4}$ pint) of strawberry pulp in place of 125 ml ($\frac{1}{4}$ pint) of milk. The pulp is added after the custard is cooked.
- *Mixed ice-cream* Balls or spoonfuls of two or more flavoured ice-creams served in individual coupes.

10 ~ Lemon sorbet

	8–10 portions
sugar	200 g (8 oz)
water	$\frac{1}{2}$ litre (1 pt)
lemons	2
egg white	1

I portion provides:

421 kJ/100 kcal
0.0 g fat
(of which 0.0 g saturated)
26.3 g carbohydrate
(of which 26.3 g sugars)
0.4 g protein
0.0 g fibre

1 Bring the sugar, water and peeled zest of lemons to the boil.

2 Remove from the heat and cool. The saccarometer reading for the syrup should be 18–20° baumé.
3 Add the juice of the lemon.
4 Add the white and mix well.
5 Pass through a fine strainer and freeze.

11 – Orange sorbet

sugar	200 g (8 oz)
water	½ litre (1 pt)
large oranges	2
lemon	1
egg white	1

Prepare and freeze as for lemon ice, 18–20° baumé.

12 – Raspberry sorbet

sugar	200 g (8 oz)
water	375 ml (¾ pt)
lemon	1
raspberry purée	125 ml (¼ pt)
egg white	1

Prepare and freeze as for lemon ice, 18–20° baumé.

—— *Egg-based sauces and creams* ——

13 – Sabayon sauce

8 portions

egg yolks	
castor or unrefined sugar	100 g (4 oz)
dry white wine	$\frac{1}{4}$ litre ($\frac{1}{2}$ pt)

1. Whisk the egg yolks and sugar in a 1 litre (2 pint) pan or basin until white.
2. Dilute with the wine.
3. Place the pan or basin in a bain-marie of warm water.
4. Whisk the mixture continuously until it increases to four times its bulk and is firm and frothy.

Note   Sauce sabayon may be offered as an accompaniment to any suitable hot sweet (pudding soufflé).

A sauce sabayon may also be made using milk in place of wine which can be flavoured according to taste: vanilla, nutmeg, cinnamon.

14 – Sabayon with Marsala (Zabaglione)

	4 portions	10 portions
egg yolks	8	20
castor or unrefined sugar	200 g (8 oz)	500 g ($1\frac{1}{4}$ lb)
Marsala	150 ml ($\frac{1}{3}$ pt)	375 ml ($\frac{3}{4}$ pt)

1. Whisk the egg yolks and sugar in a bowl until almost white.
2. Mix in the Marsala.
3. Place the bowl and contents in a bain-marie of warm water.
4. Whisk mixture continuously until it increases to four times its bulk and is firm and frothy.
5. Pour the mixture into glass goblets.
6. Accompany with a suitable biscuit, e.g. sponge fingers.

15 – Fresh egg custard sauce

	4 portions	10 portions
egg yolks (4 if using skimmed milk)	2	5
castor or unrefined sugar	25 g (1 oz)	60 g (2½ oz)
vanilla essence or vanilla pod	2–3 drops	5–7 drops
milk, whole or skimmed	250 ml (½ pt)	625 ml (1¼ pt)

> Using whole milk, four portions provides:
>
> 1666 kJ/397 kcal
> 21.7 g fat
> (of which 9.9 g saturated)
> 38.0 g carbohydrate
> (of which 38.0 g sugars)
> 14.7 g protein
> 0.0 g fibre

1　Mix the yolks, sugar and essence in a basin.
2　Whisk on the boiled milk and return to a thick-bottomed pan.
3　Place on a low heat and stir with a wooden spoon until it coats the back of the spoon. Do *not* allow to boil or the eggs will scramble.

Note　Other flavours may be used in place of vanilla:

- coffee
- chocolate
- rum
- brandy

- Curaçao
- Cointreau
- Tia Maria
- whisky.

16 – Pastry cream

eggs	2
castor or unrefined sugar	100 g (4 oz)
flour, white or wholemeal	50 g (2 oz)
custard powder	10 g (½ oz)
milk, whole or skimmed	½ litre (1 pt)
vanilla pod or essence	

> Using white flour and whole milk, this recipe provides:
>
> 4564 kJ/1087 kcal
> 31.7 g fat
> (of which 16.0 g saturated)
> 176.6 g carbohydrate
> (of which 129.3 g sugars)
> 34.8 g protein
> 2.1 g fibre

1　Whisk the eggs and sugar in a bowl until almost white.
2　Mix in the flour and custard powder.
3　Boil the milk in a thick-based pan.
4　Whisk on to the eggs, sugar and flour and mix well.
5　Return to the cleaned pan, stir to the boil.
6　Add a few drops of vanilla essence or a vanilla pod.

recipe continued ▶

7 Remove from the heat and pour into a basin.

8 Sprinkle the top with a little castor or icing sugar to prevent a skin forming.

Note Pastry cream may be varied with other flavours:

- rum
- brandy
- Tia Maria
- lime

- whisky
- orange
- lemon
- praline

- strawberry
- passion fruit
- almond
- Calvados.

Other variations include:

- *Chocolate pastry cream* Dissolve 100 g (4 oz) of couverture or 50 g (2 oz) cocoa powder in the milk and proceed as above.
- *Coffee pastry cream* Add coffee essence to taste and proceed as above.

—— *Soufflé puddings* ——

17 – Soufflé pudding (basic recipe)

	6 portions	10 portions
milk, whole or skimmed	185 ml ($\frac{3}{8}$ pt)	375 ml ($\frac{3}{4}$ pt)
flour, white or wholemeal	25 g (1 oz)	50 g (2 oz)
butter or margarine	25 g (1 oz)	50 g (2 oz)
castor or unrefined sugar	25 g (1 oz)	50 g (2 oz)
eggs, separated	3	6

Using white flour and hard margarine, 1 portion provides:

510 kJ/122 kcal
7.6 g fat
(of which 3.2 g saturated)
9.1 g carbohydrate
(of which 5.9 g sugars)
4.8 g protein
0.2 g fibre

1 Boil the milk in a sauteuse.

2 Combine the flour, butter and sugar.

3 Whisk into the milk and reboil.

4 Remove from heat, add the yolks one at a time, whisking continuously.

5 Stiffly beat the whites.

6 Carefully fold into the mixture.

7 Three-quarters fill buttered and sugared dariole moulds.

8 Place in a roasting tin, half full of water.

9 Bring to the boil and place in a hot oven at 230–250°C (Reg. 8–9; 450–500°F) for 12–15 minutes.

10 Turn out on to a flat dish and serve with a suitable hot sauce, such as custard or sabayon sauce (recipe 13).

Note   Orange or lemon soufflé pudding is made by flavouring the basic mixture with the grated zest of an orange or lemon and a little appropriate sauce. Use the juice in the accompanying sauce.

18 – Cold lemon soufflé (soufflé milanaise)

	6 portions
leaf gelatine	10 g ($\frac{1}{2}$ oz)
lemons	2
eggs, separated	4
castor sugar	200 g (8 oz)
whipping or double cream or non-dairy cream	$\frac{1}{4}$ litre ($\frac{1}{2}$ pt)

I portion provides:

1385 kJ/330 kcal
18.6 g fat
(of which 10.6 g saturated)
36.2 g carbohydrate
(of which 36.2 g sugars)
6.7 g protein
0.0 g fibre

1   Prepare a soufflé dish by tying a 8 cm (3 inch) wide strip of greaseproof paper around the outside top edge with string, so that it extends 2–4 cm (1–1$\frac{1}{2}$ inches) above the top of the dish.
2   Soak the gelatine in cold water.
3   *Lightly* grate the zest of the lemons.
4   Squeeze the juice of the lemons into a bowl.
5   Add the lemon zest, yolks, sugar and whisk over a pan of hot water until the mixture thickens and turns a very light colour.
6   Dissolve the gelatine in a few drops of water over heat, mix in, remove from heat.
7   Lightly whisk the cream until three-quarters stiff.
8   Stiffly beat the egg whites.
9   Stir the basic mixture frequently until almost on setting point.
10   Gently fold in the cream. Gently fold in the egg whites.
11   Pour into the prepared dish.
12   Place in a refrigerator to set.
13   To serve, remove the paper collar and decorate sides with green chopped almonds or pistachio nuts. The top may be similarly decorated or by using rosettes of sweetened vanilla-flavoured whipped cream.

— *Steamed puddings* —

19 – Steamed currant roll

	6 portions	12 portions
flour, white or wholemeal	300 g (12 oz)	600 g (24 oz)
with baking-powder	10 g ($\frac{1}{2}$ oz)	20 g (1 oz)
or self-raising flour	300 g (12 oz)	600 g (24 oz)
pinch salt		
chopped suet	150 g (6 oz)	300 g (12 oz)
sugar, castor or unrefined	75 g (3 oz)	150 g (6 oz)
currants	100 g (4 oz)	200 g (8 oz)
water or milk	185 ml ($\frac{3}{8}$ pt)	375 ml ($\frac{3}{4}$ pt)

1 Sieve the flour, salt and baking-powder into a bowl.
2 Mix in the suet. Mix in the sugar and currants.
3 Add sufficient water or milk to make a fairly firm dough.
4 Roll in greased greaseproof paper and a pudding cloth or foil. Tie with string at both ends. Steam for $1\frac{1}{2}$–2 hours.
5 Remove the cloth and paper and serve with a sauceboat of custard.

Note   Sultanas, raisins or dates may be used instead of currants.

20 – Steamed dried fruit pudding

	6 portions	12 portions
flour, white or wholemeal	100 g (4 oz)	200 g (8 oz)
with baking-powder	10 g ($\frac{1}{2}$ oz)	20 g (1 oz)
or self-raising flour	100 g (4 oz)	200 g (8 oz)
pinch salt		
breadcrumbs	100 g (4 oz)	200 g (8 oz)
suet	100 g (4 oz)	200 g (8 oz)
sugar, castor or unrefined	100 g (4 oz)	200 g (8 oz)
fruit (currants, raisins, dates or sultanas)	100 g (4 oz)	200 g (8 oz)
egg	1	2
milk, whole or skimmed	125 ml ($\frac{1}{4}$ pt)	250 ml ($\frac{1}{2}$ pt)

1 Mix all the dry ingredients together. Add the liquid and mix.
2 Place in a greased pudding basin, cover and steam 1½–2 hours.
3 Serve with custard sauce or vanilla sauce.

21 ⁃ Golden syrup or treacle pudding

	6 portions	12 portions
flour, white or wholemeal	150 g (6 oz)	300 g (12 oz)
with baking-powder	10 g (½ oz)	20 g (1 oz)
or self-raising flour	150 g (6 oz)	300 g (12 oz)
pinch salt		
chopped suet	75 g (3 oz)	150 g (6 oz)
castor or unrefined sugar	50 g (2 oz)	100 g (4 oz)
lemon, zest of	1	2
egg	1	2
milk, whole or skimmed	125 ml (¼ pt)	250 ml (½ pt)
golden syrup or light treacle	125 ml (¼ pt)	250 ml (½ pt)

> I portion provides:
>
> 1315 kJ/313 kcal
> 13.0 g fat
> (of which 5.9 g saturated)
> 47.8 g carbohydrate
> (of which 26.6 g sugars)
> 4.3 g protein
> 0.9 g fibre

1 Sieve the flour, salt and baking-powder into a bowl.
2 Mix the suet, sugar and zest.
3 Mix to a medium dough, with the beaten egg and milk.
4 Pour the syrup in a well-greased basin. Place the mixture on top.
5 Cover securely; steam for 1½–2 hours.
6 Serve with a sauceboat of warm syrup containing the lemon juice.

22 ⁃ Steamed sponge pudding (basic recipe)

	6 portions	12 portions
butter or margarine	100 g (4 oz)	200 g (8 oz)
castor or soft brown sugar	100 g (4 oz)	200 g (8 oz)
eggs	2	4
flour, white or wholemeal	150 g (6 oz)	300 g (12 oz)
baking-powder	10 g (½ oz)	20 g (10 oz)
few drops of milk		

1 Cream the butter or margarine and sugar in a bowl until fluffy and almost white.

recipe continued ▶

2 Gradually add the beaten eggs, mixing vigorously.
3 Sieve the flour and baking-powder.
4 Gradually incorporate into the mixture as lightly as possible keeping to a dropping consistency by the addition of the milk.
5 Place in a greased pudding basin.
6 Cover securely with greased greaseproof paper. Steam for 1–1½ hours.

Note Variations (illustrated on page 612) include
(increase the quantities two times for 12 portions):

- *Vanilla sponge pudding* Add a few drops of vanilla essence to the basic mixture, and serve with a vanilla-flavoured sauce (page 605).
- *Chocolate sponge pudding* Add 25 g (1 oz) chocolate or cocoa powder in place of 25 g (1 oz) flour, that is 125 g (5 oz) flour, 25 g (1 oz) chocolate to basic recipe. Serve with a chocolate sauce (page 624).
- *Lemon sponge pudding* Add the grated zest of one or two lemons, and a few drops of lemon essence to basic recipe. Serve with a lemon (page 622) or vanilla sauce.
- *Orange sponge pudding* Proceed as for lemon pudding, but using oranges in place of lemons. Serve with an orange sauce (page 622) or vanilla sauce.
- *Cherry sponge pudding* Add 100 g (4 oz) chopped or quartered glacé cherries to basic recipe. Serve with a custard sauce (page 623) or almond sauce (page 623).
- *Sultana/currant/raisin sponge pudding* Add 100 g (4 oz) of washed well dried fruit to basic recipe. Serve with custard sauce (page 623).

23 – Christmas pudding

6 portions

chopped suet	100 g (4 oz)
flour, white or wholemeal	50 g (2 oz)
stoned raisins	100 g (4 oz)
sultanas	100 g (4 oz)
mixed peel	50 g (2 oz)
currants	50 g (2 oz)
nutmeg	5 g (¼ oz)
mixed spice	5 g (¼ oz)
Barbados sugar	100 g (4 oz)
breadcrumbs, white or wholemeal	100 g (4 oz)
ground almonds	25 g (1 oz)
milk, whole or skimmed	60 ml (⅛ pt)

Using white flour and whole milk, I portion provides:

2037 kJ/485 kcal
19.6 g fat
(of which 8.0 g saturated)
68.7 g carbohydrate
(of which 51.4 g sugars)
6.4 g protein
4.8 g fibre

pinch of salt
eggs   2
wineglass of stout
$\frac{1}{2}$ wineglass brandy
$\frac{1}{2}$ lemon grated zest and juice
$\frac{1}{2}$ orange grated zest and juice

1   Mix all the dry ingredients together.
2   Add the liquid and mix well.
3   Leave in a cool place for 3–4 days.
4   Place into greased basins, cover with greased greaseproof paper and steam for
    6–8 hours.
5   Serve with rum or brandy cream, rum or brandy butter or custard.

—— *Pancakes* ——

24 ~ Pancakes with lemon or orange

	4 portions	10 portions
flour, white or wholemeal	100 g (4 oz)	250 g (10 oz)
pinch of salt		
egg	1	2–3
milk, whole or skimmed	$\frac{1}{4}$ litre ($\frac{1}{2}$ pt)	600 ml (1$\frac{1}{4}$ pt)
melted butter, margarine or oil	10 g ($\frac{1}{2}$ oz)	25 g (1$\frac{1}{4}$ oz)
oil for frying		
sugar, castor or unrefined	50 g (2 oz)	125 g (5 oz)

Using white flour, whole milk, hard margarine and peanut oil, 1 portion provides:

1275 kJ/304 kcal
16.2 g fat
(of which 4.8 g saturated)
35.5 g carbohydrate
(of which 16.4 g sugars)
6.1 g protein
0.9 g fibre

1   Sieve the flour and salt into a bowl, make a well in
    the centre.
2   Add the egg and milk gradually incorporating the flour from the sides, whisk to
    a smooth batter.
3   Mix in the melted butter.
4   Heat the pancake pan, clean thoroughly.
5   Add a little oil; heat until smoking.
6   Add enough mixture to just cover the bottom of the pan thinly.
7   Cook for a few seconds until brown.

recipe continued ▶

Plate 14.4a–c: Above: preparation of steamed sponge puddings
Right: steamed sponge puddings (clockwise from left): sultana, chocolate and lemon with chocolate sauce (p. 624), lemon sauce (p. 622) and custard sauce (p. 623)

8   Turn and cook on the other side. Turn on to a plate.
9   Sprinkle with sugar. Fold in half then half again.

Note   When making a batch of pancakes it is best to keep them all flat one on top of the other on a plate. Sprinkle sugar between each. Fold them all when ready for service, sprinkle again with sugar and dress neatly overlapping on a serving dish. Garnish with quarters of lemon or orange free from pips. Serve very hot, two per portion.

Plate 14.5a–d: Preparation and piping of meringues

25 – Pancakes with jam

	4 portions	10 portions
warm jam	50 g (2 oz)	125 g (5 oz)
sugar	25 g (1 oz)	60 g (2½ oz)
pancakes (recipe 24)		

1 Prepare the pancakes as above. Spread each with warm jam.
2 Roll like a swiss roll, trim the ends.
3 Dredge with castor sugar and serve.

26 – Pancakes with apple

Method I
Cook as for the basic recipe and spread with a hot purée of apple (page 672); roll up and sprinkle with castor sugar.

Method II
Place a little cooked apple in the pan, add the pancake mixture and cook on both sides. Turn out, sprinkle with castor sugar and roll up.

— *Meringues* —

27 – **Meringue** (illustrated on page 613)

	4 portions	10 portions
egg whites	4	10
castor sugar	200 g (8 oz)	500 g (1¼ lb)

This recipe provides:

3491 kJ/831 kcal
0.0 g fat
(of which 0.0 g saturated)
210.0 g carbohydrated
(of which 210.0 g sugars)
10.8 g protein
0.0 g fibre

1 Whip the egg whites stiffly.
2 Sprinkle on the sugar and carefully mix in.
3 Place in a piping bag with a large plain tube and pipe on to silicone paper on a baking sheet.
4 Bake in the slowest oven possible or in a hot plate (110°C/Reg. ¼; 225°F). The aim is to cook the meringues without any colour whatsoever.

Note To gain maximum efficiency when whipping egg whites, the following points should be observed:

- Eggs should be fresh.
- When separating yolks from whites *no* speck of egg yolk must be allowed to remain in the white; egg yolk contains fat, the presence of which can prevent the white being correctly whipped.
- The bowl and whisk must be scrupulously clean, dry and free from any grease.
- When egg whites are whipped the addition of a little sugar (15 g to 4 egg whites) will assist the efficient beating and lessen the chance of overbeating.

The reason egg whites increase in volume when whipped is because they contain so much protein (11%). The protein forms tiny filaments which stretch on beating, incorporate air in minute bubbles then set to form a fairly stable puffed-up structure expanding to seven times its bulk.

28 – **Meringue with whipped cream**

1 Allow two meringues per portion.
2 Join together with a little sweetened, vanilla-flavoured whipped cream, or non-dairy cream.
3 Decorate with whipped cream, glacé cherries and angelica, or crystallised violets or roses.

29 – Meringue and ice-cream

1 Allow 2 meringues per portion.
2 Join together with a small ball of vanilla ice-cream.
3 Serve in a coupe or ice-cream dish.
4 Decorate with whipped cream.

30 – Vacherin with strawberries and cream

A vacherin is a round meringue shell piped into a suitable shape so that the centre may be filled with sufficient fruit such as strawberries, stoned cherries, peaches, apricots, and whipped cream to form a rich sweet.

The vacherin may be prepared in one, two, four or larger portion sizes.

	4 portions	10 portions
egg whites	4	10
castor sugar	200 g (8 oz)	500 g ($1\frac{1}{4}$ lb)
strawberries (picked and washed)	100–300 g ($\frac{1}{4}$–$\frac{3}{4}$ lb)	250–750 g (10 oz–$1\frac{3}{4}$ lb)
cream (whipped and sweetened) or non-dairy cream	125 ml ($\frac{1}{4}$ pt)	300 ml ($\frac{5}{8}$ pt)

1 Stiffly whip the egg whites.
2 Carefully fold in the sugar.
3 Place the mixture into a piping bag with a 1 cm ($\frac{1}{2}$ inch) plain tube.
4 Pipe on to silicone paper on a baking sheet.
5 Start from the centre and pipe round in a circular fashion to form a base 16 cm (6 inch) then pipe around the edge 2–3 cm (1–$1\frac{1}{2}$ inches) high.
6 Bake in a cool oven at 110°C (Reg. $\frac{1}{4}$; 225°F) until the meringue case is completely dry. Do not allow to colour.
7 Allow a meringue case to cool then remove from the paper.
8 Spread a thin layer of cream on the base. Add the strawberries.
9 Decorate with the remainder of the cream.

Note Melba sauce (page 624) may be used to coat the strawberries before decorating with cream. Refer to recipe 27 notes before whipping the egg whites.

Raspberries can be used instead of strawberries.

31 – Baked Alaska

	4 portions	10 portions
sponge cake	4 pieces	10 pieces
fruit syrup	60 ml ($\frac{1}{8}$ pt)	150 ml ($\frac{1}{3}$ pt)
vanilla ice-cream	4 scoops	10 scoops
egg whites	4	10
castor sugar	200 g (8 oz)	500 g (1$\frac{1}{4}$ lb)

> 1 portion provides:
>
> 2190 kJ/521 kcal
> 16.4 g fat
> (of which 7.3 g saturated)
> 91.3 g carbohydrated
> (of which 81.2 g sugars)
> 7.7 g protein
> 0.6 g fibre

1 Neatly arrange the pieces of sponge cake in the centre of a flat ovenproof dish.
2 Sprinkle the sponge cake with a little fruit syrup.
3 Place a flattened scoop of vanilla ice-cream on each piece of sponge.
4 Meanwhile stiffly whip the egg whites and fold in the sugar.
5 Use half the meringue and completely cover the ice-cream and sponge. Neaten with a palette knife.
6 Place the remainder of the meringue into a piping bag with a large tube (plain or star) and decorate over.
7 Place into a hot oven at 230–250°C (Reg. 8–9; 450–500°F) and colour a golden brown. Serve immediately.

Note The fruit syrup for soaking the sponge may be flavoured with either rum, sherry, brandy, whisky, Tia Maria, Curaçao or any other suitable liqueur.
Variations include:

- *Baked Alaska with peaches* Proceed as for the basic recipe, adding a little maraschino to the fruit syrup and using raspberry ice-cream instead of vanilla ice-cream. Cover the ice-cream with four halves of peaches.
- *Baked Alaska with pears* Proceed as for the basic recipe, adding a little kirsch to the fruit syrup and adding halves of poached pears to the ice-cream.

— *Omelets* —

32 – Jam omelet

1 Allow 2–3 eggs per portion. Break the eggs into a basin.
2 Beat well with a fork or whisk until the yolks and whites are thoroughly combined and no streaks of white can be seen.
3 Heat the omelet pan. Wipe thoroughly clean with a dry cloth.
4 Add 10 g ($\frac{1}{2}$ oz) butter or oil. Heat until foaming but not brown.
5 Add the eggs and cook quickly, keeping the mixture moving with a fork until lightly set.
6 Remove from the heat. Add 1 tablespoon warmed jam.
7 Half fold the mixture over at right-angles to the handle.
8 Tap the bottom of the pan to bring up the edge of the omelet.
9 Tilt the pan completely over the serving dish or plate so as to allow the omelet to fall carefully into the centre of the dish.
10 Neaten the shape if necessary. Sprinkle liberally with icing sugar.
11 Brand criss-cross pattern with a red-hot poker or branding iron to caramelise the sugar.

Using 2 eggs and hard margarine, 1 portion provides:

1260 kJ/300 kcal
20.1 g fat
(of which 7.4 g saturated)
17.3 g carbohydrate
(of which 17.3 g sugars)
13.7 g protein
0.3 g fibre

Using 3 eggs and hard margarine, 1 portion provides:

1599 kJ/381 kcal
26.1 g fat
(of which 9.4 g saturated)
17.3 g carbohydrate
(of which 17.3 g sugars)
20.5 g protein
0.3 g fibre

— *Milk puddings* —

33 — Baked rice pudding

	4 portions	10 portions
rice (short or wholegrain)	100 g (4 oz)	250 g (10 oz)
sugar, castor or unrefined	50 g (2 oz)	125 g (5 oz)
milk, whole or skimmed	½ litre (1 pt)	1¼ litre (2½ pt)
butter or margarine	10 g (½ oz)	25 g (1¼ oz)
vanilla essence	2–3 drops	6–8
grated nutmeg		

> Using whole milk, hard margarine, 1 portion provides:
>
> 1006 kJ/239 kcal
> 7.0 g fat
> (of which 3.9 g saturated)
> 40.7 g carbohydrate
> (of which 19.0 g sugars)
> 5.8 g protein
> 0.6 g fibre

1 Wash the rice, place in a pie dish.
2 Add the sugar and milk, mix well.
3 Add the butter, essence and nutmeg.
4 Place on a baking sheet; clean the rim of the pie dish.
5 Bake at 180–200°C (Reg. 4–6; 350–400°F), until the milk starts simmering.
6 Reduce the heat and allow the pudding to cook slowly, allowing 1½–2 hours in all.

34 — Rice pudding

Ingredients as for baked rice pudding.

1 Boil the milk in a thick-based pan.
2 Add the washed rice, stir to the boil.
3 Simmer gently, stirring frequently until the rice is cooked.
4 Mix in the sugar, flavouring and butter (at this stage an egg yolk may also be added). A vanilla pod can be used in place of essence.
5 Pour into a pie dish, place on a baking tray and brown lightly under the salamander.

Note Candied fruit and chopped nuts may be added to the rice for menu variety.

35 – Semolina pudding

	4 portions	10 portions
milk, whole or skimmed	½ litre (1 pt)	1¼ litre (2½ pt)
semolina	35 g (1½ oz)	85 g (4¼ oz)
sugar, castor or unrefined	50 g (2 oz)	125 g (5 oz)
butter or margarine	10 g (½ oz)	25 g (1¼ oz)
lemon juice or lemon essence	2–3 drops	6–8

> Using whole milk and hard margarine, 1 portion provides:
>
> 753 kJ/179 kcal
> 6.9 g fat
> (of which 3.9 g saturated)
> 25.8 g carbohydrate
> (of which 19.0 g sugars)
> 5.1 g protein
> 0.3 g fibre

1 Boil the milk in a thick-based pan.
2 Sprinkle in the semolina and stir to the boil.
3 Simmer for 15–20 minutes.
4 Add the sugar, butter flavouring (an egg yolk if desired).
5 Pour into a pie dish. Brown under the salamander.

Note Sago, tapioca and ground rice pudding are made in the same way as for semolina pudding using sago, tapioca or ground rice in place of semolina and vanilla essence instead of lemon essence.

36 – Empress rice

	4 portions	10 portions
red jelly	125 ml (¼ pt)	300 ml (⅝ pt)
milk, whole or skimmed	½ litre (1 pt)	1¼ litre (2½ pt)
rice (short or wholegrain)	50 g (2 oz)	125 g (5 oz)
sugar, castor or unrefined	75 g (3 oz)	180 g (7½ oz)
vanilla essence or a vanilla pod	3–4 drops	7 drops
gelatine	25 g (1 oz)	60 g (2½ oz)
angelica	25 g (1 oz)	60 g (2½ oz)
glacé cherries	25 g (1 oz)	60 g (2½ oz)
lightly whipped cream or non-dairy cream	125 ml (¼ pt)	300 ml (⅝ pt)
egg whites	2	5

1 Prepare the jelly and pour into the bottom of a charlotte mould; leave to set.
2 Boil the milk; add the washed rice and simmer until tender.
3 Mix in the sugar, essence (or vanilla pod), gelatine (if leaf gelatine is used soak in cold water) and diced angelica and cherries (which may be soaked in kirsch or maraschino).

recipe continued ▶

4   Allow to cool, stirring occasionally.
5   When the setting point is almost reached fold in the whipped cream and stiffly beaten egg whites and pour into the mould.
6   Leave to set in the refrigerator. Turn out carefully and serve.

37 ~ Junket

	4–6 portions	10 portions
milk	$\frac{1}{2}$ litre (1 pt)	1 litre (2 pt)
castor sugar	10 g ($\frac{1}{2}$ oz)	20 g (1 oz)
rennet	1 tsp	2 tsp
grated nutmeg		

1 portion provides:

383 kJ/91 kcal
4.8 g fat
(of which 3.0 g saturated)
8.5 g carbohydrate
(of which 8.5 g sugars)
4.1 g protein
0.0 g fibre

1   Warm the milk to blood heat and pour into a glass dish.
2   Add the sugar and rennet, stir gently. Leave until set.
3   Sprinkle lightly with the nutmeg and serve.

Note   The addition of rennet causes the clotting or coagulation of milk.

—— *Miscellaneous* ——

38 ~ Bread pudding

	4 portions	10 portions
stale white or wholemeal bread	$\frac{1}{2}$ kg (1 lb)	$1\frac{1}{4}$ kg ($2\frac{1}{2}$ lb)
sugar, castor or unrefined	125 g (5 oz)	300 g ($12\frac{1}{2}$ oz)
currants or sultanas	125 g (5 oz)	300 g ($12\frac{1}{2}$ oz)
mixed spice	$\frac{1}{2}$ tsp	$1\frac{1}{4}$ tsp
margarine	75 g (3 oz)	180 g ($7\frac{1}{2}$ oz)
egg	1	3

1   Soak the bread in cold water until soft.
2   Squeeze the bread dry and place in a bowl.
3   Mix in four-fifths sugar and the rest of the ingredients.
4   Place in a greased baking tray. Sprinkle with the remaining sugar.
5   Bake at 180°C (Reg. 4; 350°F) for about 1 hour.

39 ~ White chocolate mousse

	4 portions	10 portions
milk, whole or skimmed	125 ml ($\frac{1}{4}$ pt)	300 ml ($\frac{5}{8}$ pt)
orange, grated zest	1	2–3
white chocolate	150 g (6 oz)	375 g (15 oz)
eggs	2	5
castor sugar	25 g (1 oz)	60 g ($2\frac{1}{2}$ oz)
leaf gelatine	6 g ($\frac{1}{4}$ oz)	12 g ($\frac{5}{8}$ oz)
whipping cream, fromage frais or natural yoghurt	250 ml ($\frac{1}{2}$ pt)	600 ml ($1\frac{1}{4}$ pt)

1 Heat the milk to boiling point with the grated zest of the orange.
2 Add the white chocolate and melt. Stir well, away from the heat.
3 Whisk the eggs and sugar together, add the hot milk and return to the saucepan.
4 Stir on the side of the stove until the mixture coats the back of a spoon but do not boil. Remove from the heat.
5 Add the soaked and squeezed gelatine and bring down to setting point.
6 Fold in the whipped cream or alternative. Carefully and immediately pour into the mould.
7 Turn out and use as required.

Note   The mousse can be prepared in individual moulds, turned out onto plates, topped with poached fruit (pears, peaches, apricots) or fresh berries (loganberries, raspberries, strawberries). It can be coated with a suitable sauce (lemon, orange, lime, strawberry, Grand Marnier, grenadine).

—— *Sweet sauces and flavourings* ——

$\frac{1}{4}$ litre ($\frac{1}{2}$ pt) = 4–8 portions.

40 ~ Jam sauce

jam	200 g (8 oz)
water	100 ml ($\frac{3}{16}$ pt)
lemon juice	2–3 drops
cornflour	10 g ($\frac{1}{2}$ oz)

recipe continued ▶

1 Boil the jam, water and lemon juice together.
2 Adjust the consistency with a little cornflour or arrowroot diluted with water.
3 Reboil until clear and pass through a conical strainer.

41 ~ Apricot sauce

apricot jam	200 g (8 oz)
water	100 ml ($\frac{3}{16}$ pt)
lemon juice	2–3 drops
cornflour	10 g ($\frac{1}{2}$ oz)

Proceed as for jam sauce above.

42 ~ Orange, lemon or lime sauce

sugar, castor or unrefined	50 g (2 oz)
water	250 ml ($\frac{1}{2}$ pt)
cornflour or arrowroot	10 g ($\frac{1}{2}$ oz)
oranges, lemons or limes	1–2

1 Boil the sugar and water.
2 Add the cornflour diluted with water, stirring continuously.
3 Reboil until clear, strain.
4 Add blanched julienne of orange zest and the strained orange juice.

Note   A little Curaçao or Cointreau may be added for additional flavour.

An example of the service of lemon sauce is illustrated on page 612.

43 ~ Syrup sauce

syrup	200 g (8 oz)
water	125 ml ($\frac{1}{4}$ pt)
lemon, juice of	1
cornflour or arrowroot	10 g ($\frac{1}{2}$ oz)

Bring the syrup, water and lemon juice to the boil and thicken with diluted cornflour. Boil for a few minutes and strain.

44 ~ Custard sauce

custard powder	10 g ($\frac{1}{2}$ oz)
milk, whole or skimmed	250 ml ($\frac{1}{2}$ pt)
castor or unrefined sugar	25 g (1 oz)

1 Dilute the custard powder with a little of the milk.
2 Boil the remainder of the milk.
3 Pour a little of the boiled milk on to the diluted custard powder.
4 Return to the saucepan.
5 Stir to the boil and mix in the sugar.

Note See also recipe 15.

> Using whole milk, this recipe provides:
>
> 1245 kJ/296 kcal
> 9.6 g fat
> (of which 6.0 g saturated)
> 47.2 g carbohydrate
> (of which 38.0 g sugars)
> 8.3 g protein
> 0.3 g fibre

45 ~ Almond sauce

cornflour	10 g ($\frac{1}{2}$ oz)
milk, whole or skimmed	250 ml ($\frac{1}{2}$ pt)
castor or unrefined sugar	25 g (1 oz)
few drops almond essence	

1 Dilute the cornflour with a little of the milk.
2 Boil the remainder of the milk. Whisk on to the cornflour.
3 Return to the pan, stir to the boil. Simmer for 3–4 minutes.
4 Mix in the sugar and essence. Pass through a strainer.

46 ~ Rum or brandy cream

Whipped, sweetened, cream flavoured with rum or brandy.

47 ~ Rum or brandy butter

Cream equal quantities of butter and sieved icing sugar together and add rum or brandy to taste.

48 – Melba sauce

Method I

raspberry jam	400 g (1 lb)
water	125 ml ($\frac{1}{4}$ pt)

Boil together and pass through a conical strainer.

Method II

raspberries	400 g (1 lb)
water	125 ml ($\frac{1}{4}$ pt)
sugar, castor or unrefined	100 g (4 oz)

Boil ingredients together, cool, liquidise and strain.

Method III

raspberries	400 g (1 lb)
icing sugar	200 g (8 oz)

Liquidise, pass through a fine sieve and add a little lemon juice.

Note   Methods II and III are also known as raspberry cullis.

49 – Chocolate sauce

cornflour	10 g ($\frac{1}{2}$ oz)
milk	250 ml ($\frac{1}{2}$ pt)
cocoa powder	10 g ($\frac{1}{2}$ oz)
or	
chocolate (block)	25 g (1 oz)
sugar	65 g (1$\frac{1}{2}$ oz)
butter	5 g ($\frac{1}{4}$ oz)

With cocoa
1   Dilute the cornflour with a little of the milk, mix in the cocoa.
2   Boil the remainder of the milk.
3   Pour a little of the milk on to the cornflour.
4   Return to the saucepan.
5   Stir to the boil.
6   Mix in the sugar and butter.

Plate 14.6: Custard sauce
(served with sultana sponge
pp. 609–610)

With chocolate
Shred the chocolate, add to the milk and proceed as above, omitting the cocoa.

Note   Chocolate sauce may be flavoured if desired with rum or Crème de Menthe.

50 – Boiled butter cream

no. 2 grade eggs	2
icing sugar	50 g (2 oz)
granulate sugar or cube sugar	300 g (12 oz)
water	100 g (4 oz)
glucose	50 g (2 oz)
unsalted butter	400 g (1 lb)

1   Beat the eggs and icing sugar until the ribbon stage (sponge).
2   Boil the granulated or cube sugar with water and glucose to 118°C (245°F).
3   Gradually add the sugar at 118°C (245°F) to the eggs and icing sugar at ribbon stage, whisk continuously and allow to cool to 26°C (80°F).
4   Gradually add the unsalted butter while continuing to whisk until a smooth cream is obtained.

recipe continued ▶

Note   Butter cream may be flavoured with numerous flavours and combinations of flavours:

- chocolate and rum
- whisky and orange
- strawberry and vanilla
- lemon and lime
- apricot and passion fruit
- brandy and praline
- coffee and hazelnut.

51 – Butter cream

icing sugar	150 g (6 oz)
butter	200 g (8 oz)

1 Sieve the icing sugar.
2 Cream the butter and icing sugar until light and creamy.
3 Flavour and colour as required.

Note   Variations include:

- *Rum butter cream* Add rum to flavour and blend in.
- *Chocolate butter cream* Add melted chocolate, sweetened or unsweetened according to taste.

52 – Praline

Praline is a basic preparation used for flavouring items such as gâteaux, soufflés, ice-creams and many other sweets.

almonds, shelled	100 g (4 oz)
hazelnuts, shelled	100 g (4 oz)
water	60 ml ($\frac{1}{8}$ pt)
sugar	200 g (8 oz)

1 Lightly brown the almonds and hazelnuts in an oven.
2 Cook the water and sugar in copper or thick-based pan until the caramel stage is reached.
3 Remove the pan from the heat.
4 Mix in the nuts.
5 Turn out the mixture on to a lightly oiled marble slab.
6 Allow to become quite cold.
7 Crush to a coarse texture using a rolling pin.
8 Store in an airtight container.

53 – Apple Charlotte

	4 portions	10 portions
stale bread (white or wholemeal)	400 g (1 lb)	1¼ kg (2½ lb)
margarine or butter	100 g (4 oz)	250 g (10 oz)
cooking apples	400 g (1 lb)	1¼ kg (2½ lb)
sugar, castor or unrefined	50–75 g (2–3 oz)	125–150 g (5–6 oz)
breadcrumbs or cake crumbs	35 g (1½ oz)	85 g (4¼ oz)

> Using hard margarine, 1 portion provides:
>
> 2163 kJ/515 kcal
> 22.3 g fat
> (of which 9.3 g saturated)
> 74.5 g carbohydrate
> (of which 23.4 g sugars)
> 9.4 g protein
> 6.1 g fibre

1 Use either one Charlotte mould or four dariole moulds.
2 Cut the bread into 3 mm (⅛ inch) slices and remove the crusts.
3 Cut a round the size of the bottom of the mould, dip into melted butter or margarine on one side and place in the mould fat side down.
4 Cut fingers of bread 2–4 cm (1–1½ inch) wide, and fit, overlapping well, to the sides of the mould after dipping each one in melted fat. Take care not to leave any gaps.
5 Peel, core and wash the apples, cut into thick slices and three parts cook in a little butter and sugar (a little cinnamon or a clove may be added), and add the breadcrumbs.
6 Fill the centre of the mould with the apple.
7 Cut round pieces of bread to seal the apple in.
8 Bake at 220°C (Reg. 7; 425°F) for 30–40 minutes. Remove from the mould.
9 Serve with apricot (recipe 41) or custard (recipe 44) sauce.

54 – Apple fritters

	4 portions	10 portions
cooking apples	400 g (1 lb)	1 kg (2½ lb)
frying batter (page 261)	150 g (6 oz)	375 g (15 oz)
apricot sauce (recipe 41)	125 ml (¼ pt)	300 ml (⅝ pt)

> Fried in peanut oil, 1 portion provides:
>
> 1034 kJ/246 kcal
> 10.2 g fat
> (of which 1.9 g saturated)
> 38.9 g carbohydrate
> (of which 25.0 g sugars)
> 2.1 g protein
> 3.0 g fibre

1 Peel and core the apples and cut into ½ cm (¼ inch) rings.
2 Pass through flour, shake off the surplus.

recipe continued ▶

3 Dip into frying batter.
4 Lift out with the fingers, into fairly hot deep fat (185°C/365°F).
5 Cook for about 5 minutes on each side.
6 Drain well, dust with icing sugar and glaze under the salamander.
7 Serve with hot apricot sauce.

Plate 14.7: Preparation of apple fritters

55 – Banana fritters

	4 portions	10 portions
bananas	4	10
frying batter (page 261)	150 g (6 oz)	375 g (15 oz)
apricot sauce (recipe 41)	125 ml ($\frac{1}{4}$ pt)	300 ml ($\frac{5}{8}$ pt)

1 Peel and cut the bananas in half lengthwise then in half across.
2 Cook and serve as for apple fritters above.

Note   Bananas may be dipped in hot pastry cream flavoured with rum, allowed to cool on an oiled tray, before passing through flour and dipping in frying batter.

56 – Pineapple fritters

	4 portions
pineapple, rings of	4
frying batter (page 261)	150 g (6 oz)
apricot sauce (recipe 41)	125 ml ($\frac{1}{4}$ pt)

Cut the rings in half, cook and serve as for apple fritters (recipe 55).

Note   Pineapple fritters may also be dipped in hot pastry cream flavoured with liqueur, allowed to cool on an oiled tray before passing through flour and dipping in frying batter.

628

57 – Baked apple

	4 portions	10 portions
medium-size cooking apples	4	10
sugar, white or unrefined	50 g (2 oz)	125 g (5 oz)
cloves	4	10
butter or margarine	25 g (1 oz)	60 g (2½ oz)
water	60 ml (⅛ pt)	150 ml (⅓ pt)

Using hard margarine, 1 portion provides:

663 kJ/156 kcal
5.1 g fat
(of which 2.2 g saturated)
29.7 g carbohydrate
(of which 29.5 g sugars)
0.4 g protein
2.7 g fibre

1 Core the apples and make an incision 2 mm ($\frac{1}{12}$ inch) deep round the centre of each. Wash well.
2 Place in a roasting tray or ovenproof dish.
3 Fill the centre with sugar and add a clove.
4 Place 5 g (¼ oz) butter on each. Add the water.
5 Bake in a moderate oven at 200–220°C (Reg. 6–7; 400–425°F) for 15–20 minutes.
6 Turn the apples over carefully.
7 Return to the oven until cooked, about 40 minutes in all.
8 Serve with a little of the cooking liquor and custard, cream or ice-cream.

Note For stuffed baked apple, proceed as for baked apples, but fill the centre with washed sultanas, raisins or chopped dates, or a combination of these.

58 – Fresh fruit salad (ilustrated on page 632)

All the following fruits may be used: dessert apples, pears, pineapple, oranges, grapes, melon, strawberries, peaches, raspberries, apricots, bananas, cherries. Kiwi fruit, plums, mangoes, paw-paws and lychees may also be used. Kirsch, Cointreau or Grand Marnier may be added to the syrup. All fruit must be ripe. Allow about 150 g (6 oz) unprepared fruit per portion.

	4 portions	10 portions
castor sugar	50 g (2 oz)	125 g (5 oz)
lemon, juice of	½	1
orange	1	2–3
dessert apple	1	2–3
dessert pear	1	2–3
cherries	50 g (2 oz)	125 g (5 oz)
grapes	50 g (2 oz)	125 g (5 oz)
banana	1	2–3

1 portion provides:

493 kJ/117 kcal
0.0 g fat
(of which 0.0 g saturated)
30.3 g carbohydrate
(of which 29.5 g sugars)
0.9 g protein
3.0 g fibre

recipe continued ▶

1 Boil the sugar with $\frac{1}{8}$ litre ($\frac{1}{4}$ pint) ($\frac{3}{8}$ litre, $\frac{5}{8}$ pint) water to make a syrup, place in a bowl.
2 Allow to cool, add the lemon juice.
3 Peel and cut the orange into segments as for cocktail.
4 Quarter the apple and pear, remove the core, peel and cut each quarter into two or three slices, place in the bowl and mix with the orange.
5 Stone the cherries, leave whole.
6 Cut the grapes in half, peel if required, and remove the pips.
7 Mix carefully and place in a glass bowl in the refrigerator to chill.
8 Just before serving, peel and slice the banana and mix in.

59 – Fruit fool

	4 portions	10 portions
Method I Apple, gooseberry, rhubarb, etc.		
fruit	400 g (1 lb)	1 kg (2$\frac{1}{2}$ lb)
water	60 ml ($\frac{1}{8}$ pt)	150 ml ($\frac{1}{3}$ pt)
granulated or unrefined sugar	100 g (4 oz)	250 g (10 oz)
cornflour	25 g (1 oz)	60 g (2$\frac{1}{2}$ oz)
milk, whole or skimmed	$\frac{1}{4}$ litre ($\frac{1}{2}$ pt)	600 ml (1$\frac{1}{4}$ pt)
castor or unrefined sugar	25 g (1 oz)	60 g (2$\frac{1}{2}$ oz)

1 Cook the fruit in water and sugar, to a purée. Pass through a sieve.
2 Dilute the cornflour in a little of the milk, add the sugar.
3 Boil remainder of the milk.
4 Pour on the diluted cornflour, stir well.
5 Return to the pan on a low heat and stir to the boil.
6 Mix with the fruit purée. The quantity of mixture should not be less than $\frac{1}{2}$ litre (1 pint).
7 Pour into four glass coupes and allow to set.
8 Decorate with whipped sweetened cream or non-dairy cream. The colour may need to be adjusted slightly with food colour.

Method II Raspberries,
strawberries, etc.

fruit in purée	400 g (1 lb)	1 kg (2½ lb)
castor sugar	100 g (4 oz)	250 g (10 oz)
fresh whipped cream	¼ litre (½ pt)	600 ml (1¼ pt)

Mix together and serve in coupes.

Method III

cornflour	35 g (1½ oz)	85 g (4¼ oz)
water	375 ml (¾ pt)	900 ml (1⅞ pt)
sugar	100 g (4 oz)	250 g (10 oz)
fruit	400 g (1 lb)	1¼ kg (2½ lb)
cream	185 ml (⅜ pt)	500 ml (1 pt)

1 Dilute the cornflour in a little of the water.
2 Boil the remainder of the water with the sugar and prepared fruit until soft.
3 Pass through a fine sieve.
4 Return to a clean pan and reboil.
5 Stir in the diluted cornflour and reboil. Allow to cool.
6 Lightly whisk the cream and fold into the mixture.
7 Serve as for Method I.

60 – Poached fruits or fruit compote

	4 portions	10 portions
fruit	400 g (1 lb)	1 kg (2½ lb)
Sugar or stock syrup		
water	¼ litre (½ pt)	600 ml (1¼ pt)
sugar	100 g (4 oz)	250 g (10 oz)
lemon	½	1

Using pears, 1 portion provides:

531 kJ/126 kcal
0.0 g fat
(of which 0.0 g saturated)
33.5 g carbohydrate
(of which 33.5 g sugars)
0.2 g protein
2.2 g fibre

Apples, pears
1 Boil the water and sugar.
2 Quarter the fruit, remove the core and peel.
3 Place in a shallow pan in sugar syrup.
4 Add a few drops of lemon juice.

recipe continued ▶

5   Cover with greaseproof paper.

6   Allow to simmer slowly, preferably in the oven, cool and serve.

Soft fruits – raspberries, strawberries

1   Pick and wash the fruit.

2   Place in a glass bowl.

3   Pour on the hot syrup.

4   Allow to cool and serve.

Stone fruits – plums, damsons, greengages, cherries

Wash the fruit, barely cover with sugar syrup and cover with greaseproof paper or a lid. Cook gently in a moderate oven until tender.

Rhubarb

Trim off the stalk and leaf and wash. Cut into 5 cm (2 inch) lengths and cook as above, adding extra sugar if necessary. A little ground ginger may also be added.

Plate 14.8: Fresh fruit salad

632

Gooseberries, blackcurrants, redcurrants
Top and tail the gooseberries, wash and cook as for stone fruit, adding extra sugar if necessary. The currants should be carefully removed from the stalks, washed and cooked as for stone fruits.

Dried fruits – prunes, apricots, apples, pears
Dried fruits should be washed and soaked in cold water overnight. Gently cook in the liquor with sufficient sugar to taste.

Note   A piece of cinnamon stick and a few slices of lemon may be added to the prunes or pears, one or two cloves to the dried or fresh apples.

61 – Pear Condé

	4 portions	10 portions
rice (short or wholegrain)	75 g (3 oz)	180 g (7½ oz)
milk, whole or skimmed	½ litre (1 pt)	1¼ litre (2½ pt)
sugar, castor or unrefined	50 g (2 oz)	125 g (5 oz)
vanilla essence or a vanilla pod	3–4 drops	6–7 drops
dessert pears	2	5
apricot glaze	125 ml (¼ pt)	300 ml (⅝ pt)
angelica	10 g (½ oz)	25 g (1¼ oz)
glacé cherries	2	5

Using whole milk, 1 portion provides:

1299 kJ/309 kcal
4.9 g fat
(of which 3.1 g saturated)
64.5 g carbohydrate
(of which 48.3 g sugars)
5.7 g protein
2.4 g fibre

1   Cook the rice in the milk, sweeten and flavour. Allow to cool.
2   Peel, core and halve the pears and poach them carefully, leave to cool.
3   Dress the rice either in a glass bowl or on a flat dish.
4   Drain the pears and neatly arrange them on top.
5   Coat with apricot glaze. Decorate with angelica and cherries.

Note   Many other fruits may be prepared as a Condé: banana, pineapple, peach. The rice can be enriched with 10 g (½ oz) butter or margarine and an egg yolk (increase the quantities 2½ times for 10 portions).

62 ~ Pears in red wine

	4 portions	10 portions
whole ripe medium sized pears	4	10
Cooking liquid		
water	250 ml ($\frac{1}{2}$ pt)	625 ml ($1\frac{1}{4}$ pt)
sugar	100 g (4 oz)	250 g (10 oz)
red wine	125 ml ($\frac{1}{4}$ pt)	300 ml ($\frac{5}{8}$ pt)
cinnamon stick	1	2–3
lemon, zest of	1	2–3
few drops of cochineal		

1 Boil all the ingredients for the cooking liquid.
2 Peel the pears. Use either whole, in which case the cores should be tunnelled out and half of the stalks left intact; or in halves or quarters with the cores and stalks removed.
3 Gently poach the pears covered with greaseproof paper in the cooking liquid.
4 The pears may be served hot or cold.
5 If an accompaniment is required this may be cream (plain or whipped), ice-cream, yoghurt or fromage frais.

Note If the pears are cut up the amount of cooking liquid may be lessened. The amount of red wine can be varied according to taste. Pears in red wine may also be used as a garnish for other dishes.

63 ~ Avocado mousse with poached pear and strawberry sauce

	4 portions	10 portions
avocado purée	250 ml ($\frac{1}{2}$ pt)	600 ml ($1\frac{1}{4}$ pt)
lemon, juice of	$\frac{1}{2}$	1
icing sugar	50 g (2 oz)	125 g (5 oz)
leaf gelatine	12 g ($\frac{1}{2}$ oz)	25 g ($1\frac{1}{4}$ oz)
whipped cream, fromage frais or natural yoghurt	125 ml ($\frac{1}{4}$ pt)	300 ml ($\frac{5}{8}$ pt)
poached pear	4 halves	10 halves

1 Add the lemon juice to the avocado purée.
2 Mix in the icing sugar.

3   Place the soaked and lightly squeezed gelatine into a small pan. Heat gently until it starts to boil.
4   Carefully add the gelatine to the purée, stirring well.
5   When setting point is reached, carefully fold in the whipped cream or alternative.
6   Pour into individual moulds and place in the refrigerator to set.
7   When set, turn out onto plates and garnish each with half a poached pear carefully fanned.
8   Mask with strawberry sauce.

⌐ *Strawberry sauce*

strawberry purée	125 ml ($\frac{1}{4}$ pt)	300 ml ($\frac{5}{8}$ pt)
white wine	125 ml ($\frac{1}{4}$ pt)	300 ml ($\frac{5}{8}$ pt)
castor sugar	50 g (2 oz)	125 g (5 oz)

Mix all the ingredients together and strain.

Note   Alternative fruit purées that can be used in the mousse are peach, apricot, mango, pawpaw, strawberry and raspberry.

Alternative sauces include raspberry, peach, apricot, lemon, orange and lime.

64 ⌐ Fruit Melba (peach, pear, banana Melba)

	4 portions	10 portions
peaches	2	5
vanilla ice-cream	125 ml ($\frac{1}{4}$ pt)	300 ml ($\frac{1}{2}$ pt)
Melba sauce (page 624)	125 ml ($\frac{1}{4}$ pt)	300 ml ($\frac{1}{2}$ pt)

> 1 portion provides:
>
> 607 kJ/145 kcal
> 2.6 g fat
> (of which 1.3 g saturated)
> 30.5 g carbohydrate
> (of which 30.2 g sugars)
> 1.6 g protein
> 1.3 g fibre

1   Dress the fruit on a ball of ice-cream in an ice-cream coupe and coat with Melba sauce. May be decorated with whipped cream.

Note   If using fresh peaches they should be dipped in boiling water for a few seconds, cooled by placing into cold water, peeled and halved.

Fresh pears should be peeled, halved and poached. Bananas should be peeled at the last moment.

65 – Pear belle Hélenè

Serve a cooked pear on a ball of vanilla ice-cream in a coupe. Decorate with whipped cream. Serve with a sauceboat of hot chocolate sauce (recipe 49).

66 – Peach cardinal

Place half a prepared peach on a ball of strawberry ice-cream in a coupe. Coat with Melba sauce; decorate with whipped cream and sprinkle with toasted almonds cut in slices, if required.

67 – Coupe Jacques

Place some fruit salad in a coupe; arrange one scoop of lemon ice-cream and one of strawberry ice-cream on top. Decorate with whipped cream if required.

68 – Glazed fruits

1 Dates stoned, stuffed with marzipan (left yellow or lightly coloured pink or green) and rolled in castor sugar.
2 Grapes (in pairs left on the stalk) or tangerine in segments, passed through a syrup and prepared as follows:

– Syrup

sugar	400 g (1 lb)
glucose	50 g (2 oz)
water	250 ml ($\frac{1}{2}$ pt)
lemon, juice of	1

1 Boil the sugar, glucose and water to 160–165°C (310–315°F).
2 Add the lemon juice, shake in thoroughly, remove from heat.
3 Pass the fruits through this syrup using a fork and place them on to a lightly oiled marble slab to cool and set.

Note   Marzipan (page 709) can be coloured and moulded into a variety of shapes. They can then be either rolled in castor sugar or glazed by dipping in a syrup as in previous recipe.

There are numerous other recipes which include fruit:

- Baked Alaska (page 616).
- Bavarois (page 599).
- Cold lemon soufflé (page 607).
- Dutch apple tart (page 675).
- Flans (page 670).
- Ice-cream (strawberry, raspberry) (page 602).
- Kiwi slice (page 688).
- Lemon curd tart (page 668).
- Lemon meringue pie (page 673).
- Meringue (page 614).
- Pancakes (page 613).
- Pies (page 667).
- Savarin (page 649).
- Sorbets (page 603).
- Soufflé puddings (page 606).
- Steamed sponge puddings (page 609).
- Tartlets and barquettes (page 678).
- Turnovers (page 680).

Many recipes also make use of dried fruit:

- Bread and butter pudding (page 595).
- Bread pudding (page 620).
- Christmas pudding (page 610).
- Mince pies (page 686).
- Steamed sponge puddings (page 609).

Prepare and cook dough products

1	Ensure that preparation and cooking areas and equipment are ready for use and satisfy health and hygiene regulations.
2	Plan the work and allocate time appropriately to meet daily schedules.
3	Ensure that the dough is prepared and cooked according to product requirements.
4	Ensure that the dough and finished products are stored in accordance with food hygiene regulations.
5	Clean preparation and cooking areas and equipment after use.

Bread and dough products basically contain wheat flour and yeast. Bread and bread products form the basis of our diet; it is not surprising, therefore, that bread is seen as a fundamental staple product in our society. 'Give us our daily bread.' We eat bread at breakfast, lunch and dinner in sandwiches, as bread rolls, as croissants, as French sticks, etc. Bread is also used as an ingredient for many other dishes, either as slices or as breadcrumbs. The basic bread dough of wheat flour, yeast and water may be enriched with fat, sugar, eggs, milk and numerous other added ingredients.

Dough consists of strong flour, water, salt and yeast which are kneaded together to the required consistency at a suitable temperature. When proving takes place the yeast produces carbon dioxide and water which aerates the dough. When baked it produces a light digestible product with flavour and colour.

Enriched doughs or enriched breads are:

- buns
- savarins
- brioche
- croissants
- Danish pastries.

Croissants and Danish pastries are enriched doughs where the fat is added by layering or lamination; a softer eating quality is obtained because the fat in the dough insulates the water molecules, keeping the moisture level higher during baking.

Flour-based products provide us with variety, energy, vitamins and minerals. Wholemeal bread products also provide roughage, an essential part of a healthy diet.

UNDERSTANDING FERMENTATION

For dough to become bread it must go through a fermentation process. This is brought about by the action of yeast, with enzymes in the yeast and dough; these convert sugar into alcohol, thus producing the characteristic flavour of bread. The action also produces carbon dioxide which makes the bread rise.

Yeast requires ideal conditions for growth; these are:

- *Warmth* A good temperature for dough production is 22–30°C (72–86°F).
- *Moisture* Yeast requires moisture; the liquid should be added at approximately 38°C (100°F).
- *Food* Yeast requires food; this is obtained from the starch in the flour.
- *Time* Time is needed to allow the yeast to grow.

Yeast is a living single-cell micro-organism and in the right conditions with food, warmth and moisture, ferments, producing carbon dioxide and alcohol while at the same time reproducing itself. It is rich in protein and vitamin B.

Yeast will not survive in a high concentration of sugar or salt and will slow down in a very rich dough with a high fat and egg content.

When mixing yeast in water or milk, make sure that the liquid is at the right temperature (38°C/100°F) and disperse the yeast in the liquid. As a living organism cannot be dissolved, we use the word disperse.

Dried yeast has been dehydrated and requires creaming with a little water before use. It will keep for several months in its dry state.

POINTS TO REMEMBER

- Yeast should be removed from the refrigerator and used at room temperature.
- Check all ingredients are weighed carefully.
- Work in a clean and tidy manner to avoid cross-contamination.
- Check all temperatures carefully.
- All wholemeal doughs absorb more water than white doughs. The volume of water absorbed by flour also varies according to the strength (protein and bran content).
- When using machines, check that they are in working order.
- Always remember the health and safety rules when using machinery.
- Divide the dough with a dough divider, hard scraper or hydraulic cutting machine.

- Check the divided dough pieces for weight. When scaling, remember that doughs lose up to 12.5% of water during baking; therefore this needs to be taken into account when scaling.
- Keep the flour, bowl and liquid warm.
- Remember to knock the dough back carefully once proved, as this will expel the gas and allow the greater dispersion of the yeast. It will once again be in direct contact with the dough.
- Proving allows the dough to ferment; the second prove is essential for giving dough products the necessary volume and a good flavour.
- Time and temperature is crucial when cooking dough products.
- When using frozen dough products always follow the manufacturer's instructions. Contamination can occur if the doughs are defrosted incorrectly.

TYPES

Enriched doughs
- *Savarin* A rich yeast dough used for savarins, babas, marignans.
- *Brioche* A rich yeast dough with a high fat and butter content.

Laminated doughs
- *Croissants* Made from a dough in which the fat content has been layered (laminated) as in puff pastry.
- *Danish* Also a laminated dough; Danish pastries may be filled with fruit, frangipane, apple, custard, cherries and many other ingredients.

Speciality doughs
- *Blinis* A type of pancake.
- *Nan bread* Unleavened bread traditionally cooked in a tandoori oven.
- *Pitta bread* Middle Eastern and Greek bread, also unleavened.
- *Chapatti* Indian unleavened bread made from a fine ground wholemeal flour.

STORAGE OF COOKED DOUGH PRODUCTS

Crusty rolls and bread are affected by changes in storage conditions; they are softened by a damp environment and humid conditions. Always store in suitable containers at room temperature and a freezer for longer storage. Do not store in a refrigerator unless you want the bread to stale quickly for use as breadcrumbs.

Staling will also occur quickly in products which contain a high ratio of fat and milk. Many commercial dough products contain anti-staling agents.

CONVENIENCE DOUGH PRODUCTS

There are many new different types of products on the market.

- Fresh and frozen preproved dough products:
  - rolls
  - croissants
  - Danish pastries
  - French breads.

- Bake-off products. These are products ready for baking, either frozen or fresh or modified atmosphere-packaged forms. This method replaces most of the oxygen around the product to slow down spoilage. These products have to be kept refrigerated:
  - garlic bread
  - rolls
  - Danish pastries.

POSSIBLE REASONS FOR FAULTS USING YEAST DOUGHS

- *Close texture:*
  - insufficiently proved
  - insufficiently kneaded
  - insufficient yeast
  - oven too hot
  - too much water
  - too little water.
- *Uneven texture:*
  - insufficient kneading
  - oven too cool
  - over-proving.
- *Coarse texture:*
  - over-proofed, uncovered
  - insufficient kneading
  - too much water
  - too much salt.

- *Wrinkled:*
  - over-proved
- *Sour:*
  - stale yeast
  - too much yeast.
- *Broken crust:*
  - under-proved at the second stage.
- *White spots on crust:*
  - not covered before second proving.

69 – Bread rolls (illustrated on page 644)

	8 rolls	20 rolls
flour (strong)	200 g (8 oz)	500 g (20 oz)
yeast	5 g ($\frac{1}{4}$ oz)	12 g ($\frac{5}{8}$ oz)
liquid (half water, half milk)	125 ml ($\frac{1}{4}$ pt)	300 ml ($\frac{5}{8}$ pt)
butter or margarine	10 g ($\frac{1}{2}$ oz)	25 g (1$\frac{1}{4}$ oz)
castor sugar	$\frac{1}{4}$ tsp	$\frac{1}{2}$ tsp
salt		

> Using white flour and hard margarine, 1 portion (2 rolls) provides:
>
> 426 kJ/102 kcal
> 1.7 g fat
> (of which 0.7 g saturated)
> 19.5 g carbohydrate
> (of which 1.0 g sugars)
> 3.4 g protein
> 1.1 g fibre

1 Sieve the flour into a bowl and warm in the oven or above the stove.
2 Cream the yeast in a small basin with a quarter of the liquid.
3 Make a well in the centre of the flour; add the dissolved yeast.
4 Sprinkle over a little of the flour, cover with a cloth, leave in a warm place until the yeast ferments (bubbles).
5 Add the remainder of the liquid (warm), the fat, sugar and the salt.
6 Knead firmly until smooth and free from stickiness.
7 Return to the basin, cover with a cloth and leave in a warm place until double its size. (This is called *proving* the dough.)
8 Knock back. Divide into even pieces.
9 Mould into the desired shape.
10 Place on a floured baking sheet. Cover with a cloth.
11 Leave in a warm place to prove (double in size).
12 Brush carefully with eggwash.
13 Bake in a hot oven at 220°C (Reg. 7; 425°F) for about 10 minutes.

Note At all times during preparation of the dough, extreme heat must be avoided as the yeast will be killed and the dough spoiled.

For variety (increase the quantities $2\frac{1}{2}$ times for 10 portions):

- Use all wholemeal flour, 1 teaspoon raw cane sugar in place of castor sugar and all water and no milk.
- Add 50 g (2 oz) each of chopped walnuts and sultanas.

> Using wholemeal flour, 1 portion provides:
>
> 379 kJ/90 kcal
> 1.6 g fat
> (of which 0.5 g saturated)
> 17.1 g carbohydrate
> (of which 1.2 g sugars)
> 3.4 g protein
> 2.3 g fibre

70 – Bun dough (basic recipe)

	8 buns	20 buns
flour (strong)	200 g ($\frac{1}{2}$ lb)	500 g ($1\frac{1}{4}$ lb)
yeast	5 g ($\frac{1}{4}$ oz)	12 g ($\frac{5}{8}$ oz)
milk and water, approximately	60 ml ($\frac{1}{8}$ pt)	300 ml ($\frac{5}{8}$ pt)
egg	1	2–3
butter or margarine	50 g (2 oz)	125 g (5 oz)
castor sugar	25 g (1 oz)	60 g ($2\frac{1}{2}$ oz)

> Using hard margarine, 1 portion (2 buns) provides:
>
> 656 kJ/157 kcal
> 6.4 g fat
> (of which 2.7 g saturated)
> 22.6 g carbohydrate
> (of which 4.0 g sugars)
> 3.6 g protein
> 1.2 g fibre

1 Sieve the flour into a bowl and warm.
2 Cream the yeast in a basin with a little of the liquid.
3 Make a well in the centre of the flour.
4 Add the dispersed yeast, sprinkle with a little flour, cover with a cloth, leave in a warm place until the yeast ferments (bubbles).
5 Add the beaten egg, butter or margarine, sugar and remainder of the liquid. Knead well to form a soft, slack dough, knead until smooth and free from stickiness.
6 Keep covered and allow to prove in a warm place.
7 Use as required.

– *Bun wash*

sugar	100 g ($\frac{1}{4}$ lb)
water or milk	125 ml ($\frac{1}{4}$ pt)

Boil together until the consistency of a thick syrup.

Plate 14.9: Shaped bread rolls with sesame seeds

71 – Fruit buns

1 Add 50 g (2 oz) washed, dried fruit (currants, sultanas) and a little mixed spice to the basic bun mixture.
2 Mould into 8 round balls.
3 Place on a lightly greased baking sheet.
4 Cover with a cloth, allow to prove.
5 Bake in hot oven at 220°C (Reg. 7; 425°F) for 15–20 minutes.
6 Brush liberally with bun wash as soon as cooked.

Using hard margarine, 1 portion provides:

728 kJ/173 kcal
6.5 g fat
(of which 2.7 g saturated)
26.9 g carbohydrate
(of which 8.0 g sugars)
3.7 g protein
1.7 g fibre

72 – Hot cross buns

1 Proceed as for fruit buns using a little more spice.
2 When moulded make a cross with the back of a knife, or make a slack mixture of flour and water and pipe on crosses using a greaseproof paper cornet.
3 Allow to prove and finish as for fruit buns.

73 – Bath buns

1 Add to basic bun dough 50 g (2 oz) washed and dried fruit (currants and sultanas), and 25 g (1 oz) chopped mixed peel and 25 g (1 oz) sugar nibs.
2 Proceed as for fruit buns. Pull off into 8 rough-shaped pieces.
3 Sprinkle with a little broken loaf sugar or sugar nibs.
4 Cook as for fruit buns.

74 – Chelsea buns

1 Take the basic bun dough and roll out into a large square.
2 Brush with melted margarine or butter.
3 Sprinkle liberally with castor sugar.
4 Sprinkle with 25 g (1 oz) currants, 25 g (1 oz) sultanas and 25 g (1 oz) chopped peel.
5 Roll up like a Swiss roll, brush with melted margarine or butter.
6 Cut into slices across the roll 3 cm (1½ inches) wide.
7 Place on a greased baking tray with deep sides.
8 Cover and allow to prove. Complete as for fruit buns.

75 – Swiss buns

1 Take the basic bun dough and divide into 8 pieces.
2 Mould into balls, then into 10 cm (4 inch) lengths.
3 Place on a greased baking sheet, cover with a cloth.
4 Allow to prove.
5 Bake at 220°C (Reg. 7; 425°F), for 15–20 minutes.
6 When cool, glaze with fondant or water icing (see below).

⁓ Water icing

	8 buns	20 buns
icing sugar	200 g (8 oz)	500 g (1¼ lb)
few drops vanilla essence		
warm water	2–3 tbsp	5–6 tbsp

1 Pass sugar through a fine sieve into a basin.
2 Gradually mix in warm water with a wooden spoon until the required consistency.

⁓ Fondant

	8 buns	20 buns
loaf sugar	200 g (8 oz)	500 g (1¼ lb)
glucose	1 tsp	2½ tsp
water	125 ml (¼ pt)	300 ml (⅝ pt)

1 Place the water, sugar and glucose in a pan and boil gently. Keep the sides of the pan clean until a temperature of 115°C (240°F) is reached. This is assessed by using a special thermometer (saccharometer).
2 Pour onto a lightly watered marble slab. Allow to cool.
3 Using a metal spatula, turn frequently.
4 Finally knead with the palm of the hand until smooth.
5 Keep covered with a damp cloth to prevent a hard surface forming.
6 To glaze Swiss buns, warm sufficient fondant in a saucepan and adjust the consistency with a little syrup (equal quantities of sugar and water boiled together) if necessary.

Note Fondant must not be heated to more than 37°C (98°F) or it will lose its gloss, because the sugar crystals increase in size and coarseness, thus reflecting less light and making the surface dull.

76 ~ Doughnuts

1 Take the basic bun dough (recipe 70) and divide into 8 pieces.
2 Mould into balls. Press a floured thumb into each.
3 Add a little jam in each hole. Mould carefully to seal the hole.
4 Cover and allow to prove on a well-floured tray.
5 Deep fry in moderately hot fat (175°C/347°F) for 12–15 minutes.
6 Lift out of the fat, drain and roll in a tray containing castor sugar mixed with a little cinnamon.

Using hard margarine and peanut oil, I portion provides:

918 kJ/218 kcal
13.3 g fat
(of which 4.0 g saturated)
22.6 g carbohydrate
(of which 4.0 g sugars)
3.6 g protein
1.2 g fibre

77 ~ Rum baba

	8 portions	20 portions
flour (strong)	200 g (8 oz)	500 g (1¼ lb)
yeast	5 g (¼ oz)	12 g (⅝ oz)
milk	125 ml (¼ pt)	300 ml (⅝ pt)
currants	50 g (2 oz)	125 g (5 oz)
eggs	2	5
butter	50 g (2 oz)	125 g (5 oz)
sugar	10 g (½ oz)	25 g (1¼ oz)
pinch salt		
small glass of rum	1	2–3

Using butter, I portion provides:

797 kJ/190 kcal
7.6 g fat
(of which 4.2 g saturated)
25.4 g carbohydrate
(of which 6.4 g sugars)
4.9 g protein
1.4 g fibre

1 Sieve the flour in a bowl and warm.
2 Cream the yeast with a little of the warm milk in a basin.
3 Make a well in the centre of the flour and add the dispersed yeast.
4 Sprinkle with a little of the flour from the sides, cover with a cloth and leave in a warm place until it ferments.
5 Add the remainder of the warm milk and the washed, dried currants and the beaten eggs, knead well to a smooth elastic dough.
6 Replace in the bowl, add the butter in small pieces, cover with a cloth and allow to prove in a warm place.
7 Add the sugar and salt, mix well until absorbed.
8 Half fill greased dariole moulds, and allow to prove.

recipe continued ▶

9   Bake in a hot oven at 220°C (Reg. 7; 425°F) for about 20 minutes.
10   Turn out when cooked, cool slightly.
11   Soak carefully in hot syrup.
12   Sprinkle liberally with rum.
13   Brush all over with apricot glaze.

Note   Babas may also be decorated with whipped cream or cream Chantilly (whipped cream which is sweetened with castor sugar and flavoured with a little vanilla essence) and finished with a glacé cherry and angelica or half walnuts or any glacéed fruit. Babas may also be flavoured with whisky or brandy in place of rum. Points about use of cream (see also page 655):

- Fresh cream must be cold when required for whipping.
- For preference it should be whipped in china or stainless steel bowls. If any other metal is used, the cream should be transferred to china bowls as soon as possible.
- If fresh cream is whipped too much, it turns to butter. This is more likely to happen in hot conditions. To prevent this, stand the bowl of cream in a bowl of ice while whisking.
- When adding cream to hot liquids dilute the cream with some of the liquid before adding to the main bulk. This helps to prevent the cream from separating.

78 – Syrup for baba, savarin and marignans

	4 babas	10 babas
sugar	100 g (4 oz)	250 g (10 oz)
bayleaf	1	2–3
rind and juice of lemon	1	2–3
water	$\frac{1}{4}$ litre ($\frac{1}{2}$ pt)	600 ml ($1\frac{1}{4}$ pt)
coriander seeds	2–3	6–7
small cinnamon stick	$\frac{1}{2}$	1–$1\frac{1}{2}$

Boil all the ingredients together and strain.

79 – Savarin paste (basic recipe)

	8 portions	20 portions
flour (strong)	200 g (8 oz)	500 g (20 oz)
yeast	5 g ($\frac{1}{4}$ oz)	12 g ($\frac{5}{8}$ oz)
milk	125 ml ($\frac{1}{4}$ pt)	300 ml ($\frac{5}{8}$ pt)
eggs	2	5
butter	50 g (2 oz)	125 g (5 oz)
sugar	10 g ($\frac{1}{2}$ oz)	25 g (1$\frac{1}{4}$ oz)
pinch salt		

1   Sieve the flour in a bowl and warm.
2   Cream the yeast with a little of the warm milk in a basin.
3   Make a well in the centre of the flour and add the dissolved yeast.
4   Sprinkle with a little of the flour from the sides, cover with a cloth and leave in a warm place until it ferments.
5   Add the remainder of the warm milk and the beaten eggs, knead well to a smooth elastic dough.
6   Replace in the bowl, add the butter in small pieces, cover with a cloth and allow to prove in a warm place.
7   Add the sugar and salt, mix well until absorbed.
8   Half fill a greased savarin mould, and prove.
9   Bake in a hot oven at 220°C (Reg. 7; 425°F) for about 30 minutes.
10   Turn out when cooked, cool slightly.
11   Soak carefully in hot syrup (see above).
12   Brush over with apricot glaze (page 671).

80 – Savarin with fruit

1   Prepare the basic savarin mixture.
2   Prove and cook for about 30 minutes in a large greased savarin mould.
3   Complete in exactly the same way as rum baba including the cream. The rum is optional for savarin.
4   Fill the centre with fruit salad.

81 – Marignans Chantilly

1 Marignans are prepared from a basic savarin mixture, and cooked in barquette moulds.
2 After the marignans have been soaked, carefully make a deep incision along one side.
3 Decorate generously with whipped sweetened vanilla-flavoured cream.
4 Brush with apricot glaze (page 671).

Prepare and cook pastry dishes

1 Ensure that preparation and cooking areas and equipment are ready for use and satisfy health and hygiene regulations.
2 Plan the work and plan and allocate time appropriately to meet daily schedules.
3 Ensure that the pastry dish ingredients are of the type, quality and quantity required.
4 Prepare, cook and finish the pastry according to dish and customer requirements.
5 Store prepared pastry and finished goods not for immediate consumption in accordance with food hygiene regulations.
6 Clean preparation and cooking areas and equipment after use.
7 Realise that competency implies knowing, understanding and applying the principles of the pastry and of baking, and that to become competent takes time as well as effort.

Ingredients

FLOUR

Flour is probably the most common commodity in daily use. It forms the foundation of bread, pastry and cakes and is also used in soups, sauces, batters and other foods.

Production of flour

The endosperm of the wheat grain contains all the material used by the baker. It consists of numerous large cells of net-like form in which starch grains are tightly packed. In addition, the cells contain an insoluble gluten protein. When flour is mixed with water it is converted into a sticky dough. This characteristic is due to the gluten which becomes sticky when moistened. The relative proportion of starch and gluten varies in different wheats, and those with a low percentage of gluten (soft flour) are not suitable for bread-making. For this reason, wheat is blended.

In milling, the whole grain is broken up, the parts separated, sifted, blended and ground into flour. Some of the outer coating of bran is removed as is also the wheatgerm which contains oil and is therefore likely to become rancid and so spoil the flour. For this reason wholemeal flour should not be stored for more than 14 days.

Types

White flour contains 72–85% of the whole grain (the endosperm only). Wholemeal flour contains 100% of the whole grain. Wheatmeal flour contains 85–95% of the whole grain. Hovis flour contains 85% of the whole grain. High ratio or patent flour contains 40% of the whole grain. 'Self-raising flour' is white flour with the addition of baking powder. Semolina is granulated hard flour prepared from the central part of the wheat grain. White or wholemeal semolina is available.

FATS

Pastry goods may be made from various types of fat, either a single named fat or a combination. Examples of fats are:

- butter
- margarine
- cake margarine
- pastry margarine
- shortening
- lard.

Butter

Butter is excellent for flavour but does not possess the same qualities of water retention or creaminess as other special manufactured fats.

Margarine

Margarine is often made from a blend of oils which have been hardened or hydrogenated (hydrogen gas is added). Margarine may contain up to 10% butterfat.

Cake margarine

This is again a blend of oils, hydrogenated, to which is added an agent which helps combine water and fat together, an emulsifying agent. Cake margarine may contain up to 10% butterfat.

Pastry margarine

This is used for puff pastry. It is a hard plastic or waxy fat which is suitable for layering.

Shortening (another name for fat used in pastry making)

This is made from oils and is 100% fat, such as hydrogenated lard, another type of shortening which is Rendered pork fat.

SUGAR

Sugar is extracted from sugar beet or sugar cane. The juice is crystallised by a complicated manufacturing process. It is then refined and sieved into several grades, such as granulated, castor or icing sugars.

Loaf or cube sugar is obtained by pressing the crystals whilst slightly wet, drying them in blocks, and then cutting the blocks into squares.

Syrup and treacle are produced during the production of sugar.

RAISING AGENTS

A raising agent is added to a cake or bread mixture to give lightness to the product. This lightness is based upon the principle that gases expand when heated. The gases used are air, carbon dioxide or water vapour. These gases are introduced before baking or are produced by substances added to the mixture before baking. When the product is cooked, the gases expand. These gases are trapped in the gluten content of the wheat flour. On further heating and cooking the product, because of the pressure of the gluten, rises and sets.

Baking powder

Chemical raising agents cause reaction between certain acidic and alkaline compounds, which produce carbon dioxide. The alkaline component is almost universally sodium bicarbonate or sodium acid carbonate commonly known as baking soda. It is ideal because it is cheap to produce, easily purified, non-toxic and naturally tasteless. Potassium bicarbonate is available for those on low sodium diets, but this compound tends to absorb moisture and react prematurely and gives off a bitter flavour.

Baking powder may be used without the addition of acid if the dough or batter is already acidic enough to react with it to produce carbon dioxide. Yoghurt and sour milk contain lactic acid and often are used in place of water or milk in such products; sour milk can also be added along with the baking soda as a separate 'natural' component of the leavening.

Baking powder contains baking soda and an acid in the form of salt crystals that dissolve in water. Ground dry starch is also added to prevent premature reactions in humid air by absorbing moisture and to dilute the powder.

Most baking powders are 'double acting', that is they produce an initial set of gas bubbles upon mixing the powder into the batter and then a second set during the baking process. The first and smaller reaction is necessary to form many small gas cells in the batter or dough, the second, to expand these cells to a size appropriate to form the final light texture, but late enough in the baking so that the surrounding materials have set preventing the escape of bubbles or the collapse of the product.

Different commercial baking powders differ mainly in the proportions of the acid salts. Cream of tartar is not normally used due to its high cost.

Carbon dioxide using baking powder

Alkali (bicarbonate of soda) + acid (cream of tartar (potassium hydrogen tartrate)).

Calcium phosphate and glucono-delta-lactose are now commonly used in place of cream of tartar.

Sodium aluminium sulphate is an acid which is only active at higher oven temperatures and has an advantage over other powders which tend to produce gas too early.

Use of water vapour

This is produced during the baking process, from the liquid content used in the mixing. Water vapour has approximately 1600 times the original volume of the water. The raising power is slower than that of a gas. This principle is used in the product of choux pastry, puff pastry, rough puff, flaky and batter products.

Points to remember

- Always buy a reliable brand of baking powder.
- Store in a dry place in an airtight tin.

- Do not store for long periods of time, as the baking powder over time loses some of its residual carbon dioxide and therefore will not be as effective.
- Check the recipe carefully, making sure that the correct preparation for the type of mixture is used; otherwise, under- or over-rising may result.
- Sieve the raising agent with the flour and/or dry ingredients to give an even mix and thus an even reaction.
- Distribute moisture evenly into the mixture to ensure even action of the raising agent.
- If a large proportion of raising agent has been added to a mixture, and is not to be cooked immediately, keep in a cool place to avoid too much reaction before baking.

What happens if too much raising agent is used

Too much raising agent causes:

- Over-risen product which may collapse giving a sunken effect;
- a coarse texture;
- poor colour and flavour;
- fruit sinking to the bottom of the cake;
- a bitter taste.

What happens if insufficient proportion of raising agent is used

Insufficient raising agent causes:

- lack of volume;
- insufficient lift;
- close texture;
- shrinkage.

EGGS

Eggs are an important and versatile ingredient in pastry work. They act as enriching and emulsifying agents. Hen's eggs are graded in seven sizes. For the recipes in this book, use grade 3 eggs.

Eggs are used in pastry work because of their binding, emulsifying and coating properties. Eggs add both protein and fat thus improving the nutritional value and flavour.

CREAM

Cream is the concentrated milk fat which is skimmed off the top of the milk and should contain at least 18% butterfat. Cream for whipping must contain more than 30% butterfat. Commercially frozen cream is available in 2 and 10 kg (4 and 20 lb) slabs. Types, packaging, storage and uses of cream are listed below.

TYPE OF CREAM	LEGAL MINIMUM FAT (%)	PROCESSING AND PACKAGING	STORAGE	CHARACTERISTICS AND USES
half cream	12	homogenised and may be pasteurised or ultra-heat treated	2–3 days	does not whip; used for pouring; suitable for low-fat diets
cream or single cream	18	homogenised and pasteurised by heating to about 79.5°C (175°F) for 15 seconds then cooled to 4.5°C (40°F). Automatically filled into bottles and cartons after processing. Sealed with foil caps. Bulk quantities according to local suppliers	2–3 days in summer; 3–4 days in winter under refrigeration	a pouring cream suitable for coffee, cereals, soup or fruit. A valuable addition to cooked dishes. Makes delicious sauces. Does not whip
soured cream	18	pasteurised/homogenised cream is soured by the addition of a starter culture of bacteria to produce a piquant acid flavour	2–3 days	suitable for savoury dishes and salad dressing
whipping cream	35	not homogenised, but pasteurised and packaged as above	2–3 days in summer; 3–4 days in winter under refrigeration	the ideal whipping cream. Suitable for piping, cake and dessert decoration, ice-cream, cake and pastry fillings
double cream	48	slightly homogenised, and pasteurised and packaged as above	2–3 days in summer; 3–4 days in winter under refrigeration	a rich pouring cream which will also whip. The cream will float on coffee or soup

TYPE OF CREAM	LEGAL MINIMUM FAT (%)	PROCESSING AND PACKAGING	STORAGE	CHARACTERISTICS AND USES
double cream 'thick'	48	heavily homogenised, then pasteurised and packaged. Usually only available in domestic quantities	2–3 days in summer; 3–4 days in winter under refrigeration	a rich spoonable cream which will not whip
clotted cream	55	heated to 82°C (180°F) and cooled for about 4½ hours. The cream crust is then skimmed off. Usually packed in cartons by hand. Bulk quantities according to local suppliers	2–3 days in summer; 3–4 days in winter under refrigeration	a very thick cream with its own special flavour and colour. Delicious with scones, fruit and fruit pies
sterilised half cream	12	homogenised, filled into cans and sealed. Heated to 115°C (240°F) for 20 minutes, then cooled rapidly	up to 2 years if unopened	a pouring cream with a slight caramel flavour
sterilised cream	23	processed as above	up to 2 years if unopened	a thicker, caramel-flavoured cream which can be spooned but not whipped
ultra-heat treated (UHT) cream	12 18 35	half (12%), single (18%) or whipping cream (35%) is homogenised and heated to 132°C (270°F) for one second and cooled immediately. Aseptically packed in polythene and foil-lined containers. Available in bigger packs for catering purposes	6 weeks if unopened. Needs no refrigeration. Usually date stamped	a pouring cream
aerosol cream		UHT cream in sterile aerosol canister. This cream starts to collapse almost immediately		suitable for squeezing on milk shakes, iced coffee and items for immediate consumption

Techniques

ADDING FAT TO FLOUR

Fats act as a shortening agent. The fat coats the sub-proteins within the flour which has the effect of shortening the gluten strands. These gluten strands are easily broken when eaten. The development of gluten in strong flour to the production of puff pastry is very important as we need long strands to trap the expanding gases which makes the paste rise.

- Rubbing in by hand: short pastry.
- Rubbing in by machine: short pastry.
- Creaming method by machine or by hand: sweet pastry.
- Flour batter method: slab cakes.
- Lamination: puff pastry.
- Boiling: choux pastry.

TERMS

Folding

As in folding puff pastry.

Kneading

Used as a term when making doughs or in the first stage of making puff pastry.

Blending

Mixing all the ingredients carefully by weight.

Relaxing

Keeping pastry covered with a damp cloth, cling film or plastic to prevent skinning. Relaxing allows the pastry to lose some of its resistance to rolling.

Cutting

- Always cut with a sharp, damp knife.
- When using cutters, always flour the cutters by dipping in flour. This will give a sharp, neat cut.
- When using a lattice cutter, use only on firm pastry; if the pastry is too soft, you will have difficulty lifting the lattice.

Rolling

- Roll the pastry on a lightly floured surface, turn the pastry to prevent it sticking. Keep the rolling pin lightly floured and free from the pastry.
- Always roll with care, treat lightly, never apply too much pressure.
- Always apply even pressure when using a rolling pin.

Shaping

Shaping refers to producing flans, tartlets, barquettes and other such goods with the pastry. Shaping also refers to crimping with the back of a small knife using the thumb technique.

Docking

Piercing raw pastry with small holes to prevent rising during baking as when cooking blind tartlets.

Glazing

Examples of glazing pastry dishes are as follows:

- Using a hot clear gel produced from a pectin source obtainable commercially for finishing flans and tartlets; always use while still hot. A cold gel is exactly the same except that it is used cold. The gel keeps a sheen on the goods and excludes all oxygen which might otherwise cause discoloration.
- Using apricot glaze, produced from apricot jam. Acts in the same way as gels.
- Using eggwash, prior to baking, to produce a rich glaze on removing from the oven.
- Dusting with icing sugar, then caramelising in the oven or under the grill.
- Using fondant to give a rich sugar glaze, which may be flavoured and/or coloured.
- Using water icing to give a transparent glaze, which also may be flavoured and/or coloured.

—— *Finishing and presentation* ——

It is essential that all products are finished according to the recipe requirements. The finishing and presentation is often a key stage in the process as failure at this point can affect the sales. The way we present goods is an important part of the sales technique. Each product of the same type must be of the same shape, size, colour and finish. The decoration should be attractive, delicate and in keeping with the product range. All piping should be neat, clean and tidy.

- *Dusting*
  This is the sprinkling of icing sugar on to a product using a fine sugar dredger or sieve, or muslin cloth.
- *Piping*
  Using fresh cream, chocolate, or fondant.
- *Filling*
  Products may be finished by filling with fruit, cream, pastry cream, etc. Never overfill as this will often given the product a clumsy appearance.

—— *Storage, health and safety* ——

- Store all goods according to the Food Hygiene (Amendments) Regulations 1993.
- Handle all equipment carefully to avoid cross-contamination.
- Take special care when using cream and ensure that products containing cream are stored under refrigerated conditions.
- All piping bags must be sterilised after each use.
- Always make sure that storage containers are kept clean and returned ready for re-use. On their return they are hygienically washed and stored.

—— *Points to remember* ——

- Check all weighing scales for accuracy.
- Follow the recipe carefully.
- Check all storage temperatures are correct.
- Fat is better to work with if it is plastic (at room temperature). This will make it easier to cream.
- Always cream the fat and sugar well before adding the liquid.
- Always work in a clean, tidy and organised way; clean all equipment after use.
- Always store ingredients correctly: eggs should be stored in a refrigerator, flour in a bin with a tight-fitting lid, sugar and other dry ingredients in closed storage containers.
- Ensure all cooked products are cooled before finishing.
- Understand how to use fresh cream; remember that it is easily overwhipped.
- Always plan your time carefully.

- Understand why pastry products must be rested or relaxed and docked. This will prevent excessive shrinkage in the oven and docking will allow the air to escape through the product thus preventing an unevenness.
- Use silicone paper for baking in preference to greaseproof.
- Keep all small moulds clean and dry to prevent rusting.

—— *Convenience pastry* ——

Convenience mixes such as short pastry, sponge mixes and choux pastry mixes are now becoming increasingly used in a variety of establishments. These products have improved enormously over the last few years. Using such products gives the chef the opportunity to save on time and labour; and with skilful imagination and creativity, the finished products are not impaired.

The large food manufacturer dominates the frozen puff pastry market. Not surprisingly even more caterers including some luxury establishments have turned to using frozen puff pastry. Frozen puff pastry is now available in 12-inch squares, ready rolled, thus avoiding the possibility of uneven thickness and waste, that can occur when rolling out yourself.

Manufactured puff pastry is available in three types, defined often by the fat content. The cheapest is made with the white hydrogenated fat which gives the product a pale colour and a waxy taste. Puff pastry made with bakery margarine has a better colour and often a better flavour. The best quality puff pastry is that which is made with all butter, giving a richer texture, colour and flavour.

Pastry bought in blocks is cheaper than pre-rolled separate sheets, but has to be rolled evenly to give an even bake. The sizes of sheets do vary with manufacturers; all are interleaved with greaseproof paper.

Filo pastry is another example of a convenient pastry product; this is available in frozen sheets of various size. No rolling out is required, once thawed; it can be used as required and moulded if necessary.

OTHER CONVENIENCE PASTRY PRODUCTS

Apart from convenience pastry mixes, there also exists on the market a whole range of frozen products suitable to serve as sweets and afternoon tea pastries. These include fruit pies, flans, gateaux and charlottes. The vast majority are ready to serve once defrosted, but very often they do require a little more decorative finish. The availability of such products gives the caterer the advantage of further labour cost reductions, while asking the chef to concentrate on other areas of the menu.

82 – Short pastry

	5–8 portions	10–16 portions
flour (soft)	200 g (8 oz)	500 g (1¼ lb)
pinch salt		
lard or vegetable fat	50 g (2 oz)	125 g (5 oz)
butter or margarine	50 g (2 oz)	125 g (5 oz)
water	2–3 tbsp	5–8 tbsp

Using ½ lard, ½ hard margarine, this recipe provides:

6269 kJ/1493 kcal
92.6 g fat
(of which 38.0 g saturated)
155.5 g carbohydrate
(of which 3.1 g sugars)
18.9 g protein
7.2 g fibre

1 Sieve the flour and salt.
2 Rub in the fat to a sandy mixture.
3 Make a well in the centre.
4 Add sufficient water to make a fairly firm paste.
5 Handle as little and as lightly as possible.

Note The amount of water used varies according to:

* the type of flour (a very fine soft flour is more absorbent);
* the degree of heat (prolonged contact with hot hands and weather conditions).

For wholemeal short pastry use ½ to ¾ wholemeal flour in place of white flour.
 Short pastry is used in fruit pies, Cornish pasties, etc.

POSSIBLE REASONS FOR FAULTS IN SHORT PASTRY

* *Hard*
  * too much water
  * too little fat
  * fat rubbed in insufficiently
  * too much handling and rolling
  * over baking.
* *Soft-crumbly*
  * too little water
  * too much fat.
* *Blistered*
  * too little water
  * water added unevenly
  * fat not rubbed in evenly.
* *Soggy*
  * too much water

- too cool an oven
- baked for insufficient time.
- *Shrunken*
  - too much handling and rolling
  - pastry stretched whilst handling.

83 – **Puff pastry** *(Illustration on page 664)*

	5–8 portions	10–16 portions
flour (strong)	200 g (8 oz)	500 g (1¼ lb)
salt		
margarine or butter	200 g (8 oz)	500 g (1¼ lb)
ice-cold water	125 ml (¼ pt)	300 ml (⅝ pt)
few drops of lemon juice		

> Using hard margarine, this recipe provides:
>
> 8997 kJ/2142 kcal
> 164.8 g fat
> (of which 70.9 g saturated)
> 150.8 g carbohydrate
> (of which 3.0 g sugars)
> 23.2 g protein
> 7.4 g fibre

1 Sieve the flour and salt; 50% wholemeal flour may be used.
2 Rub in one-quarter of the butter or margarine.
3 Make a well in the centre.
4 Add the water and lemon juice (which is to make the gluten more elastic), and knead well into a smooth dough in the shape of a ball.
5 Relax the dough in a cool place for 30 minutes.
6 Cut a cross half-way through the dough and pull out the corners to form a star shape.
7 Roll out the points of the star square, leaving the centre thick.
8 Knead the remaining butter or margarine to the same texture as the dough. This is most important; if the fat is too soft it will melt and ooze out, if too hard it will break through the paste when being rolled.
9 Place the butter or margarine on the centre square which is four times thicker than the flaps.
10 Fold over the flaps
11 Roll out 30 × 15 cm (12 × 18 inches), cover with a cloth or plastic and rest for 5–10 minutes in a cool place.
12 Roll out 60 × 20 cm (24 × 9 inches), fold both the ends to the centre, fold in half again to form a square. This is one double turn.
13 Allow to rest in a cool place for 20 minutes.

14   Half-turn the paste to the right or the left.
15   Give one more double turn; allow to rest for 20 minutes.
16   Give two more double turns, allowing to rest between each.
17   Allow to rest before using. ·

Note   Care must be taken when rolling out the paste to keep the ends and sides square.

The lightness of the puff pastry is mainly due to the air which is trapped when giving the pastry folds during preparation. The addition of lemon juice (acid) is to strengthen the gluten in the flour, thus helping to make a stronger dough so that there is less likelihood of the fat oozing out; $3\,g$ ($\frac{1}{8}$oz) ($7\frac{1}{2}$g, $\frac{1}{4}$oz for 10 portions) ascorbic or tartaric acid may be used in place of lemon juice. The rise is caused by the fat separating layers of paste and air during rolling. When heat is applied by the oven, steam is produced causing the layers to rise and give the characteristic flaky formation.

Puff pastry is used for meat pies, sausage rolls, jam puffs, etc. (See page 685 for illustrations of uses of puff pastry.)

POSSIBLE REASONS FOR FAULTS IN PUFF PASTRY

- *Not flaky*
  - fat too warm thus preventing the fat and paste remaining in layers during rolling
  - excessively heavy use of rolling pin.
- *Fat oozes out*
  - fat too soft
  - dought too soft
  - edges not sealed
  - uneven folding and rolling
  - oven too cool.
- *Hard*
  - too much water
  - flour not brushed off between rolling
  - over handling.
- *Shrunken*
  - insufficient resting between rolling
  - overstretching.

- *Soggy*
  - under baked
  - oven too hot.
- *Uneven rise*
  - uneven distribution of fat
  - sides and corners not straight
  - uneven folding and rolling.

84 – Rough puff pastry

	5–8 portions	10–16 portions
flour (strong)	200 g (8 oz)	500 g (1¼ lb)
salt		
butter or margarine	150 g (6 oz)	375 g (15 oz)
ice-cold water	125 ml (¼ pt)	300 ml (⅝ pt)
squeeze of lemon juice or ascorbic or tartaric acid		

Using hard margarine, this recipe provides:

7464 kJ/1777 kcal
124.3 g fat
(of which 53.2 g saturated)
150.8 g carbohydrate
(of which 3.0 g sugars)
23.2 g protein
7.4 g fibre

1 Sieve the flour and salt; 50% wholemeal flour may be used.
2 Cut the fat into 10 g (½ oz) pieces and lightly mix them into the flour without rubbing in.

Plate 14.10a–f: Preparation of puff pastry

3 Make a well in the centre.
4 Add the liquid and mix to a fairly stiff dough.
5 Turn on to a floured table and roll into an oblong strip, about 30×10 cm (12×4 inches), keeping the sides square.
6 Give one double turn as for puff pastry.
7 Allow to rest in a cool place, covered with cloth or plastic for 30 minutes.
8 Give three more double turns, resting between each.
9 Allow to rest before using.

85 – Sugar pastry

	5–8 portions	10–16 portions
egg	1	2–3
sugar	50 g (2 oz)	125 g (5 oz)
margarine or butter	125 g (5 oz)	300 g (12½ oz)
flour (soft)	200 g (8 oz)	500 g (1¼ lb)
pinch salt		

Using hard margarine, this recipe provides:

7864 kJ/1872 kcal
109.8 g fat
(of which 46.4 g saturated)
208.0 g carbohydrate
(of which 55.6 g sugars)
25.7 g protein
7.2 g fibre

Method I
1 Taking care not to over soften, cream the egg and sugar.
2 Add the margarine and mix for a few seconds.
3 Gradually incorporate the sieved flour and salt.
4 Mix lightly until smooth.
5 Allow to rest in a cool place before using.

Method II
1 Sieve the flour and salt.
2 Lightly rub in the margarine to a sandy texture.
3 Make a well in the centre.
4 Add the sugar and beaten egg.
5 Mix the sugar and egg until dissolved.
6 Gradually incorporate the flour and margarine and lightly mix to a smooth paste. Rest paste before using.

Note 50%, 70% or 100% wholemeal flour may be used.
  Sugar pastry is used for flans, fruit tartlets, etc.

86 ~ Suet paste

	5–8 portions	10 portions
flour (soft)	200 g (8 oz)	500 g (1¼ lb)
baking powder } or self-raising flour	10 g (½ oz)	25 g (1 oz)
pinch salt		
prepared beef suet	100 g (4 oz)	250 g (10 oz)
water	125 ml (¼ pt)	300 ml (⅝ pt)

This recipe provides:

6402 kJ/1524 kcal
89.3 g fat
(of which 40.6 g saturated)
171.3 g carbohydrate
(of which 3.0 g sugars)
19.3 g protein
7.2 g fibre

1 Sieve the flour, baking powder and salt.
2 Mix in the suet.
3 Make a well.
4 Add the water.
5 Mix lightly to a fairly stiff paste.

Note Suet paste is used for steamed fruit puddings, steamed jam rolls, steamed meat puddings and dumplings.

POSSIBLE REASONS FOR FAULTS IN SUET PASTE

- *Heavy and soggy*
  - cooking temperature too low.
- *Tough*
  - too much handling, over-cooking.

87 ~ Choux paste

	5–8 portions	10–16 portions
water	¼ litre (½ pt)	600 ml (1¼ pt)
pinch of sugar and salt		
butter, margarine or oil	100 g (4 oz)	250 g (10 oz)
flour (strong)	125 g (5 oz)	300 g (12½ oz)
eggs	4	10

Using hard margarine, this recipe provides:

6248 kJ/1488 kcal
106.6 g fat
(of which 43.3 g saturated)
99.3 g carbohydrate
(of which 4.1 g sugars)
38.9 g protein
4.5 g fibre

1 Bring the water, sugar and fat to the boil in a saucepan.
2 Remove from heat.
3 Add the sieved flour and mix in with a wooden spoon; 50%, 70% or 100% wholemeal flour may be used.

4   Return to a moderate heat and stir continuously until the mixture leaves the sides of the pan.

5   Remove from the heat and allow to cool.

6   Gradually add the beaten eggs, mixing well.

7   The paste should be of dropping consistency.

Note   Choux paste is used for éclairs, cream buns, profiteroles (illustrated on page 692).

POSSIBLE REASONS FOR FAULTS IN CHOUX PASTE

- *Greasy and heavy*
  - basic mixture over-cooked.
- *Soft, not aerated*
  - flour insufficiently cooked; eggs insufficiently beaten in the mixture; oven too cool; underbaked.

88 ~ Fruit pies

Apple, blackberry, blackberry and apple, cherry, rhubarb, gooseberry, damson, damson and apple, etc.

	4–6 portions	10–15 portions
fruit	400 g (1 lb)	1½ kg (2½ lb)
water	2 tbsp	5 tbsp
sugar	100 g (4 oz)	250 g (10 oz)
Short pastry		
flour (soft)	150 g (6 oz)	375 g (15 oz)
butter or margarine	35 g (1½ oz)	85 g (4¼ oz)
lard or vegetable fat	35 g (1½ oz)	85 g (4¼ oz)
water to mix		

> Using white flour and apple, this recipe provides:
>
> 6808 kJ/1621 kcal
> 65.0 g fat
> (of which 26.6 g saturated)
> 260.0 g carbohydrate
> (of which 144.1 g sugars)
> 15.3 g protein
> 15.0 g fibre

1   Prepare the fruit, wash and place half in a ½ litre (1 pint) pie dish.

2   Add the sugar and water and the remainder of the fruit.

3   Place a clove in an apple pie.

4   Roll out the pastry ½ cm (¼ inch) thick to the shape of the pie dish, allow to relax. Damp the rim of the pie dish and edge the rim with a strip of the pastry.

> Using 50% wholemeal flour and apple, this recipe provides:
>
> 6709 kJ/1598 kcal
> 65.6 g fat
> (of which 26.7 g saturated)
> 251.1 g carbohydrate
> (of which 144.5 g sugars)
> 17.8 g protein
> 18.8 g fibre

recipe continued ▶

5 Damp the edge of the pastry.
6 Carefully lay the pastry on the dish without stretching it and firmly seal the rim of the pie. Cut off any surplus pastry.
7 Brush with milk and sprinkle with castor sugar.
8 Place the pie on a baking sheet and bake in a hot oven at 220°C (Reg. 7; 425°F) for about 10 minutes.
9 Reduce the heat or transfer to a cooler part of the oven and continue cooking for a further 30 minutes. If the pastry colours too quickly cover with a sheet of paper.
10 Clean the pie dish, and serve with a sauceboat of custard ($\frac{1}{4}$ litre/$\frac{1}{2}$ pint); cream or ice-cream.

Note Wholemeal short paste may be used.

– *Preparation of fruit for pies*
● *Apples* Peeled, quartered, cored, washed, cut in slices.
● *Cherries* Stalks removed, washed.
● *Blackberries* Stalks removed, washed.
● *Gooseberries* Stalks and tails removed, washed.
● *Damsons* Picked and washed.
● *Rhubarb* Leaves and root removed, tough strings removed, cut into 2 cm (1 inch) pieces, washed.

89 – Jam tart

Short, sugar or wholemeal paste may be used

	4 portions	10 portions
flour (soft)	100 g (4 oz)	250 g (10 oz)
lard, margarine or vegetable fat	25 g (1 oz)	60 g (2$\frac{1}{2}$ oz)
water to mix		
butter or margarine	25 g (1 oz)	60 g (2$\frac{1}{2}$ oz)
salt		
jam	2 tbsp	5 tbsp

1 Prepare short paste (recipe 82), mould into a ball.
2 Roll out into a 3 mm thick ($\frac{1}{8}$ inch) round.

Fig 14.11: Ingredients for choux paste

3 Place carefully on a greased plate.
4 Cut off any surplus pastry. Neaten the edges.
6 Spread on the jam to within 1 cm ($\frac{1}{2}$ inch) of the edge.
7 Roll out any surplus pastry, cut into $\frac{1}{2}$ cm ($\frac{1}{4}$ inch) strips and decorate the top.
8 Place on a baking sheet and bake in a hot oven at 220°C (Reg. 7; 425°F) for about 20 minutes.

Note   A jam tart may also be made in a shallow flan ring.
    Lemon curd can be used in place of jam.

90 ~ Syrup or treacle tart

	4 portions	10 portions
syrup or treacle	100 g (4 oz)	250 g (10 oz)
lemon juice	3–4 drops	8–9 drops
white breadcrumbs or cake crumbs	15 g ($\frac{3}{4}$ oz)	50 g ($2\frac{1}{2}$ oz)
water	1 tbsp	2–3 tbsp

This recipe provides:

4364 kJ/1039 kcal
42.1 g fat
(of which 17.9 g saturated)
164.2 g carbohydrate
(of which 81.0 g sugars)
11.0 g protein
4.2 g fibre

1 Make the short paste as for jam tart.
2 Warm the syrup or treacle slightly, then mix in the remainder of the ingredients and spread onto the paste.
3 Cook as for jam tart.

91 – Flans (illustrated on page 672)

Allow 25 g (1 oz) flour per portion and prepare sugar pastry (page 665).

1 Grease the flan ring and baking sheet.
2 Roll out the pastry 2 cm (1 inch) larger than the flan ring.
3 Place the flan ring on the baking sheet.
4 Carefully place the pastry on the flan ring, by rolling it loosely over the rolling-pin, picking up, and unrolling it over the flan ring.
5 Press the pastry into shape without stretching it, being careful to exclude any air.
6 Allow a $\frac{1}{2}$ cm ($\frac{1}{4}$ inch) ridge of pastry on top of the flan ring.
7 Cut off the surplus paste by rolling the pin firmly across the top of the flan ring.
8 Mould the edge with thumb and forefinger. Decorate (a) with pastry tweezers or (b) with thumbs and forefingers, squeezing the pastry neatly to form a corrugated pattern.

Note A flan jelly (commercial pectin glaze) may be used as an alternative to apricot glaze. This is usually a clear glaze to which food colour may be added.

92 – Cherry flan – using fresh cherries

	4 portions	10 portions
sugar paste (page 665)	100 g (4 oz)	250 g (10 oz)
cherries	200–300 g (8–12 oz)	500 g (1¼ lb)
sugar	50 g (2 oz)	125 g (5 oz)
red glaze (page 676)	2 tbsp	6 tbsp

1 Line the flan ring and pierce the bottom.
2 Stone the cherries. Arrange neatly in the flan case.
3 Sprinkle with sugar.
4 Bake at 200–230°C (Reg. 6–8; 400–450°F) for about 30 minutes.
5 Remove ring and eggwash sides. Complete the cooking.
6 Brush with hot red glaze.

Note A $\frac{1}{2}$ cm ($\frac{1}{4}$ inch) layer of pastry cream or thick custard may be placed in the flan case before adding the cherries.

93 ‒ Apple flan

	4 portions	10 portions
sugar paste (page 665)	100 g (4 oz)	250 g (10 oz)
sugar	50 g (2 oz)	125 g (5 oz)
cooking apples	400 g (1 lb)	1 kg (2½ lb)
apricot glaze (page 671)	2 tbsp	6 tbsp

> 1 portion provides:
>
> 1428 kJ/340 kcal
> 13.8 g fat
> (of which 5.8 g saturated)
> 53.8 g carbohydrate
> (of which 0.0 g sugars)
> 3.5 g protein
> 2.9 g fibre

1 Line a flan ring. Pierce the bottom several times with a fork.
2 Keep the best-shaped apple and make the remainder into a purée (see below).
3 When cool place in the flan case.
4 Peel, quarter and wash the remaining apple.
5 Cut in neat thin slices and lay carefully on the apple purée, overlapping each slice. Ensure that each slice points to the centre of the flan then no difficulty should be encountered in joining the pattern up neatly.
6 Sprinkle a little sugar on the apple slices and bake the flan at 200–220°C (Reg. 6–7; 400–425°F) for 30–40 minutes.
7 When the flan is almost cooked, remove the flan ring carefully, return to the oven to complete the cooking. Mask with hot apricot glaze.

94 ‒ Apricot glaze

Prepare by boiling apricot jam with a little water and passing it through a strainer. Glaze should be used hot.

95 ‒ Apple meringue flan

Cook as for apple flan, without arranging sliced apples. Pipe with meringue (page 614) using two egg whites. Return to the oven at 200°C (Reg. 6; 400°F) to cook and colour meringue (about 5 minutes).

Note This may be finished with ordinary or Italian meringue.

Plate 14.12a–f: Making flans and slices (bands)

— *Italian meringue*

granulated sugar or cube sugar	200 g (8 oz)
water	60 ml ($\frac{1}{8}$ pt)
pinch of cream of tartar	
egg whites	4

1 Boil the sugar, water and cream of tartar to hard ball stage (121°C/250°F).
2 Beat the egg whites to full peak and while stiff, beating slowly, pour on the boiling sugar.
3 Use as required.

— *Apple purée*

	4 portions	10 portions
cooking apples	400 g (1 lb)	1 kg (2$\frac{1}{2}$ lb)
butter or margarine	10 g ($\frac{1}{2}$ oz)	25 g (1$\frac{1}{4}$ oz)
sugar	50 g (2 oz)	125 g (5 oz)

1 Peel, core and slice the apples.

672

2   Place the butter or margarine in a thick-bottomed pan; heat until melted.
3   Add the apples and sugar, cover with a lid and cook gently until soft.
4   Drain off any excess liquid and pass through a sieve or liquidise.

96 – Lemon meringue pie (economic recipe)

	8 portions	20 portions
sugar paste (page 665)	200 g (8 oz)	500 g (1¼ lb)
Lemon curd		
water	125 ml (¼ pt)	300 ml (⅝ pt)
sugar	100 g (4 oz)	250 g (10 oz)
cornflour	25 g (1 oz)	60 g (2½ oz)
butter	25 g (1 oz)	60 g (2½ oz)
lemon	1	2½
yolks	1–2	3–5
Meringue		
egg whites	4	10
castor sugar	200 g (8 oz)	500 g (1¼ lb)

> 1 portion provides:
>
> 1824 kJ/434 kcal
> 17.5 g fat
> (of which 7.8 g saturated)
> 68.3 g carbohydrate
> (of which 46.3 g sugars)
> 5.2 g protein
> 1.0 g fibre

1   Line a flan ring and cook blind.
2   Prepare the lemon curd by boiling the water, sugar and zest and juice of lemon to a syrup.
3   Thicken with diluted cornflour, remove from the heat, add the butter and whisk in yolks.
4   Place in the flan case.
5   When set, pipe in the meringue (page 614) and colour in a hot oven at 220°C (Reg. 7; 425°F).

Note   This may also be finished with Italian meringue (page 672).

– *Lemon curd*   Alternative recipe

	8 portions	20 portions
eggs, separated	2	5
castor sugar	100 g (4 oz)	250 g (10 oz)
butter	100 g (4 oz)	250 g (10 oz)
lemon	1	2

recipe continued ▶

1 Cream the egg yolks and sugar in a bowl with a whisk.
2 Add the butter, zest and juice of lemon.
3 Place in a bain-marie on a low heat and whisk continuously until it thickens (20–30 minutes).

97 – Baked jam roll

	4 portions	10 portions
short or wholemeal paste (flour with baking powder added when sifting flour, or self-raising flour) (page 661)	200 g (8 oz)	500 g (1¼ lb)
jam	2–3 tbsp	5–7 tbsp

Using white flour, 1 portion provides:

1677 kJ/399 kcal
20.9 g fat
(of which 8.9 g saturated)
50.6 g carbohydrate
(of which 12.4 g sugars)
5.3 g protein
2.2 g fibre

1 Roll out the pastry into a rectangle 30 cm × 16 cm (12 × 6 inches).
2 Spread with jam leaving 1 cm (½ inch) clear on all edges.
3 Fold over two short sides, 1 cm (½ inch).
4 Roll the pastry from the top.
5 Moisten the bottom edge to seal the roll.
6 Place edge down on a greased baking sheet.
7 Brush with eggwash or milk. Sprinkle with sugar.
8 Bake in a moderate oven at 200°C (Reg. 6; 400°F) for about 40 minutes.
9 Serve with a sauceboat of jam or custard sauce separately.

98 – Baked apple dumplings

	4 portions	10 portions
short or wholemeal paste (page 661)	200 g (8 oz)	500 g (1¼ lb)
cloves	4	12
small cooking apples (4 oz each)	4	10
sugar	50 g (2 oz)	125 g (5 oz)

1 Roll out the pastry 3 mm (⅛ inch) thick into a square.
2 Cut into four even squares. Damp the edges.

3 Place a whole peeled, cored and washed apple in the centre of each square. Pierce the apple with a clove.
4 Fill the centre with sugar.
5 Fold over the pastry to completely seal the apple, without breaking the pastry.
6 Roll out any debris of pastry and cut neat 2 cm (1 inch) fancy rounds and place one on top of each apple.
7 Egg or milkwash and place on a lightly greased baking sheet.
8 Bake in a moderately hot oven at 200°C (Reg. 6; 400°F) for about 30 minutes.
9 Serve with a sauceboat of custard, cream or ice cream.

Note Centre of apples may also be filled with different mixtures of candied fruits, dried fruits and nuts.

99 – Dutch apple tart

	6–8 portions	15–20 portions
sugar paste (page 665)	200 g (8 oz)	500 g (1¼ lb)
cooking apples	400 g (1 lb)	1¼ kg (2½ lb)
sugar	100 g (4 oz)	250 g (10 oz)
pinch of cinnamon		
lemon, zest of		
sultanas	50 g (2 oz)	125 g (5 oz)

1 Roll out half the pastry 3 mm (⅛ inch) thick into a neat round and place on a greased plate or line a flan ring.
2 Prick the bottom several times with a fork.
3 Peel, core and wash and slice the apples.
4 Place them in a saucepan with the sugar and a little water.
5 Partly cook the apples; add the cinnamon and zest of lemon.
6 Add the washed, dried sultanas and allow to cool.
7 Place on the pastry. Moisten the edges.
8 Roll out the other half of the pastry to a neat round and place on top.
9 Seal firmly, trim off excess pastry, mould the edges.
10 Brush with milk and sprinkle with castor sugar.
11 Place on a baking sheet, bake in a moderately hot oven at 200–220°C (Reg. 6–7; 400–425°F) for about 40 minutes.
12 Remove from the plate carefully before serving.

100 – Rhubarb flan

	4 portions	10 portions
sugar paste (page 665)	100 g (4 oz)	250 g (10 oz)
sugar	100 g (4 oz)	250 g (10 oz)
rhubarb	300 g (¾ lb)	1 kg (2 lb)
apricot glaze (page 671) or red glaze (see below)	2 tbsp	5 tbsp

1 Trim the roots and leaves from the rhubarb and remove the tough string. Cut into 2 cm (1 inch) pieces, wash and dry thoroughly.
2 Line flan ring and pierce.
3 Sprinkle with sugar.
4 Arrange the fruit neatly in the flan case.
5 Sprinkle with the remainder of the sugar.
6 Bake at 200–220°C (Reg. 6–7; 400–425°F).
7 When the flan is almost cooked, carefully remove the flan ring and return the flan to the oven to complete the cooking.
8 Mask with hot apricot or red glaze.

Note A ½ cm (¼ inch) layer of pastry cream or thick custard may be placed in the flan case before adding the rhubarb.

– *Red glaze*

● Boil the sugar and water or fruit syrup with a little red colour and thicken with diluted arrowroot or fecule, reboil until clear; strain.

   or

● Red jam and a little water boiled and passed through a strainer.

101 – Plum or apricot flan

	4 portions	10 portions
sugar paste (page 665)	100 g (4 oz)	250 g (10 oz)
sugar	100 g (4 oz)	250 g (10 oz)
plums or apricots	200–300 g (8–12 oz)	500–700 g (1¼–2 lb)
apricot glaze (page 671)	2 tbsp	5 tbsp

1 Line a flan ring and pierce. Sprinkle with sugar.
2 Quarter or halve the fruit. Arrange neatly in the flan case.
3 Sprinkle with the remainder of the sugar.
4 Bake at 200–220°C (Reg. 6–7; 400–425°F).
5 When the flan is almost cooked carefully remove the flan ring and return the flan to the oven to complete the cooking.
6 Mask with hot apricot glaze.

Note A ½cm (¼ inch) layer of pastry cream or thick custard may be placed in the flan case before adding the fruit.

102 – Soft fruit and tinned fruit flans

For soft fruit (strawberry, raspberry, banana) and tinned fruits (pear, peach, pineapple, cherry), the flan case is lined in the same way, the bottom pierced and then cooked 'blind': tear a piece of paper 2 cm (1 inch) larger in diameter than the flan ring, place it carefully in the flan case, fill the centre with dried peas, beans or small pieces of stale bread and bake at 200–220°C (Reg. 6–7; 400–425°F) for about 30 minutes. Remove the flan ring, paper and beans before the flan is cooked through, eggwash and return to the oven to complete the cooking. Add pastry cream and sliced or whole drained fruit. Mask with glaze. The glaze may be made with the fruit juice thickened with arrowroot, approximately 10 g (½oz) to ¼ litre (½pt).

103 – Strawberry or raspberry flan

	4 portions	10 portions
sugar paste (page 665)	100 g (4 oz)	250 g (10 oz)
fruit	200 g (8 oz)	500 g (1¼ lb)
red glaze (page 676)	2 tbsp	5 tbsp

1 Cook the flan blind, allow to cool.
2 Pick and wash the fruit, drain well.
3 Dress neatly in flan case. Coat with the glaze.

104 ~ Fruit tarts

These are made from the same pastry and the same fruits as the fruit flans. The ingredients are the same. The tartlets are made by rolling out the pastry 3 mm ($\frac{1}{8}$ inch) thick and cutting out rounds with a fluted cutter and neatly placing them in greased tartlet moulds. Depending on the fruit used, they may sometimes be cooked blind (strawberries, raspberries).

105 ~ Fruit barquettes

Certain fruits (strawberries, raspberries) are sometimes served in boat-shaped moulds. The preparation is the same as for tartlets.

Tartlets and barquettes should be glazed and served allowing one large or two small per portion.

106 ~ Banana flan (illustrated on page 681)

	4 portions	10 portions
sugar paste (page 665)	100 g (4 oz)	250 g (10 oz)
pastry cream or thick custard	125 ml ($\frac{1}{4}$ pt)	250 g (10 oz)
bananas	2	5
apricot glaze (page 671)	2 tbsp	5 tbsp

1 portion provides:

1549 kJ/369 kcal
16.0 g fat
(of which 6.9 g saturated)
53.7 g carbohydrate
(of which 30.3 g sugars)
6.0 g protein
2.9 g fibre

1 Cook flan blind, allow to cool.
2 Make pastry cream (page 605) or custard and pour while hot into the flan case.
3 Allow to set. Peel and slice the bananas neatly.
4 Arrange overlapping layers on the pastry cream. Coat with glaze.

107 ~ Mincemeat tart

	4 portions	10 portions
sugar paste (page 665)	200 g (8 oz)	500 g (1$\frac{1}{4}$ lb)
mincemeat (page 710)	200 g (8 oz)	500 g (1$\frac{1}{4}$ lb)

1 Roll out half the pastry 3 mm ($\frac{1}{8}$ inch) thick into a neat round and place on a greased plate.

2 Prick the bottom several times with a fork.
3 Add the mincemeat. Moisten the edges.
4 Roll out the other half of the pastry to a neat round and place on top.
5 Seal firmly, trim off excess pastry, mould the edges.
6 Brush with milk and sprinkle with castor sugar.
7 Place on a baking sheet and bake at 200–220°C (Reg. 6–7; 400–425°F) for about 40 minutes and serve.

108 – Cream horns (illustrated on page 681)

Makes 16

puff pastry (page 662)	200 g (8 oz)
cream	½ litre (1 pt)
few drops vanilla essence	
jam	50 g (2 oz)
castor sugar	50 g (2 oz)

Using whipping cream, 1 portion provides:

735 kJ/176 kcal
14.9 g fat
(of which 8.6 g saturated)
9.8 g carbohydrate
(of which 6.3 g sugars)
1.2 g protein
0.2 g fibre

1 Roll out the pastry 2 mm ($\frac{1}{12}$ inch) thick, 30 cm (12 inches) long.
2 Cut into 1½ cm wide (¾ inch) strips. Moisten on one side.
3 Wind carefully round lightly greased cream horn moulds, starting at the point and carefully overlapping each round slightly.
4 Brush with eggwash on one side and place on a greased baking sheet.
5 Bake at 220°C (Reg. 7; 425°F) for about 20 minutes.
6 Sprinkle with icing sugar and return to a hot oven for a few seconds to glaze.
7 Remove carefully from the moulds and allow to cool.
8 Place a little jam in the bottom of each.
9 Add the sugar and essence to the cream and whip stiffly.
10 Place in a piping bag with a star tube and pipe a neat rose into each horn.

Note These may also be partially filled with pastry cream to which various flavourings or fruit may be added:

- praline
- chocolate
- coffee
- lemon

- raspberries
- strawberries
- mango
- orange segments.

109 ~ Eccles cakes

Makes 12 cakes

Puff or rough puff pastry (pages 662/664)	200 g (8 oz)

Filling

butter or margarine	50 g (2 oz)
mixed peel	50 g (2 oz)
demerara sugar	50 g (2 oz)
currants	200 g (8 oz)
pinch mixed spice	

> I portion provides:
>
> 691 kJ/164 kcal
> 8.6 g fat
> (of which 3.7 g saturated)
> 22.1 g carbohydrate
> (of which 17.3 g sugars)
> 1.1 g protein
> 1.4 g fibre

1 Roll out the pastry 2 mm ($\frac{1}{12}$ inch) thick.
2 Cut into rounds 10–12 cm (4–5 inch) diameter.
3 Damp the edges.
4 Place a tablespoon of the mixture in the centre of each.
5 Fold the edges over to the centre and completely seal in the mixture.
6 Brush the top with egg white and dip into castor sugar.
7 Place on a greased baking sheet.
8 Cut two or three incisions with a knife so as to show the filling.
9 Bake at 220°C (Reg. 7; 425°F) for 15–20 minutes.

110 ~ Jam turnovers

Makes 12 turnovers

puff pastry (page 662)	200 g (8 oz)
jam	200 g (8 oz)

1 Roll out the pastry 2 mm ($\frac{1}{12}$ inch) thick.
2 Cut with a fancy cutter into 8 cm diameter (4 inch) rounds.
3 Roll out slightly oval 12 × 10 cm (5 × 4 inches).
4 Moisten the edges.
5 Place a little jam in the centre of each.
6 Fold over and seal firmly.
7 Brush with egg white and dip in castor sugar.
8 Place sugar side up on a greased baking sheet.
9 Bake in a hot oven at 220°C (Reg. 7; 425°F) for 15–20 minutes.

Plate 14.13: Banana flan

Plate 14.14: Cream horns

111 – Jam puffs

Ingredients as for jam turnovers, makes 8 puffs.

1 Roll out the pastry 2 mm ($\frac{1}{12}$ inch) thick.
2 Cut into 14 cm (6 inch) rounds. Moisten edges.
3 Place a little jam in the centre of each.
4 Fold over three sides to form a triangle. Finish as for jam turnovers.

112 – Cream slice (*Mille-feuilles*)

Makes 6–8 slices

puff pastry (page 662)	200 g (8 oz)
apricot jam	100 g (4 oz)
pastry cream	$\frac{1}{4}$ litre ($\frac{1}{2}$ pt)
fondant or water icing	200 g (8 oz)

1 Roll out the pastry 2 mm ($\frac{1}{12}$ inch) thick into an even-sided square.
2 Roll up carefully on a rolling-pin and unroll onto a greased, dampened baking sheet.
3 Using two forks pierce as many holes as possible.
4 Cut in half with a large knife then cut each half in two to form four even-sized rectangles.
5 Bake in a hot oven at 220°C (Reg. 7; 425°F) for 15–20 minutes; turn the strips over after 10 minutes. Allow to cool.
6 Keep the best strip for the top. Spread pastry cream on one strip.
7 Place another strip on top and spread with jam.
8 Place the third strip on top and spread with pastry cream.
9 Place the last strip on top, flat side up.
10 Press down firmly with a flat tray.
11 Decorate by feather-icing as follows:
12 Warm the fondant to blood heat and correct the consistency with sugar syrup if necessary.
13 Separate a little fondant into two colours and place in paper cornets.
14 Pour the fondant over the mille-feuille in an even coat.
15 Immediately pipe on one of the colours lengthwise in strips 1 cm ($\frac{1}{2}$ inch) apart.
16 Quickly pipe on the second colour between each line of the first.
17 With the back of a small knife, wiping after each stroke, mark down the slice at 2 cm (1 inch) intervals.

18 Quickly turn the slice around and repeat in the same direction with strokes in between the previous ones.
19 Allow to set and trim the edges neatly.
20 Cut into even portions with a sharp thin-bladed knife, dip into hot water and wipe clean after each cut.

Note At stages 15 and 16 baker's chocolate or tempered couverture may be used for marbling.

Whipped fresh cream may be used as an alternative to pastry cream. Also a variety of soft fruits may be incorporated in the layers, such as raspberries; strawberries; canned well-drained pears, peaches or apricots; kiwi fruit; caramelised poached apple slices. The pastry cream or whipped cream may also be flavoured with a liqueur if so desired such as Curaçao, Grand Marnier, Cointreau.

113 ~ Apple turnovers

Ingredients as for jam turnovers, makes 8 turnovers.

Proceed as for jam turnovers (see page 680), using a dry, sweetened apple purée.

Note Other types of fruit may be included in the turnovers, such as apple and mango; apple and blackberry; apple and passionfruit; apple, pear and cinnamon.

114 ~ Palmiers

Puff pastry trimmings are suitable for these.

1 Roll out the pastry 2 mm ($\frac{1}{12}$ inch) thick into a square.
2 Sprinkle liberally with castor sugar on both sides and roll into the pastry.
3 Fold into three from each end so as to meet in the middle, brush with eggwash and fold in two.
4 Cut into strips approximately 2 cm (1 inch) thick; dip one side in castor sugar.
5 Place on a greased baking sheet, sugared side down, leaving a space of at least 2 cm (1 inch) between each.
6 Bake in a very hot oven for about 10 minutes.
7 Turn with a palette knife, cook on the other side until brown and the sugar caramelised.

Note Palmiers may be made in all sizes. Two joined together with a little whipped cream may be served as a pastry, small ones for petits fours. They may be

recipe continued ▶

sandwiched together with soft fruit, whipped cream and/or ice-cream and served as a sweet.

115 – Puff pastry cases (*Bouchées and vol-au-vent*)

Makes 12 bouchées or 6 vol-au-vent cases.

puff pastry (page 662)	200 g (8 oz)

1 Roll out the pastry approximately ½ cm (¼ inch) thick.
2 Cut out with a round, fluted 5 cm (2 inch) cutter.
3 Place on a greased, dampened baking sheet; eggwash.
4 Dip a plain 4 cm (1½ inch) diameter cutter into hot fat or oil and make an incision 3 mm (⅛ inch) deep in the centre of each.
5 Allow to rest in a cool place.
6 Bake at 220°C (Reg. 7; 425°F) for about 20 minutes.
7 When cool remove the caps or lids carefully and remove all the raw pastry from inside the cases.

Note   Bouchées are filled with a variety of savoury fillings and are served hot or cold. They may also be filled with cream and jam or lemon curd as a pastry.

Large bouchées are known as vol-au-vent. They may be produced in one, two, four or six portion sizes, and a single-sized vol-au-vent would be approximately twice the size of a bouchée. When preparing one and two portion size vol-au-vent the method for bouchées may be followed. When preparing larger sized vol-au-vent it is advisable to have two layers of puff pastry each ½ cm (¼ inch) thick, sealed together with eggwash. One layer should be a plain round, and the other of the same diameter with a circle cut out of the centre.

Plate 14.15: Preparation of vol-au-vent (p. 684); bouchées; cream horns (p. 679); palmiers (p. 683)

684

116 – Jalousie

8–10 portions

puff pastry (page 662)	200 g (8 oz)
mincemeat (page 678), jam or frangipane (page 718)	200 g (8 oz)

1 Roll out one-third of the pastry 3 mm ($\frac{1}{8}$ inch) thick into a strip 25×10 cm (10×4 inches) and place on a greased, dampened baking sheet.
2 Pierce with a fork. Moisten the edges.
3 Spread on the filling, leaving 2 cm (1 inch) free all the way round.
4 Roll out the remaining two-thirds of the pastry to the same size.
5 Fold in half lengthwise and, with a sharp knife, cut slits across the fold about $\frac{1}{2}$ cm ($\frac{1}{4}$ inch) apart to within 2 cm (1 inch) of the edge.
6 Carefully open out this strip and neatly place on to the first strip.
7 Neaten and decorate the edge. Brush with eggwash.
8 Bake at 220°C (Reg. 7; 425°F) for 25–30 minutes.
9 Sprinkle with icing sugar and return to a very hot oven to glaze.

Plate 14.16: Puff pastry goods (from top to foreground): bouchées, vol-au-vent, palmiers, cream horns

117 – Gâteau pithiviers

	8–10 portions	20 portions
puff pastry (page 662)	200 g (8 oz)	500 g (1¼ lb)
apricot jam	1 tbsp	3 tbsp
frangipane (page 718)	using half the recipe	1½ times

1 Roll out one-third of the pastry into a round 20 cm (8 inches), 2 mm ($\frac{1}{12}$ inch) thick, moisten the edges and place on a greased, dampened baking sheet; spread the centre with jam.
2 Prepare the frangipane by creaming the margarine and sugar in a bowl, gradually adding the beaten eggs and folding in the flour and almonds.
3 Spread on the frangipane, leaving a 2 cm (1 inch) border round the edge.
4 Roll out the remaining two-thirds of the pastry and cut into a slightly larger round.
5 Place neatly on top, seal and decorate the edge.
6 Using a sharp pointed knife curved cuts 2 mm ($\frac{1}{12}$ inch) deep, radiating from the centre to about 2 cm (1 inch) from the edge.
7 Brush with eggwash.
8 Bake at 220°C (Reg. 7; 425°F) for 25–30 minutes.
9 Glaze with icing sugar as for jalousie.

118 – Mince pies

	Makes 8–12 pies
puff pastry (page 662)	200 g (8 oz)
mincemeat (page 678)	200 g (8 oz)

I portion provides:

718 kJ/171 kcal
10.2 g fat
(of which 4.5 g saturated)
17.7 g carbohydrate
(of which 10.2 g sugars)
1.3 g protein
1.0 g fibre

1 Roll out the pastry 3 mm ($\frac{1}{8}$ inch) thick.
2 Cut half the pastry into fluted rounds 6 cm (2½ inches) diameter.
3 Place on a greased, dampened baking sheet.
4 Moisten the edges.
5 Place a little mincemeat in the centre of each.
6 Cut the remainder of the pastry into fluted rounds, 8 cm (3 inches) diameter.
7 Cover the mincemeat, seal the edges.

8   Brush with eggwash.
9   Bake at 220°C (Reg. 7; 425°F) for about 20 minutes.
10 Sprinkle with icing sugar and serve warm. Accompany with a suitable sauce (custard, brandy sauce, brandy cream, etc.).

Note   Mince pies may be made with short or sugar pastry.

119 – Sausage rolls

	Makes 12 rolls	10 portions
puff pastry (page 662)	200 g (8 oz)	500 g (1¼ lb)
sausage meat	400 g (1 lb)	1 kg (2½ lb)

> 1 portion provides:
>
> 799 kJ/190 kcal
> 15.9 g fat
> (of which 5.8 g saturated)
> 7.9 g carbohydrate
> (of which 0.2 g sugars)
> 4.3 g protein
> 0.4 g fibre

1   Roll out the pastry 3 mm (⅛ inch) thick into a strip 10 cm (4 inches) wide.
2   Make sausage meat into a roll 2 cm (1 inch) diameter.
3   Place on the pastry. Moisten the edges of the pastry.
4   Fold over and seal. Cut into 8 cm (3 inch) lengths.
5   Mark the edge with the back of a knife. Brush with eggwash.
6   Place on to a greased, dampened baking sheet.
7   Bake at 220°C (Reg. 7; 425°F) for about 20 minutes.

120 – Fruit slice

These may be prepared from any fruit suitable for flans.

	8–10 portions
puff pastry (page 662)	200 g (8 oz)
fruit	400 g (1 lb)
sugar to sweeten	
appropriate glaze	2 tbsp

> 1 portion provides:
>
> 767 kJ/183 kcal
> 7.8 g fat
> (of which 3.4 g saturated)
> 28.6 g carbohydrate
> (of which 21.3 g sugars)
> 1.3 g protein
> 1.6 g fibre

1   Roll out the pastry 2 mm (1/12 inch) thick in a strip 12 cm (6 inches) wide.
2   Place on a greased, dampened baking sheet.

recipe continued ▶

3 Moisten two edges with eggwash; lay two 1½cm (⅜ inch) wide strips along each edge.
4 Seal firmly and mark with the back of a knife.
5 Prick the bottom of the slice.
6 Then depending on the fruit used, either put the fruit (such as apple) on the slice and cook together or cook the slice blind and afterwards place the pastry cream and fruit (such as tinned peaches) on the pastry. Glaze and serve as for flans.

Note Alternative methods are:

- to use short or sweet pastry for the base and puff pastry for the two side strips;
- to use sweet pastry in a slice mould.

121 – Kiwi slice

1 Cook the band blind.
2 When cool add the pastry cream.
3 Arrange the slices of kiwi fruit on pastry cream.
4 Coat with the apricot glaze.
5 Decorate with whipped cream.

Note A whole variety of fruit may be used instead of or in combination with kiwi fruit, such as banana, apricots, raspberries, mango, strawberries, pawpaw, peaches, grapes or pears.

Plate 14.17: Kiwi fruit slice

122 – Chocolate éclairs (illustrated on page 692)

Makes 12 éclairs

choux paste (page 666)	125 ml ($\frac{1}{4}$ pt)
fondant	100 g (4 oz)
whipped cream	$\frac{1}{4}$ litre ($\frac{1}{2}$ pt)
chocolate couverture	25 g (1 oz)

> 1 portion provides:
>
> 516 kJ/123 kcal
> 9.5 g fat
> (of which 5.7 g saturated)
> 8.8 g carbohydrate
> (of which 7.3 g sugars)
> 1.1 g protein
> 0.1 g fibre

1 Place the choux paste into a piping bag with a 1 cm ($\frac{1}{2}$ inch) plain tube.
2 Pipe into 8 cm (3 inch) lengths onto a lightly greased baking sheet.
3 Bake at 200–220°C (Reg. 6–7; 400–425°F) for about 30 minutes.
4 Allow to cool.
5 Slit down one side, with a sharp knife.
6 Fill with sweetened, vanilla-flavoured whipped cream, using a piping bag and small tube. The continental fashion is to fill with pastry cream.
7 Warm the fondant, add the finely cut chocolate, allow to melt slowly, adjust the consistency with a little sugar and water syrup if necessary. *Do not overheat or the fondant will lose its shine.*
8 Glaze the éclairs by dipping them in the fondant; remove the surplus with the finger. Allow to set.

123 – Coffee éclairs (ilustrated on page 692)

Add a few drops of coffee essence instead of chocolate to the fondant.

Coffee éclairs may be filled with coffee-flavoured pastry cream, page 605, or whipped non-dairy cream.

124 – Profiteroles

These are small choux paste buns which can be made in a variety of sizes:

* pea size, for consommé garnish,
* double pea size (stuffed) for garnish,
* half-cream-bun size – filled with cream and served with chocolate sauce.

125 – Cream buns

Makes 8 buns

choux paste (page 666)	125 ml ($\frac{1}{4}$ pt)
chopped almonds	25 g (1 oz)
whipped cream	$\frac{1}{4}$ litre ($\frac{1}{2}$ pt)

1 Place the choux paste into a piping bag with a 1 cm ($\frac{1}{2}$ inch) plain tube.
2 Pipe out on to a lightly greased baking sheet into pieces the size of a walnut.
3 Sprinkle each with chopped almonds. Cook, split and fill as for éclairs.
4 Sprinkle with icing sugar and serve.

126 – Profiteroles and chocolate sauce

8 portions

choux paste (page 666)	125 ml ($\frac{1}{4}$ pt)
chocolate sauce (page 624)	$\frac{1}{4}$ litre ($\frac{1}{2}$ pt)
whipped, sweetened, vanilla flavoured cream	$\frac{1}{4}$ litre ($\frac{1}{2}$ pt)

> 1 portion provides:
>
> 919 kJ/219 kcal
> 16.2 g fat
> (of which 9.7 g saturated)
> 16.4 g carbohydrate
> (of which 12.8 g sugars)
> 2.9 g protein
> 0.2 g fibre

1 Proceed as for cream buns (above), pipe out half the size and omit the almonds. Fill with cream and dredge with icing sugar.
2 Serve with a sauceboat of cold chocolate sauce.

Note   Alternatively, coffee sauce may be served and the profiteroles filled with non-dairy cream. Profiteroles may also be filled with chocolate, coffee or rum flavoured pastry cream.

127 ~ Choux paste fritters

	8 portions
choux paste (page 666)	125 ml ($\frac{1}{4}$ pt)
apricot sauce (page 622)	125 ml ($\frac{1}{4}$ pt)

1 Using a tablespoon and the finger, break the paste off into pieces the size of a walnut into a moderately hot deep fat (170°C/347°F).
2 Allow to cook gently for 10–15 minutes.
3 Drain well, sprinkle liberally with icing sugar.
4 Serve with a sauceboat of hot apricot sauce.

> 1 portion provides:
>
> 344 kJ/82 kcal
> 3.9 g fat
> (of which 1.3 g saturated)
> 11.5 g carbohydrate
> (of which 8.8 g sugars)
> 0.9 g protein
> 0.2 g fibre

128 ~ Steamed fruit puddings

Apple, apple and blackberry, rhubarb, rhubarb and apple, etc.

	6 portions
suet paste (page 666)	200 g (8 oz)
fruit	$\frac{3}{4}$–1 kg (1$\frac{1}{2}$–2 lb)
sugar	100 g (4 oz)
water	2 tbsp

1 Grease the basin.
2 Line, using three-quarters of the paste.
3 Add prepared and washed fruit and sugar. Add 1–2 cloves in an apple pudding.
4 Add water. Moisten the edge of the paste.
5 Cover with the remaining quarter of the pastry. Seal firmly.
6 Cover with greased greaseproof paper, a pudding cloth or foil.
7 Steam for about 1$\frac{1}{2}$ hours and serve with custard.

> Using apple, 1 portion provides:
>
> 967 kJ/230 kcal
> 7.4 g fat
> (of which 3.4 g saturated)
> 41.5 g carbohydrate
> (of which 27.1 g sugars)
> 1.9 g protein
> 3.0 g fibre

129 ~ Steamed jam roll

	6 portions	15 portions
suet paste (page 666)	200 g (8 oz)	400 g (1 lb)
jam	100 g (4 oz)	200 g (8 oz)

recipe continued ▶

Plate 14.18: Left: (clockwise from top): cream buns (p. 690), profiteroles and chocolate sauce (p. 689); coffee and chocolate éclairs (p. 689); Right: preparation of choux pastry goods

1 Roll out the paste into a rectangle 3 cm × 16 cm (12 × 6 inches).
2 Spread with jam leaving 1 cm ($\frac{1}{2}$ inch) clear on all edges.
3 Fold over two short sides, 1 cm ($\frac{1}{2}$ inch).
4 Roll the pastry from the top.
5 Moisten the bottom edge to seal the roll.
6 Wrap in buttered greaseproof paper and a pudding cloth or foil, tie both ends. Steam for 1$\frac{1}{2}$–2 hours.
7 Serve with jam or custard sauce.

Note　The jam may be sprinkled with finely chopped nuts (walnuts, hazelnuts, pecan, almonds).

Prepare and cook cakes and biscuits

1. Ensure that preparation and cooking areas and equipment are ready for use and satisfy health and hygiene regulations.
2. Plan the work, plan and allocate time appropriately to meet daily schedules.
3. Ensure that the ingredients are of the type, quality and quantity required.
4. Prepare, cook and finish the cakes and biscuits according to recipe and customer requirements.
5. Store prepared cakes and biscuits not for immediate consumption in accordance with food hygiene regulations.
6. Clean preparation and cooking areas and equipment after use.
7. Realise that competency implies knowing, understanding and applying the principles of the cake and biscuit making, and that to become competent takes time as well as effort.

Cake mixtures

There are three basic methods of making cake mixtures, also known as cake batters. The working temperature of cake batter should be 21°C (70°F).

SUGAR BATTER METHOD

For this method, the fat (cake margarine, butter or shortening) is blended in a machine with castor sugar. This is the basic or principal stage; the other ingredients are then usually added in the order shown below.

FLOUR BATTER METHOD

For this method the eggs and sugar are whisked to a half sponge; this is the basic or principal stage which aims to foam the two ingredients together until half the maximum volume is achieved. Other ingredients are added as shown below.

A humectant such as glycerine may be added to assist with moisture retention; if so, add at stage 2.

BLENDING METHOD

Used for high ratio cake mixtures. This uses high ratio flour, a flour which has been specially produced so that it will absorb more liquid. For this method also use a high ratio fat. This is made from oil to which a quantity of emulsifying agent has been added enabling the fat to take up a greater quantity of liquid.

High ratio cakes contain more liquid and sugar resulting in a fine stable crumb, good eating qualities, extended shelf-life and excellent freezing qualities.

The principal or basic stage is the mixing of the fat and flour to a crumbling texture as shown below.

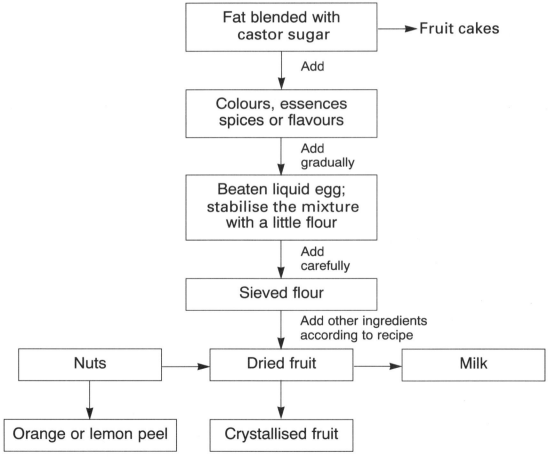

Fig 14.1: Sugar batter method

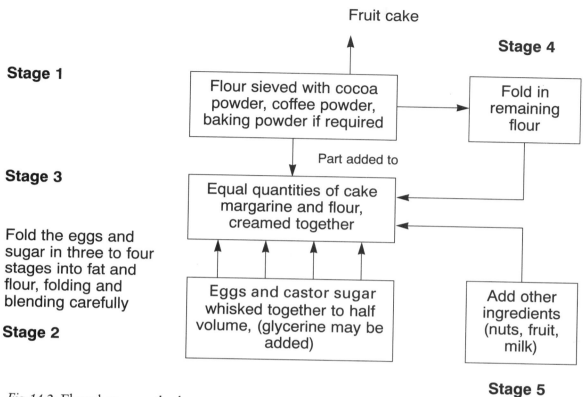

Fig 14.2: Flour batter method

It is essential that each stage of the batter is blended into the next to produce a smooth batter, free from lumps. When using mixing machines, it is important to remember to:

- blend on a slow speed,
- beat on a medium speed, using a paddle attachment.

When blending, always clear the mix from the bottom of the bowl to ensure that any first or second stage butter does not remain in the bowl.

BAKING POWDER

Baking powder may be made from one part sodium bicarbonate to two parts of cream of tartar. In commercial baking the powdered cream of tartar may be replaced by another acid product, such as acidulated calcium phosphate.

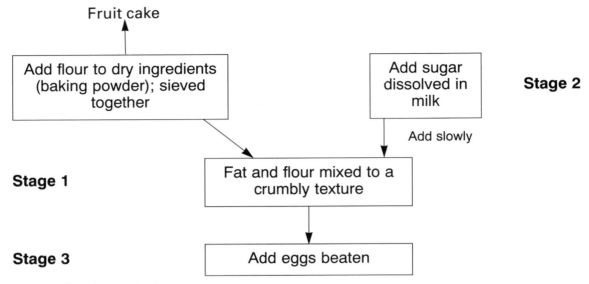

Fig 14.3: Blending method

When used under the right conditions it produces carbon dioxide gas; to produce gas a liquid and heat are needed. As the acid has a delayed action, only a small amount being given off when the liquid is added, the majority of the gas is released when the mixture is heated. Therefore cakes when mixed do not lose the property of the baking powder if they are not cooked right away.

POSSIBLE REASONS FOR FAULTS IN CAKES

- *Uneven texture*
  - fat insufficiently rubbed in
  - too little liquid
  - too much liquid.
- *Close texture*
  - too much fat
  - hands too hot when rubbing in
  - fat to flour ratio incorrect.
- *Dry*
  - too much liquid
  - oven too hot.
- *Bad shape*
  - too much liquid

- oven too cool
- too much baking powder.
- *Fruit sunk*
  - fruit wet
  - too much liquid
  - oven too cool.
- *Cracked*
  - too little liquid
  - too much baking powder.

—— *Biscuit mixtures* ——

Biscuits may be produced by the following methods:

- rubbing in
- foaming
- sugar batter
- flour batter
- blending.

RUBBING IN

This is probably the best known method and is used in producing some of the most famous types of biscuits, such as shortbread. The method is exactly the same as producing short pastry.

- Rub the fat into the flour, by hand or by machine, adding the liquid and the sugar and mixing in the flour to produce a smooth biscuit paste.
- Do not overwork the paste otherwise it will not combine and as a consequence you will not be able to roll it out.

FOAMING

This is where a foam is produced from egg whites or egg yolks or both. Sponge fingers are an example of a two foam mixture. Meringue is an example of a single foam mixture using egg whites. Great care must be taken not to overmix the product.

SUGAR BATTER METHOD

Fat and sugar are mixed together to produce a light and fluffy cream. Beaten egg is gradually added. The dry ingredients are then carefully folded in.

FLOUR BATTER METHOD

Half the sieved flour is creamed with the fat. The eggs and sugar are beaten together before they are added to the fat and flour mixture. Finally, the remainder of the flour is folded in together with any other dry ingredients.

BLENDING METHOD

In several biscuit recipes, the method only requires the chef to blend all the ingredients together to produce a smooth paste.

PRODUCTION METHODS AND EXAMPLES

- *Rubbing in*   Shortbread.
- *Foaming*   Sponge Fingers.
- *Sugar batter method*   Cats' tongues (langues du chat)   Sablé biscuits.
- *Flour batter method*   Cookies.
- *Blending method* Almond biscuits (using basic almond commercial mixture).

—— *Sponge mixtures* ——

These are produced from a foam of eggs and sugar. The eggs may be whole eggs or separated. Example of sponge products are: gâteaux, sponge fingers and sponge cakes.

The egg white traps the air bubbles by forming a semi-rigid membrane structure. When eggs and sugar are whisked together, they thicken until maximum volume is reached; then flour is carefully folded in by a method known as cutting in. This is the most difficult operation as the flour must not be allowed to sink to the bottom of the bowl, otherwise it becomes lumpy and difficult to clear. However, the mixture *must not be stirred* as this will disturb the aeration and cause the air to escape, resulting in a much heavier sponge. If butter, margarine or oil is added, it is important that this is added at about 36°C (98°F), otherwise overheating will cause the fat or oil to act on the flour and create lumps which are difficult, often impossible, to dispense.

Stabilisers are often added to sponges to prevent them from collapsing. The most common are ethylmethyl cellulose and glycerol monostearate; these are added to the eggs and sugar on the commencement of mixing.

METHODS OF MAKING SPONGES

Foaming method

Whisking eggs and sugar together to ribbon stage; folding in/cutting flour.

Melting method

As with foaming, adding melted butter, margarine or oil to the mixture. The fat content enriches the sponge, improves the flavour texture and crumb structure and will extend the shelf-life.

Boiling method

Sponges made by this method have a stable crumb texture that is easier to handle than genoise, crumbling less when cut. This method will produce a sponge that is suitable for dipping in fondant. The stages are shown below.

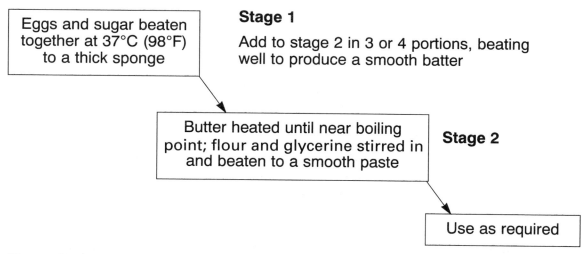

Fig 14.4: Boiling method

Blending method

High ratio sponges follow the same principles as high ratio cakes. As with cakes, high ratio goods produce a fine stable crumb, even texture, excellent shelf-life and good freezing qualities.

Creaming method

This is the traditional method and is still used today for Victoria sandwich and light fruit cakes. The fat and sugar are creamed together, beaten egg is added and finally the sieved flour with the other dry ingredients as desired.

Separate yolk and white method

This method is used for sponge fingers (page 716).

POSSIBLE REASONS FOR FAULTS IN SPONGES

- *Close texture*
  - underbeating
  - too much flour
  - oven too cool or too hot.
- *Holey texture*
  - flour insufficiently folded in
  - tin unevenly filled.
- *Cracked crust*
  - oven too hot.
- *Sunken*
  - oven too hot
  - tin removed during cooking.
- *White spots on surface*
  - insufficient beating.

POSSIBLE REASONS FOR FAULTS IN GENOESE SPONGES

- *Close texture*
  - eggs and sugar overheated
  - eggs and sugar underbeaten
  - too much flour

- • flour insufficiently folded in
- • oven too hot.
- *Sunken*
  - • too much sugar
  - • oven too hot
  - • tin removed during cooking.
- *Heavy*
  - • butter too hot
  - • butter insufficiently mixed in
  - • flour overmixed.

—— *Points to remember* ——

- Check all ingredients carefully.
- Make sure scales are accurate; weigh all ingredients carefully.
- Check ovens are at the right temperature, that the shelves are in the correct position.
- Check all work surfaces and equipment are clean.
- Check that all other equipment required, such as cooling wires, are within easy reach.
- Always sieve flour to remove lumps and any foreign material.
- Make sure that eggs and fats are at room temperature.
- Check dried fruits carefully and wash, drain and dry if necessary.
- Always follow the recipe carefully.
- Always scrape down the sides of the mixing bowl when creaming mixtures.
- Always seek help if you are unsure, or lack understanding.
- Try to fill the oven space when baking by planning production carefully; this saves time, labour and money.
- Never guess quantities. Time and temperature are important factors; they too should not be guessed.
- The shape and size of goods will determine the cooking time and temperature, the wider the cake, the longer and slower it will need to cook.
- Where cakes contain a high proportion of sugar in the recipe. This will caramelise the surface quickly before the centre is cooked. Therefore cover the cake with sheets of silicone or wetted greaseproof and continue to cook.
- When cake tops are sprinkled with almonds or sugar, the baking temperature needs to be lowered slightly to prevent over colouring of the cake crust.

- When glycerine, glucose and invert sugar, honey or treacle is added to cake mixtures, the oven temperature should be lowered as these colour at a lower temperature than sugar.
- Always work in a clean and hygienic way; remember the hygiene and safety rules, in particular the Food Safety Act.
- All cakes and sponges benefit from being allowed to cool in their tins as this makes handling easier. If sponges need to be cooled quickly, place a wire rack over the top of the tin and invert, then remove the lining paper and cool on a wire rack.

—— *The introduction of steam or moisture* ——

Because some cakes become too dry whilst baking due to oven temperature producing a dry atmosphere, some cakes require the injection of steam. Combination ovens are ideally suited for this purpose. The steam delays the formation of the crust until the cake batter has become fully aerated and the proteins have set. Alternatively add a tray of water to the oven while baking. If the oven is too hot the cake crust will form early and the cake batter will rise into a peak.

—— *Convenience cake, biscuit and sponge mixes* ——

There is now available on the market a vast range of prepared mixes, as well as frozen goods. Premixes enable the caterer to calculate costs more effectively, reduce labour costs, limit the range of stock items to be held, with less demand for highly skilled labour.

Every year more and more convenience products are introduced on to the market by large and small food manufacturers. The caterer should be encouraged to investigate these products and experiment to assess their quality.

—— *Decorating and finishing for presentation* ——

FILLING

Cakes, sponges and biscuits may be filled or sandwiched together with a variety of different types of fillings. Examples are:

- *Creams*
  - butter cream ⎱ plain, flavoured and/or coloured
  - pastry cream ⎰
  - whipped cream
  - clotted cream.
- *Fruit*
  - fresh fruit pureé
  - fruit pastries
  - preserves
  - jams
  - fruit mousses
  - fruit gels.
- *Pastes and spreads*
  - chocolate
  - nut
  - praline
  - curds.

SPREADING AND COATING TO FINISH

This is where smaller cakes and gâteaux are covered top and sides with either of the following:

- fresh whipped cream
- fondant
- chocolate
- royal icing
- buttercream
- water icing
- meringue
  - ordinary

- Italian
- Swiss
- commercial preparations.

PIPING

Piping is a skill which takes practice. There are many different types of piping tubes available. The following may be used for piping:

- royal icing
- chocolate
- fondant
- meringue
- boiled sugar
- fresh cream.

DUSTING, DREDGING, SPRINKLING

These techniques are used to give the product a final design or glaze during cooking using sugar.

- *Dusting* A light even finish.
- *Dredging* Heavier dusting with sugar.
- *Sprinkling* A very light sprinkle of sugar.

The sugar used may be icing, castor, or granulated white; demerara, Barbados or dark brown sugar.

The product may be returned to the oven for glazing or glazed under the salamander.

Remember that decorating is an art form and that there is a range of equipment and materials available to assist you in this work. An example of decorative media is as follows:

- Glacé and crystallised fruits
  - cherries
  - lemons
  - oranges
  - pineapple
  - figs.
- Crystallised flowers
  - rose petals

- violets
- mimosa
- lilac.
- Crystallised stems
  - angelica.
- Nuts
  - almonds (nibbed, flaked)
  - coconut (fresh slices, desiccated)
  - hazelnuts
  - brazil nuts
  - pistachio.
- Chocolate
  - rolls
  - flakes
  - chips
  - vermicelli
  - chocolate piping.

BISCUIT PASTES

Piped biscuits can be used for decoration:

- piped sablé paste
- cats' tongues
- almond mixture.

— *Cakes* —

130 – Scones

	Makes 8 scones	20 scones
self-raising flour	200 g (8 oz)	500 g (1¼ lb)
baking-powder	5 g (¼ oz)	12 g (⅝ oz)
pinch salt		
butter or margarine	50 g (2 oz)	125 g (5 oz)
castor sugar	50 g (2 oz)	125 g (5 oz)
milk or water	95 ml (³⁄₁₆ oz)	250 ml (½ pt)

Using hard margarine, 1 portion provides:

678 kJ/162 kcal
5.8 g fat
(of which 2.5 g saturated)
26.3 g carbohydrate
(of which 7.5 g sugars)
2.7 g protein
1.0 g fibre

recipe continued ▶

1 Sieve the flour, baking-powder and salt.
2 Rub in the fat to a sandy texture.
3 Make a well in the centre.
4 Add the sugar and the liquid.
5 Dissolve the sugar in the liquid.
6 Gradually incorporate the flour; mix lightly.
7 Roll out two rounds, 1 cm ($\frac{1}{2}$ inch) thick.
8 Place on a greased baking sheet.
9 Cut a cross half-way through the rounds with a large knife.
10 Milkwash and bake at 200°C (Reg. 6; 400°F) for 15–20 minutes.

Note 50% wholemeal flour may be used. The comparatively small amount of fat, rapid mixing to a soft dough, quick and light handling are essentials to produce a light scone.

Add 50 g (2 oz) (125 g, 5 oz for 20 portions) washed and dried sultanas to the scone mixture for fruit scones.

131 – Small cakes – basic mixture

		10 medium or 20 small cakes	25–50 portions	Using hard margarine, 1 portion provides:
flour (soft)	or self-raising flour	200 g (8 oz)	500 g (1¼ lb)	947 kJ/225 kcal
baking-powder		1 level tsp		11.6 g fat
salt				(of which 4.8 g saturated)
margarine or butter		125 g (5 oz)	300 g (12½ oz)	28.8 g carbohydrate
castor sugar		125 g (5 oz)	300 g (12½ oz)	(of which 13.4 g sugars)
eggs		2–3	5–7	3.3 g protein
				0.7 g fibre

Method I – rubbing in
1 Sieve the flour, baking-powder and salt.
2 Rub in the butter or margarine to a sandy texture.
3 Add the sugar.
4 Gradually add the well-beaten eggs and mix as lightly as possible until combined.

Method II – creaming
1 Cream the margarine and sugar in a bowl until soft and fluffy.
2 Slowly add the well-beaten eggs, mixing continuously and beating really well between each addition.

3 Lightly mix in the sieved flour, baking-powder and salt.

Note In both cases the consistency should be a light dropping one, and if necessary it may be adjusted with the addition of a few drops of milk.
 Variations include:

- *Cherry cakes* Add 50 g (2 oz) glacé cherries cut in quarters and 3 to 4 drops vanilla essence to the basic mixture (Method II) and divide into 8–12 lightly greased cake tins or paper cases. Bake in a hot oven at 220°C (Reg. 7; 425°F) for 15–20 minutes.
- *Coconut cakes* In place of 50 g (2 oz) flour, use 50 g (2 oz) desiccated coconut and 3 to 4 drops vanilla essence to the basic mixture (Method II) and cook as for cherry cakes.
- *Raspberry buns* Divide basic mixture (Method I) into 8 pieces. Roll into balls, flatten slightly, dip tops into milk then castor sugar. Place on a greased baking sheet, make a hole in the centre of each, add a little raspberry jam. Bake in a hot oven at 200°C (Reg. 7; 425°F) for 15–20 minutes.
- *Queen cakes* To the basic mixture (Method II) add 100 g (4 oz) washed and dried mixed fruit and cook as for cherry cakes.

132 – Large fruit cake

	4 portions	10 portions	
butter or margarine	125 g (5 oz)	300 g (12½ oz)	Using hard margarine, this recipe provides:
castor sugar	125 g (5 oz)	300 g (12½ oz)	
eggs	2–3	5–7	14 093 kJ/3355 kcal
flour	200 g (8 oz)	500 g (1¼ lb)	142.8 g fat
baking powder	1 level tsp	2–3 level tsp	(of which 50.7 g saturated)
dried fruit – currants, sultanas	200 g (8 oz)	500 g (1¼ lb)	504.3 g carbohydrate
glacé cherries	50 g (2 oz)	125 g (5 oz)	(of which 349.3 g sugars)
mixed spice	½ level tsp	1 level tsp	45.0 g protein
chopped peel	100 g (4 oz)	250 g (10 oz)	29.3 g fibre
almonds (peeled)	50 g (2 oz)	125 g (5 oz)	

1 Cream the fat and sugar until soft and fluffy.
2 Gradually add the beaten eggs; mix well.
3 Fold in the sieved flour and baking powder, washed and dried fruit, chopped cherries, spice and peel, combine lightly.

recipe continued ▶

4   Place in a lightly greased 18 cm (7 inch) cake tin lined with greased greaseproof or silicone paper.

5   Place the almonds on top, whole, sliced or chopped.

6   Bake at 170°C (Reg. 3–4; 325–350°F), for about 1 hour.

7   Reduce the heat to 150°C (Reg. 2; 300°F) for 30 minutes.

8   Reduce the heat to 140°C (Reg. 1; 275°F) for a further 30 minutes or until cooked.

9   Test by inserting a thin needle or skewer in the centre. If the cake is cooked it should come out clean. If not cooked, a little raw cake mixture sticks to the needle.

Note   When baking, avoid slamming the oven door; open and close it gently. An inrush of cold air checks the rising and may cause the mixture to rise unevenly. Moving or shaking the cake before it has set will cause it to sink in the middle. See also page 89.

133 – Christmas cake

butter or margarine	400 g (1 lb)
demerara sugar	400 g (1 lb)
eggs	10
mixed spice	2 tsp
currants	400 g (1 lb)
raisins	200 g (8 oz)
glacé cherries	100 g (4 oz)
sultanas	400 g (1 lb)
mixed peel	200 g (8 oz)
glass of brandy or rum	
glycerine	2 tsp
chopped almonds	100 g (4 oz)
ground almonds	100 g (4 oz)
flour (soft)	600 g (1½ lb)

Using hard margarine, this recipe provides:

48 917 kJ/11 647 kcal
499.2 g fat
(of which 171.1 g saturated)
1704.2 g carbohydrate
(of which 1243.4 g sugars)
178.6 g protein
120.4 g fibre

1   Cream the butter and sugar until light and fluffy.

2   Gradually beat in the eggs, creaming continuously.

3   Mix in spice, brandy, glycerine and chopped almonds.

4   Fold in the ground almonds and flour.

5   Correct the consistency with milk if necessary.

6   Line a 24–30 cm (10–12 inches) cake tin with silicone paper.

7   Add the mixture, spread evenly.

8   Bake at 160°C (Reg. 3; 325°F), for 1½ hours.
9   Reduce heat to 150°C (Reg. 2; 300°F), for a further 1½ hours.
10 Reduce heat to 140°C (Reg. 1; 275°F), for 30 minutes to 1 hour, or until cooked.
11 Insert a fine trussing needle or skewer into the centre of the cake; when cooked it should come out clean and free of uncooked mixture.
12 Remove from the oven.
13 Allow to set for about 15 minutes.
14 Remove the tin and paper. Allow to cool.
15 Brush with boiling apricot glaze (page 671).
16 Cover the side and top with marzipan (recipe 134).
17 Coat with royal icing (recipe 135) and decorate.

134 ~ Marzipan or almond paste
Cooked

water	250 ml (½ pt)
castor sugar	1 kg (2 lb)
ground almonds	400 g (1 lb)
yolks	3
almond essence	

Place the water and sugar in a pan and boil. Skim. When the sugar reaches 116°C (241°F) draw aside and mix in the almonds; then add the yolks and essence and mix in quickly to avoid scrambling. Knead well until smooth.

135 ~ Royal icing

icing sugar	400 g (1 lb)
whites of egg	3
lemon, juice of	
glycerine	2 dsp

Mix well together in a basin the sieved icing sugar and the whites of egg, with a wooden spoon. Add a few drops of lemon juice and glycerine and beat until stiff.

136 ‒ Mincemeat (used for mince pies)

suet (chopped)	100 g (4 oz)
mixed peel (chopped)	100 g (4 oz)
currants	100 g (4 oz)
sultanas	100 g (4 oz)
raisins	100 g (4 oz)
apples (chopped)	100 g (4 oz)
Barbados sugar	100 g (4 oz)
mixed spice	5 g ($\frac{1}{4}$ oz)
lemon grated zest and juice	1
orange grated zest and juice	1
wineglass rum	$\frac{1}{2}$
wineglass brandy	$\frac{1}{2}$

Mix the ingredients together, place in jars and use as required.

137 ‒ Rock cakes

	8 cakes	20 cakes
flour (soft) or self-raising	200 g (8 oz)	500 g (1$\frac{1}{4}$ lb)
baking powder ∫ flour	5 g ($\frac{1}{4}$ oz)	12 g ($\frac{5}{8}$ oz)
pinch salt		
margarine or butter	75 g (3 oz)	180 g (7$\frac{1}{2}$ oz)
castor sugar	75 g (3 oz)	180 g (7$\frac{1}{2}$ oz)
large egg	1	2–3
dried fruit (currants, sultanas)	50 g (2 oz)	125 g (5 oz)

Using hard margarine, 1 portion provides:

913 kJ/217 kcal
8.7 g fat
(of which 3.6 g saturated)
33.6 g carbohydrate
(of which 14.3 g sugars)
3.4 g protein
1.3 g fibre

1 Use Method I, page 706. Keep the mixture slightly firm.
2 Place with a fork into 8–12 rough shapes on a greased baking sheet; milk or eggwash.
3 Bake in a fairly hot oven at 220°C (Reg. 7; 425°F) for about 20 minutes.

— *Sponges* —

138 ~ Victoria sandwich

	4 portions	10 portions
butter or margarine	100 g (4 oz)	250 g (10 oz)
castor sugar	100 g (4 oz)	250 g (10 oz)
eggs	2	
flour (soft)	100 g (4 oz)	250 g (10 oz)
baking-powder	5 g ($\frac{1}{4}$ oz)	12 g ($\frac{5}{8}$ oz)

> Using hard margarine, this recipe provides:
>
> 6866 kJ/1635 kcal
> 94.3 g fat
> (of which 39.3 g saturated)
> 184.7 g carbohydrate
> (of which 106.6 g sugars)
> 23.3 g protein
> 3.6 g fibre

1 Cream the fat and sugar until soft and fluffy.
2 Gradually add the beaten eggs.
3 Lightly mix in the sieved flour, and baking-powder.
4 Divide into two 18 cm (7 inch) greased sponge tins.
5 Bake at 190–200°C (Reg. 5–6; 375–400°F), for 12–15 minutes.
6 Turn out on to a wire rack to cool.
7 Spread one half with jam, place the other half on top.
8 Dust with icing sugar.

139 ~ Genoese sponge

	4 portions	10 portions
eggs	4	10
castor sugar	100 g (4 oz)	250 g (10 oz)
flour (soft)	100 g (4 oz)	250 g (10 oz)
butter, margarine or oil	50 g (2 oz)	125 g (5 oz)

> Using hard margarine, this recipe provides:
>
> 5978 kJ/1423 kcal
> 65.8 g fat
> (of which 25.6 g saturated)
> 182.8 g carbohydrate
> (of which 106.6 g sugars)
> 36.5 g protein
> 3.6 g fibre

1 Whisk the eggs and sugar with a balloon whisk in a bowl over a pan of hot water.
2 Continue until the mixture is light, creamy and double in bulk.
3 Remove from the heat and whisk until cold and thick (ribbon stage).
4 Fold in the flour very gently.
5 Fold in the melted butter very gently.
6 Place in a greased, floured Genoese mould.
7 Bake in a moderately hot oven at 200–220°C (Reg. 6–7; 400–425°F) for about 30 minutes.

140 – Chocolate Genoese

	4 portions	10 portions
flour (soft)	75 g (3 oz)	180 g (7½ oz)
cocoa powder	10 g (½ oz)	25 g (1¼ oz)
cornflour	10 g (½ oz)	25 g (1¼ oz)
eggs	4	10
castor sugar	100 g (4 oz)	250 g (10 oz)
butter, margarine or oil	50 g (2 oz)	125 g (5 oz)

Sift the flour and the cocoa together with the cornflour, then proceed as for Genoese sponge.

141 – Chocolate gâteau

	4 portions	10 portions
egg chocolate genoese sponge (as previous recipe)	4	10
butter cream		
unsalted butter	200 g (8 oz)	500 g (1¼ lb)
icing sugar	150 g (6 oz)	375 g (15 oz)
block chocolate (melted in a basin in a bain-marie)	50 g (2 oz)	125 g (5 oz)
chocolate vermicelli or flakes	50 g (2 oz)	125 g (5 oz)
stock syrup (recipe 143)		

Using hard margarine and butter, this recipe provides:

20 113 kJ/4789 kcal
260.9 g fat
(of which 148.7 g saturated)
606.0 g carbohydrate
(of which 533.2 g sugars)
41.6 g protein
4.8 g fibre

1 Cut the genoese into three slices crosswise.
2 Prepare the butter cream as in recipe 51, and mix in the melted chocolate.
3 Lightly moisten each slice of genoese with stock syrup which may be flavoured with kirsch, rum, etc.
4 Lightly spread each slice of genoese with butter cream and sandwich together.
5 Lightly coat the sides with butter cream and coat with chocolate vermicelli or flakes.
6 Neatly smooth the top using a little more butter cream if necessary.

Note   Many variations can be used in decorating this gâteau; chocolate fondant may be used on the top and various shapes of chocolate can be used to decorate the top and sides.

142 – Coffee gâteau

	4 portions	10 portions
egg genoese sponge (as above)	4	10
unsalted butter	200 g (8 oz)	500 g ($1\frac{1}{4}$ lb)
icing sugar	150 g (6 oz)	375 g (15 oz)
coffee essence		
toasted, flaked or nibbed almonds	50 g (2 oz)	125 g (5 oz)
stock syrup (recipe 143)		

1 Cut genoese into three slices crosswise.
2 Prepare the butter cream as in recipe 51, and flavour with coffee essence.
3 Lightly moisten each slice of genoese with stock syrup which may be flavoured with Tia Maria, brandy etc.
4 Lightly spread each slice with butter cream and sandwich together.
5 Lightly coat the sides with butter cream and coat with almonds.
6 Smooth the top using a little more butter cream if necessary.
7 Decorate by piping the word MOKA in butter cream.
8 Coffee-flavoured fondant may be used in place of butter cream for the top.

143 – Stock syrup

	4 portions	10 portions
water	500 ml (1 pt)	$1\frac{1}{4}$ litre ($2\frac{1}{2}$ pt)
granulated sugar	150 g (6 oz)	375 g (15 oz)
glucose	50 g (2 oz)	125 g (5 oz)

1 Boil the water, sugar and glucose together, strain and cool.
2 Glucose helps to prevent crystallising.

144 ~ Swiss roll

	4 portions	10 portions
eggs	4	10
castor sugar	100 g (4 oz)	250 g (10 oz)
flour (soft)	100 g (4 oz)	250 g (10 oz)
or		
eggs	250 ml (½ pt)	600 ml (1¼ pt)
castor sugar	175 g (7 oz)	425 g (17½ oz)
flour (soft)	125 g (5 oz)	300 g (oz)

> This recipe provides:
>
> 4445 kJ/1058 kcal
> 25.3 g fat
> (of which 8.0 g saturated)
> 182.7 g carbohydrate
> (of which 106.5 g sugars)
> 36.5 g protein
> 3.6 g fibre

1 Whisk the eggs and sugar with a balloon whisk in a bowl over a pan of hot water.
2 Continue until the mixture is light, creamy and double in bulk.
3 Remove from the heat and whisk until cold and thick (ribbon stage).
4 Fold in the flour very gently.
5 Grease a Swiss roll tin and line with greased greaseproof paper.
6 Pour in genoese mixture and bake at 220°C (Reg. 7; 425°F) for about 6 minutes.
7 Turn out on to a sheet of paper sprinkled with castor sugar.
8 Remove the paper from the Swiss roll, spread with warm jam.
9 Roll into a fairly tight roll, leaving the paper on the outside for a few minutes.
10 Remove the paper and allow to cool on a wire rack.

—— Biscuits and tarts ——

145 ~ Shortbread biscuits

	Makes 12 biscuits
Method I	
flour (soft)	150 g (6 oz)
pinch of salt	
butter or margarine	100 g (4 oz)
castor sugar	50 g (2 oz)

> Using butter, 1 portion provides:
>
> 507 kJ/121 kcal
> 7.0 g fat
> (of which 4.4 g saturated)
> 14.1 g carbohydrate
> (of which 4.6 g sugars)
> 1.2 g protein
> 0.5 g fibre

1 Sift the flour and salt.
2 Mix in the butter or margarine and sugar with the flour.
3 Combine all the ingredients to a smooth paste.
4 Roll carefully on a floured table or board to the shape of a rectangle or round, $\frac{1}{2}$cm ($\frac{1}{4}$inch) thick.
5 Place on a lightly greased baking sheet.
6 Mark into the desired size and shape. Prick with a fork.
7 Bake in a moderate oven at 180–200°C (Reg. 4–6; 350–400°F) for 15–20 minutes.

Method II

soft flour, white or wholemeal	100 g (4 oz)
rice flour	100 g (4 oz)
butter of margarine	100 g (4 oz)
castor or unrefined sugar	100 g (4 oz)
egg (beaten)	1

1 Sieve the flour and rice flour into a basin.
2 Rub in the butter until the texture of fine breadcrumbs.
3 Mix in the sugar.
4 Bind the mixture to a stiff paste using the beaten egg.
5 Roll out to 3 mm ($\frac{1}{8}$inch) using castor sugar, prick well with a fork and cut into fancy shapes.
6 Place the biscuits on a lightly greased baking sheet.
7 Bake in a moderate oven at 180–200°C (Reg. 4–6; 350–400°F), for 15 minutes or until golden brown.
8 Remove with a palette knife on to a cooling rack.

Method III

butter or margarine	100 g (4 oz)
icing sugar	100 g (4 oz)
egg	1
flour (soft)	150 g (6 oz)

1 Cream the butter or margarine and sugar thoroughly.
2 Add the egg and mix in.
3 Mix in the flour.
4 Pipe on to lightly greased and floured baking sheets using a large star tube.
5 Bake at 200–220°C (Reg. 6–7; 400–425°F), for approximately 15 minutes.

146 – Sponge fingers

Makes 32 fingers

eggs	4
castor sugar	100 g (4 oz)
flour (soft)	100 g (4 oz)

1 Cream the egg yolks and sugar in a bowl until creamy and almost white.
2 Whip the egg whites stiffly.
3 Add a little of the whites to the mixture and cut in.
4 Gradually add the sieved flour and remainder of the whites alternately, mixing as lightly as possible.
5 Place in a piping bag with 1 cm (½ inch) plain tube and pipe in 8 cm (3 inch) lengths onto baking sheets lined with greaseproof or silicone paper.
6 Sprinkle liberally with icing sugar. Rest for 5 minutes.
7 Bake in a moderate hot oven at 200–220°C (Reg. 6–7; 400–425°F) for about 10 minutes.
8 Remove from the oven, lift the paper on which the biscuits are piped and place upside down on the table.
9 Sprinkle liberally with water. This will assist the removal of the biscuits from the paper. (No water is needed if using silicone paper.)

147 – Bakewell tart

8 portions

sugar paste (using 8 oz flour) (page 665)	200 g (8 oz)
icing sugar	35 g (1½ oz)
raspberry jam	50 g (2 oz)
apricot glaze	50 g (2 oz)

Frangipane

butter or margarine	100 g (4 oz)
ground almonds	50 g (2 oz)
eggs	2
castor sugar	100 g (4 oz)
flour	50 g (2 oz)
almond essence	

Using hard margarine, 1 portion provides:

2105 kJ/501 kcal
28.8 g fat
(of which 11.0 g saturated)
57.5 g carbohydrate
(of which 33.7 g sugars)
6.7 g protein
2.2 g fibre

1 Line a flan ring using three-quarters of the paste 2 mm ($\frac{1}{12}$ inch) thick.
2 Pierce the bottom with a fork.
3 Spread with jam and the frangipane.
4 Roll the remaining paste, cut into neat $\frac{1}{2}$ cm ($\frac{1}{4}$ inch) strips and arrange neatly criss-crossed on the frangipane; trim off surplus paste.
5 Brush with eggwash.
6 Bake in a moderately hot oven at 200–220°C (Reg. 6–7; 400–425°F) for 30–40 minutes.
7 Brush with hot apricot glaze.
8 When cooled brush over with very thin water icing.

148 – Frangipane for bakewell tart (alternative)

	8 portions
butter	100 g (4 oz)
castor sugar	100 g (4 oz)
eggs	2
ground almonds	100 g (4 oz)
flour	10 g ($\frac{1}{2}$ oz)

Cream the butter and sugar, gradually beat in the eggs. Mix in the almonds and flour, mix lightly.

—— Petits fours ——

These are an assortment of small biscuits, cakes and sweets served with coffee after special meals. There is a wide variety of items that can be prepared and when serving petits fours as large an assortment as possible should be offered.

Basically petits fours fall into two categories – dry and glazed. Dry includes all manner of biscuits, macaroons, meringue (see page 614) and marzipan items.

Glazed includes fruits (recipe 68) dipped in sugar, fondants, chocolates, sweets, and small pieces of neatly cut genoese sponge (recipe 139) covered in fondant.

149 – Cats tongues' (*Langues de chat*)

icing sugar	125 g (5 oz)
butter	100 g (4 oz)
vanilla essence	
egg whites	3–4
soft flour	100 g (4 oz)

1 Lightly cream the sugar and butter, add 3–4 drops of vanilla essence.
2 Add the egg whites one by one, continually mixing and being careful not to allow the mixture to curdle.
3 Gently fold in the sifted flour and mix lightly.
4 Pipe on to a lightly greased baking sheet using a 3 mm ($\frac{1}{8}$ inch) plain tube, 2$\frac{1}{2}$ cm (1 inch) apart.
5 Bake at 230–250°C (Reg. 8–9; 450–500°F), for a few minutes.
6 The outside edges should be light brown and the centres yellow.
7 When cooked, remove on to a cooling rack using a palette knife.

150 – Cornets

1 Ingredients and method to stage 3 as for cat's tongues.
2 Using a 3 mm ($\frac{1}{8}$ inch) plain tube, pipe out the mixture onto a lightly greased baking sheet into rounds approximately 2$\frac{1}{2}$ cm (1$\frac{1}{4}$ inches) in diameter.
3 Bake at 230–250°C (Reg. 8–9; 450–500°F), until the edges turn brown and the centre remains uncoloured.
4 Remove the tray from the oven.
5 Work quickly while the cornets are hot and twist them into a cornet shape using the point of a cream horn mould. (For a tight cornet shape it will be found best to set the pieces tightly inside the cream horn moulds and to leave them until set.)

151 – Piped biscuits

	20–30 biscuits
castor or unrefined sugar	75 g (3 oz)
butter or margarine	150 g (6 oz)
egg	1
vanilla or grated lemon zest	
soft flour, white or wholemeal	200 g (8 oz)
ground almonds	35 g (1½ oz)

1 Cream the sugar and butter until light in colour and texture.
2 Add the egg gradually, beating continuously, add 3–4 drops vanilla or lemon zest.
3 Gently fold in the sifted flour and almonds, mix well until suitable for piping.
4 Pipe on to a lightly greased and floured baking sheet using a medium-sized star tube (a variety of shapes can be used).
5 Some can be left plain, some decorated with half almonds or neatly cut pieces of angelica and glacé cherries.
6 Bake in a moderate oven at 190°C (Reg. 5; 375°F) for about 10 minutes.
7 When cooked, remove on to a cooling rack using a palette knife.

152 – Almond biscuits

	16–20 biscuits
egg whites	1½
ground almonds	100 g (4 oz)
castor or unrefined sugar	50 g (2 oz)
almond essence	
sheet rice paper	1
glacé cherries and angelica	

This recipe provides:

3361 kJ/800 kcal
53.5 g fat
(of which 4.2 g saturated)
62.4 g carbohydrate
(of which 62.4 g sugars)
21.2 g protein
14.4 g fibre

1 Whisk the egg whites until stiff.
2 Gently stir in the ground almonds, sugar and 3–4 drops almond essence.
3 Place rice paper on a baking sheet.
4 Pipe mixture using a medium star tube into shapes.
5 Decorate with neatly cut diamonds of angelica and glacé cherries.

6   Bake at 180–200°C (Reg. 4–6; 350–400°F), for 10–15 minutes.
7   Trim with small knife to cut through rice paper and place on to a cooling rack
    using a palette knife.

Plate 14.19: A selection of pancakes

15

SNACKS, LIGHT MEALS, SAVOURIES AND CONVENIENCE FOODS

Recipe No.			page nos.
1	Angels on horseback	Anges à cheval	727
22	Bouchées		740
20	Bruschetta		738
14	Buck rarebit		733
15	Cheese and ham savoury flan	Quiche lorraine	734
18	Cheese fritters	Beignets au fromage	736
17	Cheese soufflé	Soufflé au fromage	735
16	Cheese straws	Paillettes au fromage	735
11	Chicken liver and bacon on toast	Canapé Diane	731
21	Cocktail canapés		739
10	Creamed haddock and cheese on toast	Canapé ritchie	731
3	Devilled kidneys on toast		728
2	Devils on horseback	Diables à cheval	727
5	Fried ham and cheese savoury	Croque monsieur	729
9	Haddock and bacon on toast		730
8	Haddock on toast		730
4	Mushrooms on toast		728
7	Mushroom and soft roes on toast	Canapé quo vadis	730
19	Pizza		737
24	Sandwiches		740
23	Savouries		740
12	Scotch woodcock		732
6	Soft roes on toast		729
13	Welsh rarebit		732

Snacks, light meals, savouries and convenience foods

1 Appreciate the variety of snacks and savouries and when and where they may be needed.
2 Produce, by preparing, cooking and presenting such items to consumer requirements and satisfaction.
3 Ensure that working conditions comply with health and safety legislation.

Snacks (to be held in the hand) and light meals are a popular form of catering at any time of day or night and there is a wide variety of foods that can be offered.

Savouries can be offered usually as the last course for lunch, dinner or supper. Many savouries can also be served as a snack or light meal.

—— *Snacks* ——

- Sandwiches made with fresh bread or toasted.
- Rolls, baps, French bread, croissants, pitta bread, cut through and filled with a variety of fillings.
- Cornish pasties (page 316).
- Fried or grilled chicken pieces (pages 406, 403).
- Hamburgers (page 351).
- Kebabs (page 308).
- Potato chips, crisps and other shapes (pages 570, 571).
- Sausage rolls (page 687).
- Fruit fritters (apple, banana, pineapple) (page 627).
- Samosas (page 453).
- Tortillas (page 466).
- Barbecued spare ribs (page 379).

—— *Light meals* ——

- Soup served with a warm roll or bread.
- Selection of hors-d'oeuvre (page 153).
- Selection of salad greens served with pâté, cheese, shellfish (crab, lobster, prawns, shrimps), smoked fish (mackerel fillet, salmon, trout, eel).
- Cold meat and poultry or quiche or pie with or without salad.
- Any composed salad.
- Plate of assorted smoked fish.
- Plate of assorted preserved meats.
- An egg dish (omelet, boiled, poached, fried or scrambled eggs).
- A small dish of pasta (page 213).
- Poached smoked haddock (page 272).
- Kedgeree (page 271).
- A small portion of any fish dish.
- Kebabs (page 308).
- Barbecued spare ribs (page 379).
- Burritos (page 468).
- A small portion of any vegetarian dish.

- Baked beans on toast.
- Fried egg and chips.
- Pizza.

—— *Savouries* ——

For savouries see the recipes in this chapter.

—— *Convenience foods* ——

What makes a food or product convenient? What constitutes a convenience food? The word 'convenience' encompasses a wide range of prepared and part-prepared food. This means that certain stages or steps in the process have been eliminated thus less labour is required in their preparation.

Convenience foods can be categorised into the following:

- fresh convenience
- dried
- canned
- bottled
- frozen
- chilled
- vacuum packed
- portion controlled food, eg butter portions, jam portions

The range of convenience foods available to the caterer is expanding all the time, as new technology becomes available to the food manufacturer and there continues to be an increased demand for a wide variety of products from the caterer.

Convenience foods require a range of skills for their preparation and service. The caterer must make a full assessment of what products will be suitable to use in specific situations; will the customer accept the product you intend to use? The equipment required for preparation and service will also have to be reviewed. How is this assessment going to be carried out?

BASIC LEVEL OF CONVENIENCE

This is where the basic stages have been completed such as in peeled potatoes or carrots, but any slicing, chopping or dicing, still has to be carried out.

PRE-ASSEMBLY CONVENIENCE

There are products where all the basic stages have been completed together with the dicing, chopping, slicing, etc.

PRE-COOKING CONVENIENCE

This is where the constituents only have to be assembled prior to the cooking.

PRE-SERVICE CONVENIENCE

This is where the products only have to undergo minimal processing prior to service, such as defrosting prior to service (gâteaux), or defrosting followed by cooking and service. The products may only have to be simply cooked for a relatively short period in a conventional or microwave oven.

FULL SERVICE CONVENIENCE

This is where all the products are ready to be served, when nothing more in certain cases is required than opening a box or can.

A guide to convenience foods is shown in the table on page 726.

TYPE	PACKAGED ITEMS WHERE FOOD IS COOKED OR PREPARED	BEVERAGES	PACKAGED ITEMS WHERE FOOD IS NOT COOKED OR FULLY PREPARED
full convenience	butter portions jam portions sliced bread potted shrimps gâteaux salad dressings	fruit juices	frozen fruit
pre-service convenience	ice-cream canned fruit canned meats canned soup fruit pies	tea bags liquid coffee	frozen fruit
pre-cooking convenience	canned steak dehydrated soup sausage rolls fish fingers croquettes		uncooked frozen pies, pastries breadcrumbed scampi, scallops packet soups portioned meat supreme of chicken
pre-assembly convenience	canned steak frozen pastry fruit pie fillings pastry products	ground coffee	sponge mixes pastry mixes unfrozen scampi fish fillets portioned meat
basic convenience		coffee beans (to be ground)	peeled vegetables dried fruit jointed meats minced meat sausages

1 ~ Angels on horseback

	4 portions	10 portions
live oysters (removed from the shell)	8	20
rashers of streaky bacon (thinly batted out)	4	10
cayenne pepper		
slices toast	2	5
butter or margarine	10 g ($\frac{1}{2}$ oz)	25 g ($1\frac{1}{4}$ oz)

1 Wrap each raw oyster in half a rasher of thin streaky bacon.
2 Place on a skewer then on a baking tray.
3 Grill gently on both sides for a few minutes.
4 Sprinkle with cayenne.
5 Cut the trimmed, buttered toast into four neat rectangles.
6 Place two oysters on each and serve.

2 ~ Devils on horseback

	4 portions	10 portions
well-soaked or cooked prunes	8	20
chopped chutney	50 g (2 oz)	125 g (5 oz)
rashers of streaky bacon (thinly batted out)	4	10
butter or margarine	10 g ($\frac{1}{2}$ oz)	25 g ($1\frac{1}{4}$ oz)
slices toast	2	5
cayenne		

> Using butter, I portion provides:
>
> 754 kJ/179 kcal
> 9.5 g fat
> (of which 4.3 g saturated)
> 18.1 g carbohydrate
> (of which 10.6 g sugars)
> 6.5 g protein
> 2.4 g fibre

1 Stone the prunes carefully. Stuff with chutney.
2 Wrap each one in half a thin rasher of bacon.
3 Place on a skewer and on a baking sheet.
4 Grill on both sides under a salamander.
5 On each rectangle of buttered toast, place two prunes.
6 Sprinkle with cayenne and serve.

3 ~ Devilled kidneys on toast

	4 portions	10 portions
sheep's kidneys	4	10
salt		
butter or margarine	50 g (2 oz)	125 g (5 oz)
devilled sauce (page 124)	125 ml ($\frac{1}{4}$ pt)	300 ml ($\frac{5}{8}$ pt)
slices toast	2	5

Using butter, 1 portion provides:

791 kJ/188 kcal
12.0 g fat
(of which 7.1 g saturated)
8.9 g carbohydrate
(of which 0.9 g sugars)
11.4 g protein
0.7 g fibre

1 Prepare the kidneys as for sauté.
2 Season and quickly fry in three-quarters of the butter in a frying-pan.
3 Drain in a colander.
4 Add to the boiling sauce diable; do not reboil.
5 Mix in and serve on buttered rectangles of toast.

4 ~ Mushrooms on toast

	4 portions	10 portions
grilling mushrooms	150 g (6 oz)	375 g (15 oz)
butter or margarine	10 g ($\frac{1}{2}$ oz)	25 g ($1\frac{1}{4}$ oz)
slices of toast	2	5

1 Peel and wash the mushrooms. Place on a baking tray.
2 Season lightly with salt, brush with melted fat.
3 Gently grill on both sides for a few minutes.
4 Cut and trim the buttered toast into rectangles.
5 Neatly arrange the mushrooms on the toast.
6 Sprinkle with cayenne and serve.

5 – Fried ham and cheese savoury (*croque monsieur*)

	4 portions	10 portions
slices cooked ham	4	10
slices Gruyère cheese	8	20
slices thin toast	8	20
clarified butter, margarine or sunflower oil	50 g (2 oz)	125 g (5 oz)

Using butter, 1 portion provides:

1554 kJ/370 kcal
23.0 g fat
(of which 14.1 g saturated)
22.8 g carbohydrate
(of which 2.7 g sugars)
19.1 g protein
1.7 g fibre

1 Place each slice of ham between two slices of cheese, then between two slices of lightly toasted bread.
2 Cut out with a round cutter.
3 Gently fry on both sides in clarified butter or oil and serve.

6 – Soft roes on toast

	4 portions	10 portions
soft roes	6	15
butter or margarine	10 g ($\frac{1}{2}$ oz)	25 g ($1\frac{1}{4}$ oz)
slices toast	2	5
cayenne		

1 Pass the roes through seasoned flour.
2 Shake off all surplus flour.
3 Then either shallow fry on both sides in hot fat or grill.
4 Dress on rectangles of buttered toast, sprinkle with cayenne and serve.

7 ~ Mushroom and soft roes on toast

	4 portions	10 portions
grilling mushrooms	75 g (3 oz)	180 g (7½ oz)
soft roes	75 g (3 oz)	180 g (7½ oz)
butter or margarine	10 g (½ oz)	25 g (1¼ oz)
cayenne		

Cook the mushrooms (recipe 4) and soft roes (recipe 6) as indicated and dress neatly on rectangles of buttered toast, sprinkle with cayenne and serve.

8 ~ Haddock on toast

	4 portions	10 portions
trimmed smoked haddock fillet	200 g (8 oz)	500 g (1¼ lb)
butter or margarine	10 g (½ oz)	25 g (1¼ oz)
slices toast	2	5
cayenne		

1 Cut and trim the fish into four neat rectangles.
2 Place on a baking tray with a little butter on top.
3 Grill gently on both sides for a few minutes.
4 Place on the trimmed rectangles of buttered toast.
5 Sprinkle with cayenne and serve.

> Using hard margarine, 1 portion provides:
>
> 402 kJ/96 kcal
> 2.6 g fat
> (of which 1.0 g saturated)
> 8.1 g carbohydrate
> (of which 0.5 g sugars)
> 10.5 g protein
> 0.7 g fibre

9 ~ Haddock and bacon on toast

	4 portions	10 portions
skinned smoked haddock fillet	150 g (6 oz)	375 g (15 oz)
rashers streaky bacon (thinly batted out)	4	10
butter or margarine	10 g (½ oz)	25 g (1¼ oz)
slices toast	2	5
cayenne		

1 Cut and trim the fish into four neat rectangles.

2 Fold each one in a thin rasher of bacon.
3 Place on a baking tray.
4 Grill gently on both sides for a few minutes.
5 Place on a buttered rectangle of toast.
6 Sprinkle with cayenne and serve.

10 ~ Creamed haddock and cheese on toast

Ingredients as recipe 8 and 125 ml ($\frac{1}{4}$ pt) béchamel, 250 ml ($\frac{1}{2}$ pt) milk and water.
(Multiply $2\frac{1}{2}$ times for 10 portions.)
1 Poach the fish in the milk and water. Remove all skin.
2 Mix in the boiling béchamel. Season with cayenne.
3 Spread on rectangles of buttered toast.
4 Sprinkle with grated cheese and lightly brown under the salamander.

11 ~ Chicken liver and bacon on toast

	4 portions	10 portions
trimmed chicken livers	4	10
rashers streaky bacon (thinly batted out)	4	10
cayenne		
butter or margarine	10 g ($\frac{1}{2}$ oz)	25 g ($1\frac{1}{4}$ oz)
slices toast	2	5

Using hard margarine, 1 portion provides:

728 kJ/173 kcal
10.2 g fat
(of which 3.9 g saturated)
8.4 g carbohydrate
(of which 0.0 g sugars)
12.7 g protein
0.7 g fibre

1 Roll each half liver in half a rasher of thin bacon.
2 Place on a skewer, then on a baking tray.
3 Grill gently on both sides for a few minutes.
4 Sprinkle with cayenne.
5 Cut the trimmed, buttered toast into four rectangles.
6 Place two livers on each and serve.

12 – Scotch woodcock

	4 portions	10 portions
eggs	2–3	6–8
salt, pepper		
butter or margarine	35 g (1½ oz)	85 g (4¼ oz)
slices toast	2	5
anchovy fillets	5 g (¼ oz)	12 g (⅝ oz)
capers	5 g (¼ oz)	12 g (⅝ oz)

Using hard margarine, 1 portion provides:

611 kJ/145 kcal
10.6 g fat
(of which 4.2 g saturated)
8.1 g carbohydrate
(of which 0.5 g sugars)
5.1 g protein
0.8 g fibre

1   Break the eggs into a basin. Season with salt and pepper.
2   Thoroughly mix with a fork or whisk.
3   Place 25 g (1 oz) of butter in a small thick-based pan.
4   Allow to melt over a low heat.
5   Add the eggs and cook slowly, stirring continuously until *lightly* scrambled. Remove from the heat.
6   Spread on four rectangles or round-cut pieces of buttered toast.
7   Decorate each with two thin fillets of anchovy and four capers and serve.

Note   Adding 1 tbsp cream or milk when eggs are almost cooked will help to prevent overcooking.

13 – Welsh rarebit

	1 portion
butter or margarine	25 g (1 oz)
flour, white or wholemeal	10 g (½ oz)
milk, whole or skimmed	125 ml (¼ pt)
Cheddar cheese	100 g (4 oz)
egg yolk	1
beer	4 tbsp
salt, cayenne	
Worcester sauce	
English mustard	
butter or margarine	10 g (½ oz)
slices toast	2

Using hard margarine, 1 portion provides:

1074 kJ/256 kcal
18.6 g fat
(of which 9.7 g saturated)
11.9 g carbohydrate
(of which 2.4 g sugars)
10.1 g protein
0.7 g fibre

1   Melt the butter or margarine in a thick-based pan.

2   Add the flour and mix in with a wooden spoon.
3   Cook on a gentle heat for a few minutes without colouring.
4   Gradually add the cold milk and mix to a smooth sauce.
5   Allow to simmer for a few minutes.
6   Add the grated or finely sliced cheese.
7   Allow to melt slowly over a gentle heat until a smooth mixture is obtained.
8   Add the yolk to the hot mixture, stir in and immediately remove from the heat.
9   Meanwhile, in a separate pan boil the beer and allow it to reduce to half a tablespoon.
10   Add to the mixture with the other seasonings.
11   Allow the mixture to cool.
12   Spread on the four rectangles of buttered toast.
13   Place on a baking sheet and brown gently under the salamander and serve.

Note   Cheese contains a large amount of protein which will become tough and strong if heated for too long or at too high a temperature. A low-fat Cheddar may be used instead of the traditional full-fat variety.

14 – Buck rarebit

Prepare Welsh rarebit and place a well-drained poached egg on each portion.

Note   Variations include:

- lightly cooked slices of tomato and/or mushrooms put on the toast before adding the mixture;
- grilled back rashers or sliced, cooked ham put either under or on top of the mixture;
- the mixture spread on portions of smoked haddock, a little milk added then baked in the oven; thinly sliced tomato or mushroom can also be added.

Plate 15.1: Neapolitan pizza (see pages 737–738)

15 – Cheese and ham savoury flan (*quiche lorraine*)

	4 portions	10 portions
rough puff, puff or short pastry	100 g (4 oz)	250 g (10 oz)
chopped ham	50 g (2 oz)	125 g (5 oz)
grated cheese	25 g (1 oz)	60 g (2½ oz)
egg	1	2
milk	125 ml (¼ pt)	300 ml (⅝ pt)
cayenne, salt		

> This recipe provides:
>
> 2955 kJ/704 kcal
> 48.4 g fat
> (of which 22.6 g saturated)
> 38.1 g carbohydrate
> (of which 6.5 g sugars)
> 31.6 g protein
> 1.8 g fibre

1 Lightly grease four good-size barquette or tartlet moulds.
2 Line thinly with pastry.
3 Prick the bottoms of the paste two or three times with a fork.
4 Cook in a hot oven at 230–250°C (Reg. 8–9; 450–500°F) for 3–4 minutes or until the pastry is lightly set.
5 Remove from the oven; press the pastry down if it has tended to rise.
6 Add the chopped ham and grated cheese.
7 Mix the egg, milk, salt and cayenne thoroughly.
8 Strain into the barquettes.
9 Return to the oven at 200–230°C (Reg. 6–8; 400–450°F) and bake gently for 15–20 minutes or until nicely browned and set.

Note A variation is to line a 12 cm (6 inches) flan-ring with short paste and proceed as above. The filling can be varied by using lightly fried lardons of bacon (in place of ham), chopped cooked onions and chopped parsley.

A variety of savoury flans can be made by using imagination and experimenting with different combinations of food: Stilton and onion; salmon and cucumber; sliced sausage and tomato.

16 – Cheese straws

	4 portions	10 portions
puff or rough puff paste	100 g (4 oz)	250 g (10 oz)
grated cheese	50 g (2 oz)	125 g (5 oz)
cayenne		

> This recipe provides:
>
> 2562 kJ/610 kcal
> 48.1 g fat
> (of which 24.1 g saturated)
> 28.7 g carbohydrate
> (of which 0.6 g sugars)
> 17.4 g protein
> 1.4 g fibre

1 Roll out the pastry 60 × 15 cm (24 × 6 inches).
2 Sprinkle with cheese and cayenne.
3 Give a single turn, that is, fold the paste one-third the way over so that it covers the first fold.
4 Roll out 3 mm ($\frac{1}{8}$ inch) thick.
5 Cut out four circles 4 cm (2 inches) diameter.
6 Remove the centre with a smaller cutter leaving a circle $\frac{1}{2}$ cm ($\frac{1}{4}$ inch) wide.
7 Cut the remaining paste into strips 8 × $\frac{1}{2}$ cm (3 × $\frac{1}{4}$ inches).
8 Twist each once or twice.
9 Place on a lightly greased baking sheet.
10 Bake in a hot oven at 230–250°C (Reg. 8–9; 450–500°F) for 10 minutes or until a golden brown.
11 To serve place a bundle of straws into each circle.

Note 50% white and 50% wholemeal flour can be used for the pastry.

17 – Cheese soufflé

	4 portions	10 portions
butter or margarine	25 g (1 oz)	60 g ($2\frac{1}{2}$ oz)
flour	15 g ($\frac{3}{4}$ oz)	50 g (2 oz)
milk	125 ml ($\frac{1}{4}$ pt)	300 ml ($\frac{5}{8}$ pt)
egg yolks	3	8
salt, cayenne		
grated cheese	50 g (2 oz)	125 g (5 oz)
egg whites	4	10

> Using hard margarine, this recipe provides:
>
> 3223 kJ/767 kcal
> 60.2 g fat
> (of which 28.2 g saturated)
> 17.6 g carbohydrate
> (of which 6.1 g sugars)
> 39.7 g protein
> 0.5 g fibre

1 Melt the butter in a thick-based pan.
2 Add the flour and mix with a wooden spoon.

recipe continued ▶

3 Cook out for a few seconds without colouring.
4 Gradually add the cold milk and mix to a smooth sauce.
5 Simmer for a few minutes.
6 Add one egg yolk, mix in quickly; immediately remove from the heat.
7 When cool, add the remaining yolks. Season with salt and pepper.
8 Add the cheese.
9 Place the egg whites and a pinch of salt in a scrupulously clean bowl, preferably copper, and whisk until stiff.
10 Add one-eighth of the whites to the mixture and mix well.
11 Gently fold in the remaining seven-eighths of the mixture, mix as lightly as possible. Place into a buttered soufflé case.
12 Cook in a hot oven at 220°C (Reg. 7; 425°F) for 25–30 minutes.
13 Remove from the oven, place on a round flat dish and serve *immediately*.

18 – Cheese fritters

	4 portions	10 portions
water	125 ml ($\frac{1}{4}$ pt)	300 ml ($\frac{5}{8}$ pt)
butter or margarine	50 g (2 oz)	125 g (5 oz)
flour, white or wholemeal	60 g (2$\frac{1}{2}$ oz)	200 g (8 oz)
eggs	2	5
grated Parmesan cheese	50 g (2 oz)	125 g (5 oz)
salt, cayenne		

1 Bring the water and butter or margarine to the boil in a thick-based pan. Remove from the heat.
2 Add the flour, mix with a wooden spoon.
3 Return to a gentle heat and mix well until the mixture leaves the sides of the pan.
4 Remove from the heat. Allow to cool slightly.
5 Gradually add the eggs, beating well.
6 Add the cheese and seasoning.
7 Using a spoon, scoop out the mixture in pieces the size of a walnut; place into deep hot fat (185°C/365°F).
8 Allow to cook with the minimum of handling for about 10 minutes.
9 Drain and serve sprinkled with grated Parmesan cheese.

19 – Pizza

Pizza is a traditional dish originating from southern Italy. In simple terms it is a flat bread dough which can be topped by a wide variety of ingredients and baked quickly. The only rule is not to add wet ingredients, such as tomatoes, which are too juicy, otherwise the pizza becomes soggy. Traditionally pizzas are baked in a wood-fired brick oven but they can be baked in any type of hot oven for 8–15 minutes depending on the ingredients. A typical recipe is given here.

flour, strong white or wholemeal	200 g (8 oz)
pinch of salt	
margarine	12 g ($\frac{1}{2}$ oz)
yeast	5 g ($\frac{1}{4}$ oz)
water or milk at 24°C (75°F)	125 ml ($\frac{1}{4}$ pt)
castor sugar	5 g ($\frac{1}{4}$ oz)
onions	100 g (4 oz)
cloves garlic, crushed	2
sunflower oil	60 ml ($\frac{1}{8}$ pt)
canned plum tomatoes	200 g (8 oz)
tomato purée	100 g (4 oz)
oregano	3 g ($\frac{1}{8}$ oz)
basil	3 g ($\frac{1}{8}$ oz)
sugar	10 g ($\frac{1}{2}$ oz)
cornflour	10 g ($\frac{1}{2}$ oz)
Mozzarella cheese	100 g (4 oz)

Using wholemeal flour, 1 portion provides:

3823 kJ/910 kcal
47.1 g fat
(of which 13.1 g saturated)
103.0 g carbohydrate
(of which 20.8 g sugars)
24.8 g protein
5.9 g fibre

Using 50% wholemeal flour, 1 portion provides:

3758 kJ/895 kcal
47.6 g fat
(of which 13.1 g saturated)
97.1 g carbohydrate
(of which 21.1 g sugars)
26.5 g protein
8.4 g fibre

1 Sieve the flour and the salt. Rub in the margarine.
2 Disperse the yeast in the warm milk or water; add the castor sugar. Add this mixture to the flour.
3 Mix well, knead to a smooth dough, place in a basin covered with a damp cloth and allow to prove until doubled in size.
4 Knock back, divide into two and roll out into two 18 cm (7 inches) discs. Place on a lightly greased baking sheet.
5 Sweat the finely chopped onions and garlic in the oil until cooked.
6 Add the roughly chopped tomatoes, tomato purée, oregano, basil and sugar. Bring to the boil and simmer for 5 minutes.
7 Dilute the cornflour in a little water, stir into the tomato mixture and bring back to the boil.
8 Take the discs of pizza dough and spread 12.5 g (5 oz) of filling on each one.

recipe continued ▶

9   Sprinkle with grated Mozzarella cheese or lay the slices of cheese on top.

10   Bake in a moderately hot oven at 180°C (Reg. 4; 350°F), for about 10 minutes.

Note: The pizza dough may also be made into rectangles so that it can be sliced into fingers for buffet work.

Oregano is sprinkled on most pizzas before baking. This is a basic recipe and many variations exist, some have the addition of olives, artichoke bottoms, prawns, mortadella sausage, garlic sausage, anchovy fillets. A vegetarian pizza recipe is on page 514.

Other combinations include:

- Mozzarella cheese, anchovies, capers and garlic.
- Mozzarella cheese, pepperoni, garlic, fennel and olives.
- Mozzarella cheese, minced beef, garlic, Parmesan and olives.
- Mozzarella cheese, tomato and oregano.
- Mozzarella cheese, frankfurters, onions and olives.
- Assorted cheese and onions.
- Ham, mushrooms, egg and Parmesan cheese.
- Green peppers, onions and olives.
- Prawns, tuna, capers and garlic.
- Ham, mushrooms and olives.
- Chilli pepper, sweetcorn, anchovies and olives.
- Onions, mushrooms, garlic and olives.

20 – Bruschetta

Bruschetta is traditionally a slice of toasted or grilled bread rubbed with a fresh clove of garlic and sprinkled with extra virgin olive oil. It can then be embellished with, tomato, basil, anchovies, Ricotta cheese or almost any type of topping.

1   Toast or grill the slices of bread and rub them with garlic cloves whilst hot.

2   Cook the raw ingredients for the topping in olive oil and pile on to the bread.

3   Add final ingredients such as cheese, anchovies, herbs.

Note: Toppings include mushrooms, aubergine, onions, spinach, tomatoes, ham, rocket, olives, Parmesan, Mozzarella, anchovies. Traditionally an Italian type bread called Ciabata is used.

Fig 15.1a–b: Preparation and presentation of canapés

21 – Cocktail canapés

These are small items of food, hot or cold, which are served at cocktail parties, buffet receptions and may be offered as an accompaniment to drinks before any meal (luncheon, dinner or supper). Typical items for cocktail parties and light buffets are:

1 Hot savoury pastry patties of lobster, chicken, crab, salmon, mushroom, ham, etc. small pizzas, quiches, brochettes, hamburgers.
2 Hot sausages (chipolatas), various fillings, such as chicken livers, prunes, mushrooms, tomatoes, gherkins, etc., wrapped in bacon and skewered and cooked under the salamander. Fried goujons of fish.
3 Savoury finger toast to include any of the cold canapés. These may also be prepared on biscuits or shaped pieces of pastry. On the bases the following may be used: salami, ham, tongue, thinly sliced cooked meats, smoked salmon, caviar, mock caviar, sardine, eggs, etc.
4 Game chips, gaufrette potatoes, fried fish balls, celery stalks spread with cheese.
5 Sandwiches, bridge rolls – open or closed but always small.
6 Sweets such as trifles, charlottes, jellies, bavarois, fruit salad, gâteaux, strawberries and raspberries with fresh cream, ice creams, pastries.
7 Beverages, coffee, tea, fruit-cup, punch-bowl, iced coffee.

Note Canapés are served on neat pieces of buttered toast or puff or short pastry. A variety of foods may be used – slices of hard-boiled egg, thin slices of cooked meats, smoked sausages, fish, anchovies, prawns, mussels, etc. They may be left plain, or decorated with piped butter and coated with aspic jelly. The size of a canapé should be suitable for a mouthful.

22 — Bouchées

Prepare the puff pastry cases according to the instructions on page 684.

Bouchée fillings are numerous as bouchées are served both hot and cold. They may be served as cocktail savouries, or as a first course, a fish course or as a savoury. All fillings should be bound with a suitable sauce, for example:

Mushroom — chicken velouté or béchamel
Shrimp   — fish velouté or béchamel or curry
Prawn   — fish velouté or béchamel or curry
Chicken   — chicken velouté
Ham   — chicken velouté or béchamel or curry
Lobster   — fish velouté or béchamel or mayonnaise
Vegetable — mayonnaise, natural yoghurt, fromage frais, quark or béchamel

23 — Savouries using tartlets

There are a variety of savouries which may be served either as hot appetisers (at a cocktail reception) or as the last course of an evening meal. The tartlet may be made from thinly rolled short paste and cooked blind.

Examples of fillings

Shrimps in curry sauce,
Mushrooms in béchamel, suprême or aurora sauce,
Poached soft roes with devilled sauce.

The cooked tartlets should be warmed through before service, the filling prepared separately and neatly placed in them, garnished with a sprig of parsley.

24 — Sandwiches

Sandwiches may be made from every kind of bread, fresh or toasted, in a variety of shapes and with an almost endless assortment of fillings.

Types of bread	Types of filling	
White	Ham	Tomato
Brown	Tongue	Cucumber
Rye	Beef	Cress
Granary	Chicken	Lettuce

Wholemeal	Smoked fish	Watercress
French sticks	Tinned fish	Egg
Rolls and baps	Fish and meat paste	Cheese

Examples of combination fillings

Fish and lettuce	Roast beef and coleslaw
Cheese and tomato	Roast pork and apple sauce
Cucumber and egg	Tuna fish and cucumber
Apple and chutney	Chopped ham, celery and apple

Seasonings to flavour sandwiches *Types of spread*

Mayonnaise (egg, salmon, etc) Butter
Vinaigrette (crab, lobster, fish, egg) Margarine
English mustard (ham, beef) Peanut butter
French mustard (cheese, tongue)
Chutney (cheese, tinned meat)
Pickles

Where sandwiches are required in large quantities, the usual method is to use large sandwich loaves and remove the crusts from three sides and one end. The bread is then cut in thin slices across the loaf, using a sharp serrated knife.

The slices of bread are stacked neatly, resting on a crust of bread. They are then buttered (unless this has been done before each slice is cut) and the prepared fillings are added, so the complete loaf is made into long sandwiches. If they are to be kept for any length of time the crusts are replaced and the loaf wrapped in clean cloth, greaseproof paper or foil. When required for service the sandwiches are easily and quickly cut into any required size or shape, neatly dressed on a doily on a flat dish and sprinkled with washed and drained mustard cress. A typical set of fillings for a loaf could be: ham, tongue, smoked salmon, tomato, cucumber, egg.

Toasted sandwiches

These are made by inserting a variety of savoury fillings between two slices of hot, freshly buttered toast, e.g. scrambled egg, bacon, fried egg, scrambled egg with chopped ham, or by inserting two slices of buttered bread with the required filling into a sandwich toaster.

Club sandwich

This is made by placing between two slices of hot buttered toast a filling of lettuce, grilled bacon, slices of hard-boiled egg, mayonnaise and slices of chicken.

Bookmaker sandwich

This is an underdone minute steak between two slices of hot buttered toast.

Double-decker and treble-decker sandwiches

Toasted and untoasted bread can be made into double-decker sandwiches, using three slices of bread with two separate fillings. Treble and quadro-decker sandwiches may also be prepared. They may be served hot or cold.

Open sandwich or Scandinavian smorrëbord

This is prepared from a buttered slice of any bread garnished with any type of meat, fish, eggs, vegetables, salads, etc.

The varieties of open sandwiches can include some of the following:

1   Smoked salmon, lettuce, potted shrimps, slice of lemon.
2   Scrambled egg, asparagus tips, chopped tomato.
3   Grilled bacon, cold fried egg, tomato sauce, mushrooms.
4   Cold sliced beef, sliced tomato, fans of gherkins.
5   Shredded lettuce, sliced hard-boiled egg, mayonnaise, cucumber.
6   Cold boiled rice, cold curried chicken, chutney.
7   Minced raw beef, anchovy fillet, raw egg yolk, chopped horseradish, onion and parsley.
8   Pickled herring, chopped gherkin, capers sieved, hard-boiled egg.

When serving open sandwiches it is usual to offer a good choice. Care should be taken with finishing touches, using parsley, sliced radishes, gherkins, pickles, capers, etc., to give a neat clean look to the dish. Presentation is important.

GLOSSARY OF CULINARY TERMS

À la carte	Dishes prepared to order and priced individually
Accompaniments	Items offered separately with a dish of food
Agar-Agar	A vegetable gelling agent obtained from seaweed used as a substitute for gelatine
Ambient	Room temperature, surrounding atmosphere
Amino acid	Organic acids found in proteins
Antibiotic	Drug used to destroy disease-producing germs within human or animal bodies
Antiseptic	Substance that prevents the growth of bacteria and moulds specifically on or in the human body
Aromates	Fragrant herbs and spices
Ascorbic acid	Known as vitamin C, found in citrus fruits and blackcurrants, necessary for growth and maintenance of health
Aspic	A savoury jelly mainly used for decorative larder work
Au bleu	When applied to meat it means very underdone
Au beurre	With butter
Au four	Baked in the oven
Au gratin	Sprinkled with cheese or breadcrumbs and browned
Au vin blanc	With white wine
Bacterium (singular)	Single celled micro-organisms: some are harmful and cause food
Bacteria (plural)	poisoning; others are useful such as those used in cheese making
Bactericide	Substance which destroys bacteria
Bain-marie	• A container of water to keep foods hot without fear of burning
	• A container of water for cooking foods to prevent them burning
	• A deep narrow container for storing hot sauces, soups and gravies
Barquette	A boat-shaped pastry tartlet
Basting	Spooning melted fat over the food during cooking to keep the food moist
Bat out	To flatten slices of raw meat with a cutlet bat
Bean curd	Also known as *tofu*; a curdled, soft, cheese-like preparation made from soybean milk; it is a good source of protein
Bean sprouts	Young shoots of dried beans: mung beans, alfalfa and soybean
Beurre manié	Equal quantities of flour and butter used for thickening sauces
Blanc	A cooking liquor of water, lemon juice, flour and salt; also applied to the white of chicken – the breast and wings
Blanch	• To make white as with bones and meat
	• To retain colour as with certain vegetables

- To skin, as for tomatoes
- To make limp as for certain braised vegetables
- To cook without colour as for the first frying of fried (chip) potatoes

Blanquette	A white stew cooked in stock from which the sauce is made
Bombay duck	Small, dried, salted fish; fried, it is used as an accompaniment to curry dishes
Bone out	To remove the bones
Botulism	Rare form of food poisoning
Bouchée	A small puff paste case, literally a mouthful
Bouillon	Unclarified stock
Bouquet garni	A faggot of herbs: parsley stalks, thyme and bay leaf, tied in pieces of celery and leek
Brine	A preserving solution of water, salt, saltpetre and aromates used for meats (silverside, brisket, tongue)
Brunoise	Small dice
Butters	

- Black butter
- Brown butter: nut brown butter (beurre noisette)
- Melted butter (beurre fondu)
- Parsley butter (beurre maître d'hôtel)

Buttermilk	Liquid remaining from the churning of butter
Calcium	A mineral required for building bones and teeth, obtained from cheese and milk
Calorie	A unit of heat or energy, known as a kilocalorie
Canapé	A cushion of bread on which are served various foods, hot or cold
Carbohydrate	A nutrient which has three groups, sugar, starch and cellulose; the first two provide the body with energy; cellulose provides roughage (dietary fibre)
Carbon dioxide	A gas produced by all raising agents
Carrier	A person who harbours and may transmit pathogenic organisms without showing signs of illness
Carte du jour	Menu for the day
Casserole	An earthenware fireproof dish with a lid
Cellulose	The coarse structure of fruit, vegetables and cereals which is not digested but used as roughage (dietary fibre)
Chateaubriand	The head of the fillet of beef
Chaud-froid	A demi-glace or creamed velouté with gelatine or aspic added, used for masking cold dishes
Chiffonade	Fine shreds, eg spinach, lettuce
Chinois	A conical strainer
Chlorophyll	The green colour in vegetables
Clarification	To make clear such as stock, jelly, butter
Clostridium perfringens	Food poisoning bacteria found in the soil, vegetables and meat

Coagulation	The solidification of protein which is irreversible (fried egg, cooking of meat)
Cocotte	Porcelain or earthenware fireproof dish
Compote	Stewed (stewed fruit)
Concassé	Coarsely chopped (parsley, tomatoes)
Consommé	Basic clear soup
Contamination	Occurrence of any objectionable matter in food
Cook out	The process of cooking the flour in a roux, soup or sauce
Correcting	Adjusting the seasoning, consistency and colour
Coupe	An individual serving bowl
Court-bouillon	A well-flavoured cooking liquor for fish
Crême fraîche	Whipping cream and buttermilk heated to 24–29°C (75–84°F)
Crêpes	Pancakes
Cross-contamination	The transfer of micro-organisms from contaminated to uncontaminated hands, utensils or equipment
Credit notes	Issued when invoice contains incorrect details; credit is therefore given
Croûtons	Cubes of fried or toasted bread served with soup; also triangular pieces served with spinach, and heart-shaped with certain vegetables and entrées
Crudités	Small neat pieces of raw vegetables
Cullis (Coulis)	Sauce made of fruit or vegetable purée, eg raspberry, tomato
Danger zone of bacterial growth	Temperature range within which multiplication of pathogenic bacteria is possible. From 10–63°C (50–145°F)
Dariole	A small mould as used for cream caramel
Darne	A slice of round fish on the bone
Delivery note	Form sent by supplier with delivery of goods
Detergent	Substance which dissolves grease
Demi-glace	Equal quantities of brown sauce and brown stock reduced by half
Dilute	To mix a powder, eg cornflour with a liquid
Dish paper	A plain dish paper
Disinfectant	Substance which reduces the risk of infection
Doily	A fancy dish paper
Drain	Placing food in a colander, allowing liquid to seep out
Duxelle	Finely chopped mushrooms cooked with chopped shallots
Eggwash	Beaten egg with a little milk or water
Emulsion	A mixture of oil and liquid (such as vinegar) which does not separate on standing (mayonnaise, hollandaise)
Entrecôte	A steak cut from a boned sirloin
Enzymes	Chemical substances produced from living cells
Escalope	A thin slice such as escalope of veal

Farce	Stuffing
Fécule	Fine potato flour
Fines herbes	Chopped fresh herbs (parsley, tarragon and chervil)
First aid materials	Suitable and sufficient bandages and dressing including waterproof dressing and antiseptic; all dressings to be individually wrapped
Fleurons	Small crescent-shaped pieces of puff pastry
Flute	A 20 cm (1 inch) diameter French bread used for soup garnishes
Food borne	Bacteria carried on food
Food handling	Any operation in the storage, preparation, production, processing, packaging, transporting, distribution and sale of food
Frappé	Chilled, eg melon frappé
Freezer burn	Affects frozen items which are spoiled due to being unprotected for too long
Friandises	Sweetmeats, petits fours
Fricassée	A white stew in which the meat, poultry or fish is cooked in the sauce
Friture	A pan that contains deep fat
Fumé	Smoked, eg saumon fumé, smoked salmon
Garam masala	A combination of spices
Garnish	Trimmings on the dish
Gastroenteritis	Inflammation of the stomach and intestinal tract that normally results in diarrhoea
Gâteau	A cake of more than one portion
Ghee	The Indian name for clarified butter; ghee is pure butterfat
Glace	Ice or ice cream from which all milk solids have been removed
Glaze	To glaze
	• To colour a dish under the salamander (fillets of sole bonne femme)
	• To finish a flan or tartlet (with apricot jam)
	• To finish certain vegetables (glazed carrots)
Gluten	This is formed from protein in flour when mixed with water
Haché	Finely chopped or minced
Hors-d'oeuvre	Appetising first course dishes
Humidity	Indicates amount of moisture in the air
Incubation period	Time between infection and first signs of illness
Infestations	Insects breeding on the premises
Insecticide	Chemical used to kill insects
Invoices	Bill listing items delivered with costs of items
Jardinière	Vegetables cut into batons
Julienne	Cut into fine strips

Jus-lié	Thickened gravy
Larding	Inserting strips of fat bacon into meat
Lardons	Batons of thick streaky bacon
Liaison	A thickening or binding
Macedoine	• A mixture of fruit or vegetables • Cut into ½ cm (¼ inch) dice
Magnetron	The device which generates microwaves in a microwave oven
Marinade	A richly spiced pickling liquid used to give flavour and to assist tenderising meats
Marmite	Stock pot
Menu	List of dishes available
Micro-organisms	Very small living plants or animals (bacteria, yeasts, moulds)
Mignonnette	Coarsely ground pepper
Mildew	Type of fungus similar to mould
Mineral salts	These are mineral elements, small quantities of which are essential for health
Mirepoix	Roughly cut onion, carrots, a sprig of thyme and a bayleaf
Miso	Seasoning made from fermented soybeans
Monosodium glutamate	A substance added to food products to increase flavour
Moulds	Microscopic plants (fungi) that may appear as woolly patches on food
Mousse	A dish of light consistency, hot or cold
Natives	A menu term for English oysters
Navarin	Brown stew of lamb
Niacin	Part of vitamin B, found in liver, kidney, meat extract, bacon
Noisette (nut)	A cut from a boned-out loin of lamb
Nutrients	These are the components of food required for health (protein, fats, carbohydrates, vitamins, mineral salts, water)
Optimum	Best or most favourable
Palatable	Pleasant to taste
Pass	To cause to go through a sieve or strainer
Pathogen	Disease-producing organism
Paupiette	A stuffed and rolled strip of fish or meat
Paysanne	Cut in even thin triangular, round or square pieces
Pesticide	Chemical used to kill pests
Pests	Such as cockroaches, flies, silverfish
Petits fours	Very small pastries, biscuits, sweets, sweetmeats
pH value	A scale indicating acidity or alkalinity in food
Phosphorus	A mineral element found in fish. Required for building bones and teeth

Poppadums	Dried, thin, large, round wafers made from lentil flour, used as an accompaniment to Indian dishes
Protein	The nutrient which is needed for growth and repair
Prove	To allow a yeast dough to rest in a warm place so that it can expand
Pulses	Vegetables grown in pods (peas and beans) and dried; source of protein and roughage
Quark	Salt-free soft cheese made from semi-skimmed milk
Ragoût	Stew (ragoût de boeuf); brown beef stew
Rare	When applied to meat, it means underdone
Reduce	To concentrate a liquid by boiling
Refresh	To make cold under running cold water
Residual insecticide	Long lasting insecticide which remains active for a considerable period of time
Riboflavin	Part of vitamin B known as B_2. Sources in yeast, liver, eggs, cheese
Rissoler	To fry to a golden brown
Rodents	Rats and mice
Roux	A thickening of cooked flour and fat
Sabayon	Yolks of eggs and a little water or wine cooked until creamy
Saccharometer	An instrument for measuring the density of sugar
Salmonella	Food poisoning bacterium found in meat and poultry
Sanitiser	Chemical agent used for cleaning and disinfecting surfaces and equipment
Sauté	• To toss in fat (pommes sautées) • To cook quickly in a sauté pan or frying pan • A brown stew of a specific type, (veal sauté)
Seal	To set the surface of meat in a hot oven or pan to colour and retain the juices
Set	• To seal the outside surface • To allow to become firm or firmer (jelly)
Shredded	Cut in fine strips (lettuce, onion)
Silicone paper	Non-stick paper (siliconised paper)
Singe	To brown or colour
Smetana	A low fat product; a cross between soured cream and yoghurt
Sodium	Mineral element in the form of salt (sodium chloride); found in cheese, bacon, fish, meat
Soufflé	A very light dish, sweet or savoury, hot or cold
Soy sauce	Made from soybeans and used extensively in Chinese cookery
Spores	Resistant resting-phase of bacteria protecting them against adverse conditions such as high temperatures

Staphylococcus	Food poisoning bacterium found in the human nose and throat and also in septic cuts
Starch	A carbohydrate found in cereals, certain vegetables and farinaceous foods
Steriliser	Chemical used to destroy all living organisms
Sterile	Free from all living organisms
Sterilisation	Process that destroys living organisms
Stock rotation	Sequence of issuing goods: first into store, first to be issued
Strain	To separate the liquid from the solids by passing through a strainer
Sweat	To cook in fat under a lid without colour
Syneresis	The squeezing out of liquid from an overcooked protein and liquid mixture (scrambled egg, egg custard)
Table d'hôte	A meal at a fixed price; a set menu
Tahini	A strong flavoured sesame seed paste
Tally	Corresponds to; is the same as
Terrine	An earthenware dish used for cooking and serving pâté; also used as a name for certain products
Thiamine	Part of vitamin B known as B_1, it assists the nervous system; sources in yeast, bacon, wholemeal bread
Timbale	A double serving dish
Tofu	Low fat bean curd made from soybeans (see also bean curd)
Tranche	A slice
Trichinosis	Disease caused by hair-like worms in the muscles of meat, as in pork
Tronçon	A slice of flat fish on the bone
TVP	Texturised vegetable protein derived from soybeans
Vegan	A person who does not eat fish, meat, poultry, game, dairy products and eggs
Vegetarian	A person who does not eat meat, poultry or game
Velouté	• Basic sauce
	• A soup of velvet or smooth consistency
Viruses	Microscopic pathogens that multiply in the living cells of their host
Vitamins	Chemical substances which assist the regulation of body processes
Vol-au-vent	A large puff pastry case
Wok	A round-bottomed pan used extensively in Chinese cooking
Yeast extract	A mixture of brewers yeast and salt high in flavour and protein
Yoghurt	An easily digested fermented milk product

INDEX

almond:
  biscuits 719
  chicken 426
  paste 709
  sauce 623
Alu-Chole 451
anchovy 173:
  butter 135
  sauce 118
analysis of recipes 66
angels on horseback 727
apple:
  baked 629
  charlotte 627
  dumpling 674
  flan 671
  fritters 627
  meringue flan 671
  pancakes 613
  purée 672
  sauce 672
  turnover 683
apricot:
  flan 676
  glaze 671
  sauce 622
artichoke:
  à la greque 139
  bottoms 524
  globe 523
  Jerusalem, in cream sauce 525
  Jerusalem, purée of 525
artichokes, Greek-style 139
asparagus 526:
  points/tips 526
  soup 150
aspic jelly 165
aubergine:
  fried 527
  stuffed 528
  ratatouille 527
  ratatouille pancakes 504
avocado pear 168:
  mousse (sweet) 634

baba:
  rum 647
  syrup for 647
bacon 384:
  and chicken liver on toast 731
  and haddock on toast 730
  baked, and pineapple 387
  boiled 386
  chops, honey and orange sauce 387
  cuts uses weights 385
  fried 387
  grilled back or rashers 386
  grilled gammon rashers 389
  preparation of joints and cuts 385

quality 386
baked Alaska 616:
  with peaches 616
  with pears 616
Bakewell tart 716
baking
  definition 89
  effects 90
  method 90
  recovery time 91
  safety 91
baklavas 438
balanced diet 62
ballottine of chicken 395
banana:
  fritters 628
barbecued spare ribs of pork 379
Bath buns 645
batters, frying 261
bavarois 599:
  chocolate 599
  coffee 599
  lemon 599
  lime 599
  raspberry 600
  strawberry 600
  orange 599
  vanilla 600
beans:
  and nut burgers 492
  broad beans 541
  dried beans 541
  French beans 542
  goulash 497
  Mexican bean pot 502
  runner beans 543
  three bean salad 183
  (see also individual beans)
béchamel sauce 117
beef 324:
  dissection 324
  Bourguignonne 336
  boiled, French style 334
  boiled silverside, carrots and dumplings 333
  braised 347
  braised steak and dumplings 348
  braised steak 346
  carbonnade 345
  curried 340
  degrees for cooking 338
  do-piazza 445
  grilled 337
  hamburger American style 351
  Hamburg/Vienna steak 351
  joints, uses weights 325
  madras 446
  olives 349
  quality 327

preparation of cuts 328
preparation of beef offal 331
preparation of joints 328
ragout 335
roast 332
sauté 342
sirloin steak chasseur 338
steak pie 346
steak pudding 341
stock 113
stroganoff 342
testing for cooking 333
tournedos 340
beetroot 178, 551:
  salad 179
best end of lamb:
  boulanger 306
  roast 303
  with bread crumbs and parsley 306
biryani, vegetable 511
biscuits:
  almond 719
  cats' tongues 718
  cornets 718
  mixtures 697
  piped 719
  shortbread 714-5
bisque 136
blanc 525
blitz kuchen 478
body building foods 60
body protection foods 60
boiling 77
  definition 77
  effects 78
  method 78
  safety 89
  time and temperature 79
bones 294
bouchée 684, 740:
  preparation 684
brains, calf's 293
braising
  definition 83
  effects 85
  method 84
  safety 86
  time and temperature 85
brandy:
  butter 623
  cream 623
bread 638:
  and butter pudding (sweet) 595
  chollo 477
  dough 638
  pudding 620
  rolls 642
  sauce 131
brill 265

brine 327
broad beans 541
broccoli 529:
    broccoli sauce 498
bruschetta 738
Brussels sprouts 535:
    fried in butter 536
Bucatini Amatriciana-style 227
buck rarebit 733
buns:
    Bath 645
    Chelsea 645
    cream 690
    dough, basic recipe 643
    fruit 644
    hot cross 645
    Swiss 645
    wash 643
burritos 468
butchery
    bacon 384
    beef 324
    lamb 298
    pork 374
    veal 355
butter cream 626:
    boiled 625
butter sauce 254
butter sauces (compound) 135
butterfly pasta with crab 226

cabbage 532:
    braised 533
    braised, red 535
    stir fry with mushrooms and beansprouts
        533
cabinet pudding 597
cakes:
    Christmas 708
    decoration 703
    Eccles 680
    fruit 707
    genoese sponge 711
    mixtures 693
    small cakes, basic mix 706
    Victoria sandwich 711
calcium 59
calf's liver and bacon 372
canapés 739
cannelloni 230
carbohydrate 59:
    effects of heat on 75
carbonnade of beef 345
Caribbean fruit curry 494
Caribbean 425
carrots:
    buttered 529
    in cream sauce 530
    kugel 479
    purée 529
    Vichy 530
cats' tongues 718
cauliflower 536:
    à la greque 185
    Mornay 537
    polonaise 537
caviar 165

celeriac 181
celery 187:
    Greek-style 185
    braised 531
chantilly marignans 650
chapatis 456
charcutière sauce 127
chart roasting times 94
chasseur sauce 123
chateaubriand 330
chaud-froid sauce 164
cheese:
    and ham savoury flan 734
    braised rice with 238
    fritters 736
    cauliflower 537
    omelet 212
    quiche lorraine 734
    sauce 118
    soufflé 735
    spaghetti 219
    straws 735
Chelsea buns 645
chemmeen kari
cherry flan 670
chestnut stuffing 398
chicken 389:
    à la king 409
    boiled, with rice and suprême sauce 408
    casserole 415
    cleaning 391
    crumbed breast with asparagus 407
    curry 414
    cuts 392
    dressing 392
    food value 390
    fricassée 412
    grilled 403
    in red wine 415
    liver and bacon on toast 731
    palak 448
    pancakes 411
    pie 413
    preparation for
        grilling 394
        sauté 394
        suprême 394
        ballottines 395
    roast 399
    salad 194
    sauté 400, 401, 402, 406
    soup 147
    spatchcock 403
    stock 113
    storage 390
    suprêmes 404
    tandoori 447
    tikka 449
    types 390
    vol-au-vent 410
    liver:
        and bacon on toast 531
        with braised rice 415
    weights, portions 390
chicory 187:
    braised 540
    curled 187
    shallow fried 540

chilli con carne 484
Chinese 426
Chinese vegetables and noodles 430
Chinese-style stir-fry vegetables 493
chive and potato soup 144
chocolate:
    bavarois 599
    brownies 487
    butter cream 626
    éclairs 689
    gâteau 712
    genoese 712
    ice-cream 602
    pastry cream 606
    sauce 624
    sponge pudding 610
    white chocolate mousse 621
chop:
    bacon with honey and orange sauce 387
    lamb:
        chump braised 310
        chump grilled 309
        loin braised 310
        loin Champvallon 311
        loin grilled 309
    pork:
        charcutière 378
        flamanade 378
        grilled 380
chop suey 431
choux paste 666:
    fritters 691
chow mein 432
Christmas:
    cake 708
    pudding 610
clam chowder 486
clarification of fat 296
cleaning 34
clostridium perfringens 46
cocido madrileno 482
cocktail:
    canapés 739
    Florida 167
    fruit 168
    shellfish 170
    sauce 171
cod:
    boiled 265
    grilled 258
coffee:
    bavarois 599
    éclairs 689
    gâteau 713
    ice-cream 602
    pastry cream 606
cold foods 156
    definition 156
    equipment 157
    health, safety, hygiene 156
    techniques 157
cold meats 192
coleslaw 183
compound butter sauces 135
condé, pear 633
conduction 75
convection 75
convenience food 724

convenience pastry 660
corn on the cob 544
cornets 718
Cornish pasties 316
Cornish vegetable feast bake pie 495
cos lettuce 187
cottage pie 318
coupe Jacques 636
courgettes 539:
    deep fried 539
    ratatouille 527
    ratatouille pancakes 504
    shallow fried 539
court bouillon 189
couscous 471
crab 278:
    cocktail 170
    mayonnaise 175
crawfish 277
crayfish 275
cream 655:
    buns 690
    caramel 598
    horns 679
    pastry cream 605
    rum or brandy 623
    slice 682
cream soups (see soups)
crisps 570
crumble, vegetable 507
cucumber 179:
    salad 179
culinary terms 739
currant roll, steamed 608
curried:
    beef 340
    chicken 414
    eggs 210
    lamb 313
curry:
    beef madras 446
    sauce 129
    Thai mussaman 483
    vegetable 505
custard:
    baked egg 596
    fresh egg custard 605
    sauce 623
cutlets:
    lamb:
        breadcrumbed 307
        fried 307
        grilled 306
        mixed grill 307
        Reform 308
    potato and nut 502
    veal, fried, grilled 364

dahl 450
deep-frying
    definition 102
    effects 103
    method 102
    safety 105
    time and temperature 103-4
demi-glace sauce 122
devilled:
    kidneys on toast 728

sauce 124
    soft roes 545
devils on horseback 727
domades 437
dough 638
    types 640
doughnuts 647
dressings, salad 159
duck/duckling:
    roast 416, 417
    sizes, quality, preparation 397
    with cherries 419
    with orange salad 417
    with orange sauce 418
Dutch apple tart 675

Eccles cake 680
éclairs, chocolate and coffee 689
egg 197:
    boiled 204-5
        with sauces 205-6
    croquettes 209
    curried 210
    custard, baked 515
    custard sauce 623
    food value 199
    French fried 207
    fried 206
        and bacon 207
    health, safety, hygiene 200
    in cocotte 203
        with creamed chicken 203
        with tomato 209
    omelets 211
    poached 207
        with sauces 208-9
    purchasing 199
    sauce 118
    Scotch 210
    scrambled 201-3
    sizes 199
    Spanish omelette 190
    storage 200
    stuffed 174
    types 199
egg plant (see aubergine)
energy 60
escalope:
    veal (and variations) 365:
        breadcrumbed with ham and cheese
          366
        with cream and mushrooms 367
        with Madeira 367
        with Parma ham 368
    pork 380:
        with Calvados 381
ethnic dishes 420

fat 59
    effect of heat on 75
fennel 554
fermentation 639
fettuccine with ham and creamy cheese 226
filo pastry 439
fish:
    belle meunière 257
    bretonne 258
    cakes 273

cuts 253
    Doria 258
    fried in batter 264
    glaze 255
    grenobloise 258
    in the shell with cheese
        sauce 271
    kedgeree 271
    methods of cooking 250
    meunière 257:
        with almonds 257
    pie 274
    preparation 248
    preservation 244
    safety 247
    salad 177
    stock 114
    storage 243
    types 248
    velouté 119
    vol-au-vent with sea food 284
    (see also individual fish)
flans 670:
    apple 671
    apple meringue 671
    apricot 676
    banana 678
    cheese and ham savoury 734
    cherry 670
    plum 676
    raspberry 677
    rhubarb 676
    soft fruit 677
    strawberry 677
    tinned fruit 677
Florida:
    cocktail 167
    salad 184
flour 650
foie gras 166
fondant 646
food poisoning 54-5
fools, fruit 630
forcemeat 382
frangipane 717
French bean 542
    salad 182
French salad 188
fricassée:
    chicken 412
    chicken with onions and mushrooms 412
    veal 361
fritters:
    apple 627
    banana 628
    cheese 736
    pineapple 628
fruit 589:
    barquettes 678
    buns 465
    cake 707
    cocktail 644
    fool 630
    glazed 636
    juice 170
    Melba 635
    pies 667
    poached 631

pudding 691
salad, fresh 629
savarin 649
slice 687
scones 705-6
soft fruit flans 677
tarts 678
types
  citrus fruit 591
  food value 590
  hard fruit 591
  quality 590
  seasons 590
  stone fruit 591
  storage 591
  soft fruit 591
  tropical fruit 592
  uses 591
frying:
  deep 102
  shallow 99
frying batters 261

gado gado 457
gammon rashers 389
Gâteau Pithiviers 686
gâteau:
  chocolate 712
  coffee 713
germs 45
genoese 711:
  chocolate 712
glaze 115:
  apricot 671
  fish 255
  meat 115
  red 676
glazed vegetables 335
gnocchi:
  parisienne 233
  piemontaise 234
  romaine 234
golden syrup sponge pudding 609
goose/gosling 397
gougère 498
goulash 343
grapefruit 167:
  cocktail and variations 167
gravy 303:
  thickened 131
Greek 433
green salad 188
green sauce 162
grenadin of veal 370
grilling 96
  definition 97
  degrees of grilling chart 97
  effects 98
  method 96
  safety 99
grouse 380
gull's eggs 166

haddock:
  and bacon on toast 730
  creamed, with cheese on toast 731
  on toast 730
  poached 272

smoked 272
  halibut, boiled 265
ham 337:
  and cheese savoury 734
  and veal pie (hot) 363
  quiche lorraine 734
Hamburg Steak 351
hamburger 351
haricot bean salad 183
heads – calf, pig 293
healthy eating 57
heart 292:
  calf 292
  lamb's 292:
    braised 322
    stuffed braised 323
  ox 292
  sheep 292
herring:
  grilled 258
  soused 172
hors-d'oeuvre 153
horseradish sauce 163
hotate gai shoyu yaki 460
hotpot 317
hot veal and ham pie 363
hot water paste 195
hummus 469

ice-cream 602:
  chocolate 602
  coffee 602
  meringue with 615
  mixed 602
  regulations 601
  strawberry 602
icing:
  royal 709
  water 646
Indian and Pakistani 440
Indonesian 456
ingredient substitutes 70
Irish stew 315
Israeli 469:
  kosher foods 475

jalousie 685
jam:
  omelet 617
  pancakes 613
  puffs 682
  roll, baked 674
  roll, steamed 691
  sauce 621
  tart 668
  turnovers 680
Japanese 459
junket 620
jus-lié 131

kalamarakia yemista (stuffed squid) 435
kebab, lamb 308
kedgeree 271:
  vegetarian 508
keema matar 446
khoshaf 474
kibbeh bil sanieh 470
kidney:

calf 292
lamb 292:
  grilled 321
  sauté 321
  devilled on toast 728
pig 292
sheep 292
kiwi slice 688

knives:
  cutting wheels 34
  cutters, vegetable 33
  forks 32
  groovers 33
  knife:
    sharpening 31
    usage 30
  mechanical equipment 36
  peelers 33
  safety, rules for 27
  scissors and secateurs 34
  selection, use and care 26
  set of knives 27
  sharpening knives 31
  small equipment 26
  tongs 33
  trussing ad larding needles 34
  vegetable cutters 33
  zesters 34
koenigsberger klops 476

lamb 296:
  best end:
    boulanger 306
    roast 303
    with breadcrumbs and parsley 306
  chop:
    chump 309, 310
    loin 309, 310, 311
  curried 313
  cutlets 306–308
  fillet 311
  garnishes 311
  hotpot 317
  Irish stew 315
  kebab 308
  kashmira 444
  minced 319
  mixed grill 307
  moussaka 320
  noisettes 309,311
  pasanda
  roast (best-end, saddle etc.) 303
  roast leg of lamb 303
  shepherd's pie 318
  white stew 315
lamb and mutton:
  carving 304
  dissection 298
  joints, use and weights 297
  preparation of best-end 301
  preparation of chops 300
  preparation of joint 298
  preparation of offal 302
  preparation of saddle 299
  quality 297
  service 304

lasagne 231:
    vegetarian 509
leeks:
    Greek-style 186
    braised 552
lemon:
    bavarois 599
    curd 673
    curd tart 668
    meringue pie 673
    pancakes 611
    sauce 622
    sorbet 602
    soufflé (cold) 607
    sponge pudding 610
    water ice 646
lentil and cider loaf 499

lettuce 187:
    braised 543
    cos 187

light meals 723
liver:
    calf's, and bacon 372
    chicken, with braised rice 415
    lamb's, fried with bacon 323
    ox, braised and onions 353
lobster 276:
    cocktail 170
    cooking 277
    cleaning 277
    mayonnaise 175
    Mornay 282
    Thermidor 282
lyonnaise sauce 125

macaroni cheese 222
mackerel
    grilled 259
    soused 172
mangetout 546
marignans Chantilly 650
marrow 538:
    baby 539
    provençale 538
    stuffed 538
marzipan 709
matzo fritters 478
mayonnaise 161
meat:
    pie 346
    preservation 294
    salad 178
    storage 290
    structure 290
    (see also lamb, beef etc.)
Melbas, fruit 635
melon 169:
    charentais 170:
        with port 170
        with raspberries 170
    cocktail 168
meringue 614:
    apple meringue flan 671
    baked Alaskas 616
    with ice-cream 615
    lemon meringue pie 673

with whipped cream 614
metagee 425
methods of cookery 73
metric equivalents table vii–viii
Mexican 466
Mexican bean pot 502
microwave cookery
    applications 108
    definition 106
    safety 107
    special points 107
Middle Eastern dishes 469
milk 587:
    puddings 618
mille-feuilles 682
mince pies 686
mincemeat 710:
    tart 678
mint sauce 163
mixed:
    grill 307
    salad 188
Mornay sauce 119
moulds 43
moussaka 320:
    vegetarian 510
mousse:
    avocado (sweet) 634
    smoked mackerel 172
    white chocolate 621
mushrooms:
    grilled 532
    on toast 728:
        with soft roes 730
    pancakes:
        with chicken 411
    sauce 120, 255:
        piquant 500
        wine and mustard 491
    soup 146
    stuffed 530
    veal escalope with and cream 367
        with chicken 410
mussels 279:
mutton:
    general 296
    best-end, roast 303
    broth 138
    hotpot 317
    leg, roast 303
    minced 319
    moussaka 320
    roast 303
    shepherd's pie 318
    stew 310, 312
    stock 113
    (see also lamb)
myco-protein 295

nasi goreng 457
navarin of lamb 312:
    with vegetables 312
Niçoise salad 182
noisette of lamb:
    grilled 309
    sautéed 311
noodles 222:
    with butter 223

with eggs and bacon 223
with shredded pork 428
nut:
    and bean burgers 492
    and potato cutlets 502
    and vegetable Stroganoff 512
nutrition 57

offal 291
oil temperature chart 104
oils and fats table 71
okra 555
omelet, varieties of 212
onion:
    bhajias 452
    braised 546
    French fried 545
    fried 545
    Greek-style 185
    omelet 212
    sauce 118
        brown onion 125
orange:
    bavarois 599
    cocktail 168
    pancakes 611
    salad 184
    sauce 622
    soufflé pudding 606
    sponge pudding 610
    water ice 646
osso buco 371
oven temperature chart viii
oxtail 294:
    stewed 354
ox tongue 353:
    braised, and Madeira sauce 353
oysters 165

paella 480
pakora 453
palak lamb 442
palmiers 683
pancakes:
    apple 613
    chicken (various) 411
    jam 613
    lemon or orange 611
    ratatouille 504
paper bag cookery 106
parsley:
    and thyme stuffing 398
    butter 135
    potatoes 564
    sauce 118
parsnips 552
pasta 213
    cooking 218
    fresh egg 218
    ingredients for dishes 217
    storage 215
    stuffings 228
    types and sauces 216
pasties, Cornish 316
pastry 581
    choux 666
    filo 439
    puff 662

cases 684
rough puff 664
short 661
sugar 665
pastry cream 605:
  chocolate 606
  coffee 606
pâté (see foie gras)
peach:
  Melba 635
  cardinal 636
pear:
  belle Hélène 636
  condé 633
  in red wine 634
peas 546:
  French style 547
pease pudding 553
pecan pie 487
penne and mange-tout 225
pepper bhajee 452
pepper sauce 124
personal hygiene 16:
  dress for 17
  medical 17
pests 55
petits fours 717

phosphoras 59
picadillo 467
pie:
  chicken 413
  Cornish vegetable feast bake 495
  fish 274
  fruit 667
  lemon meringue 673
  mince 686
  pecan 487
  pork, raised 195
  steak 346
  veal and ham (hot) 363
pilaff (see rice, braised) 236
pimento 547:
pineapple fritters 628
piquant sauce 126
pithiviers 686
pizza 737:
  vegetarian 514
plaice:
  fried fillets 263
  grilled 260:
    fillets 259
plum flan 676
poaching
  definition 80
  effects 81
  method 80
  safety 81
  time and temperature 81
Pojarski 370
pork 374:
  barbecued spare ribs 379
  chop (various) 378-80
  cuts and weights 375
  dissection 375
  escalopes 380:
    with Calvados 381
  forcemeat 382

leg:
  boiled 378
  roast 377
pie, raised 195
preparation of joints 375
quality 377
roast (loin, shoulder etc.) 377
toad in the hole 382
sweet and sour 383
pork pie, raised 195
port wine sauce 126
Porterhouse steak 329
pot roasting
  definition 94
  method 94
potato 561:
  almond 567
  baked jacket 567:
    with cheese 568
  boiled 564
  brioche 566
  Byron 575
  cakes 566
  château 577
  chips 571
  cocotte 577
  crisps 570
  croquette 566
  Delmonico 578
  duchess 565
  fondant 576
  food value 563
  fried 571:
    diced 573
  hash brown 486
  latkes 475
  Macaire 575
  marquis 567
  mashed 565:
    matchstick 570
  new 579:
    rissolée 579
  noisette 577
  parisienne 578
  Parmentier 580
  parsley 564
  Pont Neuf 444
  purchasing 563
  ready packed 563
  riced 564
  rissolée 577
  roast 576
  salad 175
  sauté 569:
    with onions 570
  savoury 574
  shallow fried 569
  snow 564
  soup (see soups)
  steamed 569:
    jacket 569
  storage 563
  straw 571
  wafer 570
  wedges, deep fried 572
  with bacon and onions 578
  yield 563
potted shrimps 167

poultry 389
  (see also chicken etc.)
praline 626
prawn 275:
  cocktail 170
  mayonnaise 175
profiteroles 689
  with chocolate sauce 690
protein 59
  effects of heat on 75
puff pastry 662
pulses 556:
  cooking 558
  food value 556
  health and hygiene 557
  storage 557
  types 558
  uses 558

queen:
  cakes 707
  of puddings 594
quiche lorraine 734

radiation 74
radishes 188
ragout:
  beef 335
  oxtail 354
  veal 360
raising agents 652
raspberry:
  bavarois 600
  flan 677
  sorbet 603
  vacherin 615
  water ice 646
ratatouille 527
ravioli 229:
  filling 230
recipe analysis 66
red glaze 676
reduced stock sauces 117
reform sauce 128
rendang 458
rhubarb flan 676
ribs:
  barbecued spare (pork) 379
rice 213:
  boiled 236
  braised (pilaff) 236:
    with cheese 238
    with mushrooms 237
    with peas and pimento 237
  empress 619
  fried 239
  pudding 618:
    baked 618
  salad 181
  steamed 236
  stir fried 239
risotto 238
roast:
  gravy 303
  potatoes 576
roasting
  definition 91
  effects 92

roasting, *continued*
    method 92
    safety 94
    time and temperature 93
roasting times chart 94
Robert sauce 127
rock cakes 711
rocket 188
roes:
    soft, on toast 729
    with mushrooms on toast 730
Roquefort dressing 160
rough puff pastry 664
roux 116
royal:
    icing 709
rum:
    baba 647
    butter 623
    butter cream 626
    cream 623
runner beans 543

sabayon 254:
    sauce 604
    with Marsala 604
safety:
    accidents 6-7
    appearance 15
    artificial respiration 10
    burns 9
    cuts 9
    communicating 19
    electric shock 9
    employers responsibility for safety 11
    fainting 9
    fire blanket 4
    fire extinguishers 3
    fire hoses 3
    fire precautions 2
    fire procedures 2
    first aid 8
    equipment 8
    footwear 17
    fractures 9
    gassing 10
    HASAWA, enforcement of, 12
    hazard and accident prevention 13
    headgear 17
    Health and Safety at Work Act
      HASAWA) 10
    hygiene, personal 16
    lost property 14
    medical health officers 17
    nose bleeds 9
    personal hygiene 16
    safety 2
      legislation 10
      environment 10
    scalds 9
    shock 8
    suspicious items 5
    water sprinkler 3
sage and onion stuffing 378
sago pudding (*see* semolina)
salad dressings:
    mayonnaise 161
    Roquefort 160

thousand island 160
vinaigrette 159
salads 155
salamander 96
salami 167:
    and cooked sausages 167
salmon:
    boiled 189
    cold 189
    cutlets 273
    grilled 260
    mayonnaise 191
    smoked 166
salmonella 45
salsify 548
salt 70
samosas 453
sandwiches 740
sardines 173:
sashimi 463
sauce 116:
    almond 623
    anchovy 118
    apple 672
    apricot 622
    aurore 120
    avgothemono 438
    barbecue 379
    béchamel 117
    bread 131
    broccoli 498
    brown 121
    brown onion 125
    caper 120
    charcutière 127
    chasseur 123
    chaud-froid 164
    cheese 118
    chocolate 624
    cocktail 171
    cold 161
    cream 119
    curry 129
    custard 623
    demi-glace 122
    devilled 124
    egg 118
    fish velouté 120
    green 162
    hollandaise 134
    horseradish 163, 331
    Italian 125
    ivory 120
    jam 621
    lemon 622
    lime 622
    lyonnaise 125
    Madeira 126
    mayonnaise 161
    Melba 624
    melted butter 133
    mint 163
    mushroom 120, 255:
      with wine and mustard 491
    mustard 119
    onion 118
    orange 622
    parsley 118

    pepper 124
    piquant 126
    port wine 126
    red wine 123
    reform 128
    roast gravy 130
    Robert 127
    roux 116
    sabayon 604:
      with Marsala 604
    sherry 126
    shrimp 256
    soubise 118
    strawberry 635
    suprême 408
    sweet and sour 384
    syrup 622
    tartare 162
    tomato 132
    velouté 119
    white (béchamel) 117
    white wine, glazed 255
sauerkraut 534
sausage 382
    mixed grill 307
    rolls 687
    sauerkraut 388
    toad in the hole 382
savarin 649:
    fruit 649
    syrup for 648
    tomato 506
savouries 724, 740
scallops 280
scampi 283
scones 705:
Scotch:
    eggs 210
    woodcock 732
seafood:
    cocktail 170
    in puff pastry 284
    mayonnaise 175
sea-kale 537:
    Mornay 537
secure environment 14
security 2
self development 23, 25
semolina pudding 619
shallow fried fish:
    with almonds 257
    with belle meunière 257
    with boria 257
    with grenobloise 257
    with bretonne 257
shallow frying
    definition 99
    effects 101
    griddle 100
    method 100
    safety 102
    sauté 100
    stir fry 101
    time and temperature 101
shellfish 274
    cocktails 170
    mayonnaise 175
    quality and purchasing 275

storage 275
shepherd's pie 318:
   meatless 501
sherry sauce 126
short pastry 661
shortbread:
   piped 719
   biscuits 714
shrimp 275:
   butter 135
   cocktail 170
   mayonnaise 175
   omelet 212
   potted 167
   sauce 256
silverside 333
sirloin:
   steak with red wine sauce 339
   steak chasseur 338
strawberry sauce 635
skate with black butter 272
smoked mackerel mousse 172
snacks 723
sodium 59
sole:
   Bercy 268
   Dugléré 266
   florentine 270
   fried 264
   goujons 263
   grilled 260
   Mornay 269
   Véronique 267
   with mushrooms and bamboo shoots 429
   with white wine sauce 267
sorbet
   lemon 602
   orange 603
   raspberry 603
soubise sauce 118
soufflé:
   cold lemon 607
   cheese 735
   orange pudding 606-7
   pudding (basic) 606
soup 135:
   asparagus 150
   autumn vegetable 151
   avgolemono 434
   basic, purée and cream 149, 150
   chicken 147
   chive and potato 144
   clear (consommé) 136
   green pea 140:
      cream of 142
   haricot bean 141
   leek and potato 144
   lentil 141
   minestrone 152
   mixed vegetable 151
   mushroom 146
   mutton broth 138
   pork, ham and bamboo shoot 430
   potato 143:
      and watercress 143
   pulse 139
   royal 138
   tomato 145:

   and potato, cream of 146
   cream of 146
   fresh 146

   vegetable 148:
      cream of 148
      mixed 151
   vichyssoise 144
   yellow pea 141
soused herring and mackerel 128
spaghetti:
   bolognaise 221
   milanaise 220
   with bacon and tomatoes 225
   with cheese 219
   with tomato sauce 220
Spanish 480
spare ribs 379
spatchcock, chicken 403
spinach 540:
   purée 541
spring greens 533
spit roasting 93
sponge:
   fingers 716
   genoese 711
   mixtures 698
   steamed pudding 609
   Victoria sandwich 711
staphylococcus aureus 46
steak:
   braised 346:
      with dumplings 348
   pie 346
   pudding 341
   sirloin:
      with red wine sauce 339
      chasseur 338
steaming
   advantages 88
   definition 86
   effects 87
   method 86
   safety 89
   time and temperature 88
stewing
   definition 81
   effects 82
   method 82
   safety 83
stir fry 101:
   vegetables, Chinese style 493
stocks 111:
   fish 114
   meat (brown and white) 113
   reduced sauces 121
   reduced veal 122
   syrup 713
   vegetable (brown and white) 114, 115
stocks, soups and sauces
   health, safety and hygiene 112
strawberry:
   bavarois 600
   flan 677
   ice-cream 602
   sauce 635
   vacherin 615
   water ice 646

strudel, vegetarian 513
stuffing:
   chestnut 398
   for duck 417
   for lamb 305
   for pork (sage and onion) 378
   for veal 369
   parsley and thyme 398
substitutes – ingredients 70
succotash 487
suet paste 666
sugar 652:
   paste 665
sultana sponge pudding 610
sushi 464:
   rice 464
   bara sushi 465
sweet and sour pork 383
sweet and sour sauce 384
sweetbread 359:
   veal, escalope 373
   veal, escalope crumbed 374
sweetcorn 544
Swiss:
   buns 645
   roll 714
syrup 636:
   for baba 647
   for savarin 648
   sauce 622
   stock 713
   suet pudding 666
   tart 669

T-bone steak 329
tabbouleh 470
tacos 467
tandoori:
   chicken 447
   prawns 441
tandoori cooking
   definition 95
   method 95
taramasalata 434
tartare sauce 162
tart:
   Bakewell 716
   fruit 668
   jam 668
   lemon curd 669
   mincemeat 686
   syrup 669
   treacle 669
tempura 462
teppanyaki 463
Thai 482
thickening agents 117
thousand island dressing 160
three bean salad 183
toad in the hole 382
tomato 180:
   and cucumber salad 180
   concasse 551
   grilled 549
   juice 170
   omelet 212
   ratatouille 527:
      pancake 504

tomato, *continued*
    salad 180
    sauce 132
    savarin 506
    soups (*see* soups)
    stuffed 550
tongue, braised ox with Madeira sauce 353
tonkatsu 460
tortillas 466
tournedos 340
transference of heat 75
treacle
    pudding 609
    tart 669
trifle 594
tripe and onions 352
tuna 173
turbot 265
turkey 398:
    (*see also* chicken)
turnip:
    buttered 544
    purée 545
turnovers:
    apple 683
    jam 680
TVP – textured vegetable protein 295

USA 484

vacherin:
    raspberry 615
    with strawberries and cream 615
valentine of lamb 312
vanilla:
    ice-cream 602
    sponge pudding 610
veal 355:
    dissection 357
    and ham pie 196
    blanquette 360
    braised 362:
        shin 371

stuffed breast/shoulder 364
calf's liver and bacon 372
cutlet, fried 364
cutlet, grilled 364
escalopes 365-68
fricassée 361
joints uses weights 356
leg of veal, roast 365
Pojarski 370
preparation of joints and cuts 358
quality 360
roast:
    leg 365
    stuffed breast 370
ragoût 360
stock (brown/white) 91
sweetbreads 373–4
vegetable 517:
    and nut stroganoff 512
    biryani 511
    Cornish feast bake pie 495
    crumble 507
    curry 505
    cuts of 522
    food value 519
    glazed 335
    grilled 549
    health, safety and hygiene 520
    mixed 553:
        fried in batter 554
    moulds 555
    purchasing 519
    quality 519
    salad 177
    soup 148:
        cream of 148
        mixed 151
    stir fry, chinese style 493
    stock 114-5
    storage 520
    stroganoff 512
    types 521
vegetarian 491:

kedgeree 508
lasagne 509
moussaka 510
strudel 513
wholemeal pizza 514
velouté sauce 119
vichyssoise 144
Victoria sandwich 711
vinaigrette 159
vitamins 59
    effects of heat on 75
vol-au-vent 684:
    chicken 410:
    seafood 284

waldorf salad 182
walnut chicken 427
water 60
water ice, various 646
watercress 188
Welsh rarebit 732
white:
    chocolate mousse 621
    sauce 117
    stew, lamb 315
    stew, veal 360
    wine sauce (fish) 255
whitebait 264
whiting:
    fried 263
    grilled 259
work performance 24
    working:
        environment 1
        relationships 17
        with supervisors 18
        with others 18

yakitori 463
Yorkshire pudding 332

Zabaglione 604